BIOMETRIC SOLUTIONS
FOR AUTHENTICATION
IN AN E-WORLD

BIOMETRIC SOLUTIONS
FOR AUTHENTICATION
IN AN E-WORLD

edited by

David Zhang
The Hong Kong Polytechnic University

KLUWER ACADEMIC PUBLISHERS
Boston / Dordrecht / London

Distributors for North, Central and South America:
Kluwer Academic Publishers
101 Philip Drive
Assinippi Park
Norwell, Massachusetts 02061 USA
Telephone (781) 871-6600
Fax (781) 681-9045
E-Mail: kluwer@wkap.com

Distributors for all other countries:
Kluwer Academic Publishers Group
Post Office Box 322
3300 AH Dordrecht, THE NETHERLANDS
Telephone 31 786 576 000
Fax 31 786 576 474
E-Mail: services@wkap.nl

Electronic Services <http://www.wkap.nl>

Library of Congress Cataloging-in-Publication Data

A C.I.P. Catalogue record for this book is available
from the Library of Congress.

CONTENTS

Chapter 4

FACE RECOGNITION AND ITS APPLICATION   83

Andrew W. Senior and Ruud M. Bolle

Chapter 5

PERSONALIZE MOBILE ACCESS BY SPEAKER AUTHENTICATION   99

Ke Chen

Chapter 6

BIOMETRICS ON THE INTERNET: SECURITY APPLICATION AND SERVICES   131

Lee Luan Ling and Miguel Gustavo Lizárraga

Contents

Chapter 13

FACE VERIFICATION FOR ACCESS CONTROL   339

Wen Gao and Shiguang Shan

Chapter 14

VOICE BIOMETRICS FOR SECURING YOUR WEB-BASED BUSINESS   377

Kevin Farrell, Scott Sharp and Ron Beyner

Chapter 15

ABILITY TO VERIFY: A METRIC FOR SYSTEM PERFORMANCE IN REAL-WORLD COMPARATIVE BIOMETRIC TESTING   393

Samir Nanavati and Michael Thieme

Chapter 16

AUTOMATED AUTHENTICATION USING HYBRID   **411**
BIOMETRIC SYSTEM

Norman Poh and Jerzy Korczak

FOREWORD

Biometric authentication, or simply, biometrics refers to automatic identification of an individual based on his distinguishing physiological and/or behavioral characteristics (biometric identifiers). Because many biometric identifiers (e.g., fingerprint) are distinctive to each person, they are more reliable and more capable than knowledge-based (e.g., Personal Identification Number or password) and token-based (e.g., ID card or key) techniques in differentiating between an authorized person and an impostor. Biometric authentication is not a new topic. For example, automatic fingerprint identification systems (AFIS) have been used by the forensic communities around the world for almost 40 years! However, due to ever increasing identity fraud in welfare disbursements, credit card transactions, cellular phone calls, ATM (Automatic Teller Machines) withdrawals, visa applications, and airport security, several organizations in financial and banking services, *e*-commerce, telecommunications, and government are looking to biometric systems to enhance security, reduce fraud and improve customer satisfaction. Furthermore, as people are becoming more and more connected electronically, the ability to establish the true identity of a person at remote locations is even more critical. As a result, it is not suprising that biometric systems based on well established and proven biometric identifiers (e.g., face, fingerprint, speech and iris) as well as on relatively new identifiers (e.g., gait and facial thermograms) are being developed, tested and deployed in a number of organizations.

A number of biometrics systems are being currently used for access control and in law enforcement agencies. However, the future of biometrics technology and its impact will be determined by its successful deployment in the financial services and computer security (e.g., computer login) applications. Another major application on the horizon, that will affect our daily lives, is the national identity (ID) card. Some governments, including Hong Kong, are already developing an ID card that will store each citizen's thumb prints for authentication. Proponents of biometrics technology claim that it will not only protect our private information and our property, but it will also safeguard our lives and our society. However, there is still some concern about the tradeoff between security and privacy as a result of deploying the biometrics technology.

Biometric authentication is by no means a solved problem. Much research needs to be done to improve the perfromance (e.g., false acacptance rate and false reject rate) of these systems. Furthermore, in order for biometric systems to be deployed, they must be easy to use, fast and cost effective.

There is no question that the future of biometrcs is bright. As a pattern recognition problem, it offers challenging research topics as well opportunities to test new algroithms in a variety of high impact application domains.

This book edited by David Zhang brings contains chapters written by leading experts on major applications of biometrics technology in the "*e-*world". These applications include mobile access, network security, smart cards and *e*-commerce. Several systems that utilize multimodal biometrics to increase authentication performance are also discussed. I hope that you will enjoy reading this book and will find some useful and helpful information.

Anil K. Jain

April 2002

Pattern Recognition and Image Processing Lab
Department of Computer Science and Engineering
Michigan State University

PREFACE

In an *e*-world, there is an ever-growing need to authenticate individuals. Biometrics-based authentication is emerging as the most reliable solution. Biometrics require that the person to be identified is physically present at the point-of-authentication and rely on "something which you are or you do" to provide better security, increased efficiency, and improved accuracy. Because one's unique characteristics can not be stolen, forgotten, duplicated, shared or observed, a biometrics-based security system in an *e*-world is nearly impossible to circumvent. Currently, there are various biometrics technologies and systems for authentication, which are either widely used or under development. Some automated biometrics, such as fingerprint authentication and speech verification, have received considerable attention over the last 25 years, and some issues like face recognition and signature authentication have been studied extensively, resulting in successful deployment of biometrics systems in commercial applications.

Designing an automated biometrics system to handle large population authentication, accuracy and reliability of authentication in an *e*-world is a challenging task. Many security applications in an *e*-world can be dealt with by using biometrics solutions. Several examples include: access control, for example, a lock or an airport check-in area; immigration and naturalization; welfare distribution; military identification; banking, for example check cashing, credit card, ATM (automated teller machine); computer login; intruder detection; smart card; multi-media communication; WWW (World-Wide-Web) and an electronic purse; sensor fusion; decision fusion; categorization: for example, age and gender; industrial automation; gesture interpretation; efficient enrollment; audio-visual tracking; stock market; on-line shopping; compact embedded systems and other commercialized services. Unfortunately, because of the diverse application areas, information on these topics is available in many different journals and conference proceedings, and this scattered information causes inconvenience to researchers.

This book provides a collection of sixteen chapters containing tutorial articles and new material describing (in a unified way) the basic concepts, theories and characteristic features of integrating and formulating the different facets of biometrics solutions for authentication with recent developments and significant applicationsin an *e*-world. The articles, written by different experts from all over the world, demonstrate the various ways that this integration can be made to design efficient methodologies, algorithms, architectures and implementations for biometrics-based applications. Except for the first chapter, which is a tutorial that briefly introduces biometrics technologies/systems and applications, the authors of each of the chapters provide extensive information on the developments in their respective areas, while also maintaining cohesiveness with the other chapters. Typical technologies include exploring physical characteristics (e.g., facial features, fingerprints and palmprints authentication) and behavioral characteristics (such as a handwritten signature and voiceprint). This book provides a balanced mixture among technology, system and application. A comprehensive bibliography on the subject is also appended for the convenience of readers.

This book, which is unique in its aims, is intended to be useful to graduate students and researchers in computer science, electrical engineering, systems science, and information technology; not only as a reference book, but also as a text book for some parts of the curriculum. Researchers and practitioners in industry and R&D (research and development) laboratories working in the fields of security system design, biometrics, immigration, law enforcement, control, pattern recognition, and the Internet can also benefit from this book.

I take this opportunity to thank all the contributors for agreeing to write for the book. I owe a vote of thanks to Scott Delman, Susan Lagerstrom-Fife, Lance Wobus and Sharon Palleschi of Kluwer Academic Publisher, for taking initiative in bringing the volume out. The technical support provided by Henry Ko is also acknowledged.

David Zhang

April 2002

Biometrics Research Centre (UGC/ CRC)
The Hong Kong Polytechnic University

Chapter 1

BIOMETRICS APPLICATIONS IN AN E-WORLD

David Zhang
Biometrics Research Centre
Department of Computing
Hong Kong Polytechnic University, Kowloon, Hong Kong
csdzhang@comp.polyu.edu.hk

Abstract   This chapter briefly provides a tutorial that introduces biometrics technologies and systems. Various existing and potential applications in an *e*-world are reviewed, including user access control, smart card, mobile security, Internet/Web-based security, forensics, and so on. Also, all chapters are outlined to explain the organization of this book.

1.1. Biometrics Technologies

The advance of technology is always inspired by practical applications, and the emergence of automatic biometrics technology is exactly rooted in the requirements of *e*-world security applications. Whether this new technology can endure will be decided by how well it can solve security problems. Although biometrics technology is still in the developing stage, it has already been implemented in various applications as the most secure and convenient authentication tool because it relies on characteristics that cannot be borrowed, stolen, or forgotten, and where forgery is practically impossible. Along with the widespread applications of biometrics, more research funds and more attention are being given to this increasingly important technology [1-4,19-22,24,32-35].

Biometrics refers to the automatic authentication of a person based on his/her physiological or behavioral characteristics [19,21]. Today, a variety of biometrics technologies are used; each of them has its own particular strengths that make it more appropriate for certain types of applications. The major biometrics technologies involve finger-scan, voice-scan, facial-scan, palm-scan, iris-scan, and signature-scan, as well as integrated authentication technologies.

● **Finger-Scan Technology**

Finger-scan biometrics is based on the distinctive characteristics of a human fingerprint. A fingerprint image is read from a capture device, the features are then extracted from the image, and a template is finally created. If appropriate precautions are followed, the result is a very accurate means of authentication [7-8,23,25,27,39-41]. Fingerprint matching techniques can be placed into two categories: minutiae-based and correlation based [25]. Minutiae-based techniques first find minutiae points and then map their relative placement on the finger. However, there are some difficulties with this approach when the fingerprint image is of low quality because accurate extraction of minutiae points is difficult. Also, this method does not take into account the global pattern of ridges and furrows. In comparison, the correlation-based method is able to overcome the problems of a minutiae-based approach. However, correlation-based techniques require the precise location of a registration point and are affected by image translation and rotation. Fingerprint verification may be a good choice for in-house systems that operate in a controlled environment, where users can be given adequate explanation and training. It is not surprising that the workstation access application area seems to be based almost exclusively on fingerprints, due to the relatively low cost, small size, and ease of integration of fingerprint authentication devices. Chapters 2, 11 and 12 in this book introduce the related finger-scan technologies.

● **Voice-Scan Technology**

Of all the human traits used in biometrics, the one that humans learn to recognize first is voice characteristics [2-5,19,21,26,29]. Speech recognition systems can be divided into two categories: text-dependent and text-independent systems. In text-dependent systems, the user is expected to use the same text (keyword or sentence) during training and recognition sessions. A text independent system does not use the training text during recognition sessions. Both systems perform the following tasks: feature extraction, similarity analysis and selection. Voice biometrics has the most potential for growth, because it does not require new hardware — most PCs (Personal Computers) nowadays already come with a microphone. However, poor quality and ambient noise can affect verification. In addition, the set-up procedure has often been more complicated than with other biometrics, leading to the perception that voice verification is not user friendly. Therefore, voice authentication software needs to be improved. However, voice-scan may be integrated to finger-scan technology. Because many people see finger scanning as a higher form of authentication, voice biometrics will most likely be relegated to replace or enhance PINs (Personal Identification Numbers), passwords, or account names. Speaker identification technologies are given in Chapters 5, 12 and 14.

● **Facial-Scan Technology**

Similar to finger-scan and voice-scan biometrics, there are various methods by which facial-scan technology recognizes people [2-4,19,21,27,30,50-51]. All the methods share certain commonalities, such as emphasizing those sections of the face which are less susceptible to alteration, including the upper outlines of the eye sockets, the areas surrounding the cheekbones, and the sides of the mouth. Most technologies are resistant to moderate changes in hairstyle, as they do not utilize areas of the face located near the hairline. All of the primary technologies are designed to be robust enough to conduct one-to-many searches, that is, to locate a single face from a database of thousands, or even hundreds of thousands, of faces (see Chapters 4, 12 and 13). Face authentication analyzes facial characteristics, which requires a digital camera to capture a facial image of a user. This technique has attracted considerable interest, although many people do not completely understand its capabilities. Some vendors have made extravagant claims, which are very difficult, if not impossible, to substantiate in practice for facial recognition devices. Because facial scanning needs an extra peripheral not customarily included with basic PCs, it is more of a niche market for network authentication. However, the casino industry has capitalized on this technology to create a facial database of fraudsters for quick detection by security personnel.

● **Palm-Scan Technology**

Although research on the issues of fingerprint identification and voice recognition have drawn considerable attention over the last 25 years, and recently issues on face recognition have been studied extensively, there are still some limitations to the existing applications. For example, some people have their fingerprints worn-away due to the work they do with their hands and some people are born with unclear fingerprints. Face and voice based identification systems are less accurate and easier to overcome using a mimic. Efforts on improving the current personal identification methods will continue, and meanwhile new methods are under investigation. Unlike simple hand geometry that measures hand size and finger length, a palmprint approach is concerned with the inner surface of a hand, and looks in particular at line patterns and surface shape. A palm is covered with the same kind of skin as the fingertips, and it is also larger, hence it is quite natural to think of using a palmprint to recognize a person (see Chapter 10 for more details). Authentication of identity using a palmprint line is a challenging task, because line features (referred to as principle lines), wrinkles and ridges on a palm, are not individually descriptive enough for identification. The problem can be tackled by combining various features, such as texture, to attain a more robust verification [21,42-45]. As a new attempt, and a necessary complement to the existing biometrics techniques, palmprint authentication is considered part of the biometrics family.

● Iris-Scan Technology

Iris authentication technology leverages the unique features of the human iris to provide an unmatched identification technology. The algorithms used in iris recognition are so accurate that the entire planet could be enrolled in an iris database with only a small chance of false acceptance or false rejection [2-5,19,21,37-38,46-49]. Iris identification technology is a tremendously accurate biometric. An iris-based biometric involves analyzing features found in the colored ring of tissue that surrounds the pupil. The Iris-scan, which is undoubtedly the least intrusive of the eye-related biometrics, uses a fairly conventional camera and requires no close contact between the user and the iris-reader. In addition, it has the potential for higher than average template-matching performance. Iris biometrics work with eyeglasses in place, and it is one of the few devices that can work well in identification mode. Ease of use and system integration have not traditionally been strong points with iris scanning devices, but people can expect improvements in these areas as new products emerge.

● Signature-Scan Technology

Signature verification analyzes the way a user signs her/his name [2-5,19,21]. Signing features such as speed, velocity, and pressure are as important as the finished signature's static shape. Signature verification enjoys a synergy with existing processes that other biometrics do not. People are familiar with signatures as a means of (transaction-related) identity verification, and most people would consider nothing unusual in extending this process to include biometrics. Signature verification devices are reasonably accurate in operation, and obviously lead to applications where a signature is already an accepted identifier. Surprisingly, relatively few significant signature applications have emerged compared with the other biometrics methodologies. Some useful signature technologies are shown in Chapters 8 and 12.

● Multiple Authentication Technologies

From an application standpoint, widespread deployment of a user authentication solution requires support for an enterprise's heterogeneous environment. Often, this requires a multi-faceted approach to security, in which combinations of security solutions are deployed. An authentication solution should seamlessly extend the organization's existing security technologies. In this way, we are now interested in understanding how multiple biometrics technologies can be combined together, as well as what possible improvements this approach can produce [2,5,11,16,21,27,30]. One of the main problems for researchers of multiple biometrics is the scarcity of true multi-modal databases for testing their algorithms. Perhaps the most important resource available today is the extended M2VTS database, which is associated with the specific Lausanne protocol for measuring the performance of verification tasks. This database contains audio-visual material from 295 subjects [52]. Some related technologies for multiple biometrics are given in Chapters 9, 12, 15 and 16. As a typical example in *e-commerce* applications, a system design using integrated biometrics technologies is shown in Figure 1.1.

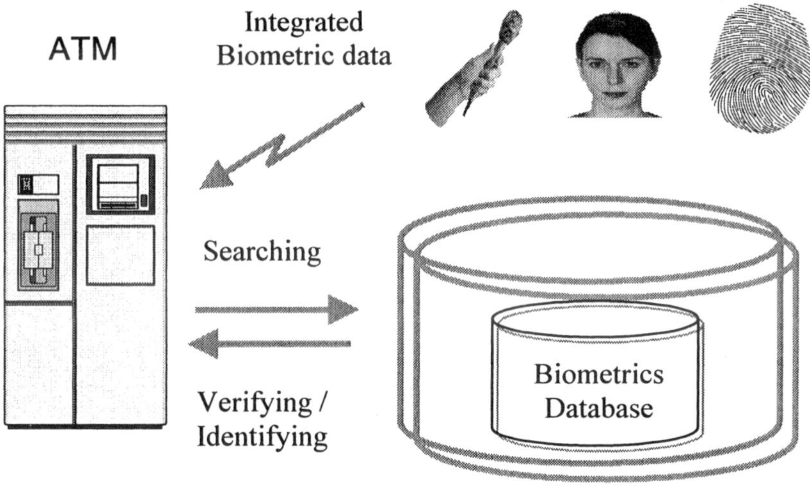

Figure 1.1. A typical system design using integrated biometrics technologies.

1.2. Biometrics Systems

The performance of a biometrics system is significantly dependent on many factors such as humidity, light, noise, the end user's attitude and familiarity with the system. Therefore, the most accurate testing should be performed in the real working environment. High levels of accuracy in one application do not qualify a system for an entirely different application. The quoted performance figures of a biometrics system are only relevant to the specific application in which they were quoted. Each application is widely different in terms of system workload and throughput, environmental factors and other variables [2,5,17-18,33,36]. For example, a fingerprint verification system may have a very high accuracy in a university restaurant although it may work badly in a village where most people have heavily worn fingerprints. However, the argument is not that the performance rules, the False Accept Rate (FAR) and False Reject Rate (FRR), are meaningless, but that the two rates may vary in diverse operating environments. FAR and FRR values provided by the system developer can be used as a guide to understand a system's general ability. In summary, a biometrics system's performance is application sensitive, and how to adapt a biometrics system to a particular application needs significant consideration.

Before applying biometrics systems, we must have a clear understanding of the business drivers. What is the main goal of the project? What are the constraints of the project, deadlines, budgets, etc.? What security level is needed? What is the current system? What are the weaknesses of the current system? Is it necessary to apply biometrics? Can biometrics solve the existing problems? Are there any other choices to secure the system? Will biometrics bring any difficulties into the system? Can biometrics integrate well with the current system? Will users of the system accept this new style of work? In summary, these many questions aim to make sure that biometrics is really needed, and this is the first step in applying this new technology.

Factors that are considered in biometrics system evaluation include:

- **Vulnerability to Fraud**

Biometrics systems aim at providing a high-level of security, so whether a biometrics trait is hard to mimic is an essential consideration in construction of these applications. In this respect, we should also be aware of future issues; for example, some movies depict defrauding a biometrics system via gouging out a victim's eye or severing a finger.

- **Ease of Use**

One springboard for the widespread adoption of biometrics system is to appeal to the general public in getting rid of the bother of remembering tens of passwords and keeping strings of keys. Therefore such a system should be really user friendly, instead of bringing greater problems than for example, losing a door key.

- **Intrusive to Human Beings**

Certain biometrics systems are seen to be more intrusive than others. For example, retina capturing has to expose eyes to a bright beam of light, while voice seems non-intrusive. However, sometimes a higher accuracy may be gained using a more intrusive approach. Places that need very high levels of security have to choose the intrusive methods. For example, workers at a nuclear power plant would probably accept the need for a degree of intrusiveness because security is such an important issue.

- **Applicability**

Physical characteristics vary and some individuals will not be able to use a biometrics system. No single biometrics system can capture and match biometrics data for the global population in all circumstances. Human beings are as diverse and unpredictable as the environments in which the systems operate. A few individuals have damaged fingers, limbs, voice boxes or eyes. This may make verification and identification using a single biometrics approach impossible; but it may be possible using multiple biometrics approaches. Also, it does not mean that a single biometrics approach is unable to perform an application where a minority of people cannot have a biometrics sample captured. It is simply the case that the minority cannot use the system automatically and must be handled in an alternative manner.

- **Speed of Verification**

Response time is a key issue for any computer system, and it also the case for biometrics systems.

- **Size of Storage for One Biometrics Template**

For an identification system, this factor directly affects the overall database size and searching speed. For a verification system, in cases where the registered template is stored in some special media such as in barcodes, magnetic cards or smart cards, this factor could determine the cost of a card.

- **Long-Term Stability**

The biometrics feature chosen to identify a person in a system should be stable for at least a while longer than the system is planned to be used, so that the system can work correctly during the period when it is active.

- **Maturity of Technology**

Some biometrics features such as a fingerprint and a signature have been used for a long time and their accuracies have been proved widely. Meanwhile, other biometrics such as face and voice are newcomers in this area and need to be proved in real-time applications.

1.3. Biometrics Applications

We have entered the age of universal electronic connectivity so that our daily life has a close relationship to various "*e*-things", such as *e*-commerce (conceptually shown in Figure 1.2), *e*-library, *e*-government, etc. In such an *e*-world, more and more activities should be related to security services. With rapid progress in electronics and Internet commerce, there has been a growing need for secure transaction processing using various biometrics technologies [5,9,11-15,18,21,52-94]. As a summary, some applications in an *e*-world are listed in Figure 1.3, where two basic types are verification (one-to-one matching) and identification (one-to-many matching).

Figure 1.2.   Electronic and Internet commerce in an *e*-world.

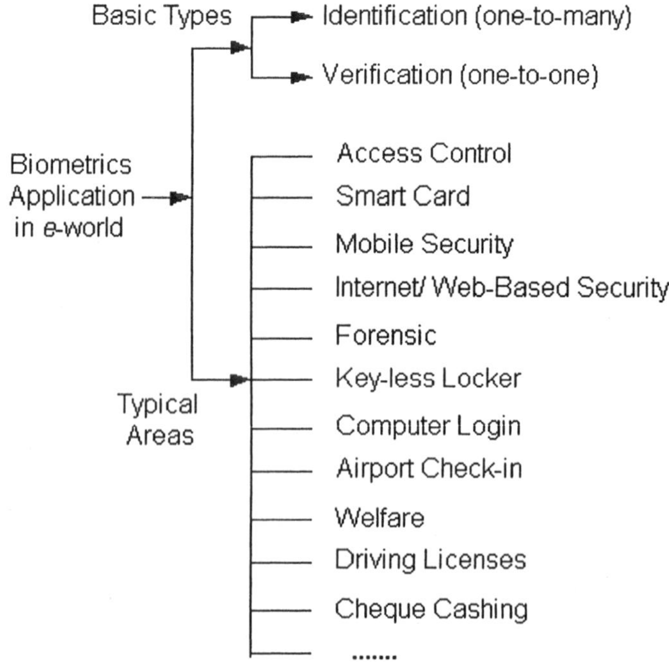

Figure 1.3.   Various biometrics applications in an *e*-world.

1.3.1 Current Applications

Some typical biometrics applications in an *e*-world are listed as follows.

- **Access Control**

For decades, many highly secure environments have used biometric technology for entry access. Today, the primary application of biometrics is in physical security to control access to secure locations (room entrance or building entrance) [1-2,5,9]. In addition, it shows that virtual access is the application that will provide the critical mass that is necessary to move biometrics for network and computer access from the realms of science-fiction devices to regular system components. At the same time, user demands for virtual access will raise public awareness of the security risks and lower resistance to the use of biometrics. A few examples of access control are given in Chapters 2, 5 and 13 in this book.

- **Internet Security**

In an *e*-world, more and more activities are related to use of the Internet. With its rapid development, have also come growing problems, such as with hackers and electronic eavesdropping. These problems threaten the prosperity and productivity of corporations and individuals. As a result, Internet security using biometrics technologies is increasingly important [14,18]. Some typical applications related to this topic are also contained in Chapters 6, 9 and 14.

- ***E*-Commerce Applications**

E-commerce developers are exploring the use of biometrics and smart cards to more accurately verify a trading party's identity (see Chapters 3 and 10). For example, many banks are interested in this combination to better authenticate customers and ensure non-repudiation of online banking, trading, and purchasing transactions [5,9,13]. Many other application issues in *e*-commerce are also given in Chapter 8.

In addition, banks may embrace various aspects of biometrics technology. Automated Teller Machines (see Figure 1.1) and transactions at the point of sale, telephone banking, Internet banking and many other banking applications are vulnerable to fraud and can be secured by biometrics. Figure 1.4 shows that we can set up various possible matching between biometrics technologies and different banking services.

- **Computer Systems**

Biometrics technology binds the authority directly with the end user and removes the need for various passwords. Voice and fingerprint recognition are now the most promising techniques in this area, and demonstrated biometrics technology for authentication solutions with portable computing devices has already been shown at the recent Comdex Chicago Show. This technology will provide enterprise systems that need to incorporate portable or hand-held devices with the ability to be secure. The company now also offers a portable fingerprint reader for the Compaq, HP and Casio hand-held units where a customer can choose authentication with or without a smart card.

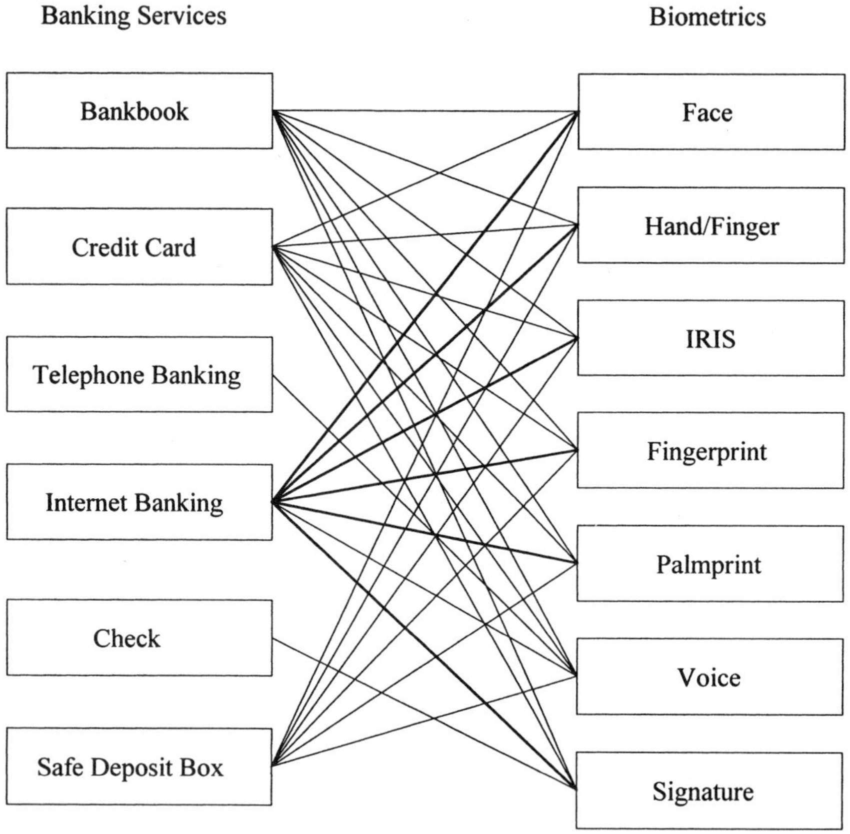

Figure 1.4. Potential biometrics applications in banking.

● **Immigration**

Terrorism, drug trafficking, illegal immigration and an increasing throughput of legitimate travelers are putting a strain on immigration authorities throughout the world. It is essential that these authorities can quickly and automatically process law-abiding travelers and identify the law-breakers. Biometrics is being employed in a number of diverse applications to make this possible. The US (United States) Immigration and Naturalization Service is a major user and evaluator of a number of biometrics systems. These systems are currently in place throughout the US to automate the flow of legitimate travelers and deter illegal immigrants. Elsewhere biometrics is used in the imagination activities of countries such as Australia, Bermuda, Germany, Malaysia and Taiwan.

- **National Identity**

Biometrics is beginning to assist governments as they record population growth, identify citizens and prevent fraud occurring during local and national elections. Often this involves storing a biometrics template on a card that in turn acts as a national identity document. Finger scanning is particularly strong in this area and schemes are already under way in Jamaica, Lebanon, The Philippines and South Africa.

- **Telephone Systems**

Global communication has truly opened up over the past decade, while telephone companies are under attack from increasing fraud. Once again, biometrics is being called upon to defend against this onslaught. Speaker ID (identification) is the technique of recognizing people by their voices. It is obviously well suited to the telephone environment and such technology is quickly becoming popular in these new markets.

- **Time, Attendance and Monitoring**

At present, some factories and companies are using punch cards to monitor the movement of their employees. When they come to work, they need to punch a hole in their cards and punch another hole when they leave. This kind of thing can be assisted by biometrics. With a biometrics system, employees may press their fingers onto a small platform when they arrive or leave. This may prevent any form of cheating. However, using this kind of system to monitor an employee's movements is still an open question because some people believe that it may undermine an employee's right to privacy.

- **Covert Surveillance**

One of the more challenging research areas involves using biometrics for covert surveillance. Using facial and body recognition technologies, researchers hope to use biometrics to automatically identify known suspects entering buildings or traversing crowded security areas such as airports. The use of biometrics for covert identification as opposed to authentication must overcome technical challenges such as simultaneously identifying multiple subjects in a crowd and working with uncooperative subjects. In these situations, devices cannot count on consistency in pose, viewing angle, or distance from the detector.

1.3.2 Potential Applications

Biometrics applications are not limited to the areas mentioned in the last section. In fact, provided that a system needs to recognize people, it can incorporate biometrics. In the law enforcement community, matching fingerprint images or parts of palmprint images is the most common method to identify suspects and bring guilty criminals to justice. Also we have seen many times in the movies where the police ask the witness to describe the criminal's physical facial features such as length, width, hair color, shape of the face, etc.; and then reconstruct a picture for the criminal and search through a database of facial images. In some movies, we may also see a criminal telephone the victim and the police record the voice of the criminal and search for the criminal according to voice identification. All these scenes are examples of identifying people using their unique physical features (e.g., fingerprints, palmprint, face, etc.) or behavioral trait (e.g., voice) and automatic biometrics can help in all these examples. It is not difficult to understand why the law enforcement community is the largest biometrics user group. Police forces throughout the world are using automatic fingerprint identification systems to assist in crime detection. There are a lot of biometrics vendors earning significant revenues in this area [9,11-15,21].

Businessmen always play an important role in developing markets for a new technology. When automatic biometrics technology becomes more and more mature in the law enforcement area, it is introduced into civilian applications by the biometrics product vendors. Usually, all civilian biometrics applications are some kind of access control. We may simply classify all the civilian biometrics applications as physical access control and data access control. Physical access control ensures only authorized individuals can physically access certain secure areas while data access control secures the access to sensitive data. Securing benefit systems from fraud, preventing illegal immigrants from entering a country or prisoners from leaving a prison, all belong to physical access control. Internet banking, telephone banking, ATM, and Web stores belong to data access control. Automatic biometrics is a rapidly expanding market. Fraud is an ever-increasing problem and security is becoming a necessity in many walks of life. Civilian access control, therefore, will not be restricted to the application areas mentioned above and it will branch out to other profitable market opportunities, as soon as a suitable need is identified.

1.4. Organization of the Book

In Chapter 2, an overview of fingerprint recognition is given. First, we present a number of applications for fingerprint recognition: physical access control, computer login, key-less locks and biometrics smart cards. Next, current fingerprint recognition technology and algorithms are introduced, as well as various new methods; technical challenges and directions for solving them are presented. Finally, it is shown that these new methods can be used to improve the performance of the selected applications.

Chapter 3 reviews the current advances and designs of biometrics for an electronic purse. In particular, the architecture of a smart card and its security issues related to commercial applications are addressed in this chapter. As a result of the rapid development of technology, the deployment of a biometrics electronic purse has moved from the laboratory to the commercial world.

Face recognition has long been a goal of computer vision, but only in recent years has reliable automated face recognition become a realistic target of biometrics researchers. In Chapter 4, the field of face recognition is reviewed, including an analysis of its strengths and weaknesses, and a description of the applications where the technology is currently being deployed and where it shows future potential. As a typical example, the IBM face recognition system and its application domains are given.

In Chapter 5, the authors envisage a bilateral user authentication framework for applications in wireless environments, which attempts to derive maximum synergy from biometrics and non-biometrics speech technologies without loss of their easy-to-access properties. Under this framework, some experiments using enabling component technologies have been conducted and the simulation results indicate that the techniques to support this framework are ready to build such an authentication system for applications to personalized mobile access.

Chapter 6 focuses on some important Internet Security issues that involve biometrics, that is, biometrics applications and services in the Internet. First of all, the authors present some important aspects regarding the security problems in telecommunications networks and the Internet. Then, a brief presentation of biometrics technologies with emphasis on biometrics encryption and standardization is given, as well as a description of a biometrics application in the Internet, named the Personal Identification Network.

The issue of how forensic scientists must report their conclusions to the judge or jury when biometrics identification techniques are used is an interesting topic. Experts must convert system identification scores into meaningful values that are useful to the Court. In this sense, the Bayesian approach is firmly established as a valid framework for any forensic discipline. In Chapter 7, the authors show the different nature of system outputs when commercial or forensic approaches are applied. A complete example of forensic characterization reporting in the speaker recognition field is also introduced.

The astonishing growth of the Internet and Intranet raises the new challenge of *e*-commerce security. With attempts to look for a low cost biometrics method as an enhancement of personal identification in the network, Chapter 8 introduces a typical system for dynamic signature verification in the Internet and Intranet, which involves such processes as dynamic signature data acquisition through the network, global and local feature extraction and matching, combined feature comparison for verification and distance measures for recognition. Some applications of on-line signature verification are also given.

In Chapter 9, the authors apply biometrics technology to the security of network access in order to overcome the limitations of the current existing password-based authentication services on the Internet. To tackle the challenge of the integration of multiple biometrics features within a single platform to satisfy the requirements of various identification purposes, a new approach to personal identification with multi-modal biometrics and data warehousing techniques is defined in this chapter. The experimental results demonstrate the feasibility of the proposed approach to network security with *e*-commerce applications.

Chapter 10 denotes a biometrics-based smart card security system by utilizing an individual's unique, reliable and stable physical characteristic – that is, a palmprint, for identification and verification. This is considered as a better solution to medium level security systems. The general process and key issues of on-line palmprint identification technology are developed. In addition, the smart card system analysis is developed and practical applications are proposed.

Chapter 11 describes secure fingerprint authentication after analyzing a pattern recognition-based threat model of a biometrics authentication system. Several solutions are proposed to alleviate the threats using conventional encryption and using novel techniques that exploit the richness of biometrics data. The authors argue that an authentication scheme with both smart card and biometrics improves the overall security of a system. The proposed methods are applicable in many application areas, including system security, *e*-commerce security, point-of-sale systems, point of entry/exit and point of access.

In Chapter 12, several biometrics recognition systems, based on voice, fingerprints, face and signature are presented. The description of the state-of-the-art technologies regarding these biometrics characteristics is presented. Minutiae extraction-based fingerprint matching, GMM-based speaker verification, on-line HMM-based signature verification, and PCA- or LDA-based face recognition are quoted. The chapter also focuses on multimodality and data fusion in biometrics systems. Finally, some application strategies and real-world demonstrations are described.

In Chapter 13, the research issues and state-of-the-art of face verification for access control are discussed. Starting from analyzing a typical face verification system for access control, the dominant technologies in the field are then developed. Some available commercial systems are also defined, and three standard performance evaluations, FERET, XM2VTS and FRVT2000, are introduced for readers to understand the statement of technology and application achievement in face verification.

The aim of Chapter 14 is to integrate biometrics technology into a Web application. As an example, the SpeakEZ Web Authentication Service provides a service-oriented solution for integrating speaker verification into an *e*-business application. Rather than forcing businesses to build monolithic applications to accomplish this added layer of security, business are able to simply utilize the Web-service to authenticate users of their *e*-business application, which provides a fast and effective means for incorporating biometrics authentication into existing and new Web-based applications.

Chapter 15 investigates a wide range of questions, including costs, compatibility, scalability, and user acceptance in biometrics IT security and *e*-commerce environments. It suggests that understanding biometrics system performance requires analysis of more than the false match rates and false non-match rates that are generally provided by the biometrics vendors. Two generally overlooked performance metrics may be critical determinants of a system's performance. These two metrics can be combined into a single metric known as the Ability to Verify (ATV), a performance measure with a direct impact on system costs, security, and convenience. Testing shows that many ATV rates can vary substantially from technology to technology, and from biometrics device to biometrics device.

The last chapter (16) proposes a framework that makes use of signal- and image-processing algorithms, together with pattern recognition techniques, which is applied to solve the problem of biometrics pattern recognition in a unified way. In general, this problem can be broken down into the following taxonomy: sensors, extractors, experts and the supervisor. Using this general schema, biometrics systems with similar fundamental problem characteristics can be processed. Based on the framework, a hybrid biometrics authentication prototype that makes use of upright frontal face-scans and text-dependent voice-scans is implemented.

Acknowledgements

The author would like to thank Dr. Jane You, Dr. Jiannong Cao and other team members in the Biometrics Research Centre for their kind collaborations. Our research is partially supported by the UGC/CRC fund, the Hong Kong Government, and the Central Fund of The Hong Kong Polytechnic University.

References

[1]   International Biometrics Industry Association (IBIA): http://www.ibia.org/.

[2]   International Biometrics Group (IBG): http://www.biometricgroup.com/

[3]   The Biometrics Consortium: http://www.biometrics.org/.

[4]   Biometrics research: http://biometrics.cse.msu.edu/.

[5]   S. Liu and M. Silverman. A Practical Guide to Biometric Security Technology, IEEE Computer Society, IT Pro – Security:

http://www.computer.org/itpro/homepage/Jan_Feb/security3.htm/.

[6]   East Shore Technologies: http://www.east-shore.com/

[7]   L. Hong, Y. Wan and A. Jain. Fingerprint Image Enhancement Algorithm and Performance Evaluation, IEEE Transactions on Pattern Analysis and Machine Intelligence, vol. 20, no. 8, pages 777-789, 1998.

[8]   J. Berry. The History and Development of Fingerprinting, in Advances in Fingerprint Technology, (H.C. Lee and R.E. Gaensslen, ed.s), CRC Press, Florida, pages 1-39, 1994.

[9]   Biometrics Collaboration Research Centre:

http://www.comp.polyu.edu.hk/~biometrics/.

[10]   The Biometrics Consulting Group: http://biometric-consulting.com/.

[11]   Association for Biometrics (AfB): http://www.afb.org.uk/.

[12]   Australian Biotechnology Association: http://vpac13.vpac.org/ausbiotech/.

[13]   Financial Services Technology Consortium: http://www.fstc.org/

[14]   Security Industry Association (SIA): http://www.siaonline.org/.

[15]   The Human Identification Project: http://www.asti.dost.gov.ph/.

[16]   GSA's SmartGov: http://policyworks.gov/smartgov/.

[17]   Biometrics in Human Services User Group: http://www.bioapi.org/.

[18]   Biometrics and Security: http://www.infosyssec.org/infosyssec/biomet1.htm/.

[19]   A.K. Jain, R. Bolle and S. Pankanti, (eds). Biometrics: Personal Identification in Networked Society, Kluwer Academic Publishers, Boston, 1999.

[20]   B. Miller. Vital Signs of Identity, IEEE Spectrum vol. 32, no. 2, pages 22-30, 1994.

[21]   D. Zhang. Automated Biometrics: Technologies & Systems, Kluwer Academic Publishers, Boston, 2000.

[22]   S. Pankanti, R.M. Bolle and A. Jain. Biometrics: The Future of Identification, IEEE Computer, vol. 33, no. 2, pages 46-49, 2000.

[23]   M. Eleccion. Automatic Fingerprint Identification, IEEE Spectrum vol. 10, no. 9, pages 36-45, 1973.

[24]   G. Lawton. Biometrics: A New Era in Security. Computer, pages 16-18, 1998.

[25]   A. Jain, L. Hong and R. Bolle. On-line Fingerprint Verification, IEEE Transactions on Pattern Analysis and Machine Intelligence, vol. 19, no. 4, pages 302-314, 1997.

[26]   J.P. Campbell. Speaker Recognition: A Tutorial, Proc. of IEEE, vol. 85, no. 9, pages 1437-1462, 1997.

[27]   L. Hong et al. Integrating Faces and Fingerprints for Personal Identification, IEEE Trans. on PAMI, vol. 20, no. 12, pages 1295-1307, 1998.

[28]   J. Daugman. High Confidence Visual Recognition of Persons by a Test of Statistical Independence, IEEE Trans. on PAMI vol. 15, pages 1148-1161, 1993.

[29]   Y. Zhang and D. Zhang. A Novel Text-independent Speaker Verification Method based on the Global Speaker Model, IEEE Trans. On Systems, Man and Cybernetics (Part A), vol. 30, no. 5, pages 598-602, 2000.

[30]   D. Sims. Biometrics Recognition: Our Hands, Eyes and Faces Give Us Away, IEEE Computer Graphics and Applications, 0272-17-16/94, 1994.

[31]   J.D. Woodward. Biometrics: Privacy's Foe or Privacy's Friend?, Proc. IEEE Special Issue on Automated Biometrics, vol. 85, no. 9, pages 1480-1492, 1997.

[32]   A. Davis. The Body as Password, Wired, July 1997.

[33]   D.R. Richards. Rules of Thumb For Biometrics Systems, Security Manage, Oct. 1, 1995.

[34]   G. Lawton. Biometrics: A New Era in Security, IEEE Computer, pages 16-18, Aug. 1998.

[35]   R. Mandelbaum. Vital Signs of Identity, IEEE Spectrum, pages 22-30, Feb. 1994.

[36]   M. Golfarelli, D. Maio and D. Maltoni. On the Error-Reject Trade-Off in Biometrics Verification Systems, IEEE Trans. Pattern Analysis and Machine Intelligence, vol. 19, no. 7, pages 786-796, 1997.

[37]   R.P. Wildes. Iris Recognition: An Emerging Biometrics Technology, Proc. IEEE Special Issue on Automated Biometrics, vol. 85, no. 9, pages 1348-1363, 1997.

[38]   C. Seal, D. McCartney and M. Gifford. Iris Recognition for User Validation, British Telecommunications Engineering, vol. 16, July 1997.

[39]   A.K. Jain, H. Lin, P.Harath and R. Bolle. An Identity-Authentication System Using Fingerprints, Proc. IEEE Special Issue on Automated Biometrics, vol. 85, no. 9, pages 1365-1388, 1997.

[40]   A.K. Jain, S. Prabhakar, L. Hong and S. Pankanti. Filterbank-based Fingerprint Matching, IEEE Transactions on Image Processing, vol. 9, no. 5, pages 846-859, 2000.

[41]   A.R. Roddy and J.D. Stosz. Fingerprint Features: Statistical Analysis and System Performance Estimates, Proc. IEEE Special Issue on Automated Biometrics, vol. 85, no. 9, pages 1390-1421, 1997.

[42] D. Zhang and W. Shu. Two Novel Characteristics in Palmprint Verification: Datum Point Invariance and Line Feature Matching. Pattern Recognition 32(4), 691-702, 1999.

[43] J. You, W. Li and D. Zhang. Hierarchical Palmprint Identification via Multiple Feature Extraction, Pattern Recognition 35, 4, 847-859, 2002.

[44] N. Duta, A.K. Jain and K. Mardia. Matching of Palmprints, Pattern Recognition Letters, vol. 23, no. 4, pages 477-485, Feb 2002.

[45] W. Shu and D. Zhang. Automated Personal Identification by Palmprint. Optical Engineering 37(8), 2359-2362, 1998.

[46] J. Daugman. High Confidence Visual Recognition of Persons by a Test of Statistical Independence, IEEE Transactions on Pattern Analysis and Machine Intelligence, vol. 15, no. 11, pages 1148-1161, 1993.

[47] M. Negin, T.A. Jr, M. Salganicoff, T.A. Camus, U.M. von Seelen, P.L. Venetianer and G.G. Zhang. An Iris Biometric System for Public and Personal Use Computer, vol. 33, no. 2, 2000.

[48] G.O. Williams. Iris Recognition, IEEE Aerospace and Electronics Systems Magazine, vol.12, no.4, pages 23-29, April 1997.

[49] C. Seal, M. Gifford and D. McCartney. Iris Recognition for User Validation, British Telecommunications Engineering Journal, vol. 16, pages 113-117, July 1997.

[50] B. Duc, S. Fischer and J. Bigun. Face Authentication with Gabor Information on Deformable Graphs," IEEE Transactions on Image Processing, vol. 8, no. 4, pages 504-516, 1999.

[51] Y. Adini, Y. Moses and S. Ullman. Face Recognition: The Problem of Compensation for Changes in Illumination Direction, IEEE Transactions on Pattern Analysis and Machine Intelligence, vol. 19, no. 7, pages 721-732, 1997.

[52] R. Sanchez-Reillo and A. Gonzalez-Marcos. Access Control System with Hand Geometry Verification and Smart Cards, IEEE Aerospace and Electronics Systems Magazine, vol. 15, no. 2, pages 45-48, Feb. 2000.

[53] M. Negin, T.A. Chmielewski, Jr., M. Salganicoff, U.M. von Seelen and P.L. Venetainer. An Iris Biometric System for Public and Personal Use Computer, vol. 33, no. 2, pages 70-75, Feb. 2000.

[54] K. Farrell and W. Mistretta. VeriNet Web-speaker Verification for the World Wide Web, Multimedia and Expo, IEEE International Conference, vol. 3, pages 1497-1500, 2000.

[55] B. Ruiz-Mezcua, D. Garcia-Plaza, C. Fernandez, P. Domingo-Garcia and F. Fernandez. Biometrics Verification in a Real Environment, Security Technology. In Proc. of IEEE 33rd Annual International Carnahan Conference, pages 243-246, 1999.

[56] R. Sanchez-Reillo and A. Gonzalez-Marcos. Access Control System with Hand Geometry Verification and Smart Cards, Security Technology. In Proc. of IEEE 33rd Annual International Carnahan Conference, pages 485-487, 1999.

[57] M. Snyderwine and D. Murray. O'Hare International Airport's Air Cargo Security Access System, Security Technology. In Proc. of IEEE 33rd Annual International Carnahan Conference, pages 210-226, 1999.

[58] A. Wahab, E.C. Tan, and S.M. Heng. Biometrics Electronic Purse, TENCON. In Proc. of the IEEE Region 10 Conference, vol. 2, pages 958-961, 1999.

[59] S. Narayanaswamy, Hu Jianying and R. Kashi. User Interface for a PCS Smart Phone, Multimedia Computing and Systems. In Proc. of IEEE International Conference on, vol. 1, pages 777-781, 1999.

[60] M. Tistarelli, A. Lagorio, M. Jentile and Grosso. Design of a Vision System for Identity Verification, E. Systems Sciences, HICSS-32. In Proc. of the 32nd Annual Hawaii, International Conference, page 9, 1999.

[61] L. Boves and E. den Os. Speaker Recognition in Telecom Applications, Interactive Voice Technology for Telecommunications Applications, IVTTA. In Proc. of IEEE 4th Workshop, pages 203-208, 1998.

[62] G.I. Davida, Y. Frankel and B.J. Matt. On Enabling Secure Applications through Off-line Biometric Identification, Security and Privacy. In Proc. of IEEE Symposium, pages 148-157, 1998.

[63] M.C. Fairhurst. Signature Verification Revisited: Promoting Practical Exploitation of Biometric Technology, Electronics & Communication Engineering Journal, vol. 9 no. 6, pages 273-280, Dec. 1997.

[64] Weicheng Shen, M. Surette and R. Khanna. Evaluation of Automated Biometrics-based Identification and Verification Systems, proceedings of the IEEE , vol. 85, no. 9, pages 1464-1478, Sept. 1997.

[65] J.L. Wayman. A Generalized Biometric Identification System Model, Signals, Systems & Computers, Conference Record of the Thirty-First Asilomar Conference, vol. 1, pages 291-295, 1998.

[66] C.J.H. Stretton. Technical Access Control Systems, The Development of a Corporate Security Strategy, Security Technology. In Proc. of IEEE 31st Annual International Carnahan Conference, pages 50-57, 1997.

[67] S.Y. Kung, Shang-Hung Lin and Ming Fang. A Neural Network Approach to Face/palm Recognition, Neural Networks for Signal Processing. In Proc. of the IEEE Workshop, pages 323-332, 1995.

[68] B. Javidi. The Role of Optics and Photonics in Encryption, Anti-counterfeiting, and Security Systems (Parts I and II), Lasers and Electro-Optics Society Annual Meeting. In Proc. of the 8th Annual Meeting Conference, vol. 1, IEEE, vol. 2, pages 255-256, 1995.

[69] D. Sims. Biometric Recognition: Our Hands, Eyes, and Faces Give us Away, IEEE Computer Graphics and Applications, vol. 14, no. 5, pages 14-15, Sept. 1994.

[70] D. Sims. Decriminalizing the Fingerprint, IEEE Computer Graphics and Applications, vol. 14, no. 4, pages 15-16, July 1994.

[71] C.G. Leedham and V.K. Sagar. Using Forensic Handwriting Analysis Techniques to Enhance Automatic Handwritten Script Recognition and Processing, Handwriting Analysis and Recognition: A European Perspective, IEE European Workshop, pages 2/1 -2/3, 1994.

[72]   D.R. Weiss. Smart Gun Technologies: One Method of Eliminating Unauthorized Firearm Use, Security Technology. In Proc. of IEEE 28th Annual International Carnahan Conference, pages 169-172, 1994.

[73]   M. Brown and S.J. Rogers. A Practical Approach to User Authentication, Computer Security Applications Conference. In Proc. of 10th Annual, pages 108-116, 1994.

[74]   R.P. Wildes, J.C. Asmuth, G.L. Green, S.C. Hsu, R.J. Kolczynski, J.R. Matey and S.E. McBride. A System for Automated Iris Recognition, Applications of Computer Vision. In Proc. of the Second IEEE Workshop, pages 121-128, 1994.

[75]   J. Carter and M. Nixon. An Integrated Biometric Database, Electronic Images and Image Processing in Security and Forensic Science, IEE Colloquium, pages 8/1-8/6, 1990.

[76]   J. Rice and B. Goodwin. Biometric Access and Use Systems, Vehicle Security, IEE Colloquium, 1990, pages 6/1 -6/6, 1990.

[77]   E.C. Driscoll and R.C. Fowler. A Comparison of Centralized versus Distributed Architectures in Biometric Access Control Systems, Security Technology. In Proc. of International Carnahan Conference, pages 193-198, 1989.

[78]   T.C. Feustel, G.A. Velius. Speaker Identity Verification over Telephone Lines: Where We are and Where We are Going, Security Technology. In Proc. of International Carnahan Conference, pages 181-182, 1989.

[79]   Brigitte Wirtz. APIs and Interoperability, Biometric Technology Today, vol. 8, no. 5, pages 8-11, 1 September 2000.

[80]   Helenice Jane Cote Gil Coury, Jorge Alfredo Léo and Shrawan Kumar. Effects of Progressive Levels of Industrial Automation on Force and Repetitive Movements of the Wrist, International Journal of Industrial, Ergonomics, vol. 25, no. 6, pages 587-595, July 2000.

[81]   Mohammad Peyravian, Stephen M. Matyas, Allen Roginsky and Nevenko Zunic SummaryPlus. Multiparty Biometric-Based Authentication, Computers & Security, vol. 19, no. 4, pages 369-374, 1 April 2000.

[82]   P. Jonathon Phillips, Alvin Martin C.L. Wilson and Przybocki Mark. Introduction to Evaluating Biometric Systems, Computer, vol. 33, no. 2, pages 56-63, 2000.

[83]   Catherine J. Tilton. Emerging Biometric API Industry Standard, Computer, vol. 33, no. 2, pages 130-132, 2000.

[84]   Sanchez-Reillo Rand and Gonzalez-Marcos Ana. Access Control System with Hand Geometry Verification and Smart Cards, IEEE Aerospace and Electronic Systems Magazine, vol. 15, no. 2, pages 45-48, 2000.

[85]   Ajit C. Tamhane and Charles W. Dunnett. Stepwise Multiple Test Procedures with Biometric Applications, Journal of Statistical Planning and Inference, vol. 82, no. 1-2, pages 55-68, 1 December 1999.

[86]   Despina Polemi. TTPs and Biometrics for Securing the Payment of Telemedical Services, Future Generation Computer Systems, vol. 15, no. 2, pages 265-276, 11 March 1999.

[87]   Chris Green. Compaq Points Fingerprints at Security Hole, Computers & Security, vol. 18, no. 1, page 76, 1999.

[88] M.M. Gifford, D.J. McCartney, C.H. Seal. Networked Biometrics Systems - Requirements Based on Iris Recognition, BT Technology Journal, vol. 17, no. 2, pages 163-169, 1999.

[89] Corien Prins. Biometric Technology Law Making our Body Identify for Us: Legal Implications of Biometric Technologies, Computer Law & Security Report, vol. 14, no. 3, pages 159-165, 6 May 1998,.

[90] David Willis. Let Your Fingers Do the Logging In, Computers & Security, vol. 17, no. 5, page 411, 1998.

[91] Thomas J. Alexandre. Biometrics on Smart Cards: An Approach to Keyboard Behavioral Signature, Future Generation Computer Systems, vol. 13, no. 1, pages 19-26, July 1997.

[92] Simson L. Garfinkel. Paring Password Pileup, Computers & Security, vol. 16, no. 8, page 677, 1997.

[93] Konen, Wolfgang. Neural Information Processing in Real-world Face-recognition Applications, IEEE Expert, vol. 11, no. 4, pages 7-8, August 1996.

[94] Kim, Hyun-Jung. Biometrics, is it a Viable Proposition for Identity Authentication and Access Control?, Computers & Security, vol. 14, no. 3, pages 205-214, 1995.

Chapter 2

ACHIEVEMENTS AND CHALLENGES IN FINGERPRINT RECOGNITION

Asker M. Bazen and Sabih H. Gerez
University of Twente
The Netherlands
{a.m.bazen,s.h.gerez}@el.utwente.nl

Abstract   This chapter gives an overview of fingerprint recognition. First, a number of applications of fingerprint recognition are presented, including physical access control, computer login, key-less lockers, and biometric smart cards. This is followed by an overview of current fingerprint recognition technology and algorithms, introducing various new methods, technical challenges, and directions on how to solve them. Finally, this chapter shows how these new methods can be used to improve the performance of the selected applications.

Keywords: Fingerprint applications, fingerprint recognition, verification, identification, matching, classification, segmentation, feature extraction, minutiae, indexing.

2.1.   Introduction

Recognition of persons on the basis of biometric features is an emerging phenomenon in our society. It has received increasing attention in recent years due to the need for security in a wide range of applications, such as replacement of the *personal identification number* (PIN) in banking and retail business, security of transactions across computer networks, high-security wireless access, televoting, and admission to restricted areas.

Traditional systems that verify a person's identity are based on knowledge (secret code) or possession (ID card). However, codes can be forgotten or overheard, and ID cards can be lost or stolen, giving impostors the possibility to pass the identity test. The use of features directly connected to a person's body significantly decreases the possibility of fraud.

Many biometric features can be distinguished: fingerprint, iris, face, voice, hand geometry, retina, handwriting, gait, and more. Among these, the fingerprint is considered one of the most practical features. Fingerprint recognition requires minimal effort on the part of the user, does not capture information other than strictly necessary for the recognition process, and provides relatively good performance. Another reason for the popularity of fingerprints is the relatively low price of fingerprint sensors. PC keyboards and smart cards with built-in fingerprint sensors are already available on the market, and the sensors can be integrated easily in wireless hardware.

Even though many academic and commercial systems for fingerprint recognition exist, there is need for further research on the subject so as to improve the reliability and performance of the systems. As this chapter will make clear, techniques to process fingerprints for recognition purposes are far from mature in spite of the extensive research already done in this field. Noise in the captured fingerprint image, plastic distortion of the skin when pressing the sensor, the partial image of a finger, large fingerprint databases: all these factors make it difficult for fingerprint recognition systems to achieve high performance. To make these systems more reliable and more widely accepted, improvement of recognition performance is necessary. Better algorithms can reduce the error rates to levels that are acceptable for wide application of biometric authentication. Furthermore, improved processing in combination with the use of low-cost sensors that can be integrated in wireless hardware or smart cards can be seen as a clear advantage.

This chapter is organized as follows. First, Section 2.2 discusses some basic issues in fingerprint recognition. Section 2.3 then presents a number of applications and summarizes the experience gained in live situations. Section 2.4 goes on to describe the methods and technologies that are used in fingerprint recognition. It also lists various challenges in fingerprint recognition, along with directions for improvement of system performance. Finally, Section 2.5 shows how the improved algorithms can contribute to a better performance of the selected applications.

2.2.   Fingerprint Recognition Issues

This section provides an overview of issues related to fingerprint recognition. It provides the background for the applications and algorithms that are described in the rest of this chapter.

2.2.1   Verification, Identification, and Classification

Several problems can be defined in the context of fingerprint recognition, being verification, identification, and classification. The term recognition is used in a general sense and encompasses all three kinds of tasks.

Verification (or *authentication*) systems use fingerprint technology to verify that someone really is who he or she claims to be. Such systems therefore receive two inputs: the claimed identity of the person requesting authentication and the fingerprint of that person. The claimed identity is used to retrieve a *reference* fingerprint stored in a database and is matched (compared) against the currently offered fingerprint (the *test* fingerprint). This results in a measure of similarity, on which the verification is based.

Identification systems, on the other hand, only receive one input, namely the *query* fingerprint. A database is searched for a matching fingerprint. This task is also referred to as one-to-many matching. If a matching fingerprint is found in the database, that identifies the person. For both verification and identification systems, *enrollment* is an important step. This is the process of taking reference fingerprints of all users and storing these in the database for comparison purposes.

Classification systems also receive a single fingerprint as input. They determine the fingerprint class that the input belongs to. A well-known set of categories is formed by the *Henry* classes. These consist of five classes related to global fingerprint patterns, shown in Figure 2.15. Classification can be an initial step in an identification task as it reduces the number of database entries to be searched.

2.2.2 Error Measures

In verification and identification systems, *matching* is an important step. This is the comparison of a particular fingerprint to another one. The result is either a 'match' or a 'non-match'. This is often achieved by assigning a numeric value, corresponding to a measure of similarity, to the result of the comparison, followed by the use of a threshold to convert this value to a match/non-match decision.

The distributions of the similarity values of genuine attempts (matching fingerprints) and impostor attempts (non-matching fingerprints) cannot be separated completely by a threshold. Instead, the distributions overlap to some extent, resulting in matching errors. This is illustrated in Figure 2.1(a). Two fingerprints are decided to match if their similarity score exceeds the threshold, while they are decided to be non-matching if their score is below the threshold.

The matching performance of fingerprint recognition systems is measured by two error measures. The *false acceptance rate* (FAR) is the probability that the system outputs 'match' for fingerprints that are not from the same finger, as shown by the dark- gray area in Figure 2.1(a). The *false rejection rate* (FRR) is the probability that the system outputs 'non-match' for fingerprints that originate from the same finger. This is shown by the light-gray area in the figure. Currently available commercial systems perform at approximately

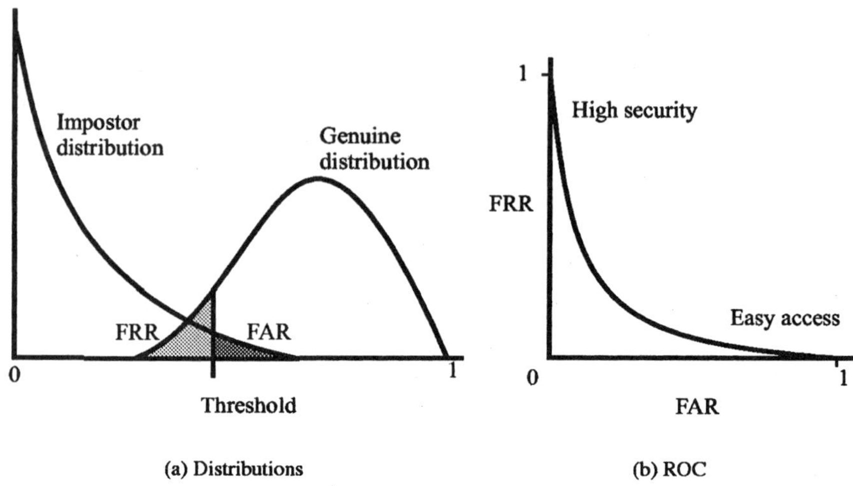

Figure 2.1.   Match and non-match distributions and ROC.

$FAR = 10^{-4}$ and $FRR = 10^{-2}$ on high-quality databases. However, for more realistic fingerprint databases, the performance easily drops below $FAR = 10^{-2}$ and $FRR = 10^{-2}$.

In most systems, the performance can be controlled by a parameter such as the threshold mentioned above. The variation in performance for different parameter settings can be visualized by plotting FAR against FRR. This plot, shown in Figure 2.1(b), is called the *receiver operating curve* (ROC). The threshold can be tuned to meet the requirements of the application for which the system is used. Some systems may require very high security (a very low FAR), while other systems may need to be very user-friendly, therefore providing easy access (a low FRR).

2.2.3   Fingerprint Features

A fingerprint is a pattern of curving line structures called *ridges*, where the skin has a higher profile than its surroundings, which are called the *valleys*. In most fingerprint images, the ridges are black and the valleys are white.

Due to all kinds of noise and distortions, fingerprints cannot be matched simply by taking the cross-correlation or the Euclidean distance of the gray scale images. Features are thus extracted from the fingerprints that are more invariant to the distortions. Commonly used features are listed below.

- The *directional field* (DF) is defined as the local orientation of the ridge-valley structures. It describes the coarse structure, or basic shape, of a fingerprint.

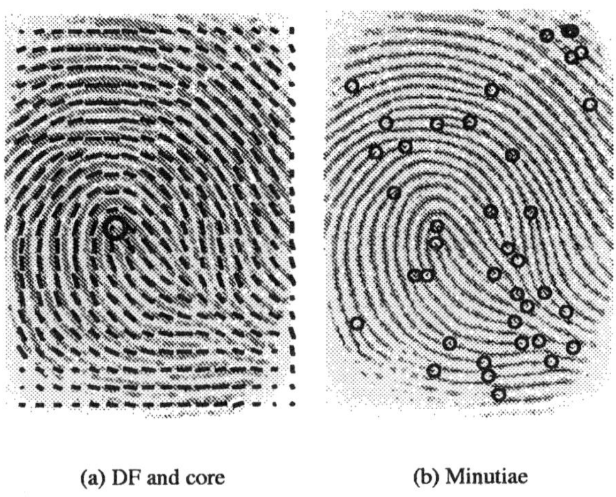

(a) DF and core   (b) Minutiae

Figure 2.2.   Fingerprint with directional field, singular points, and minutiae.

- The *singular points* (SPs) are the discontinuities in the directional field. Two types of SP exist. A *core* is the uppermost point of the innermost curving ridge, and a *delta* is a point where three ridge flows meet.

- The *minutiae* provide the details of the ridge-valley structures. Automatic fingerprint recognition systems use the two elementary types of minutiae that exist, being ridge-endings and bifurcations. Sometimes composite types of minutiae are also used.

Figure 2.2 illustrates these features for a sample fingerprint. In most fingerprint recognition systems, the directional field is used for enhancement of the fingerprint and, together with the singular points, for classification, while the minutiae are used for matching.

2.3.   Applications

This section presents a number of applications of fingerprint recognition. Physical access control, computer login and key-less lockers have been implemented by NEDAP [41], while the former company Interstrat performed experiments with biometric smart cards. Various specific aspects and practical experience with fingerprint recognition systems are discussed in this section as well. More applications and implementation issues can be found in [1].

2.3.1 Physical Access Control

Physical access control to buildings or restricted areas is one of the earliest applications of biometric techniques. The goal of this traditional application is to provide high security access control. We will discuss two situations in which fingerprints are used for physical access control.

The first situation is the more traditional setting. A bank in France has introduced fingerprint verification for access by its employees at remote locations. This particular situation involves a small number of employees who use the technology frequently, namely for each time that they require access. The users are highly motivated. They agree with the need for security measurements as the fingerprint replaces codes, and they accept that this causes inconvenience and takes some time. Since only a small number of people use the system, considerable time can be spent in training and enrollment.

The second application is situated in a city in the Netherlands, where the local authorities have decided to use fingerprint verification for access to specific departments of the city hall. In this case, the goal is to provide a secure environment for the maintenance of various kinds of information and files. The motivation is that citizens should be able to expect from their government that their information is safe.

For most departments, fingerprints are only required for access outside of working hours. During working hours, there are many employees, and strangers will not be able to obtain access without being noticed. Therefore, an ID card is enough to obtain access during the day. Within the computer department, fingerprint access applies around the clock, since access to the computer systems is much more critical.

Initially during this Dutch city hall experiment, the performance of the fingerprint verification system was somewhat disappointing. Access was refused for reasons that were unclear, and employees did not receive enough help to resolve these problems. However, improved communication and training of operators and users has led to an acceptable situation.

2.3.2 Login to Computer Network

Since access to information requires not only physical presence but also access computer systems, the city decided to secure its computer network by means of fingerprint login. All computers were equipped with a smart card reader and a fingerprint sensor. For login from different locations at a central network, both an ID card and a fingerprint are required. Furthermore, access via the Internet is also supported so as to enable teleworking at home. Computer access represents a situation that is much more controlled and relaxed than access to a building. Furthermore, feedback of the image acquisition can be

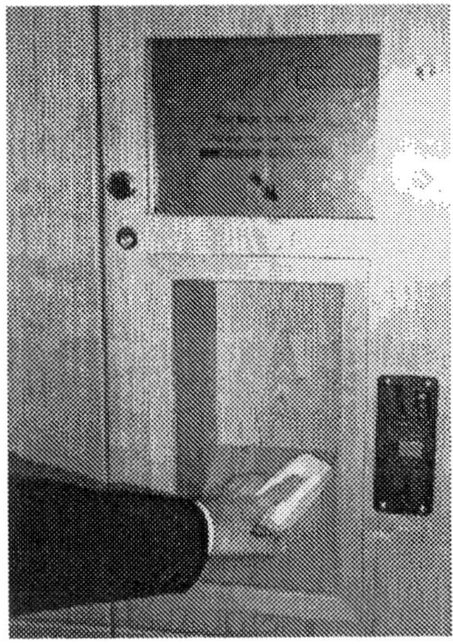

Figure 2.3.　Key-less lockers.

given on the computer screen. Therefore, the performance level of the system is much higher than in the large-scale physical access control experiment.

2.3.3　Key-less Lockers

Many swimming pools have lockers where swimmers can leave their valuables. Traditional lockers require the swimmer to carry the key during swimming. As this is quite inconvenient, the use of a fingerprint to replace the key is an attractive alternative. Furthermore, it would simplify the management of the locker system. Key-less lockers have been tested in several pilot projects. The lockers are installed in a swimming pool as an alternative to key-operated lockers. In a typical setting, a group of 100 lockers are jointly controlled by a computer that is connected to a fingerprint sensor. Figure 2.3 shows a photo of part of such a system.

This application presents several special challenges. First, the recognition of wet fingers gives rise to various problems. Fingerprint images from wet fingers lead to decreased image quality. This problem is enhanced by the fact that the layer of fat at the skin is reduced by an extended stay in the water. Various fingerprint sensors were used, but none of them yielded a satisfactory image quality. Also, water causes the skin to fit less tightly around the finger, resulting in above-average elastic distortions of the fingerprint, thereby decreasing the matching performance.

The second challenge is that users should be able to operate the lockers without the supervision of an operator. After all, correct use of the system is not the main concern of the users. They come to swim and do not want to be bothered with all kinds of procedures. Therefore, the enrollment of the fingerprint is unsupervised and involves no training. The system should give the users feedback on the correct placement of their fingers. This leads to significantly lower image quality than in a situation that involves supervised enrollment.

The final challenge is that the lockers have to be operated by the users without the use of an ID card or other token. This is an identification problem where a database of 100 fingerprints has to be searched reliably. Since no ID cards are required, it is important that the locker system is able to prevent impostor access. The goal is to keep the FAR below 1% when an impostor tries all ten fingers. After a specified number of successive impostor attempts, the system can be blocked and the operator alarmed for additional security.

Mainly because of the low image quality and the unsupervised enrollment, the system performance was much lower than in experiments involving an office situation. However, an experiment in a swimming pool with a fixed group of users that were enrolled with one-time supervision did yield satisfactory performance.

2.3.4 Biometric Smart Cards

A new application of fingerprint recognition is the biometric smart card that is used in nightclubs to offer visitors more security during their stay. Biometric smart cards are being tested in a large-scale experiment in 15 nightclubs. Visitors of the clubs have to purchase a membership card which stores a photograph and fingerprint. In order to obtain access to the clubs, their face and fingerprint are verified.

A person causing trouble at a nightclub is removed from the club. To offer security to the other visitors, such a person is added to a blacklist and will not have access to the nightclub for a specified period of time. Since all participating nightclubs have a joint blacklist, the person is also denied access to the other clubs.

New users have to be verified against the blacklist. Since suspended users may try to purchase a membership card under a false name, a fingerprint identification system is used. The identification problem is especially difficult since suspended users do not want to be recognized and may try to cause elastic deformation of their fingerprints. To deal with this issue, the FRR must be kept very low.

2.3.5 Practical Experience

This section summarizes the experience that was gained by the application of fingerprint recognition in live situations. It is clear that fingerprint recognition is much harder to implement than face, hand geometry, or iris recognition. The application of such methods is far less sensitive to untrained users and other interfering factors. However, fingerprint recognition can be applied with the very small and cheap sensors that are on the market for this technology.

The performance of a fingerprint verification system highly depends on the situation in which it is used. In the high-security bank situation, employees are well-trained and accept the fact that they have to use the system conscientiously. The system thus performs well. For computer login, people take their time as well. The login procedure takes some time anyway, and employees are relaxed as they are sitting at their desk. Therefore, this application does not cause many problems either. However, for physical access control, people may be in a hurry, or they may be cold, wet, or sweaty because of weather conditions. As a result, they may be too impatient for careful acquisition of their fingerprints. On top of that, it is more difficult to train large groups of people. In such situations, the employer must be committed to make the system a success and willing to spend time to explain the system, to train the users, and to offer continuous support.

Enrollment is another critical issue. If the enrolled fingerprints are not of high quality, system performance decreases significantly. Therefore, enough time has to be taken for the enrollment. Especially when the enrollment is unsupervised, feedback of the acquisition process is important. Users need to know whether they have to press harder or to place their fingers differently on the sensor.

In most verification systems, achievement of an extremely low FAR is not a critical issue. Impostor attempts occur only sporadically, since the impostor first has to get access to a valid ID card. If an attempt is made with a stolen ID card that has not been reported as missing yet, the fingerprint verification serves as an additional barrier. In such a case, an FAR level of 1% is satisfactory, while most algorithms offer an FAR of 10^{-3} or 10^{-4}.

Achievement of a low FRR is much bigger problem. If the FRR is too high, many users will not obtain access without knowing why. Although false rejection can also occur with high-quality fingerprints, the main cause of rejection of a fingerprint is its poor image quality (see Figure 2.8). The poor-quality fingerprint is rejected before matching with the template, so that such cases are not included in the performance figures of the software application. However, users experience such rejection as unjust.

It is generally recognized that a small percentage of a human population has very poor quality fingerprints. If those fingerprints are included in the matching performance figures, the distribution of the genuine matching score, which is shown in Figure 2.1(a), will become bimodal. It will show an additional peak near zero, caused by the poor-quality fingerprints. This will result in a heightened FRR, which cannot be resolved by means of threshold settings. The only solution is to increase the image quality by means of better sensors or enhancement algorithms.

A final remark on live systems is that a backup system has to be constructed. A backup system is needed not only when the fingerprint recognition system is out of order, but also to apply to users who are denied access by the system. Backup possibilities may consist of a code that can be used as alternative to the fingerprints, or the physical presence of operator or security staff to provide correct user access.

2.4. Fingerprint Recognition Methods and Algorithms

This section presents an overview of the methods and algorithms that are used in automatic fingerprint recognition systems. First, the general structure of a fingerprint matching system is presented, followed by a more detailed discussion of the components of the system. Next, issues related to classification and identification are discussed. Algorithms are discussed in an informal way, mostly without the use of formulae or pseudo-codes. Readers who are interested in further detail should consult the references that are shown. Whenever appropriate, opportunities to improve the algorithms are also presented.

A survey is also presented of the exciting technical challenges and of possible ways to solve them. In our opinion, the principal challenges in fingerprint recognition are:

- robust minutiae extraction from low-quality fingerprints,

- matching fingerprints that are affected by plastic distortions,

- classification methods for efficient search of fingerprints in a database.

Solving at least some of these challenges may reduce the error rates to levels that are acceptable for wide application of biometric authentication and compensate for the use of low-cost sensors.

2.4.1   System Overview

A general fingerprint matching system involves several phases. First, in the *acquisition* phase, the fingerprint is scanned using a fingerprint sensor. Next there is the *preprocessing* phase, which involves calculation of the directional field and enhancement and segmentation of the fingerprint. In the *feature extraction* phase, the positions of the minutiae are determined. Finally, in the *matching* phase, the features of the fingerprint are compared to a template that is found in the database. This entire process is illustrated in Figure 2.4. The database has been constructed earlier by applying the same steps to a set of reference fingerprints.

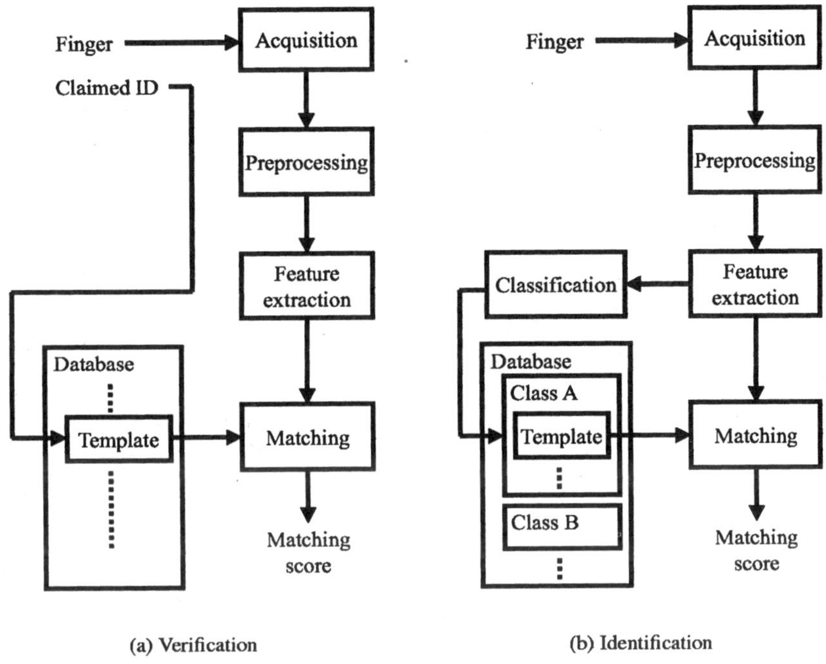

Figure 2.4.   Block diagrams of fingerprint recognition systems.

As already mentioned in Section 2.2.1, a verification system uses the claimed ID of a person to retrieve a fingerprint from a database. This situation is shown in Figure 2.4(a). An identification system, on the other hand, does not make use of a claimed ID. Instead, it has to compare the query fingerprint to all templates in the database, using some form of classification to reduce the number of matches. This is shown in Figure 2.4(b).

2.4.2   Fingerprint Sensors

The first phase in a fingerprint recognition system is the acquisition of a fingerprint. In the past, fingerprints were obtained by rolling an inked finger from nail to nail on a sheet of paper. Nowadays, however, many sensors are available that capture a fingerprint based on principles in the optical, capacitive, pressure, thermal, or ultrasound domain. They produce a digital image of the fingerprint, typically consisting of 8-bit gray-scale values.

Sensors have made the capturing process much more user-friendly since they require only a simple touch of the finger on the sensor and since no ink is involved anymore. However, the task of a fingerprint identification algorithm has become more complicated since the plain touch images (also called dab

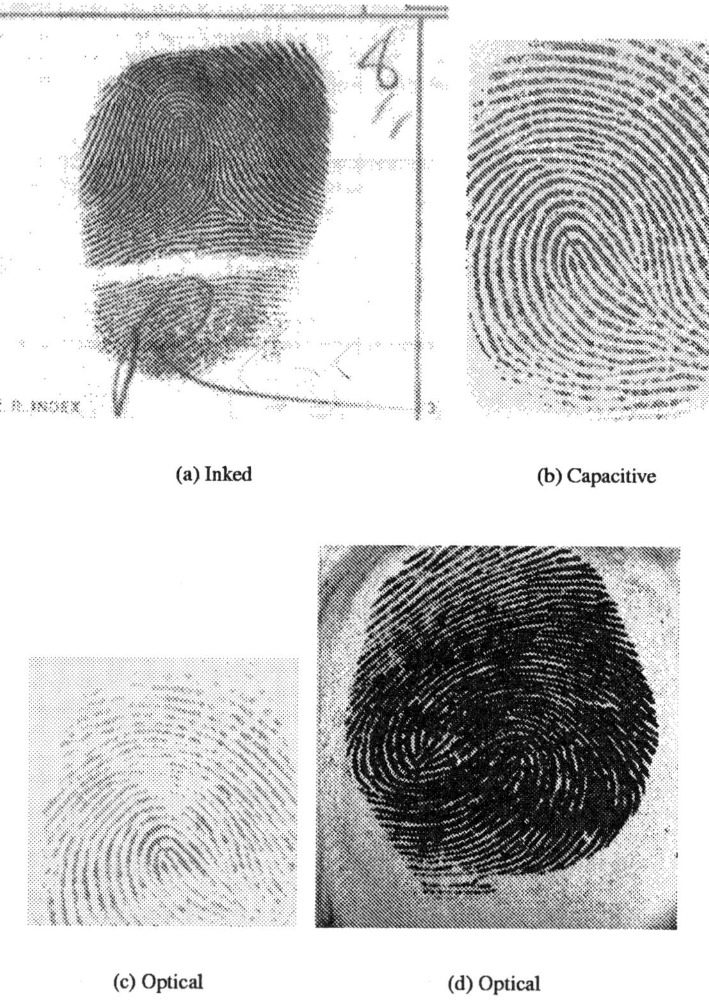

(a) Inked (b) Capacitive

(c) Optical (d) Optical

Figure 2.5. Fingerprint images that are acquired by different sensors.

images) contain a much smaller part of the entire fingerprint. Therefore, less minutiae are present, SPs may lie outside of the image area, and two images may overlap for only a very small part. Furthermore, a large amount of elastic deformation may exist between two dab images if force is applied during the acquisition. Finally, algorithms have to be tuned to the specific sensor that is used since different sensors provide images with different characteristics (see Figure 2.5).

Fingerprint mosaicking is a method that artificially constructs an approximation of a rolled image from a series of dab images. Two applications of fingerprint mosaicking are proposed. In [49], a finger is rolled over a fingerprint sensor that captures a sequence of images. These images are easily combined into a single larger image. At the Biometrics Research website at MSU [22], a method is proposed to construct a composite fingerprint image from multiple impressions that are taken at different moments. In this case, the registration is much more difficult since elastic deformations between the impressions may exist.

2.4.3   Directional field

The *directional field* (DF) describes the coarse structure, or basic shape, of a fingerprint. The DF is defined as the local orientation of the ridge-valley structures. Various methods to estimate the DF from a fingerprint are known from literature, including matched-filter approaches and 2-dimensional spectral estimation methods [53]. These approaches do not provide the same level of accuracy as gradient-based methods, mainly because of the limited number of fixed possible orientations.

In [2, 7], a method is presented for the estimation of a high-resolution DF. The main results are repeated here. The method is based on the gradient vector of the gray-scale image. The DF is, in principle, perpendicular to the gray-scale gradients. However, the gradients are orientations at pixel scale, while the DF describes the orientation of the ridge-valley structures. This requires a much coarser scale, which is not affected by local fluctuations. Therefore, the DF can be derived from the gradients by performing an *averaging* operation on the gradients, involving pixels in a specified neighborhood [35].

Gradients cannot simply be averaged in a local neighborhood, since opposite gradient vectors will then cancel each other, even though they indicate the same ridge-valley orientation. A solution to this problem is to double the angles of the gradient vectors before averaging. Opposite gradient vectors will then point in the same direction and reinforce each other, while perpendicular gradients will cancel each other. After averaging, the gradient vectors have to be converted back to their single-angle representation. The main ridge-valley orientation is perpendicular to the direction of the average gradient vector. This method was proposed by [31] and was adopted by various researchers for the estimation of the DF of fingerprints.

A difference between our method and that of other researchers is that we do not estimate the average DF for a number of blocks in the image. Instead, the DF is estimated for each pixel in the image using a Gaussian window for averaging. However, such a high resolution estimate is not needed for most DF-related tasks. In these cases, a simple *block-directional field* (BDF) with blocks of 8 by 8 pixels provides enough accuracy. The classical way to estimate a BDF is to partition the image into blocks and estimate the average squared

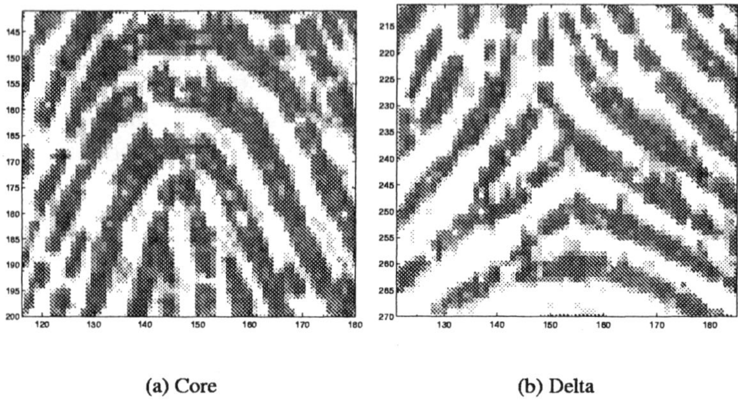

(a) Core   (b) Delta

Figure 2.6.   Segments of a fingerprint containing a singular point.

orientation as the average of the block. Sometimes, overlapping blocks are used for extra noise suppression. However, averaging with such a uniform window does not suppress the high-frequency noise sufficiently. Aliasing introduces artefacts in the DF, which in turn creates false singular points.

The cause of this problem is that the length of the averaging filter is set to the same number as the decimation rate. This can be solved by decoupling the size and shape of the averaging filter from the subsampling rate. We have proposed the use of an alternative BDF calculation method that is based on the high-resolution DF [7]. In each block, the squared orientation is estimated by means of *decimation* of the high-resolution DF. Scale-space theory tells us that averaging with a Gaussian window minimizes the amount of artefacts that are introduced by subsampling [35]. This will considerably reduce the number of false singular points in the DF. Furthermore, multi-rate signal processing tells us that the filtering and decimation steps can be implemented very efficiently using polyphase filters, by interchanging the order of decimation and filtering [44].

2.4.4   Singular Points

Singular points are the points in a fingerprint where the DF is discontinuous. Figure 2.6 shows two segments of a fingerprint, containing a core and a delta. The SPs are located near the center of the segments. However, they cannot be positioned more accurately than within the width of one ridge-valley structure in the gray-value fingerprint, which is approximately 10 pixels for this example.

Figure 2.7 shows the high-resolution DFs of the above segments. The exact SP locations can be easily determined from these DFs, with an accuracy of only

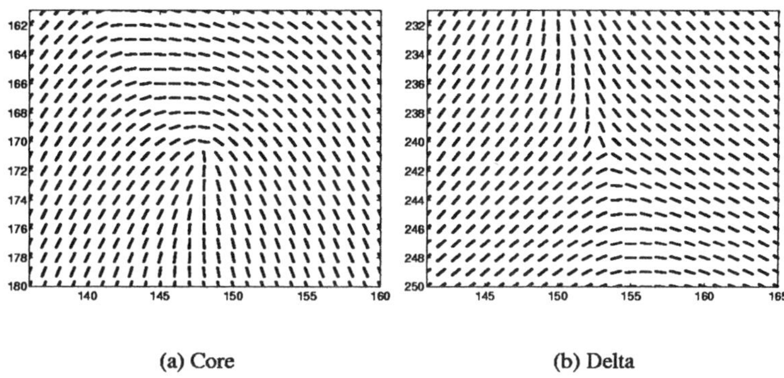

(a) Core   (b) Delta

Figure 2.7. Directional fields containing a singular point.

one pixel. Although it would seem a very straightforward task to extract the SPs from the DFs, many different algorithms for SP extraction are known from literature. Most of these methods provide somewhat unsatisfactory results, since they are not capable of consistently extracting the singular points. Instead of providing a Boolean output that indicates whether an SP is present at a particular location, they produce a continuous output that indicates to what extent the local DF resembles an SP. Postprocessing steps, like thresholds and heuristics, are necessary to interpret the outputs of the algorithms and to make the final decisions.

Our method, which is capable of pixel-accurate SP detection, is based on the Poincaré index [32]. The Poincaré index can be explained using the DFs that are depicted in Figure 2.7. Following a counter-clockwise closed contour around a core in the DF, then adding the differences between the subsequent angles, results in a cumulative change in the orientation of π; carrying this procedure out around a delta results in $-\pi$. However, when applied to locations that do not contain an SP, the cumulative orientation change will be zero.

Although the Poincaré index provides a means for consistent detection of SPs, the question arises how to calculate this measure. Apart from the problem of how to calculate cumulative orientation changes over contours efficiently, a choice has to be made on the optimal size and shape of the contour. In [3, 7], an efficient implementation of this algorithm is proposed that makes use of small 2-dimensional filters by applying Green's Theorem. The algorithm extracts *all* singular points from the DF, including false SPs that are caused by an insufficiently averaged DF. Furthermore, the algorithm can be applied to BDFs, it determines whether a core or a delta is detected, and it estimates the orientation of the singularity.

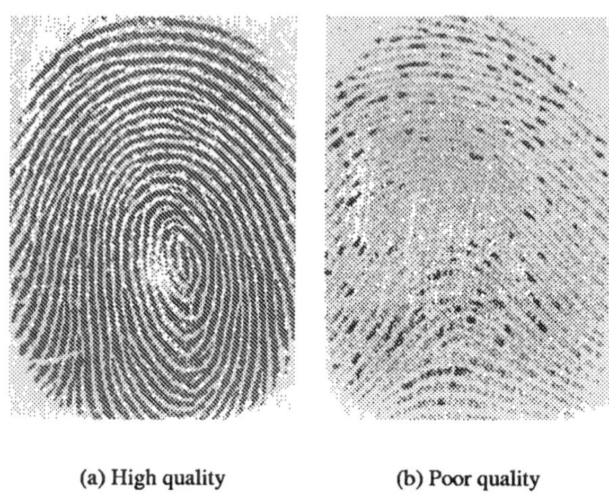

(a) High quality   (b) Poor quality

Figure 2.8.   Fingerprint images of high and poor quality.

2.4.5   Enhancement

As mentioned in Section 2.3, one of the problems in fingerprint recognition is the poor quality of fingerprint images. The task of fingerprint enhancement is to suppress the noise in the fingerprint image and to enhance the ridge-valley structures, thereby enabling more accurate minutiae extraction. Examples of a high-quality and a poor-quality fingerprint image are shown in Figure 2.8. Figure 2.9(a) shows a medium-quality fingerprint image, and Figure 2.9(b) shows an example of a fingerprint image that has been binarized using a local threshold without any enhancement. It is clear that this last image contains too much noise for reliable minutiae extraction.

Various fingerprint enhancement methods exist. The simplest enhancement method only applies a low-pass filter to the image, thus suppressing the high-frequency noise. An example of a thresholded fingerprint image that is enhanced by a low-pass filter is shown in Figure 2.9(c).

The second method makes use of FFT-based techniques [11]. The fingerprint image can be subdivided into overlapping blocks of 32 by 32 pixels, with each block being processed separately. The FFT is taken, and the result is processed non-linearly in order to enhance the ridge valley structures. Each element in the block may, for instance, be multiplied by its absolute value to some power. This enhances the spatial frequencies that are strongly present in the block and weakens the other components. The block is then transformed back to the spatial domain by means of an inverse FFT. An example of the results is shown in Figure 2.9(d).

(a) Fingerprint image

(b) No enhancement

(c) Low-pass

(d) FFT

(e) Gabor

Figure 2.9. Fingerprint images that have been enhanced by different methods and binarized for visualization purposes.

The third method makes use of oriented filters that are controlled by the DF [51, 19]. The idea is to apply a filter to each pixel that enhances those structures that agree with the local DF. For the sake of computational efficiency, the entire image is prefiltered by a number of fixed oriented filters, distributed along the unit circle. We found that four filters are sufficient, oriented at 0, $\pi/4$, $\pi/2$, and $3\pi/4$. These filters all enhance a different part of the ridge-valley structures. Next, the prefiltered images are combined according to the DF. Each pixel in the filtered image is interpolated in a linear way between the prefiltered images that correspond to the two closest orientations.

There are two critical points in this algorithm. The first is the exact shape of the filters. We use Gabor filters, which requires selection of the spatial frequency and the smoothness. The spatial frequency is tuned to the average ridge-frequency. However, since this frequency varies considerably within a single fingerprint and between fingerprints, the filters have to be rather smooth. Otherwise, the filter may construct two small ridges, where one broad ridge is in fact present in the fingerprint. Secondly, the algorithm depends heavily on the DF estimate. If the DF estimate is inaccurate, the algorithm may result in spurious ridges in the estimated DF direction.

2.4.6   Segmentation

Another important step in an automatic fingerprint recognition system is the *segmentation* of fingerprint images. Segmentation is the decomposition of an image into its components. A captured fingerprint image usually consists of two components, the *foreground* and the *background*. The foreground is the component that originated from the contact of a fingertip with the sensor. The noisy area at the border of the image is called the background. The task of the fingerprint segmentation algorithm is to decide which part of the image belongs to the foreground and which to the background, or alternatively to reject a fingerprint altogether.

Accurate segmentation is especially important for the reliable extraction of features like minutiae and singular points. Most feature extraction algorithms extract many false features when applied to the noisy background area. Therefore, the main goal of the segmentation algorithm is to discard the background and thus reduce the number of false features.

Several approaches to fingerprint image segmentation are known from literature. In [39], the fingerprint is partitioned in blocks of 16 by 16 pixels. Each block is then classified according to the distribution of the gradients in that block. Blocks with a gray-scale variance below a specific threshold are excluded. In [46] the gray-scale variance in the direction orthogonal to the orientation of the ridges is used to classify each 16 by 16 block. In [26], the output of a set of Gabor filters is used as input to a clustering algorithm that constructs spatially compact clusters.

The most important element in the design of a segmentation algorithm is the choice of the features to use for classification of a certain block or pixel. We have chosen to use three features: the coherence, which gives a measure of how well the gradients point in the same direction; the local mean gray value; and the local variance of the gray values [5]. Since sets of foreground and background features can easily be constructed, it is wise to use a supervised classification algorithm that minimizes the probability of misclassification. This is applied to classify each pixel or block of pixels of the fingerprint image. In order to

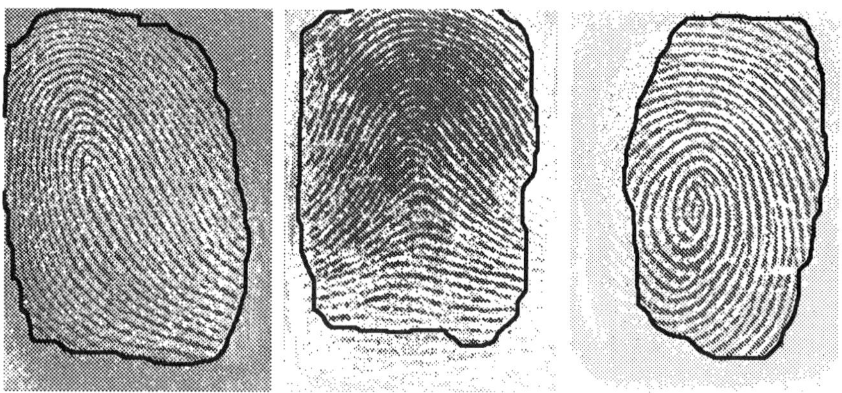

Figure 2.10.　Segmentation results.

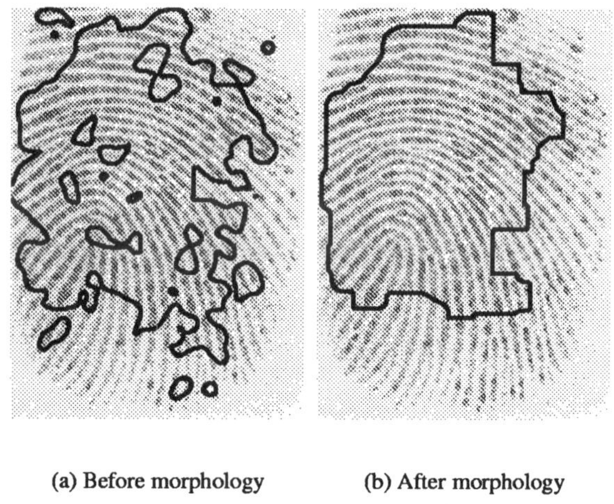

(a) Before morphology　　　(b) After morphology

Figure 2.11.　Effect of morphological postprocessing on the segmentation result.

reduce the number of misclassified pixels further and to obtain spatially compact areas, the morphological operations 'open' and 'close' are applied. This method 'repairs' the estimate by removing small areas of one class and placing them within the other class, thereby creating more compact clusters. Several results of the segmentation algorithm are shown in Figure 2.10, while the effect of the morphological operations is shown in Figure 2.11.

An alternative to the morphological postprocessing that is currently applied is the use of *hidden Markov models* (HMMs), which are widely used in speech recognition [45]. This method takes into account the context, or surroundings, for each feature vector to be classified. Using estimations of the probability of class transitions and conditional feature distributions, the segmentation is found that maximizes the likelihood of these observations. Furthermore, the use of a third class, representing low-quality regions, is likely to improve the segmentation results.

2.4.7 Minutiae Extraction

Various approaches to minutiae extraction are possible. This section discusses the traditional approach, while alternative methods are discussed in Section 2.4.9.

To extract minutiae from a gray-scale fingerprint image using the traditional approach, typical image processing transformations are applied to the fingerprint image [23]. After enhancement and segmentation, the image is binarized by a thresholding operation. This converts each pixel value to a binary value (black or white). The threshold has to be applied dynamically, which means that it is locally adjusted to the characteristics of the image, thus compensating for differences in image intensity. Some enhancement algorithms may already have taken care of this.

Next, thinning is applied to the binarized image. This is a morphological operation that reduces the width of each ridge to a single pixel, thus creating a skeleton of the image. Minutiae are then detected in the skeleton by means of a lookup-table operation. Endpoints are defined as black pixels that have only one black pixel in their 3 by 3 neighborhood, while bifurcations have three of them.

2.4.8 Postprocessing

Even after enhancement, the skeleton images of fingerprints that are corrupted by noise will generally result in a large number of false minutiae. The objective of postprocessing is to eliminate those false minutiae, while maintaining the true ones.

Most postprocessing methods operate on the ridge skeleton. They verify the validity of the extraction of minutiae using standard minutiae extraction algorithms. In [54], heuristics are constructed in order to remove minutiae that originate from frequently occurring defects such as ridge-breaks, bridges, spurs, short ridges, and islands or holes, as shown in Figure 2.12.

For instance, to repair a broken ridge, the heuristic 'two endpoints are connected if they are closer than a specified distance and facing each other' can be used. Such a heuristic is constructed for each type of false minutiae structure. An example of a skeleton image and its minutiae before and after postprocessing is shown in Figure 2.13.

Another approach is the verification of minutiae in the original gray-scale image by means of neural networks. Again, the potential minutiae are first

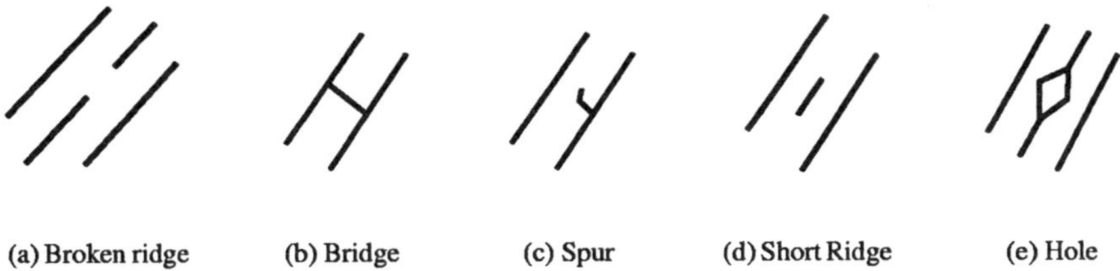

(a) Broken ridge (b) Bridge (c) Spur (d) Short Ridge (e) Hole

Figure 2.12.   Examples of false minutiae shapes.

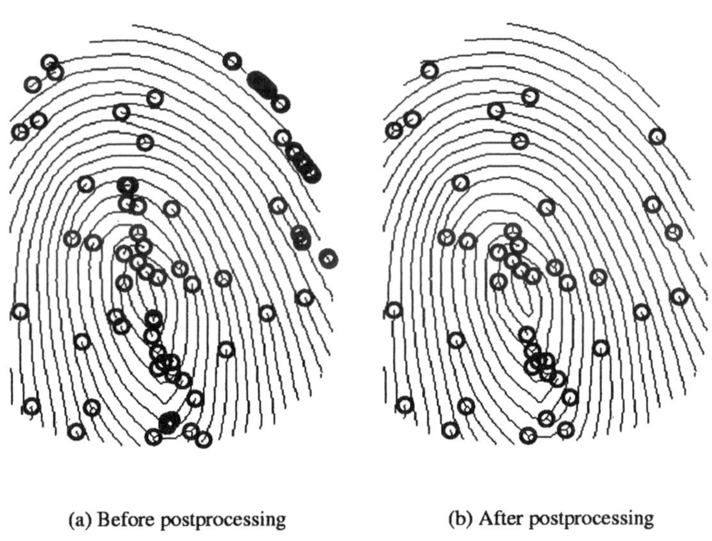

(a) Before postprocessing   (b) After postprocessing

Figure 2.13.   Skeleton image before and after postprocessing.

detected by a standard minutiae extraction algorithm. The minutiae neighborhood is then taken from the gray-scale image and normalized, for example with respect to orientation, and enhanced. In [43], this 32 by 32 neighborhood is directly fed to a learning vector quantizer (LVQ) or a Kohonen neural network. In [38] the neighborhood is first reduced to a feature vector of 26 elements by means of a Karhunen-Loève transform, after which it is classified by a multilayer perceptron.

2.4.9   Alternative Minutiae Extraction Methods

Yet another approach is to extract minutiae directly from the gray-scale fingerprint image. For this task, direct application of a neural network to each pixel neighborhood is less suited, since too many false minutiae are extracted and too much computational time is required. However, an alternative direct gray-scale minutiae detection approach is proposed in [37]. This method tracks the ridges in the gray-scale image using the directional field. The ridges are followed from a set of starting points until they terminate (endpoint) or intersect other ridge lines (bifurcation). In [29], the agent is enhanced through use of a variable step size and a directional filter for noise suppression. This results in a rather complex system, mainly to obtain robustness.

An alternative solution is to use an agent that *learns* the task. By using a variety of training examples, a robust system is obtained automatically. Van der Meulen et al. [40] used genetic programming to evolve a minutiae-extracting agent. In the approach by [8], the agent is trained by means of *reinforcement learning*. The agent is situated in the gray-scale fingerprint image and uses the DF to align its orientation with respect to the ridges. The agent learns to take large steps forward whenever possible and to take small steps to the left or the right in order to stay on the ridges. It stops when detecting an endpoint and when intersecting its own path, which indicates a bifurcation. A neural network is used to learn the optimal policy, based on the pixel values in a small neighborhood.

The above learning methods are still in development. While they may evolve in a preferred method in the future, the traditional approach remains the method of choice in current applications.

2.4.10   Minutiae Matching

The final step in a fingerprint matching system is the actual minutiae matching. This step compares two sets of minutiae and decides whether they originate from the same finger or not (match or non-match). The basic idea behind most minutiae matching algorithms is to *register* (align) both minutiae sets and then count the number of matching minutiae pairs. A pair of minutiae is considered to match if the minutiae are approximately at the same position and their orientations approximately correspond.

Problems with Minutiae Matching.   Unfortunately, there are many complicating factors in minutiae matching. First of all, both sets may suffer from false, missed, and displaced minutiae, caused by imperfections in the minutiae extraction stage. Second, the two fingerprints to be compared may originate from different parts of the same finger, which means that both sets overlap only

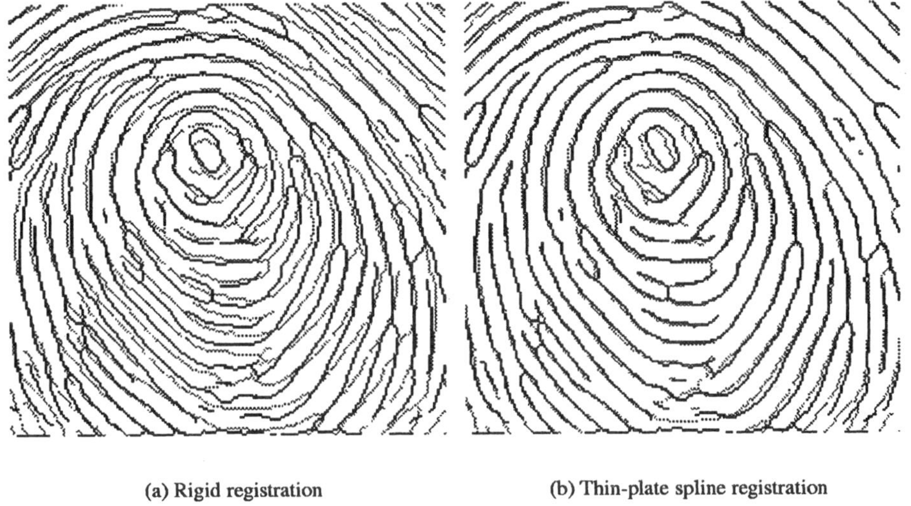

<table>
<tr><td>(a) Rigid registration</td><td>(b) Thin-plate spline registration</td></tr>
</table>

Figure 2.14.   Elastic distortions and rigid and thin-plate spline registrations.

partially. Third, the two prints may be translated, rotated, or scaled with respect to each other.

The fourth problem is the presence of non-linear plastic distortions or elastic deformations in the fingerprints, which is the most difficult problem to solve. These distortions are caused by the acquisition process itself. During the acquisition, the 3-dimensional elastic surface of a finger is pressed on a flat sensor surface. This 3D-to-2D mapping of the finger skin introduces non-linear distortions, especially when force is applied that is not orthogonal to the sensor surface. The effect is that the sets of minutiae of two prints of the same finger no longer fit exactly after registration. This is illustrated in Figure 2.14(a) where the skeletons of two prints of the same finger are optimally registered and depicted in a single figure. Of course, the fact that the two prints cannot be registered exactly decreases the matching performance.

Rigid Matching Algorithms.   Fingerprint matching algorithms may differ both in the flexibility of registration and in the method of counting corresponding minutiae pairs. For instance, a simple minutiae matching algorithm may use only rigid transformations which are a combination of rotation, translation, and possibly scaling. This may be sufficient for fingerprints that are hardly distorted. The optimal registration can be found by means of a Hough transform. Combinations of all possible minutiae pairs in both fingerprints support one set of registration parameters, and the registration that receives most support is then chosen.

After registration, the corresponding minutiae pairs are counted by defining a fixed *bounding box* or *tolerance zone* around each minutia in one set. If a minutia of the other set is located inside this box, the two minutiae are considered to be a matching pair. The matching score, which is in the range from 0 to 1, is calculated as the ratio of the number of matched minutiae to the total number of minutiae.

Such algorithms are very sensitive to plastic distortions. The rigid registration algorithm is unable to represent a registration that brings all minutiae pairs very close together, so this has to be solved in the counting stage of the algorithm. In order to tolerate minutiae pairs that are further apart because of the plastic distortions, and therefore to decrease the FRR, the size of the bounding boxes has to be increased. A side effect of this, however, is that it gives non-matching minutiae pairs a higher probability to get paired, resulting in a higher FAR. Therefore, changing the size of the bounding box around minutiae only has the effect of exchanging FRR for FAR.

Semi-Elastic and Local Similarity Algorithms.   One possible approach to this problem is the semi-elastic matching algorithm. This exploits the principle that distorted prints can be aligned well in the center of the print, while border registration is poor. The semi-elastic matching algorithm allows more displacement between minutiae pairs that are further away from the center of the print [23]. The effect is that some plastic distortions are tolerated, while the probability of pairing non-matching minutiae pairs is decreased because of smaller bounding boxes near the center of the print. However, this method only decreases the problem of the exchange of FRR for FAR, but it does not resolve it.

Another solution to the problem of plastic distortions, which also reduces the required amount of similarity, is the use of local similarity measures [28, 48]. The idea behind this method is that plastic distortions only occur over larger distances within the fingerprint. Thus, by comparing only local features in a fingerprint, like subsets of minutiae that are close together instead of the entire minutiae sets, the matching algorithm is less sensitive to plastic distortions. However, methods that decrease the required amount of similarity not only tolerate small plastic distortions, but also exchange FRR for FAR.

Topological Matching.   The least restrictive matching methods are based on topological matching. They describe the interrelationships between features in a way that is completely invariant of elastic deformations.

In [20], a graph-based fingerprint matching system is proposed. Each fingerprint is encoded in a graph, with nodes representing the ridges and edges representing the ridge adjacency information. Next, approximate graph matching is performed in three phases. Unfortunately, the performance of this graph-matching algorithm has been reported to be inferior to traditional minutiae matching algorithms.

In [4], the *intrinsic coordinate system* (ICS) is proposed as an alternative topological matching method that provides a linked multilevel description of the fingerprint. The coarse level of this description is given by the DF, and the features at the detailed level of the fingerprint are given by the minutiae. Instead of the common practice of treating the DF and the minutiae as two separate descriptions, a link between these two levels is proposed by defining the intrinsic coordinate system of a fingerprint.

The intrinsic coordinate system of a fingerprint is defined by the DF. One of its axes runs along the ridge-valley structures, while the other runs perpendicular to them. Using the ICS, minutiae positions can be defined with respect to positions in the DF, rather than using the pixel coordinates as minutiae locations, thus providing a more natural representation. If a fingerprint undergoes plastic distortions, the distortions affect the shape of the coordinate system, but the intrinsic minutiae coordinates do not change. This means that matching the intrinsic coordinates of the minutiae sets is invariant to plastic distortions. Appropriate matching algorithms based on the ICS are still being developed.

Explicitly Dealing with Plastic Distortions. Recently, some methods have been presented that deal with the problem of matching plastically distorted fingerprints more explicitly. These methods do not exchange FRR for FAR, but change the entire ROC. The first method tries to reject fingerprints that have undergone severe plastic distortions by equipping the fingerprint sensor with an additional force sensor [47]. If the measured force exceeds a certain threshold, the fingerprint is rejected and the user is asked to have his fingerprint taken again. This controlled image acquisition is especially beneficial when dealing with non-cooperative users that deliberately apply excessive force in order to create elastic deformations.

If rejection of fingerprints is not possible, the ideal way to deal with distortions would be to invert the 3D-to-2D mapping and compare the minutiae positions in 3D. Unfortunately, there is no unique way to invert this mapping. It is therefore reasonable to consider methods that explicitly attempt to model and eliminate the 2D distortion in the fingerprint image. Such methods can be expected to be stricter in the displacement allowed during minutiae matching. As a consequence, the FAR can be decreased without increasing the FRR.

In [50], a method is proposed to invert at least some of the distortions in 2D. This method first estimates the local ridge frequency in the entire fingerprint and then adapts the extracted minutiae positions in such a way that the ridge distances are normalized in the entire image. However, this normalization method only solves part of the non-linear deformations.

Since it is not known in advance whether captured fingerprints contain any distortion, true normalization of the fingerprints is not possible. The fact that no reference without distortion is available makes normalization in 2D a relative rather than an absolute matter. Instead of normalizing each fingerprint on its own, the non-linear distortions of one fingerprint with respect to the others have to be estimated and eliminated.

In [16], the physical cause of the distortions is modelled by distinguishing three distinct concentric regions in a fingerprint. In the center region, no distortions are present, since this region tightly fits to the sensor. The outer or external region is not distorted either, since it does not touch the sensor. The outer region may be displaced and rotated with respect to the inner region, due to the application of force while pressing the finger at the sensor. The region in between is distorted in order to fit both regions to each other. Experiments have shown that this model provides an accurate description of the plastic distortions in some cases. The technique has successfully been applied to the generation of many synthetic fingerprints of the same finger [12]. However, the model has not yet been used in an algorithm for matching fingerprints. Accurate estimation of the distortion parameters is still a research topic.

In [6], a minutiae-matching method is proposed that is capable of dealing with elastic distortions. The method first determines possible matching minutiae pairs by comparing local neighborhoods of the minutiae. A *thin-plate spline* model is next used to describe the non-linear distortions between the two sets of possible pairs. One of the fingerprints is deformed and registered according to the estimated model, and then the number of matching minutiae is counted. This method is able to deal with all possible non-linear distortions while using very tight bounding boxes. It has been shown to be very well able to register heavily distorted fingerprints, as illustrated in Figure 2.14(b) on page 45. This provides considerably better matching scores for deformed fingerprint.

Combining Multiple Matchers. The last issue in minutiae matching is the combination of multiple matchers [24, 42]. Since different fingerprint matching algorithms may lead to different decisions, their results can be combined in order to improve the performance [33]. There is evidence that combinations of multiple matchers are indeed able to achieve a higher performance level than the individual matchers that have been combined.

2.4.11 Alternative Fingerprint Matching Methods

Several fingerprint matching methods also exist that do not make use of minutiae sets as a basis for the matching algorithm. The ideas behind these methods are that minutiae are difficult to extract for a significant fraction of all fingerprints, and that the use of the much richer gray-scale information may improve the performance of a matching algorithm.

The FingerCode algorithm [25] filters the fingerprint image by a bank of Gabor filters that are tuned to different orientations. Next, the fixed-length feature vector, which is called FingerCode, is computed as the standard deviation in a number of predefined sectors. Each value is indicative of the overall ridge activity in a certain orientation in that sector. It is expected to capture both global and local characteristics of the fingerprint image. The matching of two FingerCodes is performed simply by taking the Euclidean distance between the two feature vectors. The matching performance can be improved by combining the decisions of the FingerCode matcher with a traditional minutiae-based system [27].

In [9], a correlation-based fingerprint verification algorithm is presented. This algorithm first selects characteristic gray-scale templates in the reference fingerprint. Template matching is then used to find the corresponding template positions in the test print. Finally, both sets of template positions are compared. Elementary decisions are subsequently made by classifying the individual template position pairs in matching or non-matching. The information of all matching template pairs is then combined in order to make a final decision whether the reference and test fingerprints match.

In [34], a verification system is presented that is based on triangular matching and dynamic time warping. Gray-scale templates are selected at the minutiae locations in the first fingerprint, and their most likely positions in the second print are found by means of template matching. Next, a technique called *triangular matching* is used to find a possible correspondence between the two prints. Finally, the match is verified using dynamic time warping to validate the gray-scale values along the lines that connect neighboring minutiae.

2.4.12 Classification

Classification systems determine which class or category the input fingerprint belongs to. Classification is an important first step in any identification system. The task of a fingerprint identification system is to find the fingerprint in a database that matches a query fingerprint. A naive identification system would simply compare the given fingerprint to all entries in the database. However, for databases of a realistic size, two closely related problems are encountered when applying this approach. Since many matches are performed, the required processing time will be excessive, and the performance will be inadequate. This is illustrated by a simple example.

Consider the identification of a fingerprint in a database of $n = 10,000$ entries. A fast matching algorithm, requiring only $t_{match} = 100$ milliseconds per match, needs almost 17 minutes for this task, and a matching algorithm with a very good performance of $FAR = 10^{-4}$ will find on average $n \cdot FAR = 1$ false match in this database. Furthermore, the probability of false acceptance over the entire database can be computed as: $FAR_{1:n} = 1 - (1 - FAR)^n = 0.63$. Obviously, these performance figures are unacceptable for any identification system.

To reduce these problems, classification is used [52]. All fingerprints in the database are classified. They are stored per class in separate databases. The query fingerprint is also classified and is only matched to the n_i fingerprints in that part of the database that contains fingerprints of the corresponding class i. The effect is two-fold, as illustrated when we carry on with the previous example. Assume that the fingerprints are classified into 100 equal-size classes and that therefore $n_i = 100$ for all i. The processing time will thus come down to 10 s, and the average number of false matches will be $n_i \cdot FAR = 0.01$ and $FAR_{1:n_i} = 10^{-2}$. However, in realistic modern fingerprint identification systems, the size of the fingerprint database is limited to a few hundred entries for reasonable performance and identification time [15].

A well-known set of categories is formed by the *Henry* classes. They consist of five classes related to global fingerprint patterns, based on the structure of the directional field. Examples of fingerprints from the five Henry classes (whorl, left loop, right loop, arch, and tented arch) are shown in Figure 2.15. Sometimes, a 4-class Henry classification is used, where arch and tented arch are combined into a single class. On the other hand, it is also possible to define more than five classes, for example adding pocketed loops, double loops, and scars.

Many ways to classify fingerprints to one of the Henry classes are known from literature. In [30], fingerprints are classified in the Henry classes by examining the relative positions of the singular points. In [13], a graph of homogeneous regions in the directional field is constructed and the graph is classified. In [21], FingerCode is used as a feature vector for Henry classification. The most popular classification approach is the application of principal component analysis (PCA) or Karhunen-Loève transform (KL) [18] to the block directional field (BDF) estimate [11]. Each element in the BDF is represented by a vector of two components that points in the direction of the local ridge orientation. The resulting vectors are concatenated to form a feature vector. Next, the dimensionality of this feature vector is reduced by the application of PCA. This method removes the redundancy and noise, while maintaining the maximum amount of information in the feature vector. The resulting small feature vector is classified by a probabilistic neural network. Multiple fingerprint classifiers can of course be combined to improve their performance [14].

There are two reasons why Henry classification is not able to reduce the size of the database to be searched very much. First, there are only five Henry classes and 90% of all fingerprints belongs to only three classes. Without classification errors, this would reduce the number of matches to 30% of the original. Second, the state-of-the-art classifiers at the moment perform at an error rate of about

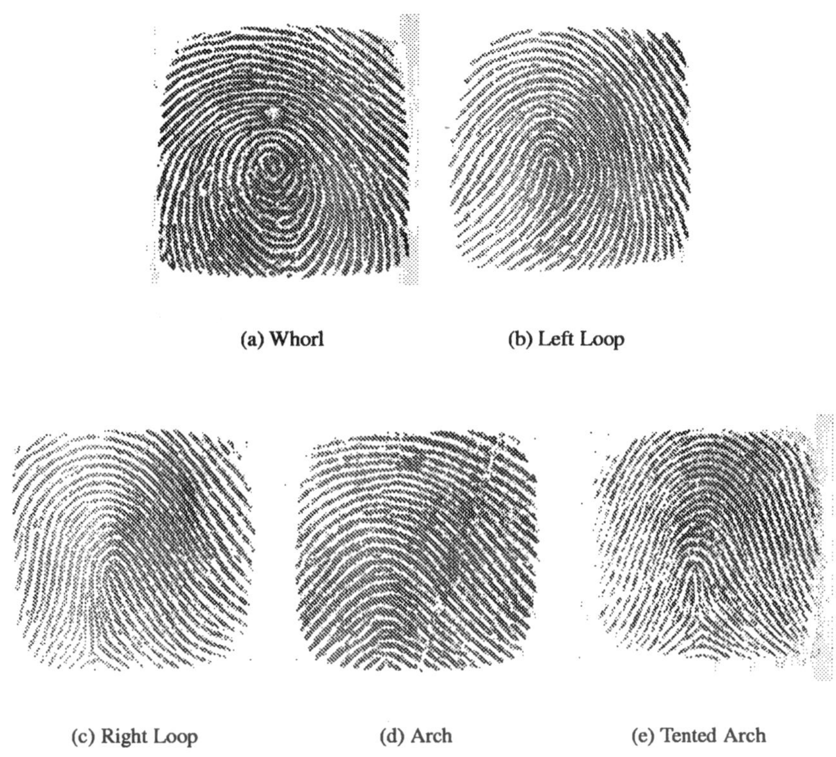

Figure 2.15. Examples of fingerprints from the five Henry classes.

6% for the Henry classes. This means that for 6% of the query prints, the corresponding print is not found correctly in the database due to classification errors. Alternatively, 20% of the query fingerprints is rejected for classification, resulting in an error rate of 1%. The effect of the rejection is that for 20% of the fingerprints the entire database has to be searched, while 1% of the prints still remains non-identified due to classification errors. One can conclude that the practical value of Henry classification is limited.

2.4.13 Indexing

To overcome some of these problems, a *continuous classification* scheme is proposed in [36]. Again, a feature vector is extracted from the fingerprints. Instead of classifying a feature vector and matching the query fingerprint to all prints in the corresponding class, the similarity of feature vectors is used as a criterion for ordering database entries. Thus, the more similar the feature vectors are, the earlier the match is performed. For this *indexing* method, the maximum part of the database to be searched is adjustable.

Most of the DF-related classification features can be used for indexing as well. Examples are the KL transform of the BDF estimate [36, 10], the multi-space KL transform of the BDF estimate [15, 14], the graph of homogeneous regions [14], and FingerCode [10].

In [17], a feature vector that is based on minutiae triplets is proposed. The algorithm first identifies all minutiae triplets in a fingerprint. Each triplet defines a triangle, from which various geometric features are extracted. One can, for instance, use the length of the sides, the angles, etc. Next, the similarity to another fingerprint is defined by the number of approximately corresponding minutiae triplets that can be found by rigid transformation. Instead of comparing the extracted triplets to each fingerprint, the authors use the Flash algorithm which constructs hash tables for fast indexing in a database.

The performance of an indexing algorithm can be visualized in a graph such as the one depicted in Figure 2.16. This graph shows the probability that the corresponding fingerprint is found versus the part of the database that is searched. From this graph, performance measures for two indexing strategies can be derived. The first strategy searches a fixed part of the database. The corresponding performance measure gives the probability that the query fingerprint is found in this part. The second strategy is much more powerful. It reduces the number of matches further by stopping the search once a match is found. The average size of the database to be searched until the matching fingerprint is found provides a second measure of the indexing performance.

Direct application of continuous classification increases the performance with respect to Henry classification, but it is still not acceptable for commercial use in large databases. In realistic modern fingerprint identification systems, the size of the fingerprint database is limited to a few hundred entries for reasonable performance and identification time [15].

Further improvement of performance is achieved by the combination of multiple features for indexing. In [14], two indexing features are combined by taking the weighted average of a non-linear function of the two feature distances. It has been shown that this increases the performance of the indexing scheme. However, the increase of performance is only significant for situations where a small part of the database is searched. This corresponds to the left-most part of the graph of Figure 2.16. When higher matching rates are required, the combination does not perform better than the individual classifiers.

Performance is improved much more when combining indexing features by means of ranked list combination. In [10], this method is used to combine the BDF estimate, FingerCode, and minutiae triplets. This approach is able to increase the performance considerably across the whole range, as shown in Figure 2.16. The average number of non-matching prints that has to be

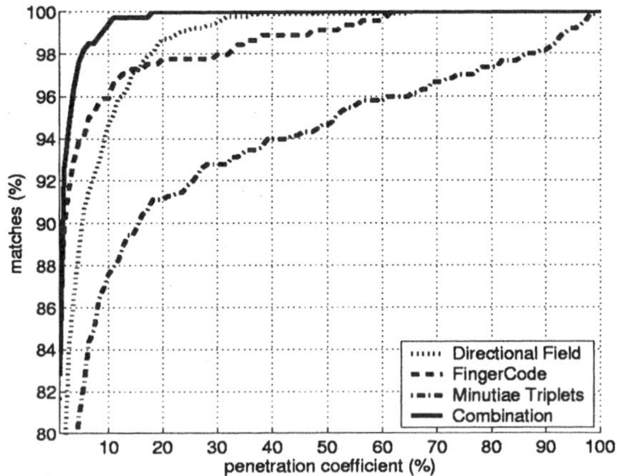

Figure 2.16. Database indexing performance for various features and their combination.

searched, which causes the increased FAR, is reduced to less than 0.5% of the database when combining features.

2.5.　Discussion

In this section, we will discuss the possibilities for performance improvement of the selected applications described in Section 2.3. We then present a summary of where the algorithms of Section 2.4 may contribute to the performance improvement. Lastly, we explore where further improvements are necessary.

High-security physical access control and computer login both perform at satisfactory levels. Of course, each new method can be used to improve performance further, but this is not strictly necessary for the adequate behavior of the systems.

One of the problems in the key-less locker application is the robust extraction of minutiae from fingerprints that are acquired from wet fingers. To improve the minutiae extraction performance to an acceptable level, all possible methods need to be used. Especially, more research in sensor technology, segmentation, enhancement, minutiae postprocessing, and alternative minutiae extraction approaches is needed.

Both in the key-less locker and in the smart card applications, elastic distortions seriously decrease matching performance. The problem in the locker applications is caused by the water of the swimming pool. The skin of fingers that have been wet for a period of time expands and is less tightly fit around the finger. This causes serious distortions of the fingerprints, even without excessive forces being applied. In the smart card application, distortions originate from users who do not want to be identified as being present on a black list.

They apply excessive forces in order to distort their fingerprint intentionally. Both applications can benefit from the distortion-invariant matching algorithm that is proposed in [6]. Furthermore, the controlled image acquisition [47] can be used to reduce deliberate distortions in the smart card application.

Key-less lockers and biometric smart cards make use of an identification system. Therefore, both applications will benefit from indexing schemes that are based on the combination of multiple features. This will reduce processing times and false acceptance rates.

2.6. Conclusions

In this chapter, we have reviewed a large range of algorithms that may belong to a fingerprint matching system. For most tasks, different methods have been presented and new potential algorithms have been introduced that will improve the performance of the system.

Not all components of a fingerprint recognition system have reached the same level of maturity. On fingerprints sensors, continuous research is performed, aiming at higher image quality and the development of smaller and lower-cost sensors. The directional field estimation and singular point extraction algorithms perform well, while enhancement and segmentation still require improvement. In minutiae extraction, improvements can be expected from the development of alternative methods, while elastic deformations are the most interesting topic in minutiae matching. Finally, many challenges remain toward improvement of indexing methods for searching large fingerprint databases.

Next, we have discussed which new algorithms can be beneficial to the selected applications and how they will improve performance. The strong demand from industry for improved performance illustrates the need for the development of more advanced fingerprint recognition algorithms.

Acknowledgments

We would like to thank Anton Kuip from NEDAP for sharing his experience with real-life applications of fingerprint recognition and for providing insight into the practical problems that are encountered in these applications.

References

[1]   J. Ashbourn. Biometrics: Advanced Identity Verification. Springer-Verlag, London, 2000.

[2]   A.M. Bazen and S.H. Gerez. Directional Field Computation for Fingerprints Based on the Principal Component Analysis of Local Gradients. In Proc. of ProRISC2000,

11th Annual Workshop on Circuits, Systems and Signal Processing, Veldhoven, The Netherlands, November 2000.

[3] A.M. Bazen and S.H. Gerez. Extraction of Singular Points from Directional Fields of Fingerprints. In Mobile Communications in Perspective. In Proc. of CTIT Workshop on Mobile Communications, pages 41–44, University of Twente, Enschede, The Netherlands, February 2001.

[4] A.M. Bazen and S.H. Gerez. An Intrinsic Coordinate System for Fingerprint Matching. In Proc. of 3rd Int. Conf. Audio- and Video-Based Biometric Person Authentication (AVBPA 2001), June 2001.

[5] A.M. Bazen and S.H. Gerez. Segmentation of Fingerprint Images. In Proc. of ProR-ISC2001, 12th Annual Workshop on Circuits, Systems and Signal Processing, Veldhoven, The Netherlands, November 2001.

[6] A.M. Bazen and S.H. Gerez. Elastic Minutiae Matching by Means of Thin-plate Spline Models. In Proc. of ICPR 2002, Quebec City, August 2002. Submitted.

[7] A.M. Bazen and S.H. Gerez. Systematic Methods for the Computation of the Directional Field and Singular Points of Fingerprints. IEEE Trans. PAMI, 24(6), June 2002.

[8] A.M. Bazen, M. van Otterlo, S.H. Gerez, and M. Poel. A Reinforcement Learning Agent for Minutiae Extraction from Fingerprints. In Proc. of BNAIC 2001, Amsterdam, October 2001.

[9] A.M. Bazen, G.T.B. Verwaaijen, L.P.J. Veelenturf, B.J. van der Zwaag, and S.H. Gerez. A Correlation-based Fingerprint Verification System. In Proc. of ProRISC2000, 11th Annual Workshop on Circuits, Systems and Signal Processing, Veldhoven, The Netherlands, November 2000.

[10] J. de Boer, A.M. Bazen, and S.H. Gerez. Indexing Fingerprint Databases Based on Multiple Features. In Proc. of ProRISC2001, 12th Annual Workshop on Circuits, Systems and Signal Processing, Veldhoven, The Netherlands, November 2001.

[11] G.T. Candela, P.J. Grother, C.I. Watson, R.A. Wilkinson, and C.L. Wilson. PCASYS - A Pattern-level Classification Automation System for Fingerprints. Technical Report NISTIR 5647, NIST, April 1995.

[12] R. Cappelli, A. Erol, D. Maio, and D. Maltoni. Synthetic Fingerprint-image Generation. In Proc. of ICPR2000, 15th Int. Conf. Pattern Recognition, Barcelona, Spain, September 2000.

[13] R. Cappelli, A. Lumini, D. Maio, and D. Maltoni. Fingerprint Classification by Directional Image Partitioning. IEEE Trans. PAMI, 21(5):402–421, May 1999.

[14] R. Cappelli, D. Maio, and D. Maltoni. Combining Fingerprint Classifiers. In Proc. of First International Workshop on Multiple Classifier Systems (MCS2000), pages 351–361, Cagliari, June 2000.

[15] R. Cappelli, D. Maio, and D. Maltoni. Indexing Fingerprint Databases for Efficient 1:n Matching. In Proc. of Sixth Int. Conf. on Control, Automation, Robotics and Vision (ICARCV2000), Singapore, December 2000.

[16] R. Cappelli, D. Maio, and D. Maltoni. Modelling Plastic Distortion in Fingerprint Images. In Proc. of ICAPR2001, Second Int. Conf. Advances in Pattern Recognition, Rio de Janeiro, March 2001.

[17] R.S. Germain, A. Califano, and S. Colville. Fingerprint Matching Using Transformation Parameter Clustering. IEEE Computational Science and Engineering, 4(4):42–49, 1997.

[18]   S. Haykin. Neural Networks, A Comprehensive Foundation. Prentice Hall International, Inc., Upper Saddle River, NJ, 1999.

[19]   L. Hong, Y. Wan, and A. Jain. Fingerprint Image Enhancement: Algorithm and Performance Eevaluation. IEEE Trans. PAMI, 20(8):777–789, August 1998.

[20]   D.K. Isenor and S.G. Zaky. Fingerprint Identification Using Graph Matching. Pattern Recognition, 19(2):113–122, 1986.

[21]   A. K. Jain, S. Prabhakar, and L. Hong. A Multichannel Approach to Fingerprint Classification. IEEE Trans. PAMI, 21(4):348–359, April 1999.

[22]   A.K. Jain. Biometrics Research Homepage at MSU. http://biometrics.cse.msu.edu/.

[23]   A.K. Jain, L. Hong, S. Pankanti, and R. Bolle. An Identity-authentication System Using Fingerprints. In Proc. of the IEEE, 85(9):1365–1388, September 1997.

[24]   A.K. Jain, S. Prabhakar, and S. Chen. Combining Multiple Matchers for a High Security Fingerprint Verification System. Pattern Recognition Letters, 20(11-13):1371–1379, November 1999.

[25]   A.K. Jain, S. Prabhakar, L. Hong, and S. Pankanti. Filterbank-based Fingerprint Matching. IEEE Trans. Image Processing, 9(5):846–859, May 2000.

[26]   A.K. Jain and N.K. Ratha. Object Detection Using Gabor Filters. Pattern Recognition, 30(2):295–309, February 1997.

[27]   A.K. Jain, A. Ross, and S. Prabhakar. Fingerprint Matching Using Minutiae and Texture Features. In Proc. of Int. Conf. on Image Processing (ICIP), Greece, October 2001.

[28]   X. Jiang and W.Y. Yau. Fingerprint Minutiae Matching Based on the Local and Global structures. In Proc. of ICPR2000, 15th Int. Conf. Pattern Recognition, vol. 2, pages 1042–1045, Barcelona, Spain, September 2000.

[29]   X. Jiang, W.Y. Yau, and W. Ser. Detecting the Fingerprint Minutiae by Adaptive Tracing the Gray-level Ridge. Pattern Recognition, 34(5):999–1013, May 2001.

[30]   K. Karu and A.K. Jain. Fingerprint Classification. Pattern Recognition, 29(3):389–404, 1996.

[31]   M. Kass and A. Witkin. Analyzing Oriented Patterns. Computer Vision, Graphics, and Image Processing, 37(3):362–385, March 1987.

[32]   M. Kawagoe and A. Tojo. Fingerprint Pattern Classification. Pattern Recognition, 17(3):295–303, 1984.

[33]   J. Kittler, M. Hatef, R.P.W. Duin, and J. Matas. On Combining Classifiers. IEEE Trans. PAMI, 20(3):226–239, March 1998.

[34]   Z.M. Kovács-Vajna. A Fingerprint Verification System Based on Triangular Matching and Dynamic Time Warping. IEEE Trans. PAMI, 22(11):1266–1276, November 2000.

[35]   T. Lindeberg. Scale-Space Theory in Computer Vision. Kluwer Academic Publishers, Boston, 1994.

[36]   A. Lumini, D. Maio, and D. Maltoni. Continuous versus Exclusive Classification for Fingerprint Retrieval. Pattern Recognition Letters, 18(10):1027–1034, 1997.

[37]   D. Maio and D. Maltoni. Direct Gray-scale Minutiae Detection in Fingerprints. IEEE Trans. PAMI, 19(1):27–39, January 1997.

[38]   D. Maio and D. Maltoni. Minutiae Extraction and Filtering from Gray-scale Images. In L.C. Jain et al., editor, Intelligent Biometric Techniques in Fingerprint and Face Recognition, pages 155–192. CRC Press LLC, 1999.

[39] B.M. Mehtre and B. Chatterjee. Segmentation of Fingerprint Images - A Composite Method. Pattern Recognition, 22(4):381–385, 1989.

[40] P.G.M. van der Meulen, H. Schipper, A.M. Bazen, and S.H. Gerez. PMDGP: A Distributed Object-oriented Genetic Programming Environment. In Proc. of ASCI Conference 2001, May 2001.

[41] NEDAP. N.V. Nederlandse Apparatenfabriek. http://www.nedap.com/.

[42] S. Prabhakar and A.K. Jain. Decision-level Fusion in Fingerprint Verification. Pattern Recognition, 2001.

[43] S. Prabhakar, A.K. Jain, J. Wang, S. Pankanti, and R. Bolle. Minutia Verification and Classification for Fingerprint Matching. In Proc. of ICPR2000, 15th Int. Conf. Pattern Recognition, Barcelona, Spain, September 2000.

[44] J.G. Proakis, C.M. Rader, F. Ling, and C.L. Nikias. Advanced Digital Signal Processing. Macmillan Publishing Company, NY, 1992.

[45] L.R. Rabiner. A Tutorial on Hidden Markov Models and Selected Applications in Speech Recognition. In Proc. of the IEEE, 77(2):257–286, February 1989.

[46] N. Ratha, S. Chen, and A. Jain. Adaptive Flow Orientation Based Feature Extraction in Fingerprint Images. Pattern Recognition, 28:1657–1672, Nov. 1995.

[47] N.K. Ratha and R.M. Bolle. Effect of Controlled Image Acquisition on Fingerprint Matching. In Proc. of 14th ICPR, pages 1659–1661, 1998.

[48] N.K. Ratha, R.M. Bolle, V.D. Pandit, and V. Vaish. Robust Fingerprint Authentication Using Local Structural Similarity. In Proc. of 5th IEEE Workshop Appl. Comp. Vision, pages 29–34, 2000.

[49] N.K. Ratha, J.H. Connell, and R.M. Bolle. Image Mosaicing for Rolled Fingerprint Construction. In Proc. of 14th ICPR, vol. 2, pages 1651–1653, 1998.

[50] A.W. Senior and R. Bolle. Improved Fingerprint Matching by Distortion Removal. IEICE Trans. Inf. and Syst., Special issue on Biometrics, E84-D(7):825–831, July 2001.

[51] B.G. Sherlock, D.M. Monro, and K. Millard. Fingerprint Enhancement by Directional Fourier Filtering. IEE Proc.-Vis. Image Signal Process., 141(2):87–94, April 1994.

[52] J.L. Wayman. Error Rate Equations for the General Biometric System. IEEE Robotics and Automation Magazine, 6(1):35–48, March 1999.

[53] C.L. Wilson, G.T. Candela, and C.I. Watson. Neural Network Fingerprint Classification. J. Artificial Neural Networks, 1(2):203–228, 1994.

[54] Q. Xiao and H. Raafat. Fingerprint Image Postprocessing: A Combined Statistical and Structural Approach. Pattern Recognition, 24(10):985–992, 1991.

Chapter 3

BIOMETRICS ELECTRONIC PURSE

Eng Chong Tan, Abdul Wahab and Su Miang Heng
School of Computer Engineering
Nanyang Technological University
Nanyang Avenue, Singapore 639798, Singapore
{asectan, asabdul}@ntu.edu.sg, shuming@ieee.org

Abstract   As a result of the rapid development of technology, the deployment of biometrics electronic purse has moved from the laboratory to the commercial world. This chapter reviews the current advances and designs of biometrics electronic purse. In particular, the architecture of a smart card and its security issues related to commercial applications are addressed.

Keywords: Biometrics, electronic purse, smart card, Java card, security

3.1.   Introduction

3.1.1   Credit Cards

Nowadays, one of the most popular ways of paying for consumer transactions offline, or online via the Internet for those companies which support electronic payment or electronic commerce (*e*-commerce), is by credit (or debit) card. Basically, a credit card is made of plastic and contains a magnetized stripe on one side which can be read by decoders designed for that purpose. Its widespread public understanding and acceptance stem from the facts that it is a well-established technology with large installed commercial infrastructure and that it is relatively inexpensive to produce and use in most online environments.

However, its disadvantages are also quite a few. A substantial number of disputes and frauds come from credit-card payments because credit cards are relatively easy to duplicate or counterfeit. In addition, credit cards have limited data storage capacity and those with low coercivity are easily damaged (i.e. stripe demagnetized). Commercially, credit cards are not acceptable or practical for all forms of transactions especially when the amount involved is too small. There are also people who do not qualify to have credit cards.

3.1.2   Smart Cards and Electronic Purse

As an effort to counteract the limitations of magnetic-stripe cards, the advent of smart cards [1], [2] provides enhanced capabilities to credit cards. A smart card is a credit-card sized plastic card (most still having the magnetized stripe) with an embedded microcomputer chip. In fact, since about five years ago, many banks have been issuing smart cards which function as credit cards as well as cashcards. A cashcard contains digital cash, allowing consumers to make small anonymous payments. The so-called digital cash is a string of digits, issued by a bank or a finance company. Every token has a digital 'stamp' that can be checked and validated by the bank when the merchant redeems the token.

An electronic purse is simply a cashcard that belongs to a pre-paid card system which avoids the use of cash money and cheques, especially meant for financial transactions of low amounts; it can be defined as: "Any card or function of a card which contains real value in the form of electronic money which someone has paid for in advance, and which can be reloaded with further funds and which can be used for a range of purposes".

When a user wants to recharge an electronic purse, he must be able to operate an ATM or card-loading terminal. Generally he needs to key in his PIN (personal identification number) before the loading process can be completed. To use the electronic purse, the user hands the card to the shop assistant who inserts the card into a terminal and keys in the amount of the transaction which is displayed to the customer. The customer confirms the amount (and keys in the PIN if necessary) and a value is debited from the card and transferred to the merchant account.

3.1.3   Security Issues of Electronic Purse

Today's network infrastructures have become so complex that their multidimensional entities require security at different levels of both network hardware and software. This is particularly true when the commercial industry has growing use and ubiquitous reliance on computer networks for electronic transactions. The commercial industry has become very interested in security of networks since, now, a favourable cost benefit can be associated with security. The problems with the electronic-purse approach might not lie in the underlying technology but in the mechanism in which this technology is deployed. One of the major concerns is identification integrity. It is difficult to check the identity of the person doing the transaction. Consumers might risk paying and not getting what they are paying for and may worry about theft or misuse of their personal and account information. The merchant on the other hand is worried about the credibility of the transaction and the true identity of the purchaser.

The prevailing technological solutions available today are based on encryption techniques such as Secure Electronic Transaction (SET) developed by MasterCard and Visa and the Secure Sockets Layer (SSL) developed by Netscape. These techniques deal with messaging integrity and provide security for Web transactions by encrypting packets of information transmitted to the Internet site but do not deal with identification, credibility or privacy. In other words, while passwords/PINs are one of the first identifiers to offer automated recognition, it is the input that is recognized, not the person who has provided it. A system which relies on passwords/PINs only is generally vulnerable to forgery and theft since passwords/ PINs can be easily compromised.

3.1.4   Particular Human Features or Behaviours

There are certain physical or physiological features of a human being, which are distinctly different from one another. The most commonly known features include fingerprint, face, hand geometry, retina and iris structures. Other distinct physiological characteristics that manifest their prominence only during actual behavioural execution are signature and voice (or speech).

Over years of extensive research and studies, scientists have used those biological features or behaviours [3], [4] as 'measured criteria' (termed biometrics) to develop various types of reliable pattern recognition systems which find applications in security. A biometric represents a unique identifier that cannot be easily transferred between individuals, and a biometric system is a pattern recognition system that establishes the authenticity of a specific physiological or behavioural characteristic possessed by a user.

A biometric system can be used either as an identification system or a verification (authentication) system. Identification requires establishing a person's identity. Verification (whether a person is who he claims he is) involves confirming or denying a person's claimed identity. Biometrics can be used in lieu of cards as a means of access to an electronic system, or they can be used in conjunction with smart cards to provide a more efficient and secure access. In this chapter, our emphasis is on the latter.

While magnetic stripe cards, such as conventional credit cards, are primarily access devices to a centralized database system of authorized users, smart cards which have biometric measurements can be used either as access devices in a centralized system, or as components of an offline decentralized system.

3.2. Smart-Card Technology

3.2.1 Overview

A smart card is a device that has both processing power and memory, and is capable of being packaged in the format defined by the International Standards Organization (ISO). The technology originated in the seventies in Germany, Japan and France. Since then, the industry has been growing at a tremendous rate, producing more than one billion cards per year since 1998.

A typical smart card has the same three fundamental elements as all other computers: processing power, data storage and a means to input and output data. The processing power is supplied by a microprocessor (actually a micro-controller, e.g. Intel 8051 or Motorola 6805, plus memory). The microprocessor is able to manipulate data and solve mathematical problems. Microprocessor chips are currently available with 8-, 16-, and 32-bit architectures. The data storage (EEPROM, FLASH, ROM, or RAM) has capacity ranges from 300 bytes to 32,000 bytes. It has at least 60 times more memory than a conventional magnetic-strip card.

The means in which data is transferred varies from card to card. In order to operate, each card must have a power source, whether in a card reader or on the card itself. A typical smart-card reader [5] is shown in Figure 3.1. It is relatively more difficult to duplicate or counterfeit a smart card because a much more sophisticated equipment is required to do so.

3.2.2 Types of Smart Cards

Depending on the access mechanism, smart cards can be classified into four types:

(1) Contact smart card – The card has embedded microelectronics with connections to contact pads on the surface of the card (usually a small gold chip about 1.5 x 1.5 cm^2 in area). The contacts enable the microcomputer to get power from, and communicate with a read/write unit. Many contact smart cards also incorporate a magnetic stripe in order to be compatible with existing equipment.

(2) Contactless smart card – It dispenses with the contact plate on the surface of a smart card and instead uses some form of electrical coupling. Generally, a contactless smart card will be placed in close proximity to a reader, less than 3 cm. An inductive (transformer) or capacitive coupling is used to transfer energy and power to the card. The clock may be internally derived and the input/output is achieved by modulating the power signal. In certain design, a contactless smart card has a miniature radio transmitter that allows the information on the chip to be read remotely.

(3) Combination smart card – It is a single card which has the features of both contact and contactless smart cards, with the additions of magnetic stripe and one-dimensional and/or two-dimensional bar-code technology incorporated into the card. This allows the card to have multi-applications if necessary. (One example of combination smart card is the "CombiCard", developed by GemPlus [6])

(4) Super smart card – It incorporates a keyboard and displays directly on the surface of the card. It can function as a standalone unit, or be connected to a computer. For this purpose, it generally has surface contacts. Disadvantages of a super smart card include high cost of production in comparison with other types of cards, difficulty in meeting ISO standards and the small size of the keypad. The primary benefit of a super smart card is its offline and self-validating functionality. (An example of a super smart card is the ULTICARD^{TM}, developed by SmartCard International Inc. in New York.)

For electronic purse applications, the contact or contactless smart card represents a more economical choice than the other two.

3.2.3   Classification of Smart Cards

Depending on their communication methods (ISO 7816-3), smart cards can be further classified as memory or intelligence cards:

(1) Memory smart card (synchronous card) – This is the most basic type of chip card. It contains a chip capable of storing data but not capable of processing information. Once linked to the outside world, it is powered, clocked and addressed totally under the control of the outside world. All that it is possible to do is directly addressing the memory on the chip. The non-processor chip that has hard wired logic to control access security, operates simply by setting an internal on/off switch based upon an equal or not equal compare of the supplied data (e.g., the PIN) with a hidden data area in the chip's memory. Once the test has been passed, the switch is set and the data is accessible or updateable according to the chip type. It is useful for stored value or electronic purse applications in which a financial value is stored on the card and debited when the card is used for a purchase.

(2) Intelligence smart card (asynchronous card) – This is a micro-processor chip card, or integrated circuit card which can add, delete, and otherwise manipulate information in its memory. It can be viewed as a miniature computer with an input/output port, a Smart Card Operating System (SCOS) which is unique to the chip or card supplier, and hard disk. The SCOS is also known as Reader Operating System (ROS). Given this capability, it is possible to drive the input/output line between the smart card and the reader as though it were a normal RS232 communication line. ISO 7816-3 defines a communication mechanism similar to RS232 operating at 9600 baud with even parity.

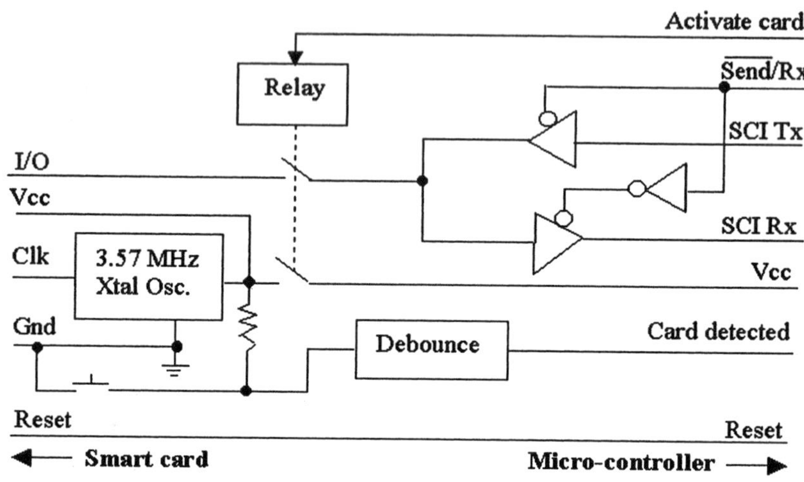

Figure 3.1. Design of a smart-card reader.

3.2.4   Java Card Technology

A Java card is a new generation of intelligence smart card that is capable of running Java programs. The Java Card API (Application Programming Interface) is part of the smallest virtual machine specification for Java. The specification is designed to allow Java to run on an 8-bit microprocessor, with 8KB of EEPROM, 16KB ROM, and 256B RAM.

The specification was first released by Schlumberger in November 1996 with its launch of the first commercial Java Card. In the following year, JavaSoft (a subsidiary of Sun Microsystems [7], [8]) released the Java card 2.0 API specification and it became an industry accepted specification for Java card. Soon, every major vendor of smart cards in the world had licensed the technology. All these vendors are in the process of building working implementations. Two of the major smart card players in the market, Schlumberger and GemPlus, already have implementations and development toolkits available for sale (GemPlus [9] even has a Java card with a 32-bit RISC core). It is expected that, by about 2002, over 700 million of the 3 billion cards sold will run the Java card virtual machine.

The limitation of conventional smart card technology is that there is no portability of applications and the flexibility to download applications into the card. In addition, knowledgeable smart card programmers are also hard to find. The unique design of Java virtual machine nevertheless offers the smart card industry a plausible solution.

As Java Applet is small, it is perfect for multiple applications to reside on a single card within a limited memory available on the card. As applets are downloadable, they can also be installed into the card dynamically via a Card Accepting Device (CAD) such as a smart card reader or even a public phone. The functionality of a Java card can be continually updated when new applications are available.

Java card uses an applet firewall to prevent individual applet from accessing the behavior or contents of objects owned by other applets so as to create a secure environment. For instance, an applet from Bank A will not be able to access any data from its competitor, Bank B's applet. On top of the security built into the platform, application developers can add their own additional layers of security in the form of data encryption or biometrics authentication.

The use of Java high-level language speeds up and simplifies the development of smart card applications so that new products can be deployed as quickly as possible. Although high-level language applications tend to run slower and consume more system resources, this should not be a problem as technology improves. In just a year since the release of the Schlumberger Cyberflex card [10], memory size has already doubled and even a 32-bit RISC core is available today.

3.2.5 Java Card Applications

With many new technologies, there is still uncertainty of what innovative products will emerge from Java cards. However, there are some clearly defined markets that will adopt Java cards in the next few years. After the introduction of Java cards, the telecommunication market is the pioneer in accepting the new technology. For example, Telecom Italia Mobile (TIM), with more than 11 million subscribers in Italy, was one of the operators that adapted Java-based platform in its future generation of SIM (Subscriber Identity Module) card for GSM (Global System for Mobile telecommunications) network.

Java's flexibility to download applets dynamically and its multi-application support allow network operators to add, remove and enhance services at any time during subscription for mobile phone services. The integration of Java with SIM card has created a new generation of "smart phone" which enables new and complex applications to be downloaded and stored in the mobile environment. In fact, Schlumbeger had demonstrated a Java-enabled SIM card (CyberFlex Simera) that worked with the latest Ericsson and Motorola cellular phones in Singapore in 1998 (Computer Times, Dec 2, 1998). After a service provider has downloaded its Java applet into the subscriber's mobile phone, the mobile phone menu will be automatically changed to reflect the new service provided.

Applications in the personal computer (PC) world are expected to take off quickly with Microsoft supporting smart cards in its latest Windows operating system and Windows CE. In addition, with PC/Smart-card specification, a smart card reader is treated by a PC just like a disk drive. As a result, we now have a reader-independent smart-card application programming interfaces. Hence, smart card is expected to be a standard "peripheral" for PC in the near future.

Scientists have also been constantly looking for more efficient algorithms which can be implemented on small word-sized microcomputers like Java cards. For example, a modulo multiplication algorithm which can be implemented on a 8-bit micro-controller [11] plays a very significant role in the context of cryptographic applications, as many of the so called "signing" operations are usually associated with such small single-chip microcomputers.

In order to support the resource hungry biometric verification algorithms, it is essential to use a Java card for the implementation of a biometrics electronic purse.

3.3. Biometric Methodologies

3.3.1 Signature Verification

This is probably one of the oldest verification methodologies of human civilization. Signature is a behavioural type of physiological characteristic owned by a user, and enjoys a synergy with existing processes that other biometrics do not. However, the uniqueness of a signature is not easily recognizable without extensive training. Although signature verification devices have proven to be reasonably accurate in operation and lend themselves to applications where the signature is an acceptable identifier, its usage alone for biometric measurement in more security-stringent applications such as electronic purse is inadequate.

3.3.2 Voice Recognition

Voice recognition is related but not exactly the same as speech recognition. Speaker recognition verifies the speaker's identity but the speech recognition interprets what the speaker say.

Speaker recognition technology can be classified into two basic types: text-dependent and text-independent. In text-dependent recognition, the speaker is required to say a predetermined phrase and thus his cooperation is needed. In text-independent recognition, the speaker need not say a predetermined phrase and need not cooperate or even be aware of the recognition system. Many of the voice recognition systems have suffered in practice because of the variability of both transducers and local acoustics. Moreover, the enrolment procedure has often been more complicated than with other biometrics. Consequently, it is difficult to deploy the current voice recognition technology for biometrics electronic purse.

3.3.3 Face Recognition

In face recognition technology, it is relatively easy to accurately match two static images, but it is much more difficult to detect and verify the identity of an individual within a group. The majority of face recognition algorithms appear to be sensitive to variations in illumination. In addition, changing facial position can have an effect on the performance of a face recognition system. While the technology might have a better success with more powerful and elaborate computer/camera set-up, its implementation for biometrics electronic purse is still immature and requires further advances in both algorithms and smart card technology (more processing power and memory).

3.3.4 Hand Geometry

Hand geometry devices measure the three-dimensional physical characteristics of a user's hand and fingers, such as the length and placement of fingers, skin translucency and hand thickness. In fact, hand geometry is one of the most established methodologies, offers good reliability, and is relatively easy to use. Furthermore, hand geometry takes up minimum storage and can be considered for biometric identification of electronic purse, but the accuracy of the method is not as good as that of fingerprint.

3.3.5 Fingerprint Recognition

One of the earliest and best-known biometric technologies is fingerprint recognition. Automatic fingerprint-based identification systems were used in the early days primarily in forensic applications for investigating criminals, but have now entered the government and commercial application domains. Some fingerprint recognition systems emulate the traditional police method of matching minutiae, while others are straight pattern matching devices. There is a greater variety of fingerprint devices available than any other biometrics nowadays. Owing to the advances in the processing algorithms, the resulting fingerprint features of a user need only a small storage space. In addition, because of the uniqueness of individual fingerprint and the high accuracy of fingerprint recognition techniques, the technology is definitely suitable for deployment in biometrics electronic purse.

3.3.6   Retina Scanning

A user needs to look into a receptacle and focus on a given point. The unique patterns of the retina are then scanned by a low intensity light source via an optical coupler. This is not particularly convenient if the user wears glasses or has concern about physical contact with the reading device. For these reasons, retina scanning has some user acceptance problems. Although retina recognition achieves high accuracy, similar to that of fingerprint, its implementation in biometrics electronic purse is less versatile.

3.3.7   Iris Scanning

It is a less intrusive eye-related biometric and uses a fairly conventional camera technology and requires no physical contact between user and reader. Iris recognition has the highest accuracy among all the biometrics at the moment. Moreover, it has been demonstrated to work with glasses in place, and is one of the few devices that can work well in identification mode. However, the technology needs more equipments and elaborate set-up. Because of higher storage requirement of a compressed iris image file (about 20 Kbytes), its deployment in biometrics electronic purse at present will be expensive, but its future is extremely promising.

3.4.   Design of Biometrics Electronic Purse

3.4.1   Applications in Mind

A design example is given here to illustrate the design of a multiple-applications Java card which can function as a biometrics electronic purse and a passport [12], in order to carry out any form of *e*-commerce transactions as shown in Figure 3.2. The card has all the corresponding applets installed on it.

For instance, a cardholder can install on-line payment, on-line booking and on-line entertainment service applets over the distributed network such as the Internet from his utilities company, telephone company, cinema and any other service providers after going through an authentication process. With the corresponding applets installed, the cardholder can now pay his bill to various billing agents, book a ticket for a movie and buy a downloadable movie from the Internet using one single card. The cardholder can also top up his electronic purse from his bank through an Internet banking applet or even the public phone.

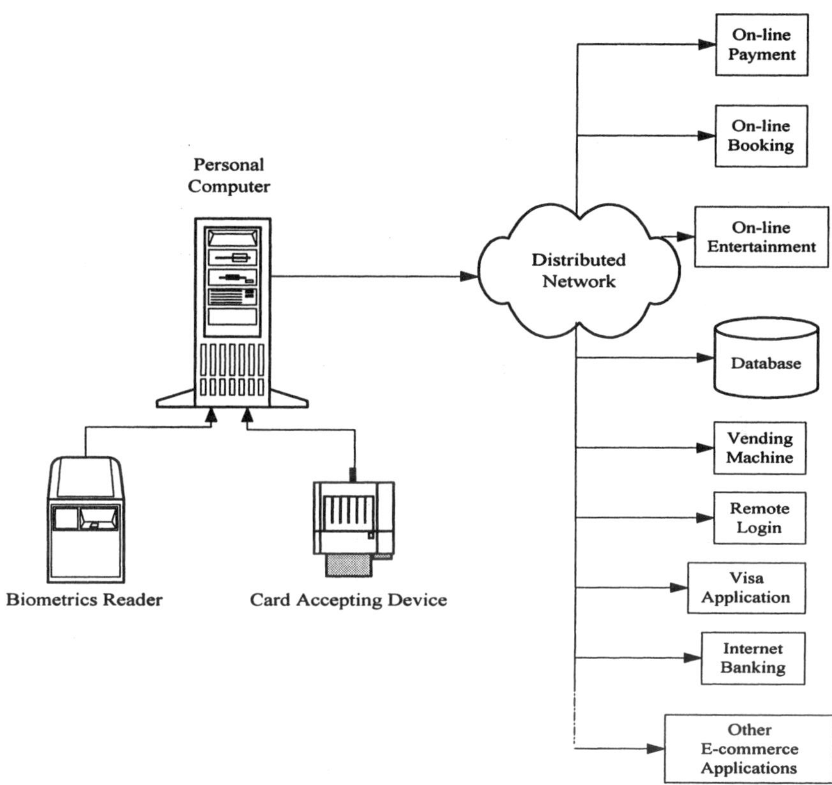

Figure 3.2. A multiple-applications Java card biometrics electronic purse.

As the world is moving towards globalization and a smart card is secure enough with biometrics authentication, a Java card can be used to implement an electronic passport as well. Upon successful application, traditional travel visa will be digitised, downloaded and installed in the Java card. As the Java card provides application and data isolation, each government agent can have their corresponding visa encrypted with an algorithm that suits their needs. Locating a visa within the card can be achieved by a standard country code. Integrating this electronic passport into the services mentioned above provides great convenience for the cardholder. Any time, anywhere, the cardholder can download and install a new service applet and access the service that it provides. The cardholder can apply for a visa, book an airline ticket and make a hotel reservation through the Internet and use the same card as a passport while travelling abroad.

3.4.2   Hardware and Software Considerations

Although there are a few types of intelligence smart cards on the market at present, the card that is sufficient to meet the basic requirements is the Schlumberger Cyberflex Multi8K Java card. It contains the SoloTM virtual machine with an operating system. The card is equipped with an 8-bit microprocessor, 8 KB of EEPROM, operating with a clock speed from 3.57 MHz to 5 MHz, and I/O rate of 9600 (standard) to 38400 bauds. Because of its portability, there are limited system resources on the card itself. The memory constraints are: 7.5 KB of application size, 1.2 KB of class library size, and 32 bytes of Java operand stack size. A development tool kit is available to help a user to create and download an applet onto the card.

In order to incorporate the biometric technology into the Java card, it is also required to implement another simple file management utilities software to upload/download biometric templates to/from the Java card.

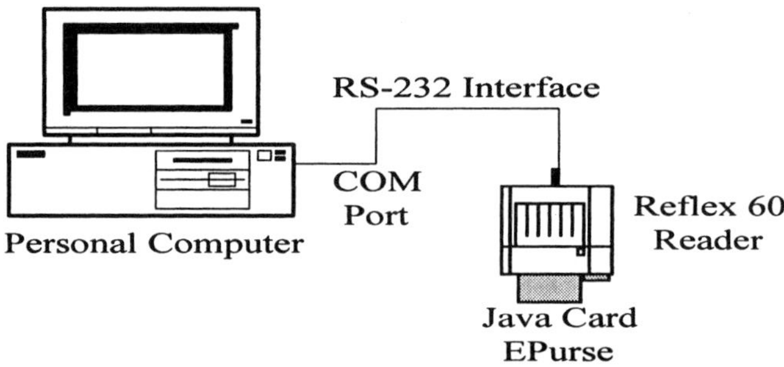

Figure 3.3.   Interface between Epurse and PC.

3.4.3   Implementation Structure of Electronic Purse

The electronic purse (EPurse) is designed to handle a full range of purse functions which include: verify key, read balance, load purse, debit purse, reset purse, and create wallet. The purse reloading is enforced by a secret key presentation. Transactions of the EPurse are performed through a terminal (such as a PC) via a card reader. Figure 3.3 shows the interface of the Epurse with a PC.

The file structure as shown in Figure 3.4 is created to implement both the Epurse and the file management utilities. Before a program file (cardlet) can be downloaded, it is necessary to create a file template for the cardlet with a File Identity (FID) and the maximum size of the file template. This template size must be at least 16 bytes (file header size) and can be more than the cardlet size but not less than the cardlet size plus the file header size (i.e.

template size > cardlet size + 16 bytes). The cardlets and data files are organized into directories and sub-directories. Under the Master File (MF, root directory), there are two DFs (Dedicated Files, sub-directories) created to store the cardlets. The Epurse and its data file (Wallet File) are stored in its DF with a size of 2000 bytes while the file management utilities cardlet resides in DF 2000. The KEY File 0011 is used for authentication and it must be located under the MF. It is important to keep track of the sequence, FID and the directory structure when a file/directory is created, as it can only be deleted in the reverse sequence in which it is created (i.e. last in first out).

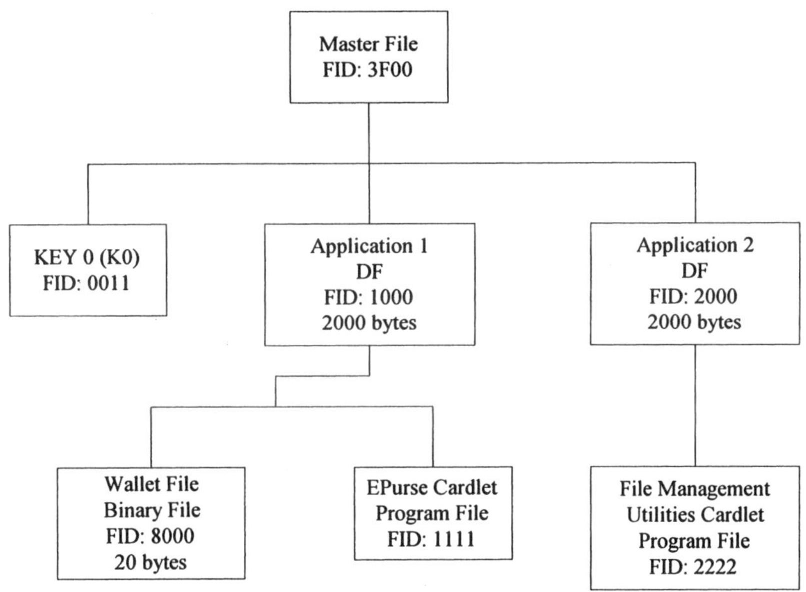

Figure 3.4.　File structure of the multi-application Java card (DF = Dedicated File, FID = File Identity).

The logical structure shown in Figure 3.5 is designed to define the interfaces and the communication protocols so that the terminal and card applications can communicate with each other to process and exchange data. The terminal application software communicates with the reader using a set of Dynamic Link Library (DLL) provided by the reader manufacturer. The basic unit of exchange with the Java card is the APDU (Application Protocol Data Unit), which is a command message sent from the application layer, and the response message returned by the card to the application layer. Communication with the card and the reader is performed with APDUs. An APDU can be considered as a data packet that contains a complete instruction or a complete response from a card.

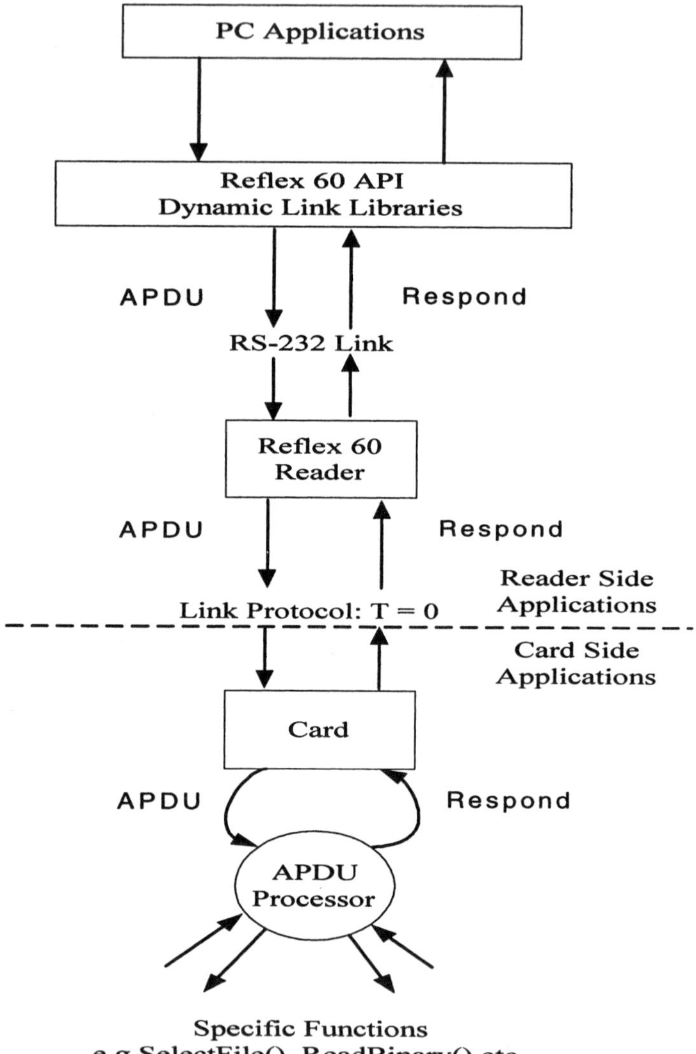

Figure 3.5. Logical structure design for Epurse (APDU =Application Protocol Data Unit).

3.4.4   APDU Commands Design for EPurse

An APDU has a well-established structure defined under the ISO-7816-4 which is very similar to the Transmission Protocol Data Unit (TPDU) defined in the ISO-7816-3. The format of a Command APDU, shown in Figure 3.6, comprises a header and a body, each of which is further subdivided into several fields. The header includes CLA, INS, P1 and P2 fields. The CLA and INS define an application class and instruction group.

The P1 and P2 fields are used to qualify specific instructions and are therefore given specific definitions by each [CLA, INS] instruction. The body of the APDU is a variable size component which is used to convey information to the card's APDU processor as part of a command. The Lc field specifies the number of bytes to be transferred to the card as part of the instruction. The Data field comprises data which must be conveyed to the card in order to allow its APDU processor to execute the command specified in the APDU. The Le field specifies the number of bytes which will be returned to the reader by the card's APDU processor in the Response APDU for this particular command. Depending on whether data is included with the command and whether response data is required, the body of the APDU can have four different forms as shown in Figure 3.7.

Figure 3.6. Format of a Command APDU.

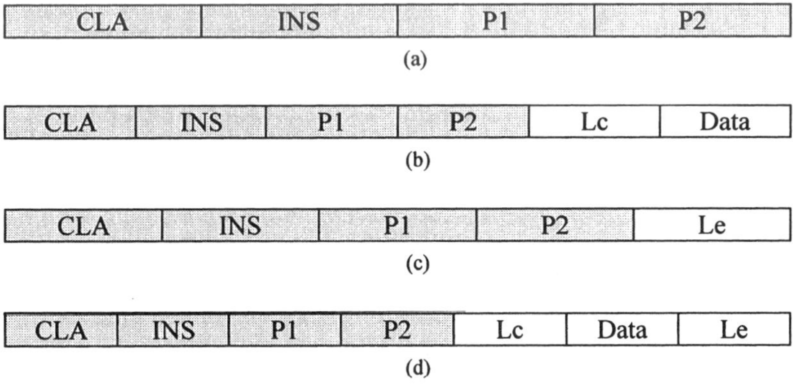

Figure 3.7. Four different forms of the body of a APDU. (a) Case 1: Command data is not present and no response is required. (b) Case 2: Command data is present but no response is required. (c) Case 3: Data is not present but response data is required. (d) Case 4: Command data is present and response data is required.

The format of a Response APDU is shown in Figure 3.8. It includes a body and a trailer. The body is either null or having a data field, depending on the specific command that it is responding to and whether or not that command is successfully executed by the card's APDU processor. The trailer comprises of two fields of status information, that are referenced as SW1 and

SW2. The card's APDU processor returns a status code according to the ISO-7816-4 clause 5.4.5 coding scheme. Generally, a status code of 9000 indicates that the command has been successfully executed.

Data Field	SW1	SW2

Figure 3.8.   Format of a Response APDU.

In a smart or Java card system, there is always a master and slave relationship between the terminal and the card. As defined under the ISO-7816, the terminal is always the master and the card is the slave. In order for the card and the terminal applications to communicate with each other, it is necessary to define an APDU command set that is common to both applications. The ISO-7816-4 clauses 5.4.1 and 5.4.2 define the coding guidelines for the CLA byte and INS byte respectively. As the EPurse provides six distinct functions, it is required to code six APDU commands for the terminal application to invoke a selected feature. The coding instruction byte (INS) is arbitrary but it follows the ISO-7816-4 standard that an instruction byte is an even number. The desired APDU commands are given in Table 3.1.

Table 3.1.   APDU commands for Epurse.

Command	CLA	INS	P1	P2	Lc	Data
VERIFY_KEY	C0	2A	00	00	08	Key
READ_BALANCE	C0	34	00	00	02	
LOAD_PURSE	C0	36	00	00	02	Top-up Value
DEBIT_PURSE	C0	38	00	00	02	Debit Amount
RESET_PURSE	C0	40	00	00	00	
CREATE_WALLET	F0	E0	00	00	10	File Header

The following provides a description of the APDU commands that are used to implement the six functions of the EPurse:

(1) VERIFY_KEY: This command is used for access control. It sends an 8-byte key code to the card to verify with the K0 store in the Key File 0011. The key must be presented prior to reset, re-loading and creating a new Wallet file.

(2) READ_BALANCE: This command is for the terminal application to retrieve the current balance in the EPurse.

(3) LOAD_PURSE: This command is used to top up the EPurse. The EPurse can hold a maximum of $300. A key needs to be entered before this transaction.

(4) DEBIT_PURSE: This command is sent to the card to reduce the card value for a purchase transaction.

(5) RESET_PURSE: This command is used by the card issuer to reset the value to $0.00. A secret key is required.

(6) CREATE_WALLET: This command is used by the card issuer when issuing a new EPurse. Before a EPurse can be used, a new Wallet File must be created for storing the value.

3.4.5   Software Development for EPurse

The logical structure in Figure 3.5 splits the entire implementation into two major software modules as card-side applications and reader-side applications.

(A) *Card-side software development*: A smart card operating system, like any other operating system, is built from a collection of modules which provide services on internal system interfaces to other modules. These internal system interfaces may change from one operating system release to the next. Application Programming Interfaces (APIs), on the other hand, are more stable interfaces. APIs are guaranteed of functionality from the programmers building the operating system to the programmers building applications to run on top of the operating system.

The Schlumberger Cyberflex 2.0 Multi8K Java card provides 63 methods on the API library in the following category:

- Communications – provide the I/O configuration and communication routines currently based on the ISO $T = 0$ protocol.
- File system – enables the manipulation of the various file types such as binary, record (fixed or variable), and cyclic files.
- Security – provides basic mechanism to handle identity and access control in files.
- Utilities – include global state management routines as well as the "Execute" functions which configure the startup program and launch a cardlet.

Figure 3.9 shows the entry point of the main program of the execution of a cardlet (program file) for the EPurse. Upon selected for execution from the terminal application, the cardlet will be processed until the card is power down or reset. During idle time, the cardlet polls the APDU processor for APDU command that comes from its counterpart, the reader-side application (terminal application), for instructions. When an APDU command is received from the APDU processor, a simple dispatcher will process the received command and launch the appropriate method to service the request based on the instruction that is encoded in the INS field of the APDU command.

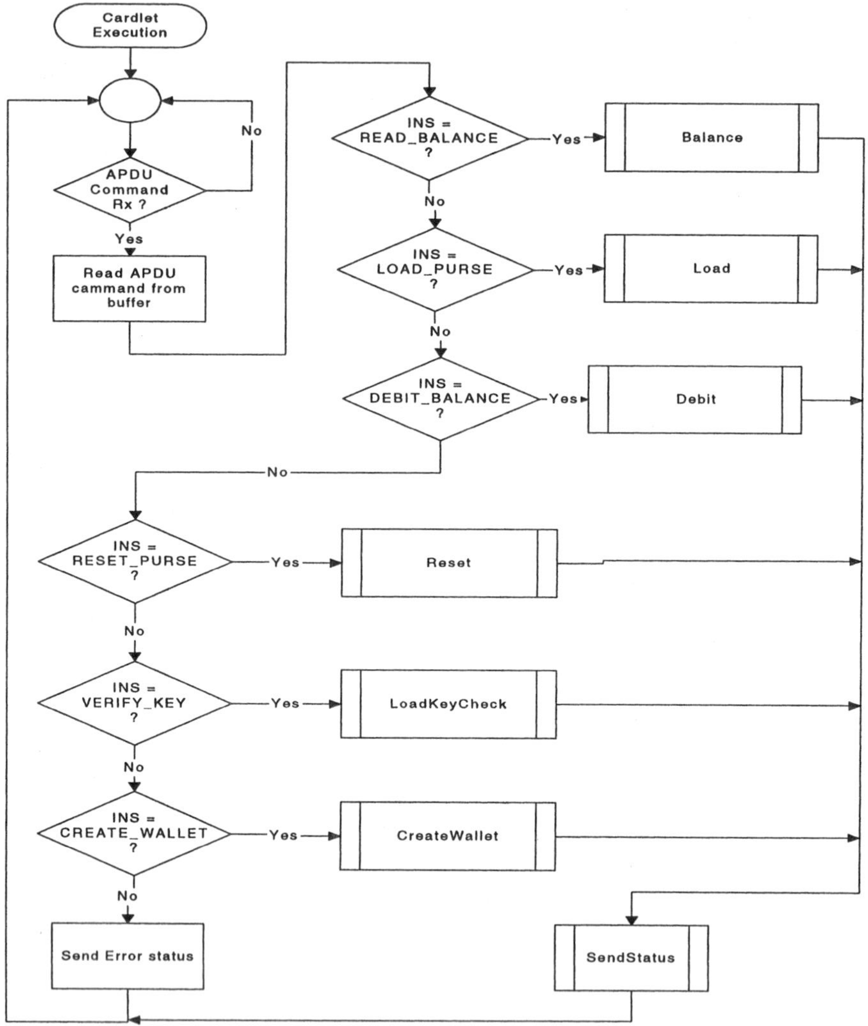

Figure 3.9.   Flow-chart for Epurse cardlet main program (INS = instruction byte).

(B) *Reader-side software development*: A set of APIs is deployed to control a Java-card (smart-card) reader so that the terminal applications can communicate with the card-side applications, i.e. the EPurse cardlets in this case. As Java-card peripherals are not as well integrated into programming languages, communicating with the reader always involve using proprietary and device-specific function libraries. In our implementation, the Schlumberger Reader API DLL is the communication layer that sits below the terminal application (Figure 3.5) to provide all the necessary functions to communicate with the reader. This DLL is compatible with the SCR60, Reflex 60 and the PCMCIA/Reflex 20 smart card readers. The reader-side applications are developed using Microsoft Visual C++ with the Schlumberger Reader API DLL.

(C) *EPurse transaction software*: This is a reader-side application software that provides the user interface for transactions to be carried out in the card over a PC. The software runs on Microsoft Windows 95 or higher and Windows NT 4.0 platforms. It provides a simple text-based interface for the card issuer with the ability to create a new Wallet File, to re-load and reset purse when a valid secret key has been successfully presented to the cardlet. Figures 3.10 and 3.12 show the main menu and flow-chart, respectively, of this application.

Before the main program can be executed, the reader will perform the required initialization and card authentication (biometrics) check. Figure 3.11 illustrates the initialization sequence for the reader to execute the EPurse cardlet that resides on the Java card. The program performs an auto-detection for the card reader from COM1 and COM2 ports. If a reader is found in either of the COM ports, the reader will be allocated to a device handler. Subsequently, the communication between the reader and the PC application will be referenced by this handler. After the reader handler has been successfully allocated, the program will then check the presence and validity of the card from the reader and execute the EPurse cardlet from the card. Transactions can then begin.

```
**************************
Java Card Electronic Purse
**************************
1.  Read Balance
2.  Top Up Purse
3.  Debit Purse
4.  Reset Wallet
5.  Create New Wallet
6.  Quit

Please enter your choice:
```

Figure 3.10.   EPurse reader-side interface (main menu).

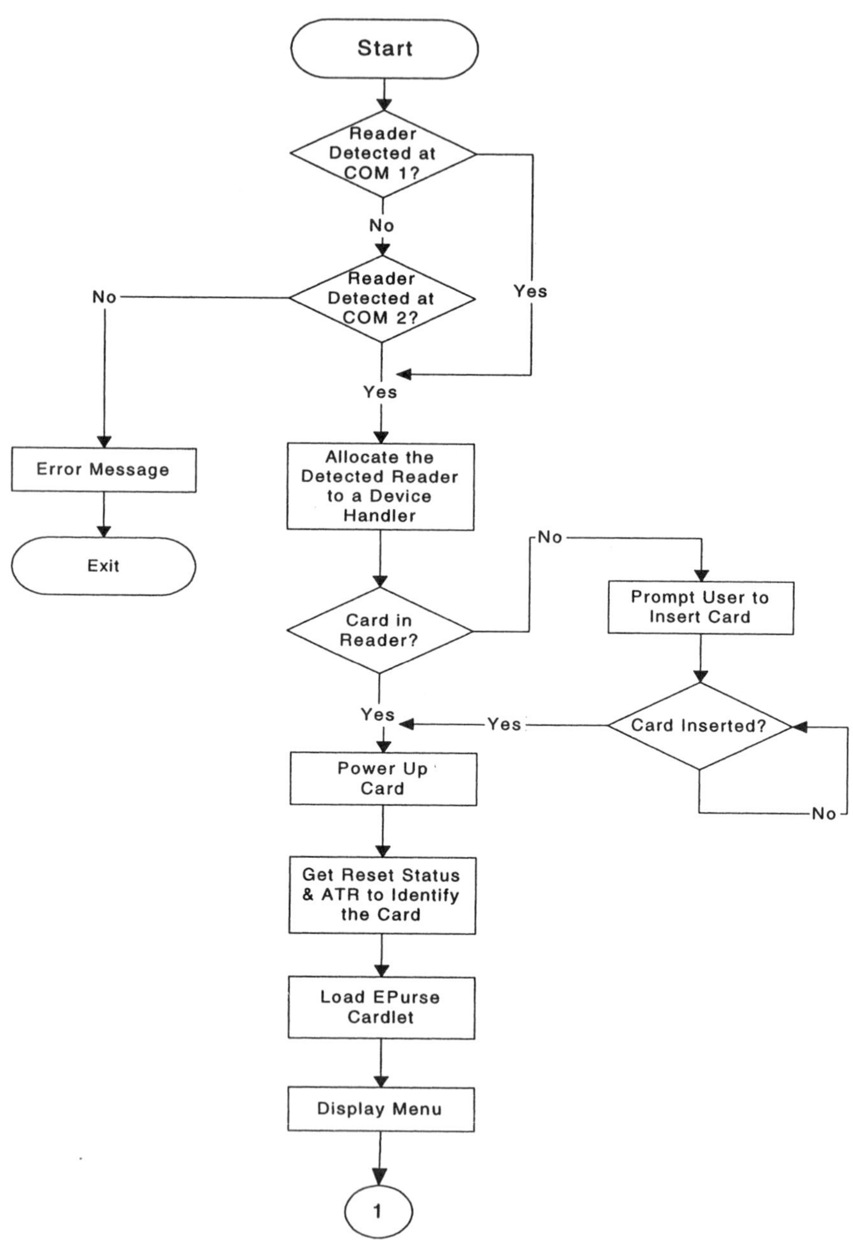

Figure 3.11. Flow-chart for reader initialization.

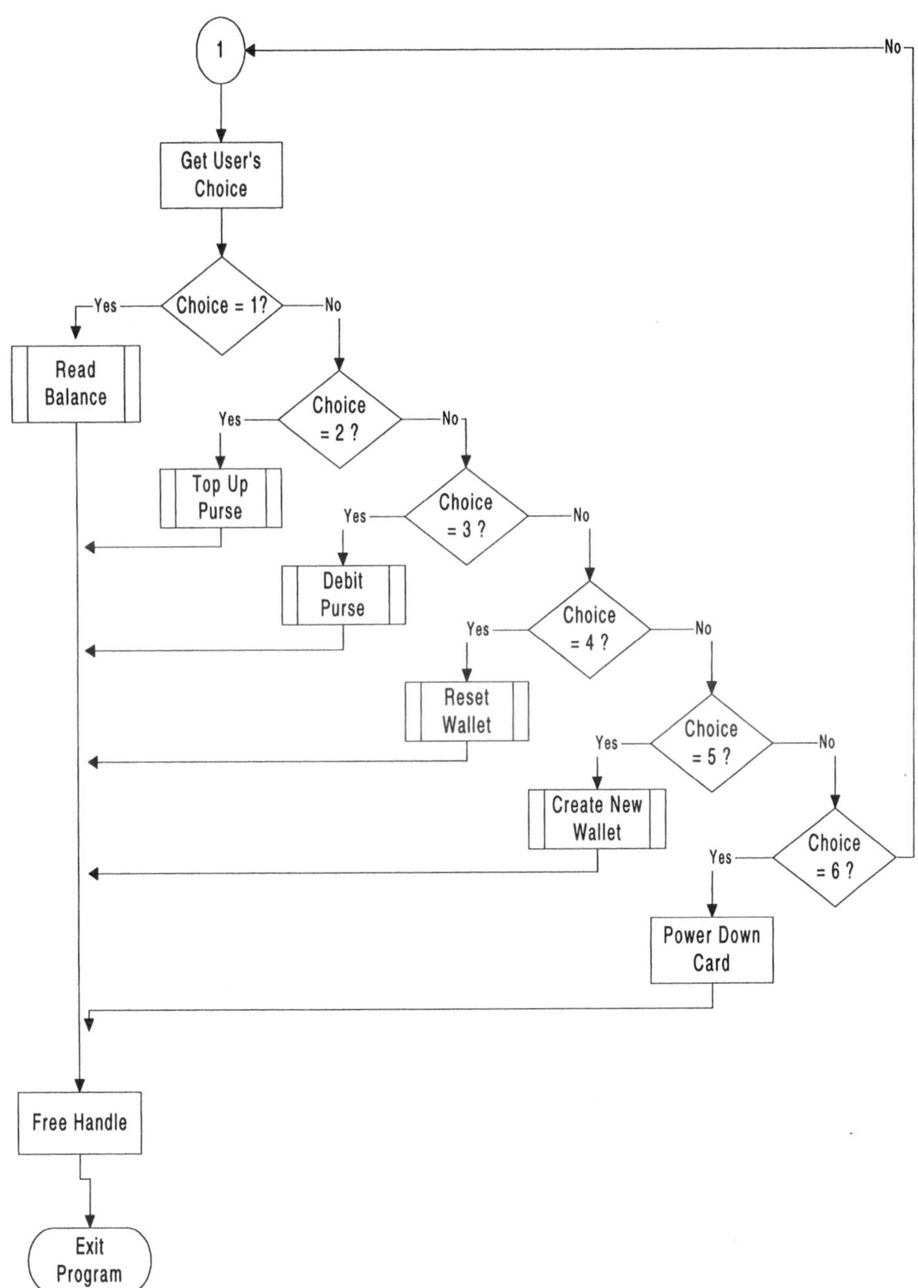

Figure 3.12.   Flow-chart for the main program (in Figure 3.10).

3.4.6   Implementation of Biometrics

Fingerprint is chosen as the biometric measurement. A user's fingerprint is processed through the following steps [13], [14]:
(1) Fingerprint scanning
(2) Histogram equalization
(3) Ridge modification
(4) Dynamic thresholding
(5) Ridge thinning
(6) Feature extraction.
The resulting extracted feature file, about 500 bytes, is then uploaded to the Java card. Compression techniques [15], [16] can be applied to further reduce the storage of the feature file if necessary. For fingerprint recognition, the stored file is downloaded from the card for matching verification in Figure 3.11 after the step, "power up card".

```
*******************************
      Java Card Management Utilities
*******************************
      Current Active File:
      File ID:  3F00
      Size:  7740 bytes
      File-type: Directory
*******************************
      1.  Execute Cardlet
      2.  Upload File
      3.  Select File
      4.  Delete File
      5.  Get File Info
      6.  Download Binary File
      7.  Get File Size
      8.  Create New Directory
      9.  Power Down Card and Exit

      Please enter your choice:
```

Figure 3.13.   Main menu of the file management utilities.

3.4.7   File Management Utilities

File management utilities are implemented so that cardlets can be dynamically added to or removed from the Java card, and multiple card applications can reside on one card and execute upon selected from the terminal. Figure 3.13 illustrates the main menu of this file management utilities application that run on a PC. At the top of the main menu, the application displays the File Identity (FID) of the current active file (selected file), its type and size. This file status provides a user with the necessary information while browsing through a directory.

A description of each function is given as follows:

(1) Execute Cardlet – launch a selected cardlet on the card.
(2) Upload File – uploads either a cardlet or binary file from a PC to the Java card. The software will determine the file size of the source file to create an appropriate file template automatically before uploading.
(3) Select File – sets a file active so that a specific action (e.g. delete file) can be performed on the file. In the case that the file is a directory, this command is similar to the "change directory" command in MS-DOS.
(4) Delete File – removes a selected file from the Java card to recover unused space. The file to be removed must be the last created file (Last-In-First-Out).
(5) Get File Info – retrieves the 16-byte header of a selected file for administrative purposes.
(6) Download Binary File – retrieves a binary file from the Java card and saves it in the PC.
(7) Get File Size – returns the file size of a selected file.
(8) Create New Directory – creates a new Dedicated File (DF). A DF can only be created under another DF or MF but not EF.
(9) Power Down Card and Exit – terminates an executing cardlet and power down the card before exiting the application.

The actual implementation of the commands in the file management utilities is similar to the design methodology in Section 3.4.4 where all fields of the APDU commands must be properly specified.

3.5.   Conclusions

Smart cards with Java card APIs represent a relatively new set of technologies with a great deal of promise. The introduction of Java cards in this rapidly expanding market offers operators, equipment manufacturers and service providers the opportunity to provide value-added services and differentiate services for their customers.

The fast growing of *e*-commerce with the integration of Java cards, PCs and the Internet not only open up a wide rang of innovative applications for smart-card Internet-computing but also create a potentially huge market for Java card applications.

By the year 2003, the demand for Java card API applications and services are expected to outstrip the current supply of resources available to the industry, thus creating a potentially lucrative market for individuals and companies who wish to specialize in smart card application development.

References

[1]   M. Hendry. Smart Card Security and Applications. Boston: Artech House, 1997.

[2]   R. Bright. Smart Card: Principles, Practice, Applications. Ellis Horwood, N.Y.: Halsted Press, 1988.

[3]   A.K. Jain, R.Bolle, S. Pankanti, eds. Biometrics: Personal Identification in Networked Society. Norwell, Mass.: Kluwer Academic, 1999.

[4]   IEEE Computer, vol. 33, no. 2, pages 46-80, 2000.

[5]   P.C. Leong and E.C. Tan. Implementation of Smart-Card Access Control with Threshold Scheme. International Journal of Electronics, vol. 87, no. 6, pages 649-657, 2000.

[6]   Gemplus: http://www.gemplus.com/application.htm

[7]   Sun Microsystems, Inc. Java Card 2.0 Language Subset and Virtual Machine Specification. October 1997.

[8]   Sun Microsystems, Inc. Java Card Applet Developer's Guide. July 1998.

[9]   Gemplus: Biometrics electronic purse:
        http://www.euroblind.org/fichiersGB/wg_elecm.htm#report
        http://www.window.state.tx.us/specialrpt.tesd/ebt26-27.htm

[10]   Schlumberger CyberFlex Live, August 1998.

[11]   P.C. Leong, E.C. Tan and P.C. Tan. Efficient Algorithm for Modular Multiplication by Micro-controller. Electronics Letters, vol. 35, no. 14, pages 1140-1141, 1999.

[12]   A. Wahab, E.C. Tan and S.M. Heng. Biometrics Electronic Purse. In Proc. of the TENCON'99, Cheju, Korea, pages 958-961, September 1999.

[13]   A. Wahab, S.H. Chin and E.C. Tan. A Novel Approach to Automated Fingerprint Recognition. IEE Proc – Vision, Image and Signal Processing, vol. 145, no. 3, pages 160-166, 1998.

[14]   L.C. Jain, et al., eds. Intelligent Biometric Techniques in Fingerprint and Face Recognition. Boca Raton: CRC Press, 1999.

[15]   D.S. Taubman and M.W.Marcellin. JPEG2000: Image Compression Fundamentals, Standards, and Practice. Boston: Kluwer Academic, 2002.

[16]   G. Held and T.R. Marshall. Data and Image Compression: Tools and Techniques. New York: John Wiley, 1996.

Chapter 4

FACE RECOGNITION AND ITS APPLICATION

Andrew W. Senior and Ruud M. Bolle
IBM T.J.Watson Research Center
P.O. Box 704
Yorktown Heights
NY 10598, USA
{aws, bolle}@us.ibm.com

Abstract   Face recognition has long been a goal of computer vision, but only in recent years reliable automated face recognition has become a realistic target of biometrics research. New algorithms, and developments spurred by falling costs of cameras and by the increasing availability processing power have led to practical face recognition systems. These systems are increasingly being deployed in a wide range of practical applications, and future improvements promise to spread the use of face recognition further still. In this chapter, we review the field of face recognition, analysing its strengths and weaknesses and describe the applications where the technology is currently being deployed and where it shows future potential. We describe the IBM face recognition system and some of its application domains.

Keywords: Face recognition, robust biometrics

4.1.   Introduction

Recognizing faces is something that people usually do effortlessly and without much conscious thought, yet it has remained a difficult problem in the area of computer vision, where some 20 years of research is just beginning to yield useful technological solutions. As a biometric technology, automated face recognition has a number of desirable properties that are driving research into practical techniques.

The problem of face recognition can be stated as 'identifying an individual from images of the face' and encompasses a number of variations other than the most familiar application of mug shot identification. One notable aspect of face recognition is the broad interdisciplinary nature of the interest in it:

within computer recognition and pattern recognition; biometrics and security; multimedia processing; psychology and neuroscience. It is a field of research notable for the necessity and the richness of interaction between computer scientists and psychologists.

The automatic recognition of human faces spans a variety of different technologies. At a highest level, the technologies are best distinguished by the input medium that is used, whether visible light, infra-red [29, 31] or 3-dimensional data [7] from stereo or other range-finding technologies. Thus far, the field has concentrated on still, visible-light, photographic images, often black and white, though much interest is now beginning to be shown in the recognition of faces in colour video. Each input medium that is used for face recognition brings robustness to certain conditions, *e.g.* infra-red face imaging is practically invariant to lighting conditions while 3-dimensional data in theory is invariant to head pose. Imaging in the visible light spectrum, however, will remain the preeminent domain for research and application of face recognition because of the vast quantity of legacy data and the ubiquity and cheapness of photographic capture equipment.

4.2.   Face as a Biometric

Face recognition (see [6, 33] for recent surveys) has a number of strengths to recommend it over other biometric modalities in certain circumstances, and corresponding weaknesses that make it an inappropriate choice of biometric for other applications. Face recognition as a biometric derives a number of advantages from being the primary biometric that humans use to recognize one another. Some of the earliest identification tokens, *i.e.* portraits, use this biometric as an authentication pattern. Furthermore it is well-accepted and easily understood by people, and it is easy for a human operator to arbitrate machine decisions — in fact face images are often used as a human-verifiable backup to automated fingerprint recognition systems.

Because of its prevalence as an institutionalized and accepted guarantor of identity since the advent of photography, there are large legacy systems based on face images — such as police records, passports and driving licences — that are currently being automated. Video indexing is another example of legacy data for which face recognition, in conjunction with speaker identification [19], is a valuable tool.

Face recognition has the advantage of ubiquity and of being universal over other major biometrics, in that everyone has a face and everyone readily displays the face. (Whereas, for instance, fingerprints are captured with much more difficulty and a significant proportion of the population has fingerprints that can not be captured with quality sufficient for recognition.) Uniqueness, another desirable characteristic for a biometric, is hard to claim at current levels of accuracy. Since face shape, especially when young, is heavily influenced by genotype, identical twins are very hard to tell apart with this technology.

With some configuration and co-ordination of one or more cameras, it is be more or less possible to acquire face images without active participation of the subject. Such passive identification might be desirable for customization of user services and consumer devices, whether that be opening a house door as the owner walks up to it, or adjusting mirrors and car seats to the driver's presets when sitting down in their car.

Surveillance systems rely on passive acquisition by capturing the face image without the cooperation or knowledge of the person being imaged. Face recognition also has the advantage that the acquisition devices are cheap and are becoming a commodity (though this is not true for non-visible wavelength devices and some of the more sophisticated face recognition technologies based on 3-dimensional data).

The main drawbacks to face recognition are its current relatively low accuracy (compared to the proven performance of fingerprint and iris recognition) and the relative ease with which many systems can be defeated (Section 4.2.1). Finally, there are many attributes leading to the variability of images of a single face that add to the complexity of the recognition problem if they can not be avoided by careful design of the capture situation. Inadequate constraint or handling of such variability inevitably leads to failures in recognition.

These include:

- **Physical changes:** facial expression change; aging; personal appearance (make-up, glasses, facial hair, hairstyle, disguise).

- **Acquisition geometry changes:** change in scale, location and in-plane rotation of the face (facing the camera) as well as rotation in depth (facing the camera obliquely, or presentation of a profile, not full-frontal face).

- **Imaging changes:** lighting variation; camera variations; channel characteristics (especially in broadcast, or compressed images).

Figure 4.1. Sample variations of a single face: in pose, facial appearance, age, lighting and expression.

No current system can claim to handle all of these problems well. In particular there has been little research on making face recognition robust to the effects of aging the faces. In general, constraints on the application scenario and capture situation are used to limit the amount of invariance of face image sample that needs to be afforded algorithmically.

The main challenges of face recognition today are handling rotation in depth and broad lighting changes, together with personal appearance changes. Even under good conditions, however, accuracy needs to be improved.

4.2.1 Robustness and Fraud

All biometric recognition systems are susceptible to accidental errors of two types which both must be minimized: False Accept (FA) errors where a random impostor is accepted as a legitimate users and False Reject (FR) errors where a legitimate user is denied access. Designers of biometric systems must also be very conscious of how the system will behave when deliberately attacked. Naturally much of biometric system design falls into the more traditional categories of physical, procedural and electronic security — preventing an attacker from circumventing the recognition system or preventing false enrollment of biometric identities into a system's database, for example. That is, purposeful and successful attempts at creating a false accept error by general means of security attacks. Nevertheless, there are a number of security attack types that are specific to biometrics.

It is very easy to change one's facial appearance to make one look very different, and so to prevent identification, *i.e.* cause a false rejection. This is particularly important in a 'non-cooperative' application where the biometric is being used to prevent a single person from obtaining a privilege (such as a vote or driving licence) more than once. While underlying bone structure is extremely difficult to change, it is also hard to measure, and all face recognition systems rely on more superficial, changeable characteristics (Section 4.3.3) making them defeasible for determined individuals.

It is also possible for some people to impersonate others with a high degree of similarity (an important vulnerability in 'cooperative' applications like physical access control). Photographs, rubber masks, video replay all allow impostor attacks — the deliberate engineering of a false acceptance error. Detection of such fake biometrics data is only superficially handled by commercial systems, though this is improving. A couple of years ago, few systems had a test to detect authenticity (rejecting objects that looked too flat to be faces rather than photographs), but a recent PC Magazine test [21] found that both systems tested could distinguish a real person from a photograph. More sophisticated shape algorithms could be devised, and elastic deformation can be used to prevent simple photograph replay attacks. (One system allows the option of requiring a change in facial expression during verification.) With computing power more abundant, the technology for detecting fake biometrics will keep improving.

The combination with other biometrics — particularly lip motion verification or speaker ID [23] reduces the exposure to impersonation attacks, but further measures are necessary to prevent video replay attacks where a pre-recorded sequence of the authorized individual is somehow injected into the system. Well established in speaker identification literature [2], prompted-text or text-independent verification can avoid a simple replay attack, at the cost of a more intrusive, complex and expensive system, but the advances in trainable speech and face synthesis algorithms [11, 15] furnish attacks on even these sophisticated systems.

4.3.   The Technology of Face Recognition

In this section we briefly review some of the technologies that have been used for face recognition. In general, face recognition systems proceed by detecting the face in an image, with the effect of estimating and normalizing for translation, scale and in-plane rotation. Given a normalized image, the features, either global or local, are extracted and condensed in a compact face representation which can then be stored in a database or a smartcard and compared with face representations derived at later times.

4.3.1   Related Fields

Face recognition is closely related to many other domains, and shares a rich common literature with many of them. Primarily, face recognition relies upon face detection described in Section 4.3.2. For recognition of faces in video, face tracking is necessary, potentially in three dimensions with estimation of the head pose [18]. This naturally leads to estimation of the person's focus of attention [9, 32] and estimation of gaze [20] which are important in human-computer interaction for understanding intention, particularly in conversational interfaces. Correspondingly there is much work on person tracking [27] and activity understanding [37] which are important guides for face tracking and for which face recognition is a valuable source of information. Recent studies have also begun to focus on facial expression analysis either to infer affective state [30] or for driving character animations particularly in MPEG-4 compression [26]. The recognition of visual speech (*i.e.* lip-reading, particularly for the enhancement of acoustic speech recognition) is also a burgeoning face image processing area [1].

4.3.2   Face Detection

Naturally, before recognizing a face, it must be located in the image. In some cooperative systems, face detection is obviated by constraining the user. Most systems use a combination of skin-tone and face texture to determine the location of a face and use an image pyramid to allow faces of varying sizes to be detected. Increasingly, systems are being developed to detect faces that are not full-frontal [13]. Cues such as movement and person detection can be used [38] to localize faces for recognition. Typically translation, scale and in-plane rotation for the face are estimated simultaneously, along with rotation-in-depth when this is considered.

4.3.3 Face Recognition

There is a great diversity in the way facial appearance is interpreted for recognition by an automatic system. Currently a number of different systems are under development, and which is most appropriate may depend on the application domain. A major difference in approaches is whether to represent the appearance of the face, or the geometry. Brunelli and Poggio [5] have compared these two approaches, but ultimately most systems today use a combination of both appearance and geometry. Geometry is difficult to measure with any accuracy, particularly from a single still image, but provides more robustness against disguises and aging. Appearance information is readily obtained from a face image, but is more subject to superficial variation, particularly from pose and expression changes. In practice for most purposes, even appearance-based systems must estimate some geometrical parameters in order to derive a 'shape-free' representation that is independent of expression and pose artefacts [8, 12]. This is achieved by finding facial landmarks and warping the face to a canonical neutral pose and expression. Facial features are also important for geometric approaches and for anchoring local representations.

Face appearance representation schemes can be divided into local and global, depending on whether the face is represented as a whole, or as a series of small regions. Most global approaches are based on a principal components representation of the face image intensities. This representation scheme was devised first for face image compression purposes [17] and subsequently used for recognition purposes [39]. The latter coined the term *eigenfaces* for this type of representation. A face image is represented as a vector of intensities and this vector is then approximated as a sum of basis vectors (eigenfaces) computed by principal component analysis from a database of face images. These principal components represent the typical variations seen between faces and provide a concise encapsulation of the appearance of a sample face image, and a basis for its comparison with other face images. This principal components representation is, like for example the Fourier transform, a decorrelating transform to an alternative basis where good representations of the salient characteristics of an image can be created from only a few low-order coefficients despite discarding many of the higher-order terms.

Other researchers have taken the approach of local representations [42, 25, 36]. Local representations have the advantage that only part of the representation is corrupted by local changes on the face. Thus, donning sunglasses only affects the local features near the eyes, but it may still be possible to recognize someone from features derived from around the nose and mouth. However, as mentioned above, inherently local representations are harder to estimate and there is a trade-off between feature estimation precision and feature size (locality of the representation).

Matching. Having processed a face and extracted the features, these are stored or transmitted as a facial code (face template), which can be as small as 84 bytes (Visionics). For each representation type, a distance or similarity measure is defined that allows 'similar' faces to be determined. Much of the art in biometrics is in the design of a model of the biometric data and, given a scheme for extracting the model parameters as a representation of the data, in creating a similarity measure that correctly discriminates between samples from the same person and samples from different people. As with any biometric system, some threshold on similarity must be chosen above which two face images are deemed to be of the same person. Altering the threshold gives different False Accept and False Rejection Rates (Section 4.2.1) — trading the one off against the other depending on the security level required. This is a trade-off between convenience and security: user-friendly matchers have a low false reject rate, while secure matchers have a low false accept rate.

4.3.4 Performance

The Face Recognition Technology (FERET) tests from Jonathan Phillips [28] provided an early benchmark of face recognition technologies. Phillips has continued the evaluation of face systems for US government agencies in the Face Recognition Vendor Tests [4]. This report provides an excellent independent evaluation of three state-of-the-art systems with concrete performance figures. The report highlights the limitations of current technology — while under ideal conditions performance is excellent, under conditions of changing illumination, expression, resolution, distance or aging, performance falls off, in some cases dramatically. Current face recognition systems are not very robust yet against deviations from the ideal face image acquisition but there is continual performance improvement.

4.4. Privacy Issues

With the widespread deployment of security cameras, and the increasing financial and technological feasibility of automating this surveillance, public fears have also increased about the potential for invasion of privacy that this technology can bring about. Notable deployments of face recognition in the London borough of Newham, in Tampa Florida [41] and at the 2001 Super bowl [40] have raised the spectre of intrusive applications of face recognition. It is now starting to become easy and cheap to connect a face recognition system to a blanket video surveillance system with great potential for crime prevention, but also bringing undreamt-of powers of control to totalitarian regimes, and the erosion of civil liberties by an ever-wakeful, omniscient 'big brother' [24] capable of tracking the activities of its citizens from cradle to grave.

Technology will have answers to assuage these fears: Cryptography will go a long way toward privacy-guarding; and rigorous rights management, to limit access to the information, will prevent privacy violations by unauthorized individuals. Automatic identity-masking controls may make these technologies in theory less privacy-intrusive than human visual surveillance systems in that an automatic surveillance system can prevent voyeurism by only allowing people access to the video when a security incident has been detected. However, it seems that this technology is a tool as any other, and only legislation, self-regulation and social pressure will guide its use to beneficial rather than oppressive aims. Inevitably, in a pluralist world, there will be applications that tend to the latter.

4.5.   Application Domain

Many applications for face recognition have been envisaged, and some of them have been hinted at above. Commercial applications have so far only scratched the surface of the potential. Installations so far are limited in their ability to handle pose, age and lighting variations, but as technologies to handle these effects are developed, huge opportunities for deployment exist in many domains.

Access Control.   Face verification, matching a face against a single enrolled exemplar, is well within the capabilities of current Personal Computer hardware. Since PC cameras have become widespread, their use for face-based PC logon has become feasible, though take-up seems to be very limited. Increased ease-of-use over password protection is hard to argue with today's somewhat unreliable and unpredictable systems, and for few domains is there motivation to progress beyond the combinations of password and physical security that protect most enterprise computers. As biometric systems tend to be third party, software add-ons the systems do not yet have full access to the greater hardware security guarantees afforded by boot-time and hard disk passwords. Visionics' face-based screen lock is one example, bundled with PC cameras. Naturally such PC-based verification systems can be extended to control authorization for single-sign-on to multiple networked services, for access to encrypted documents and transaction authorization, though again uptake of the technology has been slow.

Face verification is being used in kiosk applications, notably in Mr. Payroll's (now Innoventry) cheque-cashing kiosk with no human supervision. Innoventry claims to have one million enrolled customers. Automated Teller Machines, already often equipped with a camera, have also been an obvious candidate for face recognition systems (*e.g.* Viisage's FacePIN), but development seems not to have got beyond pilot schemes. Banks have been very conservative in deploying biometrics as they risk losing far more through customers disaffected by being falsely rejected than they might gain in fraud prevention. Customers themselves are reluctant to incur burdensome additional security measures when their personal liability is already limited by law. For better acceptance, robust passive acquisition systems with very low false rejection probabilities are necessary.

Physical access control is another domain where face recognition is attractive (*e.g.* Cognitec's FaceVACS, Miros' TrueFace) and here it can even be used in combination with other biometrics. BioId [23] is a system which combines face recognition with speaker identification and lip motion.

Identification Systems. Two US States (Massachusetts and Connecticut [3]) are testing face recognition for the policing of Welfare benefits. This is an identification task, where any new applicant being enrolled must be compared against the entire database of previously enrolled claimants, to ensure that they are not claiming under more than one identity. Unfortunately face recognition is not currently able to reliably identify one person among the millions enrolled in a single state's database, so demographics (zip code, age, name *etc.*) are used to narrow the search (thus limiting its effectiveness), and human intervention is required to review the false alarms that such a system will produce. Here a more accurate system such as fingerprint or iris-based person recognition is more technologically appropriate, but face recognition is chosen because it is more acceptable and less intrusive. In Connecticut, face recognition is the secondary biometric added to an existing fingerprint identification system. Several US States, including Illinois, have also instituted face recognition for ensuring that people do not obtain multiple driving licenses.

Surveillance. The application domain where most interest in face recognition is being shown is probably surveillance. Video is the medium of choice for surveillance because of the richness and type of information that it contains and naturally, for applications that require identification, face recognition is the best biometric for video data. though gait or lip motion recognition have some potential. Face recognition can be applied without the subject's active participation, and indeed without the subject's knowledge. Automated face recognition can be applied 'live' to search for a watch-list of 'interesting' people, or after the fact using surveillance footage of a crime to search through a database of suspects.

The deployment of face-recognition surveillance systems has already begun (Section 4.4), though the technology is not accurate enough yet [14]. The US government is investing in improving this technology [10] and while useful levels of recognition accuracy may take some time to achieve, technologies such as multiple steerable zoom cameras, non-visible wavelengths and advanced signal processing are likely to bring about super-human perception in the data-gathering side of surveillance systems.

Pervasive Computing.   Another domain where face recognition is expected to become very important, although it is not yet commercially feasible, is in the area of pervasive or ubiquitous computing. Many people are envisaging the pervasive deployment of information devices. Computing devices, many already equipped with sensors, are already found throughout our cars and in many appliances in our homes, though they will become ever more widespread. All of these devices are just now beginning to be networked together. We can envisage a future where many everyday objects have some computational power, allowing them to adapt their behaviour — to time, user, user control and a host of other factors. The communications infrastructures permitting such devices to communicate to one another are being defined and developed (*e.g.* Bluetooth, IEEE 802.11). So while it is easy to see that the devices will be able to have a well-understood picture of the virtual world with information being shared among many devices, it is less clear what kind of information these devices will have about the real physical world.

Most devices today have a simple user interface with inputs controlled only by active commands on the part of the user. Some simple devices can sense the environment, but it will be increasingly important for such pervasive, networked computing devices to know about the physical world and the people within their region of interest. Only by making the pervasive infrastructure *'human aware'* can we really reap the benefits of productivity, control and ease-of-use that pervasive computing promises. One of the most important parts of human-awareness is knowing the identity of the users close to a device, and while there are other biometrics that can contribute to such knowledge, face recognition is the most appropriate because of its passive nature.

There are many examples of pervasive face recognition tasks: Some devices such as Personal Digital Assistants (PDAs) may already contain cameras for other purposes, and in good illumination conditions will be able to identify their users. A domestic message centre may have user personalization that depends on identification driven by a built-in camera. Some pervasive computing environments may need to know about users when not directly interacting with a device, and may be made 'human aware' by a network of cameras able to track the people in the space and identify each person, as well as have some understanding of the person's activities. Thus a video conference room could steer the camera and generate a labelled transcript of the conference; an automatic lobby might inform workers of specific visitors; and mobile workers could be located and kept in touch by a system that could identify them and redirect phone calls.

4.6.   The IBM Face Recognition System

In recent years we have developed a face recognition system at IBM Research for use in a variety of projects across a number of application domains. The system is more fully described elsewhere [34, 35, 9, 22, 1] but here we present a brief overview of the approach and the application domains.

The system consists of four modules: face detection and tracking; facial feature finding; face representation; and matching. These are carried out in turn on any still image or video frame presented for recognition.

4.6.1   Face Detection

Face detection scans an image pyramid to detect faces regardless of scale and location, and uses a filtering hierarchy procedure to filter out locations that do not represent faces with successively more accurate face classifiers. A variety of face classifiers is used varying from the fast, but less accurate, Fisher's linear discriminant to a mixture of Gaussians model which is slower but is more correctly able to determine if an image region is a face or not. For colour images, the first stage of the filtering hierarchy is a skin-tone detector.

4.6.2   Feature Finding

The next stage of the system finds 29 standard features (such as corners of eyes, nose, mouth and eyebrows, some of which are shown in figure 4.2) on the face for use in anchoring the representation. Based on the location, scale and orientation of the detected face, the system uses anthropometric data gathered from a training set to predict the approximate location of the principal features (eyes, nose and mouth). The system works in a hierarchical manner to locate first these larger features, and then to locate smaller sub-features (such as the corners of eyes, nose and mouth) relative to them. Detectors (a combination of linear discriminant and Distance from feature space similar to the face detector) trained on a database of labelled face features are applied over a region close to the prediction to determine the feature's actual location, indicated by the maximum response for the detector in the search region.

Figure 4.2.   Principal facial features (in white) located by the system.

The procedure is repeated, predicting the sub-features' locations relative to the principal features and localizing them with trained detectors operating on a larger scale image. Finally the feature locations are verified with collocation statistics to reject any mislocated features, and additional anchor points are generated by geometric combinations of the visually located anchors.

4.6.3   Recognition

Recognition is carried out by finding a local representation of the facial appearance at each of the anchor points. The representation scheme used here is a vector of Gabor wavelet responses [43]. A range of 40 Gabor wavelets, with varying scale and orientations, is used to represent the local image appearance around each of the anchor features. This produces a 40-element vector, **a**, for each of the feature locations. The set of 29 vectors comprises the representation of the person's face to be stored in the face database.

Matching is carried out by comparing these features pairwise using the following similarity measure (each feature from one face with the corresponding feature from another face).

$$\mathcal{S}(\mathbf{a}, \mathbf{a}') = \frac{\sum_j a_j a_j'}{\sqrt{\sum_j a_j^2 \sum_j (a_j')^2}} \tag{4.1}$$

Each such comparison gives a similarity score. Combining all these scores gives an overall match score used to determine if the face images represent the same person. Multiple representations from successive images in a video sequence can be aggregated into a distribution capturing the facial variation, and these distributions can be compared using statistical distance measures to give a similarity score based on many frames of data.

4.6.4   Applications

The system has been designed to be generally applicable to a variety of applications, and as such accepts colour or black and white images both still and video. It has been used as a black-and-white mug shot identification system; with PC-attached cameras for computer logon from a smart-card stored database; and on broadcast video for indexing from a database of enrolled TV presenters [35]. Components of the system have also been used in a number of other projects such as audio-visual speech recognition (visual lip reading to enhance acoustic speech recognition) [1] and user intention determination (using visual cues to understand the user, particularly to whom speech is being addressed) [9].

4.7.   Conclusions

Face recognition is a technology just reaching sufficient maturity for it to experience a rapid growth in its practical applications. Much research effort around the world is being applied to expanding the accuracy and capabilities of this biometric domain, with a consequent broadening of its application in the near future. Verification systems for physical and electronic access security are available today, but the future holds the promise and the threat of passive customization and automated surveillance systems enabled by face recognition.

References

[1]   S. Basu, C. Neti, N. Rajput, A. Senior, L. Subramaniam, and A. Verma. Audio-visual Large Vocabulary Continuous Speech Recognition in the Broadcast Domain. In Multimedia Signal Processing, 1999.

[2]   H. S. M. Beigi, S. H. Maes, U. V. Chaudhari, and J. S. Sorensen. IBM Model-based and Frame-by-frame Speaker Recognition. In Speaker Recognition and its Commercial and Forensic Appications, Avignon, April 1998.

[3]   Biometrics in Human Services User Group.
URL: http://www.dss.state.ct.us/digital.htm.

[4]   Duane M. Blackburn, Mike Bone, and P. Jonathon Phillips.   Facial Recognition Vendor Test 2000 Evaluation Report.   Technical Report, Department of Defence Counterdrug Technology Development Program Office, February 2001. http://www.dodcounterdrug.com/facialrecognition/DLs/FRVT_2000.pdf.

[5]   Roberto Brunelli and Tomaso Poggio. Face Recognition: Features versus Templates. IEEE Transactions on Pattern Analysis and Machine Intelligence, 15(10):1042–1052, October 1993.

[6]   Rama Chellappa, Charles L. Wilson, and Saad Sirohey. Human and Machine Recognition of Faces: A Survey. In Proc. of the IEEE, 83(5):705–740, May 1995.

[7]   Chin-Seng Chua, Feng Han, and Yeong-Khing Ho. 3D Human Face Recognition using
       Point Signature. In International Conference on Face and Gesture Recognition, pages
       233–238, 2000.

[8]   Ian Craw and Peter Cameron. Face Recognition by Computer. In David Hogg and
       Roger Boyle, editors. In Proc. of the British Machine Vision Conference, pages 498–
       507. Springer Verlag, September 1992.

[9]   P. de Cuetos, C. Neti, and A. Senior. Audio-visual intent to Speak Detection for Human-
       computer Interaction. In Proc. of the IEEE International Conference on Acoustics,
       Speech, and Signal Processing, 2000.

[10]   Defense Advanced Research Projects Agency. Human Identification at a Distance,
       BAA00-29 edition, Feb 2000.
       URL: http://www.darpa.mil/iso2/HID/BAA0029_PIP.htm.

[11]   Robert Donovan. Trainable Speech Synthesis. PhD thesis, Cambridge University Engi-
       neering Department, 1996.

[12]   G. J. Edwards, C. J. Taylor, and T. F. Cootes. Interpreting Faces using Active Appearance
       Models. In International Conference on Face and Gesture Recognition, no. 3, pages 300–
       305, April 1998.

[13]   Raphael Feraud, Olivier Bernier, Jean Emmanuael Viallet, and Michel Collobert. A Fast
       and Accurate Face Detector for Indexation of Face Images. In International Conference
       on Face and Gesture Recognition. IEEE, March 2000.

[14]   Lee Gomes. Can Facial Recognition Help Snag Terrorists? The Wall Street Journal,
       September 21 2001.

[15]   H.P. Graf. Sample-based Synthesis of Talking Heads. In Recognition, Analysis, and
       Tracking of Faces and Gestures in Real-Time Systems, pages 3–7, July 2001.

[16]   http://www.innoventry.com.

[17]   M. Kirby and L. Sirovich. Application of the Karhunen-Loève Procedure for the Char-
       acterization of Human Faces. IEEE Transactions on Pattern Analysis and Machine
       Intelligence, 12(1):103–108, 1990.

[18]   M. La Cascia, S. Sclaroff, and V. Athitsos. Fast, Reliable Head Tracking under Varying
       Illumination: An Approach Based on Registration of Texture-mapped 3D Models. IEEE
       Transactions on Pattern Analysis and Machine Intelligence, 22(4):322–336, April 2000.

[19]   B. Maison, C. Neti, and A. Senior. Audio-visual Speaker Recognition for Video Broadcast
       News: Some Fusion Techniques. In Multi-media Signal Processing, 1999.

[20]   Y. Matsumoto and A. Zelinsky. An Algorithm for Real-time Stereo Vision Implementa-
       tion of Head Pose and Gaze Direction Measurement. In IEEE International Conference
       on Face and Gesture, page 499, 2000.

[21]   Glenn Menin. Performance Tests: Fingerprint Biometrics. PC Magazine, June 12 2001.

[22]   Chalapathy Neti and Andrew W. Senior. Audio-visual Speaker Recognition for Broadcast
       News. In DARPA Hub 4 Workshop, pages 139–142, March 1999.

[23]   Ana Orubeondo. A New Face for Security. InfoWorld.com, May 2001.

[24]   George Orwell. 1984. 1948.

[25]   P. S. Penev and J.J. Atick. Local Feature Analysis: A General Statistical Theory for
       Object Representation. Network: Computation in Neural Systems, 7(3):477–500, 1996.

[26]   E. Petajan. The Communication of Virtual Human Faces using mpeg-4 Tools. In Inter-
       national Symposium on Circuits and Systems, vol. 1, pages 307–310, 2000.

[27]   Second International Workshop on Performance and Evaluation of Tracking and Surveillance. IEEE, December 2001.

[28]   P. Jonathon Phillips, Hyeonjoon Moon, Patrick Rauss, and Syed A. Rizvi. The FERET September 1996 Database and Evaluation Procedure. In Josef Bigün, Gérard Chollet, and Gunilla Borgefors, editors, Audio- and Video-based Biometric Person Authentication, Lecture Notes in Computer Science, vol. 1206, pages 395–402. Springer, March 1997.

[29]   P. Jonathon Phillips, Patrick J. Rauss, and Sandor Z. Der. FERET (Face Recognition Technology) Recognition Algorithm Development and Test Results. Technical Report ARL–TR–995, Army Research Laboratory, October 1996.

[30]   Rosalind W. Picard. Affective Computing. MIT Press, 2000.

[31]   F. Prokoski. History, Current Status, and Future of Infrared Identification. In Proc. of IEEE Workshop on Computer Vision Beyond the Visible Spectrum: Methods and Applications, pages 5–14, June 2000.

[32]   James M. Rehg, Kevin P. Murphy, and Paul W. Fieguth. Vision-based Speaker-detection using Bayesian Networks. In Proc. of Computer Vision and Pattern Recognition, vol. 2, pages 110–116, 1999.

[33]   A. Samal and P.A. Iyengar. Automatic Recognition and Analysis of Human Faces and Facial Rxpressions: A Survey. Pattern Recognition, 25(1):65–77, 1992.

[34]   Andrew W. Senior. Face and Feature Finding for a Face Recognition System. In Second International Conference on Audio- and Video-based Biometric Person Authentication, pages 154–159, March 1999.

[35]   Andrew W. Senior. Recognizing Faces in Broadcast Video. In IEEE International Workshop on Recognition, Analysis, and Tracking of Faces and Gestures in Real-Time Systems, pages 105–110, September 1999.

[36]   Daniel L. Swets and John (Juyang) Weng. Using Discriminant Eigenfeatures for Image Retrieval. IEEE Transactions on Pattern Analysis and Machine Intelligence, 18(8):831–836, August 1996.

[37]   T. Tan, editor. Second IEEE International Workshop on Visual Surveillance. IEEE, 1999.

[38]   Jochen Triesch and Christoph von der Malsburg. Self-organized Integration of Adaptive Visual Cues for Face Tracking. In International Conference on Face and Gesture Recognition, pages 102–107. IEEE, March 2000.

[39]   M. Turk and A. Pentland. Eigenfaces for Recognition. Journal of Cognitive Neuro Science, 3(1):71–86, 1991.

[40]   Press releases http://www.viisage.com, January 20 2001.

[41]   Press releases http://www.visionics.com, June 2001.

[42]   Laurenz Wiskott, Jean-Marc Fellous, and Norbert Krüger. Face Recognition by Elastic Bunch Graph Matching. Technical Report IR-INI 96–08, Buhr-Universität Bochum, Institut für Neuroinformatik, April 1996.

[43]   Laurenz Wiskott and Christoph von der Malsburg. Recognizing Faces by Dynamic Link Matching. In Proc. of the International Conference on Artificial Neural Networks, pages 347–352, 1995.

Chapter 5

PERSONALIZE MOBILE ACCESS BY SPEAKER AUTHENTICATION

Ke Chen
School of Computer Science
The University of Birmingham
Edgbaston, Birmingham B15 2TT
United Kingdom
K.Chen@cs.bham.ac.uk

Abstract   In recent years wireless networks have been rapidly grown up, which leads to the possibility of pervasive access to information systems. At present, the most commonly available ubiquitous access device to the network is still mobile telephone. In particular, cellular phone can be used for ubiquitous access anytime and anywhere and, therefore, the only ubiquitous user access mode is spoken language. Obviously, both a cellular phone handset and any private information access or electronic transaction demand to be protected from being stolen or broken in, which paves the way for personalized services. In this chapter, we envisage a bilateral user authentication framework for applications in wireless environments. On the one hand, we use text-dependent speaker verification for handset protection as the primary stage of our security system. On the other hand, a more sophisticated speaker authentication system consisting of text-independent speaker verification and verbal information verification is located in the authentication center of a server site for further protection. Our framework attempts to derive maximum synergy from biometric and non-biometric speech technologies without loss of easy-to-access properties. Under this framework, we have conducted some experiments by enabling component technologies in terms of Mandarin Chinese. Our simulation results indicate that the enabling component techniques to support this framework are ready to build such an authentication system for applications to personalized mobile access.

Keywords: Speaker authentication, personalized mobile access, speaker verification, text-dependent, text-independent, verbal information verification, bilateral authentication, cellular phone, speech information system, server-client architecture

5.1.   Introduction

In recent years wireless networks have been rapidly developed and become indispensable components in the telecommunication world. According to the literature [11], there are over 100 million cellular and personal communication service phones in use as of mid-2000 in the United States. Even in China, a developing country, current estimates of China Telecom Inc. indicate that there are over 70 million registered cellular phone users at the mid of 2001 and, moreover, such a market will be grown up rapidly. Thus, fraud becomes a common yet serious problem that the cellular operating companies have to tackle. In this circumstance, a fraud user is able to steal handsets or the phone and serial numbers from the airwaves. Then they could use these numbers in cellular phones and make long distance and even international calls. As a result, the cellular providers may have to pay unexpected costs of millions of dollars on a monthly basis [4].

Although the world of telecommunication in the future will be the seamless integration of real-time multimodal communications in a single network, the most commonly available ubiquitous access device to the network is cellular phone for ubiquitous access anytime and anywhere. Therefore, the only ubiquitous user access mode is spoken language, a natural mechanism for information access. Given more and more services such as mobile stock quotes and transactions are popular, security upon access becomes an unavoidable problem for a speech information system of a private or confidential nature. How to authenticate a user becomes critical to prevent unauthorized users from mobile access to the private information conveyed in speech.

To solve the security problems existing in wireless environments, there are two common approaches by the use of fraud *personal identification number* (PIN) features and mathematical authentication technologies. A PIN feature is usually a string consisting of digits or alphabets, which uniquely identifies a specific person. In this way, therefore, different PINs are assigned to those authorized or registered users. When such a user would like to make an outgoing call or access a speech information system, he/she has to first unlock his/her cellular phone or pass an authentication processing prior to any access by using the PIN. On the other hand, mathematical algorithms provide a powerful tool for protecting cellular phones. In this way, the phone is identified not only by the phone number and the serial number but also by a a random key. This random key is loaded in the cellular phone by the vendor. Once a new user is registered in the network, the same random key is loaded in the authentication center. When the user makes the first call, the cellular phone performs some calculations, by certain algorithms, in terms of the phone number, the serial number, and the random key. The results generated are transmitted in the airwaves. Accordingly, the authentication center takes the same operations by using the same inputs and algorithms. As a consequence, user authentication is done by checking the consistency between bilateral results; that is, the user is allowed to make the call only if two results are identical. Although the aforementioned approaches can reduce fraud activity, there exist explicit weaknesses. The use of PIN features seems troublesome and unnatural; a user has to wait until the cellular phone is unlocked to make a call. Moreover, clones are still able to steal the user's information from the airwaves. As a result, the clones eventually will be able to crack the codes even if such algorithms may be complicated. When the handset is occupied by an unauthorized person who knows the right PIN, the immediate loss seems unavoidable.

Recently, systematic studies have shown that *biometrics* provides an alternative yet natural way for user authentication [16, 32]. Biometrics handles authentication of individuals on the basis of biological and/or behavioral characteristics. In contrast to the traditional authentication approaches, the primary advantage is that biometrics cannot be misplaced and forgotten since biometric features are always inherently associated with human beings. As summarized in the literature [16], biometrics has a number of salient and desirable properties as follows: *a)* universality, *b)* uniqueness, *c)* permanence, *d)* collectability, *e)* performance, *f)* acceptability, and *g)* circumvention. There are numerous biometric features used for authentication. However, each of them is of its strengths and limitations in terms of the above properties and has to appeal to a special authentication application. In our circumstance, voice print or speech becomes the biometric feature available only. According to perception of biometrics experts [16], voice print is of the following properties: *a)* medium universality, *b)* low uniqueness, *c)* low permanence, *d)* medium collectability, *e)* low performance, *f)* high acceptability, and *g)* low circumvention. The properties of voice print provide a two-fold insight. On the one hand, high acceptability suggests that voice print be natural and become the ideal feature for user authentication in wireless environments. On the other hand, other unsatisfactory properties indicate that the voice print itself is insufficient to be a unique feature to perform user authentication in the environments in question. Thus, it poses a dilemma to us, and a solution to this dilemma is demanded such that user authentication can be performed by using only speech without loss of its desirable advantage.

As one of automatic biometric technologies, automatic speaker recognition has been studied for several decades [15, 21]. In general, speaker recognition is classified into two categories: speaker identification, a process of identifying an unknown voice token as belonging to one of registered speakers, and speaker verification, a process of accepting or rejecting the identity claim of a speaker. Apparently, speaker verification is more appropriate to user authentication in most circumstances. Moreover, a speaker verification system often works in either of two operating modes: text-dependent and text-independent. By text-dependent, the same or known text is used for training and test. In contrast, any text is allowed to be uttered in the process of either training or test in the text-independent mode. By comparison, a text-dependent system is conceptually simple yet inflexible while a text-independent system seems complicated yet flexible. Moreover, the performance of a text-dependent system is often reasonably better than that of a text-independent system while the text-independent system can perform in a more secure way if the user is allowed to speak any random phrase. No matter what the operating mode is, speaker recognition theoretically belongs to non-verbal speech classification since the information of speaker's characteristics conveyed in speech waves plays a crucial role in this process rather than those verbal contents carried by speech waves. As a consequence, speaker verification provides a reasonably good measure of security for access to a wireless network and to private/confidential information during a personalized service.

As a matter of fact, the voice print is inherently subject to change and sensitive to environments, which leads to a classification task of miscellaneous mismatches. Thus, the use of voice print itself fails to yield the desirable performance in contrast to other biometric features. Nevertheless, speech recognition, a verbal-content based speech classification task, has been well studied and received satisfactory performance [17], which makes an automatic telephone-banking like process feasible. Borrowing the telephone-banking concept, Li *et al.* first propose an alternative speech-based authentication approach – *verbal information verification* [22]. Other than the traditional speaker recognition, verbal information verification is a process that verifies spoken utterances against the pre-registered information in a personal profile. For user authentication, a verbal information verification system mainly inspects the verbal content conveyed in speech signals while a speaker recognition system takes advantage of a speaker's characteristics represented by the speech feature vectors [23]. Although verbal information verification has nothing to do with biometrics, it has generated considerably better performance (even error free) in user authentication [23, 24] assuming that the personal information is not stolen by unauthorized people. Therefore, the combination of traditional speaker verification and verbal information verification provides a promising way for high-performance user authentication without loss of the desirable property, easy-to-access, of speech.

In this chapter, we propose a bilateral user authentication framework though the combination of speaker verification and verbal information verification for personalized mobile access to private/authorized device, e.g. cellular phone, and confidential information, e.g. electronic financial transaction. In wireless environments, client device and distributed authentication centers constitute a server-client network and, dependent upon different tasks, user authentication is performed in either of two sites or both. Considering complexity in implementation and acceptability, text-dependent speaker verification is used in client device for primary user authentication, while the combination of text-independent speaker verification and verbal information verification leads to an innovative user authentication procedure in authentication centers. Thus, the hierarchical and interactive authentication schemes constitute a new user authentication framework for personalized mobile access in wireless environments. Such a framework could provide a potential solution to the aforementioned dilemma towards an error-reduction and easy-to-access service in personalized mobile access. In terms of Mandarin Chinese dialect, we have investigated the enabling component technologies. Our experimental results indicate that the major component technologies to support this framework are ready for real use though there are challenging implementation issues to be studied in the future.

The remainder of this chapter is organized as follows. Section 5.2 presents the bilateral user authentication framework. Section 5.3 describes key enabling component technologies developed in terms of Mandarin Chinese dialect. Section 5.4 reports experimental results, and the last section draws conclusions.

5.2.   Bilateral User Authentication Framework

In this section, we present a bilateral user authentication framework to personalize mobile access. On the basis of the framework, moreover, we describe a scenario example for personalizing mobile access.

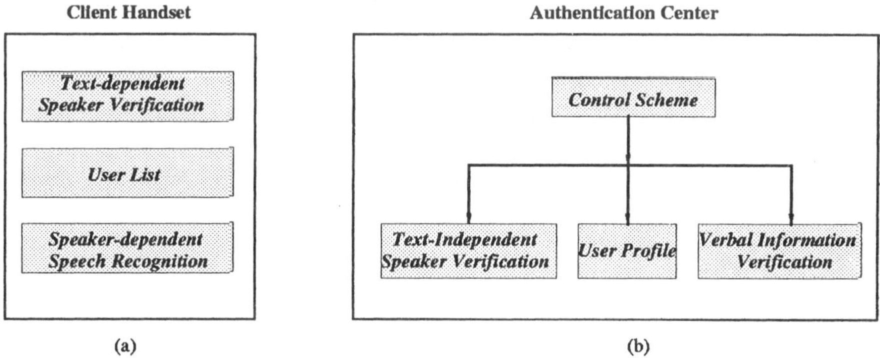

Figure 5.1.   The schematic diagram of a bilateral user authentication. (a) The client handset. (b) The authentication center.

As illustrated in Figure 5.1, the bilateral user authentication framework consists of two modules: *client device* and *authentication center*. The client device module is used for primary user authentication in order to enable the cellular phone to work for authorized users. The authentication center module works for further authentication when a user attempts to place a call of expensive cost or access to an information system containing private or personal information.

The communication between two modules is through the use of a simple yet special protocol such that the components in the authentication center can be activated.

In the client device module, there are three components related to user authentication as shown in Figure 5.1(a). A text-dependent speaker verification scheme is the key component to determine whether a user is given the right to access to the cellular phone. It should be pointed out that the claim process can be neglected since a cellular phone is usually assumed to belong to a specific user. Thus, the serial number of the phone provides a way to automatically claim identity. In case that a cellular phone may be shared by a small group of people, e.g. people belonging to a family, the user list registers those authorized users who are allowed to use this cellular phone handset. It should be stated that how to organize a user list well is a research topic and some potential solutions have been raised [6]. The speaker-dependent speech recognition scheme provides a set of simple speech recognition engines for voice-based dialing according to an address book. Note that due to the accessibility of multiple users there are an independent speaker verification/speech recognition schemes for the users enrolled in the user list. Thus, the population in the user list should not be large.

The authentication center provides a strict and final authentication mechanism for each user prior to some important mobile access. There are four schemes in the module for such authentication as depicted in Figure 5.1(b). The control scheme is used to globally control all the authentication mechanism and selectively activate an authentication scheme. Once it is activated, the text-independent speaker verification scheme always probes the specific user's identity during conversation to see if the identity of the current user occupying the cellular phone is consistent with that of its registered users claimed automatically. The user profile scheme stores the files of all the registered users served by the authentication. The contents of each file includes the personal and private information of each registered users, which provides the basis for verbal information verification. When a user is initially registered as a new user in the authentication center or the speaker verification scheme reports an inconsistent result, the verbal information verification scheme will be invoked. As a result, the current user is asked to answer a set of questions randomly selected from an elaborate questionnaire. Only if all the answers given are correct, the user will be allowed to make a continuous access. For security, the user profile could be updated regularly.

In order to intuitively understand our framework, we give a scenario example of personalized mobile access, which demonstrates how our framework works. For a new user, enrollment in the client device and the authentication center becomes the first step. In the client device site, the user is asked to utter voice-based commands and names to be dialed three times. In the authentication center, the enrollment process is to finish a user profile, through filling out a form, including personal and private information and a set of self-defined answers to some questions.

Once the enrollment has been done, the user may start the personalized access to his/her cellular phone. After the power is turned on, the user list scheme is activated, and thus, a list of authorized users are shown on the panel of the cellular phone where each authorized user is labeled by a number. The user utters the number represented him/her for identity claim. A special case is that the cellular phone is owned by one authorized user. In this circumstance, the identity claim is default and the user list is not shown. At this moment, the cellular phone is still locked. Prior to access to the phone, the user has to unlock the phone by a voice-based command. When the utterance of this command is achieved, the text-dependent speaker verification scheme is activated and authenticates the current user based on the templates stored in the enrollment process. If the user's identity is authenticated, the cellular phone is ready to enter any conversation phase. In order to be easy-to-access, a user is encouraged to make a phone call by using the voice-based dialing. Thus, the speaker-dependent speech recognition engine is activated for this task. After a conversation is performed, the phone may be locked again by the user through use of the voice-based command. There are the following cases for the client device to send a request to the authentication center: (1) the first time a user takes the cellular phone, (2) failure to unlock the phone or to dial by voice after three trails, and (3) making a long distance phone call or access to the private or personal information.

As illustrated in Figure 5.1(b), there are two authentication schemes in the authentication center. During the enrollment, users provide the corresponding user profiles such that the verbal information verification scheme can work for any registered users. When a user makes his/her first phone call, the verbal information verification scheme is activated by an automatic request from the client device. Once the user identity is verified by the verbal information verification scheme, a text-independent speaker verification model is created for this user. During the first conversation, all the utterances are automatically used to train the speaker model. That is, the second authentication scheme, text-independent speaker verification, is created based on the verbal information verification scheme during the first phone call. Once the text-independent authentication scheme is created, it would be activated by any long distance phone call request from the client device site. The text-independent authentication scheme inspects the phone call by report a verification result in a fixed interval. If the verification result indicates that an impostor is accessing the personalized client device, the phone call is immediately suspended. It is followed by a verbal information verification test. If the test is successful, the phone call is activated again. As a consequence, the utterances during the verbal information verification and conversations thereafter are used to update the text-independent speaker model. Note that in order to ensure a low error rate the text-independent speaker model is always updated in an autonomous way if the user's identity is verified. Thus, a personalized mobile access is carried out by the bilateral user authentication framework.

In the sequel, we are going to present some enabling technologies to support our bilateral user authentication framework for personalized mobile access.

5.3.   Enabling Speaker Authentication Technologies

In this section, we present enabling speaker authentication technologies to support our bilateral user authentication framework. We first describe the speaker verification technologies used in the client device and the authentication center. Then, we present a verbal information verification technology in terms of Mandarin Chinese dialect. Finally, we discuss how to derive maximum synergy for user authentication from both text-independent speaker verification, a biometric technology, and verbal information verification, a non-biometric technology.

5.3.1   Speaker Verification

Speaker verification is a biometric authentication technology. As illustrated in Figure 5.2, the critical technical components in speaker verification include speaker modeling and decision-making strategies. There are numerous approaches to speaker verification [3, 29, 13, 25, 15, 14, 5]. For the use in our framework, the speaker modeling in text-dependent speaker recognition tends to be as simple as possible and computationally efficient in the client device site, while speaker modeling in text-independent speaker recognition would be demanded to produce the error rate as low as possible. In addition, decision-making strategies used are different in the client device and the authentication center. Here, we present two enabling technologies to meet our requirements.

NFL-based Text-Dependent Speaker Verification.   Theoretically, speaker verification belongs to the category of non-verbal speech classification regardless of operating modes. However, most of text-dependent speaker verification approaches take advantage of verbal contents to capture speaker's characteristics [15], which often needs the strict temporal alignment. A temporal alignment process usually suffers from a high computational load, e.g. dynamic time warping [30]. Our previous studies showed that some instantaneous information carried by certain frames within an utterance can play a more important role in text-dependent speaker recognition and the use of transitional (interframe) information may not be involved in a strict temporal alignment [10]. Our recent studies indicated that the *nearest feature line* (NFL) is able to be a

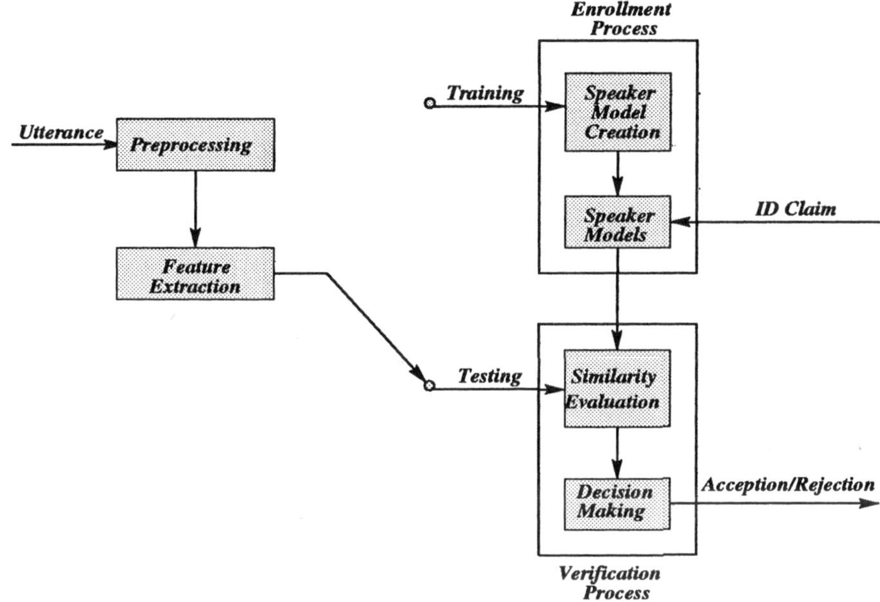

Figure 5.2. The schematic diagram of a typical speaker verification system.

text-dependent speaker verification technique without the strict temporal alignment, which does not involve in high computational load and, in particular, the performance of an NFL-based text-dependent system is better than that of a dynamic temporal warping system [9]. Thus, the NFL-based text-dependent speaker verification approach qualifies as the enabling technology in our framework.

The NFL assumes that there are at least two prototypes (in our case, two utterances of a fixed phrase) for each speaker. The line passing through two feature points, extracting from two utterances after preprocessing, can extrapolate or interpolate to form a line, named by *feature line* in the NFL approach, in the feature space. Now we consider two feature points, $\mathbf{x}_i^s$ and $\mathbf{x}_j^s$, belonging to speaker s. Thus, the distance d between the feature line $\overline{\mathbf{x}_i^s \mathbf{x}_j^s}$ passing through $\mathbf{x}_i^s$ and $\mathbf{x}_j^s$ and a query point $\mathbf{x}_q$ is calculated by

$$d(\mathbf{x}_q, \overline{\mathbf{x}_i^s \mathbf{x}_j^s}) = \|\mathbf{x}_q - \mathbf{p}_{i,j}^s\|. \tag{5.1}$$

Here $\mathbf{p}_{i,j}^s$ is a point on the feature line achieved by projecting $\mathbf{x}_q$ to $\overline{\mathbf{x}_i^s \mathbf{x}_j^s}$. As a result, such a point can be obtained by linearly combining two feature points in terms of the query point as follows:

$$\mathbf{p}_{i,j}^s = \mu \mathbf{x}_i^s + (1 - \mu)\mathbf{x}_j^s, \tag{5.2}$$

where

$$\mu = \frac{(\mathbf{x}_q - \mathbf{x}_i^s)^T (\mathbf{x}_j^s - \mathbf{x}_i^s)}{(\mathbf{x}_j^s - \mathbf{x}_i^s)^T (\mathbf{x}_j^s - \mathbf{x}_i^s)}.$$

For speaker s, any pair of his/her feature points constitute a feature line. For a given query point, $\mathbf{x}_q$, there is the nearest feature line, $\overline{\mathbf{x}_{i*}^s \mathbf{x}_{j*}^s}$, achieved by

$$\overline{\mathbf{x}_{i*}^s \mathbf{x}_{j*}^s} = \arg \min_{i,j} d(\mathbf{x}_q, \overline{\mathbf{x}_i^s \mathbf{x}_j^s}). \tag{5.3}$$

To build an NFL speaker model, we need to extract feature points or prototypes from raw speech data. In our method, each utterance, corresponding to a fixed phrase, is modeled to form a prototype (for details, see Section 5.4.2). Thus, the NFL speaker model is created by constructing the feature line space through the combination of prototypes in a pair-by-pair way. Note that the aforementioned prototypes should be normalized prior to forming the feature line space in order to facilitate the decision-making described later on.

Once a speaker model is built, the remaining task is how to make a right decision for an unknown voice token. In our circumstance, there are only enrollment data from the registered user himself/herself and no other speech data available since we allow a user to flexibly choose any phrase as the text. Obviously, we cannot use any traditional method to set a threshold and build either a background or a cohort model [15]. Cohort modeling is a typical approach to train a background model for decision-making in speaker verification. The idea underlying this approach is to build a model by the use of speakers who have acoustic characteristics similar to a specific speaker. Once a cohort model is available, the decision-making can be performed by comparing scores produced by the speaker model with that by his/her corresponding cohort model. Although a cohort model is merely available by associating with other speakers, recent studies demonstrated that the use of only enrollment data to build a background model, hereinafter named by *pseudo-cohort model*, leads to the appreciably good performance [31]. Motivated by this work, we build such pseudo-cohort models in terms of an NFL speaker model for each speaker by perturbing statistical components in his/her speaker model (for details, see Section 5.4.2). As a consequence, in our system, the decision-making on the client handset site is performed by means of the speaker and the pseudo-cohort models.

GMM-based Text-Independent Speaker Verification.   As a typical approach, Gaussian Mixture Model (GMM) has been used especially for text-independent speaker recognition to characterize speaker's voice in the form of probabilistic model. It has been reported that the GMM approach outperforms other classical methods for text-independent speaker recognition [28, 8]. Here, we briefly review the GMM-based speaker identification scheme that will be used, as a technical component in our authentication center.

For a feature vector denoted as $\mathbf{x}_t$ belonging to a specific speaker s, the GMM is a linear combination of K Gaussian components as follows:

$$P(\mathbf{x}_t|\lambda_s) = \sum_{k=1}^{K} \omega_{s,k}\, P(\mathbf{x}_t|\mathbf{m}_{s,k}, \boldsymbol{\Sigma}_{s,k}). \tag{5.4}$$

Here $\omega_{s,k}$ is a linear combination coefficient for speaker s $(s = 1, 2, ..., S)$. $P(\mathbf{x}_t|\mathbf{m}_{s,k}, \boldsymbol{\Sigma}_{s,k})$ is a Gaussian component parameterized by a mean vector, $\mathbf{m}_{s,k}$, and covariance matrix, $\boldsymbol{\Sigma}_{s,k}$ as follows:

$$P(\mathbf{x}_t|\mathbf{m}_{s,k}, \boldsymbol{\Sigma}_{s,k}) = \frac{1}{(2\pi)^{\frac{d}{2}}|\boldsymbol{\Sigma}_{s,k}|^{\frac{1}{2}}} \exp\left[-\frac{1}{2}(\mathbf{x}_t - \mathbf{m}_{s,k})^T \boldsymbol{\Sigma}_{s,k}^{-1}(\mathbf{x}_t - \mathbf{m}_{s,k})\right]. \tag{5.5}$$

Usually, a diagonal covariance matrix is used in Eq. (5.5). Given a sequence of feature vectors, $\{\mathbf{x}_1, \mathbf{x}_2, \cdots, \mathbf{x}_t, \cdots\}$, from a specific speaker's utterances, parameters estimation for $\lambda_s = (\omega_{s,k}, \mathbf{m}_{s,k}, \boldsymbol{\Sigma}_{s,k})$ $(k = 1, \cdots, K, s = 1, \cdots, S)$ is performed by the Expectation-Maximization (EM) algorithm. Thus, a specific speaker model is built through finding proper parameters in the GMM based on the speaker's own feature vectors.

To evaluate the performance, a sequence of feature vectors is divided into overlapping segments of T feature vectors for identification [28]:

$$\overbrace{\mathbf{x}_l, \mathbf{x}_{l+1}, \cdots, \mathbf{x}_{l+T-1}}^{segment\ l}, \mathbf{x}_{l+T}, \cdots\cdots$$

$$\mathbf{x}_l, \overbrace{\mathbf{x}_{l+1}, \cdots, \mathbf{x}_{l+T-1}, \mathbf{x}_{l+T}}^{segment\ l+1}, \mathbf{x}_{l+T+1}, \cdots\cdots$$

For a testing segment $X^{(l)} = \{\mathbf{x}_l, \mathbf{x}_{l+1}, \cdots, \mathbf{x}_{l+T-1}\}$, the log-likelihood function of a GMM is as following:

$$\mathcal{L}(X^{(l)}, \lambda_s) = \sum_{t=l}^{l+T-1} \log P(\mathbf{x}_t|\lambda_s) \quad s = 1, \cdots, S. \tag{5.6}$$

Thus, the likelihood value, $\mathcal{L}(X^{(l)}, \lambda_s)$, is a score produced by the speaker model corresponding to the claimed identity which will be used for decision-making.

Unlike the client handset site, there may be a large amount of data belonging to other speakers available off-line, e.g. a standard speech corpus, in the authentication center site. For the purpose of decision-making, therefore, it is feasible to utilize the data for creating a speaker-independent background model. As a result, we adopt a GMM of numerous Gaussian components and a non-diagonal covariance matrix, $P(\mathbf{x_t}|\lambda_{SI})$, to form such a background model (for details, see Section 5.4.2). Similarly, the decision-making, corresponding to a testing speech segment, is performed by means of the GMM-based speaker and background models. For an utterance of several segments, the final decision-making is achieved by a majority voting on the basis of the decision-making results with respect to all the testing speech segments comprised of this utterance.

5.3.2　Verbal Information Verification

Verbal information verification is an authentication technology recently developed in speech processing community [21, 23] where a claimed speaker is accepted/rejected by verifying spoken utterances against the information stored in a given personal data profile. Strictly to say, this technology does not belong to biometrics because it uses only the contents carried in speech for authentication. As pointed out previously, there are a number of problems as speaker verification is applied in real world, e.g., acoustic mismatch, quality of the training data, inconvenience of enrollment, and the creation of a large database to memorize all the registered speaker patterns. Obviously, the use of verbal information verification is able to enhance speaker authentication technologies. Although verbal information verification is regardless of speakers' acoustic characteristics, the technology is highly dependent on a dialect since the contents carried in speech need to be verified. Here we present the verbal information verification technology in terms of Mandarin Chinese.

General Description.　Although verbal information verification has been successful in English language, it is still questioned that such a technology is effectively applicable to other languages. Mandarin Chinese is the most widely used language in the world since there are around 1.3 billion Chinese native speakers. Previous studies [19, 20] showed that Mandarin Chinese is different from English in numerous aspects. Some salient features in Mandarin Chinese are summarized as follows. First, every word of Chinese has only one syllable and consists of explicit semi-syllable configuration; INITIAL and FINAL. INITIAL is always a consonant, while FINAL could be one of single vowels, compound vowels, and vowels along with consonants. Next, all the Chinese syllables include FINAL, while INITIAL may not be contained in a Chinese syllable. Unlike phoneme in English, INITIAL and FINAL are basic acoustic unit in Mandarin Chinese instead. Thus, we need to use them for acoustic modeling, which results in a large difference from other languages in acoustic modeling. Finally, there are a few of words that are commonly used but make no contribution to verbal information verification, such as 'year', 'month', and 'day' in Mandarin Chinese as a question about birthday is raised, since these words are always present in the answer regardless of speakers. In addition, the same meaning can be represented by an alternative word; e.g., 'day' can be spoken in two different ways in Mandarin Chinese. Such information is hardly captured from users' private data profile. All the aforementioned problems are worth studying, which causes the Mandarin verbal information verification to become a challenging task.

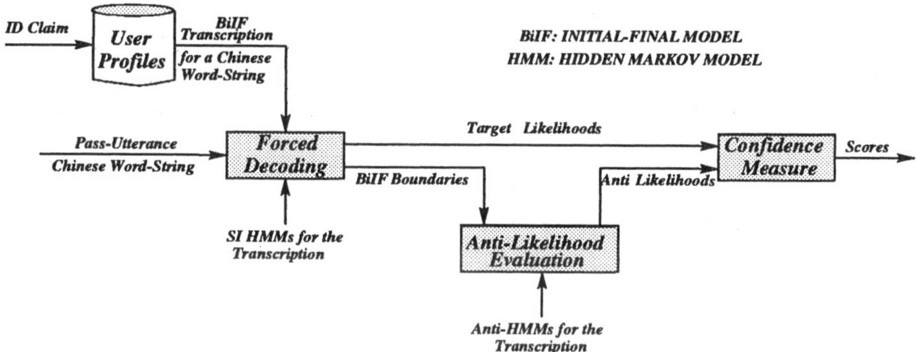

Figure 5.3. The schematic diagram of a Mandarin verbal information verification system.

For Mandarin verbal information verification, we have presented an architecture as depicted in Figure 5.3. Once an identity is claimed by a user, our system transcribes the pass-utterance from his/her private data profile. For instance, an answer to the question "What is your name?" is transcribed into a Chinese word string. During this transcription, the pass-utterance is acoustically modeled as a string consisting of INTIALs and FINALs. By the transcription, the system decodes the the pass-utterance. This process is summarized as *forced decoding* in Figure 5.3. As a result, forced decoding yields the INITIAL-FINAL's segmentation boundaries for the string. Thus, the decision-making, accepting/rejecting the claimed speaker in terms of the utterance, can be performed by a hypothesis test.

According to Chinese linguistics, there are 22 INITIALs and 37 FINALs in Mandarin Chinese dialect. In order to model the co-articulation between them, we use the right context-dependent INITIAL-FINALs as basic acoustic unit, hereinafter abbreviated by *BiIF*. In our system, we employ hidden Markov models (HMMs) to model the acoustic units. As a result, an INITIAL-based BiIF model is a left-to-right (without jump) connected HMM of three states, while a FINAL-based BiIF model is a 5-state HMM of the same structure. By combination, totally, there are 1260 BiIF models in Mandarin Chinese. It is almost impossible to collect enough training data for those models. Instead we adopt a decision-tree based clustering method to reduce the number of states and models [24]. Moreover, we use segmental K-means and import decision tree algorithms together in on iterative step during training as done in the work [27]. In contrast, such a training method is more robust than the traditional decision-tree clustering algorithm. As a consequence, the speaker-independent acoustic models are achieved by fitting the training data to HMM models by the Viterbi learning algorithm [18, 24]. Similarly, we also use the same method to achieve anti-HMM models corresponding to those BiIF models by those data used for training all the target BiIF models of the same context. More details on implementation will be described in Section 5.4.3.

Decision-Making Procedure.   Like speaker verification, decision-making is also involved into verbal information verification. In order to facilitate presentation, we first describe the verbal information verification process in a more formal way. Then, the decision-making procedure is presented based on the formal description.

Based on achieved HMMs and anti-HMMs, utterance segmentation is performed as follows. When our system prompts one single question at a moment, it knows the expected critical information, registered in his/her personal profile of the claimed speaker, to the prompted question and the corresponding subword sequence of N acoustic units, $\mathbf{S} = \{S_n\}_{n=1}^{N}$. Thus, the acoustic unit models, $\lambda_1, \cdots, \lambda_N$, in the same order of $\mathbf{S}$ are applied to decode the answer utterance in the forced decoding process. In this process, Viterbi algorithm is employed to find the maximum likelihood segmentation of the acoustic units, i.e.,

$$P(\mathbf{O}|\mathbf{S}) = \max_{t_1, t_2, \cdots, t_N} P(O_1^{t_1}|S_1) \cdots P(O_{t_1+1}^{t_2}|S_2) \cdots P(O_{t_{N-1}+1}^{t_N}|S_N), \quad (5.7)$$

where

$$\mathbf{O} = \{\mathbf{O}_1, \mathbf{O}_2, \cdots, \mathbf{O}_N\} = \left\{O_1^{t_1}, \cdots, O_{t_1+1}^{t_2}, \cdots, O_{t_{N-1}+1}^{t_N}\right\}. \quad (5.8)$$

Here $\mathbf{O}$ is a set of segmented feature vectors related to acoustic units, and $t_1, t_2, \cdots, t_N$ are the end frame numbers of acoustic unit segments. $\mathbf{O}_n = O_{t_{n-1}+1}^{t_n}$ is the segmented sequence of observations corresponding to the acoustic unit S_n from frame $t_{n-1} + 1$ to frame t_n, where $t_1 \geq 1$ and $t_i > t_{i-1}$.

For a decoded acoustic unit, S_n, in an observed speech segment, $\mathbf{O}_n$, a decision-making strategy is demanded where the acoustic unit will be assigned to either hypotheses of H_0 and H_1. Here H_0 is the hypothesis that $\mathbf{O}_n$ is consistent with the corresponding items in the personal profile and H_1 is the alternative hypothesis. According to the Neyman-Person lemma [26, 12], the hypothesis test is described as

$$r(\mathbf{O}_n) = \frac{P(\mathbf{O}_n|H_0)}{P(\mathbf{O}_n|H_1)} = \frac{P(\mathbf{O}_n|\lambda_n)}{P(\mathbf{O}_n|\bar{\lambda}_n)}. \quad (5.9)$$

Here λ_n and $\bar{\lambda}_n$ are the target HMM and the corresponding anti-HMM for the acoustic unit, S_n. Thus, the *log-likelihood ratio* (LLR) for S_n is

$$R(\mathbf{O}_n) = \log r(\mathbf{O}_n) = \log P(\mathbf{O}_n|\lambda_n) - \log P(\mathbf{O}_n|\bar{\lambda}_n). \qquad (5.10)$$

Accordingly, the averaging frame LLR, $\bar{R}_n$, is

$$\bar{R}_n = \frac{1}{L_n}\left[\log P(\mathbf{O}_n|\lambda_n) - \log P(\mathbf{O}_n|\bar{\lambda}_n)\right], \qquad (5.11)$$

where L_n is the length of the speech segment. For each acoustic unit, a decision can be made by the following rule

$$\text{Acceptance}: \bar{R}_n \geq T_n; \quad \text{Rejection}: \bar{R}_n < T_n.$$

Here either an acoustic-unit dependent threshold, T_n, or a content-independent common threshold, T, can be determined numerically or experimentally.

Since a single utterance may contain numerous acoustic units, an utterance level decision is further needed to be made as well. For this purpose, we employ a normalized confidence measure as used in the work [23]. For an acoustic-unit string characterized by the INITIAL-FINAL model, λ_n, a confidence measure is defined as

$$C_n = \frac{\log P(\mathbf{O}_n|\lambda_n) - \log P(\mathbf{O}_n|\bar{\lambda}_n)}{\log P(\mathbf{O}_n|\bar{\lambda}_n)}, \qquad (5.12)$$

where $P(\mathbf{O}_n|\bar{\lambda}_n) \neq 0$ indicates that this target score is larger than the anti-score and vice versa. Thus, a normalized confidence measure for an utterance of N acoustic units (subwords) as

$$\bar{C} = \frac{1}{N}\sum_{n=1}^{N} H(C_n) \qquad (5.13)$$

Here, $H(C_n)$ is the Heaviside step function defined as

$$H(C_n) = \begin{cases} 1, & \text{if } C_n \geq \theta, \\ 0, & \text{otherwise.} \end{cases} \qquad (5.14)$$

$\bar{C}$ is located in the fixed interval between zero and one. Due to the normalization in Eq. (5.12), the threshold, θ, is content-independent that can be determined separately. According to Eq. (5.14), an acoustic unit is accepted only if its C_n score is not less than the threshold θ. In other words, only those acoustic unit of $C_n \geq \theta$ can make a contribution to acceptance. As a result, $\bar{C}$ would be viewed as the percentage of acceptable acoustic units in an utterance. Hence, an utterance threshold may be set or adjusted in terms of the specification of our system and performance.

For verbal information verification, a test may include a number of utterances corresponding to the answers to several questions randomly selected from an elaborate questionnaire. Therefore, the sequential utterance verification must be considered for real applications. Fortunately, the above single utterance decision-making strategy, defined in Eqs. (5.12)-(5.14), can be directly extended to a sequence of subsets, which is similar to the step-down procedure in statistics [1]. Each of the subsets is an independent single utterance verification. As long as a subset is rejected, H_1 is chosen to be true and the testing procedure is terminated. In contrast, the claimed identity (user) is acceptable only if every subset passes the test, i.e., each H_0 is accepted.

5.3.3   Combination of Speaker and Verbal Information Verification

As presented in Section 5.2, the authentication center adopts a new speaker authentication strategy by combining text-independent speaker verification and verbal information verification. In such a strategy, the authentication center works in a natural way; the text-independent speaker verification scheme performs identity authentication in an automatic and transparency way, while the verbal information verification scheme is activated only if those circumstances listed in Section 5.2 occurs.

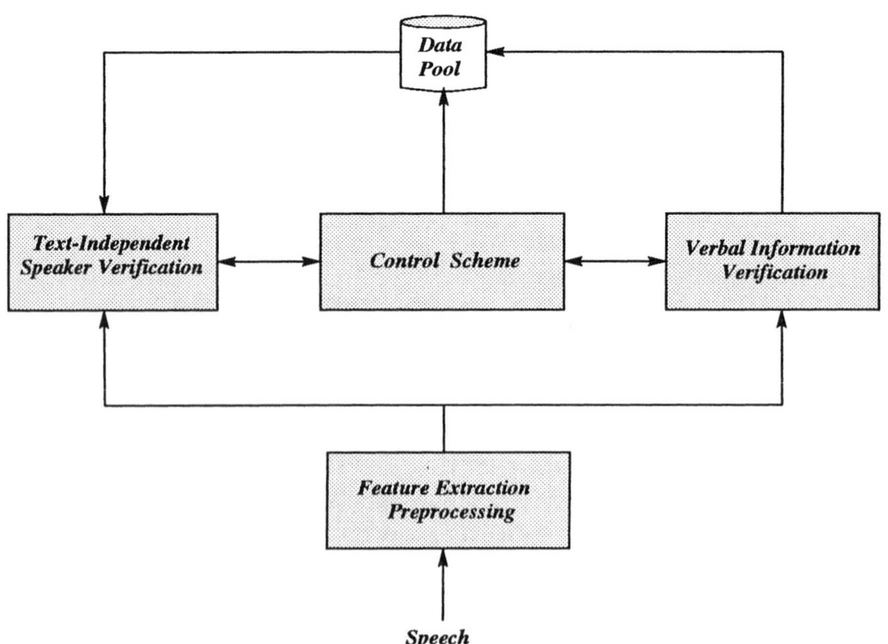

Figure 5.4.   The schematic diagram of a combination mechanism in the authentication center.

As illustrated in Figure 5.4, the control scheme is the key component of this combination scheme. When a special call request, e.g. international call, is received, the control scheme is activated and its default mode is to activate the text-independent speaker verification system based on the information of the registered caller. Thus, all the utterance in the current call is monitored by the text-independent speaker verification system during this phone call. Once a speech stream of a certain length is rejected, the system immediately breaks the call and keeps the transaction information, e.g. dialed number, in the meanwhile. Then, the control scheme suspends the text-independent speaker verification system and activates the verbal information verification system instead. Thus, a verbal information verification process proceeds; a number of questions are asked one by one and the answers from the current caller are verified based on the private profile of the handset owner. The answering utterances are stored in the data pool as shown in Figure 5.4. If any of the caller's answers is inconsistent with the corresponding item in the private profile twice, the control scheme also suspends the verbal verification system. Thus, the authentication center will terminate this call and put the memo information in the logout file. Otherwise, the control scheme redials the memorized number and makes a valid connection. In addition, the control scheme directs the speaker model in the text-independent speaker verification system to be adapted on the data available in the data pool. After the adaptation is performed, the control scheme will empty out the data pool.

It is worth mentioning that there are several differences between the combination strategy here and that proposed in the work [23]. First, two different verification systems in our combination strategy do not work simultaneously. Instead they work in an alternate way, while two verification systems in their approach have to work in a cascade way [23]. Next a text-independent speaker verification system can be used in our strategy, while a text-dependent speaker verification system is merely used for that combination [23]. Finally, automatic enrollment in the component speaker verification system is quite different. In their work [23], the speaker verification system can be trained only if the verbal verification system works for several times. In contrast, the data for automatic enrollment can be achieved while a valid user makes a local phone call. Furthermore, sufficient data can be collected from multiple calling phases such that the speaker model in the text-independent speaker verification system can be adapted regularly. Thus, the mismatch problem can be resolved by adaptation in our framework.

5.4.   Simulations

In this section, we report some simulation results on a Mandarin Chinese speech database. As addressed in Section 5.3, there are two component enabling technologies to support our bilateral user authentication framework for personalized mobile access. We report simulation results on two component technologies separately, and moreover, some speaker verification results enhanced by verbal information verification. Due to the limited space here, we report only the overall performance in all trials.

5.4.1 Database

For simulations, we use a Mandarin Chinese speech database of 50 people including 25 male and 25 female native speakers. The database consists of there sets for use in text-dependent and text-independent speaker verification as well as verbal information verification. In general, all the data in different sets are recorded in five sessions, labeled by $S_1, \cdots, S_5$, from one week to three weeks.

In the text-dependent data set, several fixed Chinese voice commands, e.g. 'unlock', 'turn on', and 'hello', are uttered three times in each session. For a voice command, thus, there are 15 fixed phrase utterances for each speaker in the set.

In the text-independent data set, we provide a set of conversation materials. In each session, a speaker in our database is asked to randomly select several sentences of over 30 seconds from the conversation set. As a result, there are the utterances of at least 30 seconds for each speaker in each session.

In the verbal information verification set, each speaker is asked to utter all the items in his/her private profiles registered in the system. Thus, there are five utterances for each item in the set. The use of five sessions is two-fold: enabling us to simulate multiple transactions and investigating the performance of our speaker-independent acoustic models, the kernel component of our verbal information verification system, in terms of voice aging. This data set will be used to test our Mandarin verbal information verification system.

As presented in Section 5.3.2, a set of speaker-independent HMMs are used for modeling Chinese acoustic units. For training the HMMs, we employ a benchmark Mandarin Chinese corpus, 863 corpus, in China. The population of this corpus is 200 people including 100 male and female speakers. For each speaker, there are a number of utterances ranging from 520 to 625 sentences elaborately selected from the database of the most famous Chinese newspaper – People Daily. Totally, all the utterances in this corpus correspond to up to 2185 sentences. Basically, almost all the phonetic information on Mandarin Chinese is covered by this corpus.

5.4.2 Speaker Verification

In this section, we report speaker verification results in terms of the text-dependent and text-independent data sets. For evaluating the performance of our methods, two different testing methods are used. one is to use *equal error rate* (EER), where the false rejection rate is equal to the false acceptance rate, without the need of a background model for decision-making. The other is to use a background model to yield real results, where we use *half total error rate* (HTER), defined as the average of the normalized false acceptance and false rejection rates, to evaluate the performance. For a specific speaker, speech data belonging to other people in the database are used as impostors' data during test.

Text-Dependent Experiments. For building an NFL speaker model, three utterances of a fixed phrase recorded in a specific session are used. Once one session is used for training, other four sessions are used for test. For reliability, we have performed five trials in the above way; five sessions are equally used as training and testing sets in five trials.

Now we present the acoustic analysis in text-dependent speaker verification. Before feature extraction, an utterance is pre-emphasized with the filter response $H(z) = 1 - 0.95z^{-1}$ and blocked into fixed-length frames. Each frame has 256 samples (2.56 ms) with 11.5 ms frame shift. The feature used is the statistical parameters of 19-order *Mel-scaled cepstrum coefficients* (MFCCs). The 19-order adaptive component weighted cepstrum coefficients [2] are superposed on MFCCs. Adaptive component weighted cepstrum is a robust feature to discriminate the speakers through emphasizing the formants of speakers.

Suppose that for an utterance belonging to speaker s, a set of N feature vectors, $X = \{\mathbf{x}_n^{(s)}\}_{n=1}^N$ where $\mathbf{x}_n = (x_{n,1}^{(s)}, \cdots, x_{n,19}^{(s)})^T$, are extracted by the above procedure. The mean and standard-deviation vectors,

$$\bar{\mathbf{x}}^{(s)} = (\bar{x}_1^{(s)}, \cdots, \bar{x}_{19}^{(s)})^T$$

and

$$\sigma_X^{(s)} = (\sigma_{X,1}^{(s)}, \cdots, \sigma_{X,19}^{(s)})^T,$$

are defined as

$$\bar{\mathbf{x}}^{(s)} = \frac{1}{N} \sum_{n=1}^N \mathbf{x}_n^{(s)}$$

and

$$\sigma_{X,i}^{(s)} = \sqrt{\frac{1}{N} \sum_{n=1}^N \left(x_{n,i}^{(s)} - \bar{x}_i^{(s)} \right)^2}, \quad i = 1, \cdots, 19.$$

Thus, a new feature vector of this utterance, by integrating two statistics, is formed as

$$\hat{\mathbf{x}}^{(s)} = \left\{ (\bar{\mathbf{x}}^{(s)}, \sigma_X^{(s)}) \right\},$$

which is viewed to be a prototype of the NFL model corresponding to this speaker.

Table 5.1.   The list of constitutions in five trails.

	Trial 1	Trial 2	Trial 3	Trial 4	Trial 5
Training Set	S_1	S_2	S_3	S_4	S_5
Testing Set	$S_2 \sim S_5$	S_1, S_3, S_4, S_5	S_1, S_2, S_4, S_5	S_1, S_2, S_3, S_5	$S_1 \sim S_4$

On the basis of such a feature vector, each speaker's NFL model consists of three prototypes and, therefore, there are three feature lines resulting from three prototypes. In order to produce the pseudo-cohort models, each prototype is perturbed by two randomly produced vectors, $\delta\bar{\mathbf{x}}^{(s)}$ and $\delta\sigma_X^{(s)}$, respectively to form two pseudo-prototypes:

$$\hat{\mathbf{x}}_+^{(s)} = \left\{ (\bar{\mathbf{x}}^{(s)} + \delta\bar{\mathbf{x}}^{(s)}, \sigma_X^{(s)} + \delta\sigma_X^{(s)}) \right\}, \quad \hat{\mathbf{x}}_- = \left\{ (\bar{\mathbf{x}}^{(s)} - \delta\bar{\mathbf{x}}^{(s)}, \sigma_X^{(s)} - \delta\sigma_X)^{(s)} \right\}.$$

Accordingly, three pairs of pseudo-prototypes are formed to construct feature lines of pseudo cohort models corresponding to the speaker. It should be stated that the above perturbation is motivated by our previous studies on setting *a prior* threshold for speaker verification[7]. As a result, an acceptance/rejection decision is made through the competition between the speaker model and his/her pseudo-cohort models.

Figure 5.5 depicts simulation results in our experiments. Figure 5.5(a) shows the EERs in different trials, as listed in Table 5.1, by using only speaker models. By the pseudo-cohort models, we examine the performance of our system and show the HTERs in Figure 5.5(b). From Figures 5.5(a) and 5.5(b), the performance of our NFL-based system is reasonable for a fixed phrase of around 1.0 second. However, such error rates are still not acceptable for practical use. Therefore, we need to further improve the performance of our NFL system.

In fact, the error may result from miscellaneous mismatches, in particular, due to voice aging. Fortunately, new speech data should be always available as long as the handset is used. The availability of new data provides possibilities to update those prototypes in both the speaker and pseudo-cohort models. In order to alleviate the mismatch effects, we present a unsupervised on-line update method as follows. When the unknown utterance U, characterized by $\hat{\mathbf{x}}_U = \{(\bar{\mathbf{x}}_U, \sigma_U)\}$, corresponding to a fixed phrase is accepted by the speaker model no matter whether this decision is right or wrong, the system will update one of the previous prototypes in the speaker and the corresponding pseudo-cohort models. Assume that $\hat{\mathbf{x}}_{i*}^{(s)}$ is the prototype satisfying the following condition:

$$i^* = \arg \min_{1 \leq i \leq 3} ||\hat{\mathbf{x}}_U - \hat{\mathbf{x}}_i^{(s)}||,$$

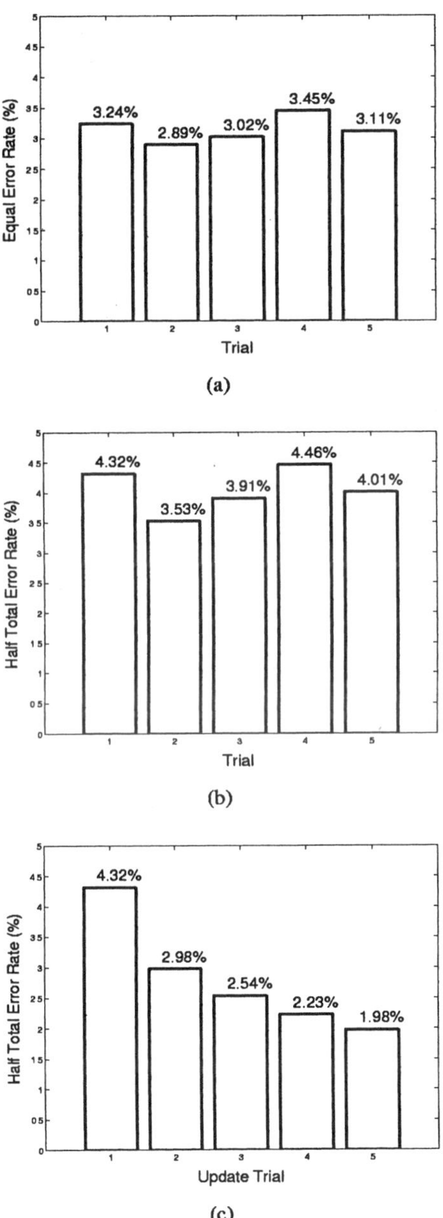

(a)

(b)

(c)

Figure 5.5.   The performance of our NFL-based text-dependent speaker verification system installed in a handset. (a) Equal error rates in different trials. (b) The performance without update in different trials. (c) The performance with update in different trials.

Table 5.2.   The list of constitutions in five update trails.

	Trial 1	Trial 2	Trial 3	Trial 4	Trial 5
Training Set	S_1	S_1, S_2	$S_1 \sim S_3$	$S_1 \sim S_4$	$S_1 \sim S_5$
Testing Set	$S_2 \sim S_5$	$S_2 \sim S_5$	$S_3 \sim S_5$	S_4, S_5	S_5

where $\| \cdot \|$ is the Euclidean norm. Then, we replace this prototype with a new prototype, $\hat{\mathbf{x}}^{(s)}$, achieved by

$$\hat{\mathbf{x}}^{(s)} = \frac{\hat{\mathbf{x}}_U + \hat{\mathbf{x}}_{i*}^{(s)}}{2}.$$

Accordingly, the corresponding prototypes, $\hat{\mathbf{x}}_{i*,+}^{(s)}$ and $\hat{\mathbf{x}}_{i*,-}^{(s)}$, in the pseudo-cohort model are updated based on the new prototype $\hat{\mathbf{x}}^{(s)}$.

To evaluate the performance of our system with the above on-line update mechanism, we conduct some experiments as listed in Table 5.2. As a result, Figure 5.5(c) illustrates the performance of our system with update. From Figure 5.5(c), it is observed that the performance in trail 1 is the same as the previous one shown in Figure 5.5(b) since there is no additional information available in trail 1. In trials 2-5, new data recorded in different sessions are available and, to some extent, the prototype update compensates for the mismatch due to voice aging. As illustrated in Figure 5.5(c), the error rate is lowered as more and more speech data recorded in different sessions are used for update. Here we emphasize that our update procedure performs autonomously and provides an alternative perspective towards the reduction of error rate in an adaptive way.

Text-Independent Experiments.   For building a GMM-based speaker model, all the utterances recorded in a session are used. For reliability, we have performed five trials in the above way; five sessions are equally used as training and testing sets in five trials. In other words, one session is used for training and other four sessions are used for test in this trial.

Prior to training of a GMM speaker model, the acoustic analysis is performed as follows: a) pre-emphasizing with filter response $H(z) = 1 - 0.95z^{-1}$, b) 32ms Hamming windowing without overlapping, c) removing the silence and unvoiced part of speech in terms of short-term average energy, and d) extracting weighted 19-order Mel-scaled cepstral feature vector from each short-term frame.

In our simulations, the GMM of 32 Gaussian components is employed to characterize each speaker and a GMM of 512 Gaussian component is used to build a world background model. The GMM models are trained by the EM algorithm. All the data in the text-independent set are used to train the

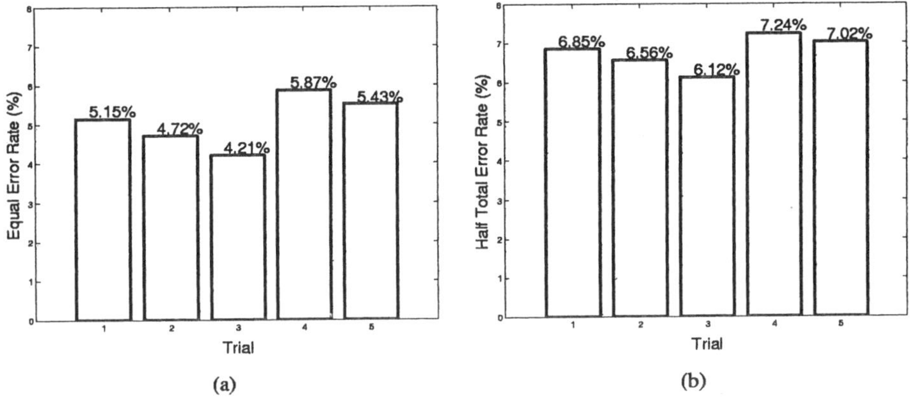

Figure 5.6. The performance of our GMM-based text-independent speaker verification system corresponding to speech segments of eight seconds. (a) Equal error rates in different trials. (b) Half total error rates in terms of the world background model.

world background model as done in the work [33]. As a result, all scores are normalized based on the world model prior to decision-making.

For decision-making, we adopt *a priori* speaker-dependent threshold setting method developed by ourselves [7]. In our method, we attempt to make a proper use of all the reliable statistics available. We believe that more reliable statistics provide more useful information, which might lead to a better threshold for decision-making. As a consequence, a speaker-dependent threshold is estimated by a linear combination of all the reliable statistics mentioned above:

$$T_S = b(\bar{\mu} + a\bar{\sigma}) + (1 - b)\mu, \tag{5.15}$$

where a and b are two speaker-independent parameters and optimized on the population of speakers used for building the world model. μ, $\bar{\mu}$, and $\bar{\sigma}$ are the statistics of normalized scores belonging to a speaker and the ensemble of impostors. Thus, Eq. (5.15) encodes the useful information conveyed by the reliable statistics, and the decision threshold becomes a monotonically increasing function of μ, $\bar{\mu}$, and $\bar{\sigma}$.

For test, we use the segment-based method presented in Section 5.3.1 to evaluate the performance of our system. Due to the limited space, we report only the results tested by speech segments of eight seconds. Figure 5.6 shows the performance of our GMM-based speaker verification system. Figure 5.6(a) depicts the EERs of our system in different trials, the same constitutions as used in the text-dependent experiments (c.f. Table 5.1), as by the use of only speaker models. In addition, the performance of our system by the use of the world background model is shown in Figure 5.6(b). From Figures 5.6(a) and 5.6(b), the performance of the GMM-based system is logic, which is consistent with other tests of a GMM-based text-dependent speaker verification system [28, 8].

As illustrated in Figure 5.6, simulation results by only text-independent speaker verification system may lead to unacceptable error rates in practice. As pointed out in this paper, such a speaker verification system needs enhancing by incorporating other technologies, e.g. verbal information verification, to reduce error rates.

5.4.3 Mandarin Verbal Information Verification

In this section, we present simulation results of verbal information verification in terms of Mandarin Chinese. Moreover, we demonstrate how the verbal information verification system can enhance text-independent speaker verification.

Verbal Information Verification Experiments. To establish a Mandarin verbal information verification system, we use HMMs to model Mandarin Chinese acoustic units, INTIALs and FINALs. By a training and pruning procedure on the 863 corpus, totally, 467 tied models and 893 tied states form our speaker-independent acoustic modeling system. As a result, the performance of our acoustic modeling system reaches the accuracy rate of 71.8% in single syllable recognition. For test, a speaker is viewed as a true speaker only if the speaker's utterances are verified against his/her provide profile. On the other hand, this speaker will be considered as an impostor when the utterances are verified against other speakers' private profiles. For each true speaker, therefore, there are K utterances and $49K$ utterances from other 49 speakers as impostors (see Section 5.4.1), where K is the number of questions that a speaker is asked to answer. In the following experiments, the sequential utterance verification method presented in Section 5.3.2 is evaluated. Since there are five sessions, the overall performance in five trials are reported here. In our experiments, different thresholds, speaker-independent and context-dependent thresholds, are used to test our system.

Figure 5.7 illustrates the performance of our verbal information verification system by a single fixed threshold as three questions are asked. Figure 5.7(a) shows a receiver operating curve where the error rates in false rejection and false acceptance are achieved by changing the threshold value. Note that the above threshold is used for the utterance-level decision-making. In this experiment, we fix the subword threshold, $\theta = 2.0$, as defined in Eq. (5.14). As a result, our system reaches an EER of 2.0% in the experiment. Indeed, the performance of our system is also dependent upon the subword threshold, θ. For evaluating the performance of our system thoroughly, we also do an experiment by varying the subword threshold value in Eq. (5.14). As a consequence, the EERs of our system are depicted in Figure 5.7(b). It is observed from Figure 5.7(b)

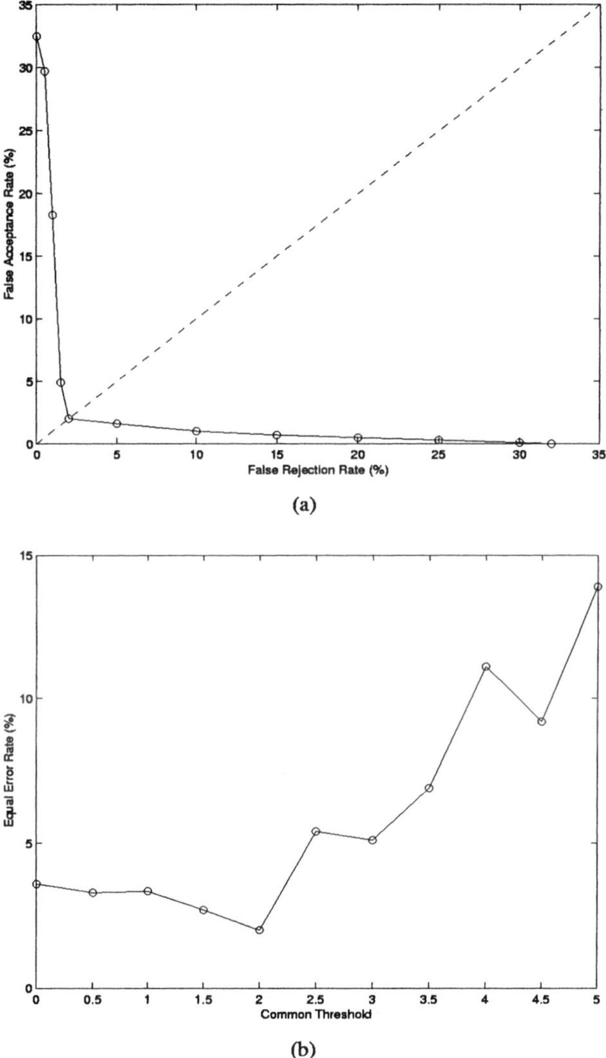

Figure 5.7. The performance of our Mandarin verbal information verification system on a population of 50 people ($K = 3$, i.e., three questions are asked for each speaker). (a) Receiver operating curve at the subword threshold $\theta = 2.0$. (b) Equal error rates as the subword threshold θ varies from 0.0 to 5.0.

that the subword threshold θ results in the different performance though the utterance-level threshold is fixed.

Although the speaker-independent threshold used in our verbal information verification leads to the satisfactory performance in contrast to speaker verification, lower error rates are demanded for enhancing speaker verification. As a

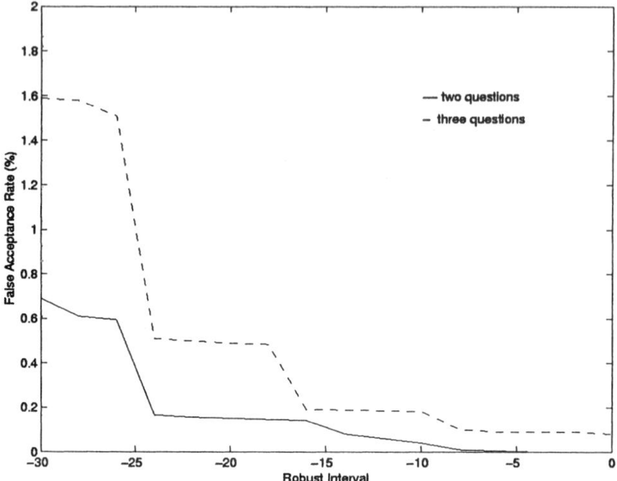

Figure 5.8.   The performance of our Mandarin verbal information verification system on a population of 50 people when a speaker-dependent threshold is used.

result, we conduct another experiment by using a context-dependent threshold in our verbal information verification system. That is, different utterances are verified by different thresholds. Thus, the decision rule becomes

$$\text{Acceptance}: U(i) \geq T(i), \quad \text{Rejection}: U(i) < T(i) \quad 1 \leq i \leq K.$$

Here $U(i)$ is the normalized confidence measure for each utterance and $T(i)$ is an original context-dependent utterance threshold. Since the variations in speech and environments lead to different testing scores for different speakers even for utterances of the same text. In order to characterize the variation and the system robustness, each utterance threshold is allowed to have a robust interval, τ. As a result, the threshold is adjusted as

$$T(i) = T(i) - \tau, \quad 0 \leq \tau \leq T(i). \tag{5.16}$$

In this circumstance, there are K thresholds associated with K questions. In our experiment, the thresholds are determined by first setting $T(i)$ such that the false rejection rate of our system is 0.0%. Then the thresholds are shifted to evaluate the false acceptance rate on different robust intervals τ as defined in Eq. (5.16). Figure 5.8 shows the relation between robust interval and false acceptance rates when two and three questions ($K = 2, 3$) are asked. As the robust interval varies, the evolutionary process of false acceptance rates are clearly shown in Figure 5.8. We can see that using two questions the system cannot reach an EER of 0.0% though some EERs are quite close to 0.0% . With three questions, our verbal information verification system yields an EER of 0.0% with 8.2%

robust interval. This three-question based result indicates that even though a true speaker's utterance scores are 8.2% lower than previous due to mismatch, the speaker still can be accepted while all the impostors in the database can be rejected correctly. Such a robust interval provides compensation for mismatch to ensure robust performance of our system, which makes the verbal information verification system qualify as a supervisor to enhance speaker verification.

Speaker Verification Enhanced by Verbal Information Verification.   In our bilateral user authentication framework, the kernel technologies include text-independent speaker verification and verbal information verification. As presented in Sections 5.4.2 and 5.4.3, the text-independent speaker verification system does not yield satisfactory results for practical use, while the verbal information verification system reaches an EER of 0.0%. On the other hand, as pointed out in Section 5.1, text-independent speaker verification can work in a transparent way, while verbal information verification has to perform by an explicit query-based way. Therefore, a synergistic integration is to enhance text-independent speaker verification by verbal information verification as presented in Section 5.3.3.

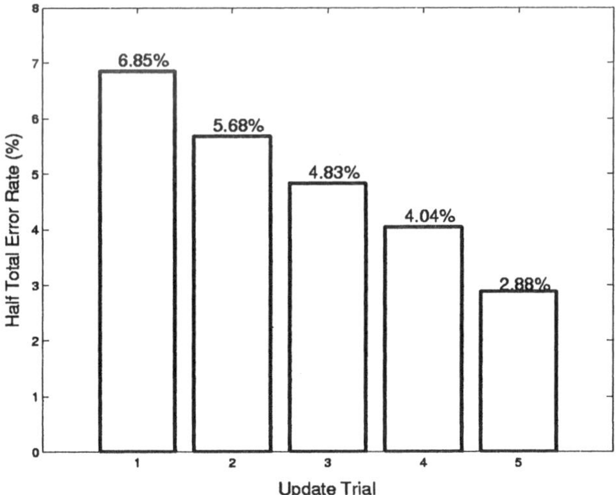

Figure 5.9.   The performance of a text-independent speaker verification system enhanced by verbal information verification in terms of testing speech segments of eight seconds.

To evaluate the performance of the combination scheme presented in Section 5.3.3, we conduct an experiment to observe how the enhanced text-independent speaker verification system performs. Given a GMM-based speaker verification system, an unknown voice token is tested by this system. If the voice token is rejected, a verbal information verification procedure is started. If the user can pass the test of verbal information verification, it implies that the previous rejection caused by text-independent speaker verification is incorrect; that is, it is a false rejection. Thus, the user's utterances in this conversation is used to update the corresponding GMM-based speaker model. Similar to the work [33], we adopt an on-line EM algorithm to retrain a GMM for fast update. In our simulation, we use the whole session to update the current GMM-based speaker model once a speech segment in this session is incorrectly rejected. In our simulation, we use the GMMs trained on session 1 as a baseline system and the three-question based verbal information verification system with context-dependent thresholds for enhancement. As a result, we show the performance of the enhanced text-independent speaker verification system in Figure 5.9. For comparison, we depict the original performance of the baseline text-independent speaker verification system in trial 1. Trials 2-5 indicate that speech data in sessions 2-5 are sequentially used for test and update. From Figure 5.9, it is evident that the error rates are dramatically reduced during such a sequential update. Here, we emphasize that the above update is error-free since our verbal verification system reaches an EER of 0.0%, which provides an effective way towards reduction of error rates in speaker verification.

5.5.   Conclusions

In this chapter, we have presented a bilateral user authentication to personalize mobile access in wireless environments where speaker verification, a biometric technology, and verbal information verification, a non-biometric technology, are integrated seamless to drive maximum synergy for user authentication. Enabling component speaker authentication technologies are described in terms of our own work. Simulations have been done separately for different enabling technologies and experimental results demonstrate that these enabling component technologies are ready for real application by building a complete bilateral user authentication system under our framework.

In our framework, we attempt to derive maximum synergy from the complementary capabilities of different speaker authentication technologies for security, easy-to-access, and friendly user interface in wireless environments. A salient feature is that such a framework can enhance the security and personalize mobile access in an adaptive way. Due to miscellaneous mismatches in voice characteristics, channels, and environments, our bilateral update strategies work efficiently towards continuous reduction of error rates in speaker authentication; the text-dependent speaker verification system in the client site is updated in an autonomous way, while the text-independent speaker verification system in the server site is updated in a supervised way by means of error-free verbal information verification. Indeed, several implementation issues for a complete bilateral user authentication system in real applications are not addressed in this chapter. Like component technologies presented in this chapter, these issues are not trivial at all and will be studied in the future development.

Acknowledgments

The partial work described here was done while the author worked at Peking University. The author is grateful to X.L. Li and T.Y. Wu for discussions and their help in simulations. The work described here was supported in part by an NSFC grant (60075017) and an MSR research grant on non-verbal speech analysis.

References

[1] T. W. Anderson. An Introduction to Multivariate Statistical Analysis. Wiley, 1984.

[2] K. T. Assaleh and R. J. Mammone. New LP-derived Features for Speaker Identification. IEEE Transactions on Speech and Audio Processing, 2: 630–638, 1994.

[3] B. Atal. Automatic Speaker Recognition Based on Pitch Contours. Journal of Acoustics Society of America, 52: 1687–1697, 1972.

[4] S. Barua. Authentication of Cellular Users through Voice Verification. In Proc. of IEEE International Conference on System, Man, and Cybernetics, pages 420–425, 2000.

[5] F. Bimbot, M. Blomberg, L. Boves, D. Genoud, H.P. Hutter, C. Jaboulet, J. Koolwaaij, J. Lindberg, and J.B. Pierrot. An Overview of the CAVE Project Research Activities in Speaker Verification. Speech Communication, 31: 1437–1462, 2000.

[6] M. J. Carey and R. Auchenthaler. User Validation for Mobile Telephones. In Proc. of IEEE International Conference on Acoustics, Speech, and Signal Processing, pages 1093–1096, 2000.

[7] K. Chen. Towards Better Making a Decision in Speaker Verification. Pattern Recognition, 35: (in press), 2002.

[8] K. Chen, L. Wang, and H. S. Chi. Methods of Combining Multiple Classifiers with Different Features and Their Applications to Text-independent Speaker Identification. International Journal of Pattern Recognition and Artificial Intelligence, 11: 417–445, 1997.

[9] K. Chen, T. Y. Wu, and H. J. Zhang. On the Use of Nearest Feature Line for Speaker Recognition. Pattern Recognition Letters, 23: (in press), 2002.

[10] K. Chen, D. H. Xie, and H. S. Chi. A Modified HME for Text-dependent Speaker Identification. IEEE Transactions on Neural Networks, 7: 1309–1313, 1996.

[11] R. V. Cox, C. A. Kamm, L. R. Rabiner, J. Schroeter, and J. G. Wilpon. Speech and Language Processing for Next-millennium Communication Services. In Proc. of The IEEE, 88: 1314–1337, 2000.

[12] M. H. DeGroot. Optimal Statistical Decisions. McGraw-Hill, 1970.

[13] G. Doddington. Speaker Recognition – Identifying People by Their Voice. In Proc. of The IEEE, 73: 1651–1664, 1985.

[14]   G. Doddington, M. A. Przybocki, A. F. Martin, and D. A. Reynolds. The NIST Speaker Recognition Evaluation – Overview, Methodology. Speech Communication, 31: 225–254, 2000.

[15]   S. Furui. Recent Advances in Speaker Recognition. Pattern Recognition Letters, 18: 859–872, 1997.

[16]   A. K. Jain, R. Bolle, and S. Pankanti. BIOMETRICS: Personal Identification in Network Society. Kluwer Academic Publishers, 1999.

[17]   B. H. Juang and S. Furui. Automatic Recognition and Understanding of Spoken Language – A First Step Toward Natural Human-machine Communication. In Proc. of The IEEE, 88: 1142–1165, 2000.

[18]   B. H. Juang and L. R. Rabiner. The Segmental K-means Algorithm for Estimating Parameters of Hidden Markov Models. IEEE Transactions on Acoustics, Speech and Signal Processing, 38: 1639–1641, 1990.

[19]   L. S. Lee. Voice Dictation of Mandarin Chinese. IEEE Signal Processing Magazine, 14: 63–101, 1997.

[20]   L. S. Lee. Structural Features of Chinese Language – Why Chinese Language Processing is Special and Where We Are. In the International Symposium on Chinese Spoken Language Processing, Singapore, 1998.

[21]   Q. Li, B. H. Juang, C. H. Lee, Q. R. Zhu, and F. K. Soong. Recent Advancements in Automatic Speaker Authentication. IEEE Robotics & Automation Magazine, 6: 24–34, 1999.

[22]   Q. Li, B. H. Juang, Q. Zhou, and C. H. Lee. Verbal Information Verification. In Proc. of EUROSPEECH, pages 839–842, 1997.

[23]   Q. Li, B. H. Juang, Q. Zhou, and C. H. Lee. Automatic Verbal Information Verification for User Authentication. IEEE Transactions on Speech and Audio Processing, 8: 585–596, 2000.

[24]   X. L. Li and K. Chen. Mandarin Verbal Information Verification. In Proc. of IEEE International Conference on Acoustics, Speech, and Signal Processing, Orlando, 2002.

[25]   J. M. Naik. Speaker Recognition – A Tutorial. IEEE Communication Magazine, 28: 42–48, 1990.

[26]   J. Neyman and E. S. Pearson. On the Use and Interpretation of Certain Test Criteria for Purpose of Statistical Inference. Biometrika, 20A: 175–240, 1928.

[27]   W. Reichl and W. Chou. Decision Tree State Tying Based on Segmental Clustering for Acoustic Modeling. In Proc. of IEEE International Conference on Acoustics, Speech, and Signal Processing, vol. 2, pages 801–804, 1998.

[28]   D. A. Reynolds. A Gaussian Mixture Modeling Approach to Text-independent Speaker Identification. Ph.D. Dissertation, Department of Electrical Engineering, Georgia Institute of Technology, 1992.

[29]   A. E. Rosenberg. Automatic Speaker Verification: Review. In Proc. of The IEEE, 64: 475–487, 1976.

[30]   H. Sakoe and S. Chiba. Dynamic Programming Algorithm Optimization for Spoken Word Recognition. IEEE Transactions on Acoustics, Speech, and Signal Processing, 27: 43–49, 1978.

[31]   O. Siohan, C. H. Lee, A. C. Surendran, and Q. Li. Background Model Design for Flexible and Portable Speaker Verification Systems. In Proc. of IEEE International Conference on Acoustics, Speech, and Signal Processing, pages 825–828, 1999.

[32]   D. Zhang. Automated Biometrics: Technologies and Systems. Kluwer Academic Publishers, 2000.

[33]   Y. Y. Zhang, D. Zhang and X. Y. Zhu. A Novel Text-independent Speaker Verification Method Based on the Global Speaker Model. IEEE Transactions on Systems, Man and Cybernetics, Part A, 30: 598–602, 2000.

Chapter 6

BIOMETRICS ON THE INTERNET: SECURITY APPLICATIONS AND SERVICES

Lee Luan Ling and Miguel Gustavo Lizárraga

Department of Communications

School of Electrical and Computing Engineering

State University of Campinas, CP. 6101

13083-970 Campinas, SP, Brazil

{lee, lizarrag}@decom.fee.unicamp.br

Abstract   Biometrics has overcome a number of fundamental technological and psychological barriers and achieved a state that enables its reliable use in many practical applications. Simultaneously, the advance of the three underlying key technologies, electronics and photonics, and software engineering, has promoted the flourish of information systems and made our society more connected than ever. Among many large information systems, the Internet certainly is the most remarkable one mainly due to its wide service variability and accessibility. Although the scientific community has struggled to make the Internet secure, the security level is still far from desirable. This chapter focuses some Internet Security issues that involve biometrics, that is, biometrics applications and services in the Internet. First of all, we presented some important aspects regarding the security problems in telecommunications networks and the Internet. Then, a brief presentation of biometrics technologies with emphasis on biometric encryption and standardization is given. In the sequel, a description of a biometric application in the Internet, named the Personal Identification Network, is given. Finally we provide a brief report about other biometric applications in the Internet.

Keywords: Internet, biometrics, network security, personal identification, encryption

6.1.   Introduction

It is a well-known fact that system security issues have a decisive influence on system performance. The rapid advance of telecommunications technologies, which have been driven by the significant progress in electronics, photonics and software engineering, has made our society more tightly interconnected than ever. Among many different network technologies, the Internet is definitely the most significant one due to its popularization that directly and indirectly affects our daily activities. The popularity of the Internet has been contributed by the surge of massive interests, low-cost computing equipment and a large variety of low-cost networking services for home, small enterprises and large corporations. Each day passes more and more people have become Internet users, and simultaneously more information is circulating and available via the Internet. Much of this information is sensitive and confidential; therefore, it is supposed that only authorized people are allowed to access it. To identify a Internet user is not a difficult task in principle but unfortunately many traditional methods for user authentication that rely on a username and password have already demonstrated their fragility, unable to reliably detect an impostor who possesses the requested information for authentication.

On the other hand, biometrics, which authenticates persons by their physical and behavioral characteristics, has gradually become a mature technology and an additional tool (or an alternative approach) for positive personal identification. Obviously it is expected that Biometrics on telecommunications systems, particularly on the Internet, is able to increase the reliability of network services like electronic mail, advertising, on-line conversation, file transfer and electronic commercial transactions. Offering a reliable protection to the Internet information, services and users via biometric methods is widely desired but still moderate in practice. Some pioneering works that seek biometric applications in the Internet have been reported [1,2,3,4,5].

This chapter deals with Internet security issues that involve biometric technologies, more specifically, biometrics for Internet applications. The organization of this chapter is as follows. In Section 6.2 we present some network topics like: the Internet and Web, applications over TCP/IP, the client-server model, network security issues and encryption. Section 6.3 focuses on some biometrics issues like: Biometric systems and mechanisms, biometric encryption and biometrics standardization. Sections 6.4 and 6.5 are dedicated to the description of some biometric applications on the Internet. Finally, in Section 6.6 we draw some conclusions and discuss future trends of biometrics on the Internet.

6.2.   Communications Networks and the Internet

The main purpose of a computer network is to permit the network resources to be shared via a communications means among computers logically connected. One sort of resources consists in electronic equipment (hardware), like printers, video cameras, scanners, etc. while other type is of application programs (software), both available for network users.

Using the internetworking concepts, "internet" is a generic name for a collection of communications networks interconnected by core network elements, bridge and /or routers. Today, the Internet is viewed as a collection of networks connecting a large number of networks around the world via the TCP/IP protocol capable of providing a huge amount of computing power.

The communications community considers that historically the Internet evolved from the first operational packet-switching network (ARPANET) developed in 1969 by the Advanced Research Project Agency (ARPA) of the U.S. Department of Defense. ARPANET began its operations only in four locations: UCLA, University of Santa Barbara, the University of Utah, and SRI (Stanford Research Institute). Today, the Internet has more than tens of millions hosts and the number of users is about the hundreds of millions with the participation of more than 200 countries. The number of connections to the Internet continues to grow as well as the number of information/service providers. The increasing demand for services in the Internet has encouraged and promoted the design and development of new and wide network applications and services. Probably the most remarkable and widely accessed network application has been the World-Wide Web or simply Web.

6.2.1   The Internet and Web

Under the context of network services, the *World-Wide Web* is regarded as a major platform for the development of distributed information systems. This is a natural approach once *Web* has the goal of offering a mechanism for the collection of information even the information is physically dispersed [6]. More formally, *Web* can be viewed as "initiatives for hypermedia information recovery that allows universal accesses to huge amount of documents" [7]. In effect *Web* has implemented an abstract knowledge space on the top of the Internet via a uniform description and access mechanism to integrate million users around the world.

Historically *Web* was initially proposed by Dr. Time Berners-Lee in 1989, a researcher at Physics and High Energy Lab of CERN in Geneva. Since then, *Web* expansion rate surpassed any other Internet supported services. *Mosaic* was the first graphically interactive interface on *Web* designed by National Centre for Supercomputing Applications (NCSA) in the United States. Mosaic became officially available in the beginning of 1993. Sooner after, many browsers were released and available for the presentation *Web* documents. In general, those browsers interact with users via some graphic interfaces that enable the presentation of hypertext documents. Moreover, recently some browsers have already had the capability of illustrating other kinds of media other than text documents, like audio and video images incorporated into hypertext.

6.2.2   Applications over the TCP/IP Protocol

A network service initiates when an application from the highest layer of the communications protocol requests the transfer of information. For the Internet, TCP/IP is the communications protocol used for the exchange of information between hosts.

TCP/IP is an abbreviation for *Transmission Control Protocol* and *Internet Protocol* which refer to the two first communications protocols taking part in the *Internet Protocol Suit*. In fact, TCP/IP is a collection (or family) of several communication protocols used in the Internet, which including also the DNS (Domain Name Service), SMTP (electronic mail), FTP (file transfer), Telnet (virtual terminal). TCP/IP is capable of establishing a network connection among any computer systems and over different transmission means [8]

The TCP/IP Reference Model does not follow directly the OSI (Open System Interconnection) Reference Model [9]. Instead, in the TCP/IP Reference Model only four layers are defined; they are: the application layer, the internet layer, the transport layer and the host-to-network layer [9].

The Application Layer: is located on the top of the transport layer and it contains all the higher-level protocols (SMTP, FTP, TELNET, DNS, NNTP, HTTP, etc.)

The Transport Layer: the layer above the internet layer in the model. Two end-to-end protocols have been defined here. The first one, TCP (*Transmission Control Protocol*) is a reliable connection-oriented protocol that guarantees a byte stream originating from one host to be delivered without error to any other host in the Internet. The second protocol, UDP (*User Datagram Protocol*), is an unreliable, connectionless protocol for applications that do not have TCP's sequencing or flow control capability.

The Internet Layer: is responsible for keeping the whole architecture together and permits hosts to introduce packets into any network and allows them to be routed independently to the destination. Such a layer typically characterizes a packet-switching network based on the connectionless concept.

The Physical Layer: The TCP/IP Reference Model does not explicitly specify much about physical connectivity protocols. Instead, TCP/IP adopts some existing standards that in fact vary largely from host to host and network to network.

6.2.3 The Client–Server Model

The *client-server* computational model is a typical application of a computational distributed system, in which an application program (*Client*) interacts with another application program (*Server*). In the conventional *client-server* model, the *server* will generate a new process to handle the communications with the client and process a request put forward by the *client* program. Normally, the communication channel will be interrupted only upon an end request received from the *client* program.

However, the *client-server* paradigm on the Internet differs from the conventional procedure above described; the *client* program will communicate with the server to send and receive data. Upon accepting inputs from user, the *client* program will establish a communications channel with the *server* for the exchange of the data. In turn, the *server* will generate a process to perform the necessary computation and manipulation on the data and return the result to the *client* program related. After that, the communications channel will be broken. This is known as the "state-less" situation where the *server* does not keep track of the state of the *client* programs [10].

6.2.4 Security Issues on Telecommunications Networks and the Internet

Security in telecommunications has always been an elusive issue. Such a situation has been contributed by the rapid evolution in telecommunications technologies and network services. Both traditional telecommunications networks, (e.g., traditional telephone systems) and the Internet have evolved over a long period and have changed dramatically their capability and the way people use them during the last decade. For the traditional telephony network the security is mainly based on the physical intactness of the infrastructure, e.g. switches and transmission equipment. Any encryption or authentication rarely is applied to the signaling protocols or the transferred data. The customers have to trust in the operators' promises and the operators have to trust in each other's promises. Even with the technological advances, such as voice digitalization, Common Channel Signaling (CCS) and Intelligent Networks (INs), little additional security measure has been introduced to this basic security model.

On the other hand, for mobile telephone networks some new security mechanisms have been designed and introduced. The security mechanism includes cryptographic authentication and authorization of users and terminal equipment. In spite of the new security features, the mobile networks still rely on the basic security model. That is, the service providers continue to be responsible for security in every level.

In terms of security, the Internet (ARPANET) in its early stage did not present any remarkable difference from its telecommunications counterparts. The major security issue was only about the availability of the infrastructure which was easily solved by connectionless dynamic routing [11]. There was no major concern about guarantee of confidentiality, authentication or integrity of data. Fortunately, the situation did not last for a long time. Sooner, the Internet community realized the importance of security measures in the Internet, and The Internet Engineering Task Force (IETF) has carried out many real actions, including the design of a number of security mechanisms and protocols. The work has been done as an open process and all specifications (RFCs) and drafts are currently available via the Internet.

In fact, there is still a lot of work to be done before we are able to declare that the Internet has achieved an acceptable security level. Security in an internet environment is an important and difficult problem because it requires the fully understanding about users, computers and every involved protocol. A single weakness can compromise the security of the entire network. Although communications protocols can support a wide diversity of users and networks, and span many political and organizational boundaries, to reach a common ground or level of trust or policies for handling data by participating individuals and organizations is definitely a non-trivial task.

6.2.5 Security Services, Information Integrity and Attacks

One way of characterizing an attack upon a computer system or communications network is to see how data is altered in terms of its flow of information. Considering a flow of information from a source (files or a region of the main memory) to a destination, one or more of the four categories of attack may occur [12]:

- **Interruption**: This kind of attack affects availability of the information by destroying a part of the system or turning information unavailable or unusable. Typical examples of this attack category include destruction of hardware (e.g. a hard disk), cuts of a communication line, or disabling of the file management system.
- **Interception**: This kind of attack breaks the confidentiality of the information and can be characterized by an unauthorized element accessing a part of the system. An unauthorized element could be a person, a program, or a computer. Typical examples of this attack type include wiretapping to capture data in a network and illegal copying of files or programs.
- **Modification**: This kind of attack destroys the integrity of the information by changing its content once the data has been intercepted. Examples of this attack type include changing values in a data file,

altering a program so that it performs differently, and modifying the content of messages being transmitted in a network.

- **Fabrication**: This attack affects the authenticity of the original object by inserting faked objects into the system. Most common examples of this kind of attack are the addition of spurious messages in networks or the insertion of records to a file.

Simmons in his paper [13] described some of the common functions traditionally associated with documents and for which analogous function for electronic documents and messages are required. These so-called *Common Information Integrity Functions* include: identification, authorization, license and/or certification, signature, witnessing (notarization), concurrence, liability, receipts, certification of original and/or receipt, endorsement, access (egress), validation, time of occurrence, authenticity (software and/or files), vote, ownership, registration, approval/disapproval, privacy (secrecy). Based on these information integrity functions, it is possible to define security services for computer and communications networks, and therefore also for the Internet. Computer and network security research and development have focused on a small number (three or four) of general security services that encompass the various functions required of an information security facilities. Although there is no unanimous agreement on the security terminology, one useful and interesting classification of security services for computer systems and telecommunications networks is the following [12]:

- **Confidentiality**: ensures that the information in a computer system and transmitted information are accessible only for reading by authorized users. This type of access includes printing, displaying, and other form of disclosure like revelation of the existence of an object.
- **Authentication**: Ensures that the origin of a message or electronic document is correctly identified and the identity is not false.
- **Integrity**: Ensures that only an authorized individual is able to modify computer system assets and send information. Modification includes writing, changing, changing status, deleting, creating, and delaying or replaying the transmitted messages.
- **Nonrepudiation**: Requires that neither the sender nor the receiver of a message be able to deny the transmission.
- **Access Control**: requires the ability to limit and control the access to host systems and applications via communications links.
- **Availability**: requires that computer system assets be available to authorized parities when needed.

6.2.6   Security Mechanisms for Internet Access

In this subsection we focus some major mechanisms widely deployed for the implementation of security services for Internet access based on the classification of the security services for computer systems and telecommunications networks listed in the previous subsection.

- **Authentication**: the authentication of a user is based on some criterions including: a) proof by knowledge (e.g., password or personal identification number), b) proof by possession (e.g., smart cards or keys), and c) Proof by property (biometrics: fingerprints or voice, etc.). For message authentication, a message authentication code (MAC) or a hash function can be used to detect possible action like message modification, delay and reordering. Notice that the digital signature can be another important option for authentication tasks.

- **Authorization**: Authorization in general is done by traffic filtering on the packet layer. A simple example of this mechanism can be a filter blockading and/or controlling the traffic flow according to some pre-established rules. The use of firewall in some routers to isolate a network domain from an external network is another well-known practice.

- **Confidentiality**: A widely deployed security tool for the confidentiality is encryption that includes conventional encryption and public-key encryption (e.g. the RSA algorithm).

- **Integrity**: Again encryption has been the most appropriate mechanism for this end.

- **Nonrepudiation**: the encryption mechanism together with the use of the private keys is one of the most efficient means for this kind of service (e.g., Digital Certification).

- **Judgeship**: Judgeship consists in providing independent record of communications activities in order to measure the efficiency of protection mechanisms and to detect suspected activities. This procedure may result in some adjustment and/or refinement of the under-investigated security systems and, in some cases, the establishment of judicial processes. In general, traps are used to catch the hackers, and the detection mechanism in real time can be used to alert the network manager.

6.2.7   Encryption

Encryption can be considered as the most important automated tool that provides desirable network and communications security. From the theoretical point of view, encryption can be defined as a mathematical process that intends to disguise the information contained in messages either being transmitted or stored in a database. Three main factors determine the degree of security of a crypto system: the complexity of the mathematical process or algorithm, the length of the encryption key used to hide or "scramble" the message, and safe storage of the key, known as *key management* [14].

There are two important classes of encryption methods commercially widely deployed: symmetric key systems (single key systems) and public key system (two-key systems). The major difference between these two encryption techniques is that a symmetric system utilizes a single key for both sender and receiver to encode and decode data, respectively, while a public encryption system uses different keys for data encoding and decoding. A widely deployed single key system (the symmetric key system) is known as DES (the Data Encryption Standard) invented by IBM in 1972. Sooner after its invention, DES was adopted worldwide as the most common single key system in the banking and financial sectors. However, it does not take long time for people to realize the fragility of the single key systems due to their high vulnerability to *interception* attack, especially in a communications network like the Internet. Since electronic commerce requires that transactions be conducted over open networks, instead of dedicated networks, and single key systems do not offer an enough security level for such transmissions, the public key systems have been developed to overcome this deficiency. Even though the public key systems in fact offer improved encryption performance with respect to the single key systems, there is another essential problem remaining as an open issue, that is, certification of the recipient of messages.

There are references in abundance on "Cryptography and Network Security." For detailed presentation and discussion of encryption techniques and their applications on computer and communications networks, refer to, for example, [12,15]. Interesting enough, advances both on network technologies (network service and security) and biometrics technologies (especially for user authentication) have promoted the synergy of these two kinds of technologies in terms of design and development of a more efficient and reliable security mechanism known as "biometric encryption". Since electronic certification of the recipient of a message deals with a personal identification problem in a network environment, no doubt can biometric encryption contribute significantly. In this case, the idea is to take advantages of biometrics' inherent nature of using the recipient's physical traits to decipher the message.

6.3.   Biometrics

In the security issue, one of the most dangerous threats is the impersonation, that is, one claims to be another person. The security service that countermeasures this threat type is known as personal recognition which can further classified into two categories: *personal identification* and *authentication*. Identification, as the name suggests, consists of a process whereby an identity is assigned to a specific person (e.g., his name) while authentication, sometimes also known as verification, is a process designed to verify one's identity. One claims that the original need for identification was social and became an economic need as transactions became more complex [16]. Authentication sometimes is viewed as the next necessary step taken after identification. In this sense, the goal of authentication is to protect a system against unauthorized use

There are many different ways to identify a person, for example, appearance, social behavior, name codes, knowledge, possession, bio-dynamics, and natural physiology and imposed physical characteristics. Each one of these identification means can be classified into one of the following approaches: proof by knowledge, proof by possession and proof by properties. [17].

Traditional technologies that use the proof of knowledge (e.g., personal information, passwords, PINs, etc.) and the proof of possession (magnetic cards, smart cards, keys, ID cards, etc.) are not sufficient to reduce the impact of counterfeiting [18]. Biometrics, the use of a person's biological information, has provided a solution to this problem based on the uniqueness of one's physical and behavioral characteristics. In principle any one of these characteristics can be a useful biometric solution. Modern biometrics found in literature are fingerprint verification, face recognition hand geometry based verification, iris pattern analysis, retina identification, automatic on-line and off-line signature verification, speaker recognition, keystroke dynamics based authentication, automatic gait recognition, odor detection, ear recognition, sweat pores analysis, DNA pattern analysis, head analysis, and infrared identification of face and body parts [16,1,3].

6.3.1   Conventional Biometrics Systems and Mechanisms

Identification of a biometric characteristic can be performed at the moment of measurement (on-line or dynamic) or later (off-line or static) that depends on the applications and offered services. A typical example is signature verification which can be either on-line or off-line.

Most biometric technologies require special hardware (sensors, A/D converters, etc.) to capture and then to convert analogue measurements (signatures, voices or patterns of fingerprints and palm prints) to digital data so that computers are able to read and process the information adequately. The cost of this specialized hardware has decreased considerably and become accessible for many home users. It is expect that in very near future the availability of the most special hardware is ubiquitous without mentioning that keyboards for keystroke based biometric systems have already had this property of ubiquitousness.

Biometric-based personal identification/authentication is a typical pattern recognition problem. A pattern recognition system consists of the following basic elements: a sensor/traducer, a feature extraction algorithm and a classification/decision algorithm [19,20]. Based on this typical pattern recognition model, a biometric-based identification system will at least contain the following component [21]:

- **Data acquisition device**: this component is responsible for measuring the user's biometric data. The acquired data is then submitted to the feature extraction unit.
- **Feature extraction unit**: this component takes the raw information as input from the acquisition device and extracts the features from the data. Often, a pre-processing is needed to prepare the raw data for feature extraction, like filtering, size normalization, etc. Many systems consider the data pre-processing as a part of the feature extraction procedure while some others not, and the pre-processing algorithm can be physically implemented inside the data acquisition device. Extracted biometric features are sent to the comparison unit.
- **Comparison unit**: is responsible for the comparison between the extracted features from the input data and the reference samples provided by the reference database and makes decision (classification).
- **Reference database**: contains the reference values of each user's biometric data that has to be stored somewhere and available whenever it is asked. The reference database can sometimes be located at the same place where the comparison unit is, but not always: in a smart card based environment, for instance, keeping each user's data on his own smart card could be preferable to a centralized and highly sensitive database. In fact, the main issue here is the data management, where data should be logically ubiquitous and secured for storage as well as for transmission.

6.3.2   Biometric Identification versus Biometric Authentication

Personal identification and Authentication via biometric features are two classical applications of biometric systems. To understand the major distinction between them notice how the comparison procedure is performed. For authentication, the system will verify the matching between a user and a stored biometric profile of this user while, for identification, the system will find, based only on the biometrics of the supposed user. In other words, the two schemes imply some differences not only in the comparison units but also the reference database. For an identification case, the reference database, which contains every biometric profile, must be centralized. For authentication, the system designer has an additional option like the database being spatially distributed, (e.g., each user's smart card). Which approach, either centralized or distributed database, offers a better solution is an application dependent problem. Sometimes convenience which implies simplicity and efficiency, can be as important as the security issue.

In terms of system performance, identification is definitely a harder problem than authentication because the biometric identification system must check two problems: is the biometric profile from a valid user and who is the true user? Two well-known performance measures are used to evaluate a biometric system: FAR (false acceptance rate) and the FRR (false rejection rate). These two performance measures are directly influenced by the quality of the measured data, the discrimination capability of the extracted features and the implemented comparison rule.

In terms of biometric decision-making, Dougman [22] investigated *"decision landscapes"* characterizing several forms of biometric decision-making. For binary decision (a verification case), he tentatively established formalism based on the Newman-Pearson (ROC) decision strategy. For a multi-biometrics system, he investigated the effect of combining two or more biometric tests into a unique enhanced test and concluded the following: *"A strong biometrics is better used alone than in combination with a weaker one when both operating at their crossover points"*. Another interesting study made by Dougman was the estimation of the degree of freedom associated with different biometrics in order to measure the randomness and complexity of their templates.

6.3.3   Choosing a Biometric System

If the degree of perfection of a system is a relative measure, definitely no biometric system is perfect. In other words, there is no totally secured biometric system. Even we know that a determined biometric method (e.g., iris pattern) offers better classification performance than some others (e.g., signature verification), selecting a biometrics method only based on some laboratory results can be highly misleading. Laboratory derived FAR and FRR are only two measures among many performance parameters that should be taken into account. Some factors that contribute to making the system selection a non-trivial problem are [23]:

- Significant difference between laboratory testing and on-field testing, due to varying environmental conditions (dirt, humidity, temperature, lighting condition, etc.) and human factors (the user's behavior or reaction);
- Device robustness and sensitivity;
- Mono or multi-biometrics approach;
- Inadequate maintenance;
- Application oriented system-operating points (e.g., user's satisfaction, loss, and cost).

Biometrics can offer high-level security access protection; However, it requires careful product selection, thoughtful on-site implementation, and constant monitoring for accuracy. In this sense, Mandell has recommended that one take the following issues into account in choosing a biometric system [23]:

- Consider biometric service rate and system response time in function of the degree of satisfaction for users;
- Consider the cost and complexity for device maintenance;
- Judge and take into account all relevant environmental factors;
- If you integrate biometrics with security databases, estimate downtime that those databases would experience;
- Make sure that the biometric system and its software have been extensive field-tested. Make sure that obtained error rates are under inside an acceptable confidence level for your application.
- Get knowledge of the degree of flexibility that the proposed system is able to support for multiple applications.
- Choose a biometric device carefully and learn in advance its protection power as well as its weakness.

6.3.4　Synergy of Technology: Biometric Encryption

Synergy of cryptography and biometrics in order to enhance security level basically can be done in two ways, not necessary mutually exclusive:

- **Keys/biometrics securing biometrics/keys**: use of encryption keys to protect biometric information (for authentication purposes) or use of biometric mechanisms to secure the privacy of encryption keys.
- **Biometric encryption**: the process of using biometric characteristics as a method to encode/decode (scramble/unscramble) data.

The basic difference between these two approaches consists in the maintenance of the integrity of biometrics and key information. That is, only for the former security strategy (Keys/biometrics securing biometrics/keys) both biometrics measures and keys are unaltered.

Currently the most widely synergy application is *"Keys securing biometrics."* The main goal of this application is to maintain and verify the integrity and authenticity of biometric information by using digital signatures. Biometric templates generated during the enrollment can be digitally signed to create a unique and reliable binding between the biometric information and some non-biometric identifiers (e.g. names, account numbers). In this manner, the authentication system can rely on the biometric template, whether the template is kept in a centralized data bank, in spatially distributed data bases, or individually recorded in a portable medium like smart cards, according to the convenience. Another application of encryption keys is the authentication of biometric devices. In this case the biometric samples captured by a given biometric device (such as fingerprint scanner, camera or microphone) is also digitally "signed" to maintain the integrity of the biometric information and to provide authenticity of the deployed biometric device. Once the biometric information is secured, the biometric applications (enrollment, verification, and identification) can rely on the biometric samples. Noticed that the encryption also preserve the privacy of the biometric information whenever it is necessary. The management of symmetric keys used to encrypt biometric information can be accomplished using PKI [24].

The length of the encryption key used to disguise the message is one important piece of the encryption process if not the most important one. Simple combinatorial exercises can show that the reliability of an encryption key is proportional to the length of the key that determines the degree of randomness (or uncertainty) of "the key metric space." In other words, the shorter the encryption key length is, the more vulnerable the data is to a "brute force" attack. "Brutal force attack" refers to an individual trying all combinations of possible passwords that would allow access to the account. Cost incurred in a "brutal force attack", can be either financial or not but normally measured in computational time, determines the reliability of the key. Prohibitive cost makes the key plausible. Notice that any additional information of the key may reduce considerably the reliability of the key, possibly making the key vulnerable or prohibitive for security applications. Therefore, key management always has been a major issue for security management, whether it is biometrically generated or not.

Biometric encryption makes the standard character encryption obsolete by replacing or supplementing the normal key characters with a personal identifier of the user that there can only be one perfect match. Without this biometric key, the information is inaccessible. Recently Peyravian, etc. presented a technique for generating unique user-dependent RSA keys utilizing users' biometrics and /or other unique user ID data. The scheme guarantees that the RSA keys generated for one user are unique and different from the keys generated for any other user [25]. The authors concluded that their new biometric technology can significantly improve the process of RSA key generation, therefore the security levels.

Safe storage of the key is the most vulnerable area in the encryption process. What would seem to be the easiest to manage becomes the most difficult because passwords or PINs can be lost, forgotten or stolen. Good encryption keys are much too long for normal individuals to easily remember so they are usually written on paper, saved in smart cards or diskettes that makes key information vulnerable to unauthorized users. Biometric encryption systems allow the user to transport the access key around without the need to make it vulnerable to be lost or stolen.

6.3.5   Ongoing Biometrics Standardization and Related Activities

There are many biometric-related industry groups and other standardization organizations directly and/or indirectly responsible for the biometrics standardization [16,26].

- ANSI X9F4 *Cryptographic Applications*: is the working group developing ANSI Standard X9.84 *Biometric Information Management and Security*, which is one of several working groups operating under the X9F *Data and Information Security* subcommittee. The standard defines the requirements for managing and securing biometric information for use in the financial industrial. In addition, the standard identifies techniques such as digital signatures and encryption to provide integrity and maintain privacy of biometric data. The standard also provides a comprehensive set of control objectives suitable for use by a professional audit practitioner to validate a biometric system.

- The BioAPI Consortium [27]: is a group of over 35 organizations that have a common interest in promoting the growth of the biometrics market. BioAPI is dedicated to developing a specification for a standardized Application Programming Interface (API) that will be compatible with a wide range of biometric application programs and a broad spectrum of biometrics technologies. The API description defines how application programmers and biometric solution vendors write to the common BioAPI interface. The BioAPI runtime frame will allow applications to interoperate with various biometric solutions. The Consortium was formed to develop a widely available and widely accepted API that will serve for several biometric technologies.

- The International Biometric Industry Association (IBIA) [28]: is a trade association founded in September 1998 in Washington, DC, to advance, advocate, defend and support the collective international interest of the biometric industry. IBIA is governed by and for biometric developers, manufacturers and integrators, and is impartially dedicated to serve all biometric technologies in all applications. The IBIA is the official register for X9.84 object identifiers and the BioAPI identifiers, which can be found at www.ibia.org/formats.htm.

- The ANSI B10 committee for Driver's Licenses/Identification [29]: ANSI B10.8 Driver's License/Identification Card Standard, through ANSI's Accredited Standards Committee. National Committee for Information Technology Standard (NCITS) is a committee dedicated to identification cards and related devices known as B10.

- The Joint Technology Committee (JCT1) Subcommittee 17 (SC17) Identification Cards and Related Devices [30]: is a joint subcommittee of the ISSO and IEC organization, whose scope includes integrated circuit card with contacts, financial transaction cards, optical memory cards, and devices and motor vehicle driver's license and related documents. SC17 has initiated a new work item to establish the data and file structures for storing biometric templates in smart cards.

- The NIST/ITL Common Biometric Exchange File Format (CBEFE) working group: The National Institute for Standard and Technology (NIST) Information Techno Laboratory (ITL) has sponsored several workshops to establish an industry specification that defines a common biometric exchange format (CBEFF) and associated metadata that will enable interoperability of biometric-based application programs and systems from different vendors.

- The Biometric Consortium [31] serves as the US Government's focal point for research, development, test, evaluation, and applications of biometric-based personal identification/verification technology. It is currently co-managed by two US Government agencies: the NIST and the National Security Agency (NSA).

- The ISSO Technical Committee 68, Subcommittee 2 (SC2) Security Management and General Banking Operations [32] has the scope of facilitating banking and related financial operations including codes, banking procedures and related security standards.

6.4. The Personal Identification Network: Biometrics Services via the Internet

Biometric identification carried out in many practical security applications (banking&finance, law enforcement, public services, physical access control, and computers&networks) is already a fact today [33,34,35,16,36]. However, most biometric identification services are still either restricted for local use or available via dedicated communications means or systems. In this section we describe a prototype of a biometric system via the Internet, named the Personal Identification Network, which has the goal of illustrating the feasibility of offering personal identification services in real time through the Internet. That is, accessing biometric personal identification services is as simple as searching any other information via *Web* without geographical limitations. For instance, in the case of credit card trade a shop clerk is able to verify the authenticity of the signature submitted by a client via the Internet. For law enforcement applications, it is expected that any local police department is able to access the desired fingerprint&face images, and/or authentication/identification services via the Internet in real time.

6.4.1   The Model of Internet Biometric Systems

The implemented prototype currently offers two types of service (1) identification of a service user, which consists in non-biometric identification, and (2) personal biometric verification requested by the user.

For the first service type, *user identification*, one important feature of the proposed prototype is the absence of geographic limitation. That is, geographically dispersed users can access the offered biometric services independently and simultaneously. Many different non-biometric identifiers, like social security number, driver license number, and a PIN, can be used according to the convenience and desired security level. Another relevant aspect of the proposed identification prototype is that it works at any network point (terminal) under any computer network environment. The prototype presents to each user the same functionality, hiding as many operational details as possible that are considered non-relevant to the users. Notice that any reference information, biometrics or not, can be found locally centralized or geographically distributed according to the convenience of the applications. It is worth mentioning that although the current prototype version does not require user biometric identification, the implementation of biometric means for user identification is straightforward once biometric facilities have already taken part of the prototype.

From a user's point of view, the prototype allows the user to interact with the Internet-based biometric system by performing the following three operations through an Internet *Web* Page, after the user being appropriately identified via the submitted *login name* and *password* [37]: *enrollment, visualization* (or *consultation*) and automatic *verification*. These three operations are represented and logically carried out by the following three network elements as illustrated by Figure 6.1.

- **Web Server**: is responsible for the management of network communications and the coordination of exchange of information among related network terminals. In addition, *Web* Server processes the requests for accessing the CGI (Common Gateway information) programs: *enrollment, consultation,* and *verification.*
- **Consulting Terminals**: through which the requests for consulting the database via *Web* Server are sent and *Web* Server then grants the access to the database for either visualization or verification service.
- **Enrollment terminals**: consist of some special hardware and software that allow the capture of biometric information.

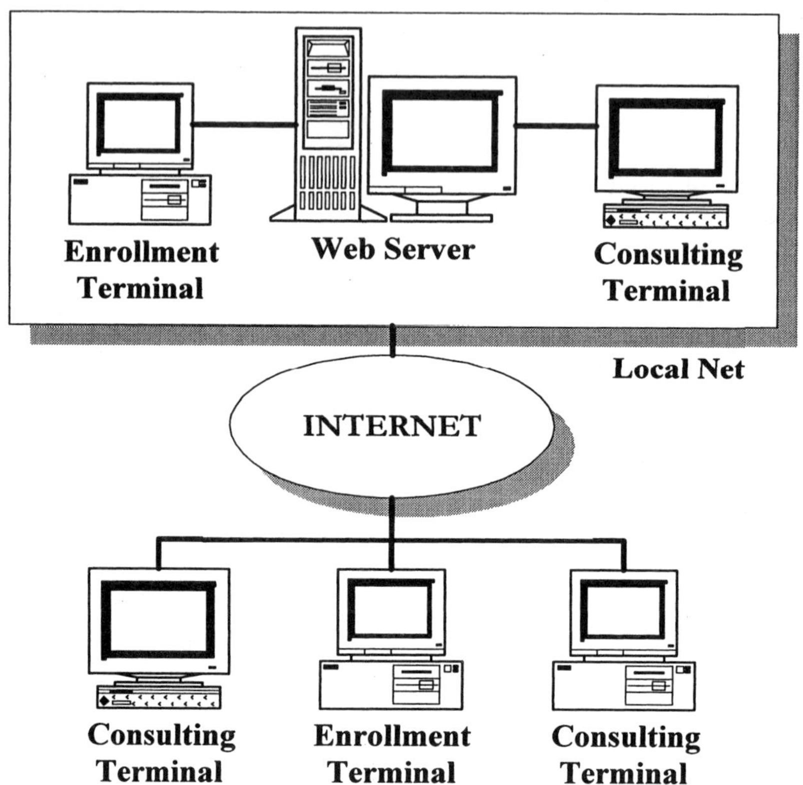

Figure 6.1. The automated Internet biometric system model for the enrollment, consultation, and verification services.

6.4.2   The System Implementation

An essential component of the proposed prototype is the *Database Manager* (DBM) responsible for maintaining the user's records and biometric data necessary for the implementation of different personal identification services. One of the interesting features of the implemented DBM is its capability of supporting both local and wide area network environments so that a large number of users are able to access in real time the personal identification services simultaneously and remotely. Another striking characteristic of DBM is its flexibility in developing independent applications for each type of biometrics. Such an independent property allows the system to be used for a large variety of purposes at the same time.

A typical example could be the situation where a local bank agency having an automated banking system available in a local area network and also connected to a long distance network where the database contains both biometric and non-biometric information about every bank client and clerk. From this local bank agency three banking services which involve in different types of personal identification could be carried out at the same time. (1) A cashier via a signature verification module accesses the database and validates the signature on a bankcheck even the check was released from other agency. (2) The authentication of a bank clerk can be done via a fingerprint module to authorize some important financial transactions and operations. (3) A client, via a face verification module attached to an automated teller machine, accesses a variety of banking services like cashing, money transfer, bill payment, etc. In this example, the advantage of maintaining a centralized database that stores all clients and clerks' biometric and non-biometric information is its easy management minimizing the possibility of database integrity violation. As an illustration, Figure 6.2 shows the interaction between the DBM and different biometric identification modules.

Each identification module consists of three sub-modules, named the *enrollment sub-module, visualization sub-module,* and *automatic verification sub-module.* A request to DBM for information by a biometric identification module is done via SQL messages.

A detailed description of the implemented algorithms for biometric signature information, feature extraction and the decision procedure for automatic signature verification can be found in [37].

For illustration purposes, next we describe how these three sub-modules were implemented and show, by illustration, how a user accesses the biometric signature services. In Subsection 6.4.3 we describe briefly the implemented algorithms for biometric signatures information, feature extraction and the decision procedure for automatic signature verification. A more detailed description can be found in [37].

The Enrollment Sub-module. This sub-module consists of five CGI programs, each one performing certain specific function [37]. The messages sent by the Enrollment Sub-Module to DBM are responsible for the creation of a profile for each new client during his enrollment (registration). If a client has not been enrolled before, a record of this client is created. This is done by sending the following client's information: *client's name* (login name), *client's identification number* (ID), three biometrics image samples, the mean vector of biometrics feature extracted from these three sample images, and the desired decision threshold value. If, on the other hand, DBM signals that the client has already been registered, the user has promptly the desired biometrics service. However, at this moment an authorized user is able to update or modify this client's personal information on the database.

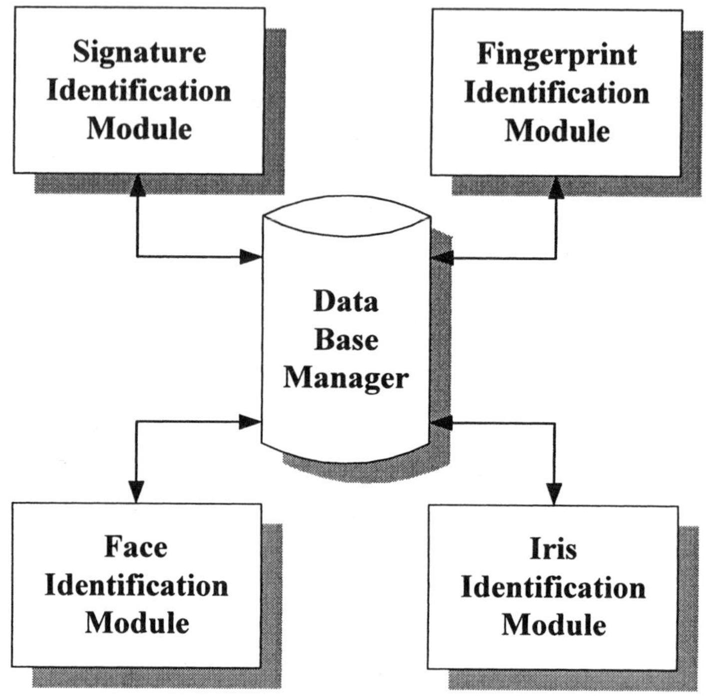

Figure 6.2.   Interaction between the Database Manager and biometric modules.

Figure 6.3 shows the very first screen in an enrollment stage where the user should submit the client's name and ID number to *Web* Server. Figure 6.4 shows a screen signaling the reception of the valid client's information by *Web* Server and requesting that three reference biometrics sample images be submitted. The *browser* screen in Figure 6.5 guides the user through the submission of the first biometric image file. A similar *browser* screen illustrated in Figure 6.5 appears twice again for the submission of other two-biometric samples. Note that each *browser* screen like that in Figure 6.5 also has the goal of acknowledging the successful transfer of the previous sample data, and the screen in Figure 6.6 indicates the end of the enrollment operation once the third biometric sample was successfully transferred to *Web* Server through the network. It is worth mentioning that on-line biometric data capture by activating the corresponding input device also could be easily implemented.

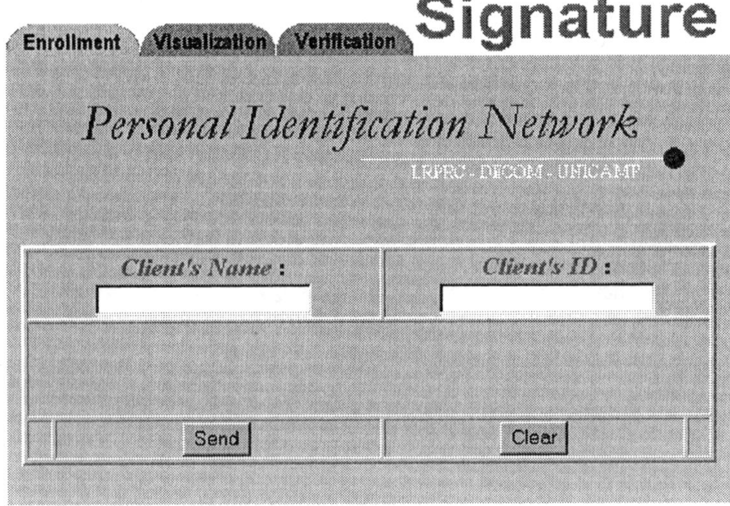

Figure 6.3. The initial screen of an enrollment procedure.

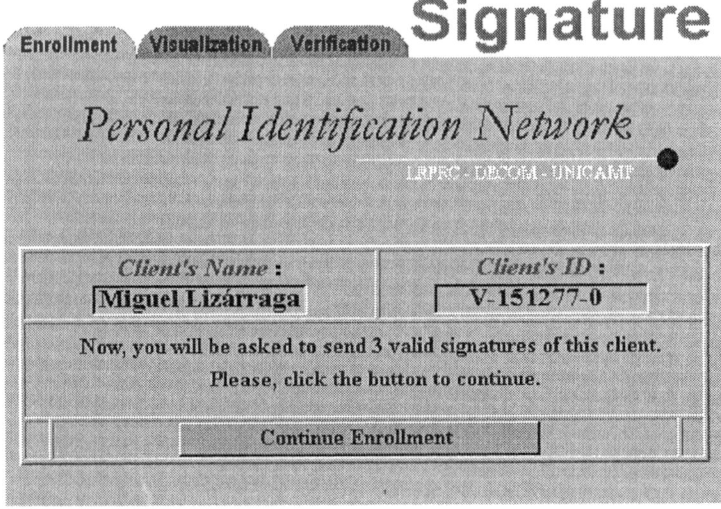

Figure 6.4. Web Server validates the received client's information and requests the continuation of the ongoing enrollment process.

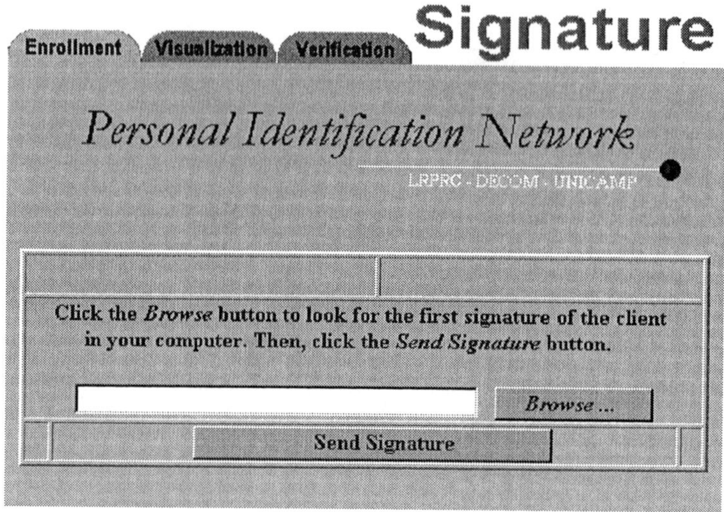

Figure 6.5.   The Browser screen for the submission of the first biometric image.

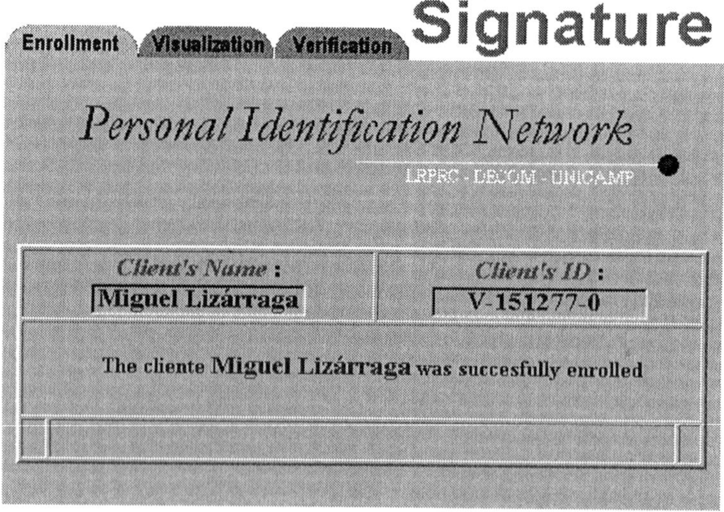

Figure 6.6.   The new client (Miguel Lizarraga) was successfully enrolled.

The visualization sub-module.   This sub-module basically consists of a CGI program that allows a user to visualize a reference biometrics image recorded in the database.

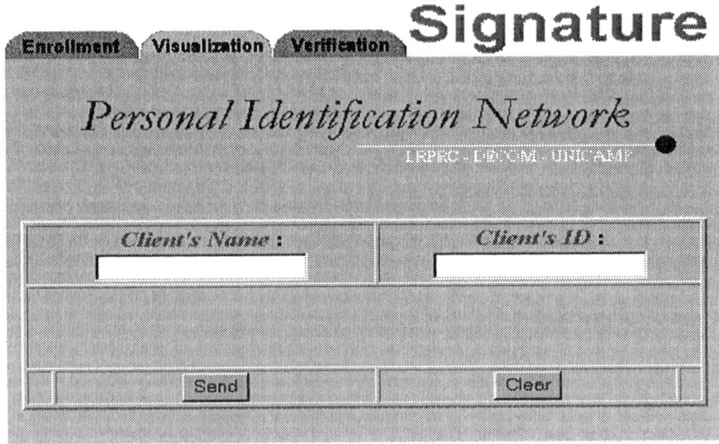

Figure 6.7.   The consultation service is activated by pressing **visualization** tab.

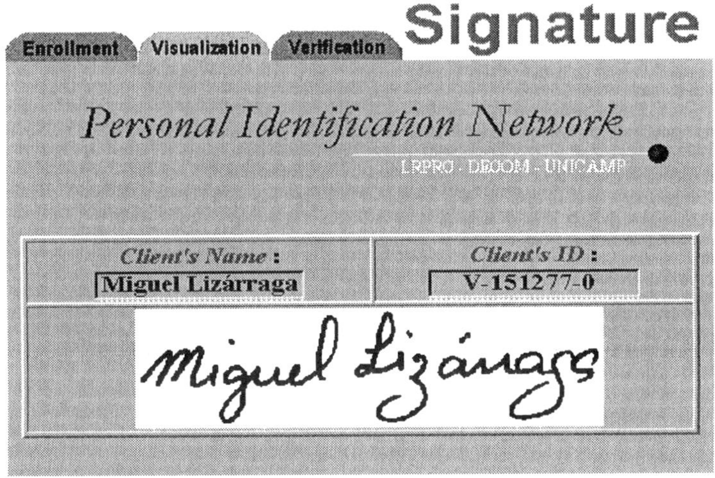

Figure 6.8.   The graphic interface displays a reference signature image.

For this end, the user first activates *visualization tab* in the graphic interface (Figure 6.7) and introduces the client's name and ID number. The submitted information is subsequently sent to the DBM for validation. Additionally, the user chooses the desired biometric visualization service by specifying the type of the biometrics ("*Signature*", "*Digital*" or "*Face*"). Then, DBM responds with an appropriate reference image according to the user's request. Figure 6.8 shows, as an example, how the biometric signature information returned by DBM is displayed on a graphic interface screen.

The Automatic Verification Sub-module.   This sub-module consists of three CGI programs. The activation of *verification tab* sets the biometric system on the *verification* mode, as illustrate by the screen in Figure 6.9.

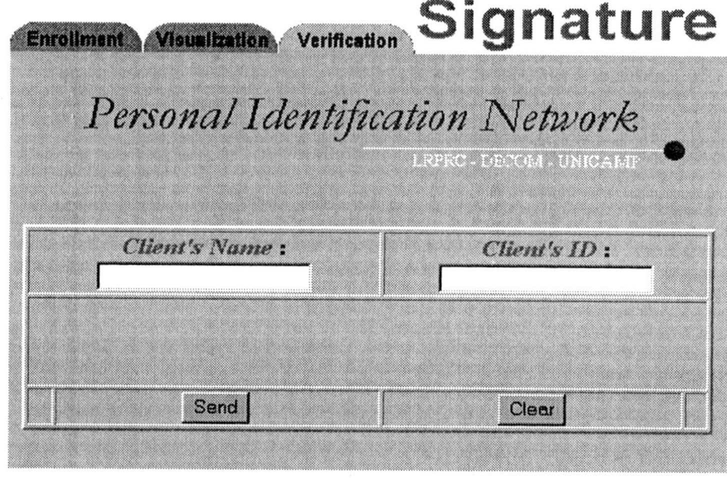

Figure 6.9.   The verification service is activated by pressing **verification** tab.

To access the identity verification service, the user introduces both client's name and ID information. After successful validation, a new screen is generated instructing the user how to precede the verification procedure. For cases of handwritten signatures, the screen in Figure 6.10 is displayed for the selection and submission of a new candidate signature image. Once *Web* Server has successfully received the submitted biometric image, it starts immediately performing the verification task. Figure 6.11 shows the result of the performed signature verification service where the submitted candidate signature being classified as a genuine one.

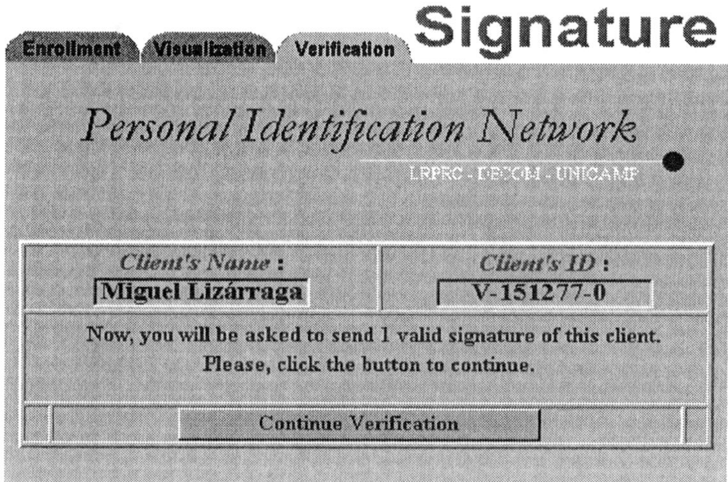

Figure 6.10. The client's information is validated and a candidate signature image is requested.

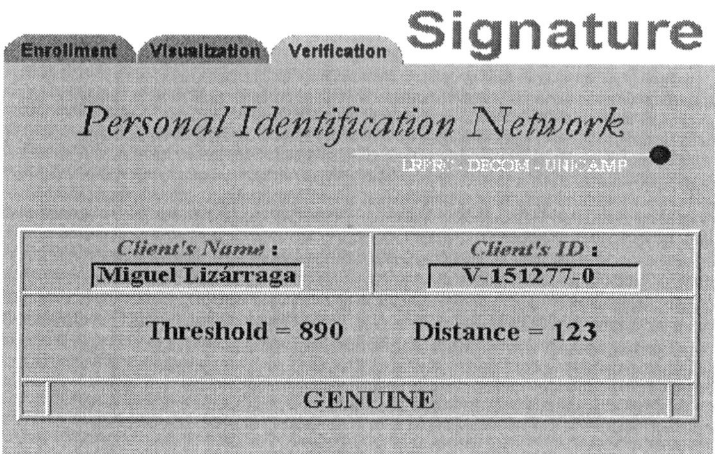

Figure 6.11. The candidate biometric signature image is classified as a genuine one.

Note that a positive verification result is plausible only if the distance measure between the reference biometrics sample and the submitted biometric candidate is less than a pre-defined threshold value. Otherwise, the candidate signature is declared as a forgery

6.4.3   Biometric Signature Verification

This sub-section describes the biometric signature verification algorithm implemented in the Personal Identification Network. The proposed approach has the following characteristics: (1) based on global/local features; (2) through a sequential, multi-expert and multi-resolution scheme; (3) using weighted Euclidean distance classifiers, and the most important, (4) on-line responses and capable of detecting both random and skilled forgeries. Simulation reveals the following system performance: false rejection error of 0.47% and false acceptance error of 2.35% for random forgeries; false rejection error of 12.75% and false acceptance error of 19.22 % for skilled forgeries.

Signature Image Preprocessing.   Three main operations are carried out in the signature pre-processing stage: signature image enclosing, normalization and frame division. The signature enclosing operation searches for the smallest box that covers the all-significant parts of a signature image. The signature size normalization operation consists of finding a suitable spatial resolution for signature representation and scaling the signature image into a standard size. The size-normalized signature image has therefore 256 pixels in width and 64 pixels in height. The signature frame division operation partitions horizontally each size-normalized signature into five partially (50%) overlapped frames. The frame division operation has the goal of isolating some significant local divided (Figure 6.12).

Signature Feature Extraction.   In this work eight sets of features are used to represent a handwritten signature for verification purposes. Some of these feature sets were selected from the literature that proves their advantages and discriminating capabilities. The first feature set basically is that proposed by Qi and Hunt in [47], which consists of global geometric and local grid features. The second and third feature sets were proposed by Bajaj and Chadhury in [48], which are composed of some statistical moments extracted from the horizontal and vertical projections of the signature image. The fourth and fifth feature sets consist of Hu invariant moments and Tsirikolias-Mertzios moments, respectively [49]. The sixth and seventh feature sets characterize a signature via the orientation of handwriting strokes and that of the envelope of a dilated signature image [50]. Finally the eighth feature set, which is of our own contribution, is called the correlation feature set.

Correlation Feature Vector Extraction.   The image correlation is a standard approach for determining the degree of match of a sub-image $w(x,y)$

of size $J \times K$ pixels within an image $f(x,y)$ of size $M \times N$, assuming $J \leq M$ and $K \leq N$. In other words, the correlation between $f(x,y)$ and $w(x,y)$ is given by

$$C(s,t) = \sum_{x=0}^{J-1} \sum_{y=0}^{K-1} f(x,y)w(x-s,y-t) \qquad (6\text{-}1)$$

taken over the image region where $f(x,y)$ and $w(x,y)$ overlap. For any fixed pair (s,t), the application of Equation 6.1 yields a unique value $C(s,t)$. Varying s and t implies moving image $w(x,y)$ in the domain defined by $f(x,y)$ that results in the function $C(s,t)$. The coordinate that grants the maximum value of $C(s,t)$ indicates the position where $w(x,y)$ best matches $f(x,y)$.

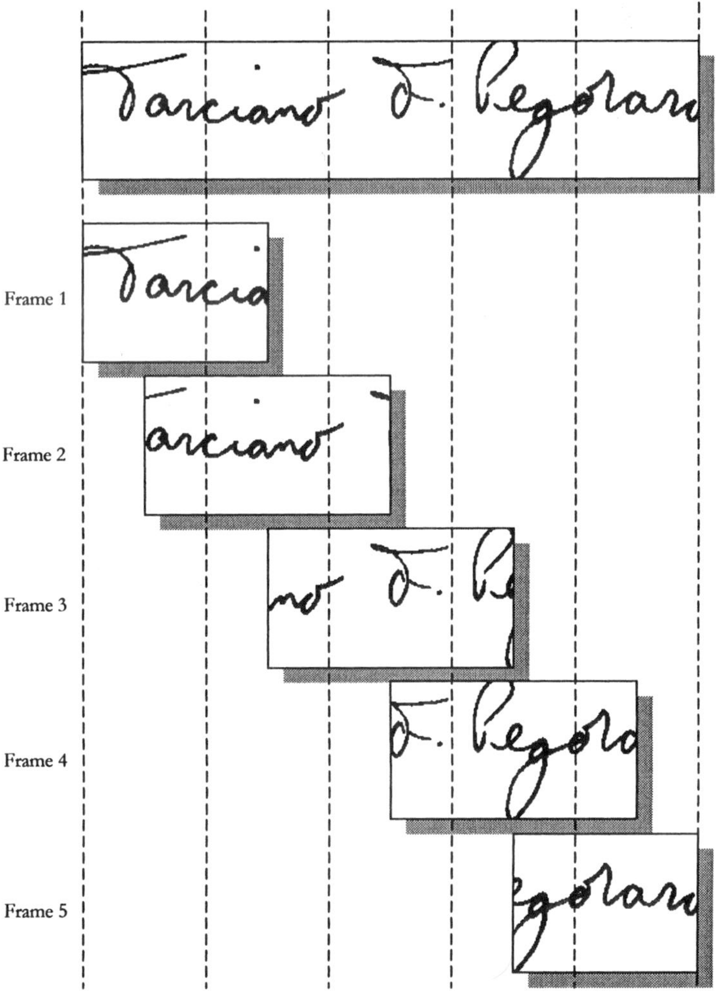

Figure 6.12.   An example of the frame division operation.

Once the best match between two images, *f(x,y)* and *w(x,y)*, is determined; the EXCLUSIVE-OR operation is carried out pixel-by-pixel between *f(x,y)* and *w(x-S,y-T)* where *(S,T)* denotes the coordinate where the best match occurs. The correlation feature vector that measures some correlation characteristics between *f(x,y)* and *w(x-S,y-T)* has the following entries: (1) the first element indicates the number of matched pixels between these two images, (2) the second element counts the number of pixels that do not match, (3) the third element is the size of the template image in pixels, (4) the fourth element is the size of the candidate image in pixels, (5) the fifth element is the number of black pixels in the candidate image, and finally (6) the sixth element is the ratio between the number of matched pixels and that of non-matched pixels.

Similarity Measure.   The following weighted Euclidean distance measure is used to evaluate the similarity between two feature vectors, that is,

$$D = \sqrt{\sum_{i=i}^{k} \frac{\left(F_{T_i} - F_{I_i}\right)^2}{\sigma^2_{\ i}}} \tag{6-2}$$

where F_{T_i} and $\sigma^2_{\ i}$ are the mean value and variance of the ith feature from the training set, respectively, and F_{I_i} is the ith feature value of the input candidate signature.

Note that Eq. (6.2) is a basic form for the measure of similarity, which can be applied directly to the correlation feature vector. When dealing with multiple frames including all other kinds of feature set other than the correlation feature vector, certain adjustment is needed. In other words, the final similarity measure between two signature images is given by the sum of all individual frame-based similarity measures

The Classification Strategy.   As mentioned before, the proposed signature verification method is an automatic, real time, and serial multi-expert and multi-resolution system. The decision process is divided into two sequential stages. The first decision stage has the goal of detecting as many random and simple forgeries as possible while the second decision stage is designed to hunt most skilled forgeries.

In the first classification stage, the feature sets 1, 2, 3, 4, 5 and 8 are deployed. Figure 6.13 shows how these feature sets are combined to obtain the first-stage final distance measure where Σ and Π represent, respectively, the addition and multiplication operators. Let D_i denote the distance measure for the ith feature, then the first-stage's final distance measure δ_l is calculated as

$$\delta_1 = \left(\sum_{i=1}^{5} D_i \right) \cdot D_5 \qquad (6\text{-}3)$$

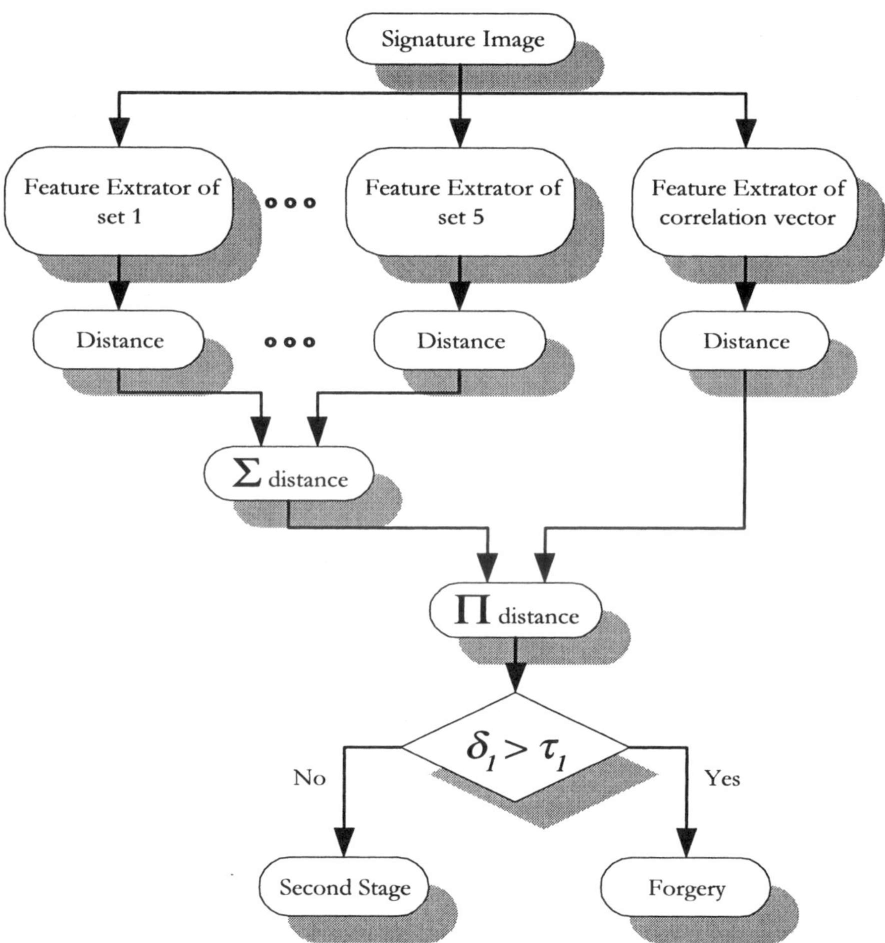

Figure 6.13. The first stage of signature verification: detection of forgeries.

The decision rule in this first stage is the following. If $\delta_1 > \tau_1$, then the input signature is regarded as forgery; otherwise, the decision procedure goes into the second stage. Here, τ_1 is the chosen decision threshold for the first classification stage.

In the second classification stage the similarity measure is calculated in a similar fashion as that in the first classification stage, however using only feature vectors 6, 7 and 8. That is,

$$\delta_2 = \left(\sum_{i=6}^{7} D_i \right) \cdot D_8 \qquad (6\text{-}4)$$

In this case if $\delta_2 > \tau_2$, then the input signature is regarded as a skilled forgery; otherwise, the input signature is declared as a genuine one. Here τ_2 is the chosen decision threshold for the second classification stage.

System Performance. The signature database used to evaluate the proposed signature verification method is composed of 2500 genuine signatures, 100 random forgeries and 750 skilled forgeries [51]. The genuine signatures were collected from 50 volunteers over a six-month period, each one contributing with his 50 genuine samples. For random forgery, fifty additional subjects were recruited, each one providing two samples of his true signature used to form the random forgery set. Finally 750 skilled forgeries were collected based on the population of 25 distinct genuine signatures. That is, 30 forgery samples were produced for each genuine type. Visual inspection reveals that our signature database contains a large variety in signature writing style, including completely incomprehensible line strokes, Chinese and Arabic signatures, and clear and neat handwriting words. All these signatures were written on white paper sheets and later digitized into binary and 200dpi digital images. Note that, in this work only 3 true signature samples for each genuine signature were used for the system training. We imposed this requirement of 3-signature-sample training set in order to simulate most real situations where only 2 or 3 signatures were stored as reference samples.

The evaluation of the system performance is done in terms of FRR_0 (false rejection rate at zero false acceptance), FAR_0 (false acceptance rate ate zero false rejection) and EER (equal error rate). Initially we evaluate each classification stage individually. Table 6.1 summarizes the result of this evaluation and reveals that two classification stages indeed have good discriminating capabilities for each dedicated forgery work.

Table 6.1. FFR$_0$, FAR$_0$ and EER obtained by single experts.

Stage	FRR$_0$(%)	FAR$_0$(%)	EER(%)
First stage, only random forgeries	3.82	2.58	0.97
Second stage, only skilled forgeries	26.62	32.65	9.72

However, in many real situations, hardly are we able to know a priori whether a signature is a random or skilled forgery. Moreover, for most real applications, only small number of genuine samples is collected for the biometric system training. In order to set the system for real applications achieving therefore meaningful results, we continue imposing that only 3 genuine samples be used for the system training. Next, we show how to determine decision thresholds τ_1 and τ_2 based only on a set of three training sample signatures.

Determination of decision thresholds τ_1 and τ_2 - Our approach for the determination of decision thresholds τ_1 and τ_2 consists in finding suitable α_1 and α_2 used in these two equations:

$$\tau_1 = \alpha_1 * (D_8) * \sum_{i=1}^{5} (D_i) \tag{6-5}$$

and

$$\tau_2 = \alpha_2 * (D_8) * \sum_{i=6}^{7} (D_i), \tag{6-6}$$

where D_i is the distance measure for feature set i between the candidate signature and the mean value based on the reference training set. For our case, experimental investigation shows that $\alpha_1 = 1000$ becomes a suitable choice to a low false rejection rate against random forgeries while $\alpha_2 = 100$ is able to guarantee a low false rejection rate against skilled forgeries. Table 6.2 shows the performances of the two classification stages using experimentally set values ($\alpha = 1000$ and $\alpha_2 = 100$).

Table 6.2. The performance of an adapted signature verification system.

Stage	ERR(%)	FAR(%)
First stage and $\alpha = 1000$	0.47	2.45
Second stage and $\alpha = 100$	12.75	19.22

6.4.4   Future Work

The proposed personal identification prototype for handwritten signatures currently is found implemented in LRPRC's *Web Page* [38]. Similar biometrics methods for fingerprint and face verification are under construction. Some encryption procedures to protect biometric information and biometric identification of users are also on the way of implementation.

6.5.   Other Biometric Topics in Internet Applications

In this section, we list some other biometrics issues that directly or indirectly related to the Internet applications. This list definitely is not exhaustive; however, it shows the increasing use of biometrics in the Internet related applications.

- A *Web*-based fingerprint verification system – Since 1998 Mitsubishi has created a fingerprint verification system that can be used over the *Web* to prevent unauthorized personal from accessing sensitive documents or gaining access to Key IT systems or to conduct *e*-commerce. The system uses a conventional fingerprint reader machine attached to a computer, working alongside a software plug-in module for Netscape's computer, which then compares the print with the fingerprint stored on the server. The system performs the online authentication using a Java based software "*agent*" downloaded from the server. It was expected that a plug-in for Microsoft's Internet Explorer browser be ready soon [39].

- In May 2000, Microsoft Corp. and I/O Software Inc. announced their cooperation to faster widespread growth of biometrics through the integration of biometric authentication technology in future versions of the Microsoft Windows operational system. Microsoft has acquired I/O Software Biometric API (BAPI) technology and SecureSuit core authentication technology to provide users with a higher level of network security based on a secure and reliable personal authorization method. The integration of biometric authentication will enable users to log on to their computers and conduct secure *e*-commerce transactions using combination of fingerprint, iris pattern or voice recognition and strong private keys, instead of a password [40].

- A research group leaded by Prof. A. K. Jain developed a prototype system that uses hand geometry to authenticate users to restrict access to *Web* pages. Some initial evaluation of the prototype system was encouraging e a similar technique can be used to authenticate people for *e*-commerce applications [41].

- Viisage Technology, Inc., a developer of face recognition technology and identification systems and solutions that improve security and protect personal privacy, has announced the creation of a new business unit to improve computing and Internet security using face-recognition technology. The new business unit will make *e*-commerce more secure by authenticating transactions via a personal computer or mobile device [42].

- A new protocol for secure electronic commerce, which is, based both on fingerprint verification and cryptography is presented [5]. The novelty of this new protocol with respect to most of the existing technique (e.g. SET protocol) is the use of fingerprint (as a secure way to authenticate customers) which requires some ad hoc managing policies in order to assure fingerprints to remain strictly confidential. The major idea of the protocol is to associate fingerprint with some cryptography techniques (DES, RSA, digital signature) so that "reserved" information like fingerprint can be kept secret and sent via Internet and used only by authorized users.

- Cyber-SIGN: is biometric signature verification software. On the Internet, Cyber-SIGN enabled applications are ideal for electronic commerce and business-to-business transactions. Cyber-SIGN may be used to create applications for increased security in electronic commerce, and these applications could include non-refutable document–personally signed electronic documents that can be trusted as tamper-proof. Cyber-SIGN is very effective when used as a secure login to a network, PC or to a secure data storage area [43].

- TRANZIX [44]: is a new digital envelope transfer protocol-based system that allows commercial exchange of electronic documents through digital transactions using customized electronic money. The system that provides very strong protection based on public-key cryptography is complemented with biometric protection on handwritten signatures. In this case, the use of biometric signatures provides additional protection to ensure authentication and also non-repudiation.

- BioNetrix [45]: The BioNetrix Authentication Suite, made by BioNetrix Systems Corp., allows organizations to centrally manage different types of biometric authentication on a Network. The authentication technologies include passwords, smart cards, token, fingerprint recognition, face recognition and voice recognition. Administrators can enforce authentication policies throughout the enterprise as well as on the World Wide Web.

- Internet security with voice and handwriting biometrics: Litronic Inc announced two additional biometric identification capabilities combined with digital signatures and smart cards, enabling stronger identity authentication for electronic data security applications. Users can now evaluate voice or handwritten signature recognition for authentication when digitally signing a document or obtaining access to secure *web* pages [46].

6.6.   Conclusions and Future Trends

Biometrics has overcome a number of substantial technological and psychological barriers if we compare its state of the art and applications today with those in two decades ago. Many factors have contributed to this break-through. From biometric product manufacturers' point of view they have faced and overcome the challenges like adopting and creating suitable standards, educating people about privacy concerns, and upgrading constantly biometric system performance according to environmental influence and real applications. From technological point of view, the advance of electronics, photonics and software engineering that contributed toward the remarkable increases in computing power and information transfer capabilities and the radical reduction of computing cost has been another major factor. Finally, massive investments in developing adequate tools to protect computers and the networks in order to protect sensitive information like intellectual properties and *e*-commerce transactions also have played a fundamental role.

In this chapter, we focus the discussion on biometrics topics in Internet applications. Firstly, we presented some important aspects regarding the security issues in telecommunications networks and the Internet. Then, a brief presentation of biometrics technology with emphasis on biometric encryption and standardization is given. In sequel, we the rest of the chapter focused on the presentation and description of the implementation of Personal Identification Network (Sections 6.3 and 6.4). Finally, a brief report on other Internet-related biometrics topics (Section 6.5).

We share the same points of view presented by many researchers with respect the future of biometrics. Increasing use of biometric methods in conjunction with other technologies like the knowledge-based authentication (e.g., passwords and PIN) is expected. The currently deployed authentication methods in the Internet (or authentication on *Web*), *Basic Authentication* (non-cryptographic methods based on password and IP address), are clearly inadequate in most situations. Its successor, *Digest Authen*tication (based on a shared secret), and secure HTTP, SSL and its successor TLS (based on public keys cryptography) although intuitively capable of improving considerably security levels, their use requires further and careful analysis. Especially for *Web*, the message integrity and confidentiality could be as essential as the authentication of users and the server [46]. Since there is no single best authentication method, biometrics is useful in the sense of adding more features to a security protocol, such as biometric encryption. The implementation of biometrics applications in the Internet requires caution because biometrics is not a simple replacement of parts of a protocol (e.g., keys or passwords). In fact, biometrics possesses some specific properties that require some special treatment. It is worth noticing that biometrics is not secure unless it is embedded in a strong cryptographic protocol [21]. The synthesis of existing encryption protocols with these probabilistic properties of biometric templates and their associated decision landscape open new avenues for research [22].

In terms of database management, the use of smart-cards could be a wise solution to many practical applications whenever the centralization of biometric data is not easy solution due to the fact that Internet users are geographically largely dispersed.

Many claim that the wireless Internet will be the future telecommunications network system (seamless interconnection solution for universal services). Clearly the design and implementation of biometric applications that adapts wireless Internet environments is another open problem that deserves investigation.

References

[1] J. Ashbourn. Biometrics – Advanced Identity Verification. Springer, London, 2000.

[2] D. Zhang. Automated Biometrics: Technologies & Systems, Kluwer Academic Publisher, USA, 2000.

[3] A. Jain, R. Bolle and S. Pankanti. Biometrics – Personal Identification in Networked Society. Kluwer, 1999.

[4] O. Ureche and R. Plamondon. Document Transport, Transfer, and Exchange: Security and Commercial Aspects. Proc. of International Conference on Document Analysis and Recognition. In Proc. of ICDAR, Bangalore, pages 585-588, September 1999.

[5] D. Maio and D. Maltoni. A Secure Protocol for Electronic Commerce based on Fingerprints and Encryption. In Proc. of ISAS, 4, pages 519-525, 1999.

[6] I. Ricarte. Introduction to Web Processing Mechanisms. (In Portuguese)
http://www.dca.fee.unicamp.br/~ricarte

[7] I. Ricarte. Hypertext Transfer Protocol -- HTTP/1.1". (In Portuguese)
http://ftp.isi.edu/in-note/erc1616.txt

[8] A. Dumas. Programming Winsock. Axcel Books, 1995.

[9] A.S. Tenenbaum. Computer Networks. Third Edition, Prentice Hall, New Jersey, 1996.

[10] M. Campione. The Java Tutorial: Object-oriented Programming for the Internet. Addison-Wesley, Reading, MA, 1996.

[11] K. Hafner and M. Lyon. Where Wizards Stay Up Late – The Origins of the Internet. Touchstone, 1996.

[12] W. Stallings. Cryptography and Network Security – Principles and Practice. Second Edition, Prentice-Hall, 1999.

[13] G. Simmons. A Survey of Information Authentication, ed. Contemporary Cryptology: The Science of Information Integrity. Piscataway, NJ: IEEE Press, 1992.

[14] S. Lewis and T. Steigerwalt. Biometric Encryption.
http://www.emory.edu/BUSINESS/et/biometric/index.htm.

[15] A.J. Menezes, P.C. van Oorschot and S.A. Vanstone. Handbook of Applied Cryptography. CRC Press, 1996.

[16] D. Polemi. Biometric Techniques: Review and Evaluation of Biometric Techniques for Identification and Authentication, including an Appraisal of the Areas where They Are Most Applicable. Final Report, Institute of Communication and Computer Systems, National Technical University of Athens, April 1997.

[17] H.M. Wood. The Use of Passwords for Controlled Access to Computer Resource. National Bureau of Standards Special Publication 500-9, US Dept. of Commerce/NBS.

[18] J. Newton. Reducing Plastic Counterfeiting. IEE Conference Publication, IEE Stevenage, England, no. 408, pages 198-201, 1995.

[19] R.O. Duda, and P.E. Hart. Pattern Classification and Scene Analysis. John Wiley & Sons, 1973.

[20] R. Schalkoff. Pattern Recognition – Statistical, Structural and Neural Approaches. John Wiley & Sons, 1992.

[21] G. Hachez, F. Koeune, and J. Quisquater. Biometrics, Access Control, Smart Cards: a not so Simple Combination. Proc. of 4th Working Conf. on Smart Card Research and Advanced Applications, Bristol-UK, 273-278, September 2000.

[22] J. Dougman. Biometric Decision Landscapes. Technical Report TR482, University of Cambridge, 1999.

[23] R.L. Mendell. Biometrics: The Tightrope Security Portal. http://securityportal.com/articles/biometrics20010220.html

[24] J. Stapleton. Biometrics. PKI Forum, May 2001. http://www.pkiforum.org

[25] M. Peyravian, S.M. Matyas, A. Roginsky and N. Zunic. Generation of RSA Keys That Are Guaranteed to be Unique for Each User. Computer & Security, vol. 19, no. 3, pages 282-288, 2000.

[26] S.M. Matyas Jr. and J. Stapleton, A Biometric Standard for Information Management and Security. Computer & Security, vol. 19, pages 428-441, 2000.

[27] BioAPI: www.bioAPI.org and/or www.bioapi.com.

[28] International Biometric Industry Association (IBIA): www.ibia.org.

[29] ANSI B10.8 Working Group for Driver License / Identification: www.aamva.org.

[30] ISO Joint Technical Committee 1 (JCT1) Subcommittee 17: www.iso.ch.

[31] Biometric Consortium: www.biometrics.org.

[32] ISO Technical Committee 68 (TC68) Subcommittee 2: www.tc68.org.

[33] T. Pegoraro. Robust Voice Recognition Algorithms Applied to Speaker Verification. MS Thesis, FEEC-Unicamp, April, 2000. (In Portuguese)

[34] M. C. Fairhurst. Signature Verification Revisited: Promoting Practical Exploitation of Biometric Technology. Electronics and Communication Engineering Journal, pages 273–280, 1997.

[35] A.K. Jain, L. Hong, and S. Pankanti. Biometrics: Promising Frontiers for Emerging Identification Market. Communications of ACM, 91–98, February 2000.

[36] L.L. Lee, T. Berger, and E. Aviczer. Reliable On-line Human Siganture Verification Systems. IEEE Trans. Pattern Recognition and Machine Intelligence, vol. 18, no. 6, pages 643-647, 1996.

[37] M.G. Lizarraga. Biometric Personal Identification via the Internet with Emphasis on Static Signature Verification. Ph.D. Thesis, State University of Campinas, Aug. 2000. (In Portuguese)

[38] LRPRC – Laboratory of Pattern Recongition and Communication Networks, School of Electrical and Computing Engineering, State University of Campinas. http://www.lrprc.feeunicamp.br/id

[39] J. Boyd. Net-Based Fingerprint Security Arrives. TechWeb News, February 6, 1998. http://content.techweb.com/wire/story/TWB19980206S0006

[40] http://www.microsoft.com/PressPass/2000/May00/BiometricsPR.asp

[41] A.K. Jain, S. Prabhakar, and A. Ross. Biometrics-based web access. Technical Report MSU-CPS-98-33, Michigan State University, 1998.

[42] http://webusers.anet-stl.com/~wrogers/biometrics/

[43] http://www.cybersign.com/

[44] M. Speir. BioNetrix delivers layered biometrics suit. http://www.fcw.com/fcw/articles/2000/0905/web-biobf2-06-05-00.asp.

[45] http://www.cybersign.com/Litronics.html

[46] J. Partanen, Authentication on the Web. Seminar on Network Security, Helsinki University of Technology, 1997. http://www.tml.jut.fi/Opinnot/Tik-110.501/1997/Web-authentication.html.

[47] Y. Qi and B. Hunt, Signature Verification Using Global and Grid Features. Pattern Recognition, vol. 27, no. 12, pages 1621-1629, 1994.

[48] R. Bajaj, S. Chaudhury, Signature Verification Using Multiple Neural Classifiers. Pattern Recognition vol. 30, no. 1, pages 1-7, 1997.

[49] L. Cordella, P. Foggia, C. Sansone and M. Vento, Document validation by signature: a serial multi-expert approach, In Proc. of ICDAR, Bangalore, pages 601 – 604, September 1999.

[50] M. G. Lizárraga. An Automatic System for Static Signature Consultation and Verification. MS. Thesis, State University of Campinas –UNICAMP, 1996. (In Portuguese)

[51] R. Sabourin and G. Genest. Off-line signature verification by local granulometric size distributions. IEEE Trans. on Pattern Analysis and Machine Intelligence vol. 19, no. 9, pages 976–988, 1997,

Chapter 7

FORENSIC IDENTIFICATION REPORTING USING AUTOMATIC BIOMETRIC SYSTEMS

Joaquin Gonzalez-Rodriguez, Javier Ortega-Garcia and Jose-Luis Sanchez-Bote
Speech and Signal Processing Group (ATVS), DIAC
Universidad Politecnica de Madrid, Spain
{jgonzalez, jortega, jbote}@diac.upm.es

Abstract
The issue of how forensic scientists must report to the judge or jury their conclusions when biometric identification techniques are used, is addressed in this contribution. Experts must convert system identification scores in meaningful values, useful to the Court. In this sense, the bayesian approach is firmly established as a valid framework for any forensic discipline. In this Chapter, we will show the different nature of system outputs when commercial or forensic approaches are used. Finally, a complete example of forensic characterization and reporting in the speaker recognition field will be shown.

Keywords: Forensic authentication, forensic reporting, forensic biometrics, forensic acoustics, speaker verification.

7.1.   Introduction

In this chapter, we will deal with the issue of how forensic scientists must report to the judge/jury their conclusions when biometric identification techniques are used (such as fingerprint, face, iris, signature, or voice recognition). In this sense, we will firstly note the difference from system characterization, that is, the identification abilities of the identification technique in use, with respect to the characterization of the forensic system that will provide objective results to the Court. This is the key issue of this contribution as forensic scientists must never arrogate the role of the judge/jury in taking decisions, and must know how to submit their results in order to comply with all the conditions of the judicial procedures, converting the system identification scores in meaningful values useful to the Court.

While commercial biometric systems performance, oriented to acceptance or rejection decisions, are widely assessed through different classical decision-based criteria (type I and II errors, ROC or DET plots) an intense debate among forensic practitioners have taken place during the last decade in order to achieve a common framework for the evaluation of evidence and its interpretation to the Court, and then how to assess the performance of forensic systems, as Figure 7.1 shows schematically.

Nowadays, the bayesian (or *Likelihood-Ratio*, LR) approach is firmly established as a theoretical framework for any forensic discipline, where systems providing its results according to this approach, from the large experience gained in DNA-based person identification, are assessed through Tippet plots. In this chapter, we will show the different nature of the outputs that automatic recognition systems must provide respectively in commercial and forensic approaches, even if the systems use the same core technology, and subsequently the need for different assessment tools specially suited for their corresponding applications.

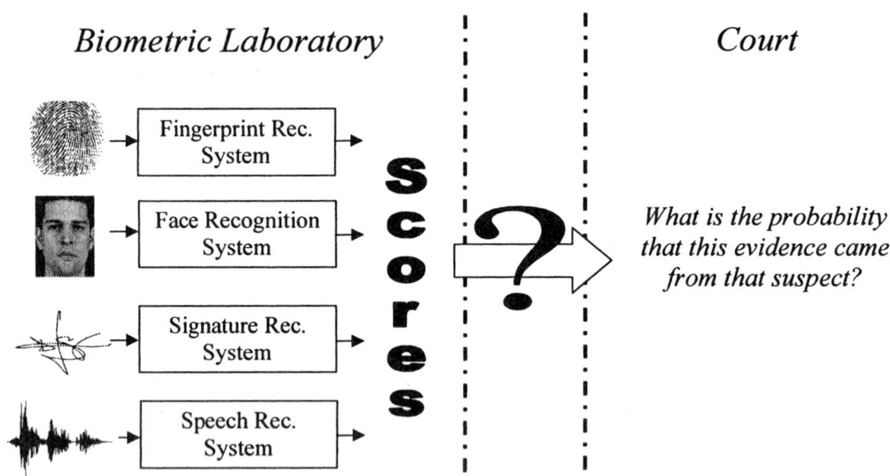

Figure 7.1. The problem of biometric score submission to Court.

The chapter is organized as follows. Firstly, we will show the different objectives of commercial biometric systems and forensic identification and the different needs of specific characterization techniques, as the outputs provided by both commercial and forensic systems will be completely different. Then we will introduce the bayesian approach for evidence analysis and forensic reporting which will perfectly suit the needs of the Court and the forensic scientist. Once the bayesian approach is understood, we will show how any biometric system can be adapted to provide its results in the form of

LRs in this bayesian environment (being so converted in a forensic identification system), and how to assess the performance of the forensic system according to the bayesian environment. Later, a whole example of forensic system characterization and reporting taken from the speaker recognition area will be shown, relating speaker recognition basic technology with bayesian analysis and reporting. This example uses NIST-Ahumada speech data, showing how easily any automatic speaker recognition system can be adapted to provide LR scores (relative to populations) instead of raw (normalized) scores. In this example, the same NIST-eval2001 raw scores are used firstly to compute DET plots, which assess the GMM-based system performance. These scores are then used again, taking into account reference populations from the same data, in order to obtain LR values which are summarized in the form of Tippet plots, assessing the forensic system based in GMM technology and reference populations.

7.2. Biometric Systems and Classical Forensic Reporting

The objective of commercial biometric systems is to accept true users and to reject impostors, usually minimizing some type of cost function as false acceptances and false rejections may occur. The usual operation mode of any biometric system is the following: in the presence of an input (unknown) pattern/model and a claimed user identity, the system will compare a reference (stored) pattern/model from the claimed user with the input pattern, giving as result a matching score which will be compared with a predetermined threshold for that specific user.

In order to assess the identification abilities of any biometric system, the system must be tested with known users and impostors, task which is usually performed thrpough the use of databases of the corresponding biometric characteristics (fingerprints, voices, signatures, faces, ...). Two types of error may occur in a detection system: false rejections (type I error), when a true user is rejected, and false acceptances (type II error), when an impostor is accepted. The probability of any of these two errors depends on the value of the threshold, in the sense that if the threshold is increased, the false acceptances will be reduced but the false rejections will be increased, and vice versa. As the same system or technology could work in different operating conditions, it is usual to show all possible operating points. This has been done classically in detection tasks by means of ROC curves, showing the tradeoff between miss (missed detections or false rejections) and false alarms (false acceptances). In order to have a single value characterizing the performance of the system, the Equal Error Rate (EER) is usually given, which is the point where the probability of a missed detection equals the probability of a false alarm, as shown in Figure 7.2.

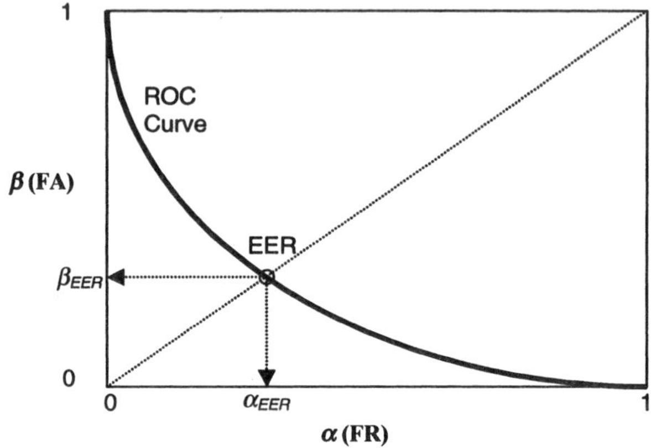

Figure 7.2.   Example of ROC detection curve and system EER, point in which $\alpha_{EER}=\beta_{EER}$.

However, as biometric systems performance increases, comparison of systems have become extremely difficult with this representation, as curves from different systems are extremely close to the lower left corner. This problem was overcome with the introduction of the DET (Detection Error Tradeoff) curve [1], which allows an almost linear representation of system performances, permitting easy observation of system contrasts (an example of DET plots will be further shown in Figure 7.10).

We want to note that this type of performance assessment (ROC/DET) perfectly suits the objective of the assessed systems, that is, to accept or reject users, because it directly shows both types of possible errors (missed detections and false alarms). Of course, and there is no doubt about this, the core technology being used within any forensic system can also be assessed through ROC/DET curves or EER values, as has been shown in the literature [2, 3].

7.2.1   Is Acceptance/Rejection the Objective of Forensic Recognition?

In the last years, the value of the different types of forensic evidence (even traditionally firmly established areas as fingerprint identification) have been severely attacked, questioning their scientific status, as is shown in influential books in the field [4, 5], specially *"...after several highly publicized miscarriages of justice in which forensic expertise played a crucial role"* [6].

Classically, there have been two different approaches to forensic reporting in "individualization of the source" areas, which includes areas as fingerprint, voice, face, signature, DNA, tool marks, paint, glass, fibers, and firearms. The first approach has been to provide just "identification" or "exclusion/elimination" decisions, which results in a very high percentage of non-reporting cases. This approach has two main drawbacks: the first one is related with the use of subjective thresholds, as these techniques does not provide absolute identifications, specially in forensic conditions, and all that the system/technique can provide is a score or a probability. Then, if the forensic scientist takes the (subjective) decision of identification or exclusion/rejection, he will be ignoring the prior probabilities related to the case (independent of the evidence under analysis), usurping the role of the Court in taking this decision, as *"... the use of thresholds is in essence a qualification of the acceptable level of reasonable doubt adopted by the expert"* [7]. The second drawback is the large amount of non-reporting cases that this identification/exclusion process induces, when *"... there is no logical reason to suppress probability statements ... because ... any piece of evidence is relevant if it tends to make the matter which requires proof more or less probable than otherwise"* [7]. The second classical approach to forensic reporting in this area consists in the use of a verbal scale of identification probabilities (typically "identification" / "very probable" / "probable" / "not conclusive" / "elimination"). This approach falls in the same errors as has just been noted, as it makes use of several subjective thresholds, but again ignores the prior probabilities (or usurp the judge/jury role if assigns it) relative to every case.

7.3. Bayesian Analysis of Forensic Evidence

Fortunately, the bayesian (or *Likelihood-Ratio*, LR) approach is now firmly established as a theoretical framework for any forensic discipline [8, 9, 10]. As an example, there are eight Working Groups (DNA, Fibers, Fingerprint, Firearms, Handwriting, Tool Marks, Paint and Glass, Speech and Audio) in ENFSI (European Network of Forensic Science Institutes) dealing with individualization of the source. All of them [11], in discussions open also to non-European participants, have dealt or are dealing with the bayesian approach, looking for common standards and procedures.

In this bayesian framework, the roles of the scientist and the judge/jury are clearly separated, because the Court wants to know the odds in favor of the prosecution proposition (C), ("the suspect has committed the crime"), given the circumstances of the case (I) and the observations made by the forensic scientist (E). These odds in favor of C are obtained from Eq. (7.1):

$$O(C|E, I) = \frac{\Pr(E|C, I)}{\Pr(E|\overline{C}, I)} \cdot O(C|I) \qquad (7.1)$$

Expressed in words, *Posterior odds = Likelihood ratio x Prior odds*, where the prior odds concern to the Court (background information relative to the case) and the likelihood ratio is provided by the forensic scientist. As a reference, in [8] a scale of likelihood ratios (LR) in the framework of DNA analysis is proposed with their respective linguistic qualifier suggesting the strength of verbal support for the evidence. This scale, as shown in Table 7.1, is actually being extended to all identification areas at British Forensic Science Service (FSS).

Table 7.1.   Scale of LR, with related linguistic qualifiers for degree of support of the evidence.

LR	*Verbal equivalent*
1 to 10	Limited support
10 to 100	Moderate support
100 to 1000	Strong support
Over 1000	Very strong support

The use of the bayesian approach is recommended because "... *assists scientists to assess the value of scientific evidence, help jurists to interpret scientific evidence, and clarify the respective roles of scientists and of members of the Court*" [7]. In this way, the scientist alone cannot infer the identity of the speaker from the analysis of the scientific evidence, but gives the Court the likelihood ratio of the two competing hypothesis (usually C, the questioned pattern *was made* by the suspect, and $\overline{C}$, the questioned pattern *was not made* by the suspect).

This LR, or Bayes factor, must be determined by the forensic scientist. In order to compute these numerator and denominator values, population data need to exist in order to determine objective probabilities. For score-based systems, as all biometric techniques, data are needed in order to model the distribution of measurements, both within and between sources, as this LR is in this case a ratio of the evaluation of probability density functions at the evidence score. A block diagram of this procedure is shown in Fugure 7.3.

Moreover, the bayesian approach allows to combine different types of evidence present in the process (blood type, fingerprint, ...) and even the incorporation of subjective probabilities related to uncertain events, as shown in [10].

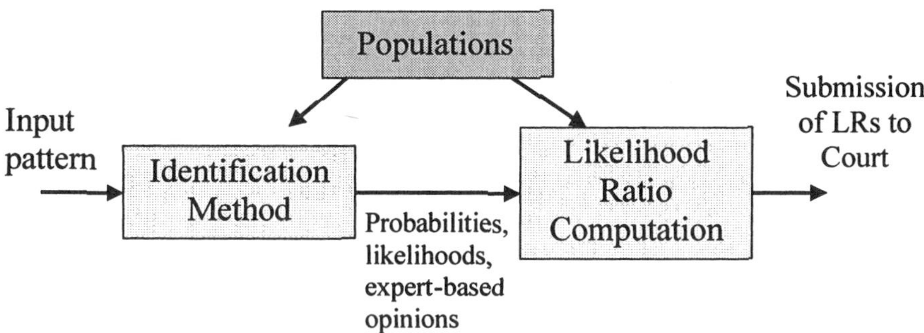

Figure 7.3. System architecture for LR Computation in the bayesian framework.

7.4.   Assessment of Forensic Biometric Systems

In order to test the abilities of systems providing their results in the form of LR values, some system calibration experiments have to be performed. In [12] and [13], a useful representation for between-source comparisons in any forensic discipline, the so-called Tippet plots, is provided, representing *proportion of cases with "LR values greater than...".* Then, we will draw in Tippet plots simultaneously two curves, one for the C hypothesis (the pattern belongs to the suspect – target), where the system should provide high LR values (LR>>1), and another one for the $\bar{C}$ hypothesis (the pattern does not belong to the suspect – non-target), where the system should provide low LR values (LR<<1). In this way, for any *x*-axis value each curve shows proportion of cases with LR greater than *x*. Then, the greater the separation between curves, the higher the discriminating power and the better the system (in an ideal system the curves should adjust respectively to the upper-right and lower-left margins of the plot). Figure 7.4 shows an example of possible Tippet plots for two different systems.

7.5.   Case Study: Forensic Speaker Recognition

In this section, we will give higher detail about the application of any biometric technique into the forensic domain. The results and details that will be given in this heading in the field of speaker recognition can be easily extrapolated to other biometric techniques, as all of them provide scores after comparing an input pattern with a claimed identity to the true user pattern/model.

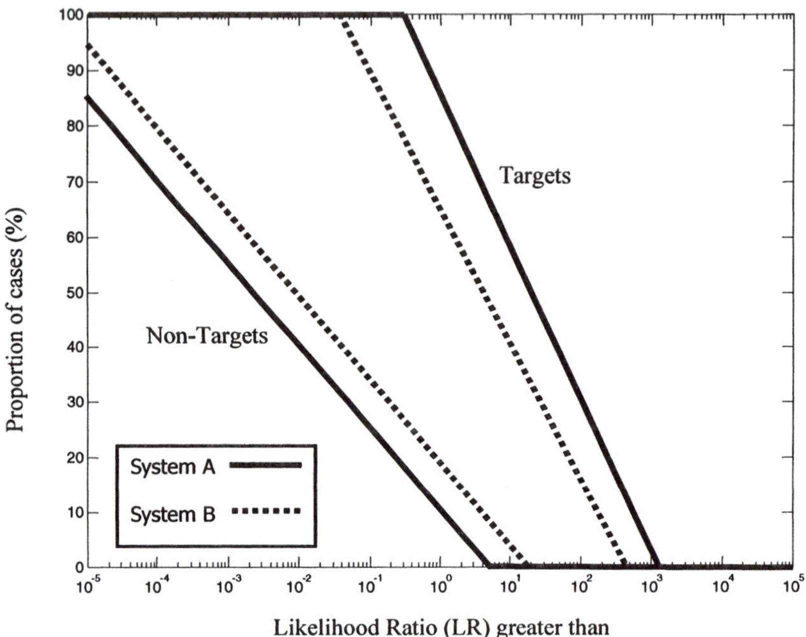

Figure 7.4. Example of possible Tippet curves for two competing systems.

Regarding forensic speaker recognition, when evidence associates an unknown voice to a suspect, the most common question to answer is: *What is the probability that this evidence (voice) came from that person?* In [7], the roles of classical commercial techniques as speaker verification (discrimination task), speaker identification (classification task) and type I and II error reporting have been properly criticized as alternatives to provide conclusions to the Court, basically because these techniques usurp the role of the judge or the jury in the process, as happens also in the assignment of prior probabilities if type I and II error reporting [14] is the selected alternative.

In the following subsections we will show how any speaker recognition system can be turned into a forensic system, and assessed as such, according to the bayesian approach for analysis of the speech evidence. Basic knowledge on automatic speaker recognition [15, 16, 17] and Gaussian Mixture Models [18] is assumed from now on.

7.5.1 Computation of Likelihood Ratios in Forensic Speaker Recognition

However, there is no closed solution to the problem of LR computation, and an agreement must be achieved in every identification area, especially in the process of selecting the characteristics of the involved populations. While it is assumed that the numerator of the LR requires an assessment of the intra-variability of the system, and the denominator is the random match probability, they can be obtained from objective or subjective measures over relative frequencies in the relevant population. One of the main problems arises from the estimation of these probabilities; specially, in open populations as in the case of fibers or tool marks.

In [19] a solution to this problem for forensic speaker recognition is proposed using automatic speaker recognition techniques. In this proposal, we have first to select the adequate population (usually from linguistic analysis or background knowledge), building speaker models (GMMs) with the selected individuals. We have also to record speech from the suspect, building a suspect speaker model (GMM) with a part of it, and obtaining some reference utterances (or *speech controls*, SC) that will be used to estimate the statistical distribution standing for the speaker intravariability. The key issue here is the computation of the probability distributions (*probability density functions, pdf*) of inter- and intra-variability, where the speech evidence, that is, the likelihood of the questioned recording with the suspect model, will be referenced. Figure 7.5. shows the complete LR computacion scheme.

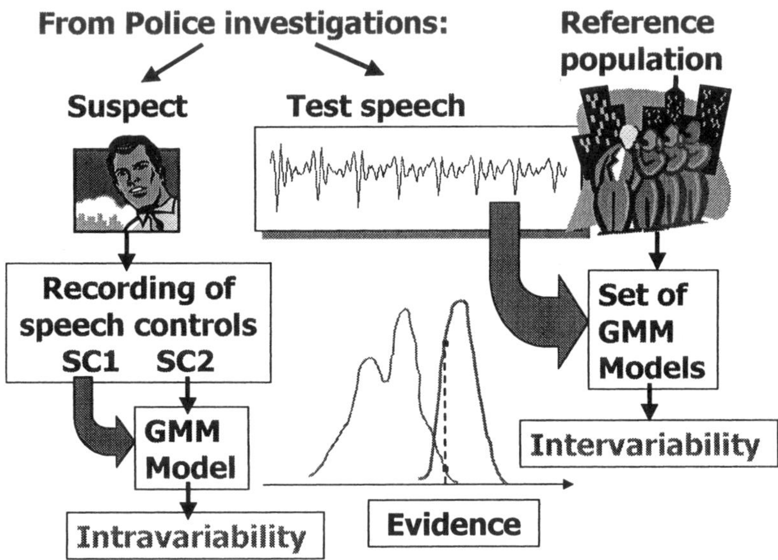

Figure 7.5. LR computation in Forensic Speaker Recognition.

The speaker intravariability is computed as the distribution, assumed to be gaussian, of the likelihoods of the speech controls (reference recordings from the suspect) with the suspect model (monomodal *pdf* in Figure 7.6). The intervariability is obtained as an statistical model of the likelihoods of the questioned recording with the models of the (selected) reference population. This is performed in [19] using kernel density estimation. In our proposal [20], this is performed by means of a multigaussian estimate (where the number of gaussians M involved is relative to the size N of the population – $M=1$ for $N<50$, $M=2$ for $51<N<100$, $M=3$ for $101<N<1000$, $M=4$ for $1001<N<10000$) in order to avoid excessive details in the distribution, as the selected population (usually hundreds or thousands of speakers) is representing all possible speakers relative to the case (language, dialect, gender, ...). Finally, the LR value is obtained as the quotient of the amplitudes of both distributions at the evidence likelihood (vertical line), as also shown in Figure 7.6.

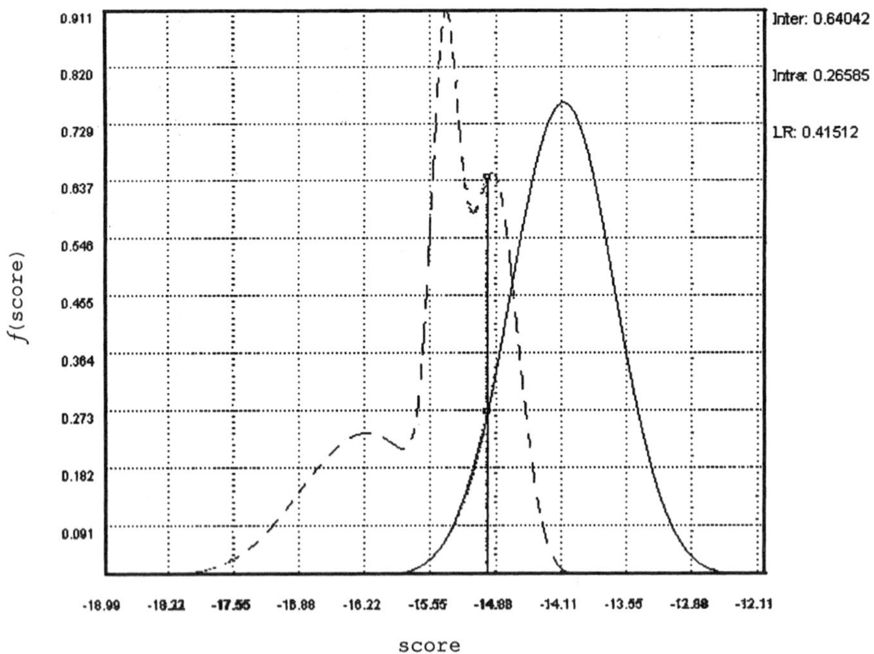

Figure 7.6. LR Computation with IdentiVox© of an impostor audio file (LR=0.41).

7.5.2 IdentiVox©: the ATVS-UPM Forensic Speaker Recognition System

IdentiVox© is a forensic tool, based in state-of-the-art Gaussian-Mixture-Modelling (GMM) text-independent speaker recognition, developed to solve the needs of forensic speech scientist. The system, perfectly suited to the bayesian approach for Forensic Speaker Recognition, operates within a user-friendly platform (Win95/98/NT/2000/ME) in a fully user-configurable environment. Speaker modeling, population management and LR computation are the main functions of the system, which also includes classical speaker identification, threshold establishment, speaker verification, channel normalization, likelihood normalization through Universal Background Models (UBMs), and user-defined parameterization (LPCC/MFCC). Figure 7.7 shows IdentiVox system structure. The work of the system user is organized in sessions (files), where the user can configure, save, open, and print reports for each individual session. In real forensic cases, the user just needs to select the test speech (directly related to the traces of the crime), the suspect speech and the reference population to be used (selected from linguistic or background knowledge), and the system will compute a LR value for every test speech file/segment.

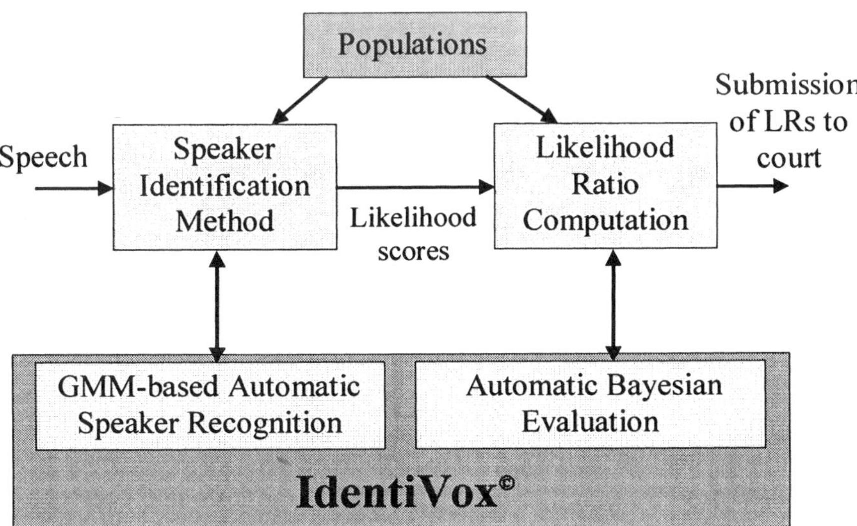

Figure 7.7. IdentiVox© system structure.

The basic technology in IdentiVox© is a proprietary implementation of Gaussian Mixture Models (GMM) and other well-known speech-related techniques, which have been shown as the best solution at the present, regarding the problem of text-independent speaker recognition, as it have been shown in last NIST evaluations [21], where our technology has been recently publicly assessed [22].

The IdentiVox[©] software is a multitask MDI (MultiDocument Interface) Windows application developed with Microsoft Visual C++. We have developed a classes library, programmed in ANSI C++ intended to the development of biometric applications (currently includes voice, fingerprint, on-line signature and face recognition).

These classes can be divided into three levels, as can be seen in Figure 7.8:

i. Basic classes: basic signal processing functions and input/output communications.

ii. Specific classes: biometric functions (modeling, likelihood computation, etc.).

iii. Session classes: communication interface with the specific classes, simplifying the development of applications.

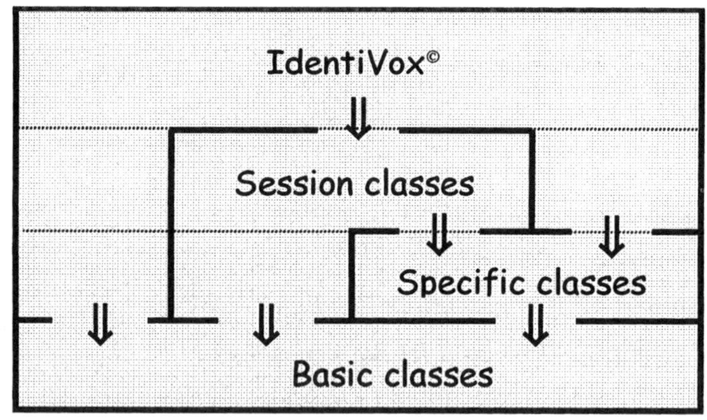

Figure 7.8. IdentiVox[©] software structure over ATVS classes library.

This structure enables us to easily update the system with new options or technology improvements. Multiple publications are available reporting the performance of the system in different conditions [2, 20, 23]. Just as an example, we can see in Figure 7.9 the graphic appearance of our forensic speaker recognition system.

7.5.3   DET and Tippet Plots with NIST-Ahumada Data

In this subsection, we will show the close relations and significant differences in the assessment of biometric systems when used in commercial or forensic applications.

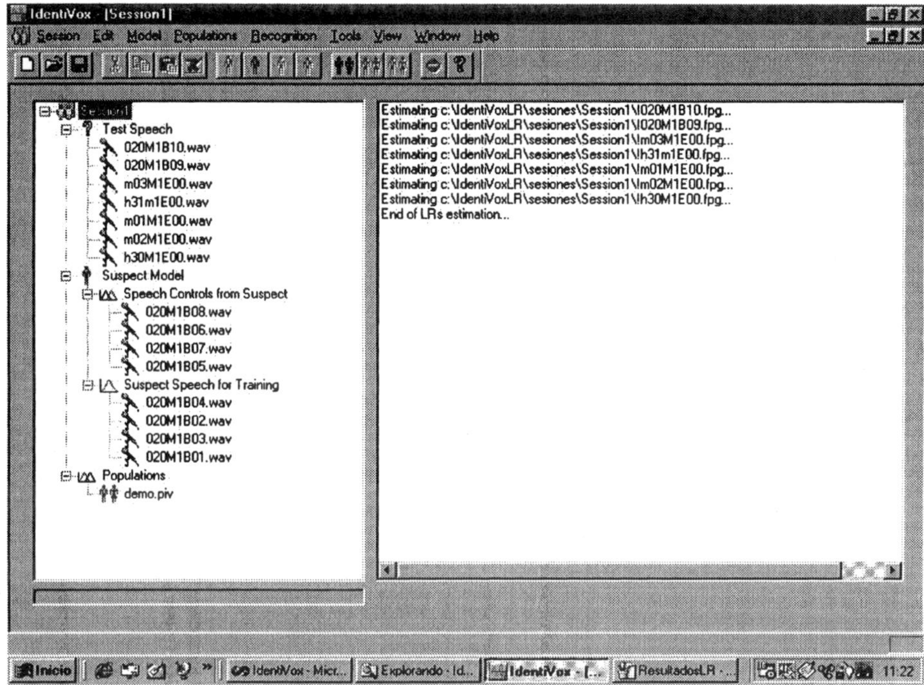

Figure 7.9. Example of an IdentiVox© session.

An interesting example is presented here, where the authors will compare the suitability and the role played by both DET and Tippet curves in different environments, yet using the same evaluation data. We have used the NIST-Ahumada [21, 24] data of 2001 evaluation, which will be used to assess respectively the technology of our research group (ATVS-UPM), as to be used in any commercial/decision application, and the forensic system we have developed, according to the bayesian approach, based in this technology.

In Figure 7.10 we show the performance of our GMM implementation with the eval'2001 NIST-Ahumada data in an extended version of the "all" condition (every two 30 s. test file per speaker is tested with all 103 male models). In eval'2001 workshop, the authors presented [22] an UBM MAP-adapted GMM system with T-Norm, with a basic coefficient vector of 8 MFCC+Δ+$\Delta\Delta$. Since last evaluation, the system has been improved as Figure 7.10 shows, by suppressing the $\Delta\Delta$ coefficients, and increasing the basic vector size to both 12 and 19 MFCC.

As it can be seen, the 19 MFCC-based system outperforms the 12 MFCC-based one, assessed from a DET curve closer to the origin of coordinates (note that the best NISTeval'01 system with these data was just 1~2% better in EER with respect to our 19 MFCC-based system). However, if we want to use any of these two systems in a forensic application, apart from the theoretical problems exposed previously (subjective thresholds and suppression of prior probabilities), the operating point of the system must have a very low (or even null) false acceptance rate, which would mean a miss detection rate much greater than 40% of the cases. Does it mean that we cannot use automatic speaker recognition technology in forensic cases?

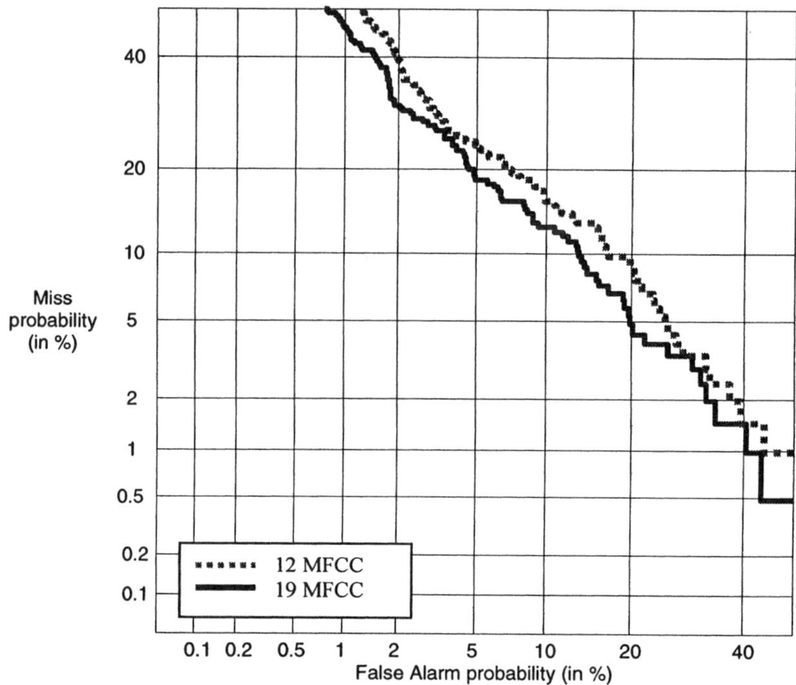

Figure 7.10. DET-plots for two versions (12 MFCC or 19 MFCC as base vector) of ATVS-system with NIST-Ahumada eval'2001data.

In this experiment, the same eval'2001 raw scores have been used to compute LR values, in order to show the performance of a GMM-based forensic system. As we have just available in this dataset one speech file per speaker to build a model, and two test files per speaker, we will always use one of the files as test file, and the other one will be used as speech control, that is, the information needed to estimate the intravariability distribution (as just one likelihood is available, it will be used as mean value of a single-gaussian distribution, and variance will be set to that of all speakers with his own test files). The intervariability is obtained as the distribution of the likelihoods of every test file with respect to all non-target models. Once we have the two distributions available for every test file, we compute the LR values and summarize them in the following Tippet plots (Figure 7.11) with both systems (12/19 MFCC). Every Tippet plot is composed of two curves, one for target speakers (103x2=206 trials) and other for non-target speakers (103x2x102= 21,012 trials):

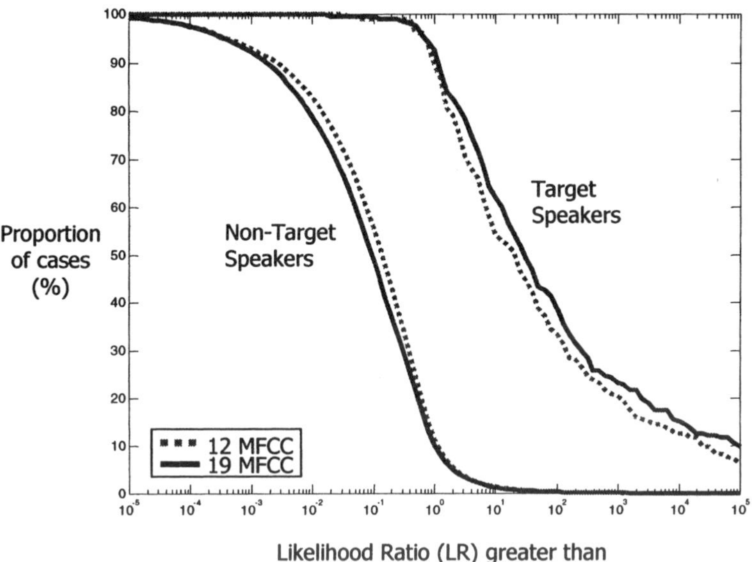

Figure 7.11.　　Tippet plots for the same two versions of ATVS-system with NIST-Ahumada eval'2001 data.

As it can be seen, the better the system the greater the separation between target and non-target curves for each system. But the most important fact here is that observing results in Figure 7.11, and independently of the system used (12/19 MFCC), we can provide a meaningful LR value for every single file, strengthening clearly the prosecution hypothesis for the case of target-speakers, and attenuating it in the case of non-target speakers, so an excellent forensic performance of the system can be derived. Moreover, the system is not assuming any prior probability nor taking any decision (which corresponds to the Court) and just limits its role to reinforce or weaken the prosecution hypothesis.

7.6.　　Conclusions

We have shown in this contribution how any biometric system can be adapted to work in the forensic environment according to the bayesian approach. In addition, the roles of ROC/DET and Tippet plots in commercial and forensic applications have been clarified. While ROC/DET curves assess system/technology performance, they cannot be used to provide conclusions to the Court as acceptance or rejection of speakers is not the goal of forensic speaker recognition, as has been shown. An interesting example is presented with NIST-Ahumada eval'2001 data, showing how easily a GMM-based system can be adapted to provide LR values according to the bayesian approach, firmly established in any forensic discipline, comparing DET and Tippet plots, the latter strongly recommended to assess LR-based systems, appropriate for forensic speaker recognition.

Acknowledgements

Authors wish to thank all people from both Speech and Signal Processing Group (ATVS) at Universidad Politecnica de Madrid, and Acoustics and Image Laboratory of DGGC. We wish to appreciate specially Julian Fierrez-Aguilar, and those directly involved in the development of the IdentiVox project, namely Marta Garcia-Gomar and Oscar Garcia-Ledesma from ATVS-UPM, and Juan-Jesus Diaz-Gomez and Jose-Juan Lucena-Molina from DGGC for extensive testing and improvement suggestions.

References

[1]   A. Martin, et al. The DET Curve in Assessment of Detection Task Performance. In Proc. of EuroSpeech'97, Rhodes (Greece), pages 1895-1898, 1997.

[2]   J. Gonzalez-Rodriguez, J. Ortega-Garcia, and J.J. Lucena-Molina. IdentiVox: A PC-Windows Tool for Text-Independent Speaker Recognition in Forensic Environments, Proc. of ENFSI (European Network of Forensic Science Institutes) Meeting, Cracow (Poland), September 2000.

[3]   H. Nakasone, and S. Beck. Forensic Automatic Speaker Recognition. In Proc. of Odyssey'2001 ISCA Speaker Recognition Workshop, Crete (Greece), pages 139-144, 2001.

[4]   B. Robertson, G.A. Vignaux. Interpreting Evidence – Evaluating Forensic Science in the Courtroom, Wiley, Chichester (UK), 1995.

[5]   K.R. Foster and P.W. Huber. Judging Science: Scientific Knowledge and the Federal Courts, MIT Press, Cambridge MA (USA), 1997.

[6]   A.P.A. Broeders. Forensic Speech and Audio Analysis: the State of the Art in 2000 AD. In Proc. of SEAF-2000 (1st National Conference of the Spanish Forensic Acoustics Society), Ed. J. Ortega-García, Madrid (Spain), 2000.

[7]   C. Champod and D. Meuwly. The Inference of Identity in Forensic Speaker Recognition, Speech Communication, vol. 31, pages 193-203, June 2000.

[8]   I.W. Evett. Towards a Uniform Framework for Reporting Opinions in Forensic Science Casework, Science & Justice, 38(3), pages 198-202, 1998.

[9]   C. Champod. Overview and Meaning of Identification, Encyclopedia of Forensic Sciences, Academic Press, pages 1077-1084, 2000.

[10]   C.G.C. Aitken. Statistical Interpretation of Evidence/Bayesian Analysis, Encyclopedia of Forensic Sciences, Academic Press, pages 717-724, 2000.

[11]   D. Meuwly. Current Discussions of the ENFSI-WG About the Use of the Bayesian Approach for the Interpretation of Evidence, Meeting of the Speech and Audio Group of ENFSI –European Network of Forensic Science Institutes-, Paris (France), 2001.

[12]   C.F. Tippet et al. The Evidential Value of the Comparison of Paint Flakes from Sources other than Vehicles, Journal of the Forensic Science Society, vol. 8, pages 61-65, 1968.

[13]   I.W. Evett and J.S. Buckleton. Statistical Analysis of STR (short tandem repeat) Data, Advances in Forensic Haemogenetics, A. Carracedo, B. Brickmann, and W. Bär, Editors. Springer-Verlag: Heidelberg, pages 79-86, 1996.

[14]   F. Taroni and C.G.C. Aitken. Forensic Science at Trial, Jurimetrics Journal 37, pages 327-337, 1997.

[15]   G.R. Doddington. Speaker Recognition – Identifying People by their Voices. In Proc. of IEEE, vol. 73, no. 11, pages 1651-1664, 1985.

[16]   R. André-Obrecht (ed.). Special Issue on Speaker Recognition and its Commercial and Forensic Applications, Speech Communication, Elsevier, pages 87-270, 2000.

[17]   R. Peres (ed.). In Proc. of "A Speaker Odyssey". The ISCA Speaker Recognition Workshop, Crete (Greece), 2001.

[18]   D.A. Reynolds. Speaker Identification and Verification Using Gaussian Mixture Models, Speech Communication, Elsevier, vol. 17, pages 91-108, 1995.

[19]   D. Meuwly and A. Drygajlo. Forensic Speaker Recognition based on a Bayesian Framework and Gaussian Mixture Modeling. In Proc. of Odyssey'2001 ISCA Speaker Recognition Workshop, Crete (Greece), 2001.

[20]   J. Gonzalez-Rodriguez, J. Ortega-Garcia and J.J. Lucena-Molina. On the Application of the Bayesian Framework to Real Forensic Conditions with GMM-based Systems, Proc. of Odyssey'2001 ISCA Speaker Recognition Workshop, Crete (Greece), pages 135-138, 2001.

[21]   http://www.nist.gov/speech/spkrinfo.htm

[22]   J. Gonzalez-Rodriguez, O. Ledesma-Garcia and J. Ortega-Garcia. ATVS Results and Presentation at NIST'2001 Speaker Recognition Evaluation, Linthicum Heights, Maryland (USA), 2001.

[23]   J. Gonzalez-Rodriguez, J. Ortega-Garcia, and J.J. Lucena-Molina. Bayesian Evaluation of Speech Evidences with IdentiVox Automatic Speaker Recognition System, Joint ENFSI-IAFP (European Network of Forensic Science Institutes – International Association of Forensic Phonetics) Meeting, Paris (France), July 2001.

[24]   J. Ortega-Garcia, J. Gonzalez-Rodriguez and V. Marrero-Aguiar. AHUMADA: A Large Speech Corpus in Spanish for Speaker Characterization and Identification, Speech Communication, vol. 31, pages 255-264, June 2000.

Chapter 8

SIGNATURE SECURITY SYSTEM FOR E-COMMERCE

Bin Li

Department of Computer Science and Technology
Harbin Institute of Technology, Harbin, China
lbn@biometrics.hit.edu.cn

David Zhang

Department of Computing
The Hong Kong Polytechnic University, Kowloon, Hong Kong
csdzhang@comp.polyu.edu.hk

Abstract   The study of human signatures has a long history, but automatic signature verification is still a new and active topic in the research and application fields of biometrics. This chapter starts with a detailed survey of recent research progress and commercial products in automatic dynamic verification. Instead of applying new and popular approaches, such as those of Artificial Neural Networks, Fuzzy Logic, or the Hidden Markov Model, this chapter proposes a low cost on-line dynamic signature verification method based on the combination of time-dependent global coordinate features and local curvature features. Global features include pen down time, pen down move, the average, maximum and standard deviation of both the velocity and acceleration, while local features make use of the time dependent relationship between adjacent curative turning points. The astonishing growth of the Internet and intranet raises the new challenge of *e*-commerce security. With the attempts to look for a low cost biometrics method as an enhancement of personal identification in the network, a typical system for dynamic signature verification in the Internet and intranet is introduced. This system involves such processes as dynamic signature data acquisition through the network, using global and local feature extraction, feature match, feature enrollment, and combined feature comparison for verification and distance measures for recognition. Finally, this chapter proposes some applications of on-line signature verification.

Keywords: *E*-commerce, signature verification, global feature, local feature, feature extraction, feature match, FRR, FAR

8.1.   Introduction

Handwriting is a skill that is personal to individuals. A handwritten signature is commonly used to authenticate the contents of a document or a financial transaction. Automatic signature verification is one of the active topics in the research and application fields of biometrics. Technologies and applications for automatic off-line (also called static) and on-line (also called dynamic) signature verification are facing a lot of real challenges. For example, there are challenges associated with how to achieve as low a false acceptance rate and a false rejection rate as possible, how to reach the highest performance with the least time and cost, and how to make the application commercially viable. However, it is never long before more new ideas and technologies are employed in this area; or useful applications and ideas are deployed out of this area. Automatic signature verification systems powered by neural networks, parallel processing, distributed computing, network and computer systems and various pattern recognition technologies, are increasingly applicable and acceptable in business areas, which are driven by the growing demands of wired and wireless business. For instance, off-line (static) signature verification can be applied in automatic bank processes, document recognition and filing systems, while on-line (dynamic) signature verification can be applied in automatic personal authentication, computer and network access control, on-line financial service and in various *e*-business applications.

8.1.1   Passwords in the Internet and Intranet

Today, with the astonishing growth of the Internet and intranet, *e*-commerce and *e*-finance have become the hottest topics on the planet. Doing business through the public network makes personal identification and data security more and more critical as well. How to protect a private identification from being pirated is a key issue that Internet and intranet clients are concerned with solving before such *e*-business can be widely accepted.

In current practices, identifying a person in the Internet and intranet depends on a password, usually stored or communicated as an encrypted combination of ASCII characters. However, no matter how strong such an encrypted security system is, such as SSL (Secure Socket Layer: 40-100bit) or the newer SET (Secure Electronic Transaction: 1024bit) with digital certificates, there are still fatal shortcomings of such conventional password approaches. For example, passwords are easy to forget, particularly when a user has to remember tens of passwords for different systems, and passwords can be stolen. So new verification techniques such as biometrics can be used to provide such authentication. Of the many possible biometrics schemes, voice is a good candidate, but it has a significant dependency on an individual's physical condition (e.g., having a cold, may degrade verification quality). Use of fingerprints is another good candidate, however, fingerprint images can be degraded when an individual perspires. The eye is yet another strong candidate, but to obtain a good iris image, an individual's eyes must be open and he/she must not wear glasses. In addition, very strong light needs to be shone onto the retina to obtain the image. The device used to capture the image of the iris or retina is also expensive. Compared with these other biometrics schemes, a signature can be easily obtained and the device is relatively cheap. Given the nature of the time, speed, pen pressure, and inclination features of a signature, which are never forgotten and difficult to steal, an on-line human signature verification system has some obvious advantages for use in personal identification. However, there are also some shortcomings of signature verification, such as instability in the signature resulting from differences in the emotions of the signer as well as the writing environment. How to overcome this potential instability and improve the precision of verification is an important topic.

8.1.2   Error Rate

In the research area of signature verification problems, two types of error rates are commonly used to evaluate a verification and recognition system: the type I error rate and type II error rate are usually called the False Reject Rate (FRR) and False Acceptance Rate (FAR), respectively. Minimizing type II errors, which represent the acceptance of counterfeit signatures (forgeries), will normally increase type I errors, which are the rejections of genuine signatures [1]. In most cases, the type II error rate is considered to be more important. However, this will obviously depend on the purpose, design, characteristic and application of the verification system. For example, credit card transactions may tolerate higher type II error rates because the customer will feel very unhappy after many rejections of their signature. This is not the case for bank account transactions, which must have the lowest type II error rate. To distinguish the relationship between type I and type II error rates, and their thresholds, an error trade-off curve is widely adopted [2], as shown in Figure 8.1. The error rate at TO is called the Equal-Error Rate (EER) when type I and type II error rates are the same.

8.1.3   Process and System

There are two types of signature verification systems: on-line systems and off-line systems. In off-line systems, the signature is written on paper, digitized through an optical scanner or a camera, and verified or recognized through examining the overall or detailed shapes of the signature. However, in on-line systems, the signature trace is acquired in real time with a digitizing pen tablet (or an instrumented pen or other touch panel specialized hardware), which captures both the static and dynamic information of the signature during the signing process. Since an on-line system can utilize not only the shape information of the signature, but also the dynamic time-dependent information, its performance (accuracy) is normally considered to be better than that of an off-line system. A typical automatic on-line signature verification and recognition process was presented by Giuseppe Pirlo in 1993 [3], and is shown in Figure 8.2. Normally the process of signature verification and recognition consists of a training stage and a testing stage. In the training stage, the system uses the features extracted from one or several training samples to build a reference signature database. These include the stages of data acquisition, preprocessing and feature extraction. During the enrollment stage, each signer gets his/her own ID (identification) linked to the signer's reference in the database. In the testing stage, on the input device, users input their ID and then sign for verification, or they sign for recognition. Then, the verification system uses this ID information to extract the reference in the database, and compares the features extracted from the input signature with the reference. Or the recognition system uses the features extracted from the input signature to compare them with those of all the signers in the database to find the most similar one. Finally the decision process checks whether the test signature is genuine or not.

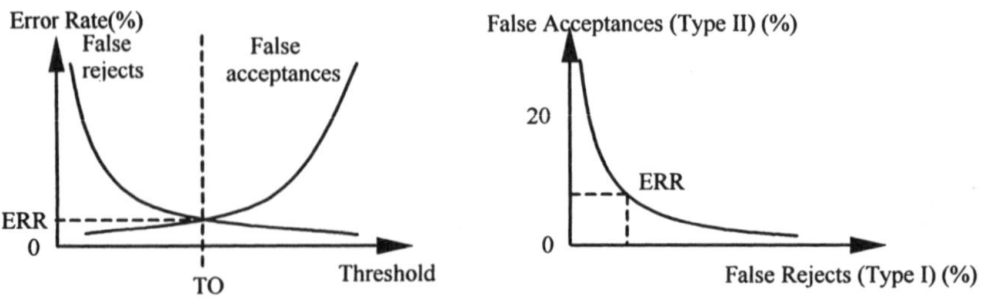

(a) Error Rate vs. Threshold

(b) False Reject Rate (Type I) vs. False Acceptance Rate (Type II)

Figure 8.1.   Error Rate Trade-off.

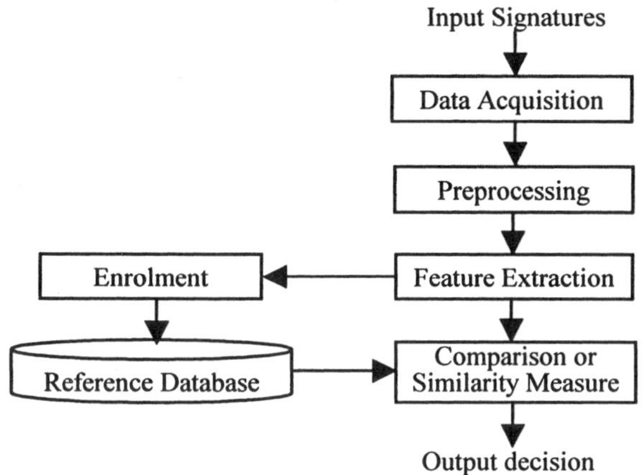

Figure 8 2. Typical automatic on-line signature verification process.

8.2. Literature Overview

A wide range of methods for on-line signature verification has been used. Depending on the signature capture device used, features such as velocity, pen pressure and pen inclination are used in addition to spatial (x,y coordinates) features. Different approaches can be categorized based on the model used for verification. In this section, several methods of signature verification are introduced. Since a signature database does not exist in the public domain, every research group has collected their own data set. This makes a comparison of the different signature verification systems a difficult task.

8.2.1 Conventional Mathematical Approaches

Mathematical approaches are still popular in the area of automatic signature verification. Below, a group of the latest mathematical methods are introduced.

Dr. Nalwa presented an approach to automatic on-line signature verification that broke with tradition by relying primarily on the detailed shape of a signature for its automatic verification rather than relying primarily on the pen dynamics during the production of the signature [4]. He challenged the notion that the success of automatic on-line signature verification hinges on the capture of velocities or forces during signature production. He contended that it was not possible to depend solely or even primarily on pen dynamics because of observed inconsistency. In his paper, he proposed a robust, reliable, and elastic local-shaped-based model for handwritten on-line curves. In particular, to support his approach, he fleshed out some key concepts, such as the harmonic mean, jitter, aspect normalization, parameterization over normalized length, torque, weighted cross correlation and warping, etc.

Consequently, he devised the following algorithm components for local and purely shape-based models, and global models based on both shape and time:

- Normalization, which made the algorithm largely independent of the orientation and aspect of a signature and made the algorithm inherently independent of the position and size of a signature.
- Description, which generated the five characteristic functions of the signature.
- Comparison, which computed a net measure of the errors between the signature characteristic and their prototypes.

His model was generated by firstly parameterizing each on-line signature curve over its normal arc-length. Then, along the length of the curve in a moving coordinate frame, he represented the measures of the curve within a sliding window. The measures of the curve were analogous to the position of the center of mass, the torque exerted by a force, and the moment of inertia of a mass distribution about its center of mass. He also suggested the weighted and biased harmonic mean as a graceful mechanism for combining errors from multiple models, of which at least one model is applicable but not necessarily more than one model is applicable. He recommended that each signature be represented by multiple models, local and global, shape based and dynamics based. With his shape-based models, his approach can also be applied to off-line signature verification. Finally, he outlined a signature verification algorithm that had been implemented and tested successfully both on databases and in a number of live experiments. Below is a list of the sample size for three different databases he used.

- Database 1 (DB1) used a Bell Laboratories in-house developmental LCD writing table with a tethered pen: a total of 904 genuine signatures from 59 signers, and a total of 325 forgeries with an equal-error rate of 3%.
- Database 2 (DB2) used an NCR 5990 LCD writing table with a tethered pen: a total of 982 genuine signatures from 102 signers, and a total of 401 forgeries with an equal-error rate of 2%.
- Database 3 (DB3) used an NCR 5990 LCD writing table with a tethered pen: a total of 790 genuine signatures from 43 signers, and a total of 424 forgeries with an equal-error rate of 5%.

Using the analysis of error trade-off curve, the false rejects rate (Type I) versus the false accepts rate (Type II), he obtained an overall equal-error rate that was only about 2.5%.

In addition, a particular system designed using his approach for automatic on-site signature verification had principal hardware components of: a notebook PC, an electronic writing table, a smart card, and a smart card reader. The threshold zero, which distinguished forgeries from genuine signatures, corresponded to 0.50 on the scale in the database experiment, and corresponded roughly to a 0.7% false rejects rate and a 1% false accepts rate.

Winston Nelson, William Turin and Trevor Hastie discussed three methods for on-line signature verification based on statistical models of features that summarize different aspects of signature shape and the dynamics of signature production. [7]

- Based on the feature statistics of genuine signatures only.
- Simpler, using a Euclidean distance error metric and using a procedure for selecting 10 out of 22 features, their experiments on a database of 919 genuine signatures and 330 forgeries showed a 0.5% Type I error rate and a 14% Type II error rate.
- Using statistical properties of forgeries as well as the genuine signatures to develop a quadratic discriminant rule for classifying signatures. The experiments on the same database showed a 0.5% Type I error rate and 10% Type II error rate.

In 1997, Ronny Martens and Luc Claesen presented an on-line signature verification system, based on 3D force patterns and pen inclination angles, as recorded during signing [8]. Their feature extraction mechanism was based on the well-known elastic matching technique. In contrast to previous work in the same area however, they emphasized the importance of the final step in the process: the discrimination based on the extracted features by choosing the right discrimination approach to improve the quality of the entire verification process drastically.

To extract a binary decision out of a previously computed feature vector, they used the following approaches for discrimination process:

- Sato's approach.
- Statistical approach.
- Mahalanobis distances.
- Kernel-approach.

Their database consisted of 360 genuine signatures from 18 signers and 615 random forgeries from 41 imitators. With a kernel function for Gaussian PDF-estimations (probability density function), they achieved a 0.4% to 0.3% equal-error rate. Their techniques, however, were not specific to signature verification, and they should be considered carefully in every process where a classification decision is made using a set of parameters.

8.2.2   Dynamic Programming Approach

Dynamic Time Warping (DTW) was a mathematical optimization technique for sequentially structured problems, which had over the years played a major role in providing primary algorithms for automatic signature verification.

Yet this useful method of non-linear, elastic time alignment still has a high computational complexity due to the repetitive nature of its operations for the optimization process. Y.J. Bae and M.C. Fairhurst proposed a parallel algorithm using a pipeline paradigm, chosen with the intention of overcoming possible deadlocks in the highly distributed network [9]. The algorithm was implemented on a transputer network on the Meiko Computing Surface using Occam2, which resulted in an order of magnitude reduction of the time complexity.

In 1996, Ronny Martens and Luc Claesen discussed an on-line signature verification system based on (DTW) [10]. They indicated that the DTW-algorithm originated from the field of speech recognition, and had been applied successfully in the signature verification area several times with few adaptations made in order to take the specific characteristics of signature verification into account. One of the most important differences was the availability of a rather large number of reference patterns, making it possible to determine which features of a reference signature were important. This extra amount of information was dealt with by disconnecting the DTW-stage and the feature extraction process,. A database containing 360 signatures from 18 different persons was used. As forgeries for a certain person, the original signatures produced by the other signers were used. The optimal classification was achieved by using Gabor transform-coefficients that described signal contents from 0Hz to +/-30Hz. As a result, the minimum ERR was 1.4%.

In their second paper on the use of the Dynamic Time Warping (DTW) technique in the signature verification area, Ronny Martens and Luc Claesen had the objective of extracting an alternative DTW-approach that was better suited to the signature verification problem [11]. They started by examining the dissimilarities between the characteristics of speech recognition and signature verification. The aim of the classical approach of the DTW-algorithm was to find an optimal time-alignment between R (Reference) and T (Test). They evaluated the algorithm using the same signature database described above. The optimized EER was about 8% using the alternative DTW comparing with about 12% using the classical DTW. They pointed out that the useful signing information was concentrated in a very small 20-30 Hz bandwidth and that a sample rate faster than 60 Hz was enough according to the Nyquist-terms in their equations.

Mark J. Paulik, N. Mohankrishnan and Micheal Mikiforuk proposed a time-varying vector autoregressive model for signature verification. They dealt with a signature as a vector random process whose components were the x and y Cartesian coordinates and the instantaneous velocity of the recording stylus [12]. This multivariate process was then represented by a time-varying p^{th} order vector autoregressive (VAR) model, which approximates the changes in complex contours typical in signature analysis. The vector structure attempts to model the correlation between the signature sequence variables to allow the extraction of superior distinguishing features. The model's matrix coefficients are used to generate the feature vectors that permit the verification of a signer's identity. A database with 100 sample signatures from 16 signers yielded an equal-error rate from 2.87% to 5.48% for experiments with different VAR (variance) or 1-D (one dimensional) global or individual thresholds.

Brigitte Wirtz presented a new technique for dynamic signature verification using a dynamic programming (DP) approach for function-based signature verification. Dynamic data such as pen writing pressure was treated as a function of positional data, and therefore evaluated locally [13]. Verification was based on strokes as the structural units of the signature. This global knowledge was fed into the verification procedure. The application of a 3-D (three dimensional) non-linear correlation of the signature signals used the stroke index as the third DP index. In conjunction with the definition of a finite state automaton on the set of reference strokes, the system could handle different stroke numbers and missing or additional strokes correctly. The correct alignment of matching strokes and the signature verification process were determined simultaneously. An additional alignment stage before the actual nonlinear correlation was obsolete. Her experimental database collected 644 genuine signatures and 669 forgeries within two months. The best equal-error rate achieved was 1% to 1.4%.

8.2.3   Hidden Markov Model Based Methods

Due to the importance of the warping problem in signature verification as well as in handwriting recognition applications, the use of Hidden Markov Models (HMMs) is becoming more and more popular in both areas. HMMs are finite stochastic automata and probably represent the most powerful tool for modeling time-varying dynamic patterns. There was a good introduction to the basic principles of HMMs in [14]. There are several papers applying HMMs in handwriting signature verification problems as well.

L. Yang et al. use the absolute angular direction along the trajectory, which is encoded as a sequence of angles, to represent the signature [15]. To obtain sequences of the same length, each signature is then quantized into sixteen levels. Another sixteen levels are introduced for pen-up samples.

Several Hidden Markov Model structures were investigated including left-to right models and parallel models. The model is trained with the forward-backward algorithm and the probabilities estimated with the Baum-Welch algorithm. In preliminary experiments, the left-to-right model with arbitrary state skips performed the best. Sixteen signatures obtained from 31 writers were used for evaluation; eight signatures were used for training and the other eight for testing. No skilled forgeries were available. The experiments also showed that increasing the number of states and decreasing the observation length lead to a decrease in the false rejects and an increase in false accepts. The best results reported are a false accept rate of 4.4% and false reject rate of 1.75%.

A method for the automatic verification of on-line handwritten signatures using both global and local features was described by R.S. Kashi, J. Hu and W. L. Nelson in their paper in 1997 [16]. These global and local features captured various aspects of signature shape and dynamics of signature production. They demonstrated that with the addition (to the global features) of a local feature based on the signature likelihood obtained from Hidden Markov Models (HMM), the performance of signature verification improved significantly. They also defined a Hidden Semi-Markov Model to represent the handwritten signature more accurately. Their test database consisted of 542 genuine signatures and 325 forgeries. The program had a 2.5% equal-error rate. At the 1% false rejection (FR) point, the addition of the local information to the algorithm, which was using only global features, reduced the false acceptance (FA) rate from 13% to 5%.

J.G.A. Dolfing, E.H.L. Aarts, van Oosterhout and J.J.G.M addressed the problem of on-line signature verification based on Hidden Markov Models (HMM) in their recent paper in 1998 [17]. They used a novel type of digitizer tablet and paid special attention to the use of pen-pressure and pen-tilt. After investigating the verification reliability based on different forgery types, they compared the discriminative value of the different features based on a linear discriminant analysis (LDA) and showed that pen-tilt was important. On the basis of "home-improved", "over-the-shoulder", and professional forgeries, they showed that the amount of dynamic information available to an imposter was important and that forgeries based on paper copies were easier to detect. In their system, training of the HMM parameters was done using the maximum likelihood criterion and applying the Viterbi approximation, followed by an LDA. Verification was based on the Viterbi algorithm which computed the normalized likelihood with respect to the signature writing time. Their database consisted of 1530 genuine signatures, 3000 amateur forgeries written by 51 individuals, and 240 professional forgeries. Their results showed an equal-error rate between 1% and 1.9%.

8.2.4   Artificial Neural Networks Approach

Along with the vigorous growth of the computing society in recent, Artificial Neural Networks (ANN) have become more and more popular in the area of automatic signature verification. ANN simplified the biometrics myth of the signature and brought a more computerized and programmable approach to this complex problem.

Luan Ling Lee described three neural network (NN) based approaches for on-line human signature verification: Bayes multilayer perceptrons (BMP), time-delay neural networks (TDNN), input-oriented neural networks (IONN). The back perceptron algorithm was used for training the network [18]. In the experiment, a signature was input as a sequence of instantaneous absolute velocities extracted from a pair of spatial coordinate time functions (x(t), y(t)). The BMP provides the lowest misclassification error rate among these three types of networks. A special database was constructed with 1000 genuine signatures collected from the same subject and 450 skilled forgeries from 18 trained forgers. The obtained equal-error rate for BMP, TDNN and IONN was 2.67%, 6.39% and 3.82% respectively.

In their paper in 1997, N. Mohankrishnan, W.S. Lee and M.J. Paulik examined the incorporation of neural network classification strategies to enhance the performance of an autoregressive model-based signature classification system [19]. They used a multilayer perceptron trained with the back-propagation algorithm for classification. They also presented and compared the results obtained using an extensive database of signatures with those from the use of a conventional maximum likelihood classifier. With 800 genuine and 800 forgery signatures, on the average, the type I and type II error rate was about 1.7% each, while they claimed their identification accuracy was about 97%.

T. Matsuura and H. Sakai presented a stochastic system representation of the handwriting process and its application to on-line signature verification [20]. Their stochastic system characterizes the motion in writing a signature as a random impulse response. The random impulse response was estimated in terms of the horizontal and vertical components of the handwriting motion, which were considered as the input and output of the system, respectively. They found that, with the random impulse response, it was possible to verify whether a signature was genuine. Their database of 2000 signatures was collected from 10 individuals over a six-month period and the equal-error rate was claimed to be 5.5%.

8.2.5   Signature Verification Product Market Survey

As a new market, the automatic signature verification system is not yet popular. However, there are several small to medium companies working on delivering the solutions and systems. These products have been adopted mostly in financial, insurance and computer system securities. Among these suppliers, Communication Intelligence Corporation, PenOp Technology and Cyber-SIGN Inc. are benchmarked to be the most popular.

Communication Intelligence Corporation (CIC) scientists patented the first mechanism for capturing the biometric qualities of a handwritten signature [22]. CIC's products include "Signature Capture", "Verification" and "Document or Mail Binding". Signatures are captured along with timing elements (e.g., speed, acceleration) and sequential stroke patterns (was the "t" crossed from right to left, and did the "i" get dotted at the very end of the signing process). They called these dynamics derived from a person's muscular dexterity as "muscle memory." Recently, IBM and CIC have announced their plan to add CIC's "Jot" handwriting recognition and "WordComplete" shorthand software applications to the IBM "ThinkPad" and "WorkPad" hardware [23].

Cyber SIGN Inc. is a worldwide market and technology leader in the area of biometrics signature verification, signature capture and display [24]. Cyber-SIGN analyzes the shape, speed, stroke order, off-tablet motion, pen pressure and timing information captured during the act of signing. The data-capturing device used is a graphic tablet with a pressure sensitive pen from WACOM [25]. It distributes its system with a software development kit, which allows the users to develop their own applications.

The system distributed by DATAVISION uses a signature pad from the same company [26]. The software is integrated with a signature display program. The software is used for account management. Five signatures are used to enroll into the system, from which a template is generated. The template can be updated. The electronic representation of the signature has a size of 108 bytes in addition to an image of the signature that is stored. The software uses both representations for verification. The capabilities of the signature pad used to capture the data are not mentioned.

PenOp Technology was founded in 1990 to be the worldwide leader in electronic signature technology that enables secure *e*-commerce [27]. PenOp owns a robust and growing portfolio of intellectual property related to electronic signatures and authentication. The PenOp signature software allows signing and authenticating documents on-line. A digitizing tablet is used to capture a stamp that is based on the captured signature. With a different user verification method (password, etc.), the signature stamp can be affixed to a document with additional information concerning when and where the document was signed. The recipient can extract and verify the signature on the document. Three signatures are used to build a signature template and the template can be updated.

SQN Signature Systems is one of the largest providers of PC based signature verification systems for banks. SQN customers range from small community banks to large commercial banks. Their signature related biometrics products include "SQN Safe Deposit Management System", "SQN VERITAS", "SQN Signature Sentry" and "SQN STOP Payment System".

Gateway File Systems Inc. is a research and development company specializing in application-specific computer Web based imaging solutions. It provides SignatureTrust™ to speed up the processing of transactions involving verification of the signing agents authority [28].

The ASV Company provides a banking technology team dedicated to electronic pattern matching solutions. The solutions group focuses on the computerized verification tools that financial institutions require in their signature verification operations, such as eBank™ DISCOVERY for bank check processing [29].

The survey in this section reveals that most of the signature verification and recognition applications are targeted at the requirements for efficiency improvement in bank processing, or for enhanced security in computer systems. Most of the applications are standalone and even if there is a client-server system, the use of the network is only for the transfer and storage of signatures, and not for real-time signature data acquisition.

8.3. A Typical On-Line Signature Verification System

8.3.1 Data Acquisition

In most of the on-line signature applications, a special pen and tablet is selected for data acquisition. This hardware is used to collect various kinds of dynamic signature information, at high resolution, such as pen-tip coordinates, velocity, acceleration, pressure and angle. However, in Internet and intranet applications, asking all clients at different locations to use the same set of special pen and tablet has unavoidable limitations on availability, calibration and cost. Network response is also an important consideration. Therefore, a practical Internet and intranet application requires a simple generic pen and tablet, and a pen independent methodology for data acquisition. To acquire pressure and pen angle information would require a more expensive and specific input instrument. Furthermore, the velocity and acceleration information can be easily calculated from the pen-tip coordinates and the related time information.

Figure 8.3.   Original signature.

In this section, signature input can be captured with any commercial mouse-like pen-tablet, such as Motorola's WisePen. To register, every signer needs to sign in a registration window five times. The pen tip coordinates *(x, y)* of every digitized sample, together with its up and down status *(z)* and correlated time to previous sample *(t)*, are recorded and stored for preprocessing and feature extraction training. The sample data is shown in Expression 8-1.

$$(t_i, x_i, y_i, z_i), i = 1,..., N \qquad (8\text{-}1)$$

Figures 8.3 and 8.4 show the original signature and the x, y coordinates of the pen tip as a function of time.

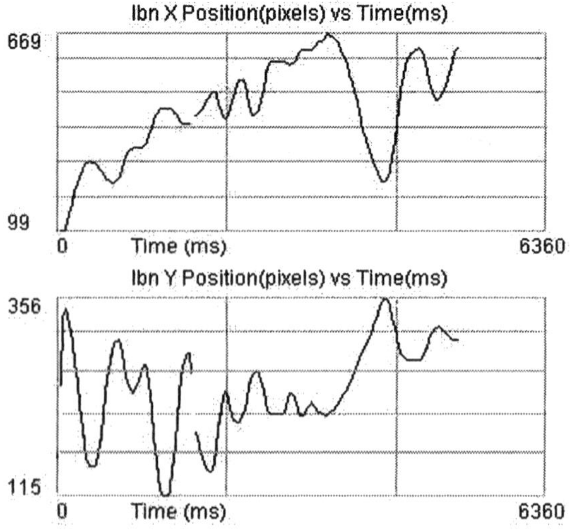

Figure 8.4.   X, Y coordinates versus time T.

There are two critical limitations of on-line signature data acquisition in a network. The first is the bandwidth limitation because the maximum data transmission speed in a public network is limited to several KBPS (Kilo bits per second) to 2 MBPS (Mega bits per second) based upon current network technology. If there is network congestion, this data transmission speed can never be consistent or guaranteed. Therefore, the server based acquisition software cannot be used because on-line signature verification requires a record of stable timing information. The second are the limitations of the client pen-tablet, the computer platform and the network browser. Each of these can vary because there are many choices in the market. Therefore, we recommend using a Java Applet, which is a platform-independent data acquisition technology. Signers using different client browses load the same applet window for signing. The sample speed only depends on the client machine instead of the server. Then, the applet sends back the processed signature information to server database.

8.3.2 Data Preprocessing

The second limitation mentioned in data acquisition, the free choice of interface (including pen-tablet, computer platform and network browser) willinduce noises into the acquired signature data. Therefore, preprocessing is an inevitable step. In order to screen out the noise that causes time stamp inconsistency, normalization preprocessing is used to re-digitize the x, y coordinates of the curve using a minimum of 20 milliseconds' time step when the pen is down (see Expression 8-2). Pen-up time is neglected because no information is available.

$$\min(t_{i+1} - t_i) = 20mS \text{, for } z_i = 1, i = 1, \ldots N \tag{8-2}$$

Smoothing preprocessing is also applied to reduce the noise of the pen-tip x, y coordinates. The smoothing preprocessing uses a moving average filter in this system, as shown in Expression 8-3.

$$\begin{cases} x_i = \dfrac{1}{3}(x_{i-1} + x_i + x_{i+1}) \\ y_i = \dfrac{1}{3}(y_{i-1} + y_i + y_{i+1}) \end{cases} \tag{8-3}$$

8.3.3 Feature Extraction and Match

There is a consensus in the on-line signature verification research area that feature extraction and classification are the most difficult parts among all the processing steps. The feature extraction process cannot be too complicated and cannot consume too much time because on-line signature verification in a network is restricted by the response requirement and network bandwidth limitations.

A multiple feature mechanism is devised. Features can be classified into two sets: global features and local features. Global features include total pen-down time, total pen-tip move, average speed, maximum speed, speed standard deviation, average acceleration, maximum acceleration and acceleration standard deviation. Global features consume less computation time, storage and transmission bandwidth, and they are useful for the top-level classification, which is applied to detect simple and random forgeries. In comparison, local features consist of detailed curvature time and coordinate information, and are especially designed to detect more sophisticated and skilled forgeries. However, they incur the major computation time and storage requirements. Now let us look into the feature extraction algorithms in detail.

- **Global Features**

For $i = 1,..., N-1$ and $z_i = 1$, we can define the following parameters.
Time between two adjacent samples: $\Delta t_i = t_{i+1} - t_i$.
Move from current sample to the next one:

$$s_i = \sqrt{(x_{i+1} - x_i)^2 + (y_{i+1} - y_i)^2}$$

Speed for each sample: $v_i = \dfrac{s_i}{\Delta t_i}$

Acceleration for each sample: $a_i = \dfrac{s_i}{\Delta t_i}$

Now we can calculate all the global features listed below.
Total Pen-Down Time:

$$T_t = \sum_{i=1}^{N-1} \Delta t_i \tag{8-4}$$

Total Pen-Tip Move:

$$S_t = \sum_{i=1}^{N-1} \Delta s_i \tag{8-5}$$

Average (Mean) Speed:

$$V_a = \frac{S_t}{T_t}$$

$$\text{(8-6)}$$

Maximum Speed:

$$V_m = \max(v_i)$$

$$\text{(8-7)}$$

Speed Standard Deviation:

$$V_s = \sqrt{\frac{\sum_{i=1}^{N-1}(v_i - V_a)^2}{N-1}}$$

$$\text{(8-8)}$$

Average (Mean Acceleration):

$$A_a = \frac{V_t}{T_t}$$

$$\text{(8-9)}$$

Maximum Acceleration:

$$A_m = \max(a_i)$$

$$\text{(8-10)}$$

Acceleration Standard Deviation:

$$A_s = \sqrt{\frac{\sum_{i=1}^{N-1}(a_i - A_a)^2}{N-1}}$$

$$\text{(8-11)}$$

- **Local Features**

Curvature information consists of local time and position features, which are designed for detecting forgeries. To abstract the time dependent curvature information from the curve, in the normalized curve of pen-tip x and y coordinates as a function of time, we select the peaks as feature points. Below, we list the detailed procedure for generating the local feature set.

Select the peaks for the feature points.For $i=1,...,N$, $j=1,...,M_x$ and $k=1,...,M_y$, we can define the feature point set based on turning points on the x and y coordinates:

$$\begin{cases} (x_j, tx_j) = (x_i, t_i) \mid \max(or)\min(x_i \mid tx_{j-1} < t_i < tx_{j+1}) \\ (y_k, ty_k) = (y_k, t_k) \mid \max(or)\min(y_k \mid ty_{k-1} < t_i < ty_{k+1}) \end{cases} \tag{8-12}$$

We then find the basic feature point, which has the biggest distance to its neighbor's points on both sides. The reason we do not select the first or the last feature point as a basic point is based on experimental findings: the edge points have bigger variation. Experimental findings also show that the points with the biggest distance to its neighboring points are also the points with least amount of noise.

For $j = 1,..., M_x$ and $k = 1,..., M_y$, we can find the basic feature point.

$$\begin{cases} (x_m, tx_m) = (x_j, tx_j) \mid \max(tx_{j+1} - tx_{j-1}) \\ (y_n, ty_n) = (y_k, ty_k) \mid \max(ty_{k+1} - ty_{k-1}) \end{cases} \tag{8-13}$$

We calculate the distance between a basic point and every feature point and record these values as feature values. Therefore for $j = 1,..., M_x$ and $k = 1,..., M_y$, we can define the feature value:

$$\begin{cases} (Dx_j, Dtx_j) = (x_j - x_m, tx_j - tx_m) \\ (Dy_k, Dty_k) = (y_k - y_n, ty_k - ty_n) \end{cases} \tag{8-14}$$

Besides the local coordinates, the local speed features are also an experimental tool to detect skilled forgeries. Local speed information includes the average speed, the maximum speed and the change of speed, such as the standard deviation.

For $j = 1,..., M_x$, $p = 1,..., P$, $k = 1,..., M_y$ and $q = 1,..., Q$, we can define the speed between adjacent feature points:

$$\begin{cases} vx_p^j = v_i^x \mid tx_j < t_i < tx_{j+1} \\ vy_q^k = v_i^y \mid ty_k < t_i < ty_{k+1} \end{cases} \tag{8-15}$$

We calculate average (Mean) speed between adjacent feature points and record these values as feature values. For $j = 1,..., M_x$ and $k = 1,..., M_y$, we can define the feature set:

$$\begin{cases} Vx_a^{\,j} = \dfrac{x_{j+1} - x_j}{tx_{j+1} - tx_j} \\[2em] Vy_a^{\,k} = \dfrac{y_{k+1} - y_k}{ty_{k+1} - ty_k} \end{cases} \qquad (8\text{-}16)$$

Next, we calculate maximum speed between adjacent feature points and record these values as feature values. For $j = 1,...,M_x$, $p = 1,...,P$, $k = 1,...,M_y$ and $q = 1,...,Q$, we can define the feature set:

$$\begin{cases} Vx_m^{\,j} = \max(|\,vx_p^{\,j}\,|) \\[1em] Vy_m^{\,k} = \max(|\,vy_q^{\,k}\,|) \end{cases} \qquad (8\text{-}17)$$

Finally, we calculate the speed's standard deviation between adjacent feature points and record these values as feature values. We can define the feature set:

$$\begin{cases} Vx_s^{\,j} = \sqrt{\dfrac{\sum\limits_{p=1}^{P-1} (vx_p^{\,j} - Vx_a^{\,j})^2}{P-1}} \\[3em] Vy_s^{\,k} = \sqrt{\dfrac{\sum\limits_{q=1}^{Q-1} (vy_q^{\,k} - Vy_a^{\,k})^2}{Q-1}} \end{cases} \qquad (8\text{-}18)$$

● **Feature Match**

There exists a mismatch between local features among the five training signatures. Such a mismatch arises from the variation between different training cases. These include a missing (existing in another case) peak point using a detection method or a missing peak by a signer as illustrated in Figure 8.5. As an unexpected result, a mismatch can affect the sequence of the feature points and result in an inaccurate or incorrect threshold set-up.

One approach used to retrieve the missing peak is by rotating the coordinates by a certain angle. After the rotation, as shown in Figure 8.6, the missing peak can be caught again. By adjusting the angle, the signing variation level can be detected. However, the best way to avoid the signer's mismatch is to let them know the importance of signing consistency during the training. The better the consistency of the signature, the stronger the resistance against possible forgery.

Mismatch on individual feature points cannot be avoided because of the natural variation in human signatures. However, we can minimize the effects of this mismatch to achieve higher verification accuracy. Compared with the previous approach to regain a missing feature, another approach is to simply neglect all of the mismatched feature points and only use the matched ones. The difficulty lies in how to judge whether a point is a mismatched case or simply a matched case affected by a time shift. Another way is to use several matching sequences and then find the best one that shows the least variation. It is not difficult to realize this approach, although it does not guarantee that a 100% match can be achieved. This **approach is called** a scan match and it is illustrated in Figure 8.7.

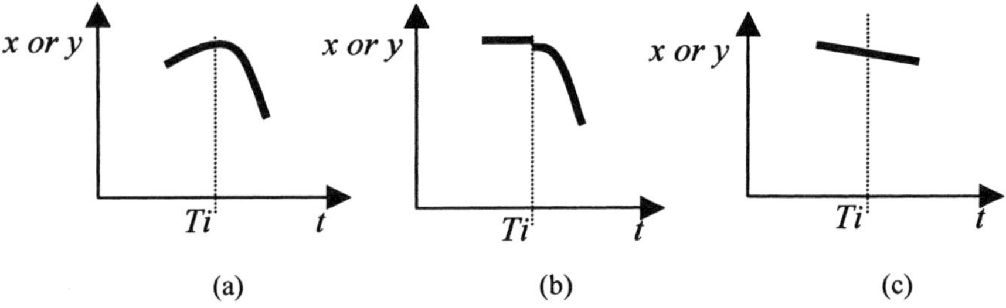

(a) Training #K (K=1...5) has a peak at *Ti*.   (b) (c) Training #L (L=1...5) has no peak at *Ti*.
Figure 8.5.   Missing peak by detection.

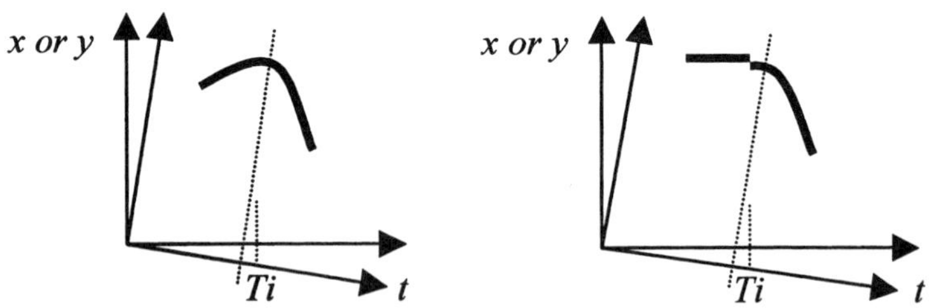

Figure 8.6.   Missing peak detected by rotation.

Referring to Figure 8.7, first in the top-level (level 1) scan, we scan the feature sequence from left to right, followed by a right to left scan, for all five training signatures simultaneously. We calculate and record the biggest variation among all the feature values for these five training signatures. Next, we scan from the middle to both ends and from both ends to the middle (level 2). We do the same calculations as we did for level 1. In the third level scan, we split the scan route into four, and start from the middle, both ends and quarter of the total distance from both ends. We do the calculations again. If we stop here, we can simply pick a route that has the smallest variation among all the features.

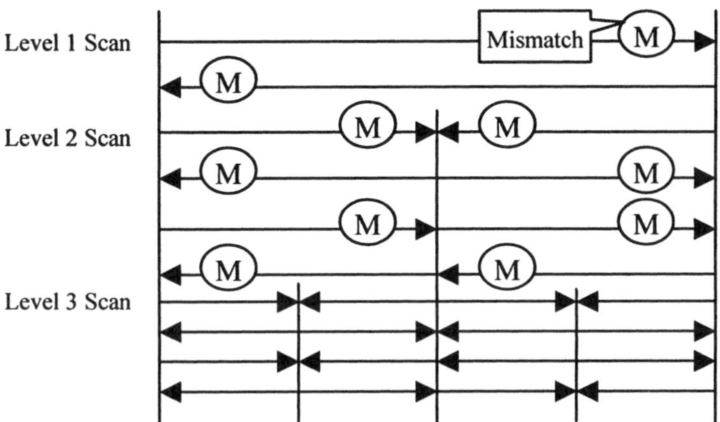

Figure 8.7. Scan for Feature Match.

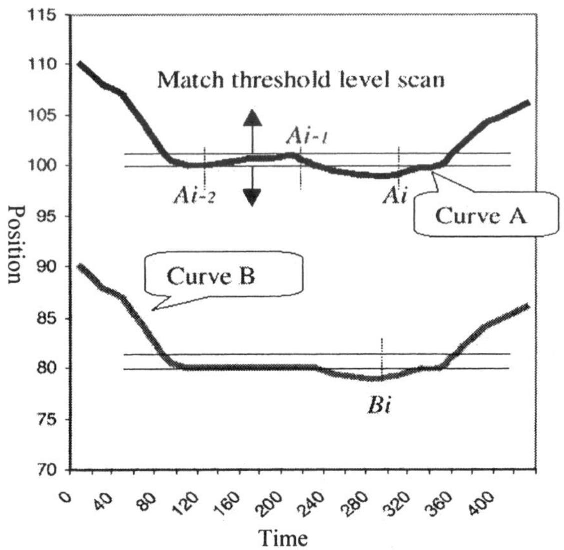

Figure 8.8. Illustration of the match threshold level scan for feature match.

Obviously, the above approach involves a great number of calculations and comparisons, which may become a burden in the on-line application. Another approach with a lower computation requirement is to scan the threshold level sensitivity for match, to smooth the curvature until the smallest mismatch is reached. As illustrated in Figure 8.8, curve A and curve B are mismatched, with A_i, A_{i-1}, A_{i-2} and B_i denoting feature points. Peak

A_i and A_{i-1} can be caused by noise. The level of sensitivity used in the match threshold level scan is enlarged until A_i and A_{i-1} are not considered to be peaks. Therefore by level scan, we are going to find a minimum difference in the number of feature points among all five training signatures.

- **Enrollment**

After the features have been abstracted and matched, thresholds need to be determined for each feature set. For the verification process, thresholds are used to set the limit for determining whether the incoming signature is genuine or a forgery. For the recognition process, the threshold is set to the gate of the minimum feature distance for determining whether the incoming signature belongs to a registered signer. Therefore, the thresholds for the verification process depend on the training signatures and vary by signer, but there is only one threshold, which is determined by the experiments, for the recognition process.

(1) Threshold Enrollment

We define the range of the feature values for each correlated feature point from the five signatures. If feature F stands for Dx, Dtx, Dy or Dty, we have the range R (see Expression 8-19) after the subtraction of maximum and minimum values, where $j=1...M$ is the sequence of feature and $i=1...5$ is the sequence of the five training signatures. For global features, M should be eight, while for local features M depends on the number of peaks after the feature match.

$$R_j = \max(F_j^i) - \min(F_j^i) \qquad (8\text{-}19)$$

Next, we determine the threshold by multiplying the range by a threshold factor K for later verifications. K is to be adjusted by each verification system according to the experimental results. For minimum storage and transfer, only TH_j is required:

$$TH_j = k \bullet R_j \qquad (8\text{-}20)$$

Figure 8.8 illustrates the thresholds for global features and local features. LTH and UTH denote the lower threshold and upper threshold. The all zero crossing point is the (so-called) basic feature point. It may be noticed that, for some feature points, the thresholds are too loose because noise and variation remains in the training signatures after they have gone through the normalization, smoothing and matching process.

(2) Averaging and Indexing Enrollment

We define the average of the feature values for each correlated feature point from the five signatures. For $j=1...M$ and $i=1...5$, we have the feature average calculated and enrolled for future recognition:

$$A_j = \frac{\sum_{i=1}^{5} F_j^i}{5} \tag{8-21}$$

Enroll the index of all the registered signers in the database that is linked to each signer's own signature feature sets.

- **Comparison for Verification**

As shown in Figure 8.9, if the features of an incoming test signature are within the threshold range, the signature is considered to be genuine; otherwise, it is rejected as a forgery. As presented in the threshold calculations above, the threshold factor K is adapted by the system to adjust the tightness or looseness of the range. Since there are different levels of noise and variation in data acquisition for training and verification processes, one or several errors should be allowed in the comparison. Such errors cannot be avoided by adjusting K. The criteria used for how many feature points can be allowed outside of the threshold range depends on the design requirements of an individual system.

8.4. Proposed On-Line Dynamic Signature Verification Applications

8.4.1 System Password Authentication

On-line signature verification provides a brand new and reliable method for system password authentication. Actually, this is not a completely new idea because there have been several proposals and systems in this field. For example, George S.K. Fung, Rynson W.H. Lau and James N.K. Liu proposed a novel signature based password authentication system [21]. Their approach comprised five processes: signature data acquisition and feature extraction, discretization, feature selection, password encoding process, and password comparison and evaluation. The survey in Section 8.2 also presents several applications in this market. However, it is definitely a new methodology is the user is able to login using on-line signature recognition without requiring a user name.

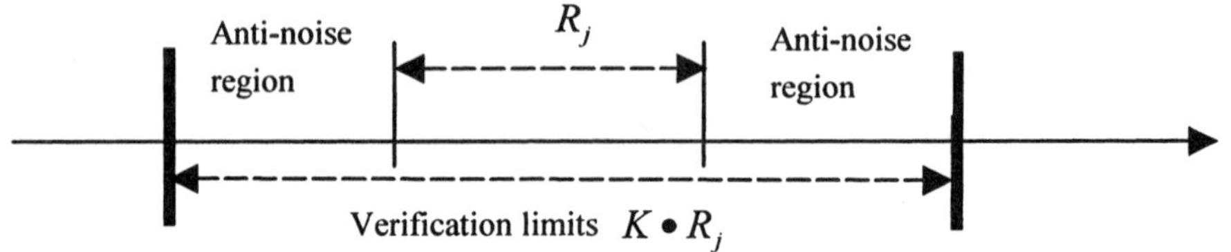

Figure 8.9.   Threshold used for the verification process.

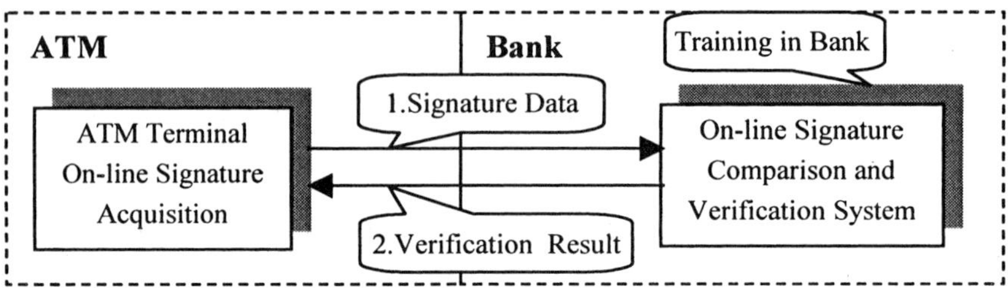

Figure 8.10.   On-line Signature Verification Scheme for ATM application.

8.4.2   ATM Application

On-line signature verification can be very useful in the ATM application
to achieve better security in transactions. Figure 8.10 shows the process of
such an application.

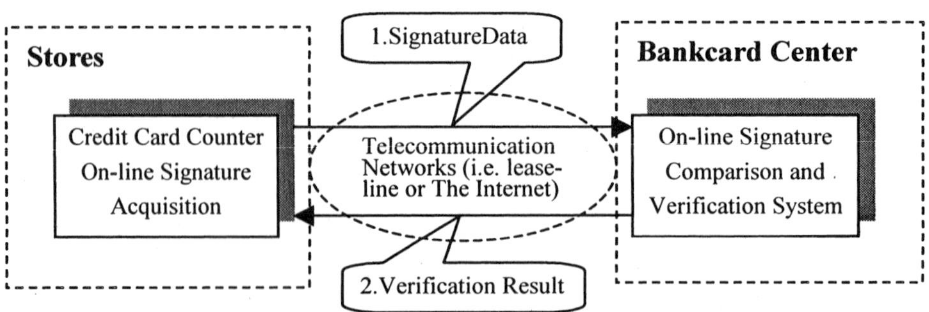

Figure 8.11.   On-line Signature Verification Scheme for On-site Credit Card Check.

8.4.3   On-site Credit Card Verification

To prevent the use of stolen or fake credit cards, an on-line signature based credit card verification system is proposed (as shown in Figure 8.11), because the dynamic signing features of a person are more difficult to trace or fake. In such an application, smart card technology can be used as well.

8.4.4   Internet *E*-commerce Application

As discussed above, the fast growing area of *e*-commence is affected by Internet security issues in personal identification especially credit card verification where the number of cases of illegal useof credit cards information is rising with the growth of *e*-commerce. Therefore, a Web-based on-line signature verification system via the Internet and intranet is proposed in this chapter to provide a higher level of security in personal identification for *e*-commerce. As a security enhancement, a combination of traditional character-based password and dynamic signature verification can be applied. Public key based digital signatures are also an important personal information protection method in such network security.

Figure 8.12 shows one interpretation of such a system. If we define a trade transaction as a process, the pre-process, such as pre-trade registration and agreement, should be performed first. These include the following necessary steps.

- **Pre-process: (see Figure 8.12 a)**
    1. The standards and contracts of the signature verification approaches are agreed among all parties - card center, Internet store and cardholder.
    2. The Internet store enrolls and acquires the access to the bankcard center server.
    3. The cardholder enrolls in the bankcard center server by training and storing her/his dynamic signature information in the server database.
    4. The cardholder registers herself/himself in the Internet store.
    5. As an enhancement, the cardholder may require a traditional password as well. After the successful pre-process, the Internet trade transaction can be performed.

- **Process: (see Figure 8.12 b)**
    1. The cardholder inputs an order into the store server.
    2. The cardholder inputs card information into the store server.
    3. The store sends the signing window using a Java applet to the cardholder.
    4. The cardholder signs on the window of his browser.

5. The Java applet sends the captured signature to the card center.

6. The card center routes confirmation or rejection information to the cardholder.

7. The card center routes the confirmation or rejection information to the store as well.

8. The store accepts or rejects the order based on the signature verification result.

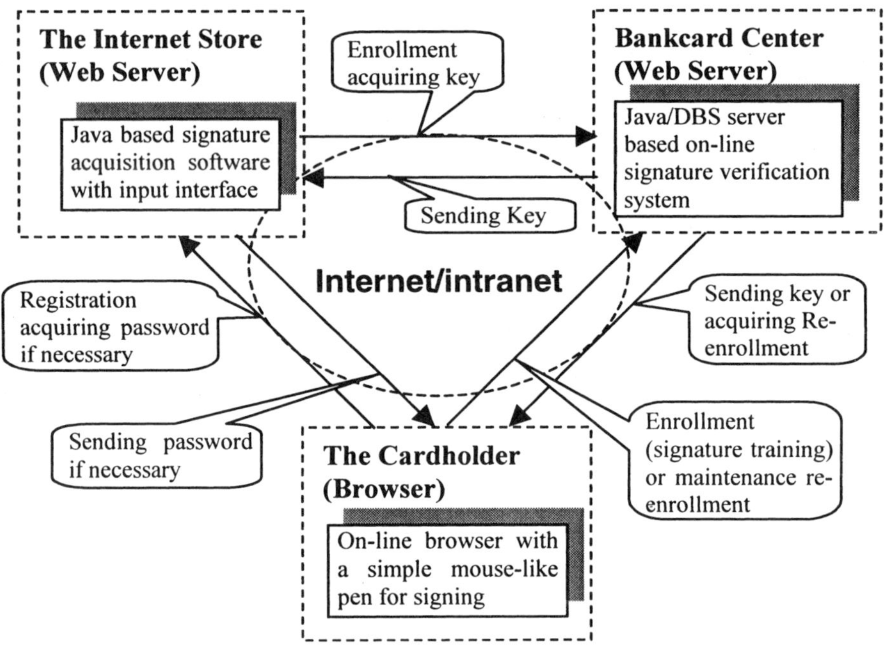

(a) Pre-process and Maintenance.

Figure 8.12.   (cont).

As a means of security maintenance, many password-protected systems have the common practice that obliges users to change their password regularly, for example once per quarter. A similar practice may be applied to the dynamic signature verification system. This is not only because the signature information might be stolen, but also the signing behavior of the user may change slightly over time. Therefore, regular re-enrollment into the bankcard server database cannot be avoided.

The other issue is the network security itself. Every transaction in the above system must use an encryption method to prevent the personal data from been intercepted by criminals. The popular public-key based digital signature encryption methods can be applied (we do not discuss the details of digital signatures in this chapter).

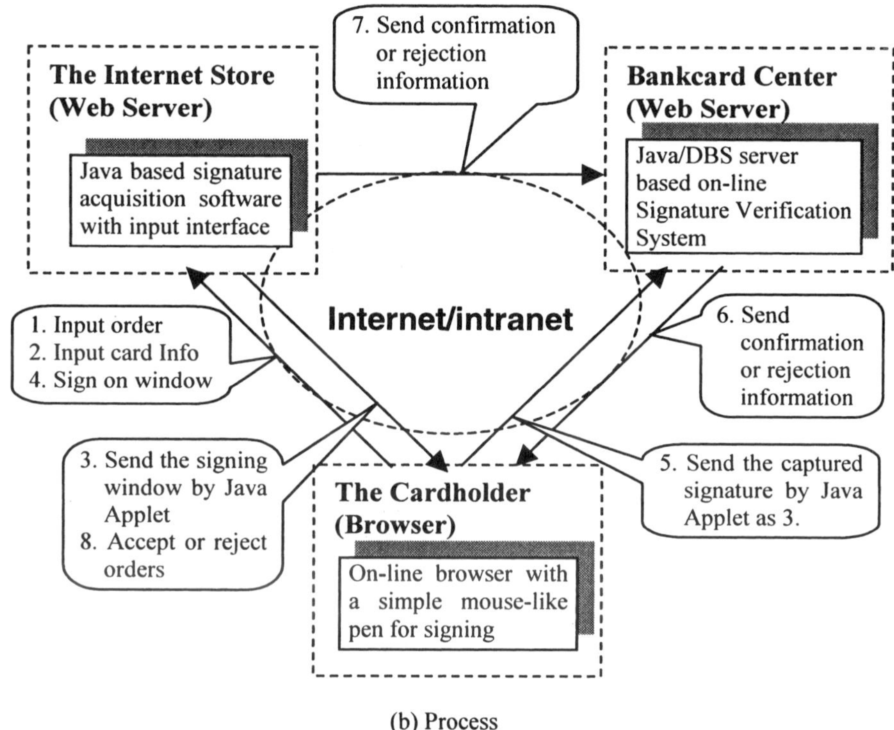

Figure 8.12. Proposed signature verification application for *E*-commerce.

In the applications market, it is not difficult to find products that are based on automatic signature verification, but most of these are standalone systems. In other words, the signer and the verification system execute on the same hardware. With the dramatic growth of the Internet, these applications are not suitable for *e*-commerce where a customer and supplier are located in different places.

However, the above system for Internet commerce would be able to deal with geographically separate customers and suppliers. There are a lot of advantages in such a system that uses technology such as Java applet, CGI (Common Gateway Interface), Java Servlets, JDBC (Java Database Connectivity), a DBMS (database management system) and the Internet. Different customers can use different input interfaces such as pen, mouse or touch screen, for signing, provided he/she can keep on using this tool after their signature is recorded in the signature server. Internet stores can serve customers worldwide without worrying about the correctness of the credit card information. Such a system can be ported and installed on any Internet server and run on any popular browsers that support Java, such as NS (Netscape) Communicator 4 or MS (Microsoft) Internet Explorer 5.

However, there is still an unsolved issue: security in the Internet. This is a side topic that we believe will be either balanced with Internet business demands or settled in the near future.

8.5.　　Conclusions

With the development and popularization of the network, signature verification in *e*-commerce has become a hot topic. This chapter has introduced recent progress in automatic signature verification research. Because of the limitations of the application of signature verification in Internet or intranet, some complex methods, such as Hidden Markov Models and Artificial Neural Networks, and some new capture devices cannot be used. A low cost on-line signature verification system that uses only conventional mathematical methods and a common writing tablet has been introduced in detail. Lastly, several application approaches for on-line signature verification systems are presented. This chapter foresees the great potential of signature verification in the Internet, such as in Internet commerce.

With the vigorous growth of computing and networking technology, the application of automatic signature verification will become increasingly accepted in the real world.

References

[1]　R. Plamondon and G. Lorette. Automatic Signature Verification and Writer Identification – The State of the Art, Pattern Recognition, 22, 2 (1989) 107-131, 1989.

[2]　F. Leclerc and R. Plamondon. Automatic Signature Verification: The State of the Art – 1989-1993, Progress in Automatic Signature Verification, Singapore: World Scientific, pages 3-20, 1994.

[3]　Giuseppe Pirlo. Algorithms for Signature Verification, Fundamentals in Handwriting Recognition. In Proc. of the NATO Advanced Study Institute on Fundamentals in Handwriting Recognition, France: Springer-Verlag, pages 435-455, 1993.

[4]　Vishvjit S. Nalwa. Automatic On-line Signature Verification. In Proc. of The IEEE, vol. 85, no. 2, pages 215-239, February 1997.

[5]　Rejean Plamondon and Sargur N. Srihari. On-line and Off-line Handwriting Recognition: A Comprehensive Survey, IEEE Transactions on Pattern Analysis and Machine Intelligence, vol. 22, no. 1, January 2000.

[6]   Friederike Dorothea Griess, Project Report: On-line Signature Verification, Michigan State University Department of Computer Science and Engineering, May 2000.

[7]   Winston Nelson, William Turin and Trevor Hastie. Statistical Methods for On-line Signature Verification, Progress in Automatic Signature Verification, Singapore: World Scientific, pages 109-130, 1994.

[8]   Ronny Martens and Luc Claesen. On-line Signature Verification: Discrimination Emphasised. In Proc. of ICDAR, Ulm, IEEE 1997.

[9]   Y.J. Bae and M.C. Fairhurst. Parallelism in Dynamic Time Warping for Automatic Signature Verification. In Proc. of ICDAR, Ulm, IEEE, 1995.

[10]   Ronny Martens and Luc Claesen. On-line Signature Verification by Dynamic Time Warping. In Proc. of 13th International Conference on Pattern Recognition, 1015-4651/96, 1996.

[11]   Ronny Martens and Luc Claesen. Dynamic Programming Optimization for On-line Signature Verification. In Proc. of 4th ICDAR '97. 0-8186-7898-4/97, 1997.

[12]   Mark J. Paulik, N. Mohankrishnan and Micheal Mikiforuk. A Time Varying Vector Autoregressive Model for Signature Verification. In Proc. of The IEEE, 0-7803-2428-5/95, 1995.

[13]   Brigitte Wirtz. Stroke-Based Time Warping for Signature Verification. In Proc. of ICDAR, Ulm, IEEE 1995.

[14]   L.R. Rabiner and B.H. Juang. An Introduction to Hidden Markov Models, IEEE ASSP Magazine, pages 4-16, 1986.

[15]   L. Yang et al. Application of Hidden Markov Model for Signature Verification, Pattern Recognition, vol .28, no. 2, pages 161-170, 1995.

[16]   R.S. Kashi, J. Hu and W. L. Nelson. (Bell Labs, Lucent Technologies), On- line Handwritten Signature Verification using Hidden Markov Model Features, In Proc. of ICDAR, Ulm, IEEE 1997.

[17]   J.G.A. Dolfing, E.H.L. Aarts, van Oosterhout and J.J.G.M.. On-line Signature Verification with Hidden Markov Models. In Proc. of 14th International Conference on Pattern Recognition, 1998.

[18]   Luan Ling Lee. Neural Approaches for Human Signature Verification. In Proc. of ICDAR, Ulm, IEEE 1995. 3rd International Conference on Signal Processing, 1996.

[19]   N. Mohankrishnan, W.S. Lee and M.J. Paulik. Multi-Layer Neural Network Classification of On-line Signatures, IEEE 39th Midwest symposium on Circuits and Systems, 1996.

[20]   T. Matsuura and H. Sakai. On Stochastic System Representation of Handwriting Process and Its Application to Signature Verification, 3rd International Conference on Signal Processing, 1996.

[21]   G.S.K. Fung, R.W.H. Lau, and J.N.K. Liu. A Signature Based Password Authentication Method. In Proc. of 1997 IEEE International Conference of System, Man and Cybernetic, pages 631-636, October 1997.

[22]   http://www.cic.com/

[23]   http://www.newsfactor.com

[24]   http://www.cybersign.com/

[25]   http://www.wacom.com/

[26]   http://www.datavisionimage.com/

[27]   http://www.sqnsigs.com/

[28]   http://www.gwfs.bc.ca/

[29]   http://www.thediscovery.net/

Chapter 9

WEB GUARD: A BIOMETRICS IDENTIFICATION SYSTEM FOR NETWORK SECURITY

Jane You and David Zhang

Department of Computing

The Hong Kong Polytechnic University, Kowloon, Hong Kong

{csyjia, csdzhang}@comp.polyu.edu.hk

Abstract　　With the fast development of E-commerce, there is an immediate need for an efficient and effective personal identification and verification system for the security of network access. To overcome the limitations of the current existing password-based authentication services on the Internet, we apply biometrics computing technology to achieve high performance. To tackle the challenge of the integration of multiple biometrics features within a single platform to satisfy the requirements of various identification purposes, we introduce a new approach to personal identification with multimodal biometrics and data warehousing techniques. In contrast to the existing systems which employ a fixed mechanism for data representation and similarity measurement, we extend the concepts of conventional data warehouse and biometrics database to biometrics data warehouse for effective data representation and storage. In addition, we propose a fuzzy neural network to provide automatic and autonomous classification for the verification and identification outputs by integrating fuzzy logic technology and the Back Propagation Feed Forward (BPFF) neural network. To increase the speed and flexibility of the process, we use mobile agents as the steering tool for parallel processing in a distributed environment, which includes hierarchical biometric feature representation, multiple feature integration, dynamic biometric data indexing and flexible search. An agent development tool named "Aglet" is used as a programming framework to illustrate the combination of multiple biometrics features in a hierarchical structure for fast and reliable identity verification and identification. The experimental results demonstrate the feasibility of the proposed approach to network security with *e*Commerce applications.

Keywords:　　Personal identification, biometrics computing, data warehousing, feature extraction and indexing, fuzzy neural network, mobile agent, parallel processing, distributed computing

9.1.   Introduction

The rapid growth of the Internet and the World Wide Web has stimulated the emergence of electronic commerce. The global economic forces have created an environment that fosters electronic commerce. The technology advances in computer industry have led to the fast development of *E*-commerce applications. Nowadays, *E*-commerce is playing an important role in reducing costs, improving product quality, reaching new customers or suppliers, and creating new ways of selling existing products. Such a rapid growing *E*-commerce environment involves communication, business transaction, service and on-line processing [16]. According to [23], *E*-commerce is characterized as an interdisciplinary area which covers a wide range of issues including security, trust, law, payment mechanisms, advertisement, on-line catalogs, multimedia shopping experiences and intermediaries. However, a significant barrier to effective exploitation of these web-based business activities has been created by the lack of powerful authentication techniques. The wide *E*-commerce applications require high security with reliable identification and verification of users who access to the services. The process of identifying and/or verifying a user's identity is known as authentication. However, the traditional security measures such as passwords, PIN (Personal Identification Number) and ID cards hardly satisfy the high security requirements because the use of passwords, PINs and ID cards are very insecure – they can be lost, stolen, forged or forgotten. More importantly, the password-based methods would become powerless on computer networks, especially the Internet, where attackers can monitor network traffic and intercept passwords or PINs. The incident of invasion to the information system of USA Defense Ministry is one example of such failures. Therefore, there is an urgent need to authenticate individuals in various domains in today's automated, geographically mobile, increasingly electronically wired information society [13].

Biometric technology provides a totally new and yet effective solution to effective authentication, which would change the conventional security and access control systems by recognising individuals based on their unique, reliable and stable biological or behavioral characteristics, such as fingerprints, palmprints, iris patterns, facial features, speech patterns and handwriting styles. This new security technique overcomes many of the limitations of the traditional automatic personal identification technologies [22].

The ultimate goal of developing a personal identity verification system is to achieve the best possible performance in terms of accuracy, efficiency and cost. With the prices of biometrics sensors continue to fall, it is widely believed that biometrics will become a significant component of the identification technology. A biometric system uses one or more sensors to acquire a sample of a physical or behaviour characteristic of someone to be identified and then classifies the sample in some unique way and compares it with the information about the individual or a related group of people in a database. Both biometric verification and biometric identification techniques will be used. In the verification process, biometric data are obtained from a person under identification and compared to stored data for the actual person to answer the question "Am I whom I claim I am?". On the other hand, biometric identification intends to answer the question "Who am I?" by reading a person's biometric characteristics and trying to find a match from data stored for hundreds or even thousands of validated persons.

How to achieve high performance for personal identification from a large collection of biometric data remains a challenging task. In general, the design of such an automated biometric system involves biometric data acquisition, data representation, feature extraction, matching, classification and evaluation. Although the recent advances in computer technology have made it possible for industry to develop affordable automated biometrics identification and verification systems, these systems are based on single biometric and application oriented. Therefore, they are not able to meet the general practical requirements including variations, distortions and noise. Recent studies show that the fusion of multiple sources of evidence would improve the system performance and increase the robustness of verification. Consequently, it is desirable to utilise and integrate multiple biometric features to improve system accuracy and efficiency. However, a comprehensive integrated and fully automatic biometric verification and identification system has not yet been fully exploited.

To meet the challenge and immediate need for a high performance Internet authentication service to secure Internet-based E-commerce applications and overcome the limitations of the current existing password-based authentication services on the Internet, we apply biometrics computing technology to achieve fast and reliable personal identification. Considering the reliability and convenience of biometric data collection from users, eight biometric features, *i.e..* fingerprints, palm-prints, hand geometry, iris, ear, face, signature and voice are considered in our proposed multimodal system. We adopt a dynamic feature selection scheme for the application-oriented authentication tasks. In other words, the user will determine the level of authentication – either single feature based by using individual features such as fingerprints, palm-prints, hand geometry, iris, ear, face, signature and voice; or multiple feature based by integrating multiple features in a hierarchical structure for coarse-to-fine matching. Thus, the rapid growth in the size and diversity of online biometric information systems will have a great impact on network security.

It is noted that most of the existing techniques for biometrics information processing are based on the use of conventional database structures to handle large collections of high-dimensional biometric data. Although the recent research on multimedia database systems [10], [17], [27] has made advances in creation of large multimedia databases with effective facilities for query processing, it is mainly focused on data modeling and structuring. Object-oriented models have the capacity for retrieving one or more media samples by satisfying a particular set of conditions, however, when faced with large quantities of data that are stored at a low level of information granularity, they can be very slow. Although the application of knowledge discovery techniques to relational databases has made it possible for biometric data mining, it is difficult to integrate multiple biometrics features for flexible indexing and dynamic search.

Recently the combination of data mining and data warehousing has emerged as an innovative and totally new approach to information management [5], [9]. Data mining provides the capacity for the discovery of hidden knowledge, unexpected patterns and new rules from large databases. A data warehouse is not only a central store of data that has been extracted from operational data, it also contains the process managers that make information available, enabling users to make informed decisions [3]. In other words, data warehousing is concerned with summation, reduction and transformation of data and storing it in a materialized relation available for direct querying. Therefore, it can speed up queries by using a materialized view, and deal with noisy and incomplete data. Consequently, with a data warehouse, we will have clean data, complete data and carry out data reduction and summarization for fast querying with knowledge discovery. Although there have been many successful data mining and data warehousing systems, little has been done on date warehousing and mining for image database for biometrics information systems.

Based on a comprehensive study of the requirements, existing techniques and problems for biometrics based personal identification, we propose a multimedia data warehouse structure to facilitate flexible indexing, dynamic querying processing and hierarchical searching for biometric information retrieval and identification. The proposed data warehousing model allows users to integrate multiple biometric data streams in a top-down manner. Instead of using a fixed similarity measure to search for the best match, we adopted a dynamic scheme which generates the matching criteria in accordance with the type of query, the selection of a feature, and the level of the search. More specifically, the proposed algorithms include: 1) to extend the concepts of a conventional data warehouse and a multimedia database to multimedia data warehouses for effective data representation and storage; 2) to develop a multimedia starflake schema to integrate multiple data streams for hierarchical data representation and indexing; 3) to introduce a dynamic similarity measurement scheme based on statistical feature selection criteria; 4) to apply data aggregation techniques for decision support to speed up query processing and searching procedures; 5) to use fuzzy neural network for data classification. In addition, the new system architecture is implemented by using mobile agents in a distributed computing environment, which can simultaneously extract useful biometrics information from different data collection sources on the network with flexibility. Furthermore, a case study is presented to illustrate the feasibility of the proposed approach to biometrics based network security.

This chapter is organized as follows. Section 9.2 outlines the proposed concept of a biometrics data warehouse for dynamic data indexing. The use of statistical feature selection criteria for hierarchical search and fast query processing is described in Section 9.3 and Section 9.4 respectively. The generation of a fuzzy neural network for data classification is summarized in Section 9.5. Section 9.6 briefly summarises the mobile agent techniques for parallelism in a distributed environment. A case study of multiple biometrics system for web-based personal identification is highlightened in Section 9.7. Finally, Section 9.8 presents our conclusions and proposals for future work.

9.2.   Biometrics Data Warehouse

Data warehouse is viewed as a technology which not only functions as a data superstore, but also processes data to create a data warehouse, operational data store, or data mart stored on traditional servers, Intranet servers, or Internet servers. In other words, data warehouses are not just large databases; they are large, complex environments that integrate many technologies. A major gain of using a data warehouse consists of being able to store data at different levels of granularity along different dimensions such as data type, time, etc. Thus, they require a lot of maintenance and management.

Developing a data warehouse is similar to other software projects. Schema was initially used in database design. It is a representation of a database, which gives semantics to the data to model the database. In relational databases, there are two types of schema – conceptual schema and logical schema. A conceptual schema often refers to an entity-relationship diagram, and logical schema represents the structure and connection of the relational tables. In object-oriented databases, conceptual models are usually used. A schema is also adopted to construct a data warehouse. Facts and dimensions are two basic concepts related to data warehouse schema.

Although the concept of data warehouse originated from the traditional business information systems, it can be extended to biometrics information systems. In this chapter, we focus on the establishment of a biometrics data warehouse for web-based personal identification for network security. The description of an individual's identity is regarded as fact data in a biometrics data warehouse, and multiple biometric features constitute dimension data. For a general description of an individual, fingerprints, palmprints, hand geometries, face, iris, ear, signature, voice and so on are considered as dimension data, where each individual biometric feature can be further represented by its own basic components. For example, fingerprints consist of four basic features such as global ridge pattern distribution (fingerprint class), local ridge patterns, fingerprint minutiae (ridge endings and bifurcations) and other salient points (core and delta points). Figure 9.1 demonstrates these basic features for fingerprint representation, and Figure 9.2 illustrates a snow-flake star schema which shows the relationship between fact data and dimension data, where the center table represents the fact table (individual's identity) and the surrounding (reference) tables are dimension tables (**individual's biometric features**).

Figure 9.1.   Basic features for fingerprint representation.

It is noted that in real life, it may be difficult to restructure all the components within the biometrics data model into a set of distinct dimensions. In other words, there are situations where there are several components or relationships that span one or more dimensions. To more effectively represent data, the starflake schema allows a degree of crossover between dimensions. In our proposed system, the fact table defines seven major data streams of the multiple biometric content, namely face, fingerprints, palmprints, hand geometry, iris, signature and voice. Note the fields in the dimension table for palmprints are the features that describe the content of a palmprint image. Each of the sequences in the starflake schema corresponds to a relational table. Table 9.1 is a typical image dimension table for palmprint description. For other biometrics data streams such as face, fingerprint, hand geometry, iris, signature and voice, the corresponding dimension tables can be constrctured in a similar way.

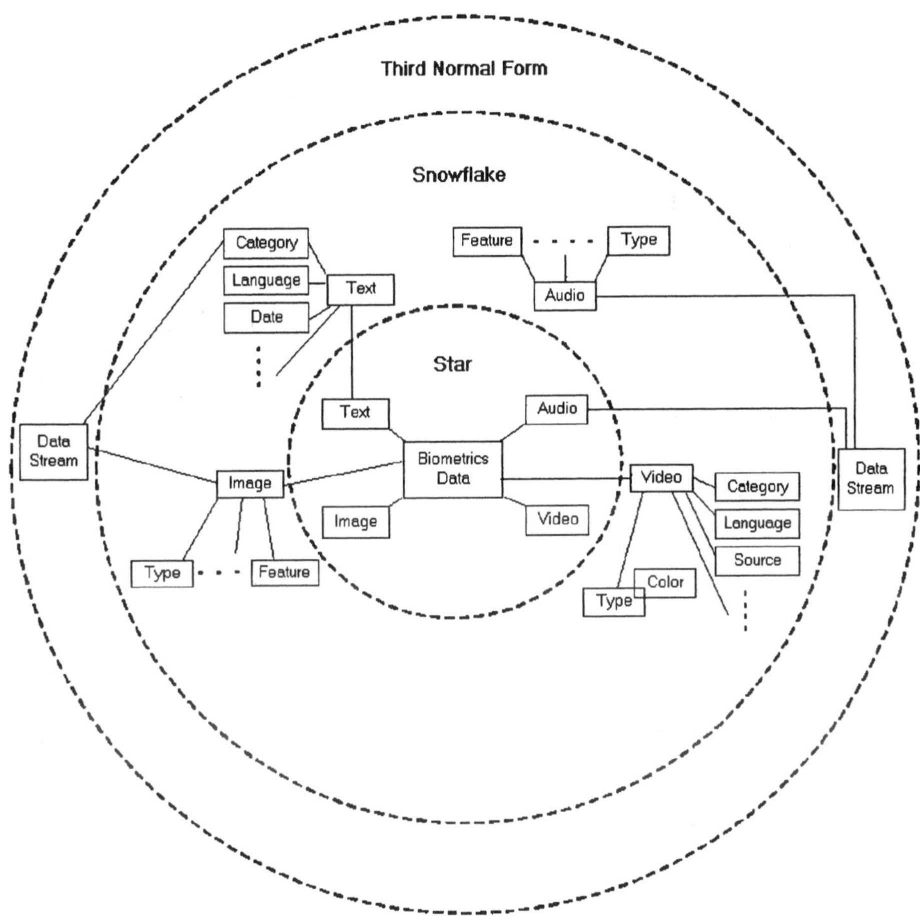

Figure 9.2.   A snow-flake star schema for biometrics based identity representation.

Table 9.1.   The major fields used for palmprint dimension table.

Category	Age Group	Gender	Location	Feature	Date
White	elderly	male	continent	color	year
Asian	adult & female	country	X-ray	texture	month
African	child		region	shape	day
others			city	lines	
			district	feature points	

To facilitate the management and decision support for the data warehouse, the above starflake schema, which uses a combination of denormalized star and normalized snowflake schemas, is adopted. In these cases, a series of combinatory database views is created in order to allow user access tools to treat the fact table partitions as a single, large table for fast information retrieval. In addition, key reference data is structured into a set of dimensions, which are referenced from the fact table. Each dimension is stored in a series of normalized tables (snowflake), with an additional denormalized star dimension table. The following summarizes the major features of the proposed data structure:

- Support multiple biometrics data streams by different dimensions,

- Represent biometrics data in a hierarchical structure by normalized snow-flake schemas at different levels.

- Integrate multiple biometrics features by crossover between dimensions.

- Speed up biometrics data query and manipulation processing by data partitioning.

9.3.   Dynamic Feature Selection

Feature extraction is a key issue for identity verification and identification. It is very difficult, if not impossible, to use one feature model for pattern matching with high performance in terms of accuracy, efficiency and robustness. Although the research reported in [7] resulted in a more reliable approach to palmprint feature point detection than the line matching algorithm detailed in [28], the issues of efficiency and robustness remain untackled. The technique detailed in [7] involves one-to-one feature point based image matching, which requires high computation resource for a large palmprint database. In addition, the matching lacks flexibility because only one similarity measurement is applied. To speed up the search process for the best match with reliable features and flexible matching criteria, we introduce a statistically based feature selection scheme to rank different features for dynamic feature selection and flexible similarity measurement. Instead of using a fixed feature extraction mechanism and a single matching criterion as in [7], [28], we extend a statistical approach to select and integrate the most relevant features to generate a decision tree for a hierarchical search.

The use of a feature selection criterion to determine the ranking of the input attributes was initially proposed by Carter and Catlett in 1987 [4]. Recently feature selection criteria based on statistical measures have been extensively studied. These statistically based criteria include the Chi-square criterion, Asymmetrical Tau and Symmetrical Tau [29]. A comprehensive description and comparison of these criteria is given in [21]. Chi-square statistic provides a test of significance with regard to the independence between variables, however, it does not give a measure of the degree of association between the variables. Goodman and Kruskal proposed their measure of association, the Asymmetrical Tau [12], to overcome the limitations of the Chi-square criterion for cross-classification tasks in the statistical area. The Asymmetrical Tau is a measure of the relative usefulness of one variable in improving the ability to predict the classifications of members of the population with respect to a second variable. Nevertheless, when this approach was used directly as a feature selection criterion for constructing decision trees, it tended to favor features with more values. To improve this approach, Zhou and Dillon defined their Symmetrical Tau criterion [29] by combining a proportional-reduction-in-error (PRE) measure and a cost-complexity heuristic to obtain a balanced statistical-heuristic criterion for building multi-branching decision trees. According to Zhou and Dillon [29], the Tau criterion has a number of major merits:

- It is a measure of association and has a built-in statistical strength to cope with noise.

- Dynamic error estimation conveys potential uncertainties in classification and is crucial for probabilistic decision tree induction.

- Tau processes multi-valued features fairly. There is no bias favoring features with many or few values. This improvement is not at a cost of computational efficiency.

- The Tau criterion is not proportional to the sample size and its proportional-reduction-in-error (PRE) nature makes it not only a stepwise measure of different features' abilities, but also an overall measure of a particular feature's sequential variation in predictive ability. This provides a basis for deleting the features that have become less useful for prediction and helps to prevent splitting when no useful feature remains.

- The criterion has a middle cut tendency that separates a node into two balanced subsets.

- It is able to deal with Boolean combinations of logical features.

It should be pointed out that all of the approaches discussed above originated from research in the area of machine learning and employ a top-down, divide-and-conquer strategy to represent the acquired knowledge as decision trees. The proposed criteria focus on the examination of individual features for classification. They have been used in many applications such as pattern recognition, taxonomy, switching theory, databases, machine diagnosis and decision table programming. However, these individual feature based methods are not suitable for visual information system because of the complexity of image data. In general, to process a match, the system gives each sample a relevance score in terms of the given similarity measure, and search for the candidate with the best similarity measure. Although there are searches on limited domains where one image feature or model may always be the best, in general, the one-feature solution will be too brittle, and an integration of multiple features or models will give the better performance. We extend the use of the Symmetrical Tau criterion to guide the selection and integration of the appropriate features from multiple biometrics features for similar palmprint pattern grouping. The major steps are summarized as below:

- Step 1: Identify all of the individual features to be used for retrieval and obtain their feature vectors. For n features f_i ($i = 0, 1, ..., n - 1$), there will be n individual feature vectors v_i ($i = 0, 1, ..., n - 1$).

- Step 2: Apply Gaussian normalization to the above feature vectors.

- Step 3: Initialize a set of weights α_i ($i = 0, 1, ..., n - 1$) and obtain the corresponding combined feature vector $v_c = \sum_{i=0}^{n-1} \alpha_i v_i$.

- Step 4: Calculate the corresponding Symmetrical Tau using the following formula [29]:

$$Tau = \frac{\sum_{j=1}^{J} \sum_{i=1}^{I} \frac{P(ij)^2}{P(+j)} + \sum_{i=1}^{I} \sum_{j=1}^{J} \frac{P(ij)^2}{P(i+)} - \sum_{i=1}^{I} P(i+)^2 - \sum_{j=1}^{J} P(+j)^2}{2 - \sum_{i=1}^{I} P(i+)^2 - \sum_{j=1}^{J} P(+j)^2} \tag{9.1}$$

where

  - the contingency table has I rows and J columns;
  - $P(ij)$: probability that a variable belongs both to row i category and to column category j;
  - P(i+) and P(+j) are the marginal probabilities in row category i and column category j, respectively.

- Step 5: Adjust the set of weights, obtain a new combined feature vector v'_c and calculate the corresponding Tau.

- Step 6: Repeat Step 5 for all of the given adjustment weight sets.

- Step 7: Find the maximum value of Tau from the sequences of Tau obtained in the previous stage.

- Step 8: Choose the combined feature with the maximum Tau value.

9.4. Hierarchical Search

To avoid a blind search for the best fit between the queried media data and all of the sample patterns stored in the multimedia data warehouse, a guided search strategy is essential to reduce the computational burden. In conventional data warehouses, various methods of partitioning have been developed to improve the efficiency for query processing. The idea behind this is to break up a single entity into multiple 'smaller' sub-entities by slicing the table into smaller pieces. Most of the existing methods fall into two major categories – horizontal partitioning and vertical partitioning. In general, the way in which a fact table will be split depends on the type of query. However, there is no guidance for the optimal selection of features to process a query. We propose here to partition along a dimension to facilitate a coarse-to-fine media data matching scheme for multimedia information retrieval. A hierarchical image matching scheme based on wavelet transforms in a pyramid structure is reported in [26]. We further extend this idea by constructing a decision tree to guide the search for the candidate with the best similarity.

Unlike the existing methods which use a single decision tree throughout the decision making process, we propose to develop a dynamic decision tree cluster in conjunction with the starflake data warehouse structure to achieve a fast search for the best candidate in a hierarchical structure. To be dynamic, the statistically based Symmetrical Tau criterion is adopted to guide the selection of the relevant features in constructing different decision trees with respect to different query types. For example, individual features are used to build a decision tree to classify individual dimension tables associated with the fact table for the core operation within the star. The combination of different features will be considered to create a decision tree for further data processing in the partitioned or summarized data tables in correspondence to the snowflake stage. More trees with reference to combined features will be generated if there is any crossover between dimensions in the third normal form. In summary, the proposed hierarchical scheme for fast searching has the following characteristics: 1) the construction of a decision tree cluster to handle a diversity of queries; 2) the use of multiple features and their combinations in constructing various decision trees at different levels; 3) the adoption of the statistically based Symmetrical Tau criterion for the selection of features; and 4) the combination of dynamic decision tree clusters with the starflake structure to achieve hierarchical search.

9.5. Robust Classification via Fuzzy Neural Network

The combination of fuzzy set theory with neural network computation, genetic algorithms, evolutionary computation, and other advanced methodological tools has laid the foundation for a diversity of successful applications in areas such as expert systems, database and information retrieval systems, pattern recognition and clustering, signal and image processing, speech recognition, risk analysis, robotics, medicine, psychology, chemistry, ecology, and economics. A comprehensive survey of applications of fuzzy set theory is presented in [18]. In this chapter, we employ fuzzy neural network to achieve robust classification for multimedia information retrieval.

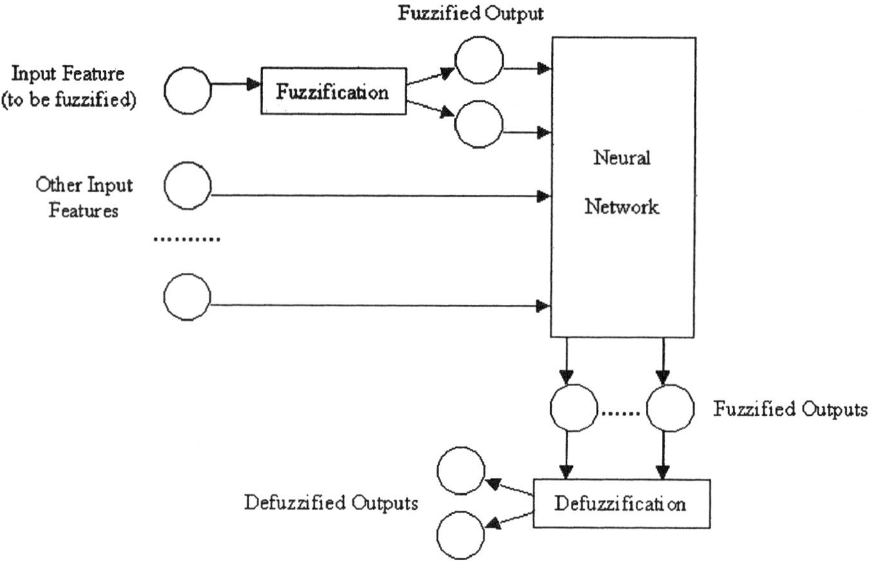

Figure 9.3.   A fuzzy neural network model.

In contrast to the traditional decision support systems, fuzzy systems deal with information in imprecise terms and provide decision support based on the fuzziness measurement of set members [6]. Therefore, the development of a fuzzy system requires the specification of fuzzy sets and the relevant fuzzy membership functions. However, these two key issues are traditionally predefined by the system designers (experts). Consequently, such a fuzzy system will lack flexibility to handle unspecified cases. To equip a fuzzy system with learning capabilities, an alternative approach is to integrate fuzzy sets with other learning models. Many researchers have proposed the use of neural networks in fuzzy systems. Wong and Wang proposed a "FuzzyNet model" [25]; Enbutsu *et al.* developed a hybridization scheme to extract fuzzy rules from a multilayered neural network [8]; Janikow suggested to use genetic algorithm for learning fuzzy controller [14]. To tackle the uncertainties in practice for multimedia information retrieval such as user requirement, query data specification, feature selection, similarity measurement, search strategy, classification and performance evaluation, we integrate fuzzy set theory with the Back Propagation Feed Forward (BPFF) neural network to achieve flexibility and robustness for automatic and autonomous decision support for classification. A schematic diagram for the fuzzy neural network model is shown in Figure 9.3.

When a feature image is regarded as a fuzzy set x of size $M \times N$ and L levels of feature measurements, we extend Pal and Rosenfeld's fuzzy compactness approach [20] to determine the optimal threshold value for classification by minimizing the measurement of fuzziness. They introduced the index of fuzziness to reflect the average amount of ambiguity (fuzziness) present in an image I by measuring the distance between its fuzzy property $\mu_{\mathbf{X}}$ and the nearest two-level property $\mu_{\overline{\mathbf{X}}}$. A linear index of fuzziness is defined below:

$$v_l(\mathbf{X}) \;=\; \frac{2}{MN} \sum_{i=1}^{M} \sum_{j=1}^{N} |\mu_{\mathbf{X}}(x_{ij}) - \mu_{\overline{\mathbf{X}}}(x_{ij})| \tag{9.2}$$

$$=\; \frac{2}{MN} \sum_{i=1}^{M} \sum_{j=1}^{N} \mu_{\mathbf{X} \cap \overline{\mathbf{X}}}(x_{ij}) \tag{9.3}$$

$$=\; \frac{2}{MN} \sum_{i=1}^{M} \sum_{j=1}^{N} \min\{\mu_{\mathbf{X}}(x_{ij}), (1 - \mu_{\mathbf{X}}(x_{ij}))\} \tag{9.4}$$

where $\mu_{\overline{\mathbf{X}}}(x_{ij})$ denotes the nearest two-level version of $\mathbf{X}$ such that

$$\mu_{\overline{\mathbf{X}}}(x_{ij}) \;=\; 0 \quad \text{if } \mu_{\mathbf{X}}(x_{ij}) \le 0.5$$
$$=\; 1 \quad \text{otherwise}$$

In contrast to the conventional measurement of fuzziness in a gray scale image detailed above, we extended this approach by applying the distance measurement to feature image rather than the measurement of fuzziness of the image in gray scale. Accordingly, $\mathbf{X}$ refers to the feature set and x_{ij} represents the certain feature measurement. Instead of processing the gray scale image, we consider the minimization of fuzziness in image feature to select appropriate threshold value for classification output. Such an algorithm is summarized as follows:

- Step 1: Convert the original biometrics data (fact table in the biometrics data warehouse) to feature image (dimension tables associated with the fact table) by its relevant measurement (color, texture or shape). The maximum and minimum values are l_{max} and l_{min} respectively.

- Step 2: Construct the "feature image" membership $\mu_{\mathbf{X}}$, where

$$\mu_{\mathbf{X}}(l) = S(l; a, l_i, c), \quad l_{min} \le l, l_i \le l_{max} \tag{9.5}$$

and

$$
\begin{aligned}
S(l; a, b, c) &= 0 & l \le a, \\
&= 2[(l-a)/(c-a)]^2, & a < l \le b, \\
&= 1 - 2[(l-c)/(c-a)]^2, & b < l \le c, \\
&= 1 & l > c
\end{aligned}
$$

with cross-over point $b = l_i = (a+c)/2$ and bandwidth $\triangle b = b - a = c - b$.

- Step 3: Obtain the linear index of fuzziness in image feature image $\mathbf{X}$ by computing

$$v_l(\mathbf{X}) = \frac{2}{MN} \sum_l T_i(l) h(l) \tag{9.6}$$

where

$$T_i(l) = \min\{S(l; a, l_i, c), 1 - S(l; a, l_i, c)\} \tag{9.7}$$

and $h(l)$ denotes the number of occurrences of the level l.

- Step 4: Vary l_i from l_{min} to l_{max} and choose $l_i = l_c$ which corresponding to the minimum of $v(X)$.

Figure 9.4 shows a general structure of the proposed FFBP network for multimedia data classification. The network consists of two parts: fuzzy module and Feed Forward Back Propagation (FFBP) neural network module. The fuzzy module provides the network with a collection of fuzzy variables as input nodes. The FFBP neural network is a multi-layer neural network responsible for biometrics pattern classification for identity identification.

9.6.   System Implementation

Parallel computation has been used successfully in many areas of computer science to speed up the computation required to solve a problem. In the field of image processing and computer vision this is especially appropriate since it appears that the biological model for vision is a parallel model. In contrast to the conventional parallel implementation where either the dedicated hardware or the software are required, the parallel implementation of our parallel biometrics computing is carried out in a distributed computing environment. This section briefly describes the use of Mobile Agents for the system implementation.

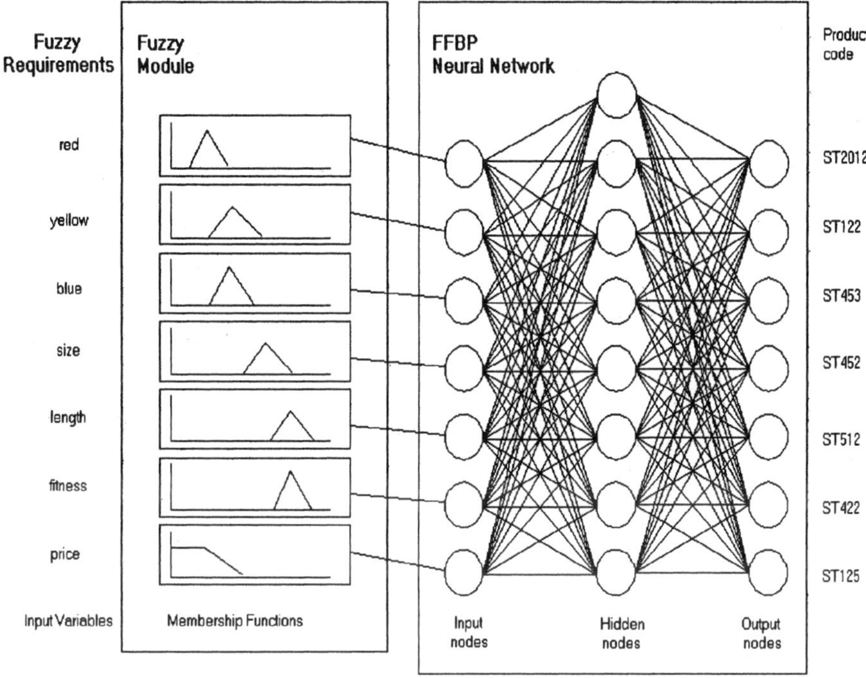

Figure 9.4. Fuzzy Forward Back Propagation Network for identity identification.

9.6.1 System Environment

Internet provides an ideal platform to support web-based E-commerce. The current Internet-based systems are mainly based on a client and server architecture, where all transactions are made by many request /response interactions over the network. However, a user may experience communication difficulties with long response time. To reduce the communication overheads, a mobile agent based approach becomes more appropriate for E-commerce applications. A mobile agent based system utilizes different techniques to send a mobile software agent to a remote system so as to conduct multiple interactions with the software resident on the remote system. The outputs are sent back to the user on the completion of the interaction. An agent can also interact with other agents on the Internet before returning to its original system. Therefore, mobile agent based systems are more flexible for web-based E-commerce applications than the existing client/server systems. The current agent technologies include IBM Aglets [2], ObjectSpace Voyager Agents [24], FTP Software Agent [11], General Magic Odyssey Agent System [19], Java Agent Template Lite (JATLite) [15] and Agent Builder Environment from IBM [1]. Figure 9.5 shows the movement of an agent with a specific computing task, where an agent jumps from machine to machine and interacts with resources on each machine.

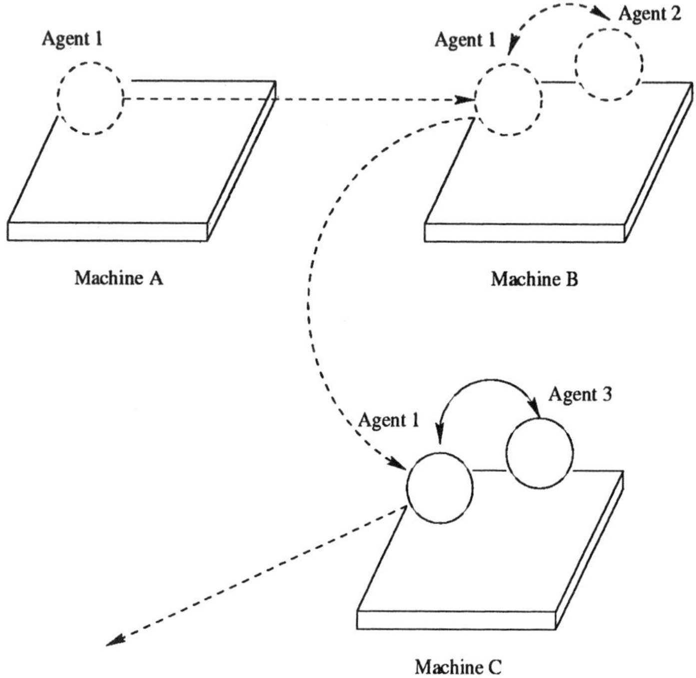

Figure 9.5. The abstraction of mobile agent.

There are several advantages of using mobile agent technologies for *E*-commerce applications. The following summarizes the major issues.

- Network load

  Distributed systems heavily rely on communication protocols for multiple interactions for a given task. By contrast, mobile agents reduce the load by packing a conversation and dispatch it to a destination host, where the interaction can take place locally.

- Network latency

  E-commerce applications such as on-line shopping, price negotiation and *E*-auction require real-time interactions. The normal network does not meet such real-time requirements because of its significant network latencies. However, mobile agents can overcome this limitation because they can be dispatched from a central controller to function locally and directly execute the controller's operations.

- Asynchronous and autonomous issues

  The traditional mobile applications rely on expensive and fragile network connections. Therefore, it is not feasible to keep the connection open between mobile device and the selected network site for a certain task. Nevertheless, mobile agent technology facilitates asynchronous and autonomous operations by embedding tasks into mobile agents and dispatching them into network again on completion.

- Flexibility

  One of the major advantages of agent technology is the dynamic adjustment of its operation with respect to its execution environment and react to the changes autonomously. Therefore, multiple mobile agents can distribute themselves among the hosts over the network so as to maintain the optimal configuration for any Internet-based operations.

- Heterogeneous issues

  In general, network computing is fundamentally heterogeneous from both hardware and software perspective. Since mobile agents are computer and transport-layer independent, they are dependent on their execution environment only. Consequently, mobile agent based systems are positioned for seamless system integration.

- Robustness and fault-tolerant

  Robustness and fault-tolerant are two crucial issues for any Internet-based *E*-commerce applications. The nature of flexibility and dynamic adjustment to the execution environment make it feasible for mobile agents to provide the solid base for the development of robust and distributed *E*-commerce systems.

9.6.2   System Platform

Mobile agent via IBM Aglets is adopted as the system platform for the implementation of our biometrics based personal identification system. IBM Aglets is a Java-based framework for implementing mobile agents [2] with the following features: 1) provides an object-oriented programming interface; 2) offers mechanisms for moving codes, data and state information from one machine to another; 3) creates a platform-independent development and runtime environment; 4) secures security mechanisms.

The basic functionalities and runtime properties of Aglets are defined by the Java Aglet, AgletProxy and AgletContext classes. The abstract class Aglet defines the fundamental methods that control the mobility and life cycle of an aglet. It also provides the access to the inherent attributes of an aglet, such as creation time, owner, code-base and trust level, as well as dynamic attributes, such as the arrival time at a site and address of the current context.

The main function of AgletProxy class is to handle the access to the aglet. All of the communication among aglets are through their proxies. In addition, AgletProxy also provides location transparency by forwarding requests to remote hosts and returning results to the local host.

The AgletContext class provides the runtime execution environment for aglet within the Tahiti server. When an aglet is dispatched to a remote site, it is detached from the current AgletContext object, serialized into a message bytestream, sent across the network, and reconstructed in a new AgletContext. As a result, the same execution environment will be created at the remote site.

Security issue is another critical component of the Aglet environment. Aglets provide a security model in the form of an AgletSecurityManager, which is a subclass of the "standard" Java SecurityManager.

9.6.3 Implementation Strategies

To facilitate the implementation of each components of the system, we adopt a hybrid agent computing paradigm. There are two classes of agents – global agents and local agents. The global agents will handle inter-image coordination, query processing and reasoning. Each global agent may consist of a few of sub-agents. The following lists five global agents and their associated sub-agents proposed in our system:

- *Coordinator Agent:* coordinating other global and image agents

- *Query Agent:* processing users' complex query with three sub-agents, namely,

  – query understanding: categorising query based on the selection of biometrics features and determine the corresponding dimensional feature table

  – query reasoning: extracting the component features from the dimensional table for feature grouping

  – query feature formation: determining the statistically based feature selection criteria such as Symmetric Tau for multiple biometrics feature integration

- *Feature Agent:* generating multiple biometrics feature representation and integration with three sub-agents:

  – wavelet transform : decomposition of an image into a series for sub-band images for image hierarchy

  – feature representation: individual feature vector in terms of wavelet coefficients

- feature integration: combination of multiple feature vectors with adjusted weights

- *Fuzzy Agent:* creating analytical tools for fuzzification and defuzzication with two sub-agents:

  - fuzzy feature representation

  - fuzzy neural network

- *Verification/Identification Agent:* performing hierarchical feature matching for identity verification and identification with two sub-agents:

  - matching criterion selection: selection of similarity measures

  - feature matching: hierarchical image matching

- *User Interface Agent:* managing all user interactions

The local agents are referred to as *Image Agents*, which are responsible to perform relevant biometrics computing tasks on each individual image.

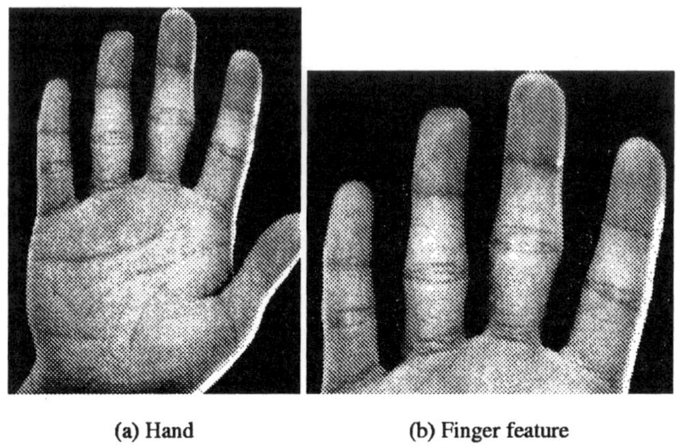

(a) Hand   (b) Finger feature

Figure 9.6.   An example of multiple feature integration for hand representation.

9.7.   Experimental Results

The prototype system Web Guard is developed using IBM Aglets on both Linux and unix platforms. The biometrics image samples used for the testing are 232×232 size with the resolution of 125 dpi and 256 grayscales. Three types of biometrics features, namely hand geometries, fingers, and palmprints are associated with each individual. Our biometrics image data warehouse integrates three individual image databses of hand geometries, fingers and palmprints. A total of 2,000 images from 500 individuals are stored. These biometrics samples are collected from both female and male adults with the age range from 18 to 50. A special electronic sensor is used to get digitized samples on-line. Figure 9.6 illustrates the samples of digitized hand boundry, fingers and palmprints of one hand, and Figure 9.7 shows the samples of different palmprint patterns from different individuals. A series of experiments have been carried out to verify the high performance of the proposed algorithms.

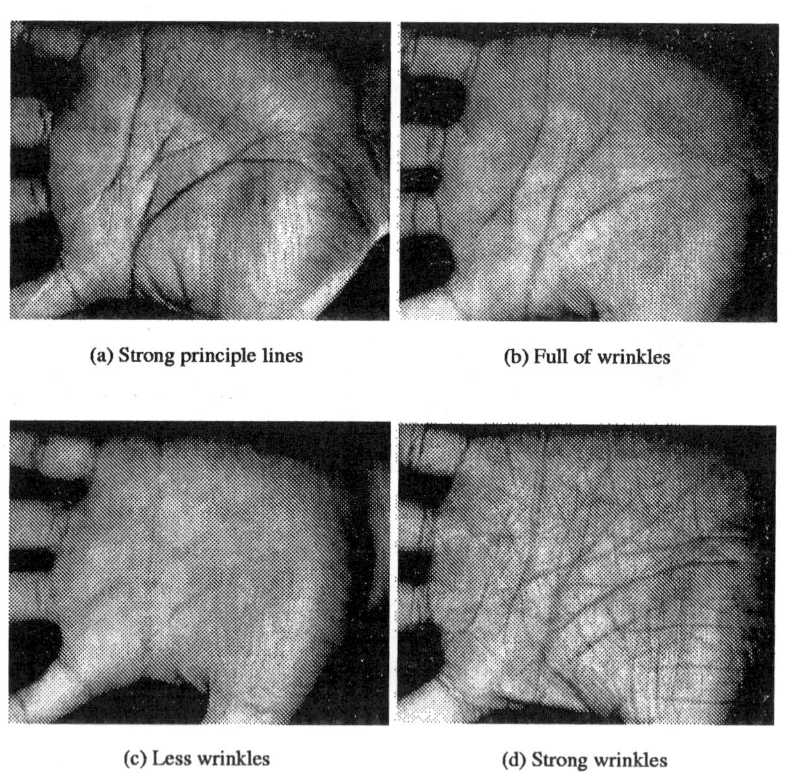

(a) Strong principle lines   (b) Full of wrinkles

(c) Less wrinkles   (d) Strong wrinkles

Figure 9.7.   Samples of different palmprint patterns.

The shape of a hand boundary can be used as a global biometrics feature for coarse matching. This feature data can be can be presented by a data cube, and each dimension corresponds to a particular feature entity. The following lists the relevant features as dimensions for hand shape classification: (1) list of boundary feature points, sorted in the anti-clock order along the hand boundary; (2) parameters which control the active contour along the hand boundary; (3) measures of invariant moments, sorted in descend order; (4) list of coefficients of a B-Spline curve; (5) time when the image was taken; and (6) list of individual's identity details.

The above multi-dimensional structure of the data cube offers flexibility to manipulate the data and view it from different perspectives. Such a structure allows quick data summarization at different levels and the application of OLAP operations (On-line Analytical Processing) to view and analyze the data from different aspects as specified. The OLAP operations include drill-down, roll-up, slice and dice. The statistical data resulted from the OLAP operation is used to discover the hidden patterns or implicit knowledge to speed up the task of hand pattern classification. In other words, we adopted association rules as the technique for data mining to guide the classification. For a collection of 200 hand image samples, 80% candidates are excluded after the coarse level selection.

The dynamic selection of biometrics features is further demonstrated by multi-level palmprint feature extraction for personal identification and verification. The experiment is carried out in two stages. At stage one, the global palmprint features are extracted at coarse level and candidate samples are selected for further processing. At stage 2, the regional palmprint features are detected and a hierarchical image matching is performed for the final retrieval output. Figure 9.8 illustrates the multi-level extraction of a palmprint features. Figure 9.8(a) shows a sample of a palm, Figure 9.8(b) detects global principal lines, Figure 9.8(c) represents the global palmprint texture feature and Figure 9.8(d) details the regional palmprint texture features for local feature representation at a fine level. The average accuracy rate for classification is 97%.

Such a guided search scheme can be further extended to fuzzy matching in a hierarchical manner for the categorization of candidates for on-line personal identification to secure network access. Below illustrates examples of fuzzy membership function used for face feature selection (color and degree of fitness).

$$Color(color) = \{red, yellow, blue\}$$

$$\underline{color} = \left\{ \begin{array}{l} Light, Normal, Deep \mid \forall \mu_{\underline{color}}(Light), \\ \mu_{\underline{color}}(Normal), \mu_{\underline{color}}(Deep) \in [0,1] \end{array} \right\}$$

$$\mu_{\underline{color}}(Light) = \left\{ \begin{array}{ll} 1 & \text{if } 0 \leq x \leq 64 \\ \frac{96-x}{32} & \text{if } 64 < x \leq 96 \\ 0 & \text{otherwise} \end{array} \right.$$

$$\mu_{\underline{color}}(Normal) = \left\{ \begin{array}{ll} \frac{x-64}{32} & \text{if } 64 \leq x \leq 96 \\ 1 & \text{if } 96 < x \leq 160 \\ \frac{192-x}{32} & \text{if } 160 < x \leq 192 \\ 0 & \text{otherwise} \end{array} \right.$$

$$\mu_{\underline{color}}(Deep) = \begin{cases} 1 & \text{if } x > 192 \\ \frac{x-160}{32} & \text{if } 160 \leq x \leq 192 \\ 0 & \text{otherwise} \end{cases}$$

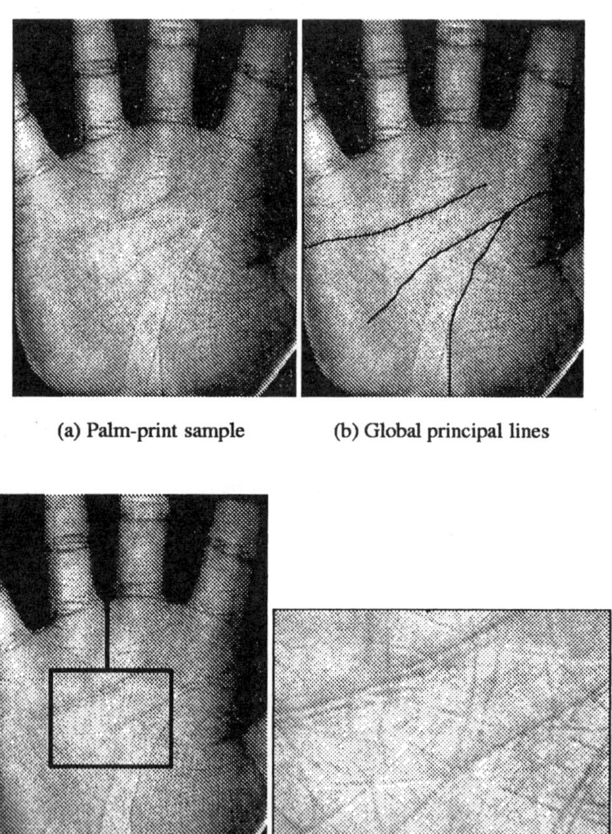

(a) Palm-print sample   (b) Global principal lines

(c) Palm texture feature   (d) Local texture feature

Figure 9.8.   Hierarchical palmprint feature extraction.

The evaluation of system efficiency is judged by Round Trip Time (RTT) test. Instead of calculating the difference between the arrival and departure time to/from the server, the RTT test uses the total round trip time for the agents involved , which is determined by all of the time fragments spent on each component during the operation staring from the collection of user requirement(UR), fuzzification(RFS), to the fuzzy feature selection(FFSS), defuzzification scheme(DFS) and evaluation scheme(ES). Two Tahiti servers are used

Table 9.2.   System efficiency evaluation – average RTT for 100 trials.

Server Location	Execution Time (ms) Server 1	Execution Time (ms) Server 2
A. Client Machine		
UR		
RFS	310	305
B. Server Machine		
FDM	320	2015
FFSS	4260	4133
C. Client Machine		
DFS	320	330
ES	251	223
TOTAL RTT	5461	7006

in this test. Server 1 is located on the same LAN of the client machine while Server 2 is situated at a remote site with the campus for simulation. Table 9.2 shows the average execution time at different stage for 100 trials. It is noted that most of the execution time is spent on FFSS for fuzzy decision making(FDM). In practice, the network traffic should be considered for real applications.

9.8.   Conclusions

This paper explores the integration of data warehousing, biometrics computing, agent technology and fuzzy neural network to provide efficient and effective security support for today's fast growing E-commerce applications. To tackle the key issues such as biometrics data representation, storage, integration, indexing, similarity measures, searching methods and query processing, we propose a new approach of using a biometrics data warehouse. The extension of the conventional data warehouse to a biometrics data warehouse offers a promising alternative for effective data representation and storage. The use of a multimedia starflake schema facilitates dynamic data integration and indexing. The use of a statistically based feature selection criterion, the symmetrical Tau, for flexible similarity measures provides a base to guide the search in a hierarchical structure. The development of a fuzzy neural network which combines fuzzy logic technology with the Back Propagation feed Forward (BPFF) neural network provides an effective alternative to deal with the uncertainties in practice for identity identification. To meet the need for an autonomous, mobile and robust system which can offer decision-making support to secure network access, the proposed multi-agent based web-mining approach outperforms the traditional mobile systems by reducing network load, overcoming network latency, providing an asynchronous, autonomous and heterogeneous environment, and increasing system flexibility, robustness and fault-tolerance.

The prototype system Web Guard demonstrates the feasibility of the proposed techniques for other *E*-commerce applications.

References

[1]   ABE, URL: http://www.networking.ibm.com/iag

[2]   Aglets, URL: http://www.trl.ibm.co.jp/aglets

[3]   S. Anahory and D. Murray. Data Warehousing in the Real World – A Practical Guide for Building Decision Support Systems, Addison-Wesley, 1997.

[4]   C. Carter and J. Catlett. Assessing Credit Card Applications Using Machine Learning, IEEE Expert, Fall, pages 71-74, 1987.

[5]   M.S. Chen, J. Han and P.S. Yu. Data Mining: An Overview from a Database Perspective, IEEE Trans. Knowledge and Data Engineering, vol. 8, pages 866-883, 1996.

[6]   D. Dubois and H. Prade. Fuzzy Sets and Systems: Theory and Applications, Academic Press, 1990.

[7]   N. Duta, A.K. Jain and K.V. Mardia. Matching of Palmprints, Paper under review in IEEE Trans. Pattern Anal. Machine Intell., currently downloadable from http://biometric.cse.msu.edu, 2001.

[8]   L. Enbutsu, K. Baba and H. Hara. Fuzzy Rule Extraction from a Multilayered Neural Network, Int'l Joint Conference on Neural Networks (IJCNN'91), pages 794-799, 1991.

[9]   U.M. Fayyad, G. Piatetsky-Shapiro, P. Smyth and R. Uthurusamy. Advances in Knowledge Discovery and Data Mining, AAAI/MIT Press, 1996.

[10]   M. Flickner, H. Sawhney, W. Niblack and J. Ashley. Query by Image and Video Content: The QBIC system, IEEE Computer, vol. 28, pages 23-32, 1995.

[11]   FTP Software Agents, URL: http://www.ftp.com

[12]   L.A. Goodman and W.H. Kruskal. Measures of Association for Cross-classifications, J. Amer. Statist. Assoc., vol. 49, pages 732-764, 1954.

[13]   A. Jain, R. Bolle and S. Pankanti. Biometrics: Personal Identification in Networked Society, Kluwer Academic Publishers, 1999.

[14]   C.Z. Janikow. Learning Fuzzy Controllers by Genetic Algorithms, Proceedings of ACM Symp. on Applied Computing, ACM Press, New York, pp. 1105-1112, 1994.

[15]   JATLite, URL: http://java.stanford.edu/java-agent/html

[16]   R. Kalakota and A.B. Whinston. Electronic Commerce, Addison-Welsey, 1997.

[17]   S. Khoshafian and A.B. Baker. Multimedia and Image Databases, Morgan Kaufmann Publishers, 1996.

[18]   G.J. Klir, U.H.S. Clair and B. Yuan. Fuzzy Set Theory: Foundations and Applications, Prentice Hall, 1997.

[19]   Odyssey, URL: http://www.genmagic.com

[20]   S.K. Pal and A. Rosenfeld. Image Enhancement and Thresholding by Optimization of Fuzzy Compactness, Patt. Recog. Lett., vol.7, pages 77-86, 1988.

[21]   S. Sestito and T.S. Dillon. Automated Knowledge Acquisition, Sydney, Prentice Hall, 1994.

[22] W. Shen, M. Surette and R. Khanna. Evaluation of Automated Biometrics-based Identification and Verification Systems. In Proc. of the IEEE, vol. 85, pages 1464-1478, 1997.

[23] E. Turban, J. Lee, D. King and H.M. Chung. Electronic Commerce: A Managerial Perspective, Prentice Hall, 2000.

[24] Voyager, URL: http://www.objectspace.com/voyager

[25] F. Wong and P.Z. Wang. Fuzzy Neural Systems for Decision Making. In Proc. of the Int'l Joint Conference on Neural Networks (IJCNN'91), pages 497-505, 1991.

[26] J. You and P. Bhattacharya. A Wavelet-based Coarse-to-fine Image Matching Scheme in a Parallel Virtual Machine Environment, IEEE Trans. Image Processing, vol. 9, pages 1547-1559, 2000.

[27] O.R. Zaiane. Resource and Knowledge Discovery from the Internet and Multimedia Repositories, Ph.D Thesis, Simon Fraser University, 1999.

[28] D. Zhang. Automated Biometrics: Technologies and Systems, Kluwer Academic Publisher, 1999.

[29] X. Zhou and T.S. Dillon. A Statistical-heuristic Feature Selection Criterion for Decision Tree Induction, IEEE Trans. Patt. Anal. Machine Intell., vol. 13, pages 834-841, 1991.

Chapter 10

SMART CARD APPLICATION BASED ON PALMPRINT IDENTIFICATION

Guangming Lu

Department of Computer Science and Engineering
Harbin Institute of Technology, Harbin, China
lgm@biometrics.hit.edu.cn

David Zhang

Department of Computing
The Hong Kong Polytechnic University, Kowloon, Hong Kong
csdzhang@comp.polyu.edu.hk

Abstract   There has been an ever-growing need to authenticate individuals at various occasions in our modern and automated society. Unfortunately, the traditional security measures such as passwords and identity cards cannot satisfy various security requirements. This chapter describes a biometrics-based smart card security system by utilizing an individual's unique, reliable and stable physical characteristic, their palmprint, for identification and verification. This is considered a better solution for medium level security systems. In Section 10.2, we present the general process and key issues of on-line palmprint identification. The smart card system architecture is described in Section 10.3. The system analysis and applications are proposed in Section 10.4. In Section 10.5, we describe our conclusions.

Keywords: Biometrics, smart card, palmprint identification.

10.1.   Introduction

Smart Cards, also called integrated circuit cards (ICCs), which are embedded with a special type of hardware logic or a microprocessor to store the security information, offers a higher level of security than traditional authentication methods, such as personal identification number (PIN), integrated circuit card and magnetic strip card.

Smart card based applications have been widely used in many fields. The Smart-Universe suite addresses five smart card application areas comprising: electronic payments (Smart-Wallet), customer loyalty (Smart-Shopper), secure identity (Smart-Identity), ticketing (Smart-Show), and physical access control (Smart-Access). Especially, with the rapid growth of the Internet, Electronics Commerce (EC) has now become an important part of worldwide business activities, and this area also offers a very broad set of applications. Smart cards will play an important role in the development of the EC security infrastructure.

A smart card based on biometrics has become a new research trend in recent years. Smart cards provide a convenient method for storing biometrics templates. Equally, biometrics can also be used to protect access to information stored on smart cards, or used in combination with a smart card to provide access to network services.

Since the biometrics identification system and smart card system all have wide application prospects, and they can be combined in many application fields; many companies and research groups have paid much attention to these technologies. Now, various kinds of application systems have been developed and marketed. Litronic Inc., a provider of PKI (Public Key Infrastructure) based Internet security solutions, has announced the demonstration of a three-factor identification system. This combines iris biometrics with digital signatures and smart cards, which enables stronger identity authentication for electronic data security applications. The digital signature system incorporates an iris scan identification before the smart card is permitted to digitally sign a document. French smart card manufacturer, Oberthur Card Systems, has presented a smart card based fingerprint authentication solution that applies biometrics to the PKI architecture. Developed with id3 Semiconductors, the cards are designed to create digital signatures once an individual has been successfully authenticated through fingerprint matching. Recently, a new smart card has appeared on the market, which can pick out and recognize a voice in almost any circumstances; for example, with background noise, whilst eating, under the influence of alcohol, or even when you have a cold.

There are many different biometric technologies developed in different places. Although fingerprint identification is more popular and accepted by the public, for some special applications like construction sites, the workers could not use the fingerprint sensor because of dirt on their hands, also, some people do not have clear fingerprints due to the nature of their physical work, or they may simply have problematic skin. Iris and retina recognition can provide a very high accuracy but this approach suffers from the high cost of the input devices, and they are more intrusive to the user. Recently, many researchers have focused on face and voice identification; nevertheless, the accuracy obtained is still far from satisfactory. The accuracy and uniqueness of using 3-D (3 dimensional) hand geometry for authentication is still an open question. Therefore, the development and investigation of palmprint approaches are very valuable. Because the surface area of a palmprint is larger than a fingerprint, the stability of a palmprint is higher and the chance of it being damaged (beyond use in authentication) is lower than that of a fingerprint. It would certainly be helpful that more information is available from a palmprint to verify or identify a person.

More importantly, people feel that it is easy and convenient to capture their palmprint images. People only need to put their hands on the capture device, and it is comfortable for users to enroll. For iris and retina recognition, when capturing the iris or retina images, the users need to control the position of their heads in the capture process to fix the position of the captured image. Also, the eyes have to be opened wide enough to capture the whole iris or retina image. Users might be tired after the image capturing process, because they need to keep their eyes wide open for a reasonable period of time.

Similar to fingerprints, palmprint have been used in law enforcement as a powerful means of criminal identification because of its stability and uniqueness. The rationale for choosing the palmprint as the basis for personal identification originates in its user friendliness, flexibility in the application environment, and its discriminating ability. Normally, people do not feel uneasy about having their palmprint image taken for testing. More importantly, these palmprint features are stable and uniquely represent each individual's identity. Consequently, it is essential to develop an effective approach to automate palmprint identification and verification for security applications.

In this chapter, we describe the smart card system based for palmprint identification. As a replacement for a conventional PIN, the smart card uses the authorized cardholder's palmprint to enter a security system. Once the user's palmprint has been scanned and processed, the new solution stores the palmprint feature set within the smart card. With this solution, the only way to gain full access to the security system is to compare the stored palmprint sample with all the samples registered in the database to find if the user is a legal enrollee. If the comparison result is positive, then the user is granted access rights to the system.

The rest of this chapter is organized as follows. In Section 10.2, we present the general process, and the key issues of on-line palmprint identification. The smart card system architecture is described in Section

10.3. The system analysis and applications are proposed in Section 10.4. In Section 10.5, we present our conclusions.

10.2.   On-line Palmprint Identification System

Automatic biometrics identification or verification systems are either on-line or off-line, which are differentiated by the data acquisition method. In an on-line system, samples are acquired in real time with digital devices during the identification or verification process. In an off-line system, samples are acquired before the identification or verification process.

The on-line palmprint identification system scans the palmprint in real-time, and performs on-line comparison of the currently captured palmprints with those stored in the database. Then, the system can display a message to let the user know whether his/her identity is authenticated by the system (see Figure 10.1).

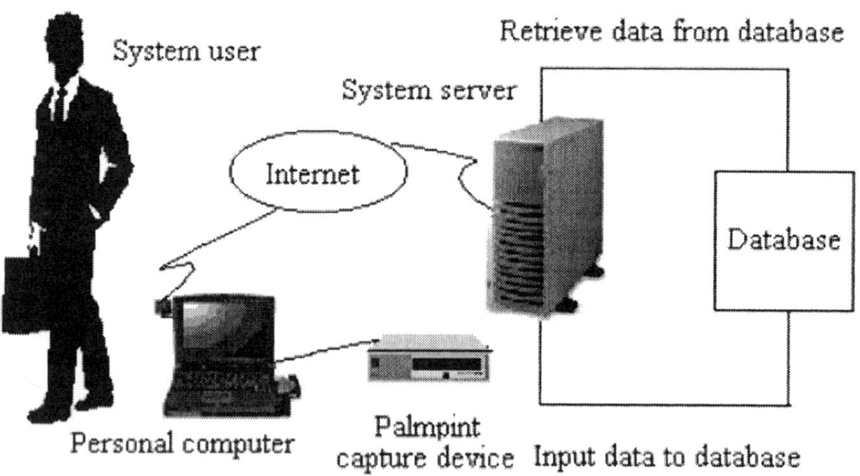

Figure 10.1.   The architecture of the on-line palmprint identification system.

10.2.1   Smart Card and Palmprint Identification

Normally, palmprint identification starts with the capturing process, and proceeds by extracting the unique information or data from one palmprint of a user. Next, the system compares the extracted data with those stored in the database to see if there is any match. However, in a smart card based palmprint identification system, the palmprint sample of a user is stored in the smart card, and it can be read using a smart card reader, so there is no need to capture the user's palmprint in real-time. When the user wants access to any secure systems in which he has been registered, the system will read the feature sample from the smart card and then match it with all of the candidates in the server's database. If the matching result is positive, then the user will be permitted to enter the system; otherwise, he/she will be regarded as an impostor. Figure 10.2 shows the processes of such a system.

From the architecture of a palmprint-based smart card system, we can see that palmprint identification involves the following main processes: image preprocessing, feature extraction and feature matching. Image preprocessing is used to normalize the original palmprint images. The captured palmprint images may exhibit small rotations and/or shift in palm positions, and the size of different palms are not the same; therefore, the original images are processed before feature extraction. After the image preprocessing, any rotation and/or shift are corrected, and a fixed size sub-image is extracted so that different palmprints are converted into the same size images for feature extraction. During feature extraction, a palmprint image is presented with a feature set, which is derived using a feature extraction algorithm. Feature matching is used to compare the feature sets of palmprint images so that a decision can be made as to whether two palmprints are from the same palm.

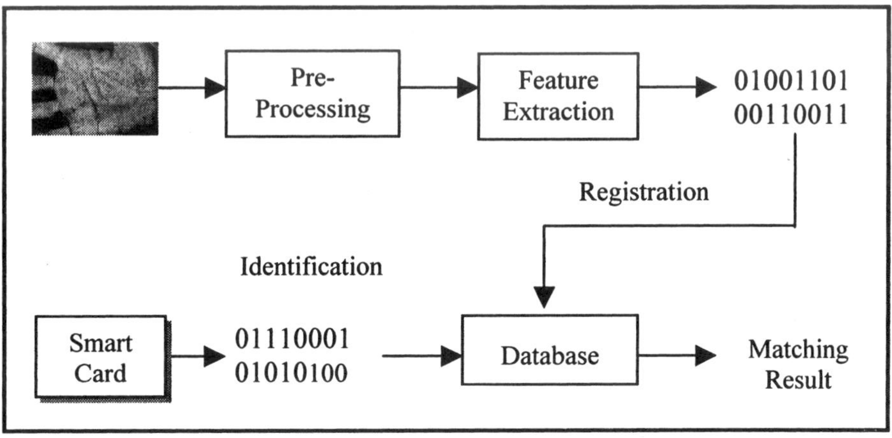

Figure 10.2. The process of palmprint based smart card identification system.

Preprocessing. For a series of palm images, the position, direction and the degree of stretching may vary over time. Therefore, even palmprint images taken from the same palm may exhibit a little rotation and/or shift. Also, the sizes of palms vary. Therefore, it is necessary to align all the palmprints and normalize their sizes for feature extraction and matching.

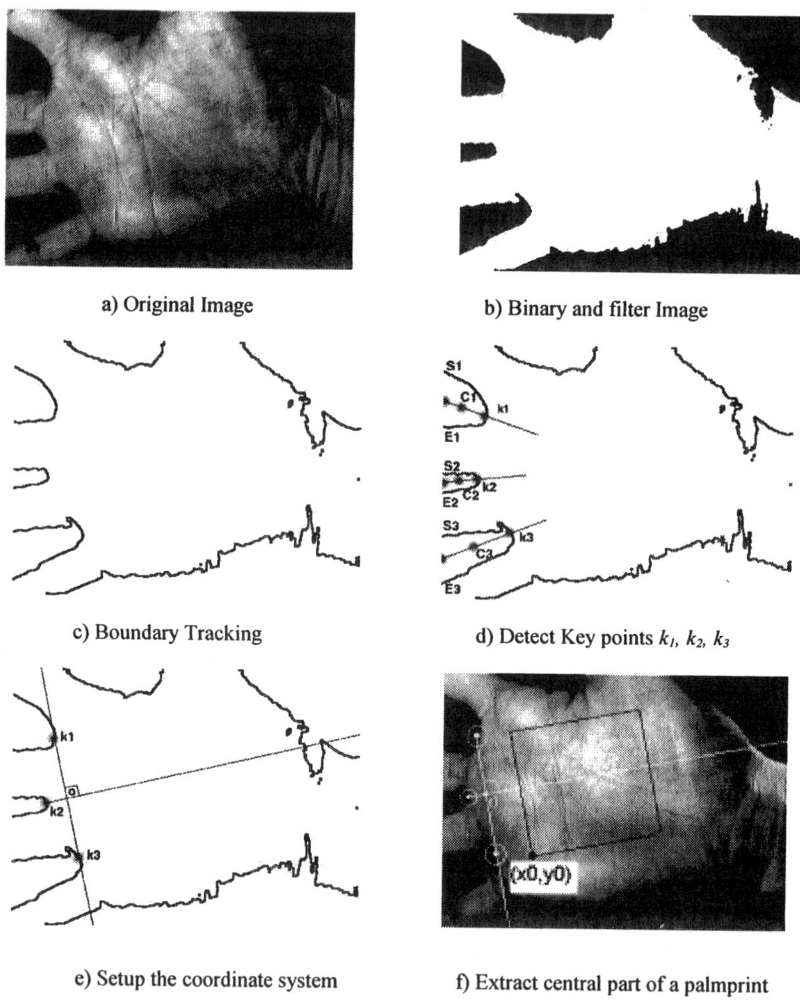

a) Original Image
b) Binary and filter Image
c) Boundary Tracking
d) Detect Key points k_1, k_2, k_3
e) Setup the coordinate system
f) Extract central part of a palmprint

Figure 10.3. Main steps of preprocessing palmprint images.

To solve this problem, a right angle coordination system can be defined, which is based on three key points between fingers; and only a sub area of a palmprint image is used in feature extraction. Within each of the palmprint images, a specific part of the image is selected, which is a fixed size sub-image from the same location. The size and location of the sub-image are determined through many observations. The principle used to decide the size and location of the sub-image is simply based on making sure that most palmprint features are retained within this area, and that all palmprints contain that sub-image. The basic steps of palmprint alignment are shown in Figure 10.3, and described in detail below.

a. Using a threshold to convert the original gray scale image into a binary map, and using a low-pass filter (such as Gaussian filter) to smooth the binary map, see Figure 10.3(b).

b. Tracing the boundary of the holes between fingers, see Figure 10.3(c).

c. Calculating the center of gravity of the holes and deciding the three key points: k1, k2, k3, see Figure 10.3(d).

d. Aligning k1 and k3 to determine the Y-axis of the palmprint coordination system and making a line through k2 that is perpendicular to the Y-axis to determine the origin of the palmprint coordination system. This coordinate system can be used to align different palmprint images. See Figure 10.3(e).

e. Extracting the sub-image. Upon on the coordination system, a certain part of a palmprint image with fixed size is extracted and used in feature extraction. The sizes of palmprints are normalized after sub-image extraction. See Figure 10.3(f).

Feature Extraction.   Feature extraction is used to describe a palmprint image as a concise feature set. How to define the features is the key issue of palmprint identification. Well-chosen features must distinguish the palmprint from others, and also establish the similarity of images taken from the same person's palmprints. The sub-image derived from palmprint preprocessing has a great many textural characteristics. However, it is very difficult to extract these textural features directly from low-resolution images. Hence, an effective feature extraction algorithm plays a very important role in the process of image identification and verification.

Indeed, there are many features that can be mined in a palmprint image. For example, the three principal lines caused by flexing the hand and wrist in the palm, which are named the heart line, the head line and the life line. Figure 10.4 shows the layout of a palm where a palm is divided into three regions: finger-root region (I), inside region (II) and outside region (III). The three (marked) curves, 1, 2 and 3, represent the three principal lines of the heart line, head line and life line, respectively. There are a many large wrinkles and ridges that remain unchanged with respect to rotation of the hand and the passing of time. Therefore, these feature lines are regarded as reliable and stable features that can be used to distinguish one person from another. The following list presents these key features and the relevant line patterns.

- Geometry Features: width, length and area are the geometry features in accordance with a palm's shape.
- Principal Line Features: very important physiological characteristics to distinguish different individuals because of their stability and uniqueness.

- Wrinkle Features: thin and irregular lines and curves that are different from the three principal lines.
- Minutia Features: significant feature measurement of ridges existing in a palm.
- Delta Point Features: the center of a delta-like region in a palmprint, which is normally located in the finger-root region and outside region.
- Texture Features: the skin patterns on a palm.
- Structure Features: such as the principal lines' lengths, positions, directions and the distances between them.

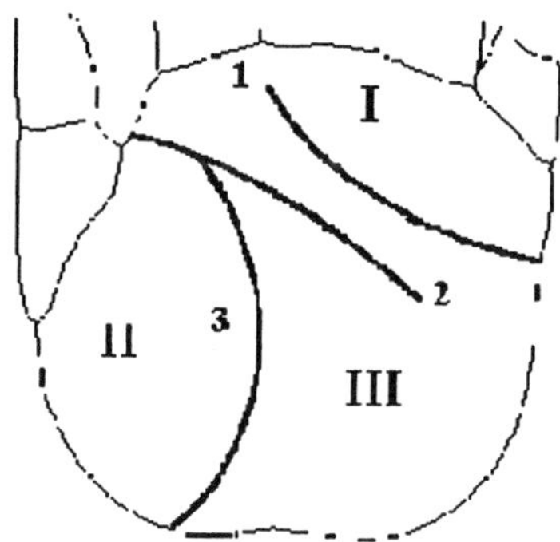

Figure 10.4. The layout of a palmprint. Regions: (I) finger root region, (II) inside region, and (III) outside region; Principal Lines: (1) heart line, (2) head line, and (3) life line.

The palmprint features listed above fall into three categories: point features, line features and texture features. Point features include delta point and minutiae, which can only be extracted from high-resolution palmprint images. Principle lines and wrinkle lines belong to line features, which can be extracted in low-resolution palmprint images. Skin texture is a kind of statistical feature that can be extracted from both low-resolution and high-resolution palmprint images. Since we are using a low-resolution palmprint image to do the identification, the line and texture based feature extraction methods are used. Our research group has been devoted to this field for several years, and it has presented several different palmprint identification models that use different feature extraction algorithms.

Feature Matching.   Feature matching is actually a process of classification, so various classification approaches can be applied to palmprint matching. In this palmprint based smart card identification system, feature matching computes the distance between two palmprint samples. Now, if we assume that a palmprint feature is represented by a 256-byte code, feature matching involves calculating the degree of similarity between two 256-byte codes. Let D_{xy} represent the distance between two codes $(x_1, x_2, ..., x_n)$ and $(y_1, y_2, ..., y_n)$. Assuming that X is the feature code inside the smart card and Y is the feature code of the authenticated individual. The definition of distance D_{xy} is given as:

$$D_{xy} = (1 - r_{xy}) \times 100 \qquad (10\text{-}1)$$

where

$$r_{xy} = \frac{l_{xy} l_{xy}}{l_{xx} l_{yy}} \qquad (10\text{-}2)$$

and

$$l_{xx} = \sum_{i=1}^{n} (x_i - \bar{x})^2 , \; l_{xy} = \sum_{i=1}^{n} (x_i - \bar{x})(y_i - \bar{y}) \qquad (10\text{-}3)$$

$$\bar{x} = \frac{1}{n} \sum_{i=1}^{n} x_i , \; \bar{y} = \frac{1}{n} \sum_{i=1}^{n} y_i \qquad (10\text{-}4)$$

The range of D_{xy} is between 0 and 100 (i.e., the smallest distance is 0, and the largest distance is 100). If D_{xy} is less then a given threshold T_d, then we can say that the two palmprints come from the same person, and the matching result is positive; otherwise, the palmprints are considered to be from different people, and authentication of that individual is denied.

10.2.2   Palmprint Capture Device Design

In the past, off-line palmprint identification and verification were previously conducted using samples that were collected by smearing ink onto the palm and making a palmprint on a sheet of white paper. After the ink dried, the palmprint image was then converted to an electronic image using a scanner and stored in a computer. An example of this kind of off-line palmprint image is shown in Figure 10.5.

Indeed, researchers who collected samples from people found that it was not easy to convince these people to help them, and allow them to capture their palmprint images; because of the convenience in the way it made the palm dirty. In addition, the palmprint images collected had different kinds of shape because different people made their palmprint on the paper using different amounts of force. Hence, the palmprints might be larger and darker when someone pushed harder on the paper, or smaller and lighter when less force was used.

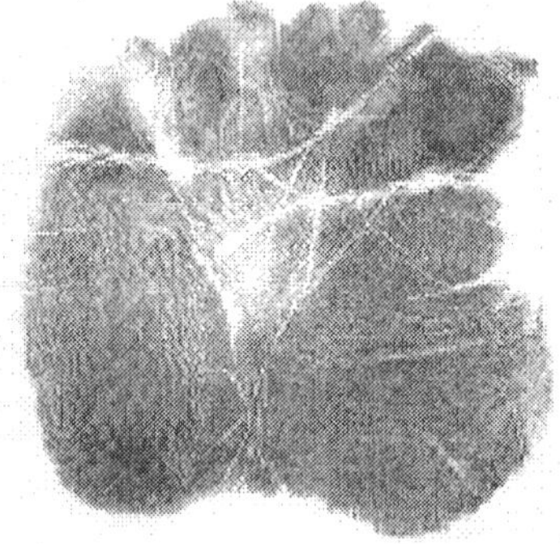

Figure 10.5. The palmprint image that was obtained by smearing ink onto the palm.

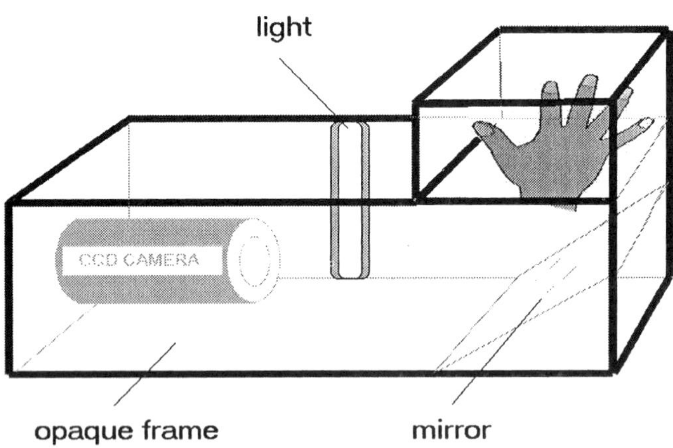

Figure 10.6. The design of the palmprint capture device.

So for an on-line palmprint identification system, it is very important but technically challenging to design a device that can capture a palmprint image in real-time. The CCD (charge coupled device) camera is the best choice. It can photograph a palmprint and directly transfer a high quality gray-scale image to a computer system (see Figure 10.6). The novel feature of the design shown in Figure 10.6 is that we do not need the hand to be pressed against a glass panel, so that the inner surface of the palm remains in its natural shape; and a suitable light can be used and shone onto the palm using the mirror. Also, the palmprint images are obtained using a low resolution. Some typical sample images are shown in Figure 10.7.

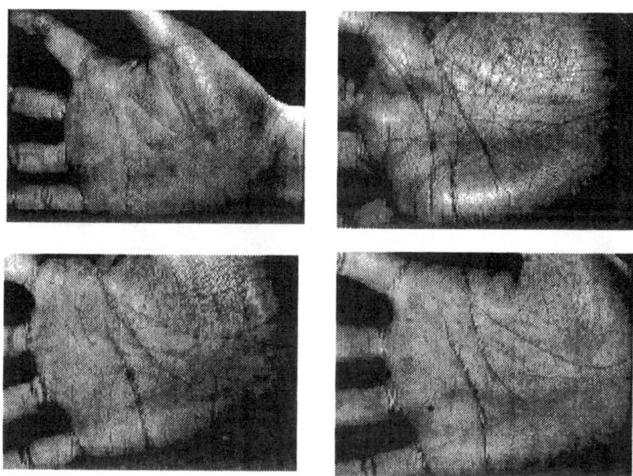

Figure 10.7.   Some typical palmprint samples captured by the above device.

10.3.   Smart Card Architecture

There are two basic kinds of smart cards. The first type of card is often called a memory card. Memory cards are primarily information storage cards that typically these contain a stored value that represents money that the user can "spend" in a payphone, retail outlet, vending machines or related transactions; similar to credit cards and ATM cards. These cards have been used, for example, automating payment in mass transit railway systems throughout the world.

The second type of card is an "intelligent" smart card that contains an embedded microprocessor chip. The central processing unit has the ability to store and secure information and make decisions, as required by the card issuer's specific application needs.

In most of the biometrics based smart card systems, the smart card always refers to the latter type, since it can offer a read/write capability, and biometrics feature sets can be well protected inside the card. However, in some low-security systems the memory card is also a good choice, since it is cheaper than the microprocessor embedded smart card.

10.3.1   Physical Architecture

The physical structure of a smart card is specified by the International Standards Organization (ISO) in standards documents 7810, 7816/1 and 7816/2. Generally, it is made up of three elements. The plastic card is the most basic one and has the dimensions of 85.60mm x 53.98mm x 0.80mm. A printed circuit and an integrated circuit chip are embedded in the card. Figure 10.8 shows an overview of the physical structure of a smart card.

The printed circuit conforms to ISO standard 7816/3, which provides five connection points for power and data. The circuit is fixed in the recess provided on the card and it is burned onto the circuit chip, filled with a conductive material, and hermetically sealed with contacts protruding. The printed circuit protects the circuit chip from mechanical stress and static electricity. Communication with the chip is accomplished through contacts that overlay the printed circuit.

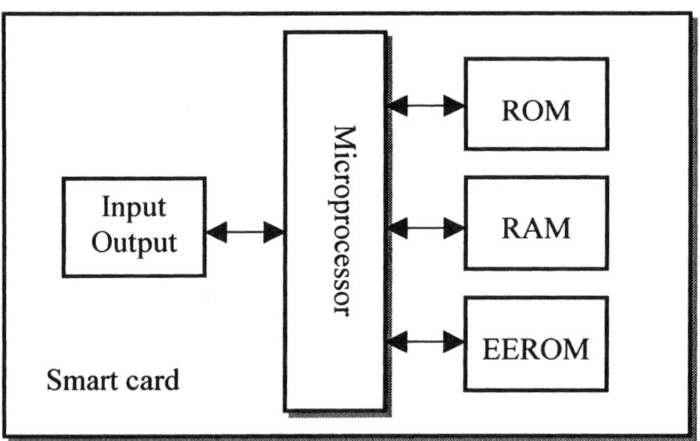

Figure 10.8.   The physical architecture of a smart card.

Typically, an integrated circuit chip consists of a microprocessor, read only memory (ROM), random access memory (RAM) and electrically erasable programmable read only memory (EEPROM). RAM is used as cache memory and typically serves to calculate results and as stack memory. The system ROM holds basic I/O (input/output) test and security functions and the user ROM stores the operating system, fixed data, standard routines, and lookup tables. The EEPROM serves to store information that must not be lost when the smart card is not connected to a power source (the terminal or card reader or card writer) and stores information that will be modified for individual users over the life of the card. The EEPROM is programmed by an on-chip charge pump that is controlled by the CPU, and it is not accessible directly by external command. The current circuit chips are made from silicon, which is not flexible and particularly easy to break. Therefore, to avoid breakage when the card is bent, the chip is restricted to only a few millimeters in size.

Furthermore, the physical interface which allows data exchange between the integrated circuit chip and the card acceptor device (CAD) is limited to 9600 bits per second. The communication line is a bi-directional serial transmission line, which conforms to ISO standard 7816/3. All the data exchanges are under the control of the central processing unit in the integrated circuit chip. Card commands and input data are sent to the chip, which then responds with status words and output data upon receiving commands and data. Information is sent in half duplex mode, which means transmission of data is in one direction at a time. This protocol together with the restrictions on the bit rate prevent a massive data attack on the card.

In general, the size, the thickness and bending requirements for the smart card are designed to protect the card from being spoiled physically. However, this also limits the memory and processing resources that may be placed on the card. As a result, the smart card always has to cooperate with other external peripherals to operate. For example, it may require a device to provide and supply user input and output, time and date information, power and so on. These limitations may degrade the security of the smart card in some circumstances where the external elements are suspect and precarious.

10.3.2   Smart Card Data Security

To protect the palmprint data during registration and identification, we need the provision of security for palmprint data storage, processing and delivery. Recently, a great deal of research has focused on this topic. The key issue is how to ensure that the user can trust the access equipment, including the smart card reader and the associated computer platform; since they allow the possibility of stealing (leaking) the users' authenticated palmprint data. There are two methods of using cards for data system security, host-based and card-based. The safest systems employ both methodologies.

Host-Based System Security.   A host-based system treats a card as a simple data carrier. Because of this, straight memory cards can be used very cost-effectively for many systems. All protection of the palmprint data is done via the host computer. The palmprint data may be encrypted but the transmission to the host can be vulnerable to attack. A common method of increasing the security is to write in the clear (not encrypted) a key that usually contains a date and/or time along with a secret reference to a set of keys on the host. Each time the card is re-written the host can write a reference to the keys. In this way, each transmission is different. However, parts of the keys are in the clear for a potential hacker to analyze. Security can be increased by using smart memory cards that employ a password mechanism to prevent unauthorized reading of the data. Unfortunately the passwords can be sniffed (electronically intercepted) in the clear. Access is then possible to the main memory. These methodologies are often used when a network can batch the palmprint data regularly and compare values and card usage and generate a problem card list.

Card-Based System Security. These systems are typically microprocessor card-based. A card, or token-based system treats a card as an active computing device. The Interaction between the host and the card can be a series of steps to determine if the card is authorized for use in the system. The process also checks if the user can be identified, authenticated and if the card will present the appropriate credentials to conduct a transaction. The card itself can also demand the same from the host before proceeding with a transaction. The access to specific information in the card is controlled by the card's internal operating system and the preset permissions set by the card issuer.

There are predominately two types of card operating systems. One type of card OS (operating system) is the most cost-effective in many businesses because you only pay for the size and functions that you specify. This classical approach treats each card as a secure computing and storage device. The issuer sets the permissions on the files in advance. The only access to the card is through the operating system. There are no back doors, and no commands for reconfiguration of file structures on the card. Data is read or written to the card through permissions set only by the issuers. The operating system performs a set of "applications" such as authentication and encryption, as requested through commands sent to the card. The CardLogix M.O.S.T. is one example of this type of operating system.

The second methodology is the disk drive approach to card operating systems. The card is a computing device with an active memory manager and this allows it to be loaded with specific applications and files. The card's operating system allows for active file allocation and management. It is designed for cards that are expected to have a long life (e.g., 4 years). Java Cards and the Microsoft Windows Card OS are examples of this approach. These cards have a much higher risk of tampering due to the ability to introduce active applets and or viruses onto the card. Conceivably, someone could replace a purse or file containing a low monetary value with a new purse that has the same identification and a higher monetary value.

Initial issuance of these cards is costly, due to the sophistication of the OS. The advantage of this approach is that card replacement costs can possibly go down through the use of upgrades on existing cards. This card architecture requires a larger memory to allow for future (as yet unplanned) upgrades, and a larger program memory to upload applets. This translates to larger semiconductors at higher cost. These approaches may also come with a software-licensing burden that is ultimately paid by the card issuer. Also, the security infrastructure costs are much higher to manage due to the multiple points of entry to the card system functions.

10.4. System Analysis and Applications

In 2000, the biometric industry managed to generate revenues of about US\$ 196 million. By the end of 2001, this is expected to be about US\$ 350 million. By 2003, it is anticipated that revenues will exceed one billion dollars.Make no mistake; this industry is moving forward at lightning speed.

10.4.1 The Market Overview of the Smart Card

The growth in demand for smart cards during 2001 will be over 20%, as forecasted by Schlumberger in its annual market review. Growth will be driven largely by wireless applications, and the start of m-commerce will add a new dimension to this segment.

Despite substantial silicon shortages, card shipments in 2000 grew 27.86% to reach 1790 million units. This trend will probably continue until the expected increases in semi-conductor capacity come on-stream at the end of 2001(See Table 10.1).

Table 10.1. World smart card consumption and forecast for 1999-2001.

By market (million units)	1999	2000	2001	Growth 2000/1999	Growth 2001/2000
Payphone	920	1080	1190	17.4%	10%
Mobile Communications	160	350	500	118.75%	43%
Banking	135	120	150	-11%	25%
Healthcare	60	65	70	8.3%	8%
Transport	25	30	45	20%	50%
Others	100	145	215	45%	48%
Totals	1400	1790	2170	27.86%	21%

The outstanding application sector for smart cards was, as expected, SIM (subscriber identity module) cards for mobile phones, which expanded by more than 118.75% from 1999 to 2000. Banking cards (the next largest market sector for microprocessor smart cards) will achieve healthy double-digit growth in 2001. Among other microprocessor card applications, pay–

TV and ID cards grew strongly. Take-up of digital TV and the emergent need for PC, intranet and Internet security contributed to this growth. The health cards sector remained fairly static, because of its cyclical nature and reliance on large projects; indeed two of these projects –(the French and German health insurance schemes) are close to being completed. Payphone cards, the major application category for memory chip-based cards, accounted for well over half of the industry's total card shipments: over a billion units in terms of volume, but only one-sixth of the industry's revenue. This segment remained stable and predictable. Nevertheless, there are many bright spots to look forward to in 2001.

10.4.2   Applications

Bill Gates, the chairman of Microsoft, has recently called for the industry to reduce the cost of smart card and biometric technologies, so that over time, their use will increase the security of computing by eliminating the need for passwords and by making PKI more pervasive. Microsoft's commitment to smart cards and biometrics has recently been visibly demonstrated with the acquisition of I/O Software's Biometric API and its Secure Suite core authentication technology.

Although figures for the number of systems using smart cards and biometrics are not readily available, many governments and institutions are interested in this kind of system (a selection of which are listed below). Several of the applications chose fingerprint, face or hand geometry as the characteristic, but the palmprint is also a suitable replacement for these approaches.

In Finland, the Makropilotti social security smart card, which is currently being piloted in Pori, will contain health and social security data and will contain a biometric identifier.

In the Netherlands, Bell Group PLC has announced the involvement of its smart card software subsidiary, Bell ID, in two new security contracts for the Schiphol Group at Schiphol Airport, Amsterdam. First, an iris recognition-based scheme for frequent travelers from most European countries (and airport staff who work in secure areas) and second, a multi-application, smart card scheme embracing the 80,000 employees of numerous organizations and businesses who work across the entire airport site.

In the Netherlands, the Minister of Justice opened the new border passage system on 23 October year which is being implemented by the Schiphol Group as part of its Privium service program. Automatic passage is allowed after comparison between a passenger's iris scan and iris data held on the chip of a personal smart card.

In USA, the immigration bureau uses the biometric based smart card for border control. A notable example is the INSPASS system in which travelers were issued with a card enabling them to use strategically placed biometric terminals and bypass long immigration queues.

The European Commission is looking into the combined use of smart cards and biometrics through its FASME (Facilitating Administrative Services for Mobile Europeans) project. This research project is investigating the use of Java Cards and biometrics to support people moving round Europe and to make access to local government services easier. The aim is to automate processes such as citizen registration, car registration and driver license applications.

In Spain, TASS, the Spanish social security smart card, also stores fingerprint templates, allowing cardholders to access on-line benefits information at kiosks and to receive benefit payments at ATMs.

In Israel, the Ministry of Defence's Basel project will see the distribution of smart cards carrying face and hand geometry templates to 200,000 non-Israeli workers who cross the Israeli border to go to work. The group installing the system is headed by EDS Israel. The company Recognition Systems provides the hand geometry technology and the facial recognition technology.

In the USA, the smart card-based electronic purse scheme at Fort Sill in Oklahoma involves 20,000 US army recruits storing fingerprint templates on their electronic purse cards for authentication at the point of sale. The General Services Administration Smart Access Common ID project will also involve biometric templates stored on smart cards.

10.4.3   System Analysis

Palmprint identification, like other biometrics, is not a 100% perfect system. Standard error rates (FAR and FRR) are defined. FRR (Fault Reject Rate) is the probability that a biometric system will fail to identify an enrollee, or fail to verify a legitimately claimed identity of an enrollee, and is also known as a 'Type I error rate' or 'False Non-Match Rate'. FAR (Fault Accept Rate) is the probability that a biometric system will incorrectly identify an individual or will fail to reject an impostor, and is also known as the 'Type II error rate' or 'False Match Rate'. The FRR and FAR are stated as follows:

$$FRR = \frac{number\ of\ false\ rejections}{number\ of\ enrollee\ attempts} \tag{10-5}$$

$$FAR = \frac{number\ of\ false\ acceptances}{number\ of\ impostor\ attempts} \tag{10-6}$$

Both rates must be as low as possible, but they are actually antagonists and part of an intricate balancing act. If you make the system more difficult to enter for an impostor (reducing FAR) you also make the system more difficult to enter for a true enrollee (by raising the FRR); and vice versa.

For a given system, this is a question of relative probabilities, and a company deploying these systems will generally adjust the matching threshold depending on the level of security needed. For instance, to enter a safe, a bank needs a very secure system, so it would adjust the threshold to a very high level to reach an FAR that is as close to zero as possible. However, the bank employees will have to accept more false rejections: and they may have to repeat the entry procedure several times.

Besides the FAR and FRR, another key issue involved in palmprint identification is efficiency (time consumption), which reflects how fast the final output can be given. It depends on efficient searching and matching algorithms, especially for a large database. Obviously, the higher the efficiency that can be achieved by an identification system the better it meets the needs of the users.

Palmprint images were collected in our laboratory from 500 persons using our self-designed capture device that was introduced in Figure 10.6 (Image size=320*240 pixels). Six samples were captured for the right palm of each person. Thus, we set up a palmprint database with a total of 3,000 images. During the testing we used 3 samples from each person to calculate the mean feature set, then, the remaining 3 samples for authentication. The feature extraction algorithm was based on the wavelet transform, and the length of the feature set was 256 bytes. Based on this scheme, the FAR is almost equal to zero and the FRR is less than 2%. At the same time, the time taken for the entire authentication process is less than 2 seconds.

10.5.   Conclusions

In this chapter, we have discussed the smart card system based on palmprint identification, which combines the two popular research topics of smart cards and biometrics. This has better security performance than traditional authentication methods such as PINs and ID cards. In this chapter, we introduced the general procedure and key issues in palmprint identification and explained the architecture of the smart card system in detail. We then gave the system performance analysis of a palmprint identification based smart card system. We believe that this kind of security system will be widely accepted and used in various fields, especially, in *e-*world applications.

References

[1]   W. Shu and D. Zhang. Palmprint Verification: An Implementation of Biometric Technology. In Proc. of 14th International Conference on Pattern Recognition (ICPR'98), Brisbane, Australia, 219 – 221, 1998.

[2]   D. Zhang, W. Shu. Two Novel Characteristics in Palmprint Verification: Datum Point Invariance and Line Feature Matching, Pattern Recognition, 32(1999) 691-702, 1999.

[3]   A.K. Jain, H. Lin, P.Harath, and R. Bolle. An Identity-Authentication System Using Fingerprints. In Proc. of IEEE Special Issue on Automated Biometrics, vol. 85, no.9, Sept. 1997.

[4]   A. Jain, R. Bolle and S. Pankanti. Biometrics Personal Identification in Networked Society, Kluwer Academic Publishers, 1999.

[5]   A.R. Roddy, J.D. Stosz. Fingerprint Features – Statistical Analysis and System Performance Estimates. In Proc. of IEEE Special Issue on Automated Biometrics, vol. 85, no. 9, Sept. 1997.

[6]   D. Zhang. Automated Biometrics Technologies and Systems, Kluwer Academic Publishers, 2000.

[7]   Q. Xiao, Z. Bian. An Approach to Fingerprint Identification by Using the Attributes of Feature Lines of Fingerprint, IEEE, CH2342-4/86/0000/0063$01.00, 1986.

[8]   K. Morita, K. Asai. Automatic Fingerprint Identification Terminal for Personal Verification, Hybrid Image Processing, vol. 638, 1986.

[9]   S.Y. Kung, S.H. Lin and M. Fang. Neural Network Approach to Face/palm Recognition. In Proc. of the 1995 IEEE Workshop on Neural Networks for Signal Processing, Cambridge, MA, USA, pages 323-332, 1995.

[10]   J. You, W. Li, D. Zhang. Hierarchical Pamlprint Identification via Multiple Feature Extraction, to appear in Pattern Recognition, 2001.

[11]   W. Shi, D. Zhang. Automatic Palmprint Verification, International Journal of Image and Graphics, vol. 1, no. 1, pages 135-152, 2001.

[12]   K. Matsumoto. Palm-recognition Systems: An Ideal Means of Restricting Access to High-security Areas, Mitsubishi Electric Advance, vol. 31, pages 31-32, 1985.

[13]   M. Shiono, H. Ishikawa and H. Shimada. An Experiment on Personal Identification for Gate Security using Hand Shape and Palm-print, Transactions of the institute of Electronics, Information and Communication Engineering D- II, vol. J74, no. 6, pages 688-697, 1991.

[14]   X. Shen, M. Cheng, Q. Shi, and G. Qiu. A New Automated Fingerprint Identification System, Journals of Computer Science & Technology, vol. 4, no. 4, 1989.

[15]   L. O'Gorman and J. V. Nickerson. An Approach to Fingerprint Filter Design, Pattern Recognition, vol. 22, no. 1, pages 29-38, 1989.

[16]   Q. Xiao, H. Raafat. Fingerprint Image Postprocessing: A Combined Statistical and Structural Approach, Pattern Recognition, vol. 24, no. 10, pages 985-992, 1991.

[17]   J. Zhang, Y. Yan and M. Lades. Face Recognition: Eigenface, Elastic Matching, and Neural Nets, Special Issue on Automated Biometrics, Proceedings of the IEEE, vol. 85, no. 9, 1997.

[18]   D. Mcelroy, E. Turban. Using Smart Card in Electronic Commerce, International Journal of Information Management, vol. 18, no. 1, pages 61-72, 1998.

[19]   S. Moon, H.C. Ho and K.L. Ng. A Secure Card System with Biometrics Capability, In Proc. of the 1999 IEEE Canadian Conference on Electrical and Computer Engineering, 261-266, 1999.

[20]   Abdul Wahab, E.C. Tan and S.M. Heng. Biometrics Electronic Purse, IEEE Tencon, 958-961, 1999.

[21]   L.C. Guillou, M. Ugon and J.J. Quisquater. Cryptographic Authentication Protocols for Smart Cards, Computer Networks, 437-451, 2001.

[22]   Editorial. Current Directions in Smart Cards. Computer Networks, 377-379, 2001.

[23]   David M' Raihi and Moti Yung. E-Commerce Applications of Smart Cards, Computer Networks, 453-472, 2001.

[24]   Raul Sanchez-Reillo. Smart Card Information and Operations Using Biometrics, IEEE AESS Systems Magazine, 3-6, April 2001.

[25]   Q. Xiao and H. Raafat. Combining Statistical and Structural Information for Fingerprint Image Processing, Classification and Identification. Pattern Recognition: Architectures, Algorithms and Applications, 1991.

[26]   A. Jain, H. Lin, and R. Bolle. On-Line Fingerprint Verification, IEEE Transactions on PAMI, vol. 19, no. 4, April 1997.

[27]   R.A. McLaughlin, M.D. Alder and C.J.S. DeSilva. Inference of Structure: Hands. Pattern Recognition Letters, Oct. 1994.

[28]   Survey. The Smart Card Market in 2000. Card Technology Today, 14-15, March 2000.

[29]   Survey. The Smart Card Market in 2000. Card Technology Today, 13-14, Feb. 2001.

[30]   Bob Carter. Implementation Implications of Biometrics, Information Security Technical Report, vol. 3, no. 1, 60-69, 1998.

Chapter 11

SECURE FINGERPRINT AUTHENTICATION

Nalini K. Ratha, Jonathan H. Connell and Ruud M. Bolle
Exploratory Computer Vision Group
IBM Thomas. J. Watson Research Center
Hawthorne, NY 10532, USA
{ratha, jconnell, bolle}@us.ibm.com

Abstract   Biometrics-based authentication systems offer advantages over the present practices of knowledge and/or possession-based authentication systems. However, when using biometrics, the overall authentication architecture needs to be reexamined to ensure that no new weak security points are introduced. After analyzing a pattern recognition-based threat model of a biometrics authentication system, this chapter describes secure fingerprint authentication. Several solutions are proposed to alleviate the threats using conventional encryption as well as novel techniques that exploit the richness of biometrics data. The proposed methods are applicable in many application areas. These includes system security, electronic commerce security, point of sale, point of entry/exit and point of access. We also argue that an authentication scheme with both smart card and biometrics improves the overall security of a system.

Keywords: Authentication, identification, smart card, encryption, biometrics

11.1.   Introduction

Person identification is an important and fundamental task in our day-to-day life. Humans identify family, friends, acquaintances and business associates effortlessly. With the rapid growth of the transportation and communication industries, however, the phenomena of a community where everyone knows one another and without much effort identifies each other is disappearing. Communities are not limited by geography anymore, and this makes the task of person identification difficult and the outcome unreliable if left to the human. Automated systems, providing robust person authentication and identification services are therefore of increasing importance. Remote positive user authentication is also increasingly important in our ever more networked world.

Robust person identification has unfortunately become a necessity of modern life. The consequences of a compromised insecure authentication system in a corporate or enterprise environment can be catastrophic, often leading to loss of confidential information, service denials, and issues with integrity of data and information content. Reliable user authentication is not just limited to computer, network or other type of electronic access. Many other activities in everyday life require positive person authentication. These include customer authentication at points of sale, physical access control of buildings, restricted points of exit/entry (e.g., airports), vehicle ignition control, etc. All these areas will benefit from enhanced biometrics security, although different applications may have different requirements and should be looked at separately. This chapter examines inherent strengths and weaknesses of biometrics and does not study biometrics for a particular application.

11.1.1   Authentication and Repudiation

Today's prevailing techniques for machine *user authentication* mainly involve passwords and user IDs, or magstripe magnetic cards and PINs. Here the user ID or magstripe card lays claim on an identity and supplying the correct PIN suffices as authentication of this identity. Sometimes the scenario is even more lax and the mere possession of a magstripe card, or even an account number, is accepted as authentication method, e.g., purchasing gas at the gas station.

These methods suffer from several limitations. One of the main problems is that such systems can be fooled relatively easily. First, passwords, PINs and magstripe cards can be shared among genuine users of a system or resource and, worse, they can be shared with unauthorized individuals. Moreover, passwords and PINs can be illicitly acquired by direct covert observation. Once an unauthorized individual has acquired a password, this person has complete access to the associated resources.

Hence, another major problem with current authentication technology is that there is no way to positively link the usage of a system to the actual user. This is the issue of "repudiation" – an individual can simply deny that it was *he* who used the system. Biometrics technology is particularly attractive because it provides true (irrefutable) user authentication.

Similarly, while critical credit card transaction information is sent over the Internet using secure encryption methods, the present practice is not capable of assuring that the rightful owner presents the credit card. In a networked environment, where the access points to systems and resources are widely distributed geographically, remote authentication policies based on a simple combination of user ID and password, or, worse, simply based on possession, have become, or are rapidly becoming, inadequate. Automated biometrics system technology in general, and fingerprint technology in particular, provides much more accurate and reliable user authentication methods.

11.1.2 Biometrics

The area of biometrics is rapidly advancing and is concerned with identifying people based on their physiological or behavioral characteristics. Rather than checking the knowledge or possessions of the user, the user is authenticated by checking physiological or behavioral traits that are more or less unique to an individual and invariant over time. Roughly, physiological biometrics, such as fingerprint, face and iris do not depend on the emotional of physical state of an individual. Behavioral biometrics, on the other hand, often depend on the particular state of an individual (e.g., tired, sick). These biometrics include speech pattern and written signature.

An advantage of biometrics signals is that they are much larger than a password or pass phrase. Biometrics signals range from several hundred bytes to over a megabyte. Typically, the information content of the signals is more or less proportional to the size of the signal. For passwords, one could simply extend the length of traditional passwords to get equivalent bit strength, but that presents significant usability problems. After all, it is nearly impossible to remember a phrase of 2,000 characters and it would take an impractically long time to enter such a phrase (especially without errors) at the keyboard. Automated biometrics authentication provides the security advantages of long passwords while retaining the speed and simplicity of short passwords.

Automated biometrics system will help to ease the problems associated with the existing methods of user authentication. But of course, vulnerable weak points in such systems will be found by ethical hackers and hackers with more malicious intentions. Password based systems are prone to brute-force dictionary attacks [30]. Substantially more effort is required to attack a biometrics system in a straightforward brute-force manner [21]. Although standard encryption techniques are useful in many ways to prevent breaches of security, there are several new types of attacks possible in the biometrics domain. If biometrics authentication is used in human supervised mode, this may not be a concern. But in remote unattended applications, such as web-based *e*-commerce applications, hackers may have the opportunity and ample time to make several attempts, or even physically violate the remote client before being noticed. These biometrics oriented attacks need special solutions as standard encryption techniques are not able to address them.

11.1.3   Chapter Overview

Summarizing, the following observations can be made:

- Today's societies are highly networked and mobile, which means that distances are getting shorter and communities are getting larger. The driving forces here are the enormous advances in communication and transportation technologies.

- The prevailing methods of identification and authentication are rapidly becoming insufficient and outdated. Identification by humans demands perceptual discriminations which the human is not particularly good at making. Moreover, today's automated authentication methods suffer from the above mentioned repudiation problems.

- The new 'electronic economy' lacks face-to-face communication and requires different secure authentication methods. Somehow, the remote server or service has to positively verify the user's true identity. It is obvious that biometrics is an answer here. When applying biometrics authentication, however, the system has to be carefully analyzed for any new security holes.

We will discuss in more detail the problems that are unique to biometrics authentication systems and propose solutions to several of these problems. Though our analysis is very general and applies to other biometrics, we will focus on fingerprint recognition in this chapter as an example. In Section 11.2, we model a generic biometrics system as a pattern recognition system and use this model to help identify possible attack points. In Section 11.3, we introduce the stages of automated fingerprint authentication and we give some special consideration to machine representations of fingerprints. These sections form the basis for the following discussions. In Section 11.4, we describe techniques to alleviate some of the threats described in Section 11.2. We conclude with a discussion of our observations in Section 11.5.

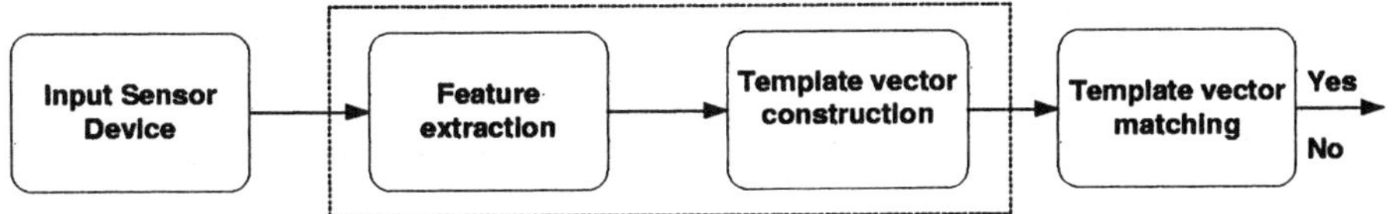

Figure 11.1. The different stages of an authentication viewed as a pattern recognition system.

11.2.   Biometrics-Based Authentication Systems

As shown in Figure 11.1, a biometrics-based authentication system can be cast as a pattern recognition system. Excellent introductions to such biometrics systems can be found in [11, 15]. We will examine the security aspects based on this system architecture.

11.2.1   Biometrics as Pattern Recognition

Looking at Figure 11.1 in more detail, a biometrics based authentication system consists of several stages, or modules, that can be found in many pattern recognition system. These modules are:

- An input device that captures and digitizes a sample of the biometrics signal, i.e., the signal acquisition module. For fingerprints, this can be a stand-alone fingerprint scanner connected to a client through an input port, or it can be a fingerprint sensor that is more tightly integrated with the client. Either way, some live phenomena is sampled and digitized. In statistical terms this is called a sample of a random variable where the variable in this case is the three-dimensional fingerprint itself. Limitations in measurement techniques distort the true input signal thus the measurement therefore is a random variable whose parameters depend on the biometrics.

- A feature extraction and representation module that computes "landmarks" from this sample biometrics. A fingerprint image, for example, consists of a flow pattern of ridges and valleys where the ridges have endings and bifurcations. A module for constructing an invariant representation (called template in the case of fingerprints) uses these features to build a compact representation of the biometrics sample. Typically, the sample acquired from a user varies significantly from presentation to presentation. For this reason, this stage attempts to model the biometrics signal in an invariant fashion by eliminating known classes of variations.

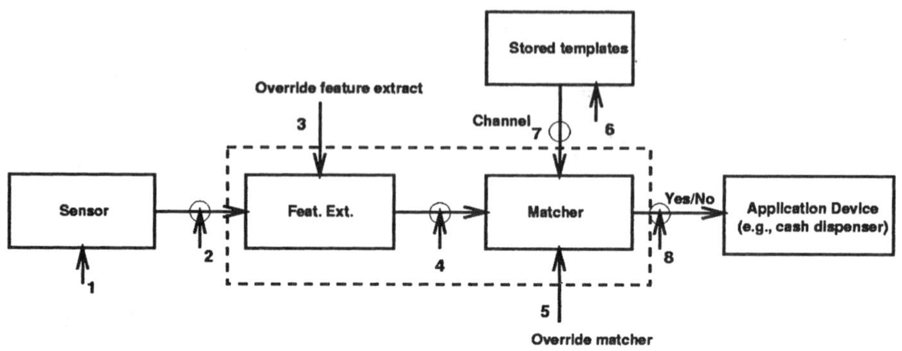

Figure 11.2. Possible attack points in a generic biometrics-based system.

- To authenticate a user against a claimed identity, the corresponding stored template is retrieved and matched against the newly computed template from the current input sample supplied by the user. The output of this module is either *YES* when the two templates are closely matching, or *NO* when the templates are substantially different. The match decision is often based on some score measure that represents the degree of match, i.e., some similarity measure. Such similarity measures can take into account linear and nonlinear geometric transformations from sample to sample, lighting changes, and other variations in signal acquisition.

11.2.2 Threat Model

Enrolling a person in a biometrics authentication or identification system requires the measurement of a biometrics sample, and ideally measuring the biometrics as precisely as possible. A good quality result can often be obtained because a person is generally enrolled by an authorized and knowledgeable supervisor. During the enrollment, an invariant template is extracted and stored in a database representing the particular individual, This database can be centralized, or can be an ultimately distributed database that uses smart cards to store individual biometrics templates.

The subsequent process of biometrics authentication is generally very complex, both from a pattern recognition point of view and from a security point of view. Schneier [27] describes several types of security problems specific to biometrics systems. In this chapter, we look at an additional eight points of attack on biometrics-based authentication systems as shown in Figure 11.2. In particular we examine the following issues:

- *Attack point 1:* An unauthorized person may present a fake biometrics at the sensor. In this mode of attack, a reproduction or copy of the biometrics is presented as input to the pattern recognition sensing system. Examples include a fake finger, a copy of a written signature, a voice impersonation and even a simple face mask.

- *Attack point 2:* Digitally pre-recorded biometrics signals are somehow electronically presented to the input sensing system. In this mode of attack (replay attack), a recorded signal is replayed to the authentication system, bypassing the sensor. Examples here include the presentation of an old copy of fingerprint image or injecting a recorded audio signal of a speaker.

- *Attack point 3:* The feature extraction process is somehow overridden with fake data. For example, the feature extraction module could be attacked with a Trojan horse so that it produces feature sets pre–selected by attackers, such as stolen templates associated with authorized users.

- *Attack point 4:* The biometrics feature representation is somehow tampered with. After the features have been extracted from the input signal, these features are replaced by a different synthesized, tampered feature set. Here the attacker has to know the techniques for encoding the biometrics feature set into the representation.

- *Attack point 5:* The heart of the system is attacked by corrupting the module that matches biometrics representations. The biometrics template matcher is manipulated so that it always produces artificially high or low match scores, depending on the desire and intent of the attacker.

- *Attack point 6:* Tampering or manipulating the stored templates. The database of enrolled individuals is either locally or remotely accessible. The database may also be distributed over several servers. An unauthorized individual may try to modify one or more biometrics representations in the database, which may result in authorization of fraudulent individuals or, at least, the denial of service to authorized users.

- *Attack point 7:* The channel between the stored templates and the matcher could be attacked. When operating with a central database of stored templates, these templates are sent to the matcher through a secure channel. This channel could be attacked to modify the content of the templates before they are received by the matcher. Here, again, the attacker must know how the biometrics feature sets are encoded in the biometrics representation.

- *Attack point 8:* It may be possible to manipulate the authentication system by overriding the final match decision. If the final decision can be intercepted and altered, this obviously becomes quite dangerous. Even if the actual pattern recognition system has excellent performance characteristics, it has been rendered useless by the simple exercise of illicitly overriding the final matching result.

Notice that many of the threats outlined in Figure 11.2 have parallels in password-based authentication systems. For instance, all the channel attacks on biometrics systems are the same as the channel attacks on password based systems. One difference in a password based system is that there is no direct equivalent to the fake biometrics detector. Yet if a password is in some standard dictionary or other password bank, it might be deemed "fake" or at least suspicious. Also, many systems apply password rules; for example, a password should contain at least one digit. Login attempts with passwords that do not follow the rules could also be considered quite suspicious. Another difference is that in a password or token-based authentication system, no attempt is made to thwart replay attacks since there is no expected variation of the authentication "signal" from one presentation to the next. A possible analogue would be if the password matching module is forgiving and (say) lets the user transpose two characters and still declare a match. A sudden consistent use of the password with two characters transposed might then be interpreted as an indication of replay attacks.

11.3.   Fingerprint Recognition

Fingerprints are claimed to be unique to a person and, except for cuts and bruises, the prints remain invariant over the lifetime of a subject. Somewhat suprisingly, identical twins have different fingerprints because the ridges are the result of a morphogenesis process, not genetically predetermined. The overall flow pattern of these ridges as well as local perturbations form the basis for discriminating between different fingerprints.

11.3.1   Processing

As the first step in the fingerprint authentication process, an impression is acquired, typically using an inkless scanner. Several scanning technologies are available as recently surveyed by O'Gorman [18]. Fig-

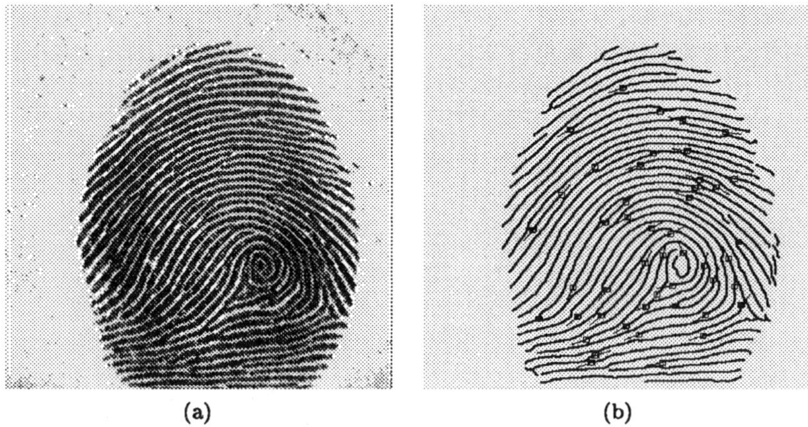

Figure 11.3. Fingerprint recognition. (a) input image. (b) features.

ure 11.3a shows a scanned fingerprint obtained using an optical sensor. A typical scanner digitizes the fingerprint impression at 500 dpi with 256 gray levels per pixel.

As with the true three-dimensional finger, the digital image of the fingerprint contains a number of unique features in terms of ridge bifurcations and ridge endings, collectively referred to as *minutiae*. While human experts use up to 18 types of fingerprint features for matching, most automated fingerprint matching algorithms use only these two types: ridge endings and ridge bifurcations.

The next stage in processing locates these minutiae features in the fingerprint image, as shown in Figure 11.3b. The ridge pattern of the fingerprint image is extracted by judicious image processing algorithms that localize the ridges in the image. A further processing step determines the ridge endings and ridge bifurcations. Minutiae features are commonly represented by their location (x, y) and the ridge direction θ at this location. This set of measurements forms the matching template for the finger. However, due to sensor noise and other variability in the imaging process, the feature extraction stage may miss some minutiae and may generate spurious minutiae. Further, due to the elasticity of the human skin, the relationship between minutiae may be distorted, almost randomly, from one impression to the next.

In the final stage, the matcher subsystem attempts to arrive at a degree of similarity between two sets of features. To do this the matcher needs to compensate for the rotation, translation, scale, and elastic distortions between the newly derived template and the stored template. For fingerprints, the use of the Hough transform (as in [23]) or the exploitation of edit distances (as in [12]) are examples of methods for matching minutiae. The similarity is often expressed as a score, where a high score indicates a good match. Based on this score, a final decision of *match* or *no-match* is made.

11.3.2   Issues

The operational issues in a fingerprint recognition system are somewhat different from those of more traditional password based systems. First, there is a system performance issue known as the "fail to acquire" rate to be considered. For instance, some people have very faint fingerprints (or no finger ridges at all), which renders a fingerprint authentication system useless to them. A related issue is "failure to enroll", typically arising from a "reject" option in the system based on input image quality. That is, a sufficiently poor quality input will not be accepted by the system during enrollment and authentication. Note that poor quality inputs can be due to non-cooperative users, improper usage, dirt on the finger and poor quality input scanners. These have no analogues in a password system.

Further, there is the fact that in a biometrics-based system the matching decision is not clear-cut. A strict matching password system always provides a correct response – if the passwords match, it grants access but otherwise it refuses access. However, in a biometrics system, the overall accuracy depends on the quality of input and enrollment data along with the basic, inherent accuracy characteristics of the underlying feature extraction and matching algorithm.

For fingerprint systems, and biometrics recognition systems in general, there are two basic types of errors: the false accept rate (FAR) and the false reject rate (FRR). If a non-matching pair of fingerprints is accepted as a match, it is called a false accept. On the other hand, if a mated pair of fingerprints is rejected by the system, it is called a false reject. Often the interplay of the two errors is presented by plotting FAR against FRR with the decision threshold as the free variable. This plot is called the ROC (Receiver Operating Characteristic) curve [7]. The two errors are complimentary in the sense that if an effort is made to lower one of the errors by varying the threshold, the other error rate automatically increases. The FRR is also called the false negative rate (FNR) and the FAR is called the false positive rate (FPR). Or sometimes a false negative is labelled a *Type I* error and a false positive is a *Type II* error.

For a biometrics-based authentication system, the relative false accept rate and false reject rate can be set by choosing a particular operating point (i.e., matching threshold) on the ROC. Very low (close to zero) error rates for *both* the errors (FAR and FRR) are not possible at the same time, since as of yet, no biometrics has matured to guarantee 100% accuracy. By setting a high threshold, the FAR error can be close to zero, and similarly by setting a significantly low threshold, the FRR rate can be close to zero.

A meaningful operating point for the threshold is decided based on the requirements of the application, and the FAR versus FRR error rates at that operating point may be quite different for different applications. To provide high security, biometrics systems are usually operated at a low FAR (not an equal error rate). The probability that the fingerprint signal is supplied by a genuine person given a good matching score is then high enough to accept that the two prints are the same. The certainty about the decision here will of the same order of magnitude as the certainties required in a courts of law. This high confidence generally provides better non-repudiation support than obtained with passwords.

11.4. Techniques to Improve Security

There exist several security techniques to thwart attacks at the eight weak points indicated in Figure 11.2.

In this section, we outline what can be done to further improve the security of a biometrics authentication system. In the course of the exposition we will describe interesting solutions for some of the problems specific to biometrics, e.g., liveness detection and replay attacks. For instance, finger conductivity or fingerprint pulse at the sensor can stop simple attacks at point 1. These problems have no counterpart in traditional password-based authentication system.

11.4.1 Conventional Precautions

Standard cryptography [25] can provide additional security as it does for traditional password based systems. Any communication channel between a client and server in the generic architecture should use encryption to avoid unwanted exposure of the data being exchanged. The final match decision should also be encrypted to avoid an attack at point 8. However, encryption might also be used at a lower level than the network. For example, a sensor may decide to use a hardware encryption method to send a signal to the client where it is decrypted for processing.

The simplest way to stop attacks at points 5, 6 and 7 is to have the matcher and database reside at a secure location. Also, the two main subsystems, feature extraction and matching, if not at the same site should at least be carried out in a secure mode. In particular, if feature extraction is performed at the client, the features should be digitally signed [26] to make sure that the template generated is authentic (attack point 4). A secure coprocessor [29] should be employed if possible. In general, one needs to be wary of a rogue system acting as a genuine client (e.g., a fake ATM trying to acquire biometrics and other details of users) and creating security holes in the overall process. Of course, even the most stringent precautions cannot prevent attacks in which there is collusion.

There are also brute force attacks to consider. With inter-operability in mind, several standards are being developed for exchanging information between systems using the same biometrics. For example, if fingerprints are used by several related institutions, they could probably share minutia representation and allow matching against each other's users by swapping templates. Though this is a requirement for inter-operability, care must be taken to prevent rogue systems from methodically generating and testing fingerprint templates in a sequential fashion. As mentioned above, the matcher should only accept digitally signed copies of templates with proper protocols. Other simple steps can also help safeguard the system against random template attacks, like a policy of locking the account if a predetermined number of rejections are noticed.

11.4.2   Liveness Detection

Most applications of biometrics-based systems require that the subject is a living human being. (A notable exception here is the identification of John Doe's at the morgue.) Hence, the use of fake biometrics such as facemasks, contact lenses with fake iris patterns, and synthetic fingers should be rejected right at the stage of biometrics signal acquisition. In a supervised operation, this is not so much of an issue, as the operator can presumably make sure the body part being used is a real and alive. However, in a remote transaction operation, the system should have the intelligence to reject fake biometrics itself. With progress made in the area of prosthetics, there may be very little visible difference between fake and real biometrics.

In optical scanners, as the finger touches an optical prism it is easy to scan even photographs of fingerprints. Brownlee [3] describes a novel method of detecting fingerprint such reproductions using two light sources. The object (finger in this case) is imaged twice using two different light sources. The first light source directs light to the prism platen and images where the skin is in contact using the standard frustrated total internal reflection technique. The second light source beams light straight up through the prism to produce an image where the areas with no skin contact are illuminated. If the sum of the difference of the two images is greater than a threshold, the finger is claimed to be from a live human being.

Interestingly, the human body has other associated signals that can be used to differentiate a fake simulacrum from a living body part. In this context, fingerprint and other biometrics that involve contact based sensing present easier problems than non-contact biometrics like face or voice. For fingerprints, often a simple heart beat detector will suffice for checking liveness. In the field of biomedical engineering there is also interest in measuring bioimpedance [8]. Setlak [28] presents a novel fingerprint sensor based on this idea to detect spoof fingers. It uses electrical impedance sensing to check if the conducitivity and capacitance of the object on the sensor is close to the expected impedance of a living subject. This method works with an active inkless scanner where the finger is in touch with the sensor directly.

Other clever methods have also been developed. Martinsen et al. [13] propose a method to measure moisture content in skin. This can be used to detect a fake finger pattern overlaid on a real finger. Fukuzumi describes a living body discriminating apparatus [6]. In this method, the finger muscle potential differences are measured using several electrodes. Still other methods use body temperature measurements and/or skin conductivity to activate a switch that enables imaging of the finger. Such techniques are novel but can be fooled relatively easily.

In general, there is no absolute fake finger detector. Methods such as those described above can only make a system much harder, and therefore much more expensive, to attack. This results in greater deterrence against spoofing of the biometrics authentication system.

11.4.3 Replay Attacks

One of the drawbacks of biometric authentication systems is their vulnerability to replay attacks. That is, the authentication system may be fraudulently supplied with pre-recorded biometrics signals or templates in an attempt to gain access. In this section, we present two solutions based primarily on the idea of challenge-response systems, but with challenges applicable to the biometrics domain.

Acquisition Validation. One serious class of threat is where an imposter poses as a real user to the server. In this type of attack, it is assumed that the perpetrator has somehow obtained a valid biometrics signal or template. This is possible since the biometrics signal or template must be transmitted from the client to the server. While this would typically be done in compressed and encrypted form, it may somehow be possible to compromise.

We propose a new method to thwart such attempts based on a modified challenge/response system. Conventional challenge/response systems are based on challenges C_u to the user, such as requesting their mother's maiden name, or challenges to a physical device C_d, like a special-purpose calculator that computes a numerical response. That is,

$$\text{the challenge is } C; \text{ the response is } f(C), \tag{11.1}$$

where the function f is only known to the user or the physical device. Here, for example,

$$f(C_u) = f(\text{''mother's maiden name?''}) = \text{maiden\_name}.$$

Note, however, that for a biometrics authentication system the challenge (11.1) only proves that the responder (the user or physical device) knows the function f. It does *not* ensure that the biometrics signal itself was acquired shortly before the response is verified.

Our approach is based on posing challenges C_s to the sensor instead. As shown in Figure 11.4, the sensor itself is assumed to have enough intelligence to respond to the challenges. For example, many silicon fingerprint scanners [18, 24] can exploit the proposed method since a processor can be integrated without much effort (as indicated by the integrated sensor and processor in the figure).

Our system differs in that it computes a response string, which depends not only on the challenge string, but also on the content of the returned biometrics template or signal. The dynamic challenges ensure that the biometrics signal was acquired, or the biometrics template was derived, after the challenge was issued. The dependence on signal or template values meanwhile guards against substitution of data after the response has been generated.

Our solution is diagrammed in Figure 11.4. When a transaction is initiated at the user terminal or system, the server generates a pseudo-random challenge C_s for this particular transaction. Note that we assume that the transaction server itself is secure. The client system then receives this challenge and passes it on to the intelligent sensor. Now, the sensor first acquires a new signal, and then computes a response to the challenge based in part on the newly acquired biometrics signal or derived biometrics template $\mathcal{B}$. That is, unlike the conventional challenge/response system of (11.1), we have

$$\text{the challenge to the sensor is } C_s; \text{ the response is } f(C_s, \mathcal{B}). \tag{11.2}$$

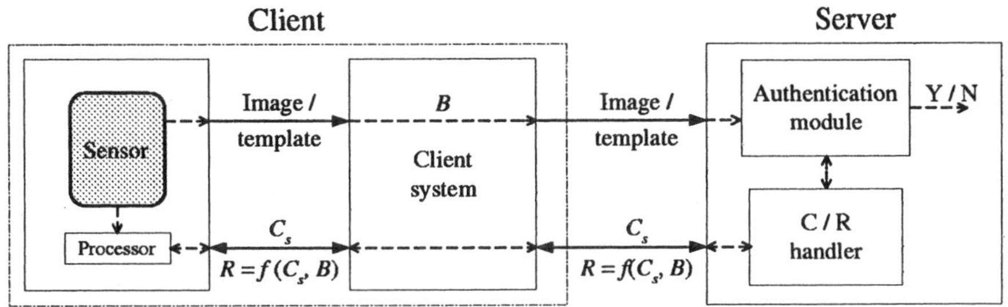

Figure 11.4. The client-server model with challenge/response biometrics signal validation.

Because the response processor is tightly integrated with the sensor (preferably on the same chip), the signal channel into the response processor *is assumed ironclad and inviolable.* It is just about impossible to inject a fake signal or template under such circumstances.

As an example of an image-based response, consider the function "$x1+$" which operates by appending pixel values of the fingerprint image (in scan order) to the end of the challenge string. A typical challenge might be "50, 100, 500". In response to this, the integrated processor selects the 50th, 100th, and 150th pixel value to generate an output response composed of gray levels such as "233, 129, 176." The complete image as well as the response is transmitted to the server where the response can be verified and checked against the image.

Other examples of responder functions include computing a checksum of a segment of the signal, a set of pseudo-random samples, a hash of signal values, a block of contiguous samples starting at a specified location with a given size, or a specified known function applied to selected samples of the signal. Of course, a combination of these functions can be used to achieve arbitrarily complex responder functions. The important point here is that the response depends on the challenge *and* the biometrics signal itself.

Note that standard cryptographic techniques do not provide adequate solutions. While they are mathematically strong, they are also computationally intensive and require maintaining secret keys for a large number of sensors. Moreover, encryption techniques cannot check for liveliness of a signal. An old stored signal can be given to the encrypter and it will simply encrypt it. Similarly, a digital checksum of a signal only ensures its integrity, not its liveliness.

WSQ-based Data Hiding.   Yet another way to enhance security is to use data-hiding techniques to embed additional information directly in compressed biometrics signals. For instance, if the embedding algorithm remains unknown, the service provider can look for the appropriate standard watermark to check that a submitted image was indeed generated by a trusted machine (or sensor). Several techniques for hiding digital watermarks in images have been proposed in the literature [14, 19]. Hsu and Wu [10] describe a method for hiding watermarks in JPEG (Joint Photographic Experts Group) compressed images. Excellent surveys of data-hiding techniques are presented in Bender et al. [1] and Swanson et al. [31]. Petitcolas et al. [19] also provide a nice survey and taxonomy of information hiding techniques.

The data hiding approach described here is motivated by the desire to create online fingerprint authentication systems for commercial transactions that are secure against replay attacks. To achieve this, the service provider issues a different verification string for each transaction. The string is mixed in with the fingerprint image before transmission. When the provider receives back the image it can be decompressed and the image can be checked for the presence of the correct one-time verification string. This guards against resubmission of stored images. The method hides such messages with minimal impact on the decompressed appearance of the image. Moreover, the message is not hidden in a fixed location (which would make it more vulnerable to discovery) but is deposited, instead, in different places *based on the structure of the image itself.* Although our approach is presented in the framework of fingerprint image compression, it can be easily extended to other biometrics such as wavelet compressed facial images.

Due to bandwidth limitations, for both Web-based and other online transaction processing systems, it is undesirable to send raw fingerprint images to the server. A typical fingerprint image is on the order of 512×512 pixels with 256 gray levels, resulting in an image size of 256 KBytes. This would take nearly 40 seconds to transmit at 53 Kbaud. Thus it is desirable to compress the fingerprint image before transmission. Unfortunately, many standard compression methods, such as JPEG, have a tendency to distort the high-frequency spatial structure of a fingerprint image. It is exactly this detail, the ridges, that is used in most automated fingerprint matching algorithms. Therefore several research efforts regarding domain-specific compression methods were proposed. As a result, the Wavelet Scalar Quantization (WSQ) Gray-scale Fingerprint Image Compression Algorithm developed by the Federal Bureau of Investigations [5] has become the *de facto* standard in the industry. This yields low image distortion even at high compression ratios (over $10 : 1$). Yet, because of the open compression standard, transmitting a WSQ compressed image over the Internet is not partic-

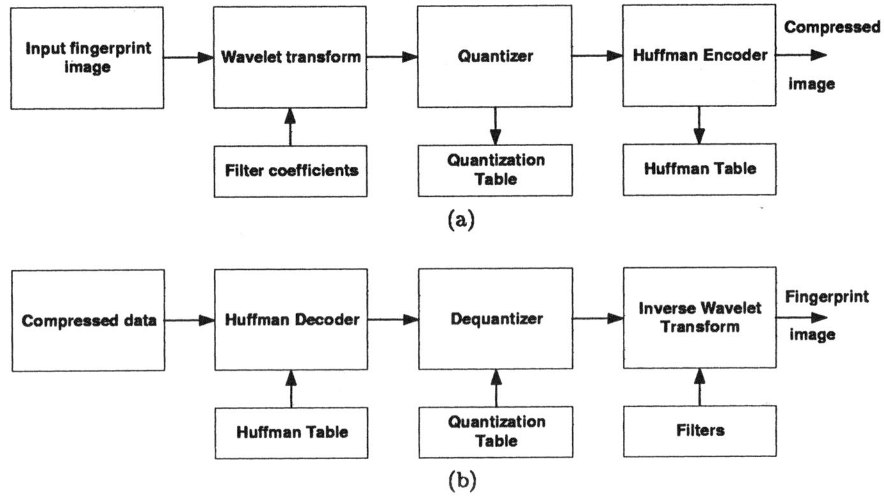

Figure 11.5. WSQ algorithm stages. (a) encoder. (b) decoder.

ularly secure. If a compressed fingerprint image bitstream can be freely intercepted (and decrypted), it can then be decompressed using readily available software. This potentially allows the signal to be saved and fraudulently reused (attacks at points 2 and 4 in Figure 11.2).

Our information hiding scheme works in conjunction with the WSQ fingerprint image encoder and decoder. In the first step of the WSQ compression, the input image is decomposed into 64 spatial frequency subbands using perfect reconstruction multi-rate filter banks [2] based on discrete wavelet transformation filters. The filters are implemented as a pair of separable 1D filters. The subbands are the filter outputs obtained after a desired level of cascading of the filters as described in the standard. The 64 subbands of the gray scale fingerprint image shown in Figure 11.6(a) are shown in Figure 11.6(c).

There are two more stages to WSQ compression. The second stage is a quantization process where the Discrete Wavelet Transform (DWT) floating-point coefficients are transformed into integers with a small number of discrete values. This is accomplished by uniform scalar quantization of each subband. There are two characteristics for each band k: the zero of the band (Z_k) and the width of the bins (Q_k). These parameters must be chosen carefully to achieve a good compression ratio without introducing significant information loss that will result in distortion of the images. The Z_k and Q_k for each band are transmitted directly to the decoder. The third and final stage is Huffman coding of the integer indices representing the DWT coefficients. For this pur-

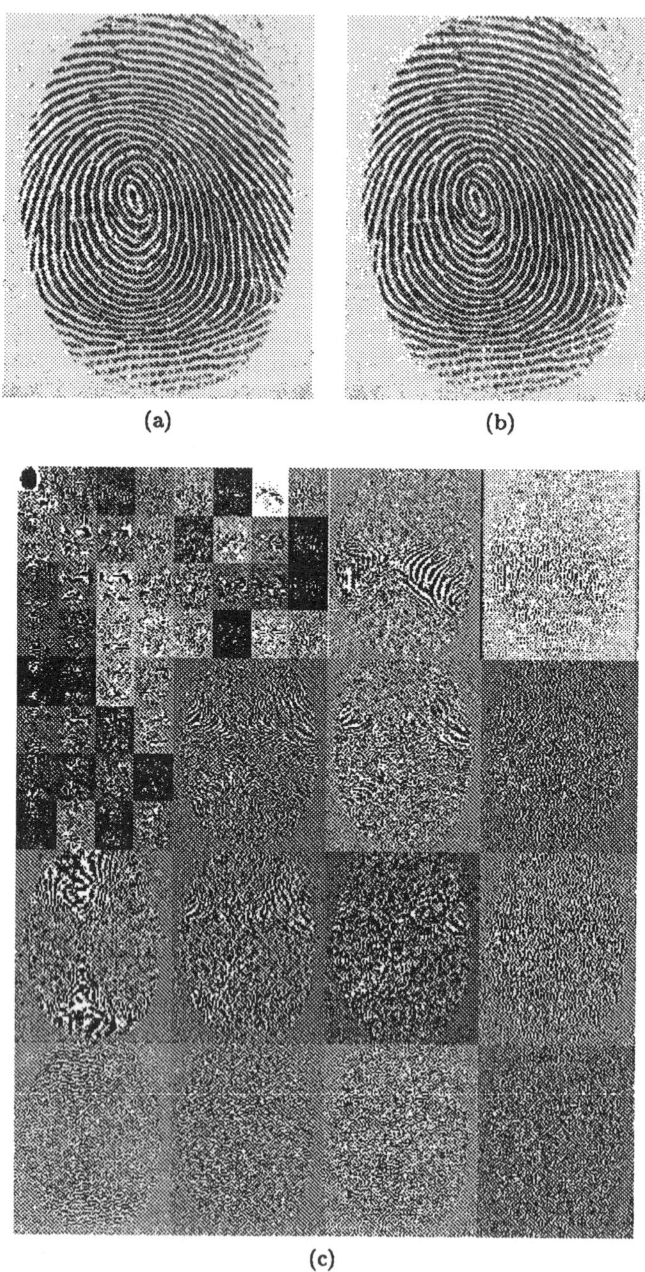

(a)   (b)

(c)

Figure 11.6. WSQ results. (a) fingerprint image. (b) reconstructed image with embedded message. (c) its 64 subbands.

pose, the bands are grouped into three blocks. In each block, the integer coefficients are re-mapped to numbers between 0-255 as prescribed by the translation table defined in the standard [5]. This translation table encodes run lengths of zeros and run lengths of ones and performs Huffman coding of the results. Negative coefficients are translated in a similar way by this table.

Our data-hiding algorithm works on the quantized indices before this final compression. We assume the message size is very small compared to the image size (or, equivalently, the number of DWT coefficients). The basic principle is to find and only slightly alter certain of the DWT coefficients. However, care must be taken to avoid corrupting the reconstructed image. Note however that the Huffman coding characteristics and tables are not changed; the tables are computed as for the original coefficients, not after the coefficient altering steps described next. To hide a message during the image encoding process, we perform three (or, optionally, four steps) basic steps:

- Selecting a set S of sites. Given the partially converted quantized integer indices, this stage collects the indices of all possible coefficient sites where a change in the least significant bit is tolerable. Typically, all sites in the low frequency bands are excluded. Even small changes in these coefficients can affect large regions of the image. For the higher frequencies, candidate sites are selected if they have coefficients of large magnitude. Making small changes to the larger coefficients leads to relatively small percentage changes in the values and, hence, minimal degradation of the image. Note that among the quantizer indices there are special codes to represent run lengths of zeroes, large integer values, and other control sequences. All coefficient sites incorporated into these values are avoided. In our implementation, we only select sites with translated indices ranging from 107 to 254, but excluding 180 (an invalid code).

- Generating a seed for a random number generator for choosing sites from S for modification. Sites from the candidate set S, which will be modified, are selected in a pseudo-random fashion. To retain predictability in encoder and decoder, the seed for the random number generator is based on the subbands that are not considered for alteration. For example, in the selection process, the content of subbands 0-6 are left unchanged in order to minimize distortion. Typically, fixed sites within these bands are selected and used as the seed, although, in principle, any statistic from these bands may be computed and used. Selecting the seed in this way ensures that the message is embedded at varying locations, based on the image content. It further ensures that the embedded message can only be read if the proper seed selection algorithm is known by the decoder.

- Hiding the message at selected sites by bit setting. The message to be hidden is translated into a sequence of bits. Each bit will be incorporated into a site chosen pseudo-randomly by the random number generator seeded as described above. That is, for each bit a site is selected from the set S based on the next output of the seeded pseudo-random number generator. If the selected site has already been used, the next randomly generated site is chosen instead. The low order bit of the value at the selected site is then changed to be identical to the current message bit. On average, half the time this results in no change at all to the coefficient value.

- Optionally appending the changed bits to the coded image. All the original low order bits of the effected sites can be saved and appended to the compressed bit stream as a user comment field (an appendix). The appended bits are a product of randomly selected low-order coefficient bits and hence these bits are uncorrelated with the hidden message.

The modified decoder performs three steps (optionally four steps) that mirror those of the encoder. The first two steps are identical to the first steps of the encoder. These steps construct the same set S and compute the same seed for the random number generator. The third step uses the pseudo-random number generator to select specific sites in S in the prescribed order. The least significant bits of the values at these sites are extracted and concatenated to recover the original message.

If a restoration appendix is included, the decoder can optionally restore the original low-order bits while reconstructing the message. This allows perfect reconstruction of the image (up to the original compression), despite the embedded message. Because the modification sites S are so carefully selected, the decompressed image even with the message still embedded, will be nearly the same as the restored decompressed image. In practice, the error due to the embedded message is not perceptually significant, and does not affect subsequent processing and automated authentication. Figure 11.6(a) and (b) show the original image and the reconstructed image where data was hidden in the WSQ encoded image.

When using this data hiding technique, only a specialized decoder can locate and extract the message from the compressed image during the decoding process. This message might be a fixed authentication stamp, personal ID information that must match some other part of the record (which might have been sent unencrypted), or some time stamp. If the bit stream does not contain an embedded message or the bit stream is improperly encoded, the specialized decoder will fail to extract the expected message and hence can reject the image.

Many implementations of the same algorithm are possible by using different random number generators or partial seeds. This means it is possible to make every implementation unique without much effort; the output of one encoder need not be compatible with another version of the decoder. This has the advantage that compromising one version will not affect any other version.

11.4.4   Smart Cards

A typical smart card consists of a processor and memory as shown in Figure 11.7. The tamper proof design and low power consumption with even 128-bit hardware encryption makes them an attractive candidate for many secure authentication applications. Over the years, smart cards have evolved from simple memory cards to more complex systems with 32-bit CPUs and hardware encryption engines to carry out secure computations. Data stored in smart card memory is protected by combined hardware and software mechanisms. Special on-board electronics protects data from unwanted alterations during memory read or write operations. Chemical and electrical corruption of memory content are detected using hardware memory integrity checks and in software using checksums. Illegal tape-out reading of smart card data is protected using hardware and software techniques. In addition standard encryption techniques can be combined to encrypt the data. The hardware encryption engine makes the card a reliable storage device. These measures make smart cards a strong candidate to support the privacy of stored data. More details about smart cards can be obtained from [20, 4].

Smart cards can play an important role in making biometrics-based authentication ultimately secure. While biometrics is the pinnacle of reliable authentication, smart cards are the model of highly secure storage. Thus the two might be combined in many applications to enhance security. For instance, many smart cards use a PIN to enable the card. An application waits for the user to enter the PIN before the stored contents can be accessed. Biometrics can replace this step.

In a hybrid system a user would need a card and the related biometrics to authenticate to a system. Arguably one would use a simple magstripe card to store basic information to claim an identity (e.g., name, account number, etc.) anyhow, as this is a much more convenient method than

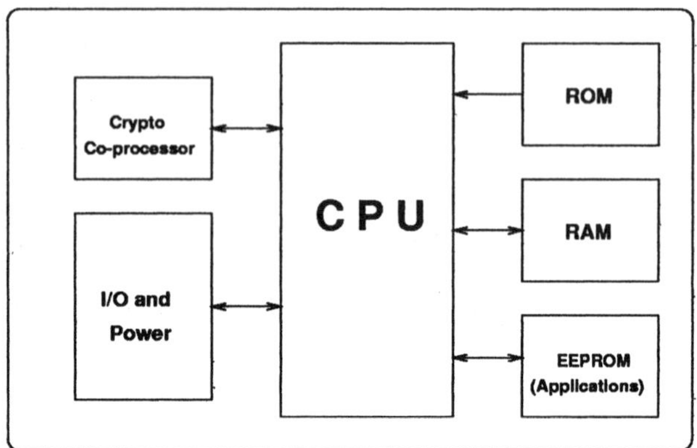

Figure 11.7. System architecture of a smart card.

having the user type the information in. Smart cards are then a more attractive option because of their built in security features that makes even the basic information secure. A two factor authentication consisting of a valid card and a valid enrolled biometrics is always more secure than any one single factor system. However, if the user loses the card, access is prohibited until a new replacement card is obtained. The lost card, even when falls into wrong hands, does not pose any threat to the system as one also needs the biometrics also to successfully pass the authentication system.

Actually storing biometric information in the smart card has the added advantage of privacy. (Other privacy related enhancements are presented in [22].) As pointed out earlier, with the central storage of a biometrics, there is the possibility of misuse of the biometrics for purposes unknown to the owner of the biometrics. Large collection of biometrics data can be sold or given away to unlicensed parties who can use the information however they choose. Yet smart cards provide a way of decentralizing the database into millions of pieces and thus giving the owners (enrollees) control. Furthermore, there is no central database which, if compromised (attack point 6), invalidates the complete system. That is, the authentication system does not store the biometrics on its central database anymore, rather the biometrics data can be stored on the smart card in encrypted form.

In this model, during the enrollment the user's biometrics is collected and the features are extracted from the biometrics signal after ensuring the quality of the input signal. The template is then stored in the smart card. For authentication of the user, the smart card and the live biometrics are presented to the system. The system generates the matching template from the presented biometrics, decrypts the stored template from the smart card, and examines the similarity between the two templates. The two steps in this proposed method are shown in Figure 11.8. Notice that having all the data local significantly cuts down on communication with the server.

Once a secure storage site is available, many other kinds of information can also recorded. Of course textual information such as personal name and account number can be part of the stored data. In a fingerprint-based authentication system, the fingerprint features along with, say, the threshold to be used during matching might be stored in the smart card. Similarly, in a face recognition-based system, the face template and the expected ranges of variation in its parameters can be stored. For speech systems, this method can provide extra benefit. In addition to storing a representation of the user's voiceprint, a generic voice model can also be saved. These parameters can then be restored by the service machine and used by a speech recognition driven menu system, thus resulting in improved interface performance.

The smart cards above are not assumed to have a significant amount of memory and processing power. A high-end smart card can have up to 64 KB of ROM memory and run at 32 MHz clock rate [9]. However, the RAM space is quite limited and often only on the order of 1-2 KBytes. This, for the present, prohibits running any high compute-intensive applications such as signal processing of biometrics input. However, by proper design, some or all of the *matcher* can be made to run on the smart card even now. The applications running on a smart card are virtually attack free by design. A secure protocol would be used to read the verdict computed by the card. By running the matcher on the smart card, the enrolled template never has to leave the card and hence further enhancing security. Moon et al. [16] describe such a collaborative fingerprint authentication method using a trusted host and smart cards.

With the size and cost of biometrics sensors, in particular fingerprint sensors, on the decline, very soon every person might have their personal smart card with both processing and a built-in fingerprint sensor. Noore [17] describes just such a smart card with a fingerprint scanner on it. Such a smart card system could directly run the image-based challenge-response and WSQ compression data hiding techniques described earlier. As such, it would be the ultimate authentication tool for use in many remote applications such as home banking, brokerage access control, and electronic commerce.

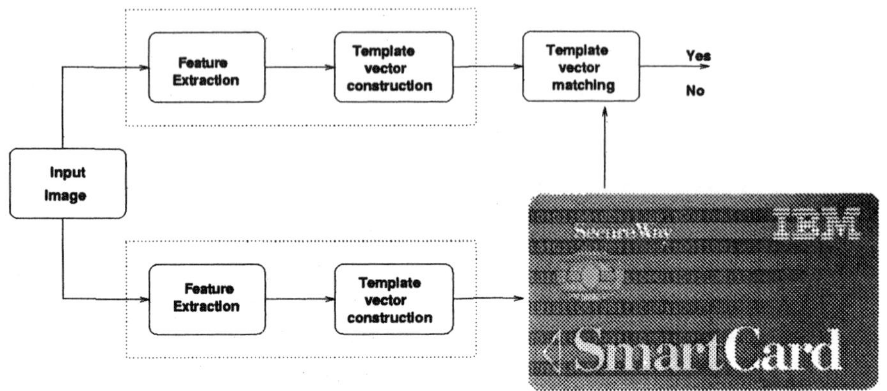

Figure 11.8. System architecture using biometrics and smart card.

11.5. Conclusions

Biometrics based authentication has many usability advantages over traditional systems such as authentication systems that use passwords. Among these are the facts that the user can never lose his biometrics and the fact that the biometrics signal is difficult to steal or forge. Yet, all systems, including biometrics systems, are vulnerable when unauthorized people are determined enough. We have highlighted eight weak attack points of a generic biometrics system and have discussed possible attacks and then suggested several ways to alleviate some of these security threats. In particular, replay attacks can been addressed using data hiding techniques to secretly embed a telltale mark directly in the compressed fingerprint image. And a challenge/response method can be used to check the liveliness of the biometrics signal acquired from an intelligent sensor. Finally, smart cards have been discussed as a means for protecting the template database and enhancing privacy.

References

[1]   W. Bender, D. Gruhl, N. Morimoto and A. Lu. Techniques for Data Hiding. IBM Systems Journal, 35(3&4):313–335, 1996.

[2]   C. Brislawn, J. Bradley, R. Onyshczak and T. Hopper. The FBI Compression Standard for Digitized Fingerprint Images. In Proc. of the SPIE, vol. 2847, pages 344–355, 1996.

[3]   K. Brownlee. Method and Apparatus for Distinguishing a Human Finger from a Reproduction of a Fingerprint. US Patent Number: 6,292,576, 2001.

[4]   J.F. Dhem and N. Feyt. Hardware and Software Symbiosis Helps Smart Card Evolution. IEEE Micro, (Nov.-Dec.):14–25, 2001.

[5]   FBI. WSQ Gray-scale Fingerprint Image Compression Specification. Technical
       Report CJIS FBI, IAFIS-IC-0110v2, Federal Bureau of Investigation, 1993.

[6]   S. Fukuzumi. Living Body Discriminating Apparatus. US Patent Number:
       6,181,808, 2001.

[7]   R. Germain. Large Scale Systems. In Jain, A., Bolle, R. and Pankanti, S.,
       editors, Biometrics: Personal Identification in Networked Society, Kluwer Aca-
       demic Press, Boston, pages 311–326 , 1999.

[8]   S. Grimnes and G. Martinsen. Bioimpedance and Bioelectricity Basics. Aca-
       demic Press, New York, 2000.

[9]   E. Hamann, H. Henn, T. Schack and F. Seliger. Securing e-business Applica-
       tions Using Smart Cards. IBM Systems Journal, 40(3):635–647, 2001.

[10]   C.T. Hsu and J.L. Wu. Hidden Digital Watermarks in Images. IEEE Trans.
       on Image Processing, 8(1):58–68, 1999.

[11]   A. Jain, L. Hong and S. Pankanti. Biometrics Identification. Communications
       of the ACM, 43(2):91–98, 2000.

[12]   A. Jain, L. Hong, S. Pankanti and R. Bolle. An Identity Authentication System
       Using Fingerprints. Proceedings of the IEEE, 85(9):1365–1388, 1997.

[13]   O. Martinsen and S. Grimnes. Measurement of Moisture Content in Skin. US
       Patent Number: 5,738,107, 1998.

[14]   N. Memon and P.W. Wong. Protecting Digital Media Content. Communica-
       tions of the ACM, 41(7):35–43, 1998.

[15]   B. Miller. Vital Signs of Identity. IEEE Spectrum, 31(2):22–30, 1994.

[16]   Y.S. Moon, H.C. Ho, K.L. Ng, S.F. Wan and S.T. Wong. Collaborative Fin-
       gerprint Authentication by Smart Card and a Trusted Host. In Proc. of the
       2000 Candian Conf. on Electrical and Computer Engineering, pages 108–112,
       2000.

[17]   A. Noore. Highly Robust Biometric Smart Card Design. IEEE Transactions
       on Consumer Electronics, 46(4):1059–1063, 2000.

[18]   L. O'Gorman. Practical Systems for Personal Fingerprint Authentication.
       IEEE Computer, 33(2):58–60, 2000.

[19]   F.A. Petitcolas, R.J. Anderson and M.G. Kuhn. Information Hiding – A Sur-
       vey. In Proc. of the IEEE, 87(7):1062–1078, 1999.

[20]   N. Ratha and R. Bolle. Smart Card Based Authentication. In A. Jain, R.
       Bolle and S. Pankanti, editors, Biometrics: Personal Identification in Networked
       Society, Kluwer Academic Press, Boston, pages 369–384, 1999.

[21]   N. K. Ratha, J. H. Connell and R.M. Bolle. An Analysis of Minutiae Matching
       Strength. In Proc. of IEEE 3rd Int. Conf. Audio- and Video-Based Biometric
       Person Authentication, AVBPA 2001, pages 223–228, 2001.

[22]   N.K. Ratha, J.H. Connell and R.M. Bolle. Enhancing Security and Privacy in
       Biometrics-based Authentication Systems. IBM Systems Journal, 40(3):614–
       634, 2001.

[23]   N.K. Ratha, K. Karu, S. Chen and A. Jain. A Real-time Matching System for
       Large Fingerprint Database. IEEE Trans. on Pattern Analysis and Machine
       Intelligence, 18(8):799–813, 1996.

[24]   T. Rowley. Silicon Fingerprint Readers: A Solid State Approach to Biometrics. In Proc. of the CardTech/SecureTech, vol. 1, pages 152–159, 1997.

[25]   B. Schneier. Applied Cryptography. Wiley, New York, 1996.

[26]   B. Schneier. Security Pitfalls in Cryptography. In Proc. of the CardTech/SecureTech, pages 621–626, 1998.

[27]   B. Schneier. The Uses and Abuses of Biometrics. Communications of the ACM, 42(8):136, 1999.

[28]   D. Setlak. Fingerprint Sensor having Spoof Reduction Features and Related Methods. US Patent Number: 5,953,441, 1999.

[29]   S. Smith and D. Safford. Practical Sever Privacy with Secure Coprocessors. IBM Systems Journal, 40(3):683–695, 2001.

[30]   W. Stallings. Network and Internetwork Security. Prentice Hall, Englewood Cliffs, 1995.

[31]   M.D. Swanson, M. Kobayashi, and A.H. Tewfik. Multi-media Data Embedding and Watermarking Technologies. In Proc. of the IEEE, 86(6):1064–1087, 1998.

Chapter 12

FROM BIOMETRICS TECHNOLOGY TO APPLICATIONS REGARDING FACE, VOICE, SIGNATURE AND FINGERPRINT RECOGNITION SYSTEMS

Javier Ortega-Garcia, Joaquin Gonzalez-Rodriguez, Danilo Simon-Zorita and Santiago Cruz-Llanas
Biometrics Research Lab – ATVS
Universidad Politecnica de Madrid (UPM), Spain
{jortega, jgonzalez, dsimon, cruzll}@diac.upm.es

Abstract   In this chapter, several biometric recognition systems, based on voice, fingerprint, face and signature are presented. The description of the state-of-the-art technologies regarding these biometric characteristics is widely faced. Minutiae extraction-based fingerprint matching, GMM-based speaker verification, on-line HMM-based signature verification, and PCA- or LDA-based face recognition are quoted. We will also focus on multimodality and data fusion in biometric systems; finally, some application strategies and some real-world demos are described.

Keywords: Biometrics, person recognition, person authentication, speaker recognition, face recognition, fingerprint matching, on-line signature verification, data fusion, multimodal systems, biometric applications.

12.1.   Introduction

In this chapter, we will present the problem of personal recognition by means of multiple biometric characteristics [1-10]. We will be concerned with four basic biometric characteristics, namely, voice, on-line signature, face and fingerprint. Two of them are physiological ones (fingerprint and face), and the other two are behavioral ones (voice and on-line signature). Our Biometrics Research Lab.-ATVS at Universidad Politecnica de Madrid, Spain (www.atvs.diac.upm.es), has been in the last decade involved with biometric signal processing, in both commercial and forensic applications. We will focus on these four biometric characteristics for different reasons: a) regarding fingerprint, due to its uniqueness and high discriminative capability [11-12]; b) regarding face, for its direct visualness with respect to in situ human interaction [13-14]; c) regarding voice, for its widespread availability in telephone networks [15-17]; and d) regarding signature, for its personal, social and legal acceptability as an identification procedure [18-19].

The Chapter is organized as follows: in Section 12.2, automatic speaker recognition systems are described; from speaker information involved in the speech signal to a global description of automatic recognition systems; moreover, some speaker recognition results, specifically those from NIST 2001 Speaker Recognition Evaluation, will be presented. In Section 12.3, automatic face recognition is described, from facial image processing to the inherent problems of face recognition; performance of face recognition systems will be shown, including results derived from the FERET competition. In Section 12.4, fingerprint matching systems, based on minutiae extraction, are presented; a complete image enhancement scheme will be described, permitting the final goal of minutiae extraction. Once this minutiae pattern is extracted, the complete pattern matching process is accomplished, making use of edit distance. In Section 12.5, on-line signature verification, based on Hidden Markov Models, is presented; the complete dynamic signature parameterization process will be described. After some specific parametric normalization techniques, the signature model generation process and the database employed will be also presented. Finally, on-line signature verification results will be shown.

Section 12.6 is dedicated to the problem of Multimodality and Data Fusion in Biometric Systems [20-22], as far as in many real-world commercial applications, and in order to improve single-system results, two or more biometric characteristics can be used together to enhance the complex output decision. Finally, in Section 12.7, some application strategies, in order to develop real biometric recognition systems from technology, will be discussed. We will also describe our voice, face, fingerprint and on-line signature demos in this final Section.

12.2.   Automatic Speaker Recognition

12.2.1   The Speaker Information in the Speech Signal

The process of communication by means of speech is the most usual form of transmitting information among people. This speech signal carries, besides the message we want to transmit, a lot of additional information as emotions, language, or identity of the speaker. Humans can easily recognize familiar voices [23], but where is this speaker-identity underlying information in the speech signal?

The identity information in the speech signal resides in both the low-level information, related with the acoustic and phonetic characteristics of the speech production process in the speaker, and the high-level information, related with psycho-linguistic peculiarities of the speaker. While humans can recognize speakers mostly focused in high-level characteristics, (and this information is crucial in classical Forensic Acoustics [24]), automatic speaker recognition systems are based in low level information, usually parameterized in the form of LPCC (Linear Predictive Cepstral Coefficients) or MFCC (Mel-Frequency Cepstral Coefficients). These coefficient vectors extract the segmental information of the vocal tract characteristics, and the use of delta (velocity) and delta-delta (acceleration) coefficients take into account the suprasegmental information, related with the short-term variation of the segmental information [25].

12.2.2   Speaker Recognition Systems

The goal of automatic speaker recognition techniques is to obtain reliable methods and procedures which are able to make decisions about the identity of a certain speaker without any kind of human supervision.

In automatic systems there are three different operating phases:

1. *Training* – models, patterns or templates corresponding to each one of the users of the system must be obtained (on- or off-line).
2. *Testing* – comparison between models, patterns or templates and input speech signals are accomplished in order to make decisions about the speaker identity.
3. *Updating* – the system must be able to incorporate new speakers, to delete users, and optionally to improve models, references and thresholds corresponding to the actual users of the system.

Speaker recognition systems are usually classified according to different approaches:

- **Text dependence:**
    1. *Text-dependent systems*: the test and training utterances used for each speaker correspond to the same 'text' (PIN, phrase, etc.).
    2. *Text-independent systems*: the test utterance is independent from the training speech.

- **Task dependence:**
    1. *Speaker identification*: the system classifies known speakers, in terms of what is the likelihood for each of them to produce the input testing speech. We have to make a distinction between *closed-set identification*, where the input speech is always

assigned to the most likely speaker, and *open-set identification*, where an additional output ("none of the known speakers") is possible, if the likelihood for the best classified speaker does not exceed a predefined threshold.

2. *Speaker verification*: in this case, the user of the system claims to be known. Then, the function of the verification system is to compare the input speech signal with the claimed identity model, taking an acceptance or rejection decision. Two types of users will be considered, true users (targets) and impostors (non-targets), and two types of errors must be considered in such decision systems: false rejections (miss detections or type I error), where a true user is not accepted, and false acceptances (false alarms or type II error), where an impostor is falsely accepted.

3. *Forensic speaker recognition*: an especial task must be considered here, where the objective is not to identify or verify speakers, but to answer to the Court question: "What is the probability that this voice came from that suspect?" (this task is issued in detail in Chapter 7 of this book [26]).

Regarding degrading elements in automatic speaker recognition, two main factors have been identified, namely, the time interval between enrolment and access trials (*multisession variability*); and the use of different communication channels as different microphones/telephone handsets or the presence of noise and reverberation (*channel variability*). In order to assess the performance of any speaker recognition system, databases with speech from known speakers are needed, taking into account these variability factors in order to test the systems in realistic conditions [27-28].

12.2.3   Speaker Recognition Algorithms

Different automatic techniques have been used for speaker recognition in the last thirty years, but all of them somehow can be included in one of the four following groups. We are not going to describe here each one of the algorithms in depth, but rather refer their operating principles, give some references, and show the applications where can be used as basic recognition technique.

Dynamic Time Warping (DTW).   This technique [25] has been used in text-dependent systems, as it compares in a time-dependent mode different realizations of given utterances. In this sense, a high likelihood score (small distance) will be provided for different realizations of the same password from the same speaker. The algorithm searches the best alignment path by means of dynamic programming techniques between the input and the reference utterance, where the cost of this best path will act as the distance between these two utterances.

There are two main factors affecting the performance of DTW-based text dependent systems, namely the end-point detection and the use of local path constraints. Because of the simplicity of the system it is very easily applicable to tasks like access control. However, it cannot be used in text-prompted applications, as the system needs an uttered reference for every possible required password. Additionally, the system is highly dependent of the reference utterance, not allowing variability in the speech signal.

Vector Quantization (VQ).		In Vector Quantization [29], each N-dimensional input vector (a point in the N-dimensional space) is represented by the closest 'codevector' or 'centroid' from a small group of vectors ('codebook') highly representative of the input vectors distribution in the N-dimensional space. These vectors of the 'codebook' are chosen as the best representatives of the different 'clusters' in which the input data can be divided.

In this way, the necessary elements to build a speaker recognizer by means of Vector Quantization are the following:

1. *Training data:* obtained from the parameterization of the speakers database.
2. *Similarity measure:* this is the basic measure that allows to carry out the assignments of the input vectors to the different classes or 'clusters'.
3. *Grouping algorithm:* it allows to divide the input data space in classes, which will be represented in the 'codebook' through their respective centroids.
4. *Assignment of vectors:* it determines the search procedure of the nearest codevector for any input vector.

The most extended similarity measure is the euclidean distance, which has a direct geometric sense in the N-dimensional space of characteristic vectors. The training of the 'codebook' is typically performed by means of the widespread Lloyd algorithm, also known as 'k-means' or LBG (standing for its authors Linde, Buzo and Gray), or by means of binary splitting. The procedure of vector assignment is usually carried out by means of Nearest Neighbor search, or by means of tree-search in the case of binary-splitting.

In order to apply VQ to speaker recognition, usually one different codebook per speaker is built, minimizing the distortion of the training speech for their respective codebooks. In the case of speaker identification, the distortion of the input speech with every speaker model is computed, and the lowest distortion will give us the identified speaker. In the case of speaker verification, the distortion of the test speech with respect to the claimed speaker model is computed and compared with a threshold. If this distortion is smaller than the threshold, the input speech will be accepted. Multiple VQ-based speaker recognition systems have been reported according to this general scheme [30].

Neural Nets (NN).   Neural Nets [31] are computational models emulating the human brain behavior by means of topologies resembling the interconnection of the nervous cells. A neural net consists on a group of 'neurons' (also called perceptron, nodes or cells) that are interconnected by means of weighted paths. In this way, each neuron is a processing element performing a function giving a single output from multiple inputs, usually controlled through an activation function.

Three architectures have been used for direct classification in speaker recognition obtaining good results in moderate complexity tasks:

- Multi-Layer Perceptron (MLP) [32]: the training will be carried out according to a cost function. The most usual form of training a multilayer network is by means of the 'back-propagation' algorithm (which is an application of the LMS algorithm to the training process). Introducing into the net the sequential nature of the speech signal, Recurrent Neural Networks (RNN) have also been used in speaker recognition, which are basically MLPs where recurrent connections of neurons in the same and different layers are permitted.

- Radial Basis Functions (RBF) [33]: RBFs are two layer networks with gaussian functions in the first layer and lineal output units. RBFs form a basis for the input space, where the activation of one of the RBF nodes is a function of its proximity to the current input pattern. In contrast to MLP sigmoids, the gaussian functions of the RBFs have localized receptive fields and will only respond to a specific part of the input space.

- Vector Learning Quantization (LVQ) [34]: the LVQ architecture uses several output cells for each class. It is quite similar to the vector quantization as it is based on the nearest neighbor classification principle. However, the reference vectors are not from the input patterns but rather they are learned according to a classification objective, allowing to identify the frontiers of the classes with more precision than with VQ and with much less references.

All these systems, based on direct classification, have serious inconveniences, being the most important that the complexity of the system increases dramatically with the number of speakers. A form of breaking this complexity is to introduce a-priori knowledge directly in the architecture of the system.

Hidden Markov Models (HMM). Nowadays, HMM-based systems are the selected alternative in almost every speech and speaker recognition system, based in their ability to model the different variability sources that appear in the speech signal and in the excellent results that are obtained with a moderate level of complexity.

Hidden Markov Models [25], initially used in word recognition, have been extended to almost every area in speech-related recognition, from continuous speech recognition and language modeling to speaker recognition. Text-dependent systems have used word models, or sub-word units as PLU (Phone Like Units) or ASU (Acoustic Segment Units), where each unit is modeled with a two or three state left-to-right model with continuous densities based in one to three gaussian mixtures. Speech-recognition-based systems have also been used in text-dependent systems, and extensively also in text-independent systems, looking for suppression of the dependence with the message and focusing in the speech production characteristics of the speaker. In [35] an ergodic (fully connected) HMM was used, where each utterance is characterized by a sequence of transitions on a fully connected HMM, representing each state one of a set of generic phonetic categories. In [36], it is shown that the transitional information among states does not contribute to the recognition, which is only related with the total number of mixtures of the model, that is, *number of states* x *number of mixtures per state*, independently of the number of states.

- **Gaussian Mixture Models (GMM)**

A very interesting case is that of the 1-state ergodic HMM, known as Gaussian Mixture Model (GMM) [15], as segmentation into states or maximum likelihood path sequence search are not further needed. The classical training process of the GMM is usually carried out by means of Maximum Likelihood estimation (ML) through a two steps algorithm known as Expectation Maximization (EM).

- **Likelihood Normalization**

Likelihood or score normalization is usually performed in speaker verification systems in order to improve the performance of the decision system. Different approaches have been proposed [37-38], but the idea of using a Universal Background Model (UBM) [39-40] as normalization term is almost a standard in current speaker verification systems. Additionally, speaker models can be obtained [41] via MAP (Maximum a Posteriori) [42] adaptation from speaker independent UBMs. Moreover, score-based normalization techniques as H-Norm and T-Norm provide further robustness to channel mismatch. The use of GMM-UBM with H-Norm and T-Norm is the approach that has obtained the best results in last Odyssey Speaker

Recognition and NIST Evaluations [43, 44], usually from male and female separate task-specific UBMs.

12.2.4   Some Speaker Recognition Results

In order to have an objective evaluation of our technology at ATVS, we participated in the one-speaker detection task of NIST 2001 Speaker Rec. Evaluation [45]. The submitted system, developed in our lab from basic signal processing to MAP model adaptation in our own classes library (C++), used the current parameterization of Telefonica platforms in their speech recognition deployed systems, analyzing with 32 ms. windows overlapped 16 ms., pre-emphasis of 0.97 with 16 mel-spaced (0-4 kHz) magnitude filters, obtaining 27 coefficients ((c0 + 8MFCC) + Δ + $\Delta\Delta$) per analysis frame. A single 1024 ML UBM have been used in the three submitted one-speaker tasks. Training speech for the UBM was extracted from the impostor subcorpus of Gaudi-Ahumada database [46], which includes about 400 speakers (200 male and 200 female) (the male impostors are partly the same as the 122 speakers of Ahumada NIST development data). This Gaudi-Ahumada database was GSM coded in order to simulate cellular conditions. Then, the training material for the single UBM used in this evaluation was balanced in four subsets: Gaudi male, Gaudi female, Gaudi-cellular male and Gaudi-cellular female, with a total amount of about 6 hours of speech. Speaker models are 256 mixtures GMM adapted with MAP from a 1024 UBM. To perform the adaptation, in the first MAP iteration the 768 (1024 − 256) less significant mixtures are discarded to build the model, enabling faster training and a smaller size of the models. Likelihood normalization is also used in three different ways, using the Gaudi-UBM, and the T-Norm and H-Norm techniques. Results are usually shown in the form of DET curves [47] where system performances are observed much clearer than in ROC curves. Recently, we have repeated the 2001 Ahumada task with a different parameterization using 38 coefficients (19MFCC + Δ), and with a 512-mixture UBM, obtaining similar results to the best results reported in 2001 evaluation, as shown in Figure 12.1, where solid lines represent Ahumada NIST 2001 eval. and dashed line current ATVS system in the 'all' condition.

12.3.   Automatic Face Recognition

12.3.1   Facial Image Processing

In order to make a comprehensive understanding of the problem of face recognition, firstly we will mention some technologies and potential applications related to 'facial image processing', namely:

- **Face recognition** has applications in *security* and *forensics* as a cheap and non-intrusive modality. Automatic *indexation and retrieval of people from images and video* is an emerging application.
- **Face coding** and **reconstruction** for visual communications.
- **Expression** or **gender recognition, age estimation** or **lipreading**.
- **Synthetic faces** and **animation**.

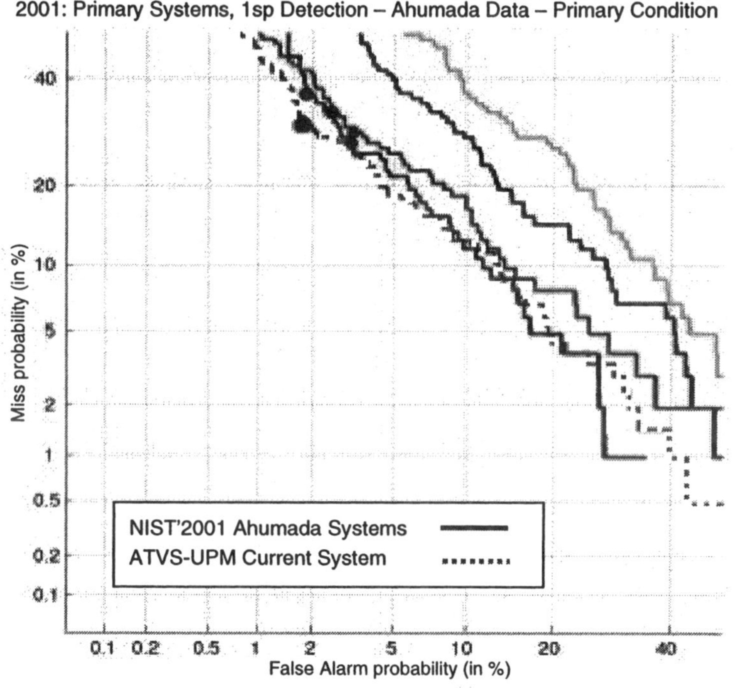

Figure 12.1. Ahumada NIST2001 eval (solid lines) and current ATVS system (dashed line).

12.3.2   Inherent Problems in Face Recognition

Face recognition is not a simple problem. Extensive surveys on face recognition are [13, 48]. Additional information can be found in [14, 49, 50]. The face of the same subject can look very different in different images. Considering the faces as rigid objects, they can appear at different locations, scales or orientations. But faces are not rigid objects: facial expressions, gestures or speech also affect the appearance of the face. Other important sources of variability are illumination, artificial (make-up, sunglasses) or natural (beards, moustaches) artifacts appearing at the face, ageing, image format coding, etc. Some sources of variability are illustrated in Figure 12.2.

An inconvenient for face recognition is that, for computers, images are only bidimensional arrays of a great amount of pixels and this representation is very sensitive to the sources of variability already described: illumination, facial expression, etc. Some methods use this low original level of representation for perfoming directly the recognition onto it (*correlation* or *template-based methods*), while others try to access higher levels of representation which simplify the problem (*model-based or feature-based methods*). A comparison between these two options was originally done in [51], but successful face recognition systems working nowadays do integrate both approaches. Higher levels of representation (features or models) are usually considered in order to attempt the following goals:

- Reduction of the dimension of the data.
- Enhancement of the discriminating power. The new level of representation should be independent of the undesired causes of varibility (illumination, translations, etc.) and highly dependent of the identity. A brief description of a system will be accomplished using a particular model (*Elastic Graph Matching*) as an example, but there are other successful models, such as [52], which will not be described here.

Figure 12.2.   Illumination, facial expression and pose as sources of variability (male from Yale database, http://cvc.yale.edu/projects/yalefaces/yalefaces.html, female from PICS database, http://pics.psych.stir.ac.uk/).

12.3.3   Dimensionality Reduction

For the purpose of face recognition we need a training database, usually consisting of M images of the same size N (N will denote the number of pixels). Each image in this training database can be expressed as a N-dimensional column vector y_i, obtained by scanning the pixels of the image in a prefixed way. So, all the training database can be expressed in a compact way as the NxM matrix $Y=[y_1\ y_2\ ...\ y_M]$. For template-based methods, assessing the identity of a new incoming image y would imply to compute its distances to all the columns of Y. All the face images are similar, in the sense that all of them contain a fixed object (the face) with a fixed structure (eyes, nose, etc.). So, it could be thought that the true dimension of the face-space tends to be much smaller than M. We will call M' this new reduced dimension of the face-space. The key idea is to preprocess Y so that its dimension is reduced from M to M'(<<M).

Firstly, this idea was applied for facial image processing in image coding [53]. But quickly the idea was extended to face recognition. The pioneer contribution of [54] introduced the concept of *eigenfaces*, which has become a standard in the face recognition literature. Eigenfaces are the M' vectors which span the face-space.

They are usually obtained in the following way. First, Y is centered in the mean (i.e, the mean vector $\mathbf{m} = (1/M)\sum_{i=1}^{M}\mathbf{y}_i$ is substracted to all the columns $\mathbf{y}_i$). As a result, we obtain the centered matrix X=[$\mathbf{x}_1$ $\mathbf{x}_2$ ... $\mathbf{x}_M$]. The span of the columns of this matrix is (M–1)-dimensional (we have lost one dimension when substracting the mean). The purpose is to find the NxM' matrix W=[$\mathbf{w}_1$ $\mathbf{w}_2$ ... $\mathbf{w}_{M'}$], whose columns are called *eigenfaces*, fulfilling the following conditions:

- The columns of W form an orthonormal set: $W^T W = I_{M'}$ ($I_{M'}$ is the identity matrix of dimension M').
- The reconstruction error E is minimum over W. E is defined as $E = \sum_{i=1}^{M}\|\mathbf{e}_i\|^2$, where $\mathbf{e}_i$ is the reconstruction error for each sample of the training set: $\mathbf{e}_i = (\mathbf{y}_i - \mathbf{m}) - WW^T(\mathbf{y}_i - \mathbf{m})$.

With these requirements an analytical solution exists for W. Consider the matrix $S = (1/M)XX^T$. It is a *biased covariance matrix* from the samples in Y. The solution W is a subset of the eigenvectors of S. We remind that $\mathbf{w}$ is an eigenvector of S if $S\mathbf{w} = \lambda\mathbf{w}$, with λ being the associated eigenvalue. This is the reason for the elements of W to be called *eigenfaces*. The eigenvectors chosen for the subset are the M' ones whose associated eigenvalue λ (which is always real and positive) is higher. Once W has been obtained, a generic face image can be reduced to the dimension M' by projecting it onto the M'-dimensional face-space by means of the operation $W^T(\mathbf{y} - \mathbf{m})$.

What we have presented so far is only a particular case of *Principal Component Analysis* (PCA) or the *Discrete Karhunen-Loève Transform*. The term *principal components* describes quite well what eigenfaces are: the axis along which the variation of the data is more important. The relative importance of each component is determined by the associated eigenvalue, which corresponds to the variance of the data when projected onto this principal component.

Figure 12.3 shows some examples of eigenfaces for a given training set (composed of 3 images of each of 100 subjects). Some preprocessing (alignment of manually marked facial features, resizing and cropping, illumination normalization) has been applied before PCA.

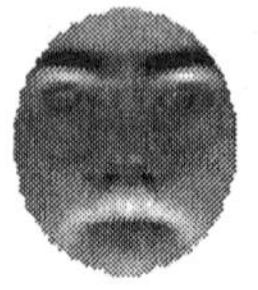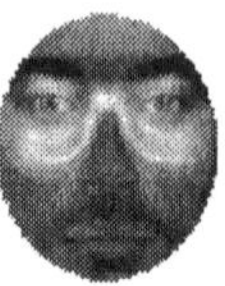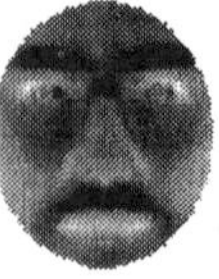

Figure 12.3. Some eigenfaces of a given training set.

Figure 12.4 shows some synthetic faces obtained from these eigenfaces. Each column reconstructs variations around the mean (second row) in both directions along the corresponding eigenface. Some important causes of variation in the training data set are observed (fringe/non-fringe, sunglasses, male/female).

The basic technique of eigenfaces has been extended in a number of ways during the last years, trying to improve the recognition performance. We will summarize some of the practical or theoretical aspects which have emerged from eigenfaces.

One of the most succesful is the *fisherfaces* technique [55], also called *Most Discriminating Features*. Now we look for a subspace where the instances of the same subject are as close as possible, keeping as far as possible the images from different subjects. Mathematically, instead of considering only the covariance matrix, we take into account two covariance-type matrices: the *within-class* and *between-class* matrices, defined, respectively as Eq. (12.1) and Eq. (12.2):

$$S_W = \frac{1}{M}\sum_{i=1}^{c}\sum_{x \in C_i}(\mathbf{x}-\mathbf{m}_i)(\mathbf{x}-\mathbf{m}_i)^T \qquad (12.1)$$

$$S_B = \frac{1}{M}\sum_{i=1}^{c}M_i(\mathbf{m}_i-\mathbf{m})(\mathbf{m}_i-\mathbf{m})^T \qquad (12.2)$$

where C_i is the set of M_i images of the subject i in the training set (whose mean is $\mathbf{m}_i$), c is the number of subjects and $\mathbf{m}$ is the global mean.

When applying a matrix W to the data in the original N-dimensional space, these matrices become, respectively W^TS_WW and W^TS_BW. An usual criterion is to choose W so that it accounts for separation between classes as Eq. (12.3):

$$W = \arg\max_{W} \frac{\left|W^T S_B W\right|}{\left|W^T S_W W\right|} \qquad (12.3)$$

Again, an analytic solution exists and it is given by the generalized eigenvalue problem: $S_B W = S_W W \Lambda$, with Λ being a diagonal matrix of eigenvalues. Because of singularity problems with the analytic solution that we have presented, a PCA step is previously performed in [55, 56] and the technique is applied to the PCA features instead to the original images. The joint transformation of PCA and LDA (standing for *Linear Discriminant Analysis*, the statistical technique underlying this solution) produces *fisherfaces* as a representation. Figure 12.5 shows the first 4 fisherfaces (as for eigenfaces, they are usually ranked by the associated eigenvalue) of the same training set than before.

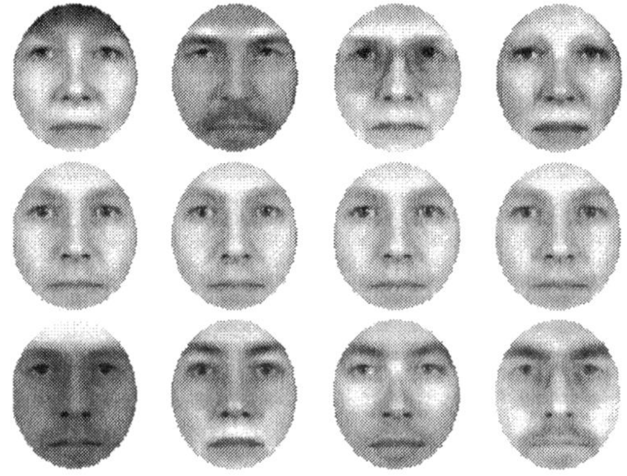

Figure 12.4.   Some synthetic faces obtained from eigenfaces at Figure 12.3.

Figure 12.5.   First 4 fisherfaces of the same training set used for Figure 12.3.

Principal Components as well as Linear Discriminant Analysis can have richer interpretations if probabilistic models are employed. In [56], for instance, the distribution of the columns of Y (following the same notation of the eigenface case) is assumed to be a multivariate normal $\aleph(\mathbf{m}, \Sigma)$, where $\mathbf{m}$ is the mean of the training set. Ordinary Principal Component Analysis produces the eigendecomposition of the estimated covariance matrix as $\hat{\Sigma} = S = W \Lambda W^T$. But the novelty in [57] is that the estimate of Σ is not just the one obtained with principal components, but include also an additive constant term (a kind of 'white-noise' term) for the non-principal components. Given an image $\mathbf{y}$ and the notation used throughout this section for N, M', W (now, W_{pca} again), λ and $\mathbf{m}$, we define:

Centered image: Face-space representation: Distance from face-space:

$$\mathbf{x} = (\mathbf{y} - \mathbf{m}) \in \Re^N \qquad \mathbf{v} = W^T\mathbf{x} \in \Re^{M'} \qquad d^2_{dffs}(\mathbf{x}) = \left\| (I_N - WW^T)\mathbf{x} \right\|^2$$

The estimated gaussian *pdf* used in [57] is expressed in (12.4) as:

$$\hat{P}(\mathbf{x}) = \left[\frac{\exp\left(-\dfrac{1}{2}\displaystyle\sum_{i=1}^{M'} \dfrac{\mathbf{v}_i^2}{\lambda_i}\right)}{(2\pi)^{M'/2}\displaystyle\prod_{i=1}^{M'}\lambda_i^{1/2}} \right] \cdot \left[\frac{\exp\left(-\dfrac{d^2_{dffs}(\mathbf{x})}{2\rho}\right)}{(2\pi\rho)^{(N-M')/2}} \right] = \hat{P}_{DIFS}(\mathbf{x})\hat{P}_{DFFS}(\mathbf{x}) \quad (12.4)$$

The parameter ρ can be interpreted as the variance of the white noise that we mentioned before along the non-principal components. In [57] it is shown that its optimal value is the mean of the eigenvalues of the non-principal components. Placing the problem in a probabilistic framework like the one described has shown to be advantageous. In [58] this formulation is used to probabilistically model *extra-personal* and *intra-personal* variations. A dual set of eigenfaces is so employed. The use of the likelihoods obtained with the two models allows a bayesian formulation of the problem which outperforms the original eigenfaces technique.

Other promising dimensionality reduction techniques applied to face recognition are *Independent Component Analysis* [59] or *non-linear approaches* [60-61].

12.3.4   Elastic Graph Matching

Elastic Graph Matching (EGM) receives this name because a *labeled graph* is the high-level structure chosen for representing the face. This structure is composed by a set of *nodes*, which, physically, correspond to the position of some well-defined facial features previously defined or *fiducial points* (e.g. the tip of the nose) and a set of *edges* connecting the nodes belonging to the same facial features (e.g. the mouth) or having constrained topological relations. *Elasticity* is required to be able to fit or *match* the graph to whichever face image.

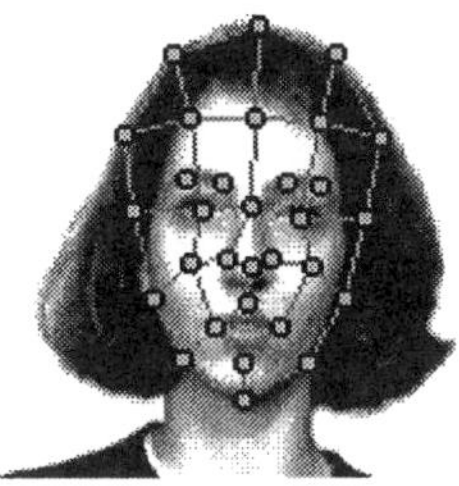

Figure 12.6. Example of a graph matched to a face image.

To include *texture properties* in the description each node is attributed a vector called *jet*. The description consists in the responses of a set of filters (Gabor filters) at the given node. A family of Gabor filters indexed by their central frequencies $\mathbf{k}_j$ is applied. σ^2 is a variance parameter:

$$\psi_j(\mathbf{x}) = \frac{k_j^2}{\sigma^2} \exp\left(-\frac{k_j^2 x^2}{2\sigma^2}\right)\left[\exp(i\mathbf{k}_j \mathbf{x}) - \exp\left(-\frac{\sigma^2}{2}\right)\right] \qquad (12.5)$$

Figure 12.7 shows the filtered images for a given image (left) and bank of Gabor filters. 3 scales (rows) and 4 orientations (columns) composed the filter bank.

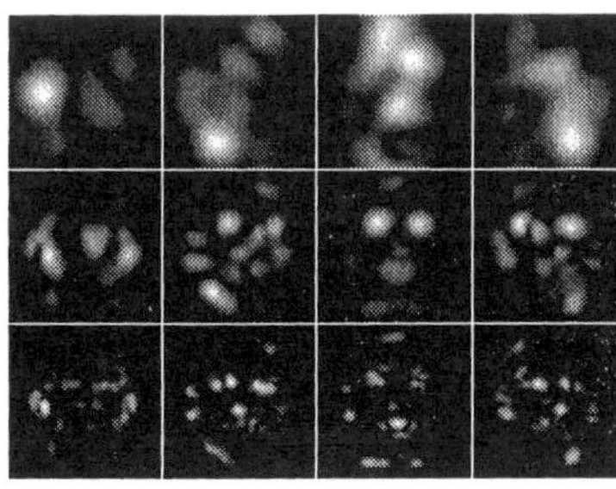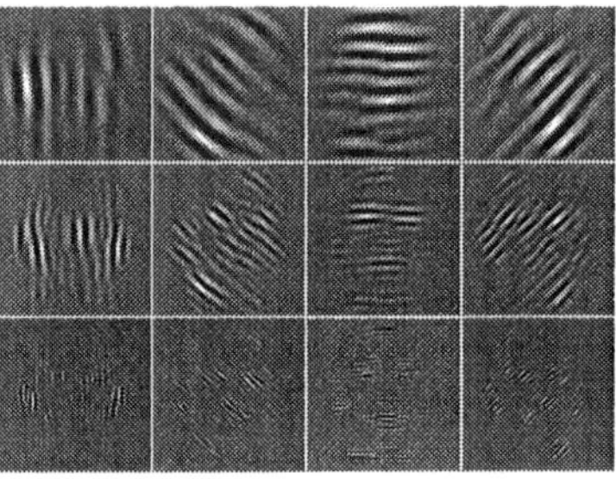

Figure 12.7. Image at the left (from PICS database), filtered by Gabor filters. Center: magnitudes of the responses; Right: real part. Levels of frequency shown along raws and orientations along columns.

In [62] a generic graph structure (the *Face Bunch Graph*) containing, at each node, all the jets of a given training set is matched to a new incoming image. Once matching has been performed, the recognition is done by means of the comparison between the obtained graph and the graphs stored in a training database. In both matching and recognition stage, a measure of the *similarity* between two graph structures is crucial. Exact details and formulae for this similarity are given in [62].

The system described has its roots in [63]. This basic scheme based on Gabor wavelets has known lot of extensions and variants [64-65].

12.3.5   Performance of Face Recognition Systems

At the time of this writing, the biggest public effort that has been accomplished in order to test the performance of face recognition systems in controlled conditions (same datababe and same protocol) is the FERET competition. It is designed to give performances for the two usual tasks in biometrics: identification [66] and verification [67].

Among the ten algorithms tested, the following 3 techniques (outlined here) seemed to work better than the others: probabilistic PCA, a particular Linear Discriminant approach and Elastic Graph Matching. Elastic Graph Matching performed exceptionally well in identification experiments, whereas the Linear Discriminant technique was the top performer for verification. As expected, the results were extremely dependent on the difference in the conditions between the gallery images and the probe images. For instance, for the EGM in identification, the identification dropped from approximately 95% when the reference and tested images were taken in the same conditions (frontal images, same session) to 59% when they were taken in different sessions. FERET experiments confirm that illumination and pose are very challenging factors for face recognition systems.

Another important effort for making standards for measuring face verification performance is that of the Lausanne protocol [68] over the extended M2VTS database [69]. This database is multimodal, containing audio and video.

The 'classic' face recognition system, as described so far, works on still gray-level images of a fixed size. We could think whether we could obtain better results whithout constraining the problem so much and considering other sources of information. Complementary sources of information could be *color*, the *3-D nature* of the head or *video of movement*. Some of these cues are being very useful for locating faces and facial features, but it is still an open problem how to consider them for recognition.

12.4.   Minutiae-Based Fingerprint Recognition Systems

Regarding fingerprint automatic recognition, three different stages can be clearly specified, namely:

    a. *Data acquisition:* fingerprint images are acquired by means of a sensor.

b.   *Characteristics extraction*: fingerprint characteristics are extracted from the acquired image in order to generate a biometric pattern.

c.   *Pattern matching*: test (input) fingerprint pattern is compared with the previously registered/stored patterns.

Once the first step is accomplished and in order to be able to extract the fingerprint information, a complete image enhancement scheme has to be applied. Next, we will describe this image processing procedure.

12.4.1   Image Enhancement Scheme

The aim of image enhancement is to provide a fingerprint image, with enough quality, so that the extractor of characteristics may obtain the most reliable biometric pattern. One of the most common biometric patterns used in current systems, due to its high reliability, is the minutiae pattern [7, 8, 11, 12, 70-78]. A point in the fingerprint image is designated as a minutia if it belongs to an ending, beginning or bifurcation of a ridge. Accordingly, a single minutia will be basically determined by its spatial coordinates on the image. Even so, the entire minutiae pattern usually consists of: a) the spatial coordinates of every minutia, b) the oriented angles of the ridges associated with every minutia, and c) the spatial coordinates of a finite number of sampled points obtained from the associated ridges.

Commonly, acquisition process introduces undesired noisy information in the biometric pattern. Image imperfections may cause genuine minutiae deletion and spurious minutiae generation by the extraction algorithm. Imperfections may induce too miscalculations in determining the spatial coordinates of each minutiae and its relative orientation in the image. Consequently, the reliability of the whole recognition system decreases significantly, since fingerprint recognition is based on the comparison, within some tolerance limits, between the incoming biometric pattern to the system and the biometric patterns previously stored in the system database. All these reasons make necessary an image enhancement stage previous to the characteristics extraction stage. Figure 12.8 shows the general block diagram of the biometric pattern extraction of a fingerprint. Next, the improved sequence of stages in which the complete outlined process consists is described.

Image Normalization.   The objective of this stage is to increase the dynamic range of the gray scale between ridges and valleys of the image in order to facilitate the processing of the following stages. The normalization factor is calculated according to the mean and the variance of the image. Figure 12.9 shows, as an example, the original NIST "f05" image and the normalized fingerprint.

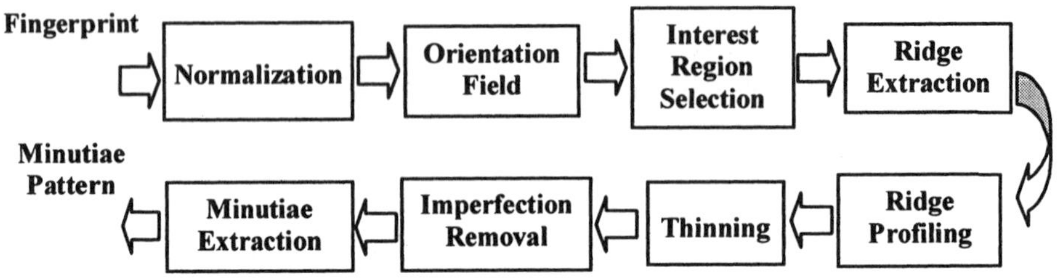

Figure 12.8. Complete firgerprint pattern extraction process.

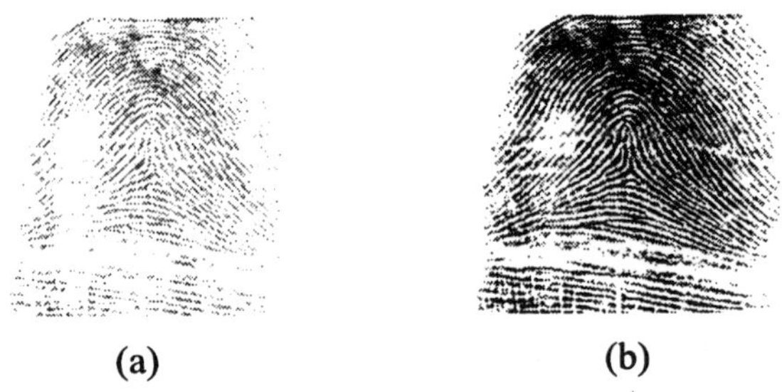

(a)   (b)

Figure 12.9. (a) NIST "f05" original image. (b) Normalized fingerprint.

Calculation of the Orientation Field. The orientation field represents the local orientation of the ridges contained in the fingerprint. In order to estimate it, the image is divided in 16x16 pixel blocks and the gradient is calculated at every pixel, in x and y coordinates. From the gradient information the orientation angle is estimated through the minimum square adjustment algorithm given in [70, 72]. Often, in some blocks, the orientation angle is not correctly determined, due to background noise and damages in ridges and valleys, caused by impression lacks of certain image areas. Therefore, as significant local angle variations between adjacent blocks cannot exist, a new spatial low-pass filtering is applied to the estimated oriented field to correctly re-align all the segments. The size of the filter mask (of unit sum) used is 5x5 blocks. Figure 12.10(a) shows the resulting orientation field obtained from gradient calculation. Figure 12.10(b) shows the re-aligned field obtained after the spatial low pass filtering. This orientation field will fix the adaptive filter parameters in successive stages.

Selection of the Interest Region. In order to determine the exact limits of the firgerprint trace in the whole file, the image area defined by all the 16x16 blocks, in which a high variance of the gray level in the normal direction of the ridges exists, is selected. Thus, the normal orientation field of the ridges is previously estimated. After that, the noisy area of the image, to be excluded in the following steps, is defined by low variance in all directions [71].

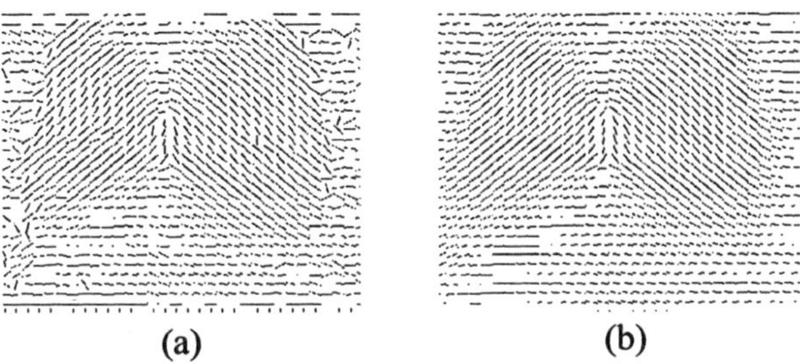

(a)   (b)

Figure 12.10. (a) Initial orientation fields. (b) Re-aligned fields.

Ridge Extraction. In order to decide whether a single pixel belongs or not to a given ridge, it is necessary to filter the fingerprint image with two adaptive masks, both capable to increase the gray level in the normal direction of the ridge [70]. The orientation of the mask is adapted within each 16x16 block, depending on the angles obtained from the orientation field of figure 12.10(b). If the gray level of a pixel exceeds a threshold in the two filtered images, it is considered that the pixel belongs to a ridge; otherwise, it is assigned to a valley, producing a binary image of the fingerprint. The size of the masks is *LxL*, and they are defined by the functions given in Eq. (12.6), where $E[\cdot]$ stands for "integer value of":

$$h_1(u,v) = \begin{cases} \dfrac{1}{\sqrt{2\pi}\,\delta}\, e^{-\left(\frac{u-u_0}{\delta}\right)^2}, & \text{if}: u_0 = E[(v_c - v)ctg(\theta) + u_c] \\ 0, & \text{otherwise} \end{cases}$$

$$h_2(u,v) = \begin{cases} \dfrac{1}{\sqrt{2\pi}\,\delta}\, e^{-\left(\frac{v-v_0}{\delta}\right)^2}, & \text{if}: v_0 = E[(u_c - u)tg(\theta) + v_c] \\ 0, & \text{otherwise} \end{cases}$$

(12.6)

$\forall\, u, v \in [1, L]$, where u and v are the coordinates of a pixel in the mask; (u_c,v_c), is the center of the mask; θ, is the orientation angle of the ridge in each image block, and δ, is a parameter to adjust the function mask to the width of the ridge. Figure 12.11(a) shows the filtered image with one of the spatial masks. Figure 12.11(b) represents the binary image obtained after a threshold is applied, producing smoother ridge borders. For good quality fingerprint images, as in scanned fingerprints, the previous filtering process is simplified using just a single mask, with an spatially-oriented impulse train (unit amplitude and zero width function), also spatially adapted to the angle of the ridges, and then also binarized through a threshold [75].

Ridge Profiling.   To simplify the processing of the following steps, a new image filtering to profile the fingerprint ridges and eliminate the stains of certain areas is applied. In order to accomplish this process, the low frequency components are first extracted and then subtracted to the original image, providing the high frequency components necessary to profile the ridges, as can be derived from Eq. (12.7):

$$p[u,v] = f[u,v] + \lambda \cdot f_H[u,v] = f[u,v] + \lambda \cdot (f[u,v] - f_L[u,v]) \qquad (12.7)$$

where $p[u,v]$, is the resulting profiling image; $f[u,v]$, is the binary image; $f_H[u,v]$ and $f_L[u,v]$ are, respectively, the high and low frequency images; and λ is a factor ($\lambda > 0$), that determines the degree of profiling. An additional filtering can be applied to eliminate the spurious ridges due to stains in the image. Thus, a unit impulse train mask is used, capable to locally adapt its orientation to the ridge orientation.

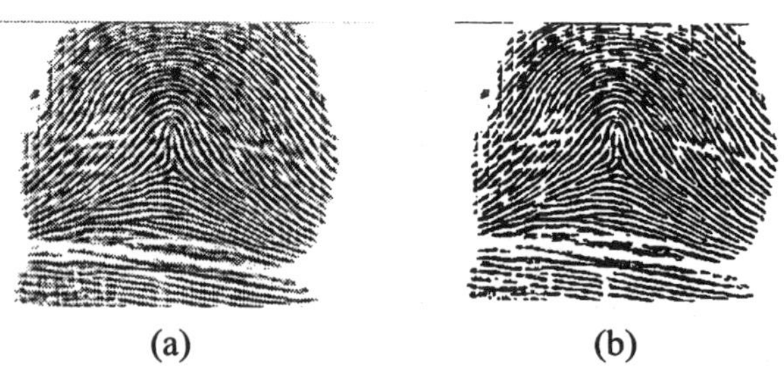

(a)   (b)

Figure 12.11.   (a) Filtered image with a spatial mask. (b) Binary image.

12.4.2   Extraction of Characteristic Information

Thinning.   In this step two consecutive fast parallel thinning algorithms are applied [79], in order to reduce to a single pixel the width of the ridges in the binary image. These operations are necessary to simplify the subsequent structural analysis of the image for the extraction of the fingerprint minutiae. The thinning must be performed without modifying the original ridge structure of the image. During this process, the algorithms cannot miscalculate beginnings, endings and/or bifurcation of the ridges, neither ridges can be broken.

Imperfection Removal. After thinning, depending on the image quality, the structural imperfections of the original fingerprint remain in certain degree. This results in breaking ridges, spurious ridges and holes; therefore, it is necessary to apply an algorithm for removing all the lines not corresponding to ridges and an algorithm to connect all the broken ridges. Figure 12.12(a) shows the thinned image obtained once the algorithms for thinning and imperfection removal are applied.

Minutiae Extraction. In the last stage, the minutiae from the thinning image are extracted, obtaining accordingly the fingerprint biometric pattern. This process involves the determination of: *i*) whether a pixel, belongs to a ridge or not and, *ii*) if so, whether it is a bifurcation, a beginning or an ending point, obtaining thus a group of candidate minutiae. Next, all points at the border of the interest region are removed. Then, since the minutiae density per unit area cannot exceed a certain value, all the candidate-point clusters whose density exceed this value are substituted by a single minutia located at the center of the cluster. Figure 12.12(b) shows the resulting minutiae after cluster elimination.

(a)   (b)

Figure 12.12. (a) Image after thinning and imperfection removal. (b) Minutiae after cluster elimination.

12.4.3   Pattern Recognition

One of the most important objectives of fingerprint automatic verification systems is to achieve a high reliability in comparing the input biometric pattern to the system (test pattern) with respect to the different system database patterns. Given two biometric patterns, testing and stored patterns, the recognition algorithm must determine if the corresponding fingerprints belong or not to the same individual (finger). Therefore, a similarity measure between the comparing patterns must be established. In addition, when talking about verification systems, a threshold to decide the matching result is required [12, 70, 73, 74, 80-82].

Generally, the different acquisitions of a fingerprint do not represent exactly the same region of the finger. So, the two comparing patterns must be aligned before deciding if the two corresponding fingerprints belong to the same individual. Also, the acquired image often present stains due to dirtiness on the scanner surface and scratches of the finger. These noise artifacts cause the generation of spurious minutiae in the extraction stage of characteristics. Besides, the pressure of the finger over the scanner surface, or over the paper in the case of inked fingerprints, may produce elastic deformations of the skin, which result in the variation of the true relative position of the minutiae in the image.

Normally, the minutiae patterns are aligned, and later, the matching process is accomplished looking for correspondence between the two aligned structures. Since the solution of the two problems, alignment and correspondence, are interrelated, both are implicitly and simultaneously solved. Alignment problem can be solved by means of several strategies referred in the literature. Generally, solution of translation and rotation problems between test and database patterns is accomplished together with the alignment process. Techniques based on the structure of the ridges of the fingerprint use the correlation between the two compared images to align the patterns [83-85]. Alignment, in systems based on minutiae detection, is achieved, considering the relative position of the minutiae of the image [12, 70,73,86-88].

Once the alignment process is accomplished, the two biometric patterns are matched. A score is defined to describe the similarity between them. The elastic techniques for minutiae comparison, permit a certain spatial tolerance margin (tolerance box) in the matching procedure [12, 70, 73]. The adaptive elastic techniques employ a tolerance box capable to adapt its size depending on the spatial coordinate values of the explored minutiae, to compensate the nonlinear elastic deformations of the skin. Figure 12.13 shows a diagram of the different pattern recognition stages.

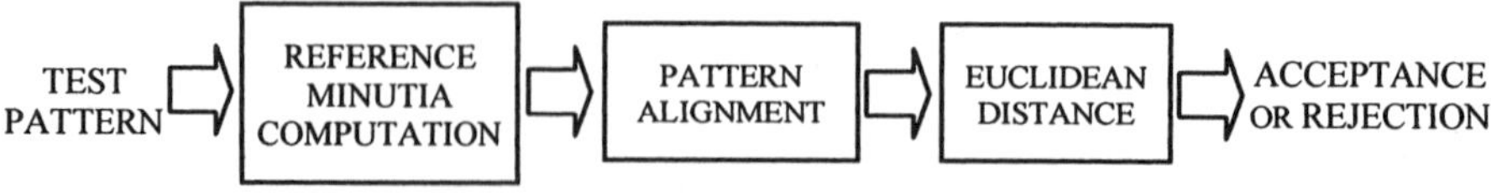

Figure 12.13. Minutiae pattern verification process.

Minutiae Alignment. As it was described before, biometric patterns are defined by the x and y coordinates of each minutia, and the resulting spatially sampled points obtained from each ridge associated to each minutia. The alignment process is accomplished in the following stages: *a) Calculation of the reference minutia.* Due to the skin elasticity, non-linearities among fingerprints of the same individual acquired in different moments usually appear. Therefore, a point-to-point correspondence in each matching procedure between test and database pattern must be established. The spatial distribution of the two point-patterns are analyzed to determine the reference minutiae, one from each pattern, which present the maximum similarity between them. *b) Calculation of translation and rotation parameters* between the two reference minutiae previously determined. *c) Application of the calculated translation and rotation parameters to all the points in the test pattern.* All the test minutiae are translated and rotated to be aligned with the database minutiae. The equations for this operation are given in Eq. (12.8):

$$\begin{pmatrix} x_{ai} \\ y_{ai} \\ \theta_{ai} \end{pmatrix} = \begin{pmatrix} \Delta x \\ \Delta y \\ \Delta\theta \end{pmatrix} + \begin{pmatrix} \cos\Delta\theta & \mathrm{sen}\Delta\theta & 0 \\ \mathrm{sen}\Delta\theta & -\cos\Delta\theta & 0 \\ 0 & 0 & 1 \end{pmatrix} \cdot \begin{pmatrix} x_i - x_{ref} \\ y_i - y_{ref} \\ \theta_i - \theta_{ref} \end{pmatrix} \qquad (12.8)$$

where: $(\Delta x, \Delta y, \Delta\theta)^T$, are the translation and rotation parameters; $(x_i, y_i, \theta_i)^T$, are the spatial coordinates and the associated orientated angle of the i-*th* database minutia; $(x_{ref}, y_{ref}, \theta_{ref})^T$, is the reference minutia; and $(x_{ai}, y_{ai}, \theta_{ai})^T$, is the corresponding i-*th* aligned minutia.

Non-linear deformations of the fingerprints cause two biometric patterns of the same individual not to be exactly coincident once they have been aligned. Therefore, an elastic matching algorithm must be implemented, capable to establish the correspondence between points under certain tolerance limits.

Pattern Matching. Pattern matching algorithm is performed in two stages. In the first one, minutiae of the two compared patterns are sorted to produce both strings of points in polar coordinates. The use of this coordinate system is justified because non-linear deformations of fingerprints are consistent in a given region of the image, loosing this characteristic while getting further away from this region in the radial directions. In the second stage, the string matching algorithm transforms ("edits") the test pattern string into the database pattern string. The number of edit operations needed in the transformation establishes the similarity between the two strings. Edit operators model the possible modifications introduced during image acquisition. Given all the possible editions which transform the test pattern string into the database pattern string, the algorithm selects the transformation which provides the minimum cost.

Other matching algorithms are elastic and adaptive, permitting so to survey and to correct all the possible alignment looses and non-linear deformations between both strings. This characteristics are achieved by adapting, within each pair of minutiae, the size of the tolerance box when the previous pair of compared minutiae mismatch.

12.5. On-Line HMM-Based Signature Verification System

In this section, a complete on-line signature verification [18,89-91] system is described, including experiments over a realistic database. In order to accomplish this verification process, several stages are completed. Firstly, we will describe the whole signature acquisition process, being a dynamic procedure [92] in the sense that instantaneous information is sampled at 100 Hz; including here the acquisition tool developed for this purpose. After acquisition, parameterization stage will be described, including a complete set of dynamic coefficients and derivating from these velocity and acceleration functions. Once this extraction of characteristic information is done, dynamic modeling of signature signal is realized by means of Hidden Markov Models (HMM), a powerful tool to characterize random variables as those derived from previous stage [93-97]. Lastly, verification experiments will be presented, showing excellent results when tests are accomplished making use of score-domain normalization.

12.5.1   On-line Signature Acquisition Process

Acquisition Device.   The complete acquisition process is accomplished through an acquisition device plus a software processing module; the hardware device is in our case a low-cost standard WACOM® digitizing tablet, model INTUOS A6 USB, with the following features: *a) acquisition area:* 127x106 mm, *b) pressure levels:* 1,024, *c) resolution:* 2,540 lines/inch (100 lines/mm), *d) precision:* +/- 0.25 mm, *e) detection heigth:* 10 mm, and *f) sampling frequency:* 100 pps (points –spatial samples- per second). The tablet provides the following instantaneous information (at 100 pps) about the signature [dynamic range of each parameter is specified]: a) *x position* (x_k) [0-12700], b) *y position* (y_k) [0-9700], c) *pressure* (z_k) [0-1024], d) *pen azimuth* (az_k) [0-3600], and e) *pen altitude* (in_k) [300-900]. Figure 12.14 shows graphically the referred azimuth and altitude angles.

With all this information, the signature will be characterized as a vector sequence, where each vector contains the parameters acquired at each sampling instant, beginning at instant $t=1$, and ending at instant $t=T$, being therefore T the duration of each signature [97], as it can also be seen in Figure 12.14.

In order to carry out the signature acquisition process, we have developed a software application, *SignCapture©*, that controls the tablet operation via *Wintab 1.1* interface. *SignCapture* interface visual appearance is shown in Figure 12.15.

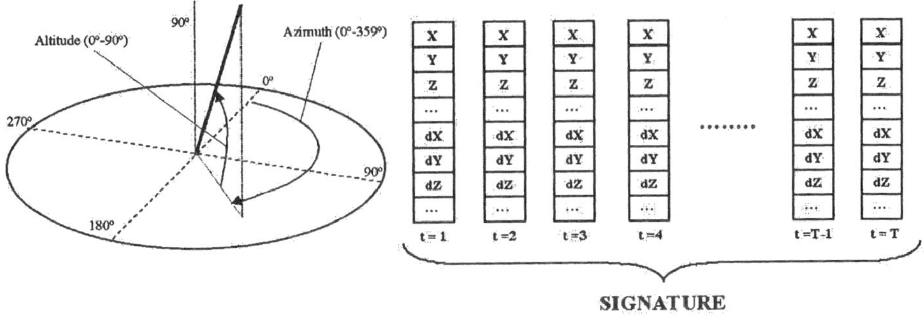

Figure 12.14. Pen azimuth and altitude (left). Instantaneous vector characterization of on-line signature acquisition process (right).

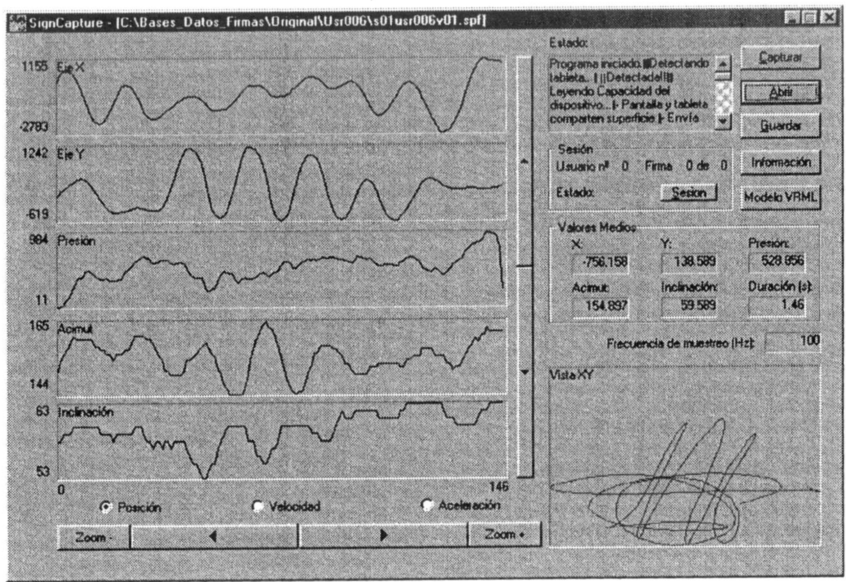

Figure 12.15. SignCapture Interface.

Preprocessing. Before extracting from acquired instantaneous information relevant characteristics, we need to preprocess it in order to remove useless information, correct wrong values and set common reference values for all the signatures captured. The different preprocessing schemes carried out on the acquired information are described below.

- ### *Initial Point Alignment*

The main goal of this task is to make information independent from the position on the tablet where the signature is initially performed. To achieve this, we have set as coordinate origin the first point acquired for the signature; or in other words, all the signatures will be aligned with respect to the initial point, that will be the coordinate origin $(x_0, y_0) = (0,0)$. This will warp signature geometry and allow a correct matching process.

- ### *Signature Segmentation*

Concerning signature segmentation, that is, automatic decision of whether a determined point is or is not signature information (determination of the beginning and ending of signing), we have set as signature beginning the first sample where pressure information is not null (first pen-down). Signature ending is settled as the last sample where pressure information was not null (last pen-up). Because few pen-ups can be found in a signature, we have established a maximum pen-up duration (3 seconds in our system), so that if a pen-up exceeds this time threshold, the acquisition is stopped and the last sample with not null pressure is considered the signature ending.

- ### *Azimuth Correction*

Due to azimuth encoding carried out by the tablet (see Figure 12.14), when azimuth varies around 0° during signing process (usual case in left-handed people), the acquired values will jump from 0° to 359° and viceversa, and will result in a discontinuous waveform for this parameter. In this framework, small rotations of signatures will produce jumps in different parts of the azimuth waveform and degrade system efficiency. To prevent this effect, azimuth conversion according to negative angle notation has been used, and discontinuities are corrected. Figure 12.16 shows this restoring process.

12.5.2   Signature Parameterization

In addition to the five instantaneous parameters acquired directly by the tablet (x, y, pressure, azimuth and altitude), other parameters can be derived from these in order to exploit all the dynamic information that signing process contains. Furthermore, instantaneous velocity and acceleration of variation of each parameter has been used, guiding to a more robust and accurate signature representation.

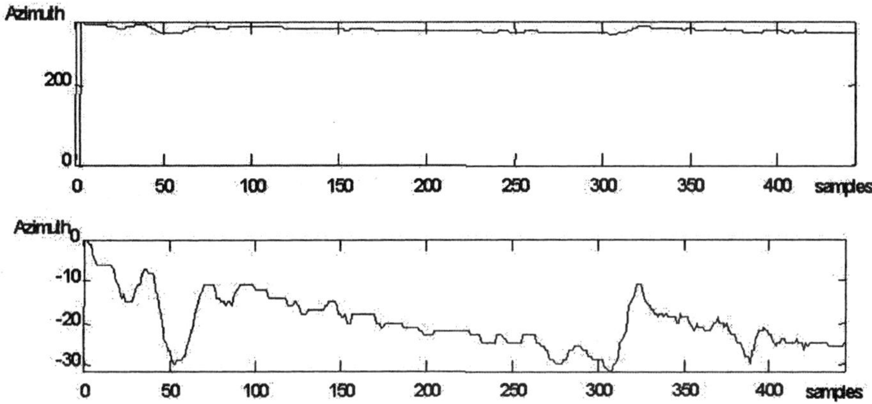

Figure 12.16. Acquired azimuth function (up). Restored azimuth function (down).

Velocity and Acceleration of Each Parameter. In order to compute parameter velocities and accelerations [98] we have approximated the derivative function through second order regressions instead of differences between consecutive samples. The reason for this procedure is that using differences between samples results in a sample by sample resolution and sample-level variations of velocity or acceleration are associated, among other factors, to the characteristics of the rubbing between pen and paper. Instead, if derivatives are calculated through regressions, the so obtained curves present softened waveforms, and these small noisy variations are removed. The general expression of the order N regression calculated in the instant t for parameter q is:

$$reg[q_t, N] = \frac{\sum_{\tau=1}^{N} \tau(q_{t+\tau} - q_{t-\tau})}{2\sum_{\tau=1}^{N} \tau^2} \tag{12.9}$$

Figure 12.17 shows the derivative functions obtained from original parameter set, when computing derivatives as sample differences or as regressions.

Then, velocity and acceleration for parameter q at instant t can be computed as:

$$\Delta_{q_t} = reg[q_t, 2], \qquad \Delta\Delta_{q_t} = reg[\Delta_{q_t}, 2] \tag{12.10}$$

Additional Parameter Computation. Many efforts have been made in order to obtain the optimal parameter representation of signing process [89, 90, 99, 100]. In our scheme, several other parameters have been derived from initial set, in order to test their influence in the verification system, using second order regression in order to obtain derivatives:

- ***Instantaneous Trajectory Angle (th_k)***

The angle (th_k) formed by the pen trajectory with respect to the signature longitudinal axis in a given instant k is calculated as:

$$th_k = arctg\left(\frac{y_k - y_{k-1}}{x_k - x_{k-1}}\right) \quad \Rightarrow \quad th_k = arctg\left(\frac{reg[y_k,2]}{reg[x_k,2]}\right) \qquad (12.11)$$

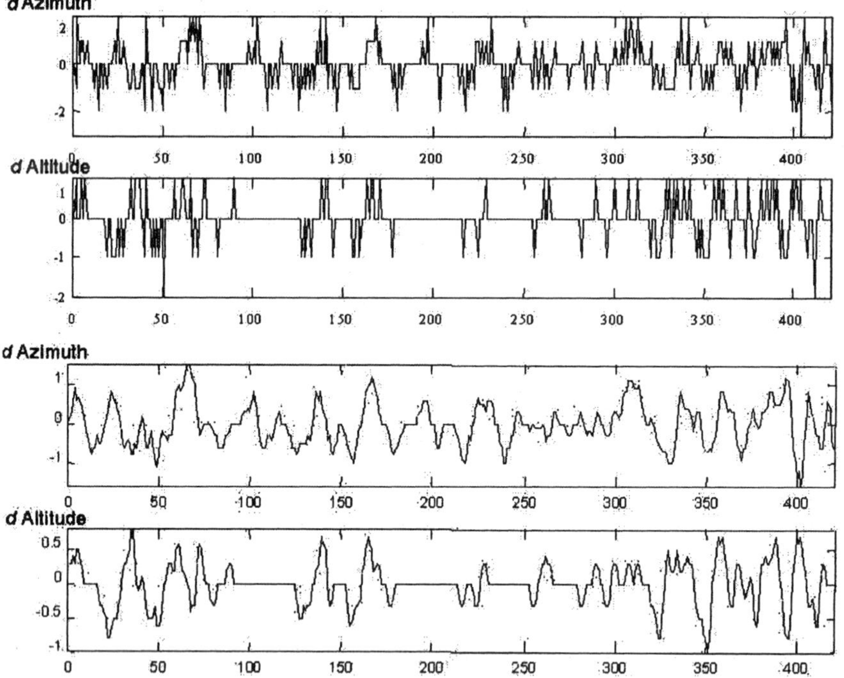

Figure 12.17.   Derivative functions (azimuth and altitude), computed as sample differences (up) or regressions (down).

- ***Instantaneous Displacement (vl_k)***

The instantaneous displacement of the pen during the signing process is defined as the distance between the current and the previous point. It is given by

$$vl_k = \sqrt{(x_k - x_{k-1})^2 + (y_k - y_{k-1})^2} \quad \Rightarrow \quad vl_k = \sqrt{reg[x_k,2]^2 + reg[y_k,2]^2} \qquad (12.12)$$

- ***Tangential Acceleration (at_k)***

Tangential acceleration of the pen movement is given by the expression below:

$$at_k = vl_k - vl_{k-1} \quad \Rightarrow \quad at_k = reg[vl_k, 2] \qquad (12.13)$$

- ***Curvature Radius (rc_k)***

Curvature radius is computed as

$$rc_k = \frac{at_k}{\omega_k - \omega_{k-1}} \quad \Rightarrow \quad rc_k = \frac{at_k}{reg[\omega_k, 2]} \qquad (12.14)$$

where ω_k is obtained by

$$\omega_k = th_k - th_{k-1} \quad \Rightarrow \quad \omega_k = reg[th_k, 2] \qquad (12.15)$$

Due to the huge dynamic range of curvature radius in a signature (acute angles with $rc_k \to 0$, and rectilinear parts with $rc_k \to \infty$), we will use the log magnitude of Eq. (12.14), $\log|rc_k|$.

- ***Centripetal or Normal Acceleration (an_k)***

Centripetal acceleration is computed as

$$an_k = rc_k(\omega_k - \omega_{k-1})^2 \quad \Rightarrow \quad an_k = rc_k reg[\omega_k, 2]^2 \qquad (12.16)$$

Since centripetal acceleration is proportional to curvature radius, its dynamic range could be also huge, and we will use the logarithmic expression of it $\log|an_k|$.

Parametric Normalization Techniques. Besides the addition of new parameters to the signature parameter vector we have used some normalization techniques, in order to minimize intra-signer variability, set reference values, limit dynamic ranges, etc.

- ***Limiting Signature Size***

The first normalization is embedded in the acquisition process. Forcing the user to sign into a predetermined grid, we are limiting *a priori* the maximum size of the signature and so, the size variability for the signatures of each user.

- ***Initial Point Alignment***

This normalization is carried out in the preprocessing phase. Its objective is to make the geometric information (x,y) independent from the initial position where the signature is executed. To reach this, after acquiring the signature, each sample is referenced to the (x,y) value of the first one in the signature, which means in other words, aligning all signature beginnings with the relative (to each signing grid) coordinate origin. This is computed through expression Eq. (12.17).

$$\begin{array}{ll} x'_k = x_k - x_0 \\ y'_k = y_k - y_0 \end{array} \quad \Rightarrow \quad \begin{array}{ll} x'_0 = 0 \\ y'_0 = 0 \end{array} \qquad (12.17)$$

where (x_k, y_k) are x and y acquired coordinates at k instant, and (x'_k, y'_k) are the aligned x and y coordinates. Since this alignment is carried out just after the acquisition, any signature will be as default aligned with the coordinate origin in its first sample, as it can be seen in Figure 12.18.

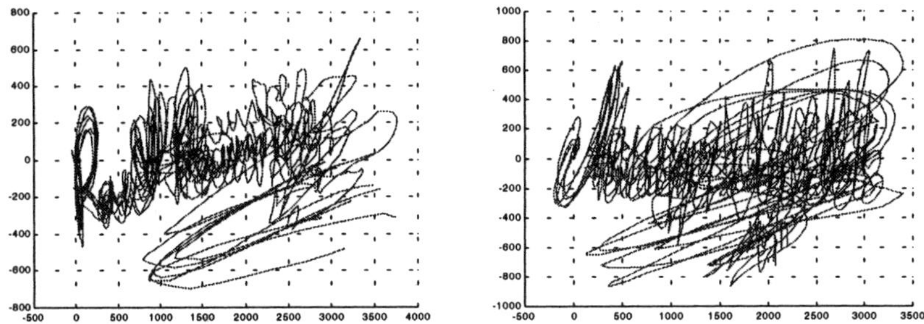

Figure 12.18. Examples of initial point alignment for several realizations of the same signatures.

12.5.3   Database and Signature Model Generation

- ***Database Description***

The signature database used below for tests comprises 75 signers (users), captured under the same conditions in a single-session scheme. Each signer has been requested to realize *15 original signatures* and *15 trained forgeries*; specifically, trained forgeries for the current user have been produced by the three following users, each of them producing five forgeries of the three preceding users. This makes a total of *1,125 original signatures* and *1,125 trained forgeries* in the database.

- ***Signature Model Generation***

As it has been previously stated, each signature is characterized by a time-varying set of parameters. In order to preserve this complete dynamic information, Hidden Markov Models (HMM) have been used as a powerful technique to model random dynamic variables, including signature dynamics [93-96]. This means that every input signal will be modeled through a double stochastic process, characterized by a number of states with transition probabilities among them and, being in each state, observation probabilities modeled through a continuous density multivariate gaussian mixture. The reader is referred to [25], in order to find a complete HMM description. Concerning the HMM configuration, and specifically to left-to-right topology, number of states per model, order of the gaussian mixture and number of realizations (repetitions) of each signature that train the model are parameters to adjust. In order to determine the optimal combination of these three variables, a preliminary test has been accomplished.

12.5.4   Signature Verification Results

Preliminary Signature Verification Tests.   Two main goals have been sought in the preliminary system tests, namely:

- ***Finding the Optimum HMM Configuration***

Finding the best number of states and mixtures and the minimum number of training signatures needed to obtain good verification results.

- ***Finding the Best Signature Parameterization***

In order to get a signature representation as robust against forgeries as possible.

In order to accomplish preliminary tests, a subset of 22 signers has been used. A fixed signature parameterization is set (x, y, pressure, azimuth and altitude, $+\Delta$, $+\Delta\Delta$), which means an instantaneous 15-parameter set is calculated at a 100 samples per second rate, varying the number of states x of the HMM (Nx), the number of mixtures y per state (My), and the number z of training signatures (Rz), to set the optimum HMM configuration. Verification results are provided, in terms of average EER (%), without applying any likelihood normalization techniques, and also using best-reference score normalization [16]. Table 12.1 sumarizes these preliminary tests.

We will denote, from now on, HMM model configuration as XYZ, (number of states, number of mixtures per state and number of signature repetitions per model). The best result derived from Table 12.1 corresponds to a HMM 486 configuration, using NBest normalization technique, and obtaining an average $EER_{486} = 2.62\%$. This is the model configuration selected to be used in the following tests. 484 configuration ($EER_{484} = 3.39\%$)

will be used in the following tests too, since it does not degrade much the efficiency in verification, and results in a faster training.

Table 12.1. Preliminary tests verification results.

EER(%)		R2		R4		R6	
		No norm	Best ref	No norm	Best ref	No norm	Best ref
	M2	13.69	8.07	14.07	7.05	14.36	6.54
N2	M4	15.70	6.89	14.30	4.96	14.64	6.38
	M8	15.66	7.78	13.97	4.03	14.70	4.29
	M2	13.78	7.42	13.82	5.89	14.94	4.98
N4	M4	13.82	6.69	14.51	4.26	13.45	4.65
	M8	14.37	6.72	11.43	3.39	12.05	2.62
	M2	12.41	6.31	11.42	4.58	11.43	3.38
N8	M4	13.25	7.44	10.46	3.56	9.98	2.69
	M8	12.76	7.83	9.21	3.05	9.15	2.99
	M2	10.65	6.88	9.23	3.67	9.16	2.88
N16	M4	12.66	9.69	8.34	3.69	7.64	3.43
	M8	12.36	9.76	9.44	4.21	7.44	3.40

Optimal Signature Verification Tests. Once the HMM configuration is optimally established, some tests have been carried out, starting with a basic representation of the signature (x,y) and adding parameters to the feature vector. In this framework, the parameters added resulting in a system improvement, will remain as a fixed part of the vector for the following tests. Four tests have been performed for each parameterization, two of them using four training signatures, and other two using six signatures, varying the training set, and then obtaining a more objective evaluation.

The base parameters of the signature are denominated as: *x*: x position. *y*: y position. *z*: pressure. *az*: azimuth. *in*: altitude. *th*: trajectory angle. *lrc*: log curvature radius. *lan*: log centripetal acceleration. *at*: tangential acceleration. *vl*: instantaneous displacement.

Results on the 75 user database are presented in Table 12.2. in terms of average EER of all the users (user-dependent decision threshold) and joint EER (user-independent threshold). In order to calculate joint EER, a likelihood normalization for each user is performed (by means of *z-norm* normalization [43, 44], aligning impostor distribution for each user to mean 0 and variance 1).

12.5.5   Conclusions

A complete on-line verification system has been described. A preliminary verification experiment has determined that an HMM with *4 states, 8* mixtures and *6 training signatures* using best reference score normalization technique, has obtained an average $EER_{486} = 2.62\%$. After this optimal HMM setting, the final experiments shown in Table 12.2 were performed in order to establish which parametric set produced the best results on our database of 75 signers database, including 1,125 real signatures and 1,125 trained forgeries; an optimal set including x position, y position, pressure, trajectory angle, tangential and log normal acceleration, log curvature radius, and displacement, together with first and second order derivatives have shown to reach average EER of 0.5%, which constitutes an excellent result compared with previous signature verification systems [19].

Table 12.2. On-line signature verification results, showing EER (in %), considering different instantaneous parameter sets, with both individual and global thresholds, and considering no likelihood normalization procedure *(no Norm)* or best reference normalization *(Bref)*.

Dynamic Vector of Parameters	# train Rep.	Individual Threshold		Global Threshold	
		EER (Bref)	EER (no Norm)	EER (BRef)	EER (no Norm)
(x, y)	R4	8.03	12.82	13.66	20.41
	R6	9.03	11.82	16.38	20.10
(x, y, z)	R4	6.75	11.56	13.56	20.58
	R6	4.93	10.28	10.55	18.23
(x, y, z, az)	R4	9.95	13.85	21.71	26.22
	R6	8.57	12.98	20.57	25.22
(x, y, z, in)	R4	13.10	15.63	19.65	24.37
	R6	11.22	13.91	17.68	23.38
(x, y, z, th)	R4	4.40	8.08	9.46	16.67
	R6	3.66	7.36	8.59	15.06
(x, y, z, th, lrc)	R4	3.67	6.33	8.69	14.39
	R6	3.18	5.77	8.52	13.69
(x, y, z, th, lrc, lan)	R4	3.12	5.87	10.02	15.36
	R6	2.72	5.46	7.90	12.93
(x, y, z, th, lrc, lan, at)	R4	2.77	5.73	8.45	13.36
	R6	1.99	5.35	7.53	12.64
(x, y, z, th, lrc, lan, at, vl)	R4	1.93	4.23	6.75	10.81
	R6	1.73	4.13	6.69	10.29
(x, y, z, th, lrc, lan, at, vl) $+ \Delta(\cdot)$	R4	0.50	4.51	4.05	11.25
	R6	0.89	3.25	6.30	12.30
(x, y, z, th, lrc, lan, at, vl) $+ \Delta(\cdot) + \Delta\Delta(\cdot)$	R4	1.15	5.71	5.41	15.11
	R6	1.04	4.43	5.80	13.05

12.6. Multimodality in Biometric Systems

In the preceding sections we have been concerned mainly about technological development of monomodal biometric systems (in our case, face, speech, fingerprint and signature). It is now interesting to face how multimodal biometric systems operate and the possible improvements they can produce.

Multimodality can be studied under the general frame of *data fusion,* as the particular case when the nature of the data to be fused is different. Data fusion [20,101] is a very broad and active field of research, with applications in robotics, target detection, etc.

In this section we will try to find connections of our particular biometric problem with this field of data fusion, but we can not forget that the original biometric problem is also a pattern recognition problem. So we will deal with various subjects simultaneously (mainly, data fusion and pattern recognition). In the biometric recognition problem more than a fusion or combination of original data (face images, speech signals and so on) we would rather combine the classifiers themselves or the decisions that they take individually. We refer to some particular works where the combination of classifiers is addressed [21,102].

In [102] important aspects of the theory of combination of classifiers are settled and three techniques are described for combination (voting, bayesian formulations and Dempster-Schafer formulations). The examples in [102] are monomodal from our point of view, because all the classifiers take the same input in a handwriting recognition problem. But it is important to note that *monomodal* fusion can be important in biometrics too in order to improve, with several systems, the performance on a single modality. There are many studies dealing with combination of classifiers with a single modality. For example, see [103] for speaker recognition or [104] for fingerprint recognition.

In [21], the task of combining classifiers in a probabilistic bayesian framework is referred, and, moreover, an example of multimodal biometric verification under this framework is provided (single modalities are speech, frontal and profile images). Each classifier is supposed to give an estimate of the *a posteriori* probability of the classes. To be more specific, let us consider R modalities and K classes (K would be two, for a *verification* problem where the classes are acceptance/rejection; and the number of subjects, for an *identification* problem). Given a feature vector $\mathbf{x}_r$ for modality r, the classifiers should give the *a posteriori* probability for each class k: $P(\omega_k \mid \mathbf{x}_r)$. We would like to obtain, for each class, a single measure accounting for all the modalities 1, 2, ..., R. Two basic rules are derived in [21] from the Bayes theorem and certain hypothesis:

- **The Product Rule:** $P^{-(R-1)}(\omega_k)\prod_{i=1}^{R} P(\omega_k \mid \mathbf{x}_i)$ (12.18)

- **The Sum Rule:** $(1-R)P(\omega_k)+\sum_{i=1}^{R} P(\omega_k \mid \mathbf{x}_i)$ (12.19)

From these original rules, other combination schemes (max, min, median and majority vote) are proposed. In a real world scenario, it is impossible to work with the true posteriors $P(\omega_k \mid \mathbf{x}_r)$, but, rather, we can work with *estimated posteriors* $\hat{P}(\omega_k \mid \mathbf{x}_i)$, where an analysis of the sensitivity of errors is important. In [21] it is shown that the sum rule is more robust to errors than the product rule. As an example of the possible improvements obtained with this multimodal approach, we reproduce in Table 12.3 the results of [21] for the multimodal approach (you can verify that only the sum rule outperforms clearly the individual modalities):

Table 12.3.   Comparative results of some multimodal approaches.

Method	EER(%)
Frontal	12.2
Profile	8.5
Speech	1.4
Sum	0.7
Product	1.4
Maximum	12.2
Median	1.2
Minimum	4.5

We have seen that these combination rules are very simple and can produce improvements, but they do not take into account the reliability of the individual classifiers. Including in the scheme this kind of information, as pointed out in [105] for a generic fusion approach, could still improve the results.

You can consult [106] for a quite complete updated overview on combination schemes. Here we will only mention some works that have been carried out related to multimodal biometrics. Some pioneer works in this field are [107-111].

One of the most remarkable and recent works in multimodal biometrics is [112]. Somehow, this work comprises and summarizes some of the main points of previous works of the same authors. One important idea behind these works is that the problem of fusion of modalities can be addressed as a pattern recognition problem at a higher level, and, so, pattern recognition solutions can be applied to solve it. It is a pattern recognition problem because the final goal is to obtain labels (accepted/rejected for verification, the identity in the identification case) and it is high-level because we do not work directly onto the original data, but rather with the scores given by the individual experts modalities. Under this point of view, multiple pattern recognition techniques can be applied to address the problem. The following possibilities are explored (they are sorted in decreasing performance order for the tests): *Logistic Regression, Maximum a Posteriori, k-Nearest Neighbors classifiers, Multilayer Perceptrons, Binary Decision Trees, Maximum Likelihood, Quadratic Classifiers* and *Linear Classifiers*. Logical operators (AND, OR and MAJORITY) were also tried. Three modalities (speech, frontal and profile face) were used again in a verification problem. All the methods (except the OR combination) outperformed clearly the best single modality (speech). Even if not totally supported by the statistical analysis that the authors do, they claim that Logistic Regression is the best technique, at least for this experiment. The best performing techniques (logistic regression, and Maximum a Posteriori), with the Maximum Likelihood approach, are close relatives to the bayesian product rule described before. In a recent contribution [113] the paradigm of Support Vector Machines has been compared with all the mentioned techniques carrying the same experiments, outperforming all of them.

One of the main problems for researches in multimodal biometrics is the scarcity of true multimodal databases for testing the algorithms. The multimodal biometrics experiments mentioned so far [21,112-113] have been carried out over the M2VTS database [114]. This database comprises 37 different persons and provides 5 shots for each person. The shots consisted in the registration of audio and video of the person counting from 0 to 9, and rotating the head in the sequence [0, -90, 0, 90] degrees. Perhaps the most important resource available nowadays is the extended M2VTS database [69], which is associated to the specific Lausanne protocol for measuring the performance on verification tasks [68]. This database contains audio-visual material from 295 subjects. Four sessions per subject were taken, each of them containing two shots.

A recent report giving results on multimodal recognition on X2MVTS is [115]. The methods reported are (again, sorted in decreasing performance for the tests): *Bayesian Scheme based on the Product Rule, Polynomial Support Vector Machines, Radial Basis Functions Support Vector Machines, Decision Trees, Multilayer Perceptrons* and *Fisher Linear Discriminants*.

Considering what has been previously exposed, and taking into account the results obtained in the mentioned experiments, bayesian methods and Support Vector Machines have been shown to be the best techniques for performing multimodal biometric recognition. Bayesian methods are theoretically optimal, but they need lot of data to have reliable estimates. For Support Vector Machines the amount of data is not so important. It could be the reason that it performs better in [112], as the size of the M2VTS is much smaller than the XM2VTS database in [115]. It should be noted that in these two last studies the sum rule (and its variants such as averaging or weighted averaging) has not been considered (only a promising result for linear pooling is reported in [116]). A system using also a product rule for combination and working on three modalities (fingerprint, face and speech) is presented in [117].

12.7.   From Technology to Applications

12.7.1   Application Strategies

Some strategies have to be considered in order to develop real-world applications from biometric recognition technologies. We will concisely mention some of them.

- ***Intra-User Variability***

Some biometric characteristics are implicitly highly changing, like speech or face; others, like fingerprints or iris patterns are less exposed to change. In any case, some factors of variability may always occur, due not only to signal/image variability, but also to acquisition requirements and devices. In general, it can be stated that for almost unchangeable patterns, variability should be controlled by controlling the operating framework. The region of interest in fingerprint or iris matching should be fixed, and the iris illumination should be well pre-defined.

Regarding voice, signature of face, where variability is always existing, some factors have to be controlled (type of microphone and position; illumination and pose, etc.), but many others have to be included in the model or pattern to be used, like inter-session variability, channel variability or feature normalization.

- ***Model Training***

Biometric characteristics require the use of some kind of feature extraction procedure. Regarding speaker verification, cepstral coefficients of input speech are computed for each analysis frame; with respect to on-line signature verification, some dynamic information, like instantaneous displacement, velocity, acceleration or pressure is extracted from each sampling period information; in fingerprint matching, minutiae are extracted in order to generate a fingerprint pattern. After these extraction procedures, in many cases features are statistically modeled: that is the case for speech features or signature dynamics, where HMMs are frequently used; or for face recognition, in which eigenface decomposition is accomplished.

Regarding model training, some factors have to be taken into account, like model consistency or model updating. For model consistency we understand the statistical representativeness of the identity of the user (client) included in the model; in practice, consistency is strongly related with variability factors included in the training sessions, with number of repetitions (realizations) of each biometric characteristic included in the model, or with number of sessions employed to acquire the training material. Regarding model updating, the model should be able to adapt to changes with time of the input features.

- ***Verification Threshold Setting***

a) False Acceptance and False Rejection Errors. The process of setting verification thresholds is a complex process, where two types of errors are involved: *i)* the error of accepting an impostor as a user, or false acceptance error (E_{fa}), and *ii)* the error of rejecting a user as an impostor, known as false rejection error (E_{fr}). Systems can be globally characterized in terms of ROC or DET curves, or also through any characteristic points, as equal error rate (EER), or even expressing the FR value for a given FA value ($E_{fr} = x|_{@\,Efa=y}$) or viceversa. If our application requires a restrictive (high) threshold, E_{fa} will diminish, but E_{fr} will be increased, producing the annoying effect of rejecting a user. Other applications should admit a less restrictive operating point, decreasing in this case E_{fr} but increasing E_{fa}.

b) Cost Detection Function. E_{fa} and E_{fr} are not the only parameters to be considered in threshold setting. We have to consider the complete detection cost of the system [47], described by the function:

$$c_{det} = c_{fr} \cdot E_{fr} \cdot P_{us} + c_{fa} \cdot E_{fa} \cdot \left(1 - P_{us}\right) \qquad (12.20)$$

where: a) c_{det}, is the global cost (to be minimized) of the decision of a determined application, b) c_{fr} and c_{fa}, evaluate the cost of false rejection related to the cost of false acceptance (for instance, c_{fr}=10 y c_{fa}=1, shows that false rejection cost is considered to be ten times more relevant than false acceptance cost), and c) P_{us}, is the *a priori* probability of a user entering the biometric system; $1-P_{us}$ will be consequently associated to the *a priori* probability of having a real impostor accessing to the system.

c) User-specific Thresholds vs. Universal Thresholds. Some matching algorithms produce user-independent scores, like edit distance in fingerprint matching; nevertheless, in other matching procedures, like HMMs, scores are user-dependent. This means that although user-specific thresholds can be used, in real applications user-independent (universal or common) thresholds are more convenient, as the whole system compares with a single value. Some score normalization algorithms, like Z-Norm, T-Norm or H-Norm [43, 44], contribute to set universal thresholds, permitting the system to be directly represented in terms of DET or ROC curves.

d) Practical Estimation of E_{fr} and E_{fa}. In real applications, although for E_{fa} we may use as many impostor files as we need (even from separate off-line impostor populations), in the case of E_{fr} a problem arises, as usually we will have small number of user realizations in order to estimate the false rejection curve. Additionally, in many cases these realizations will come from the same session, and will hence incorporate small intra-variability. In this case, the use of score normalization techniques [43,44] is a good alternative in order to fix verification thresholds.

12.7.2 Biometric Recognition Demos at ATVS

- ### *Speaker Recognition System*

Speaker Recognition at our Biometrics Research Lab.-ATVS is accomplished by means of GMM technology (see Section 12.2). Some utterances are used for training the GMM identity model, and other utterances for testing, computing though the normalized likelihood score between test utterance and trained model. Our system is able to work in both text-dependent (pre-fixed utterance as, i. e., a PIN) and text-independent (free speech) modes. Figure 12.19 shows the speaker verification on-line demo input screen.

- ### *Face Recognition System*

Face Recognition at ATVS is accomplished by means of eigenface decomposition. Figure 12.20 shows the on-line face capture interface, in order to accomplish the real-time eigenface decomposition process. No special illumination or pose conditions are required, and low-resolution web-cam based acquisition is used; on the contrary, spatial restrictions are applied, as the user must situate his face inside the capture rectangle.

- ### *On-Line Signature Recognition System*

On-line signature recognition at ATVS, as it has been previously stated in Section 12.5, follows the perspective of HMM with left-to-right topology considerations. Our system uses dynamic information, and a 24-parameter vector is used at 100 Hz sampling rate. Figure 12.21 shows an identification procedure in which the pattern is compared with the test signature, giving raise to several log-scores for 4 different users. It has to be clarified that when using HMMs, the pattern signature means training signature; for our system, between 4 and 6 repetitions of signature are used for training.

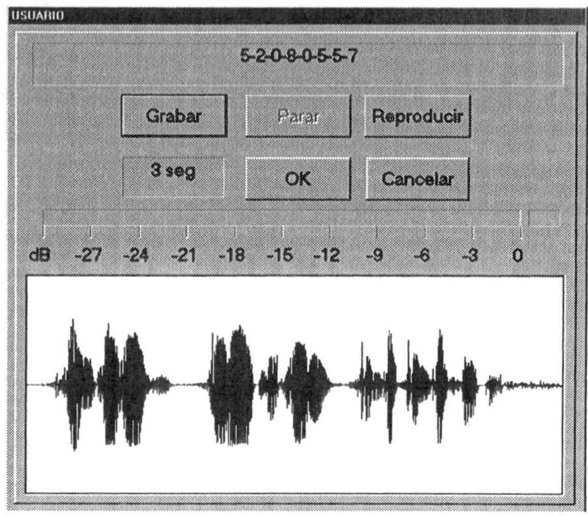

Figure 12.19. Demo of PIN-based speaker verification system at ATVS.

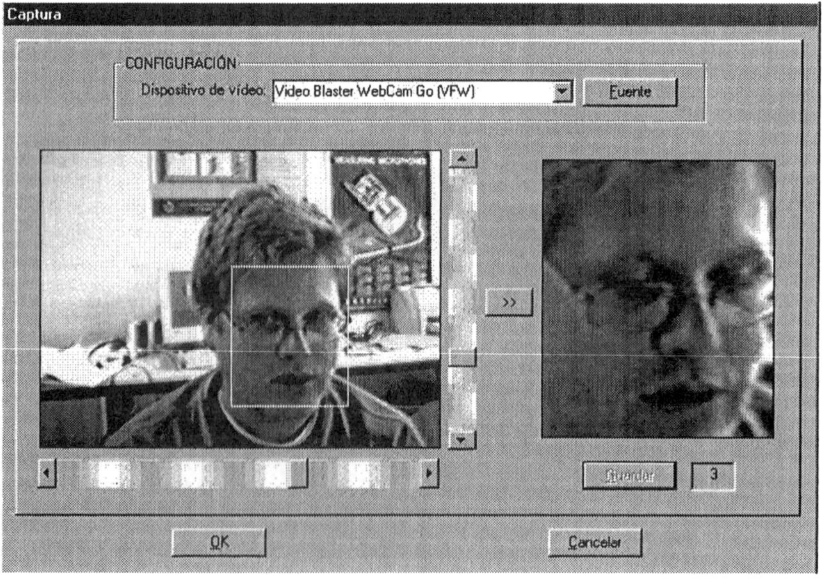

Figure 12.20. On-line face acquisition interface.

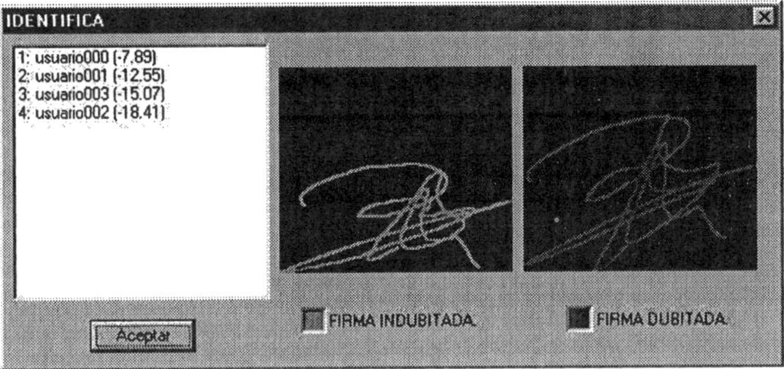

Figure 12.21. On-line signature dynamic identification, by means of HMMs. Stored (*"firma indubitada"*) and test (*"firma dubitada"*) patterns are compared, and several log-scores are presented.

- ### *Fingerprint Matching System*

Regarding fingerprint matching, our system is a minutiae-pattern based system. In order to set the template to be compared, a complete minutae extraction procedure is accomplished (see Section 12.4). After the storage of this pattern, any testing can be realized by extracting the minutiae pattern of the test fingerprint and by using pattern matching techniques; in our case, an elastic cost function through edit distance is used. Figure 12.22 shows the computed minutiae pattern superimposed on the ridge structure of an extracted fingerprint.

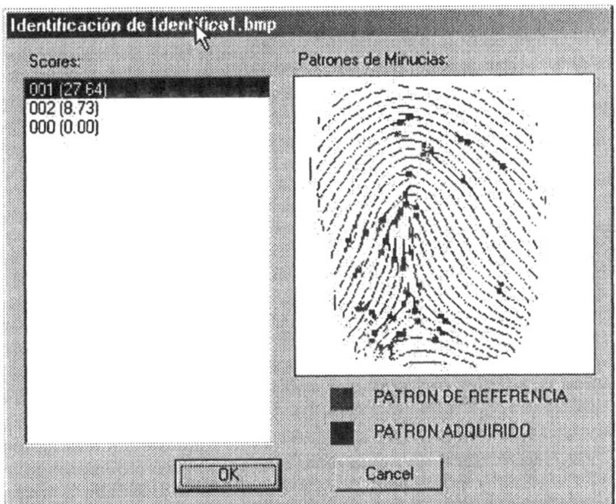

Figure 12.22. On the right, ridge structure of a fingerprint and its minutiae pattern superimposed. Two different minutiae patterns are shown: the reference pattern (*"patron de referencia"*), and the test pattern (*"patron adquirido"*).

Acknowledgments

This work has been partially supported by Spanish Ministry of Science and Technology under project TIC00-1669-C04-1. Authors wish to thank Jorge Martin-Rello, Julian Fierrez-Aguilar, Marta Sanchez-Asenjo and Daniel Garcia-Romero for their valuable development work.

References

[1]   B. Miller. Vital Signs of Identity [Biometrics], IEEE Spectrum, vol. 31, no. 2, pages 22-30, Feb. 1994.

[2]   D. Sims. Biometric Recognition: Our Hands, Eyes, and Faces Give Us Away, IEEE Computer Graphics and Applications, vol. 14, no. 5, pages 14-15, Sept. 1994.

[3]   Weichen Shen, M. Surette, and R. Khanna. Evaluation of Automated Biometrics-Based Identification and Verification Systems. In Proc. of the IEEE, vol. 85, no. 9, pages 1464-1478, Sept. 1997.

[4]   M. Golfarelli, D. Maio, and D. Malton. On the Error-Reject Trade-Off in Biometric Verification Systems, IEEE Trans. On Pattern Analysis and Machine Intelligence, vol. 19, no. 7, pages 786-796, July 1997.

[5]   J. D. Woodward. Biometrics: Privacy's Foe or Privacy's Friend?, In Proc. of the IEEE, vol. 85, no. 9, pages 1480-1492, Sept. 1997.

[6]   G. Lawton. Biometrics: A New Era in Security, Computer, vol. 31, no. 8, pages 16-18, Aug. 1998.

[7]   A. Jain, R. Bolle, and S. Pankanti (eds.). Biometrics – Personal Identification in Networkwed Society, Kluwer Academic Publishers, 1999.

[8]   D. D. Zhang. Automated Biometrics – Technologies and Systems, Kluwer Academic Publishers, 2000.

[9]   P. J. Philips, A. Martin, C L. Wilson, and M. Przybocki. An Introduction Evaluating Biometric Systems, Computer, vol. 33, no. 2, pages 56-63, Feb. 2000.

[10]   C. J. Tilton. An Emerging Biometric API Industry Standard, Computer, vol. 33, no. 2, pages 130-132, Feb. 2000.

[11]   D. Maio and D. Maltoni. Direct Gray-Scale Minutiae Detection in Fingerprints, IEEE Trans Pattern Anal. and Machine Intell., vol. 19, no. 1, pages 27-40, 1997.

[12]   A. Jain, S. Pankanti. Automated Fingerprint Identification and Imaging Systems, Book Chapter from "Advances in Fingerprint Technology", 2nd Edition, Elsevier Science, NY, 2001.

[13]   R. Chellappa, C.L. Wilson and S. Sirohey. Human and Machine Recognition of Faces: A Survey. In Proc. of the IEEE, pages 705-740, 1995.

[14]   Special Issue on Face and Gesture Recognition, IEEE Trans. Pattern Analysis and Machine Intelligence, vol. 19, no. 7, July, 1997.

[15]   D. A. Reynolds. Speaker Identification and Verification using Gaussian Mixture Speakers Models, Speech Communication, vol. 17, pages 91-108, 1995.

[16]   S. Furui. An Overview of Speaker Recognition Technology, ESCA Workshop on Automatic Speaker Recognition, Martigny (Switzerland), pages 1-9, April 1994.

[17]   J. Ortega-Garcia, J. Gonzalez-Rodriguez, and S. Cruz-Llanas. Speech Variability in Automatic Speaker Recognition Systems for Commercial and Forensic Purposes, IEEE Aerospace and Electronics Systems Magazine, vol. 15, no. 11, pages 27-32, Nov. 2000.

[18]   F. Leclerc and R. Plamondon. Automatic Signature Verification: The State of the Art, 1989-1993, International Journal of Pattern Recognition and Machine Intelligence, vol. 8, no. 3, pages 643-660, 1994.

[19]   R. Plamondon and S. N. Srihari. On-Line and Off-Line Handwriting Recognition: A Comprehensive Survey, IEEE Trans. on Pattern Analysis and Machine Intelligence, vol. 22, no. 1, pages 63-84, January 2000.

[20]   Special Issue on Data Fusion. In Proc. of the IEEE, vol. 85, no. 1, January 1997.

[21]   J. Kittler, M. Hatef, R.P.W. Duin and J. Matas. On Combining Classifiers, IEEE Trans. Pattern Analysis and Machine Intelligence, vol. 20, no. 3, pages 226-239, March 1998.

[22]   R. W. Frischholz and U. Dieckmann. BioID: A Multimodal Biometric Identification System, Computer, vol. 33, no. 2, pages 64-68, Feb. 2000.

[23]   H.J.M. Steeneken and D.A. van Leeuwen. Speaker Recognition by Humans and Machines. In Proc. of Eurospeech'97, pages 2319-2322, 1997.

[24]   H.J. Künzell. Current Approaches to Forensic Speaker Recognition. In Proc. of ESCA Workshop on Automatic Speaker Recognition, Identification and Verification, Martigny, Switzerland, pages 135-141, 1994.

[25]   J.R. Deller, J.G. Proakis and J.H.L. Hansen. Discrete-time. In Proc. of Speech Signals, Prentice Hall, New Jersey, 1993.

[26]   J. Gonzalez-Rodriguez, J. Ortega-Garcia and J.L. Sanchez-Bote. Forensic Identification Reporting using Automatic Biometric Systems, Chapter 7.

[27]   J. Godfrey, D. Graff and A. Martin. Public Databases for Speaker Recognition and Verification. In Proc. of ESCA Workshop on Automatic Speaker Recognition, Identification and Verification, Martigny, Switzerland, pages 39-42, 1994.

[28]   D. Gibbon, R. Moore and R. Winski, eds.. Handbook of Standards and Resores for Spoken Language Systems, EAGLES Spoken Language Working Group, Mouton de Gruyter, Berlin, 1997.

[29]   A. Gersho and R.M. Gray. Vector Quantization and Signal Compression, Kluwer Academic Publishers, 1991.

[30]   A.E. Rosenberg and F.K. Soong. Evaluation of a Vector Quantization Talker Recognition System in Text Independent and Text Dependent Modes, Computer, Speech and Language, 22, pages 143-157, 1987.

[31]   D.B. Morgan & C.L. Scofield. Neural Networks and Speech Processing, Kluwer Academic Publishers, 1991.

[32]   J. Oglesby and J.S. Mason. Optimization of Neural Models for Speaker Identification. In Proc. of IEEE Intl. Conf. Acoust. Speech and Signal Proc. (ICASSP'90), pages 261-264, 1990.

[33] J. Oglesby and J.S. Mason. Radial Basis Function Networks for Speaker Recognition, In Proc. of IEEE Intl. Conf. Acoust. Speech and Signal Proc. (ICASSP'91), pages 393-396, 1991.

[34] Y. Bennani, F. Fogelman and P. Gallinari. A Connectionist Approach for Speaker Identification. In Proc. of IEEE Intl. Conf. Acoust. Speech and Signal Proc. (ICASSP'90), pages 265-268, 1990.

[35] N.Z. Tishby. On the Application of Mixture AR Hidden Markov Models to Text Independent Speaker Recognition, IEEE Trans. on Acoustics, Speech and Signal Proc., vol. ASSP-30, no. 3, pages 563-570, 1991.

[36] T. Matsui and S. Furui. Comparison of Text-Independent Speaker Recognition Methods Using VQ-Distortion and Discrete/Continuous HMMs. In Proc. of IEEE Intl. Conf. Acoust. Speech and Signal Proc. (ICASSP'92), vol. 2, pages 157-160, 1992.

[37] A. Higgins et al. Speaker Verification Using Randomized Phrase Prompting, Digital Signal Processing (Academic Press), vol. 1, pages 89-106, 1991.

[38] A.E. Rosenberg et al.. The Use of Cohort Normalized Scores for Speaker Verification, In Proc. of the International Conference on Spoken Language Processing (ICSLP'92), pages 599-602, 1992.

[39] M.J. Carey and E.S. Parris. Speaker Verification Using Connected Words. In Proc. of Institute of Acoustics, vol. 14, no. 6, pages 95-100, 1992.

[40] T. Matsui and S. Furui. Similarity Normalization Method for Speaker Verification Based on a Posteriori Probability. In Proc. of ESCA Workshop on Automatic Speaker Recognition, Identification and Verification, Martigny, Switzerland, pages 59-62, 1994.

[41] D. A. Reynolds, T.F. Quatieri and R.B. Dunn. Speaker Verification Using Adapted Gaussian Mixture Models, Digital Signal Processing, vol. 10, no. 1-3, pages 19-41, January/April/July 2000.

[42] J.L. Gauvain and C.H. Lee. Maximum a Posteriori Estimation for Multivariate Gaussian Mixture Observations of Markov Chains, IEEE Trans. on Speech and Audio Processing, vol. 2, pages 291-298, April 1994.

[43] M.A. Przybocki and A. Martin. Odyssey Text Independent Evaluation Data. In Proc. of Odyssey'2001 Speaker Recognition Workshop, pages 21-23, Crete (Greece), 2001 .

[44] A. Martin and M.A. Przybocki. The NIST Speaker Recognition Evaluations: 1996-2001. In Proc. of Odyssey'2001 Speaker Recognition Workshop, Crete (Greece), pages 39-42, 2001.

[45] J. Gonzalez-Rodriguez, O. Ledesma-Garcia, J. Ortega-Garcia. ATVS Results and Presentation at NIST'2001 Speaker Recognition Evaluation, Linthicum Heights, Maryland (USA), 2001.

[46] J. Ortega-Garcia, J. Gonzalez-Rodriguez and V. Marrero-Aguiar. AHUMADA: a Large Speech Corpus in Spanish for Speaker Characterization and Identification, Speech Communication 31, pages 255-264, 2000.

[47] A. Martin. The DET Curve in Assessment of Detection Task Performance. In Proc. of Eurospeech'97, pages 1895-1898, Rhode (Greece), 1997.

[48]   A. Samal and P.A. Iyengar. Automatic Recognition and Analysis of Human Faces and Facial Expressions: A Survey, Pattern Recognition, vol. 25, pages 65-77, 1992.

[49]   http://www.cs.rug.nl/~peterkr/FACE/face.html.

[50]   In Proc. of the several (one to four) International Conferences on Automatic Face and Gesture Recognition, Ed. IEEE Computer Society.

[51]   R. Brunelli and T. Poggio. Face Recognition: Features versus Templates, IEEE Trans. Pattern Analysis and Machine Intelligence, vol. 11, no. 6, pages 567-585, 1989.

[52]   A. Lanitis, C.J. Taylor and T.F. Cootes. Automatic Interpretation and Coding of Face Images Using Flexible Models, IEEE Trans. Pattern Analysis and Machine Intelligence, vol. 19, no. 7, pages 743-756, July 1997.

[53]   L. Sirovich and M. Kirby. Low-dimensional Procedure for the Characterization of Human Faces, Journal of the Optical Society of America, vol. 4, pages 519-524, 1987.

[54]   M. Turk and A. Pentland. Eigenfaces for Recognition, Journal of Cognitive Neuroscience, vol. 3, pages 71-86, 1991.

[55]   P.N. Belhumeur, J.P. Hespanha and D.J. Kriegman. Eigenfaces vs. Fisherfaces: Using Class Specific Linear Projection, IEEE Trans. Pattern Analysis and Machine Intelligence, vol. 19, no. 7, pages 711-720, July 1997.

[56]   D. L. Swets and J. Weng. Using Discriminant Eigenfeatures for Image Retrieval, IEEE Trans. Pattern Analysis and Machine Intelligence, vol. 18, no. 8, pages 831-836, Aug. 1996.

[57]   B. Moghaddam and A. Pentland. Probabilistic Visual Learning for Object Representation, IEEE Trans. Pattern Analysis and Machine Intelligence, vol. 19, no. 7, pages 696-710, July 1997.

[58]   B. Moghaddam, W. Wahid and A. Pentland. Beyond Eigenfaces: Probabilistic Matching for Face Recognition. In Proc. of the Third IEEE Int'l Conf. On Automatic Face and Gesture Recognition, pages 30-35, 1998.

[59]   M.S. Bartlett and T.J. Sejnowski. Independent Component Representations for Face Recognition. In Proc. of the SPIE: Conference on Human Vision and Electronic Imaging III, vol. 3299, pages 528-539, 1998.

[60]   D. Valentin, H. Abdi, A.J. O'Toole and G.W. Cottrell. Connectionist Models of Face Processing: A Survey, Pattern Recognition, vol. 27, pages 1208-1230, 1994.

[61]   M-H Yang, N. Ahuja and D. Kriegman. Face Recognition Using Kernel Eigenfaces, IEEE Conf. on Image Processing (ICIP 2000), vol. 1, pages 37-40, Sept. 2000.

[62]   L. Wiskott, J.M. Fellous, N. Krüger and C.V.D. Malsburg. Face Recognition by Elastic Bunch Graph Matching, IEEE Trans. Pattern Analysis and Machine Intelligence, vol. 19, no. 7, pages 775-779, July 1997.

[63]   M. Lades, J.C. Vorbruggen, J. Buhman, J. Lange, C.V.D. Malsburg, R.P. Wurtz and W. Konen. Distortion Invariant Object Recognition in the Dynamic Link Architecture, IEEE Trans. on Computers, vol. 42, no. 3, pages 300-310, March 1993.

[64]   R.P. Wurtz. Object Recognition Robust under Translations, Deformations, and Changes in the Background, IEEE Trans. Pattern Analysis and Machine Intelligence, vol. 19, no. 7, pages 769-775, July 1997.

[65]   C.L. Kotropoulos, A. Tefas and I. Pitas. Frontal Face Authentication Using Discriminating Grids with Morphological Feature Vectors, IEEE Trans. On Multimedia, vol. 2, no. 1, pages 14-26, March 2000.

[66]   P.J. Phillips, H. Moon, S.A. Rizvi and P.J. Rauss. The FERET Evaluation Methodology for Face-Recognition Algorithms, IEEE Trans. Pattern Analysis and Machine Intelligence, vol. 22, no. 10, pages 1090-1103, Oct. 2000.

[67]   S.A. Rizvi, P.J. Phillips and H. Moon. The FERET Verification Testing Protocol for Face Recognition Algorithms, Technical Report NISTIR 6281, Nat'l Inst. Standards and Technologyhttp://www.nist.gov/itl/div894/894.03/pubs.html#face.1998, 1998.

[68]   J. Luettin and G. Maitre. Evaluation Protocol for the Extended M2VTS Database (Lausanne protocol)", Technical Report 98-05 at IDIAP, ftp.idiap.ch/pub/reports/1998/com98-05.ps.gz, 1998.

[69]   K. Messer, J. Matas, J. Kittler, J. Luettin and G. Maitre. XM2VTSDB: The Extended M2VTS Database, Audio-and Video-based Biometric Person Authentication, AVBPA'99, pages 72-77, March 1999.

[70]   A. K. Jain, L. Hong and R. Bolle. On-line Fingerprint Verification, IEEE Trans. Pattern Anal. and Machine Intell., vol. 19, no. 4, pages 302-314, 1997.

[71]   N. Ratha, S. Chen and A. K. Jain. Adaptive Flow Orientation-based Feature Extraction in Fingerprint Images, Pattern Recognition , vol. 28, no. 11, pages 1657-1672, 1995.

[72]   L. Hong, Y. Wan and A. K. Jain. Fingerprint Image Enhancement: Algorithm and Performance Evaluation, IEEE Trans. Pattern Anal. and Machine Intell., vol. 20, no. 8, pages 777-789, 1998.

[73]   L. Hong, A. Jain, S. Pankanti and R. Bolle. Identity Authentication Using Fingerprints. In Proc. of the First Audio and Video-Based Person Authentication, Crans-Montana, Switzerland, 12-14 March 1997.

[74]   R. Roddy and J. D. Stosz. Fingerprint Features – Statistical Analysis and System Performance Estimates. In Proc. of IEEE, vol. 85, no. 9, pages 1390-1421, 1997.

[75]   D. Simon, J. Ortega, S. Cruz, J. L. Sanchez and J. Glez. An Improved Image Enhancement Scheme for Fingerprint Minutiae Extraction in Biometric Identification, In Proc. of the Third Audio and Video-Based Person Authentication, Halmstad, Sweden, 6-8 June, 2001.

[76]   A. Ross, S. Prabhakar and A. K. Jain. Fingerprint Matching Using Minutiae and Texture Features, International Conference on Image Processing (ICIP), Greece, October 7-10, 2001.

[77]   V. S. Srinivasan and N. N. Murthy. Detection of Singular Points in Fingerprint Images, Pattern Recognition, vol. 25, no. 2, pages 139-153, 1992.

[78]   D.C.D. Hung. Enhancement and Feature Purification of Fingerprint Images, Pattern Recognition, vol. 26, no. 11, pages 1661-1671, 1993.

[79]   A. Mandalia, A. Pandya and R. Sudhakar. Modified Fast Parallel Thinning Algorithm for Noisy Handprinted Characters, Department of Computer Science and Engineering, Florida Atlantic University, 1993.

[80] R. Bolle, N. K.Ratha and S. Pankanti. Evaluating Techniques for Biometrics-Based Authentication Systems. In Proc. of 15th IAPR International Conference on Pattern Recognition, Barcelona, Spain, Sep 3-8, 2000.

[81] A. K. Jain, L. Hong and Y. Kulkarni. A Multimodal Biometric System using Fingerprint, Face, and Speech, Proc. 2nd Int'l Conference on Audio- and Video- based Biometric Person Authentication, Washington D. C., pages 182-187, 1999.

[82] L. Hong and A. K. Jain. Integrating Faces and Fingerprints for Personal Identification, IEEE Trans. Pattern Anal. and Machine Intell., vol. 20, no. 12, pages 1295-1307, 1998.

[83] A. K. Hrechak and J. A. McHugh. Automated Fingerprint Recognition Using Structural Matching, Pattern Recognition, vol. 23, pages 893-904, 1990.

[84] L. Coetzee and E. C. Botha. Fingerprint Recognition in Low Quality Images, Pattern Recognition, vol. 26, no. 10, pages 1441-1460, 1993.

[85] A. K. Herchak and J. A. McHugh. Automated Fingerprint Recognition Using Structural Matching, Pattern Recognition, vol. 23, no. 8, pages 893-904, 1990.

[86] R. Cappelli, A. Lumini, D. Maio and D. Maltoni. Fingerprint Classification by Directional Image Partitioning, IEEE Trans Pattern Anal. and Machine Intell., vol. 21, no. 5, pages 402-421, 1999.

[87] D. Isenor and S. Zaky. Fingerprint Identification Using Graph Matching, Pattern Recognition, vol. 19, pages 113-133, 1986.

[88] X. Quinghan and B. Zhaoqi. An Approach to Fingerprint Identification by Using the Attributes of Feature Lines of Fingerprints. In Proc. of Eighth Int. Conf. Pattern Recognition, pages 663-665, Oct. 1986.

[89] R. Plamondon and G. Lorette. Automatic Signature Verification and Writer Identification – The State of the Art, Pattern Recognition, vol. 22, no. 2, pages 107-131, 1989.

[90] W. Nelson, W. Turin and T. Hastie. Statistical Methods for On-Line Signature Verification, Int. Journ. Pattern Rec. and Mach. Intell., vol. 8, no. 3, pages 749-770, 1994.

[91] V.S. Nalwa. Automatic On-Line Signature Verification. In Proc. of IEEE, vol. 85, no. 2, pages 215-240, 1997.

[92] K. Huang and H. Yan. On-Line Signature Verification Based on Dynamic Segmentation and Global and Local Matching, Optical Eng., vol. 34, no. 12, pages 3480-3488, 1995.

[93] L. Yang, B. K. Widjaja and R. Prasad. Application of Hidden Markov Models for Signature Verification, Pattern Recognition, vol. 28, no. 2, pages 161-170, 1995.

[94] R. S. Kashi, W. Turin and W. L. Nelson. On-Line Handwritten Signature Verification Using Stroke Direction Coding, Optical Eng., vol. 35, no. 9, pages 2526-2533, 1996.

[95] R. Martens and L. Claesen. Utilizing Baum-Welch for On-Line Signature Verification. In Proc. of the Sixth International Workshop on Frontiers in Handwriting Recognition (IWFHRVI), Taejon, Korea, pages 389-397, August 1998.

[96]   J. G. A. Dolfing, E. H. L. Aarts and J.J.G.M. Van Oosterhout. On-Line Verification Signature with Hidden Markov Models. In Proc. of the 14th International Conference on Pattern Recognition, pages 1309-1312, Brisbane, Australia, August 1998.

[97]   D. Sakamoto et al.. On-Line Signature Verification Algorithm Incorporating Pen Position, Pen Pressure and Pen Inclination Trajectories, IEEE Intl. Conf. on Acoust. Speech and Signal Proc., ICASSP-01, vol. 2, pages 993-996, 2001.

[98]   F. K Soong and A.E. Rosenberg. On the Use of Instantaneous and Transitional Spectral Information in Speaker Recognition, IEEE Trans. on Acoust., Speech and Signal Proc., vol. ASSP-36, no. 6, pages 871-879, 1988.

[99]   R. Baron and R. Plamondon. Acceleration Measurement with an Instrumented Pen for Signature Verification and Handwriting Analysis, IEEE Trans. On Instrumentation and Measurement, vol. 38, no. 6, December 1989.

[100]   W. Nelson and E. Kishon. Use of Dynamic Features for Signature Verification, IEEE Intl. Conf. on Systems, Man and Cybernetics, vol. 1, pages 201-205, 1991.

[101]   Information Fusion. Multi-Sensor, Multi-Source, Information Fusion., Ed. Elsevier.

[102]   L. Xu, A. Kryzak and C.Y. Suen. Methods of Combining Multiple Classifiers and Their Application to Handwriting Recognition, IEEE Trans. on Systems, Man and Cybernetics, vol. 22, no. 3, pages 418-435, May-June 1992.

[103]   K, Chen and H. Chi. A Method of Combining Multiple Probabilistic Classifiers through Soft Competition on Different Feature Sets, Neurocomputing, no. 20, pages 227-252, Elsevier, 1998.

[104]   S. Prabhakar and A.K. Jain. Pattern Recognition, 2001, http://biometrics.cse.msu.edu/publications.html.

[105]   J.A. Benediktsson and P.H. Swain. Consensus Theoretic Classification Methods, IEEE Trans. on Systems, Man and Cybernetics, vol. 22, no. 4, pages 688-704, Jul.-Aug. 1992.

[106]   A.K. Jain, R.P.W. Duin and J. Mao. Statistical Pattern Recognition: A Review, IEEE Trans. Pattern Analysis and Machine Intelligence, vol. 22, no. 1, pages 4-37, Jan. 2000.

[107]   R. Brunelli and D. Falavigna. Person Identification using Multiple Cues, IEEE Trans. Pattern Analysis and Machine Intelligence, vol. 17, no. 10, pages 995-966, Oct. 1995.

[108]   U. Dieckmann, P. Plankensteiner and T. Wainer. Sesam: A Biometric Person Identification System using Sensor Fusion, Pattern Rec. Letters, vol. 18, no. 9, pages 827-833, Sept. 1997.

[109]   E. Bigun, J. Bigun, B. Duc and S. Fisher. Expert Conciliation for Multimodal Person Authentication Systems by Bayesian Statistics. In Proc. of the First Int'l Conference on Audio-and Video-based Biometric Person Authentication, Ed. Springer Verlag, pages 327-334, March 1997.

[110]   P. Jourlin, J. Luettin, D. Genoud and H. Wassner. Acoustic-labial Speaker Verification. In Proc. of the First Int'l Conference on Audio-and Video-based Biometric Person Authentication, Ed. Springer Verlag, March 1997.

[111]   L. Hong and A. Jain. Integrating Faces and Fingerprints for Personal Identification, IEEE Trans. Pattern Anal. and Machine Intelligence, vol. 20, no. 12, pages 1295-1307, Dec. 1998.

[112] P. Verlinde, G. Chollet and M. Acheroy. Multi-modal Identity Verification using Expert Fusion, Information Fusion, no. 1, pages 17-33, Ed. Elsevier, 2000.

[113] B. Gutschoven and P. Verlinde, Decision Fusion using Support Vector Machines (SVM). In Proc. of the 3rd International Conference on Information Fusion, July, 2000.

[114] S. Pigeon and L. Vandendorpe. The M2VTS Database (release 1.0), http://www.tele.ucl.ac.be/M2VTS, 1996.

[115] S. Bengio, J. Mariethoz and S. Marcel. Evaluation of Biometrics Technology on XM2VTS, Technical Report 01-21 at IDIAP, ftp.idiap.ch/pub/reports/2001/com01-21.ps.gz.

[116] S.Ben-Yacoub, J. Luettin, K.Jonsson, J. Matas and J. Kittler. Audio-visual Person Verification. In Proc. of the IEEE Computer Society on Computer Vision and Pattern Recognition (CVPR'99), 1999.

[117] A. Jain, L. Hong and Y. Kulkarni. A Multimodal Biometric System Using Fingerprints, Face, and Speech. In Proc. of the Second Int'l Conference on Audio-and Video-based Biometric Person Authentication, March 1999.

Chapter 13

FACE VERIFICATION FOR ACCESS CONTROL

Wen Gao[1,2,3] and Shiguang Shan[1,3]

1. Institute of Computing Technology, Chinese Academy of Sciences

2. Department of Computer Science, Harbin Institute of Technology

3. Graduate School, Chinese Academy of Sciences

{wgao,sgshan}@ict.ac.cn

Abstract   In this chapter, we discuss the research issues and state-of-the-art of face verification for access control. We start by analyzing a typical face verification system for access control, and then explore the dominant technologies in the field. We introduce most of the typical and popular algorithms, listing the open research issues or technical challenges. Some available commercial systems in this field are also listed, and three standard performance evaluations, FERET, XM2VTS and FRVT2000 are simply introduced.

Keywords: Face recognition, Access control, Face detection, Face verification, Template Matching, Deformable template, Principle Component Analysis, Eigenface, Fisherface, linear subspace, Active shape model, Active appearance model, Illumination cones, Photometric alignment, Elastic graph matching, Hidden Markov Models, Quotient image, linear object class

13.1.   Introduction

The human face is another attractive source of biometric information, from which discriminatory measurements can be acquired intuitively and naturally without much user interaction relative to other biometric information. The recognition of faces has been a well-established field of research, with a large number of algorithms proposed in the past thirty years. Some commercial systems have also emerged in recent years. Several survey papers are available [12,14,23,26,70].

Though it an easy task for human beings to recognize a person from just one or several photos, this is not the case for computers. Automatic face recognition has been recognized as one the most challenging tasks in pattern recognition and artificial intelligence. In this section, we briefly introduce some background and definitions of face verification, from a computational perspective.

13.1.1   Motivation

Verification of identity based on biometric information is essential for many security applications, since the conventional authentication approaches, e.g. user/password mechanisms, have proved unreliable and inconvenient. Examples include access control to physical facilities, security systems or information databases. Suspect tracking, surveillance and intrusion detection are also potential applications [26].

In addition to the wide range of commercial and law enforcement applications mentioned above, there are many emerging fields that can benefit from face verification technology, such as the new generation of intelligent human-computer interfaces and *e*-services, including tele-shopping and tele-banking.

There exist many optional biometric cues for identity verification, such as the iris, fingerprint, voice, handprint, signature, and retina. The human face plays an irreplaceable role in biometrics technology due to some of its unique characteristics. First, most cameras are non-invasive; therefore face verification systems are one of the most publicly acceptable verification technologies in use. Another advantage is that face recognition systems can work mostly without the cooperation of the user concerned, which is therefore very convenient for the general users. Furthermore, they can even work in the situation where the subject concerned is not aware of the procedure. This point greatly facilitates applications such as criminal hunting, surveillance, tracking shoplifters, suspect tracking and investigation, etc. This is why the U.S. has decided to install the FaceFINDER™ real-time face recognition system at an undisclosed major U. S. airport, after the 9.11 terrorism attacks.

13.1.2   Computational Solutions to Access Control Based on Face
Verification

Access control is an important application of Biometric products. It is obvious that controlling the access to confidential physical buildings or information systems/databases, potentially dangerous vehicles (such as aeroplane, huge ship etc.), nuclear and biochemistry weapons etc., is essential for public security. However, conventional identity authentication mechanisms such as passwords or identification cards have proved unreliable. Biometrics is expected to solve these kinds of access control problems.

The general computational the machine recognition of faces can be formulated as follows: *given still or video images of a scene, identify one or more persons in the scene using a stored database of faces* [26]. Strictly speaking, there are two categories of applications in face recognition: face recognition/identification and face verification/authentication. In a recognition application, the input to the system is a face image, and the system reports the decided identity from a database of known individuals, whereas in verification application, the system confirms or rejects the claimed identity according to the input face image.

The basic architecture of face verification solutions for access control is illustrated in Figure 13.1. Here, one can see that an access control system based on face verification is commonly divided into several modules, including face detection, feature extraction, and face verification etc. The following sections describe these modules in detail.

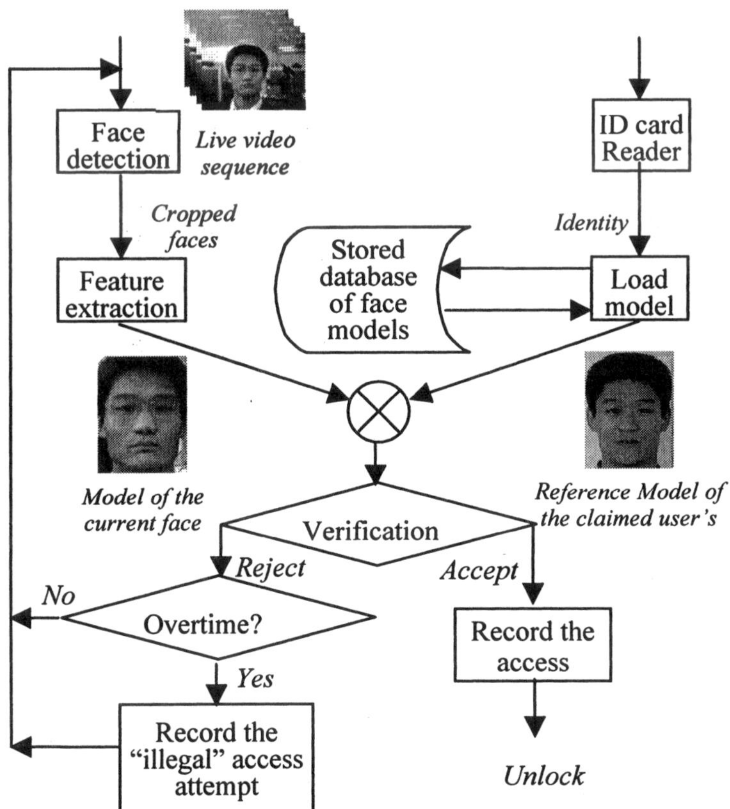

Figure 13.1. Access control system based on face verification.

13.1.3   Organization of this Chapter

The remainder of the chapter is organized as follows. First, a short review on face detection is given in Section 13.2. Then we describe three distinct aspects of face verification in detail in Section 13.3: models of identify, feature extraction, and classification. The solutions to illumination and pose problems are discussed in Section 13.4. An example access control system based on face verification is presented in Section 13.5. Several commercial systems are introduced and some famous evaluation protocols are addressed in Section 13.6. Some conclusions are drawn in last section.

13.2.   Face Detection

Face detection aims to determine whether there are faces in an image, and, if any, determine how many there are and where each face is. The approaches to face detection may be divided into four categories [83]: knowledge based methods, template matching, invariant feature methods, and statistics/learning based methods. Although the boundaries between them are not always clear, we can still briefly review most of the approaches to face detection under this taxonomy.

1. Knowledge Based Methods

The classical work in this category is the multiple-rule based method proposed by Yang and Huang [22]. The main problem with knowledge-based methods is the difficulty of transforming human knowledge into rules described in computer languages, especially for 3-D rotated faces in different poses.

2. Template Matching Methods

Miao and Yin, et al. [67] proposed a mosaic Gravity-Center Template matching method. It can be observed that the main components of an upright human face, such as double eyebrows, double eyes, nose bottom and mouth, almost all orient in a horizontal direction and that the vertical scale of the features are approximately equal.

3. Invariant Feature Methods

There are many works using various invariant features including gray values, edges, textures, color or a combination of these features. Among them, color is most widely used for both face detection and lip-reading [84]. However, color information is not enough to correctly locate faces, although non-upright and non-frontal faces can be easily detected as candidates. It is therefore usually combined with other features such as edges or textures.

4. Statistics/Learning Based Methods

The methods in this category are the most widely used ones by a majority of researchers. They include the use of Eigenfaces [2,5,49], Fisherfaces [51],

Neural Networks [59-60], and Support Vector Machines (SVMs) [41,61,75, 76]. SVMs were first introduced by Osuna, Freud and Girosi [41] for face detection. Their system reports better performance than some neural network systems.

By using the segmentation techniques mentioned in above, given a still image or a live video sequence, faces can be cropped out and fed into the following face verification modules.

13.3.   Face Verification

It is difficult to thoroughly review all the face verification technologies developed by thousands of researchers since the 1970s. Instead of discussing individual face recognition approaches in this chapter, we summarize the relevant technologies in terms of three aspects: the models of identity, feature extraction methods, and classification methods.

13.3.1   Models of Identity

Models of identity answer questions about what kind of representation should be exploited for faces, that is, what kind of "template" T should be extracted to represent a face. Typical models of identity are discussed below.

Geometric Features.   Geometric features of a face were often exploited by early researches such as Poggio [8,14] etc. The idea is to describe a face as the relative position of distinctive facial features such as eyes, mouth, nose and chin, as well as other parameters. Systems using geometric features for face recognition can be found in [8-10,12,14,50]. Since pure geometry is not sufficient for recognition, it is generally combined with other features, such as gray-level templates etc.

Holistic or Analytic Templates.   In the simplest version of template matching, the face is represented as a bi-dimensional array of intensity values sampled from the whole face region, that is, a template. A probe template is then compared using a suitable metric (typically the Euclidean distance) with stored ones [14,28,50,71]. Several full templates per face may be used to account for the recognition from different viewpoints, as Beymer has done in [28]. Another variation is to use multiple templates to cover different illumination variations, even for a single viewpoint.

Iso-Density Maps.   Iso-density lines are the boundaries of constant gray level areas after quantifying an image. To understand the concept of iso-density lines better, one can consider the following analog from geology: If the brightness of a picture is viewed as the height of a mountain, then the equal altitude contour lines correspond to iso-density lines [4].

To extract isodensity lines, the gray level histogram is utilized. In [4], the histogram is divided into eight areas. Contour line tracing on iso-density levels is performed, and outlines based on 4-connectivity pixels are extracted as the iso-density lines, to represent the 3D structure of the face.

Statistical Principal Components. Eigenface, proposed by Turk and Pentland in 1991 [5], is a well-known model in the face recognition community, which is essentially PCA or KLT in a certain context. The basic idea is to regard face images as points in a high dimensional image space. These points approximately form a subspace, so called "face subspace", in the image space. A group of orthogonal bases of the "face subspace" can be estimated by eigenspace decomposition of the covariance matrix derived from a set of training face images. The bases are called "Eigenfaces" for their visual similarity to true faces. Any face image can then be represented approximately as a linear combination of Eigenfaces. The coefficients of the linear combination, computed by projecting the face image onto the subspace, are conventionally used as the features and can be fed into any classifier for recognition. Eigenfaces have been widely used in a variety of systems [4-5, 19,34,37,39,49,56,62,70,72-73], including some commercial systems.

Singular Values. Singular values of an image intensity array imply algebraic features of the face image, and can be used to represent the face. The Singular Value Decomposition (SVD) decomposes a matrix A into its left singular vectors L, right singular vectors R and the corresponding singular values V. It has been shown that the singular vectors represent "shape" information while the singular values are representative of the "gain" in the image.

In [3], Hong shows that the singular values (SVs) extracted by SVD perform well as shape descriptors. He also proves their stability and invariance to proportional variation of image intensity in the optimal discriminating vector space, and to transposition, rotation, translation and reflection. When an image is represented as an n-dimensional SV feature vector, the recognition problem can be solved in an n-dimensional feature space.

2D Shape Model. It is believed that the contours of the whole face and its salient features (eye, nose and mouth) are important for recognition in the biological vision system. This is why many choose to represent a face by its shape.

One model for shape is the Point Distribution Model (PDM) [22]. In PDM, shape is generally represented by a vector of length *2n*, consisting of the concatenation of the *x* and *y* coordinate values of *n* predefined landmarks in the object image. The PDM models assume the existence of a set of *M* annotated examples from which to derive a statistical description of shape variation. As a powerful shape description, a PDM can subsequently be used to locate new instances of such shapes in other images. It is most useful for describing shapes that have a well understood "general" configuration, but which cannot be easily described by a rigid model [22,53,55,65,77]. Obviously, a PDM sets up a sparse correspondence among shapes, while optical flow derives a pixel-wise, dense correspondence between shapes. However, both descriptions can be vectorized as a shape variable, denoted as *x*. It can be represented compactly by performing a Principal Component Analysis (PCA) as $b_s = P_s^T (x - \bar{x})$ *and* $x = x + P_s b_s$, where P_s is the principal component matrix. The linear combination coefficients, b_s, are named statistical shape parameters [22,53,55,65,77].

Another available model to represent face shape utilizes correspondence field, e.g. *optical flow*, which describes the relative shape of an image measured with respect to an image with a standard reference shape. Optical flow is a pixel-wise representation for shape, defining a feature point at each pixel in a sub-image containing a face. The shape vector can be visualized as a vector field of correspondences between a face of standard shape and the given image being represented [28,29,45].

Statistical Texture Parameters. Texture is the geometrically normalized version of the facial image, or shape-free gray-level face patch. That is, geometrical differences among face images, i.e. spurious texture variation due to shape differences, are factored out by warping images to a predefined standard reference shape. This can be done by warping an example image so that its control points match the mean shape [22,53,55,65,77]. Figure 13.2 shows results from our experiments, where shape is modelled by a PDM.

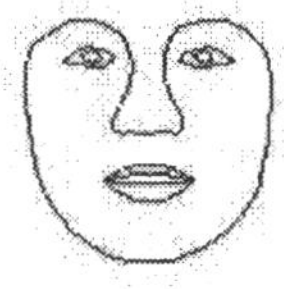 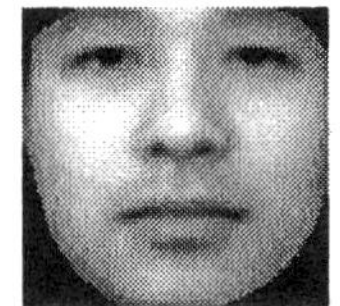 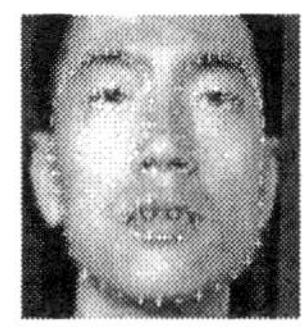 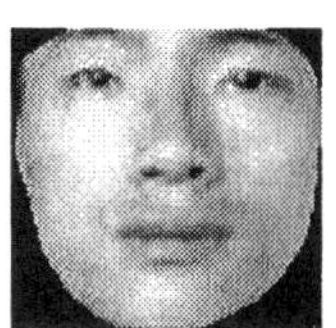

(a) Reference shape   (b) Reference texture   (c) Annotated face   (d) Getting texture

Figure 13.2. Image warping and texture.

Generally, texture is statistically modelled by PCA. Any texture can be represented by statistical texture parameters, bg, as follow: $b_g = P_g^T(g - \overline{g})$ and $g = \overline{g} + P_g b_g$, where P_g is the principal component matrix. In this case, the linear combination coefficients, bg, are called statistical texture parameters.

Statistical Appearance Model. Shape and texture are two distinct aspects of facial appearance. They can be combined together appropriately to model a face for representation and/or recognition.

If both shape and texture are modeled with PCA, the shape and texture of any example can be summarized by its shape parameter vector and texture parameter vector. Since there may be correlations between shape and texture variations, a further PCA can be applied to the data. For each example, a vector can be generated by concatenating the shape and texture parameters with weights applied to each shape parameter, allowing for difference in units between shape and texture models. Then PCA can be applied on these vectors to build a combined model [55,65,77].

Formally, for each example, the shape parameter bs and the texture parameter b_g are combined as: $b = \begin{pmatrix} w_s b_s \\ b_g \end{pmatrix} = \begin{pmatrix} w_s p_s^T(x - \overline{x}) \\ p_g^T(g - \overline{g}) \end{pmatrix}$, where w_s is a diagonal matrix of weights for each shape parameter. PCA is further applied to generate $b = Qc$ and $Q = \begin{pmatrix} Q_s \\ Q_g \end{pmatrix}$, where Q is a matrix composed of eigenvectors and c is a vector of appearance parameters combined with the shape and texture information. Then one can express shape and texture as functions of c by: $x = \overline{x} + P_s W_s Q_s c$ and $g = \overline{g} + P_g Q_g c$.

Statistical appearance models can be used for both image analysis and image synthesis. Active appearance models (AAMs) [55,65,77], in which statistical appearance models have been applied to image analysis and synthesis by T.F.Cootes and Taylor, has attracted more and more attention in both the computer graphics and face recognition community in recent years.

Labelled Graph. Faces can be represented as labelled graphs [33,46,49], with nodes positioned at fiducial points and labelled with local texture information, and edges labelled with the 2D distance between fiducial points. Typical local texture features are Gabor wavelet features, in which each node contains a set of complex Gabor wavelet coefficients, known as a *jet*. A jet can be expressed as $J_j = a_j \exp(i\phi_j)$, where magnitudes, $a_j(\vec{x})$, vary slowly with position, and phases, $\phi_j(\vec{x})$, rotate at a rate approximately determined by the frequency of the kernel.

Theoretically, the labelled graph is an attractive model to represent a face, since it not only models geometric (configurable) information derived from the landmarks, but local features corresponding to predefined fiducial points and their neighbours.

Surface Property (Normal & Albedo). Ideally, the face surface can be approximated using Lambertian model. The image brightness of a Lambertian surface element illuminated by a point light source is $e(x) = n(x) \bullet s$, where $n(x) = \rho(x) \cdot \hat{n}(x)$ is the normal vector, $\rho(x)$ is the local surface albedo, and $\hat{n}(x)$ is the local unit surface normal. Similarly, $s = b \cdot \hat{s}$ is the source vector, where b represents the intensity of the source and $\hat{s}$ is a unit vector in the direction of the source. In Lambertian model, the intensity of a pixel in a face image depends on three factors: the surface normal, the albedo and the direction of the light source. Among them, the first two are inherent to the face surface, while the last one has nothing to do with the face property. Therefore, it is acceptable to recover the normal and albedo at each surface point from one or more images of a face viewed from a fixed viewpoint.

By factoring out the useless effect of lighting conditions in the face images, it is a theoretically perfect model to represent the face using illumination-free face properties such as surface normal and albedo, but it is more challenging to recover these surface properties. Nevertheless, the recent developments in shape-from-X (shading, motion, texture, contour etc.), illumination cones [82], and photometric stereo [43] will greatly facilitate the application of the model.

3D Face Model. By providing a prior knowledge, 3D face models can facilitate the face recognition in both facial image analysis and virtual view generation. A technique to derive a specific person's 3D face model from a general 3D face model and two images (frontal and lateral) of the person is described in [80]. The model fitting procedure is illustrated in Figure 13.3 (a,b,c). Once a 3D model is generated, virtual views can be re-rendered for both analysis and synthesis. Figure 13.3 (e, f) shows two synthesized views from the 3D face model generated in Figure 13.3(c) after texture mapping [80].

Summary. This section surveys the representation problems of face images. Eleven distinct face models are introduced, from basic principles to main applications, from geometry to radiometry. A trend that can be seen clearly is that statistical appearance models are emerging as dominant models.

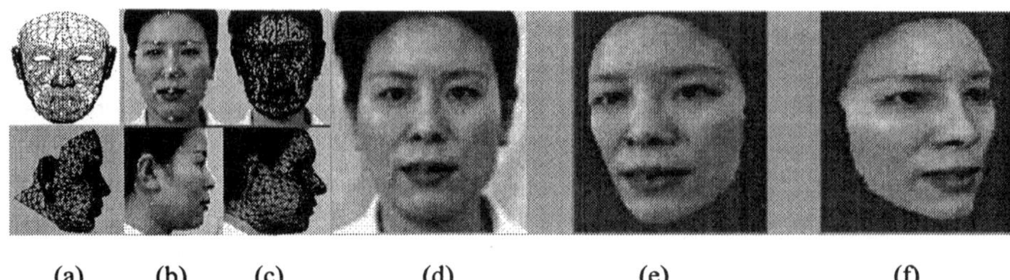

Figure.13.3.   Warping a Generic 3D-Face Model to an Individual One (a) Generic 3D-Face Model. (b) Extracted Feature Points in Frontal and Lateral Images. (c) Fitted Individual 3D-face model. (d) Input Given Person's Frontal Image. (e, f) Synthetic Face Rotated 20 Degree to the left and right respectively.

13.3.2   Feature Extraction

Models of identity deal with the problem of how to model a face. In this section, we concentrate on how to build and apply the models mentioned in above. Obviously, one-to-one correspondence between models of identity and model-building algorithms is difficult to setup. Specific models of identity may be built by using several different feature extraction algorithms, while one algorithms for feature extraction may provides results that can be used to build several different models of identity.

Template Matching.   Template matching is one of the most typical techniques for feature extraction. Correlation is commonly exploited to measure the similarity between a stored template and the window image under consideration. Templates should be deliberately designed to cover variety of possible image variations. During the search in the whole image, scale and rotation should also be considered carefully to speed up the process [14].

Beymer [28] exploited template matching to locate salient features (eyes, nose and mouth) in a face image. Affine transforms are introduced to process matching with pose variations.

Hough Transform.   The Hough Transform (HT) is a well-accepted feature detection method. It requires an explicitly chosen class of objects for detection (e.g., lines, circles, or ellipses) and the parameterization of this class that describes all possible "ideal" instances of the object. Since in the contour of a face, few "ideal" mathematical curves exist, its application in face recognition is limited. However, it can be used to detect the irises of the eyes in the detected face region.

Deformable Template. Deformable template (DT), proposed by Yuille [6,11], is a feature extraction algorithm that extracts geometric features from an image. As an algorithm that makes use of the global information, DT is effective in accurately and robustly extracting the locations and the shapes of salient facial organs such as eyes, mouth and chin against noises. In DT, templates are specified by a set of parameters that enables the priori knowledge about the expected shape of the features to guide the detection process. The templates are flexible enough to change their sizes and other parameters to match themselves to the data. The final values of the parameters are used to describe the features. This method works despite of the variations in scale, tilt, rotation and lighting conditions. Variations of the parameters allow the template to fit any normal instance of the feature.

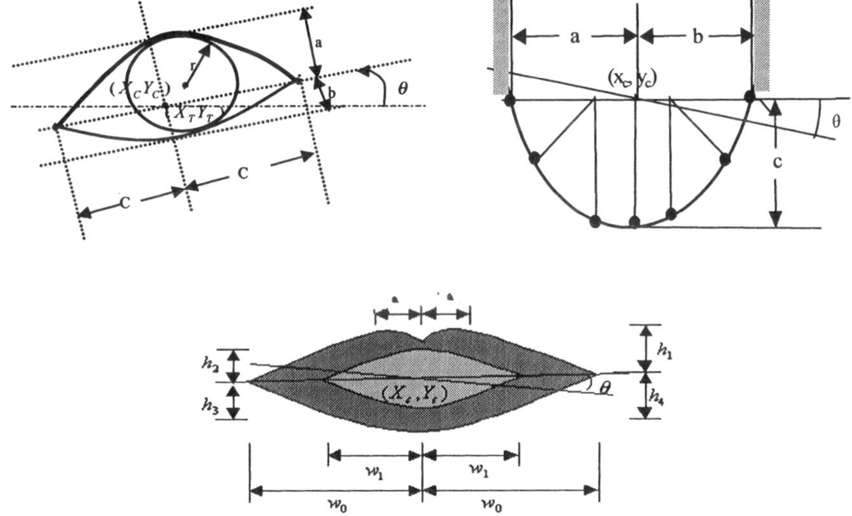

Figure 13.4. Template for the eyes, chin and mouth.

The deformable templates interact with the image in a dynamic manner. An energy function is defined, which contains terms attracting the template to salient features, such as edges, peaks, valleys and the intensity itself. The minimum of the energy function corresponds to the best fit of the image. The parameters of the template are then updated using steepest descent or other optimal algorithms. This corresponds to following a path in parameter space, and contrasts with traditional methods of template matching, which would involve sampling the parameter space to find the best match. Changing these parameters corresponds to altering the position, orientation, size and other properties of the template. The initial values of the template are determined by a preprocessing [6,11]. Typical templates for the eyes, mouth and chin are illustrated in Figure 13.4.

Active Contour.   Active Contour Model proposed by Kass et al. [1] is a sophisticated approach to contour extraction in image understanding. It is defined as an energy minimizing process of a contour. If the contour is described parametrically by $v(s) = [x(s), y(s)]$, where $x(s), y(s)$ are x, y coordinates along the contour and $s \in [0,1]$, the energy function is defined as follows:

$$E_{snake} = \int_0^1 E_{snake}(v(s))ds = \int_0^1 [E_{int}(v(s)) + E_{image}(v(s)) + E_{con}(v(s))]ds$$

where E_{con} represents external constraint forces and E_{int} represents the internal energy of the contour. Generally, E_{int} is defined as $E_{int} = \alpha(s)|\frac{dv}{ds}|^2 + \beta(s)|\frac{d^2v}{ds^2}|^2$, where $\alpha(s)$, $\beta(s)$ specify the elasticity and stiffness of the active contour. The second term E_{image} is the image energy that attracts the contour to the desired feature in the image. As an example, the following definition of E_{image} will attract the active contour to lines, edges, and terminations: $E_{image} = \omega_{line}E_{line} + \omega_{edge}E_{edge} + \omega_{term}E_{term}$.

In face recognition, it is important to extract the whole face from the image so that the changing background will not influence the recognition results. While the contour of a face is usually difficult to be parameterized, the active contour model is suitable to extract the contour of a face.

Principal Component Analysis (PCA).   PCA estimates a group of orthogonal and linearly independent bases of the "face subspace" using eigenspace decomposition of the covariance matrix derived from a set of training face images. Formally, let $\mu_1, \mu_2, \cdots, \mu_m$ be the leading eigenvectors corresponding to the first m maximum eigenvalues $\lambda_1 > \lambda_2 > \cdots > \lambda_m$ of the covariance matrix, thus $U_f = [\mu_1 \mu_2 \cdots \mu_d]$ expands the "face subspace". Then any face image Φ can be approximately represented as a linear combination of the Eigenfaces. The coefficients of the linear combination can be computed by projecting the face image to the subspace through $W = U_f^T \Phi$.

Conventionally, $W = [\omega_1 \omega_2 \cdots \omega_d]$ is used as the features extracted from the input face image Φ and can be fed into any classifier (Nearest Neighbours, Linear Discriminant Analysis (LDA) [39, 62, 70], Support

Vector Machine (SVM) [75] and Artificial Neural Network (ANN) etc.) for recognition.

It is well known that Eigenface transform is the optimal transform in the sense of Minimum Square Error (MSE), but not Most Discriminating Features (MDF). Many efforts have been done to seek MDF from the grey-level information or the Eigenface transforms [51,62,70]. LDA is the most popular one.

In practice, face images should be processed carefully to align all the training examples as well as the new given images under recognition. To alleviate the influence of background, translation, rotation, lighting, scale variance, geometric and intensity normalization should be carefully adopted.

Active Shape Model. Active shape model [22,53] is an optimal procedure to extract 2D shape representation from an input facial image based on the statistical shape model trained by PCA from a set of annotated facial images.

Given a rough starting approximation, an instance of a shape model can be fitted to a new given image by searching in the space of shape parameters. An iterative approach is employed to improve the fitting of the instance to an image. In practice, one can look along profiles normal to the model boundary at each model point. If we expect the model boundary to correspond to an edge, we can simply locate the strongest edge (including the orientation if known) along the profile. This position indicates a new location for the model point. PCA is then conducted to revise the new shape according to the statistical prior. To speed up the searching procedure, multi-resolution strategy should be adopted as in [22,53]. An example of ASM is illustrated in Figure 13.5, where 55 landmarks are used.

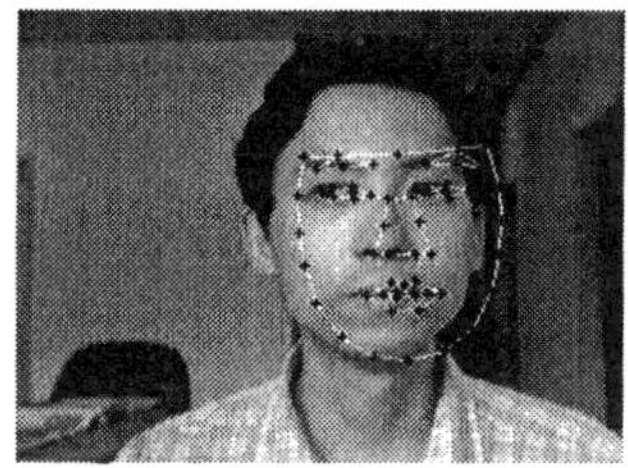 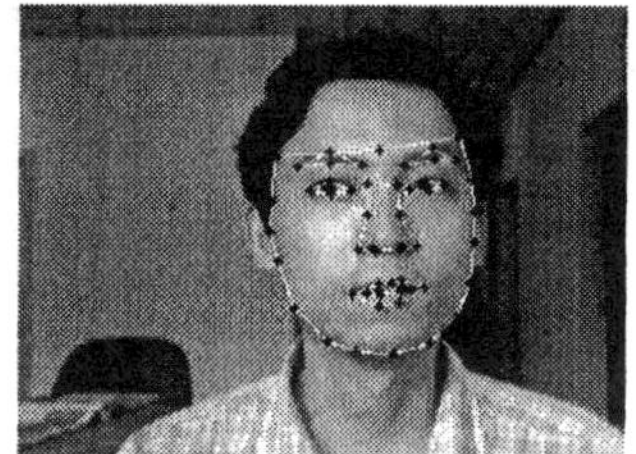

(a) Initial shape   (b) Result of ASM search

Figure.13.5. Active Shape Model.

Active Appearance Model. By training on a set of facial image annotated by predefined landmarks, statistical appearance model is finally modeled as:

$$x = \bar{x} + P_s W_s Q_s c, \quad g = \bar{g} + P_g Q_g c, \quad Q = \begin{pmatrix} Q_s \\ Q_g \end{pmatrix},$$

where c is the final appearance model.

Active Appearance Model (AAM) [55,65] then deals with the kernel problem: given an image to be interpreted, an appearance model described above and a reasonable starting approximation, AAM adjusts the model parameters to generate a synthetic example that matches the new image as much as possible. Basically, AAM is an optimization algorithm that searches in both the parameter space of the appearance model and the global transformation parameter space. The interpretation procedure can be considered as an optimization, where the difference between the new given image and the model image synthesized by the appearance model is minimized. A difference vector δI can be defined as $\delta I = I_n - I_m$, where I_n is the vector of grey-level values in the new given image, and I_m is the vector of grey-level values for the current model parameters. Then, searching the best match between the model and the given image is equivalent to minimizing the magnitude of the difference vector, $\Delta = \|\delta I\|^2$, by varying c, the model parameters. Cootes etc. [55,65,77] further proposed to learn some priori knowledge about how to adjust the model parameters during an image search to speed up the search procedure. Their method is to model the relationship between δI and δc by using a linear regression model: $\delta c = \Phi \delta I$. Then δc is used in the iterative algorithm for minimizing Δ. Figure 13.6 illustrates the procedure of AAM and the final experimental results.

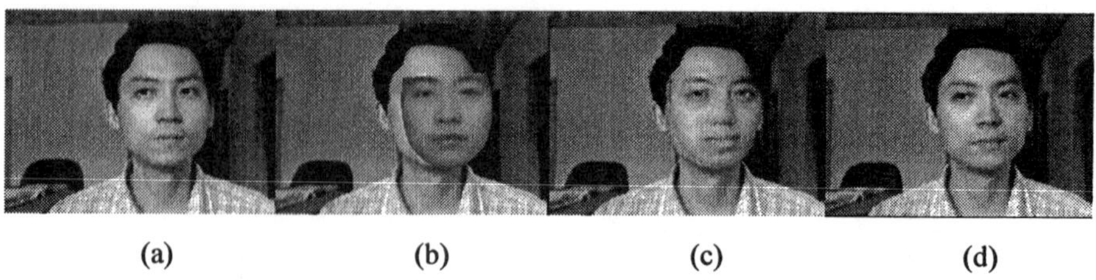

(a)   (b)   (c)   (d)

Figure 13.6. AAM procedure and results (a) Input new given image. (b) Initial model image overlapped. (c) Intermediate model image overlapped. (d) Final model image overlapped.

Optical Flow-Based Shape and Texture Extraction. Beymer [29] proposed an algorithm, named *Vectorizer*, to build the correspondence field between a new given image and a pre-defined reference image with standard shape. In other words, it tries to extract the relative shape representation of the face and its shape-free grey-level intensity.

The algorithm is first initialized by optical flow to build the pixel-wise correspondence between the new given image and the reference image. Then an iterative process of interleaving shape and texture computation is carried out to tune the correspondence. The face *Vectorizer* alternates back and forth between the shape computation and texture computation. The key idea here is to couple the two computations so that each of them uses the other's output, that is, the texture computation uses shape for geometrical normalization, and the shape computation uses the texture analysis to synthesize a "reference" image for finding correspondence.

Since the *Vectorizer* finally builds a pixel-wise dense correspondence between the two images, it can be applied to the problems of facial feature detection and registration of two arbitrary faces.

Elastic Bunch Graph Matching. To extract a graph model from a face, a data structure named Face Bunch Graph (FBG) is developed to represent the faces in general [46]. FBG is constituted by multiple face graphs. Each graph has the same topologic structure, with the nodes referring to the identical fiducial points from different faces. A set of *jets*, referring to the same fiducial points from different faces, is called a bunch. To represent wide ranges of local features, different jets should be stored at each node. The graph edges are labelled with the averages of the distance between the fiducial points. Generally, FBG is constructed manually or self-automatically by deliberately designing a bootstrapping algorithm.

So far, a face is modelled as a labeled graph, and faces in general are represented by FBG as mentioned above. Then, given a new image, the goal of Elastic Bunch Graph Matching (EBGM) is to build its labeled graph by finding the fiducial points, and thus to extract a graph from the image which maximizes its similarity with the Face Bunch Graph based on certain similarity function.

In practice, a heuristic algorithm is generally needed to approach the optimum within a reasonable time. A coarse to fine approach can be adopted by introducing the degrees of freedom of the FBG progressively: translation, scale, aspect ratio, and local distortion.

Photometric Stereo. Assuming a known reflectance function, photometric stereo recovers surface orientation unambiguously. Take a particular Lambertian surface with varying albedo $\rho(x,y)$ as an example. The key idea of photometric stereo is to look at the surface from one fixed viewing direction while changing the direction of incident illumination. Suppose we have three or more such Lambertian surface images, the surface normal can be uniquely determined based on the shading variations of the observed image.

In traditional photometric stereo, to recover shape and albedo under Lambertian surface assumption, we need at least three images illuminated by three different point light sources with known intensities and incident directions. Quite recently, Georghiades, Belhumeur and Kriegman [52,54,57, 82] proposed the illumination cone technology to relax these constraints. Their method is to reconstruct the shape and albedo for each face by using seven face images taken in a fixed pose but illuminated by point light sources at varying, unknown positions. The surface geometry and albedo map is estimated up to a generalized bas-relief (GBR) transformation. The symmetries and similarities in faces can be utilized to solve the three parameters specifying the GBR transformation.

Summary.   In this section, techniques for building the face models described in Section 13.3.1 are further discussed. Typical features extraction algorithms include template matching, Hough transform, deformable template, active contour, active shape model and EGBM. They all can be used to extract geometric features and/or 2D shape models. Both AAM and *Vetorizer* can provide the information needed to build the statistical appearance model. SFS and Photometric aim at the recovery of surface properties.

13.3.3 Classification

In Section 13.3.1 and 13.3.2, we discussed the problem of modeling a face. So far, we are able to model both training images and testing images. In this section, we will concentrate on how to classify a testing image by comparing it with the stored models.

Nearest Neighbour (NN).   The simplest classification scheme is the nearest neighbor classifier in the model space. Under this scheme, an image in the test set is recognized by assigning it the label of the closest point in the learning set. Here, distances are measured in the model space.

This procedure, which is also referred as correlation, has several well-known disadvantages. First, if the images in the learning set and test set are collected under varying lighting conditions, then the corresponding points in the image space will not be tightly clustered. Second, correlation is computationally expensive. Third, it requires large amount of storage since the learning set must contain numerous images for each person who registered.

Bayesian Inference. Moghaddam et al. [34,37,56,73] formulate a probabilistic similarity measure based on the probability of the image intensity differences, denoted by $\Delta = I_1 - I_2$, that is, the characteristic of typical variations in appearance of the same object. Two mutually exclusive classes are defined: within-class differences Ω_I and between-class differences Ω_E.

In terms of the within-class differences, given a posterior probability determined by Bayesian rules, the similarity measure between two facial images can be directly defined as $S(I_1, I_2) = P(\Delta \in \Omega_I) = P(\Omega_I | \Delta) = \dfrac{P(\Delta|\Omega_I)P(\Omega_I)}{P(\Delta|\Omega_I)P(\Omega_I) + P(\Delta|\Omega_E)P(\Omega_E)}$, where the priors $P(\Omega_I)$ and $P(\Omega_E)$ can be set as default setting of equal priors. Moghaddam et al. model each of the classes as Gaussian density [73], and the class-conditional densities are defined as:

$$P(\Delta | \Omega_I) = \frac{1}{(2\pi)^{d/2}|\Sigma_I|^{1/2}} \exp\left(-\frac{1}{2}\Delta^T \Sigma_I^{-1} \Delta\right), \quad P(\Delta | \Omega_E) = \frac{1}{(2\pi)^{d/2}|\Sigma_E|^{1/2}} \exp\left(-\frac{1}{2}\Delta^T \Sigma_E^{-1} \Delta\right).$$

An alternative probabilistic similarity measure can be defined in a simpler form by only exploiting the within-class likelihood using the ML rule instead of the MAP rule. It is represented as $S(I_1, I_2) = P(\Delta|\Omega_I)$.

For identification problem, there is a gallery $\{g_j\}$ of K known individuals and a to-be-identified probe p. The similarity score between p and each g_j is $S(p, g_j)$. The probe is identified as person k who has the maximum similarity score, that is, $k = \arg\max_j S(p, g_j)$.

The performance advantage of the probabilistic matching technique has been demonstrated in an independent double-blind test on a large (800+) database as part of ARPA's September 1996 "FERET" competition, where Bayesian similarity outperformed competing algorithms [71-72].

Artificial Neural Network (ANN). The application of Artificial Neural Networks (ANN) in face recognition has addressed several problems: gender classification, face recognition and classification of facial expressions [9,23, 48-49,59,69]. In [48], Lawrence applies a Convolutional Neural-Network approach to face recognition.

Theoretically, any models of identity can be fed into a Neural Network for classification. Geometric features, templates, statistical shape/texture/ appearance models and singular values etc. can all be trained by NN for face verification.

Nearest Feature Line Method.   The basic assumption of the nearest feature line (NFL) method is that at least two distinct prototype feature points are available for each class. This is usually satisfied in most cases. Working in a feature space, NFL method uses a linear model to interpolate and extrapolate each pair of prototype feature points that belong to the same class. More specifically, two prototype feature points are generalized by a feature line (FL) that passes through the two feature points. The FL approximates variants of the two prototypes under variations in poses, illuminations and expressions, i.e. all face images that could possibly derived from the prototypes. It virtually provides an infinite number of prototype feature points of the class. The capacity of the prototype set is thus expanded. The classification is done using the minimum distance between the feature points of the query and the FLs. The classification result also provides a quantitative position number as a by-product, which can be used to indicate the relative changes (in terms of poses, illuminations and expressions) between the query face and the two associated faces [85].

Linear Subspace Method.   In [51], a linear subspace method is proposed based on the observation that for a Lambertian surface without self-shadowing, the images of a particular face lie in a 3-D linear subspace. For each face, three or more images are taken under different lighting directions to construct a 3-D basis for the linear subspace. To perform recognition, simply compute the distances between the new image and each linear subspace and choose the face with the shortest distance. This method is actually a variant of the photometric alignment method in [43].

In [86-87], a variant of the linear subspace method is proposed. It estimates the class conditional probability of each class based on the computations of linear subspace for each face. A face-unlock screen saver is developed in the spirit of this method. In [88-89], by deriving multiple virtual images from one face image, the subspace method is further extended to accommodate the case when only one sample image is available for each face.

Linear Discriminant Analysis (LDA).   To use the class membership information and find eigenfeatures that emphasize the variations of different faces images while de-emphasize the variations of the same face due to different illuminations and facial expression etc., Linear Discriminant Analysis (LDA) was proposed in [51]. This method is class specific. It chooses an optimal projection W_{opt} as follows:

$$W_{opt} = \arg \max_{W} \frac{\left| W^T S_B W \right|}{\left| W^T S_W W \right|}$$

where S_B is the between-class scatter matrix and assumed to be non-singular, S_W is the within-class scatter matrix. In the projected space, the points corresponding to the images of the same face are clustered while those corresponding to the images of different faces are separated.

When LDA is applied to the face recognition, one difficulty arises: the within-class scatter matrix S_W is always singular. More specifically, the rank of S_W is at most $N - c$ with N being the total number of learning images and c being the number of different faces, but in general, N is much smaller than the pixels number n in each image. To overcome this difficulty, PCA is first used to reduce the dimension of the feature space from n to $N - c$ or less before the standard LDA method is used. This combined method is known as Fisherfaces. It partly solves the generalization problem and has demonstrated excellent performance [39,62,70].

Support Vector Machines (SVMs). Support Vector Machines (SVMs) have been recently proposed by Vapnik and his co-workers as a very effective method for general-purpose pattern recognition. Intuitively, given a set of points belonging to two classes, a SVM finds the hyper-plane that separates the largest possible fraction of points of the same class to the same side while maximizing the distances from either class to the hyper-plane. This hyper-plane is called Optimal Separating Hyper-plane (OSH). It minimizes the risk of misclassifying not only the samples in the training set but also the unseen samples in the test set [75].

The application of SVMs to computer vision area has emerged recently. Osuna et al. [41] train a SVM for face detection, where the discrimination is between two classes: face and non-face, each with thousands of samples. Guo and Stan [75] show that the SVMs can be effectively trained for face recognition and is a better learning algorithm than the nearest center approach.

Graph Matching. After all images, including the gallery images and the probe images, are extracted using EBGM procedure, the faces are represented as labelled face graphs. The matching procedure then involves the distance computation of the jets between different graphs, which is represented as:

$$S_a(J, J') = \frac{\sum_j a_j a_j'}{\sqrt{\sum_j a_j^2 \sum_j a_j'^2}}$$

On the FERET dataset, the algorithm performs impressively well for the frontal images with recognition accuracy of 98%. For half rotated and profile images, the performance degrades to 57% and 84%, respectively; however, since these are difficult cases in face detection and recognition systems, the results are still comparatively good [71].

Hidden Markov Models (HMMs).   HMMs are generally used for the statistical modelling of non-stationary vector time series. By considering the facial configurable information as a time varying sequence, HMMs can be applied to face recognition [25].

The most significant facial features of a frontal face image, including the hair, forehead, eyes, nose and mouth, occur in a natural order from top to bottom, even if the image has small rotations in the image plane, and/or rotations in the plane perpendicular to the image plane. Based on this observation, the image of a face may be modelled using a one-dimensional HMM by assigning each of these regions a state as illustrated in Figure 13.7 [25].

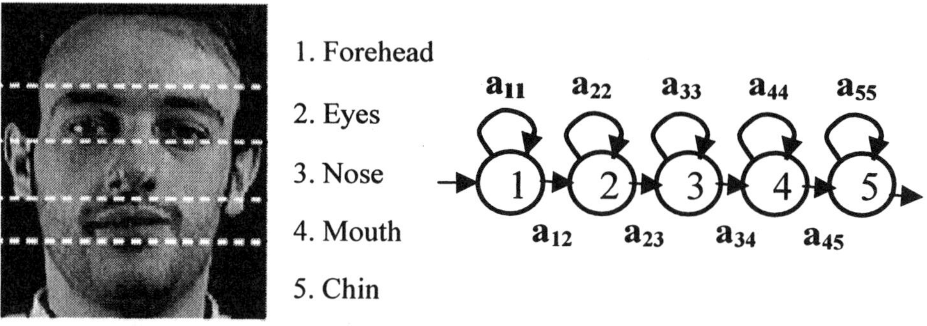

Figure 13.7.   A Top-to-Bottom 5 states HMM in [25].

Given a face image for one subject in the training set, the goal of the training stage is to optimise the parameters to best describe the observation. Recognition is carried out by matching the test image against each of the trained models. To complete this procedure, the image is converted to an observation sequence and the likelihood is computed for each stored model. The model with the highest likelihood reveals the identity of the unknown face.

The HMM approach has shown the ability to yield satisfactory recognition rates. However, HMMs are processor intensive models, which implies that the algorithm may run slowly.

Summary.   We have discussed several classifiers in this section. It should be noted that, except the graph matching and HMMs-based approaches, the input to other classifiers generally could be any of the models of identity discussed in Section 13.3.1. Therefore, many face recognition systems can be easily setup by combining different models with various classifiers. Such examples include PCA+NN, PCA+LDA, PCA+SVM, PCA+ANN, PCA+Bayesian, AAM+LDA, AAM+SVM, AAM+ANN etc. Among these algorithms, PCA-based Bayesian inference [73], PCA-based LDA [70] and PCA-based SVM [75] have demonstrated impressive performance in the experiments.

13.4. Major Challenges

Robust face recognition is still a challenging problem, even many techniques have been proposed, and some significant progress has been made. Up to now, at least two major challenges need to be emphasized [71], that is, **Illumination Variation Problem** and **Pose Variation Problem**. Either one of the problems can cause serious performance degradation in most of the existing systems. An even more difficult situation would be from the combined problem of pose and illumination variations. Unfortunately, this often happens when face images are acquired in an uncontrolled practical environment such as in the case of surveillance [70].

In addition, occlusion and make-up are other sources of appearance variation. Glasses, especially black-frame glasses or sunglasses, will greatly change the appearance of a face image, not to say the modern make-up techniques such as pasting black beards or other accessories. Since quite little work has been done in this area, this section will mainly concentrate on the solutions to these problems.

13.4.1 Illumination Problem

Solutions to illumination problem include invariant features-based methods, parameterized illumination manifold, photometric alignment, linear illumination subspace, quotient images and illumination cones etc.

Invariant Features-Based Methods. Some image representations are considered to be illumination invariant to some extent. These include edge maps, derivatives of the grey level, images filtered with 2D Gabor-like functions, and a representation that combines a log function of the intensity with these representations [47]. But none of these representations is sufficient to overcome the image variations.

Illumination and Pose Manifolds. Murase and Nayar [17] proposed a continuous and compact representation of object appearance, the ***parametric***

eigenspace, which is parameterized by the variables, namely, object pose and illumination.

In this method, an image set of the object is first obtained by varying pose and illumination in small increments. The image set is then normalized in brightness and scaled to achieve invariance to sensor magnification and illumination intensity. The eigenspace for the image set is constructed and all object images (learning samples) are projected onto this space to obtain a set of points. These points lie on a *manifold* that is parameterized by pose and illumination and can be constructed from the discrete points using spline interpolation [27].

Recognition, pose and illumination direction estimation can then be achieved as follows: given an image consisting of an interested object, the segmented object region is normalized in scale and brightness such that it has the same size and brightness range as the images used in the learning stage. This normalized image is projected onto the eigenspace. The closest manifold reveals the identity of the object, and exact position of the closest point on the manifold determines pose and illumination direction.

Photometric Alignment.   Proposed by Shashua et al. in [43], the basic idea of photometric alignment is to find an algebraic connection between all images of an object taken under varying illumination conditions. In [43], they prove that "an image of an object with an order k linear reflection model, $I(p) = x(p) \cdot \alpha$, can be represented as a linear combination of a fixed set of k images of the object". The Lambertian model of reflection is a typical case of order *3* linear reflectance models, and face surface can be approximated as a Lambertian model. Therefore, assume we take three pictures of a face I_1, I_2, I_3 from light source directions s_1, s_2, and s_3, respectively, then, any new given image I of the face, taken from a new given setting of lighting sources, can be simply represented as a linear combination of the three pictures, that is, $I(p) = \alpha_1 I_1(p) + \alpha_2 I_2(p) + \alpha_3 I_3(p)$, for some coefficients $\alpha_1, \alpha_3, \alpha_3$. The coefficients can be solved by observing the grey-values of three points. Using more than three points will provide a least squares solution. The solution is unique, offering that $s1$, $s2$, and $s3$ are linearly independent, and the normal directions of the three sampled points span all other surface normalization.

Alignment-based recognition under changing illuminations can then proceed in the following way. Let the images I_1, I_2, I_3 be the model images of the face. For any new given image I, rather than matching it directly to previously seen images (the model images), a number of points (at least 3) is first selected to solve the coefficients $\alpha_1, \alpha_3, \alpha_3$, and then synthesize an image by $I' = \alpha_1 I_1(p) + \alpha_2 I_2 + \alpha_3 I_3$. If the image I is of the same face, and the only change is in illumination, then I and I' should perfectly match (the matching is not necessarily done at the image intensity level, one can match the edges of I against the edges of I', for example). This procedure has factored out the effects of changing illuminations from the recognition process without recovering scene information, i.e. surface albedo or surface normal, and without assuming knowledge of directions of light sources. Another property of this method is that one can easily find a least squares solution for the reconstruction of the synthesized image, thereby being less sensitive to errors in the model or noise in the input.

Shashua et al. [43] further address the problems that arise when some of the objects points are occluded from some of the light sources, when the surface reflects light specularly, and when spectral composition of light sources is changing.

3D Linear Illumination Subspaces. This method, as a variant of photometric alignment methods, also exploits the observation that, for a Lambertian surface without self-shadowing, the images of a particular face lie in a 3-D linear subspace [51]. For classification, this observation suggests a simple classification algorithm to recognize Lambertian surfaces invariant to different lighting conditions. For each face, use three or more images taken under different lighting directions to construct a 3-D basis for the linear subspace. To perform recognition, we can simply compute the distances between the new image and each linear subspace and choose the face corresponding to the shortest distance. This recognition scheme is called Linear Subspace method.

If there were no noise or self-shadowing, Linear Subspace algorithm would achieve error-free classification under any lighting conditions, provided that the surfaces obey the Lambertian reflectance model. Nevertheless, there are several compelling reasons to look elsewhere. First, due to self-shadowing, specularities and facial expressions, some regions of the face may have variability that does not satisfy the linear subspace model. Second, to recognize a test image, we must measure the distance in the linear subspace for each person's data. While this is an improvement over a correlation scheme that needs a large number of images for each class, it is still computationally expensive. Finally, from the storage point of view, the linear subspace algorithm must keep three images in memory for every person, which is space intensive.

Quotient Images Based Method. More recently, Shashua et al. [81] propose a Quotient images based method to address the problem of "class-based" image-based recognition and rendering with varying illumination. Their key result is based on the definition of an illumination invariant signature image, which enables an analytic generation of the image space with varying illuminations.

They show that the set of all images, generated by varying lighting conditions on a collection of Lambertian objects that have the same shape but different surface albedoes, can be characterized analytically using images of a prototype object and an illumination invariant "signature" image per object of the class. The Cartesian product between the signature image of an object y and the linear subspace determined by the images of the prototype object generates the image space of y. They also show how to obtain the signature image from a database of example images of several objects, and prove that the signature image obtained is invariant to illumination conditions.

The method works remarkably well on real face images using a very small set of example objects, as few as two example objects. In many cases, the re-rendering results are indistinguishable from the "real" objects, and the recognition results outperform conventional methods by far.

Illumination Cones.   In the last few years, Belhumeur and Kriegman et al. [52,54,57,82] have proposed a generative appearance-based method, named illumination cones, for recognizing human faces under variations of lighting and viewpoint. Their work is well summarized in [82].

Belhumeur et al. [52] first prove that the set of images of an object in a fixed pose, seen under all possible illumination conditions, is a convex cone in the space of images. Particularly, the illumination cone of a convex object with Lambertian reflectance can be completely determined by several properly chosen images. Although faces are neither Lambertian surfaces nor convex, experimental results show that the illumination cone of a face can be also established from a few images acquired under different lighting conditions. To construct the illumination cone of a face, its shape and albedo should be recovered first. Georghiades et al. [47] use seven images of a face in a fixed pose, but under different and unknown lighting conditions, to reconstruct its surface geometry and albedo map. In turn, this reconstruction serves as a generative model to render or synthesize images of the face under new given poses and illumination conditions. The pose space is then sampled and, for each pose, the corresponding illumination cone is approximated by a low-dimensional linear subspace whose basis vectors are estimated using the generative model.

Once the illumination cone of a specific face is constructed, recognition can be achieved by assigning to a test image the identity of the closest approximated illumination cone, based on Euclidean distance within the image space. Because illumination cones represent the whole image set of an object under all possible configurations of point light sources at infinity, nearly perfect recognition rates can be still achieved even under extreme illumination conditions.

13.4.2   Pose Problem

Various methods have been proposed to handle the pose problem. Basically, these methods can be divided into three categories: 1) multi-view based methods when multiple images per person are available, 2) hybrid methods when multiple training images are available for training but only one test image per person is available for recognition, and 3) single image based methods when no training is carried out. Up to now, the second type of approach is most popular [70].

Multi-View Based Methods. One of the earliest efforts in multi-view based methods was from Beymer in [28], where a multi-view component template-based correlation-matching scheme was proposed. In his work, pose estimation and face recognition are coupled in an iterative loop. For each hypothesized pose, the input image is aligned to the database images with a selected pose. The alignment is first carried out through 2D affine transformation based on three key feature points (eyes and nose), and then optical flow is used to refine the alignment of each template. The correlation scores of all pairs of matching templates are used to perform recognition.

View-based Eigenface [19] is another approach of the multi-view strategy. It explicitly encodes the pose information by constructing an individual eigenspace for each pose, and uses these pose eigenspaces for a given image to estimate the pose of the face and thus recognizes in a subspace specific to the estimated pose.

Linear Object Classes. The work described in [44-45] by Vetter and Poggio is based on the idea of linear object classes. Linear object classes are 3D objects whose 3D shape can be represented as a linear combination of a sufficiently small number of prototypical objects. They have the property that new orthographic views of any object of the class under uniform affine 3D transformations, and in particular rigid transformations in 3D, can be generated exactly if the corresponding transformed views are known for the set of prototypes. Based on this property, it is possible to "learn" a direct mapping from standard pose to a particular virtual pose as follows. Using multiple prototype objects, first de-compose the new given face as a linear combination of prototypes at the standard pose, yielding a set of linear prototype coefficients. Then, by taking the linear combination of prototype objects at the virtual pose using the same set of coefficients, the new given face at the virtual pose can be synthesized.

This approach accomplishes more than just object recognition tasks. It can provide additional artificial example images of an object when only a single image is given. On the other hand, the coefficients, which result from a decomposition of shape and texture into example shapes and textures, provide a representation of the object that is invariant to any affine transformations.

In [58], Vetter et al. further extend the Linear Object Class to combine the prior knowledge of 3D shape by introducing a generic 3D model of human head. Example images are used to "learn" a pose-invariant shape and texture description of a new face. And 3D model is used to solve the correspondence problem between images with faces in different poses.

Parallel Deformation. Parallel deformation is another example-based technique to represent prior knowledge by using 2D example views of prototype faces under different poses and apply the rotation seen in the prototypes to "rotate" the given single real view [29-30].

It works as follows: using only one prototype object, measure the 2D deformation of object features from the standard to virtual view. Then map this 2D deformation onto the new given object and use the deformation to distort, or warp the new given image from the standard pose to the virtual one.

3D Model. Generic 3D models of the human face can be used to predict the appearance of a face under different poses, expressions and lighting conditions. 3D face shape is represented either by a polygonal model or by a more complicated multi-layer mesh that simulates tissue. Once a 2D face image is texture mapped onto the 3D model, the face can be considered as a traditional 3D object in computer graphics subjecting 3D rotations or changes in light source positions. Faces are texture mapped onto 3D model either by specifying corresponding facial features in both the image and 3D model or by recording both 3D depth and color image data simultaneously by using specialized equipment like the Cyberware scanner.

A generic 3D model could then be applied to the scenario of pose-invariant face recognition from one example view. The single view of each person could be texture mapped onto a 3D model, and then the 3D model could be rotated to novel poses to generate multiple virtual views for recognition purpose.

13.5. An Example Access Control System Based on Eigenface

This section will describe an example access control system based on Eigenface method, which, as mentioned above, is one of the most popular face recognition methods. In Eigenface method, a training set containing enough number of face examples are needed. The training set is also expected to cover all kinds of variations due to different lighting conditions, slight facial expressions and head poses.

In addition, to alleviate the influence of translation, ration, lighting and scale variance, geometric and grey normalization should be adopted. As to geometric normalization, generally, the two irises are fixed at specific locations using affine transformation. And a mask, as shown in Figure 13.8 (b), is covered over the face region to eliminate the alterable background and hairstyle. Finally, all faces are warped to a fixed size as shown in Figure 13.8 (c). Histogram equalization is also conducted to normalize illuminations, and all face data are vectorized to the unit length before they are fed into training or testing procedure.

(a) A face image

(b) Face mask

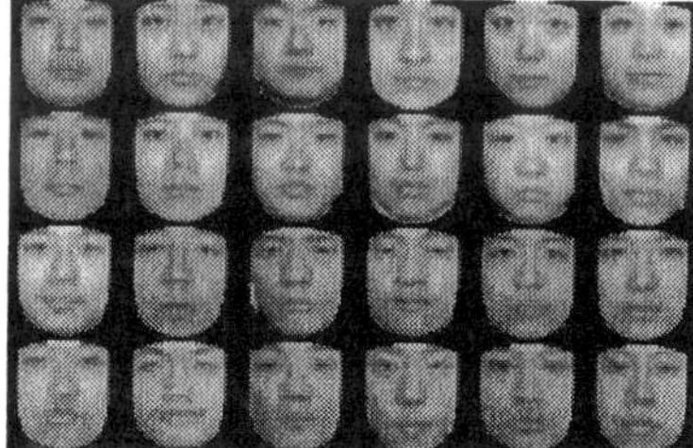
(c) Faces in the training set

Figure 13.8. Normalization and training set.

Given such a training set containing m training samples denoted as $\{f_1, f_2, \cdots, f_m\}$, Eigenfaces are learned as follows:

First, compute the covariance matrix of the training set as:

$$C = \sum_i (f_i - \bar{f})(f_i - \bar{f})^T .$$

C is then decomposed by SVD as:

$$C = UDU^T , \text{ or } C\mu_i = \lambda_i\mu_i \text{ for } i=1,2\ldots, m \text{ and } \lambda_1 < \lambda_2 < \cdots < \lambda_m,$$

where $U = [\mu_1, \mu_2, \cdots, \mu_m]$ and $D = \begin{pmatrix} \lambda_1 & 0 & 0 \\ 0 & \lambda_i & 0 \\ 0 & 0 & \lambda_m \end{pmatrix}$.

In Eigenface method, $\mu_1, \mu_2, \cdots, \mu_m$ are called "Eigenfaces" because of their visual similarities to the face pattern. (In fact, it can be shown mathematically that each of them is the linear combination of the training images, which explains the similarity.) Some Eigenfaces learned from a training set are illustrated in Figure 13.9.

Figure 13.9. Leading Eigenfaces learnt from a training set of 350 faces.

Then, any input face f can be represented as the linear combination of these Eigenfacesby:

$$W = U^T (f - \bar{f}).$$

In turn, f can be reconstructed by the inverse procedure as:

$$f' = \bar{f} + UW.$$

This procedure is visually illustrated in Figure 13.10.

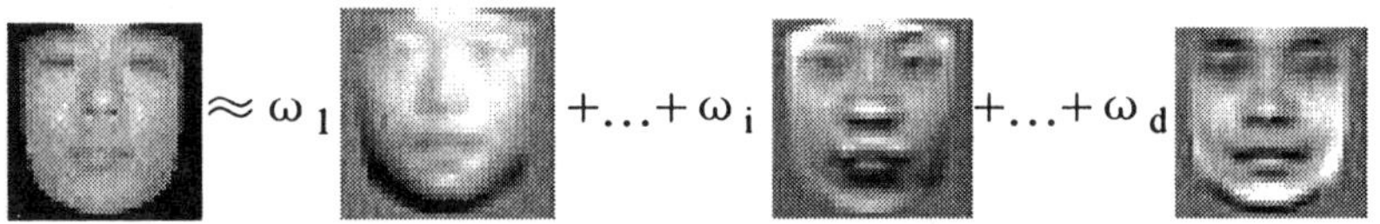

Figure.13.10.   *One face image is represented as the linear combination of m leading Eigenfaces.*

The vector W computed in the equation described above is generally used as the feature of the input face f. Any classifier can be conducted on these features to achieve face recognition. Commonly, the similarity between two Eigenface features W_1 and W_2 can be defined as:

$$S(W_1, W_2) = \frac{<W_1, W_2>}{\|W_1\| \cdot \|W_2\|},$$

where "$<W_1, W_2>$" denotes the dot product of the two vectors, and "$\|.\|$" is the L_2 of the vector.

Finally, to determine whether the two Eigen-features W1 and W2 are from the same face or not, a threshold T_k for each face should be learnt. This can be done by a simple Bayesian minimum probability of error rule, as illustrated in Figure 13.11.

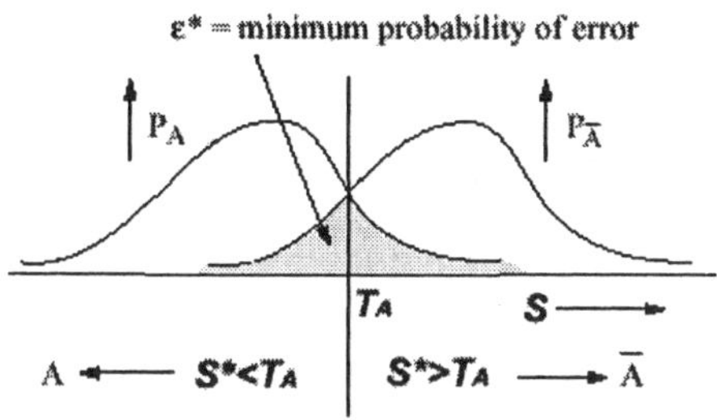

Figure 13.11.   Determining threshold to Bayesian minimum probability of error rule.

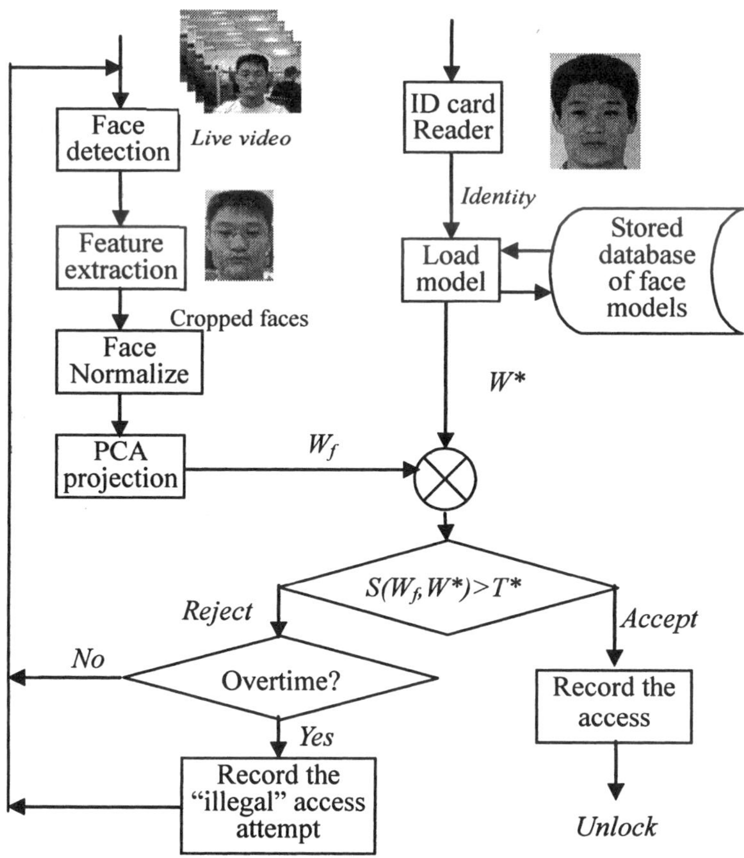

Figure. 13.12.   Face verification for access control based on Eigenface method.

The architecture of the face verification system for access control based on Eigenface method is shown in Figure 13.12.

Note that, in the figure, the stored database of known face models is commonly trained offline. In addition, the records should be saved in the case that someone has passed the verification or cannot be verified in the given time. This would be quite useful for the later reference.

13.6.   Commercial Systems and Performance Evaluation

Since the middle of the 1990s, some commercial face recognition products have emerged based on the techniques mentioned above. Along with the emergence of these commercial systems, how to evaluate these systems is attracting more and more attentions from researchers. In this section, we will present several commercial face recognition systems and a few performance evaluation benchmarks.

13.6.1   Existing Commercial Systems

FaceIt® is developed by Visionics Corporation. It is based on the Local Feature Analysis (LFA) method proposed by Atick [35] in Rockfeller University. It achieves excellent performance in the first FERET testing and is also highly ranked in the recent FRVT2000 testing.

FaceFINDER™ is from Viisage Technology Inc. Viisage developed a series of face recognition systems including FaceFINDER, FaceEXPLORER, FacePIN, FacePASS, FaceTOOLS etc. These systems are based on the well-known Eigenface method. *FaceFINDER™* has recently been selected to deploy the first face-recognition technology system for security in a U.S. airport after the US 9.11 terrorism attacks.

Hunter™ is a facial recognition surveillance system from LAU Technologies. It is also based on the MIT Eigenface techniques. It participated the FRVT2000 evaluation.

FaceSnap® RECORDER is a turnkey solution for video surveillance, monitoring and law enforcement developed by C-VIS Computer Vision and Automation Gmbh. The kernel techniques are Elastic Graph Matching [46], which has been recognized as one of the most promising technologies in FERET testing [71].

TrueFace is developed by the eTrue Inc. and uses neural network technology. It has found several partners in *e*-commerce industry including Microsoft. The eTrue service has been chosen as the first biometric authentication service in Microsoft .NET enterprise servers.

In addition to the systems mentioned above, there are many other face recognition commercial systems available in the Biometrics market, including **SpotIt!** from ITC-irst (initialized by Roberto Brunelli), **Banque-Tec International, FaceVACS** from Cognitec AG, **BioID** (a system adopting sensor-fusion approach using face, speech and lip movement analysis by DCS AG, Germany) and ZN-Face etc.

13.6.2 Performance Evaluation

Given the numerous theories and techniques, as well as commercial systems that are applicable to face recognition, it is clear that evaluation of these algorithms is crucial. Obviously, large sets of test images are essential for adequate evaluation, while it is also extremely important that the sample be statistically as similar as possible to the images that arise in the application being considered. Scoring should be done in a way that reflects the costs or other system requirements.

During the past decade, some publicly available large face databases have been collected and corresponding evaluation protocols have been designed. Among them, in US, the series of FERET evaluations [71] have attracted many institutions and companies to participate. However, in Europe, (X)M2VTS evaluation is more attractive.

FERET.   To facilitate the evaluation of various algorithms in a set-up very close to a real-world setting, and to identify potential problems that have not revealed in the researchers' small-scale tests, the FERET program was initiated, emphasizing the evaluation of FRT algorithms. Under the FERET program, a large number of face images were collected, and testing procedures were established. Up to date, 14,126 images from 1199 individuals are included in the FERET database [71].

Overall, three algorithms perform very well: Elastic Graph Matching from USC [46], Probabilistic Eigenface from MIT [56] and Subspace LDA from UMD [62]. On frontal images taken the same day, typical first-choice recognition accuracy is over 95%. For images taken with a different camera under various lighting conditions, typical accuracy drops to 80%~90%. For images taken one year later, the typical accuracy is approximately 50% [71, 72].

(X)M2VTS.   The M2VTS project (Multi Modal Verification for Televices and Security Applications) deals with access control using multi-modal identification of human faces among different European ACTS (Advanced Communications Technologies & Services) projects. The M2VTS database contains 37 subjects and 5 shots for each person. The XM2VTS [69] multi-modal database is an expansion of the original M2VTS multi-modal database.

The XM2VTS database contains four recordings of 295 subjects taken over a period of four months. Each recording contains a speaking headshot and a rotating headshot. Sets of data taken from this database are available, including high-quality color images, 32 KHz 16-bit sound files, video sequences and a 3D model at production cost.

FRVT2000.   The DoD Counter-drug Technology Development Program Office initialized the FRVT2000 in May and June 2000 to evaluate the performance of the commercial systems available in U.S. biometrics market. Besides the testing inherited from the FERET, FRVT2000 has further tested the performance of different system on the eight variations: compression, distance, expression, illumination, media, pose, resolution and temporal. Furthermore, FRVT2000 conducts a product usability test: access control with live subjects.

The results of the FRVT 2000 show that progress has been made in temporal changes, but developing algorithms that can handle temporal variations is still a necessary research area. In addition, developing algorithms that can compensate for pose variations, illuminations and distance changes are noted as other areas for future researches.

13.7.   Summary and Conclusions

In this chapter, we survey the up-to-date technologies of automatic face verification for access control. We have focused on models of identify, features extraction and classification of the face verification problem. Major challenges and their corresponding solutions are discussed. An example access control system based on Eigenface is presented. Some commercial systems available in the industry market are introduced briefly along with the introductions of several famous evaluation projects on face recognition. As a summary based on the previous discussion, we've come to the following conclusions:

- Geometric feature based methods and template matching methods used to be popular technologies, in 1990s, *appearance* based technologies have become the dominant methods. While much recently, *photometry* based approaches have attracted much attention for their ability to deal with illumination and pose problems;

- Among these diverse techniques, those based on *Eigenface* have been recognized as the most popular and successful techniques. Eigenface based LDA, SVM and Bayesian inference are all among the techniques being and to be further studied. Recently, SVM has again provided a good development opportunity for Eigenface;

- The most promising techniques should perfectly combine the 2D shape, local features and holistic appearance features. Both *Active Appearance Models* and *Elastic Graph Matching* have achieved great success and attracted more and more attention.
- The state-of-the-art of Face Recognition Technology is still far from the public expectations, mainly due to the *pose and illumination varying problems*. The most possible solutions to those open issues include illumination cone, linear subspace, illumination/pose manifolds, linear object class, photometric stereo, shape-from-shading, 3D models and Quotient image based methods.
- Industry calls for the face verification systems. Several face recognition *commercial systems* have been available in the Biometrics industry. Latest improvement in face recognition is expected to provide the industry more robust and reliable commercial systems.

Acknowledgment

This work is supported by National Science Foundation of China, National Hi-Tech Development Programm of China, 100 Outstanding Scientists foundation of Chinese Academy of Sciences, and YCNC Co. Ltd. The authors want to express thanks to these organizations.

Also, the authors would like to express their gratitude to Dr. Xilin Chen, Dr. Debin Zhao, Mr. Yan Liu, Ms. Hongxun Yao, Mr. Jun Miao, Ms. Ying Liu, Ms. Wenjie Sun, Dr. Jie Yan, Mr. Bo Cao, Mr. Pin Liao, Ms. Xiujuan Chai, Mr. Wei Wang, Mr. Guoqin Cui, Mr. Gang Deng, Mr. Feng Jiao, Ms. Wenjuan Lian and Mr. Hongming Zhang for their contributions on technical discussions, system implementation, materials preparation and revision for this chapter. Authors also would like to thank Sonya Allin for proofreading the manuscript.

References

[1]   M. Kass, A. Witkin and D. Terzopoulos. Snakes: Active Contour Models. Int. Journal of Computer Vision, pages 321-331, 1988.

[2]   M. Kirby and L. Sirovich. Application of the Karhunen-Loeve Procedure for the Characterization of Human Faces, IEEE Trans. on PAMI, 12(1), 103-108, 1990.

[3]   Zi-Quan Hong. Algebraic Feature Extraction of Image for Recognition. Pattern Recognition, 24(3), pages 211-219, 1991.

[4]   Osamu Nakamura, Shailendra Mathur, and Toshi Minami. Identification of Human Faces Based on Isodensity Maps. Pattern Recognition, 24(3), pages 263-272, 1991.

[5]   M. Turk and A. Pentland. Eigen-faces for Recognition Journal of Cognitive

Neuroscience, 3(1), pages 71-86, 1991.

[6]   A.L. Yuille. Deformable Templates for Face Detection, J. Cog. Neu. 3, 59-70, 1991.

[7]   A. Shashua. Geometry and Photometry in 3D Visual Recognition, PhD thesis, Massachusetts Inst. of Technology, Cambridge, 1992.

[8]   R. Brunelli and T. Poggio, Face Recognition Through Geometrical Features. In Proc. of ECCV '92, pages 792-800, 1992.

[9]   R.Brunelli and T. Poggio. HyperBF Networks for Gender Classification. In Proc. of DARPA Image Understanding Workshop, pages 311-314, 1992.

[10]   B.S. Manjunath, R. Chellappa and C.V.D. Malsburg. A Feature Based Approach to Face Recognition. In Proc. of IEEE Computer Soc. Con. On Computer Vision and Pattern Recognition, pages 373-378, 1992.

[11]   A.L. Yuille, P.W. Hallinan and D.S. Cohen. Feature Extraction from Faces Using Deformable Templates. International Journal of Computer Vision, 8, 99-111. 1992.

[12]   Ashok Samal and A. Prasana. IyenGar Automatic Recognition & Analysis of Human Faces & Facial Expressions: A Survey, Pattern Recognition, 25(1), pages 65-77, 1992.

[13]   Martin Lades, Jan C. Vorbruggen, J. Buhmann, J. Lange, C.V.D. Malsburg, R.P. Wurtz and W. Konen. Distortion Invariant Object Recognition in the Dynamic Link Architecture, IEEE Trans. On Computers, 42(3), pages 300-311, 1993.

[14]   R. Brunelli and T. Poggio. Face Recognition: Features vs. Templates. IEEE Trans. on PAMI, 15(10): 1042-1052, 1993.

[15]   G. Chow and X.B Li. Towards a System for Automatic Facial Feature Detection. Pattern Recognition, 26(12), pages 1739-1755. 1993.

[16]   Ke Liu, Yongqing Cheng and Jingyu Yang. Algebraic Feature Extraction for Image Recognition Based on an Optimal Discriminant Criterion. Pattern Recognition, 26(6): 903~911, 1993.

[17]   S.K. Nayar and H. Murase. Dimensionality Of Illumination Manifold In Eigenspace, TR-CUCS-021-94, Columbia University, 1994.

[18]   Peter W. Hallinan. A Low-dimensional Representation of Human Faces for Arbitrary Lighting Conditions. In Proc. of IEEE Computer Society Conf. Computer Vision and Pattern Recognition, Seattle, WA, 995~998, 1994.

[19]   Alex Pentland, Baback Moghaddam and Thad Starner. View-Based and Modular Eigenspaces for Face Recognition, IEEE Conference on Computer Vision & Pattern Recognition, 1994.

[20]   G.Z. Yang and T.S. Huang, Human Face Detection in a Complex Background, Pattern Recognition, 27(1), 43-63, 1994.

[21]   X. Xie, R. Sudhakar and H. Zhuang. Improving Eye Feature-extraction Using Deformable Templates. Pattern Recognition, 27(6), 791-799, 1994.

[22]   A. Lanitis, C.J. Taylor, and T.F. Cootes. An Automatic Face Identification System Using Flexible Appearance Models. In British Machine Vision Conference, BMVA Press, 1: 65~74. 1994.

[23]   D. Valentin, H. Abdi, A.J.O. Toole and Garrison W.Cottrell. Connectionist Models of Face Processing: A Survey, Pattern Recognition. vol.27, pages 1209-1230, 1994.

[24]   S.R. Gunn and M.S. Nixon. A Dual Active Contour. BMVC 94, September, York, U.K. 305-314, 1994.

[25]   F.S. Samaria. Face Recognition Using Hidden Markov Models. PhD Thesis, Trinity College, University of Cambridge, Cambridge, 1994.

[26]   Rama Chellappa, Charles L. Wilson and Saad Sirohey. Human and Machine Recognition of Faces: A Survey. In Proc. of the IEEE, vol.83, no.5, pages 705-740, 1995.5.

[27]   H. Murase and S. Nayar. Visual Learning and Recognition of 3D Object from Appearance, Int. J. Computer Vision, 14:5-24, 1995.

[28]   D. Beymer and T. Poggio. Face Recognition from One Example View. In Proc. of Int'l Conf. Computer Vision, pages 500-507, 1995.

[29]   David Beymer. Vectorizing Face Images by Interleaving Shape and Texture Computation, A.I. Memo, no. 1537, 1995.9.

[30]   David Beymer and Tomaso Poggio. Image Representations for Visual Learning, Science, vol.272, pages 1905-1909, 1995.

[31]   R. Epstein, P. Hallinan, and A. Yuille. 5+/-2 Eigenimages Suffice: An Empirical Investigation of Low-Dimensional Lighting Models, Proc. Physics-Based Modeling Workshop in Computer Vision, session 4, 1995.

[32]   P. Hallinan, A Deformable Model for Face Recognition under Arbitrary Lighting Conditions, PhD Thesis, Harvard Univ., 1995.

[33]   T. Leung, M. Burl and P. Perona. Finding Faces in Cluttered Scenes Using Labeled Random Graph Matching. In Proc. of Int'l Conf.Computer Vision, pages 637-644, 1995.

[34]   B. Moghaddam and A. Pentland. Probabilistic Visual Learning for Object Detection, In Proc. of Int'l Conf. Computer Vision, pages 786-793, 1995.

[35]   P.Penev and J.Atick. Local Feature Analysis: A General Statistical Theory for Object Representation, Network: Computation in Neural Systems, vol.7, pages 477-500, 1996.

[36]   Liu Mingbao and Gao Wen. A Hierarchical Approach To Human Face Detection In a Complex Background. the First International Conference on Multimodal Interface, Beijing, 1996.

[37]   Babak Moghaddam, Chahab Nastar and Alex Pentland. A Bayesian Similarity Measure for Direct Image Matching, International Conference on Pattern Recognition, Vienna, Austria, August 1996.

[38]   C.H. Lee, J.S. Kim and K.H. Park. Automatic Human Face Location in Complex Background Using Motion and Color Information, Pattern Recognition, 29(11), 1877-1889, 1996.

[40]   Daniel L. Swets and John Weng. Using Discriminant Eigenfeatures for Image Retrieval. IEEE Trans. on PAMI, 18(8): 831~836, 1996.

[41]   S. Nayar and H. Murase. Dimensionality of Illumination Manifolds in Appearance Matching. In Proc. of Int'l Workshop Object Representations for Computer Vision, pages 165, 1996.

[42]   E. Osuna, R. Freund and F. Girosi. Training Support Vector Machines: An Application to Face Detection. In Proc. of CVPR, 130-136, 1997.

[43]   A. Yuille and D. Snow. Shape & Albedo from Multiple Images Using Integrability, In Proc. of IEEE Conf. Computer Vision and Pattern Recognition, pages 158-164, 1997.

[44]   A.Shashua. On Photometric Issues in 3D Visual Recognition from a Single 2D Image, International Journal of Computer Vision, 21(1/2), 99-122, 1997.

[45]   Thomas Vetter and Tomaso Poggio. Linear Object Classes and Image Synthesis from a Single Example Image, IEEE Trans. On PAMI, vol.19, no. 7, pages 733-742, 1997.

[46]   Thomas Vetter, Michael J. Jones and Tomaso Poggio. A Bootstrapping Algorithm for Learning Linear Models of Object Classes, IEEE CVPR, Puerto Risco, USA, pages 40-46, 1997.

[47]   Laurenz Wiskott, Jean Marc Fellous, Norbert Kruger and Christoph von der Malsburg. Face Recogniton by Elastic Bunch Graph Matching, IEEE Trans. on PAMI, vol.19, no. 7, pages 775-779, 1997.

[48]   Yael Adini, Yael Moses and Shimon Ullman. Face Recognition: The Problem of Compensting for Changes in Illumination Direction, IEEE Trans. on PAMI, vol.19, no.7, pages 721-732, 1997.

[49]   Steve Lawrence, Lee Giles, Ah Chung Tsoi and Andrew D. Back. Face Recognition: A Convolutional Neural-Network Approach, IEEE Trans. on Neural Network, vol.8, no.1, Jun. 1997.

[50]   Jun Zhang, Yong Yan and Martin Lades. Face Recognition: Eigenface, Elastic Matching and Neural Nets. In Proc. of the IEEE, vol.85, no. 9, pages 1422-1435, Sep. 1997.

[51]   K.M.Lam and H.Yan. An Analytic-to-Holistic Approach for Face Recognition Based on a Single Frontal View", IEEE Trans. on PAMI, vol.20, no.7, July, 1997.

[52]   P.N.Belhumeur, J.P.Hespanha and etc. Eigenfaces vs Fisherfaces: Recognition Using Class Specific Linear Projection. IEEE Trans. on PAMI, vol.20, no.7, July, 1997.

[53]   P. Belhumeur, D. Kriegman, and A. Yuille. The Bas-Relief Ambiguity, In Proc. of IEEE Conf. Computer Vision and Pattern Recognition, pages 1040-1046, 1997.

[54]   A. Lanitis, C.J. Taylor and T.F. Cootes. Automatic Interpretation and Coding of Face Images Using Flexible Models. IEEE Transactions on Pattern Analysis & Machine Intelligence, vol.19, no.7, pages 743-56, July 1997.

[55]   P. Belhumeur and D. Kriegman. What Is the Set of Images of an Object Under All Possible Illumination Conditions, Int'l J. Computer Vision, vol. 28, no. 3, pages 245-260, July 1998.

[56]   T.F. Cootes, G.J. Edwards and C.J. Taylor. Active Appearance Models, Proc. European Conf. Computer Vision, vol. 2, pages 484-498, 1998.

[57]   Baback Moghaddam, Wasiuddin Wahid and Alex Pentland. Beyond Eigenfaces: Probabilistic Matching for Face Recognition, the 3rd IEE Int. Con. On Auto. Face- and Gesture- Recognition, Nara, Japan, 1998.4.

[58]   A.S. Georghiades, D.J. Kriegman and P.N. Belhumeur. Illumination Cones For Recognition Under Variable Lighting: Faces. Proc. of IEEE CVPR, pages 52-58, 1998.

[59] Thomas Vetter, Synthesis of Novel Views from a Single Face Image, IJCV, 28(2), pages 103-116, 1998.

[60] H.A. Rowley, S. Baluja, and T. Kanade. Neural Network-based Face Detection, IEEE Trans. on PAMI, 20(1), 23-38, 1998.

[61] K.K. Sung and T. Poggio. Example-based Learning for View-based Human Face Detection, IEEE Trans. on PAMI, 20(1), 39-50, 1998.

[62] M. Pontil and A. Verri. Support Vector Machines for 3D Object Recognition, IEEE Trans. On PAMI, 20: 637-646, 1998.

[63] W. Zhao, R. Chellappa and A.Krishnaswamy. Discriminant Analysis of Principal Components for Face Recognition. In Proc. of Inter. Conf. On Auto. Face and Gesture Recognition, pages 336-341, 1998..

[64] D.W.Jacobs, P.N. Belhumeur and R. Basri. Comparing Images under Variable Illumination. In Proceedings of IEEE Conference on Computer Vision and Pattern Recognition, pages 610-617, 1998.

[65] Ruo Zhang, Ping-Sing Tai, James Edwin Cryer and Mubarak Sha. Shape from Shading: A Survey, IEEE Trans. On PAMI, 21(8), pages 690-706, 1999.

[66] G. Edwards, T. Cootes, and C. Taylor. Advances in Active Appearance Models. In Proc. of Int'l Conf. Computer Vision, pages 137-142, 1999.

[67] Volker Blanz and Thomas, Vetter. A Morphable Model For the Synthesis of 3D Faces, SIG'GRAPH'99, 1999.

[68] J. Miao, B.C. Yin and K.Q. Wang, et al. A Hierarchical Multiscale and Multiangle System for Human Face Detection in a Complex Background Using Gravity-center Template, Pattern Recognition, 32(7), 1999.

[69] K. Jonsson, J. Matas, and J. Kittler. Learning Salient Features for Real-time Face Verification. In S. Akunuri and C. Kull-man,editors, AVBPA'99, pages 60–65, 1999.

[70] K. Messer, J. Matas, J. Kittler, J. Luettin, and G. Maitre. XM2VTSDB: The Extended M2VTS Database. In Proc. of International Conference on Audio- and Video-Based Person Authentication, pages 72-77, 1999.

[71] W. Zhao and R. Chellappa. Robust Image-Based 3D Face Recognition, CAR-TR-932, N00014-95-1-0521, CS-TR-4091, Center for Auto Research, UMD, 2000.1.

[72] P.J. Phillips, H. Moon and etc. The FERET Evaluation Methodology for Face-Recognition Algorithms, IEEE Trans. on PAMI, vol.22, no.10, pages 1090-1104, 2000.

[73] Alex Pentland. Looking at People: Sensing for Ubiquitous and Wearable Computing, IEEE Trans. On PAMI, vol.22, no.1, pages 107-119, Jan. 2000.

[74] Baback Moghaddam, Tony Jebara and Alex Pentland. Bayesian Face Recognition, Pattern Recognition vol.33, pages 1771-1782, 2000.

[75] Constantine L. Kotropoulos and Anastasios Tefas. Ioannis Pitas Frontal Face Authentication Using Discriminating Grids with Morphological Feature Vectors, IEEE trans. On Multimedia, vol.2, no.1, pages 14-26 March, 2000.

[76] G. Guo, S.Z. Li and K. Chan. Face Recognition by Support Vector Machines. In Proc. of 4th Int. Conf. on Auto. Face and Gesture Recognition, Grenoble, pages 196-201, 2000.3.

[77]   K. Jonsson, J. Matas, J. Kittler and Y.P. Li. Learning Support Vectors for Face Verification and Recognition. In Proc. of the 4th International Conference on Face and Gesture Recognition, Grenoble, France, pages 208-213, 2000.3.

[78]   T.F. Cootes, K. Walker and C.J. Taylor. View-based Active Appearance Models. In Proc. of the 4th International Conference on Face and Gesture Recognition, Grenoble, France, pages 227-232, 2000.3.

[79]   Wenyi Zhao and Rama Chellappa. SFS Based View Synthesis for Robust Face Recognition. In Proc. of the 4th International Conference on Face and Gesture Recognition, Grenoble, France, pages 285-292, 2000.3.

[80]   Baback Moghaddam and Ming-Hsuan Yang. Gender Classification with Support Vector Machine. In Proc. of the 4th International Conference on Face and Gesture Recognition, Grenoble, France, pages 306-311, 2000.3.

[81]   Shiguang Shan, Wen Gao, Jie Yan and etc. Individual 3D Face Synthesis Based on Orthogonal Photos and Speech-driven Facial Animation. In Proc. of the International Conference on Image Processing (ICIP'2000), Vancouver, BC, Canada, pages 238-242, vol. 3, 2000.9.

[81]   A. Shashua and T. Riklin-Raviv. The Quotient Image: Class-Based Re-Rendering and Recognition with Varying Illuminations, IEEE Trans. on PAMI, 23(2): pages 129-139, 2001.2.

[82]   Athinodoros S. Georghiades, Peter N. Belhumeur and David J. Kriegman, From Few to Many: Illumination Cone Models for Face Recognition Under Variable Lighting and Pose, IEEE Trans. on PAMI, 23(6) pages 643660-139, 2001.6.

[83]   M.H. Yang, N. Ahuja, D. Kriegman. Detecting Faces in Images: A Survey, IEEE Trans. on PAMI, vol.24, no.1, 2002.1

[84]   Hongxun Yao, Wen Gao and etc. Face Detection and Location Based on Skin Chrominance and Lop Chrominance Transformation from Color Images Pattern Recognition, 2000.10.

[85]   Stan Z. Li and Juwei Lu. Face Recognition Using the Nearest Feature Line Method, IEEE Transactions On Neural Networks, 10(2), pages 439-443, MARCH, 1999.

[86]   Shiguang Shan, Wen Gao, Xilin Chen and Jiyong Ma. Novel Face Recognition Based on Individual Eigen-subspaces. In Proc. of International Conference on Signal Processing, ICSP2000, Beijing, China, vol. 3, pages 1522-1525, 2000.

[87]   Shiguang Shan, Wen Gao and etc. A Face-Unlock Screen Saver by Using Face Verification Based on Identity-Specific Subspaces. In Proc. of the Pacific-rim Conference on Multimedia (PCM'01), Beijing, China, pages 1096-1101, 2001.

[88]   Shiguang Shan and Wen Gao. Unified Framework For Classifying Facial Images Based On Facial Attribute-Specific Subspaces And Minimum Reconstruction Error, Proc. of ACCV'2002, Melbourne, Australia, vol. 2, pages 858-863, Jan. 2002.

[89]   Shiguang Shan, Wen Gao and Debin Zhao. Face Identification From A Single Example Image Based On Face-Specific Subspace (FSS), to appear in proc. of ICASSP2002, Orlando, Florida, USA, May 2002.

Chapter 14

VOICE BIOMETRICS FOR SECURING YOUR WEB-BASED BUSINESS

Kevin Farrell, Scott Sharp and Ron Beyner
SpeakEZ Incorporated
Greenwood Village, Colorado, USA
{Kevin.Farrell, Scott.Sharp, Ron.Beyner}@speakezinc.com

Abstract   As the explosive growth of *e*-business applications over the Internet continues, so does the need to integrate a higher level of security than traditionally obtained through a text password or personal identification number. Speaker verification is the most practical biometric technology available to accomplish this extra layer of security. Not only is the human voice non-obtrusive to the end user, but the required voice collection hardware is readily available on most personal computers being distributed today. However, integrating biometric technology into a web application is no easy task. User management issues, security, and technology integration are just a few of the pieces that must be designed and built into an *e*-business solution involving voice biometrics.

The SpeakEZ Web Authentication Service provides a service-oriented solution for integrating speaker verification into an *e*-business application. Rather than forcing businesses to build monolithic applications to accomplish this added layer of security, business are able to simply utilize the web-service to authenticate users of their *e*-business application. This provides a fast and effective means for incorporating biometric authentication into existing and new web-based applications.

Keywords: Speaker verification, *e*-business, internet security

14.1.   Introduction

It is common knowledge that millions of new individuals populate the Internet each year and that the increases will continue for some time. It is also common knowledge that while millions of people browse the network there are still only a precious few who actually buy products and conduct business on the Internet itself. Why, because as survey after survey tells us, people are still afraid to give personal information and credit card information over the Internet. At the head of every survey is a call for more and better security. We want less intrusive yet more effective security!

It may be that Corporations will lead the way to solving this dilemma. The two primary goals of every corporation will never change. How can we continue to increase profits and continue to decrease costs at the same time? When you couple these two fundamental goals of every corporation with the fact that our society becomes more remote each and every day, it becomes very clear that corporations must learn how to become business partners with the Internet.

Corporate security used to be tied primarily to doors and locks because we conducted business face to face. Today we live in a virtual society where many of the people we deal with we have never seen. We like this because the cost savings of doing business this way is tremendous. It also gives us a chance to reach many more people so the opportunity to increase revenue also presents itself. So who are these people? They are employees working in remote offices, business partners, customers, our suppliers, and yes they are even our competitors. With the possible exception of our competitors, we would like to see the Internet become a larger portion of our content delivery to our employees, partners, customers, and suppliers. In order to do this we must have an effective authentication method to insure we are delivering the correct data content to the correct person.

Speaker Verification is an effective way to provide more effective security in a less intrusive fashion and the technology has proven that it is ready for primetime in recent independent studies. It has always been regarded as the least intrusive and easiest to use of the biometric technologies and recent studies now verify that the performance is as good as or better than other more intrusive biometrics. Speaker Verification is the only Biometric that can cost effectively deliver applications to the entire Enterprise in the three common delivery points; telephony, desktop, and network security. Even within the network and the Internet there are many applications where speaker verification will provide excellent results.

This chapter explores several internet-based business opportunities for speaker verification. We continue this chapter with a general discussion of speaker verification technology along with the details of the SpeakEZ technology that will be referred to through the remainder of this chapter. We then present several business opportunities for speaker verification on the internet and then describe the system architecture that addresses these. Last, we provide results for a technical evaluation that we performed over the internet and then conclude this chapter.

14.2. Speaker Verification

Speaker verification consists of determining whether or not a voice sample provides sufficient match to that of a claimed identity. People's voices are unique primarily due to the physiological differences between people's vocal tracts. Additional differences are also due to speaking mannerisms, such as prosody and accent. Speaker verification by computer is generally accomplished by first analyzing the frequency content of the actual voice data. The differences between lengths and shapes of people's vocal tracts will generally show differences in the frequency spectrum. Representations of this data, known as features, are then used to train pattern classifiers such that a future decision can be made regarding the match of the features extracted from the voice data during enrollment and verification. There are numerous variations of speaker verification that are offered by different technology vendors. These will be discussed in the following subsection.

14.2.1 Speaker Verification Technology Differentiators

One differentiator of speaker verification technologies is whether the technology is text-independent or text-dependent. Text-independent speaker verification systems do not place any constraints on the phrase used for enrollment or verification and are intended to authenticate the individual regardless of the spoken phrase. Text-dependent speaker verification requires that the same password be used for both enrollment and verification.

Text-independent speaker verification systems are more flexible with respect to the phrases used for enrollment and verification, however, there are some tradeoffs. One tradeoff is that more enrollment data is required for text-independent systems than for text-dependent systems. This is necessary to train a pattern recognition system to successfully recognize all of the different sounds that a given person will use when speaking. Another tradeoff is that text-dependent technologies will generally outperform text-independent technologies with respect to accuracy when given the same data as they can take advantage of the temporal aspects of the speech whereas text-independent technologies cannot. Also, when using text-dependent speaker verification technology, an imposter must guess the proper password to even have a remote possibility of impersonating the true user whereas in text-independent speaker verification this is not necessary.

Another differentiator of technologies in the case of text-dependent speaker verification is the constraint on input vocabulary. One scheme is to have users enroll with spoken digits. Here, verification will then consist of the user repeating that set of digits. Another scheme is to have users enroll with spoken digits and then have the verification consist of speaking those digits in a random, prompted order. Other systems require that the user speak a specific phrase, such as "My voice is my password", and then verify with this same phrase. We will refer to these systems as fixed-text systems. Finally, there are systems that use user-selectable passwords where a user can choose his or her password without having any vocabulary or language constraints.

There are certain advantages and disadvantages that come with each of these password selection options. The advantage of using spoken digits is that a speaker verification system can use transcription information to aid in segmentation and classification. This can be achieved by having a speaker-independent digit recognizer preprocess the incoming speech to label the data with respect to the corresponding digits. Normalization techniques, such as "cohort normalization", can then be applied to improve the recognition accuracy. There are several disadvantages to using only digits for text-dependent speaker verification. One disadvantage is that the user will now have to remember this information, similar to memorizing a personal identification number (PIN). If the system tries to overcome this by prompting the user for this digit sequence, then there will be some compromise in the security provided by the speaker verification technology. This is due to the fact that the false accept error will be higher for cases where the correct password is known than it will for cases where the password is unknown. Another disadvantage of using spoken digits is that the system will have to be customized for all supported languages. These advantages and disadvantages are also applicable to fixed-text systems.

The advantage of user-selectable password systems is that a user can choose a password that is easier to remember than a digit string and which also can be more difficult to "guess" by an imposter. Applications also have more flexibility in that they can use passwords based on personal information, such as place of birth, mother's maiden name, etc. Another advantage is that systems with user-selectable passwords do not require custom configurations for different languages. The SpeakEZ speaker verification technology consists of text-dependent technology that allows for user-selectable passwords. The technology is described in more detail in the following subsection.

14.2.2   SpeakEZ Speaker Verification Technology

The overall speaker verification algorithm that is used by the SpeakEZ speaker verification technology is illustrated in Figure 14.1. Most speaker verification systems will be similar to some extent in that they have components for performing feature extraction and classification. The purpose of the feature extraction component is to determine characteristics of the speech signal that are unique for a speaker. The classification component will then take those features and apply them to a pattern recognizer to determine speaker authenticity.

There are several technical innovations that have been integrated into the SpeakEZ speaker verification algorithm. One such innovation that is used is within the feature extraction component. Here, pole-filtered cepstrum are used as the feature for recognition [1]. When computing the pole-filtered cepstrum, an estimate is made of the channel. This estimate is then used to form an inverse filter that removes the channel contribution to the signal. This makes the technology more robust to changes in the recording device, such as different microphones and telephones.

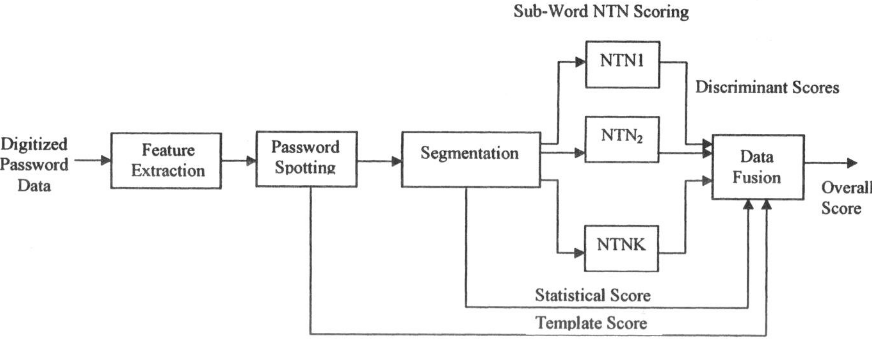

Figure 14.1. SpeakEZ speaker verification process.

After feature extraction, we apply a patent-pending method for locating the password within the recorded speech. This allows for the removal of extraneous sounds from the beginning or ending of the password. Another innovation is in the segmentation component of the SpeakEZ verification algorithm. Here, a "blind segmentation" algorithm is used to decompose the spoken password into different segments where each segment contains data from a different sound within the password [2]. This decomposition makes data modeling simpler when it comes time to train a classifier [3].

Our modeling phase also has several novel aspects. One is the Neural Tree Network (NTN). The NTN is a hierarchical model that uses a tree architecture to implement a sequential linear decision strategy [4]. The NTN learns to contrast the feature data from the enrolling speaker with feature data from other users such that unique portions of a person's password can be identified. Another novel aspect of our modeling phase is that we incorporate scores from several different models. The password-spotting algorithm we use is based on a template matching approach that yields a speaker verification score as a by-product. The blind segmentation algorithm also produces a speaker verification score that is based on a statistical measurement. The NTN provides a discriminative-based speaker score. Since the measurements from these different modeling approaches are all based on different criteria, i.e., template matching, statistical, and discriminant, they tend to make different errors [5]. Hence, a consensus-based decision that combines information from all three of these methods using data fusion can yield error rates far lower than that achieved by any of the modeling approaches used individually. These innovations all attribute to the accuracy of the SpeakEZ speaker verification technology.

14.2.3   Other Biometrics

There are numerous other biometrics that have been used for authentication purposes. These include fingerprint, hand geometry, face, iris, retina, vein, signature and DNA. Biometrics are generally categorized as being either physiological or behavioral. Physiological biometrics are based on characteristics that don't really change from one session to the next, such as fingerprint, hand geometry, face, iris, retina, and DNA. Behavioral biometrics, such as signature and voice, can exhibit differences from one measurement to the next based on mood, stress, and other external influences. Though voice is generally categorized as a behavioral biometric, the main characteristics are still derived from physiological traits, namely the vocal tract.

There are three metrics that are commonly used to compare different biometrics. These are accuracy, cost, and intrusiveness. Accuracy is typically quantified as the equal error rate. Cost refers to the cost of the sensor or device that is required to acquire the biometric data plus the cost of the software. The intrusiveness refers to the level of discomfort people will have when using a particular biometric. With respect to intrusiveness and cost, voice has frequently been cited as being the choice biometric [6]. However, with respect to accuracy voice is typically considered to be less accurate than most of the traditional physiological biometrics such as fingerprint, hand, and face. Most of these claims, including accuracy, have been based on subjective criteria. For example, since voice is categorized as a behavioral biometric, it must therefore be less accurate than physiological biometrics. However, a recent scientific evaluation [7] of different biometrics showed this not to be the case. Numerous biometrics were evaluated including fingerprint, face, iris, hand geometry, and vein, and the results showed voice to be one of the more accurate biometrics. When combined with the obvious benefits of low cost and low intrusiveness, this makes voice a very practical choice of biometric.

14.3. Business Opportunities on the Web using Speaker Verification

The SpeakEZ speaker verification technology has numerous applications in security. Additionally, it is complementary to other forms of security such as smart cards, digital certificates, and passwords. Most other forms of security rely on information of "What you know" as in the case of passwords and "What you have" as in the case of smart cards. Biometrics use information regarding "Who you are" which can be used with other security measures to provide extremely secure systems.

What makes voice especially attractive for business opportunities on the web is the availability of the voice acquisition device, namely the microphone. Virtually all personal computers and laptops that are shipped today contain sound acquisition hardware and a microphone. Other biometric sensors, such as fingerprint readers and video cameras, generally require a separate purchase and are not standard equipment on today's computers.

The advantages of voice from the standpoint of cost, intrusiveness, and accuracy discussed thus far in this chapter make it a very attractive technology for use in internet applications. Two specific business applications will now be discussed. The first is for protecting web content and the second is for eBusiness applications. These are discussed in the following subsections.

14.3.1   Protecting Web Content

All companies look for ways to attract people to their web site but as discussed earlier depending on who that person is we want them to see different things. We would like employees to have access to vital company information so they can be as productive from outside the office as they would be if they are physically there, yet we do not want others to be able to access that data. We want Business Partners to have access to pricing and product information that we do not want in the hands of our competitors. And the list goes on and on. Speaker Verification is a great tool for allowing a person to access web content that is intended for them only. The ROI (Return On Investment) of using Speaker Verification for protecting web content is tremendous. It allows your users easy non intrusive yet more secure entry to your web site which allows you to conduct more and more of your business through the Internet. The more business we do through the Internet the lower our cost of doing business. The more security we have on the Internet the more our Customers and Partners will want to do business with us in this fashion because it is also a great cost saving for them as well as a convenience to do business with us.

14.3.2   *e*Business

The other application that would offer a powerful business case is using speaker verification to authenticate an Internet purchase. As mentioned earlier there are millions of people who window shop on the Internet but a precious few who actually make the purchase on line. The primary reason is their fear of giving credit card and other personal information on line. Credit card information as well as other personal information could easily be stored in data base profiles so that a user could simply authorize the sale with their voice. This would be a great benefit to both parties. For the purchaser, they can complete their purchase in a single session and for the vendor the sale is completed on line requiring no human interaction for the sales process. Speaker Verification will allow customers the ease of use yet secure feeling that will allow more people to finish their purchase while on line. In most organizations, simply gaining an additional 5% of your business to be done in this fashion would result in a ROI that would more than justify the purchase of the system and we believe that 5% would be a very low goal to set.

14.3.3   SpeakEZ Web Authentication Products

SpeakEZ web authentication products are available now and come in two delivery methods in order to meet the demands of everyone. For large Enterprise users the hardware, software, and professional services support can be sold directly to the user and maintained by them directly. The cost of such a system provides great value when you compare it to other types of security available. The software would be licensed to the customer and priced per user based on the number of users in a given application and the number of servers needed. Per user costs could be as low as a few dollars per user based on the volume and can be purchased on a one-time basis or an annual basis depending on the need of the customer.

When you compare the cost of Speaker Verification to tokens, smart cards, and other devices that a person must physically carry the cost is more than impressive and Voiceprints cannot be lost or stolen. When you add the fact that the speaker verification software adds a greater security feature because it directly identifies the user and not just information about the user, the value proposition becomes overwhelming.

When you compare the cost of Speaker Verification to other Biometrics like face, finger printing, and others, the results are similar. Speaker Verification requires no special hardware, is less intrusive, easer to use, and recent studies verify just as accurate. Again the value proposition becomes overwhelming.

For the smaller companies who have the same needs, they can receive the same benefits by enrolling in a hosted service. The pricing for a hosted service would be a monthly fee based on the number of users and the application. An architectural discussion of the SpeakEZ Authentication Web service is provided in the following section.

14.4.   SpeakEZ Web Authentication Service

The SpeakEZ Authentication Web Service provides a service-oriented solution for integrating speaker verification into an *e*-business or web application. Before going into the specific details of the overall system architecture, we need to briefly discuss some of the high-level details of the web service itself.

The key element in the web service architecture is the definition of the actual services that are provided. The Authentication Web Service provides three services to clients of the system: enrollment, verification and user management. Before speaker authentication can be accomplished, users of the system must build a voice print model by enrolling in the system. Enrollment is accomplished by submitting a collection of enrollment voice utterances and associated user information to the enrollment service. Once a voice print model has been created and stored in the system, clients can authenticate users by providing claimed user identification information and associated utterance data to the verification service for validation. The user management service is simply an administrative service for managing users. This includes adding, removing, enabling, and disabling user accounts associated with a given client. Each of these services and their associations with the different components of the Authentication Web Service will be described in greater detail below.

To help ease the integration of the services described above into an *e*-business or web application, a set of ActiveX controls are provided to clients of the system. These controls expose the interfaces to the Authentication Web Service at a high level and encapsulate the operational services, XML-based interface definitions, encryption algorithms and HTTP protocols needed to utilize the authentication service. By providing a high level interface to the Authentication Web Service, businesses are able to easily add speaker verification to *e*-business applications without having to design and implement components for communicating with the Authentication Web Service.

A browser side ActiveX control and a Netscape LiveConnect Plugin are also supplied to clients of the Authentication Web Service. The browser side components encapsulate the full enrollment and verification processes including data collection, speech quality checks, and all end-user interactions necessary for the authentication process. The browser side components also utilize speech pre-processing strategies for reducing the overall size of the speech data necessary for enrollment and verification. Reducing the overall size of data transmitted by pre-processing speech data helps increase the performance of the system in terms of bandwidth and distributed processing.

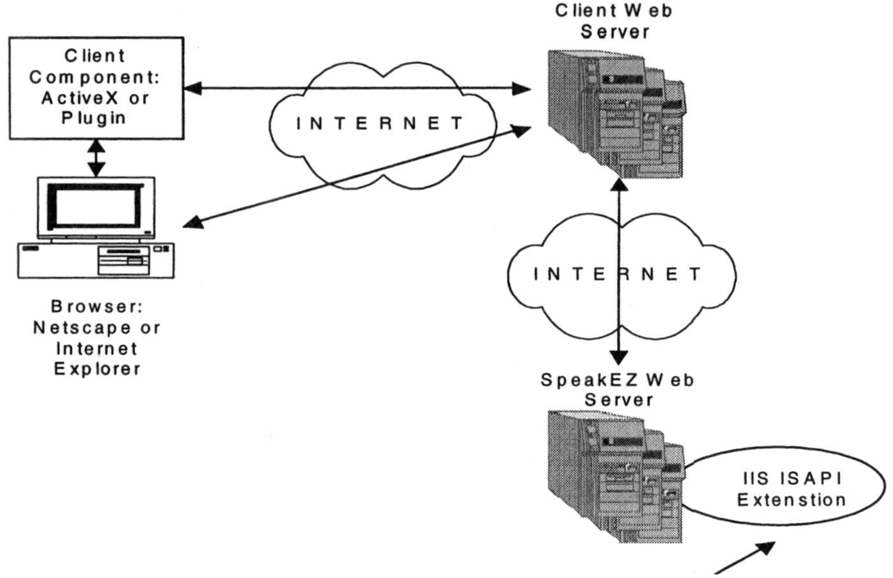

Figure 14.2. Authentication Web Service System Architecture.

Figure 14.2 illustrates the overall system architecture for the Web Authentication Service. Each component of the system is described below.

Client Browser - a standard commercial Web browser. Currently, Internet Explorer and Netscape Navigator are supported. All end-user interactions are performed through this browser including user enrollment and user verification.

Browser Component - a standardized component that allows speaker enrollment and verification to be performed through the client browser. Currently, a single LiveConnect Plugin is used for Netscape Navigator, and the ActiveX control is used for Internet Explorer. These client components encapsulate the full enrollment and verification processes including data collection, speech quality checks, and all user interactions. These interactions are performed through a graphics user interface (GUI) that the components provide. All data collected and pre-processed by these components is encrypted and sent to the Client Web Server Component where they are forwarded to the Authentication Web Server for processing. Figure 14.3 and 14.4 illustrates screens in this interface for collecting speech recordings from the user.

Client Web Server - the web server hosting the client specific *e*-business application. This is where the business-to-business relationship with the Authentication Web Service takes places. Using the supplied server-side ActiveX controls, this server places user enrollment, verification, and management requests to the authentication service and makes appropriate application decisions based on the results of each request.

Authentication Web Server - the Microsoft Internet Information Server (IIS) web server(s) hosting the Authentication Web Service.

Authentication Web Server Extension – a standard IIS ISAPI extension responsible for forwarding authentication service requests to the appropriate Enrollment Verification Server.

Enrollment Verification Server (EVServer) – a server component that provides the actual enrollment, verification and user management processing. Each EVServer can be configured to reside on a separate processing node, allowing the architecture to easily scale as the service requests increase.

EVDB – the database used to store user information and voice print models as well as other information associated with authentication service. Each EVServer interacts with this database to retrieve necessary information to perform enroll, verify, and user management functions.

NOTE: the network traffic between all components of the system is encrypted for added security on a public network. Additionally, the use of aged security tokens is also integrated into all communication requests and responses in the system. This is done to discourage fraudulent attempts to violate the service.

As previously discussed, the Authentication Web Service supports three services: enrollment, verification, and user management. Each of these services is described in detail below.

User Management: The user management service is a mechanism in which clients can administer their respective users. The administrative functions include adding users, removing users, enabling users, and disabling users. All user information and associated client or group information is stored in the EVDB and is used during the enrollment and verification processing. The interfaces for these administrative functions are supplied to the client in the form of an ActiveX control. Internally, the ActiveX control encrypts the information, attaches a unique security token, builds the necessary XML stream, and submits the request to the Authentication Web Service for processing. The actual processing of the request occurs on the EVServer and the EVDB is updated accordingly.

Enrollment: During enrollment, the client collects information necessary to complete a user enrollment. To help with this data collection, the supplied browser-side component interacts with the end-user to obtain a list of repeated password phrases. Figure 14.3 illustrates a screen used to collect enrollment password phrases. As mentioned earlier, the speech data collected from the end-user is pre-processed to reduce the total network traffic. Once speech data is collected from the end-user, the client submits the speech data and associated user information to the Authentication Web Service using the provided server-side ActiveX control. Internally, the ActiveX control encrypts the information, attaches a unique security token, builds the necessary XML stream and submits the enrollment request to the Authentication Web Service for processing. The actual processing of the request occurs on the EVServer. If the user is valid (i.e. the user is enabled and exists in the EVDB), the EVServer uses the supplied speech data to generate a voice print model for the user. This voice print model is then stored in the EVDB for future verification requests.

Verification: During verification, the client collects information necessary to complete verification of a user. To help with this data collection, the supplied browser-side component interacts with the end-user to obtain a password utterance that will be used to verify against an enrolled voice print model. Figure 14.4 illustrates a screen used to collect a verification password phrase. As mentioned earlier, the speech data collected from the end-user is pre-processed to reduce the total network traffic. Once speech data is collected from the end-user, the client submits the speech data and associated user information to the Authentication Web Service using the provided server-side ActiveX control. Internally, the ActiveX control encrypts the information, attaches a unique security token, builds the necessary XML stream and submits the verification request to the Authentication Web Service for processing. The actual processing of the request occurs on the EVServer. The EVServer retrieves the voice print model associated with the given user and attempts to verify the user using the supplied speech data. The results of the verification are then returned to the client.

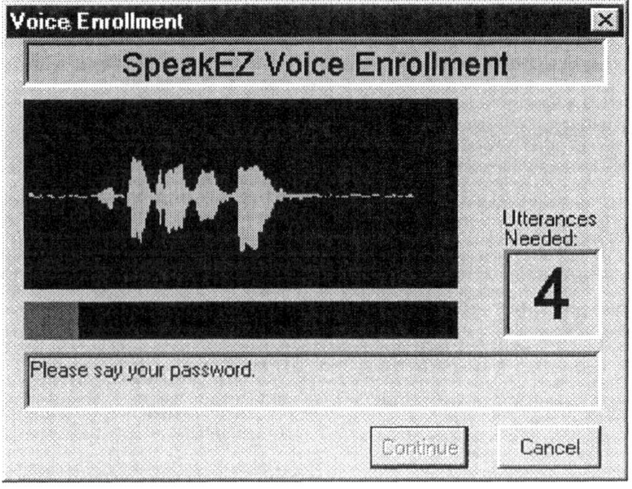

Figure 14.3. Enrollment data collection screen.

14.5. Speaker Verification Performance

A trial of the SpeakEZ speaker verification technology was performed over the web to evaluate its accuracy and usability.   There were a total of 31 participants that included 16 females and 15 males. Roughly half of these participants had minimal to no experience in using speech technology.

The results reported here are compiled from the first three phases of the web trial.   The first phase was for user enrollment. Each person was instructed to enroll with the passwords "American dollar", "Miami, Florida", and the person's full name. The enrollment consisted of four repetitions of each password. The second phase was conducted to measure the false reject error. Here, each person was instructed to perform four verifications for each of their three passwords using their correct password. This would result in 12 authentic user trials for each speaker. These verification attempts were performed using the same microphone type as that used during enrollment. The third phase was conducted to measure the false accept error. Here, each person was provided a list of 10 other users of the same gender to impersonate.   The users were instructed to provide two impersonation attempts for each of the three passwords. This would result in 60 imposter attempts issued by each speaker.   All impersonations used the correct password of the user. Hence, this represents a worst-case scenario as in a fielded application the password may not necessarily be known by the impersonator.

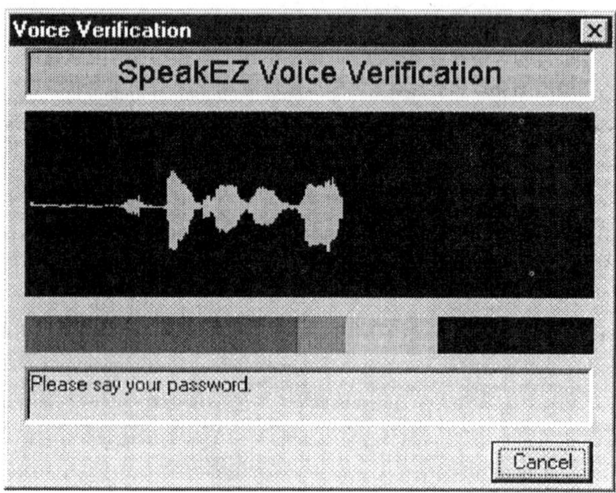

Figure 14.4. Verification data collection screen.

If all of the data were successfully collected, there would be 372 authentic user trials and 1860 imposter trials. Not all of the participants completed the full data collection for each of these three phases. In addition, there were some users that provided extra data for their true user trials and imposter trials. Hence, the final number of trials was 426 true user trials and 1787 imposter trials.

The verification threshold was set to a value that was estimated to yield an operating point near the equal error rate. For the 426 true speaker trials there were a total of 14 false rejects corresponding to a false reject rate of 3.3%. For the 1787 imposter trials there were a total of 22 false accepts corresponding to a false accept error of 1.2%.

All of the audio data from the web trial was then annotated to determine if the participants had properly conducted the trial. From this annotation, there were a number of cases found where the user did not use the proper password for either the correct user attempt or for the imposter attempt. There were also cases where some phases were not collected for certain users. Three labeled databases were constructed from this data where users that did not have all the phases collected were deleted and also data where the wrong password was uttered was deleted. The details of the databases constructed from the annotation results are provided in Table 14.1.

Table 14.1. Statistical information for databases.

Password	# Users	# True trials	# Imposter trials
Miami, FL	31	133	588
American $	28	118	534
Full name	23	114	448

Table 14.2. Equal error rates on annotated databases.

Password	Miami, FL	American $	Fullname	Average
EER	3.01	4.94	4.33	4.09

Off-line experiments were then performed on these databases to determine the equal error rate (EER) for each password. This was done by setting the same verification threshold for all speakers and then incrementing it until the false reject error and false accept error were approximately equal. Note that this is different than adjusting the threshold individually for each speaker, which generally gives a lower EER estimate. The results of these trials are shown in Table 14.2.

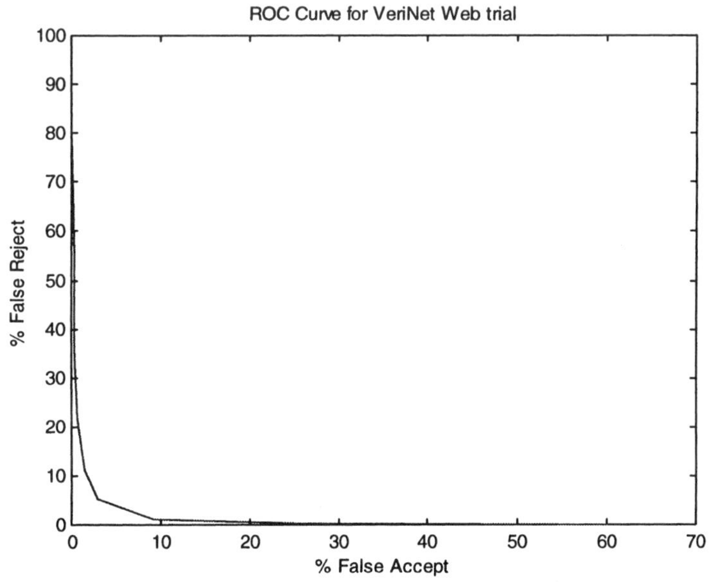

Figure 14.5. Receiver operating characteristic curve for web trial.

The scores from these trials were combined and a receiver operating characteristic (ROC) curve was generated. Figure 14.5 displays this ROC. The equal error rate for the compilation of these trials is 3.91%.

14.6. Summary

This chapter discussed speaker verification technology along with its application to internet security with respect to web page protection and *e*Business. Speaker verification provides a powerful, convenient, and complementary means for supplementing today's existing security measures. As internet security issues remain to be one of the main obstacles for broad acceptance of *e*Business applications, a solution to this could provide extensive benefits. We believe that speaker verification as provided in the Authentication Web Service provides a viable solution to internet security.

References

[1]   D. Naik and R.J. Mammone. Pole-filtered Cepstral Mean Subtraction. In Proc. of IEEE International Conference on Acoustics, Speech and Signal Processing (ICASSP), pages 157-160, 1995.

[2]   M. Sharma and R.J. Mammone. Subword-based Text-dependent Speaker Verification System with User-selectable Passwords. In Proc. of IEEE International Conference on Acoustics, Speech and Signal Processing (ICASSP), pages 93-96, 1996.

[3]   H-S Liou and R.J. Mammone. A Subword Neural Tree Network Approach to Text-Dependent Speaker Verification. In Proc. of IEEE International Conference on Acoustics, Speech and Signal Processing (ICASSP), pages 357-360, 1995.

[4]   K.R. Farrell, R.J. Mammone and K.T. Assaleh. Speaker Recognition using Neural Networks and Conventional Classifiers, IEEE Transactions on Speech and Audio Processing, vol. 2, no. 1, part II, pages 194-205, January 1994.

[5]   K.R. Farrell, R.P. Ramachandran and R.J. Mammone. An Analysis of Data Fusion Methods for Speaker Verification. In Proc. of IEEE International Conference on Acoustics, Speech and Signal Processing (ICASSP), pages 1129-1132, 1998.

[6]   http://biometric-consulting.com/bio.htm

[7]   http://www.cesg.gov.uk/technology/biometrics

Chapter 15

ABILITY TO VERIFY: A METRIC FOR SYSTEM PERFORMANCE IN REAL-WORLD COMPARATIVE BIOMETRIC TESTING

Samir Nanavati and Michael Thieme
International Biometric Group
1 Battery Park Plaza
New York, NY 10004, USA
{samir, mthieme}@biometricgroup.com

Abstract   Institutions considering biometric deployments in IT security and *e*-commerce environments must investigate a range of questions, including costs, compatibility, scalability, and user acceptance. However, there are essential performance-related questions which can only be answered by looking at comparative, independent testing of biometric technologies: How susceptible are biometrics to "accepting" impostors and "rejecting" authorized users? What is the likelihood of false matching and false non-matching for different technologies and different solutions? What percentage of users will be able to enrol in a given biometric solution? Analysis of IBG Comparative Biometric Testing results from different biometric technologies – including finger-scan, facial-scan, voice-scan, signature-scan, iris-scan, and keystroke-scan - suggests that understanding biometric system performance requires analysis of more than false match rates and false non-match rates generally provided by biometric vendors. Two generally overlooked performance metrics may, in many cases, be critical determinants of a system's overall effectiveness: failure to enrol rates and false non-match rates over time. These two metrics can be combined into a single metric known as Ability to Verify (ATV), a performance measure with a direct impact on system costs, security, and convenience. Testing shows that many ATV rates can vary substantially from technology to technology, and from biometric device to biometric device.

Keywords: Biometric testing, performance, accuracy

15.1.   Introduction

The requirement for strong user authentication in the enterprise is increasing steadily as a result of two trends in today's computing environments:

- Increasing amounts of sensitive data are accessible through internal and external networks.
- The number and aggregate value of electronic transactions continues to grow at an extremely rapid pace.

Whether in the growth of B2B activity, the need to secure internal networks and intranets, or end-user applications such as online banking and financial services, most new developments in day-to-day corporate or end user computer usage highlight the need for strong user authentication. Biometric technology is expected to play a large role in many of these computing environments, as its core function is to provide strong user authentication.

Traditional authentication methods such as passwords and PINs are proving inadequate to new challenges involved in user authentication, as they are highly vulnerable to compromise, unauthorized sharing, and intercept. In addition to more obvious risks such as fraud and theft, outmoded authentication methods can contribute to loss of personal and private information, especially in an Internet environment. By comparison, biometric technologies provide greatly increased security and convenience. For end users, biometrics can eliminate the need to manage a large number of passwords; for enterprise environments, biometrics reduce the overhead dedicated to managing passwords for thousands of users.

The question facing potential deployers is not whether biometrics are a worthwhile solution, but which biometric solution is best suited to their needs and what percentage of users will be able to interact with the technology on a daily basis.

Addressing the need in the biometric market for independent performance results, IBG's Comparative Biometric Testing provides False Match Rates, False Non-Match Rates, and Failure to Enrol Rates for leading biometric systems. Understanding these metrics, and having access to real-world performance data, is critical to any deployer considering biometrics for employees, customers, or citizens. Independent testing of leading biometric solutions across a variety of disciplines helps determine which technologies are best suited for deployment in IT security and *e*-commerce environments.

15.2.   Test Methodology

IBG has developed a detailed Comparative Test methodology to reflect the expectations and requirements of typical deployers in an *e*-commerce and IT security environment. These deployers have relatively limited tolerance for elongated enrolment processes, and generally have operational requirements for fairly rapid verification. In addition, these deployers utilize 1:1 matching as opposed to 1:N identification, ensuring rapid matching and increasing user accountability due to the use of a unique, user-specific identifier. There is also a moderate amount of user guidance involved during enrolment, but not during verification. Such a methodology would require some modification for applications such as locating duplicate enrolments in a public benefits database or physical access to high-risk facilities. However, this methodology is highly applicable to deployment environments such as financial institutions, health care providers, and general corporate enterprises.

Careful control of test conditions is an essential component of IBG's biometric testing. Factors such as background noise, lighting, temperature, positioning of acquisition devices, and information visible to test subjects are carefully controlled for each biometric technology system tested.

15.2.1   Defining "Enrolment Attempts and "Verification Attempts"

A critical issue in comparative testing is how to define "enrolment attempts" and "verification attempts". If a user is given an infinite number of attempts to enrol and verify, the system's performance will "increase" accordingly, although in most real-world applications this would be unacceptable. In IBG's testing, both verification and enrolment attempts are limited through standard protocols which accommodate the operational differences between core technologies. This ensures that reasonable comparisons can be made across technologies which may otherwise be difficult to compare from an operational perspective.

For example, when testing verification in most finger-scan, voice-scan, and signature-scan systems – which in nearly all cases require consecutive, iterative presentations of biometric data - users are given three attempts to verify (both legitimately and fraudulently) at each security level. Depending on the technology, an "attempt" can be a finger placement, a spoken phrase or word, or a signed phrase or word. When testing facial-scan and iris-scan technology – in which data is acquired when the subject is within a given range of an acquisition device – an "attempt" is defined as a user interaction with an acquisition device for one full verification cycle, with an imposed time limit of approximately 10 seconds. Inability to verify within three attempts for iterative technology, or one full cycle for range-driven systems, is deemed a non-match. Additional limits may, in certain cases, by placed on technologies with abnormally long verification or enrolment processes.

For enrolment testing, users are allowed a total of six "attempts" to enrol in iterative systems such as finger-scan, voice-scan, and signature-scan systems. Again, this means that the user can provide up to six finger placements, spoken phrases, or signed phrases. The systems themselves may require 1, 2, 3, or 4 attempts for enrolment, but the limit of six placements represents a reasonable requirement of biometric system deployers. In range-driven systems, such as facial-scan and iris-scan, users are allowed to interact with an acquisition device for one full enrolment cycle, with an imposed time limit of approximately 25-30 seconds. Inability to enrol within three attempts for iterative technology, or one full cycle for range-driven systems, is deemed a failure to enrol.

While it may seem that the multiple attempts permitted in iterative systems would grant these systems an advantage in limiting false non-match rates and failure to enrol rates, range-driven systems may acquire dozens of images within a singe acquisition cycle.

15.2.2   Primary Visit Protocols

The test's first visit ("Primary Visit") involves extensive testing of approximately 240 subjects of various demographic, age, ethnic, and employment backgrounds.

Over the course of one hour, subjects attempt to enrol in each biometric system. Those who are able to enrol are then verified against their enrolment; for systems with security thresholds, this verification begins at high security. If unable to verify, attempts are made to verify the subject at medium then low security settings.

Subjects then attempt "fraudulent verification" in each of the systems by posing as one of several pre-enrolled test users. For systems with security thresholds, false verification testing begins at low security, then moves to medium and high security. Finger-scan systems are given an additional false verification test: users attempt verification with their middle finger against their enrolled index fingers, again moving from low to medium and high security in the case of a false match.

For those systems which use varying accuracy thresholds, the "high-medium-low" settings are provided by the vendors. The large majority of vendors provide thresholds for test purposes; a handful prefer that their technology only be tested at one security level.

The following principles are followed regarding user interaction with the biometric systems:

- A specific limit is established on attempts to enrol and verify, in order to ensure that no more than a moderate amount of time and effort is necessary to enrol or verify in a given system.
- Scripted instructions are given before subjects interact with the systems.
- If necessary, a small amount of placement or usage advice is permitted during the first user enrolment attempt with each system.
- Subsequent attempts at enrolment and verification permit minimal placement or usage advice, as preliminary explanation and specific advice, if necessary, have already been offered by this point.

Every effort is made to ensure that the user interaction with the system is representative of what is reasonable in an IT security or *e*-commerce environment.

In addition, for test rounds in which one or more of the systems tested utilizes neural net technology, the test order is changed slightly: false verification attempts precede enrolment attempts. This is to prevent the introduction of impostor data into the neural net cells prior to false verification attempts.

15.2.3   Effect of Time: Supplemental Visit

To provide an additional, often-overlooked measure of system performance, International Biometric Group retests the majority of subjects from its Primary Visit approximately six weeks after their original test date. This long-term true verification testing ("Supplemental Visit") determines the ability of systems to verify users when a delay is introduced between enrolment and verification.

In an IT security or *e*-commerce environment, long-term performance is a critical measure of a system's capabilities. The ability to immediately verify a user after enrolment is important, but there may be situations in which a user enrols but does not use the biometric system for several weeks. This is especially true in an *e*-commerce environment, where transactions are likely to occur sporadically. Users may interact with the system in a slightly different fashion, leading to changes in the presentation of biometric data. Even if systems are used daily, changes in behavioural or physiological characteristics can affect the ability of many technologies to verify users. Time can magnify the impact of these changes.

The Supplemental Visit testing consists of true verification, meaning that users are asked to verify against their previous enrolment. As in the Primary Visit testing, users attempt verification at high security, and progress to medium security then low security if necessary (this applies only to systems with thresholds).

15.3.   High-level Test Results

The following test results are for three systems tested in recent IBG Comparative Testing Rounds. Each system represents a different production biometric technology, configured for 1:1 verification. While the specific systems and technologies which correspond to these results are held confidential, Systems A and C are iterative technologies (finger-scan, voice-scan, signature-scan, or keystroke-scan); System B is a range-driven technology (iris-scan or facial-scan technology). The findings below are generally representative of system performance for many leading biometric systems, but should by no means be taken as representative of every solution's capabilities. The more robust systems tested have generated lower error rates, and the less robust systems tested have generated higher error rates, than those indicated here.

15.3.1   System A: Results and Analysis

Failure to Enrol Rate – PRIMARY VISIT		System A
Total Subjects	236	
System FTE: 5.09%		
False Match Rates – Primary Visit *(Each subject attempted to verify against two different enrollees. Testing begins at low security and moves to medium then high)*		
High Security FMR: 0.00%	Medium Security FMR: 0.50%	Low Security FMR: 1.74%
False Non-Match Rates – Primary Visit *(Testing begins at high security and moves to medium then low)*		
High Security FNMR: 0.00%	Medium Security FNMR: 0.00%	Low Security FNMR: 0.00%
False Non-Match Rates – Supplemental Visit *(Testing begins at high security and moves to medium then low)*		
High Security *FNMR: 12.57%*	*Medium Security* *FNMR: 1.26%*	*Low Security* *FNMR: 0.63%*

Figure 15.1.   System A: High-Level Primary Visit Results.

Primary Visit.   System A performed extremely well in the Primary Visit, with extremely low FMR and FNMR - even at low security - and a respectable 5.09% FTE. When one considers that this technology has historically been prone to accuracy and performance problems, these results are impressive. In contrast to past *ad hoc* testing and usage of this biometric discipline, where false non-match was a very common problem, System A had zero false non-matches at high security.

In many biometric systems, low FNMR often corresponds to higher false match rates. Such was not the case with System A, which returned false match rates of 1.74%, 0.50%, and 0.0% for low, medium, and high security, respectively.

Both the FMR and FNMR were very low, in contrast to the FTE rate of 5.09% which is slightly higher than one encounters in many biometric systems. This suggests that the system is stringently checking the sample quality before allowing a subject to be enrolled, contributing to the low FMR and FNMR at the expense of a higher FTE rate.

Supplemental Visit. Supplemental Testing shows that at medium security, the FNMR is 1.26%, a strong score. At low security, the cumulative FNMR is 0.63%, again quite impressive. The high security FNMR of 12.57% is a large increase from the original 0%, which may indicate that the high security setting is best reserved for applications where the risks of false matching far outweigh the inconvenience associated with false non-matching.

Although the FNMR increases at all three security settings in comparison to Primary Visit Testing, the performance is still quite strong at the medium and low levels. Given that the Primary Testing did not return any false matches at any security level, lowering the security thresholds of the system may reduce the high security FNMR without severely impacting the low-security FMR. These two metrics are inversely related, such that adjusting thresholds to decrease FNMR results in increased FMR, and vice versa.

15.3.2 System B: Results and Analysis

Primary Visit. Aside from a 5% FTE, which is somewhat higher than one may expect from a range-driven technology given the strictly controlled enrolment and verification environment, System B performed very well, with slightly over 2% FMR and FNMR at medium thresholds. At high security, the technology had no false matches along with a false reject rate of 6.11%. At low-security settings, the system had a 1.31% false reject rate at low settings, to go with a 7.17% FMR. In either case, these ratings indicate that the technology can perform well in various environments, and that the system thresholds are accurate indicators of the technology's capabilities at various security settings.

Supplemental Visit. The false non-match rates are much higher than one would expect, even on low-security settings. Over half of enrolled subjects were not identified at high security. Furthermore, over 20% of returning subjects were incapable of being verified on low-security, whereas in the Primary Test, approximately 1% of subjects could not be verified on low-security. Given that the acquisition conditions - including distance to camera, angle of facial capture, composition of background, and lighting conditions - were uniform between enrolment and verification, it is fair to conclude that other factors related to biometric data or its presentation may have had an impact on the system's ability to verify users over time.

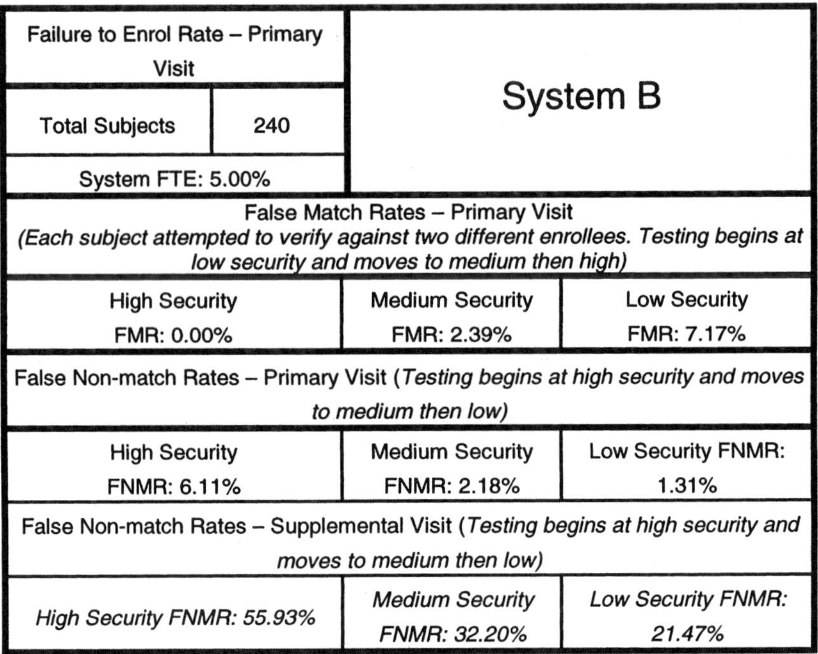

Failure to Enrol Rate – Primary Visit		System B	
Total Subjects	240		
System FTE: 5.00%			
False Match Rates – Primary Visit *(Each subject attempted to verify against two different enrollees. Testing begins at low security and moves to medium then high)*			
High Security FMR: 0.00%	Medium Security FMR: 2.39%	Low Security FMR: 7.17%	
False Non-match Rates – Primary Visit *(Testing begins at high security and moves to medium then low)*			
High Security FNMR: 6.11%	Medium Security FNMR: 2.18%	Low Security FNMR: 1.31%	
False Non-match Rates – Supplemental Visit *(Testing begins at high security and moves to medium then low)*			
High Security FNMR: 55.93%	*Medium Security FNMR: 32.20%*	*Low Security FNMR: 21.47%*	

Figure 15.2. System B: High-Level Primary Visit Results.

15.3.3 System C: Results and Analysis

Primary Visit. In Primary Visit testing, System C suffered from an unusually high FTE of over 12%, but performed very well in false match testing. Its FNMR progressed from approximately 2%-4% moving from low to high thresholds.

The system's low security FMR was over 8% when each subject attempted to verify his or her middle finger versus his or her index finger, but the FMR moved to below 1% for medium thresholds. This suggests that System C is able to establish distinct performance levels when moving from threshold to threshold. The FMR of subjects attempting to verify against different subjects was 0% for medium and high security.

Supplemental Visit. System C's low security FNMR increased by over 400%, from 2.37% to 10.63%, between the Primary and Supplemental Visits.

This would seem to indicate that either the low security threshold is too restrictive to successfully account for temporal changes, or that the core matching algorithms may not accommodate such temporal changes.

Failure to Enrol Rate – Primary Visit		System C
Total Subjects	240	
System FTE: 12.08%		
False Match Rates – Primary Visit *(Each subject attempted to verify against two different enrollees. Testing begins at low security and moves to medium then high)*		
High Security FMR: 0.00%	Medium Security FMR: 0.00%	Low Security FMR: 1.89%
False Non-match Rates – Primary Visit *(Testing begins at high security and moves to medium then low)*		
High Security FNMR: 4.74%	Medium Security FNMR: 3.32%	Low Security FNMR: 2.37%
False Non-match Rates – Supplemental Visit *(Testing begins at high security and moves to medium then low)*		
High Security FNMR: 20.63%	*Medium Security FNMR:* *15.00%*	*Low Security FNMR:* *10.63%*

Figure 15.3. System C: High-Level Primary Visit Results.

15.4. Ability to Verify (ATV)

For a biometric system to be deployed successfully in typical IT security and *e*-commerce environments, it must be capable of reliably verifying a large percentage of users on a daily basis. Biometrics are seen as a convenience and cost-saving tool as well as a security tool; providing consistent functionality will be a necessary condition of enterprise-level deployments. In this light, an interesting way to view the capabilities of systems tested is to assess the systems' Ability to Verify (ATV). Deriving a single performance metric from a system's FTE and FNMR, ATV represents the percentage of an enterprise's users a biometric system will be capable of verifying reliably on a daily basis.

ATV is rendered as follows:

$$\text{ATV} = 1-((1-\text{FTE})*(1-\text{FNMR}))$$

This metric can be thought of as representing the group of users who cannot enrol (FTE) along with users falsely rejected by the system (FNMR). None of the systems tested to date has generated a 100% ATV rate, but in general, a high ATV rate will make for a more effective system.

To illustrate, a system administrator of a 1,000-person domain can reasonably assume that a system with an ATV of 97.5% will be capable of verifying 975 on a typical day. On average, 25 users unable to be verified by the system would either need to utilize a different biometric or a different authentication technology. The same administrator considering a system with an ATV of 85% would need to accommodate 150 users outside of the primary biometric – a much more challenging task.

Special ATV considerations are necessary when assessing the viability of utilizing multiple biometrics in an application. Such applications may require verification using more than one biometric technology; others may allow users to verify on one of multiple technologies. In both cases lower ATV rates may be the result of implementing "layered" biometrics.

15.4.1   ATV: Primary vs. Supplemental Visits

Comparison of Primary and Supplemental Visit ATV rates for systems A, B, and C demonstrate the effect of time on system performance. Because test protocols call for control over a wide variety of external factors, the decreased ability to verify is most likely attributable to changes in biometric data or to changes in how this data is presented by the subject.

System	FTE	Primary Visit		Ability to Reject Impostors (1-FMR)
		Low Security FNMR	*Ability to Verify*	
System A	5.08%	0.00%	94.92%	98.26%
System B	5.00%	1.31%	93.76%	92.83%
System C	12.08%	2.37%	85.84%	96.05%

Figure 15.4. Low Security Primary Visit ATV.

System	FTE	Supplemental Visit		Ability to Reject Impostors (1-FMR)
		Low Security FNMR	*Ability to Verify*	
System A	5.08%	0.63%	94.32%	98.26%
System B	12.08%	10.63%	78.57%	96.05%
System C	5.00%	21.47%	74.60%	92.83%

Figure 15.5. Low Security Supplemental Visit ATV

System	FTE	Primary Visit		Ability to Reject Impostors (1-FMR)
		Medium Security FNMR	*Ability to Verify*	
System A	5.08%	*0.00%*	*94.92%*	100.00%
System B	5.00%	*2.18%*	*92.93%*	97.61%
System C	12.08%	*3.32%*	*85.00%*	99.84%

Figure 15.6. Medium Security Primary Visit ATV.

System	FTE	Supplemental Visit		Ability to Reject Impostors (1-FMR)
		Medium Security FNMR	*Ability to Verify*	
System A	5.08%	*1.26%*	*93.72%*	100.00%
System B	5.00%	*32.20%*	*65.36%*	97.61%
System C	12.08%	*15.00%*	*74.73%*	99.84%

Figure 15.7. Medium Security Supplemental Visit ATV.

System	FTE	Primary Visit		Ability to Reject Impostors (1-FNMR)
		High Security FNMR	*Ability to Verify*	
System A	5.08%	*0.00%*	*94.92%*	100.00%
System B	5.00%	*6.11%*	*89.20%*	100.00%
System C	12.08%	*4.74%*	*83.75%*	100.00%

Figure 15.8. High Security Primary Visit ATV.

System	FTE	Supplemental Visit		Ability to Reject Impostors (1-FMR)
		High Security FNMR	*Ability to Verify*	
System A	5.08%	*12.57%*	*82.99%*	100.00%
System B	12.08%	*20.63%*	*69.78%*	100.00%
System C	5.00%	*55.93%*	*41.87%*	100.00%

Figure 15.9. High Security Supplemental Visit ATV.

15.4.2 ATV in *E*-Commerce Applications and IT Security

There is no "minimum" ATV score necessary for success in a given environment - every deployment has different authentication requirements. However, a basic framework can be established for IT security and *e*-commerce deployments. These guidelines assume that a reasonable balance is struck between security and convenience, but that user convenience is a more compelling day-to-day driver than absolute security.

More importantly, the following guidelines assume that *e*-commerce deployments are "opt-in", whereas IT security deployments are not. The use of biometrics in an *e*-commerce environment will likely be a decision left to the consumer – it is difficult to envision a company making biometric usage a precondition of doing business online for all customers. Because *e*-commerce presupposes a mix of biometric and non-biometric users, a high ATV is not quite as essential in *e*-commerce: the system security already accounts for the presence of non-biometric users; accordingly the system is no more difficult to maintain. However, in IT security, where an employer can mandate the usage of biometrics, employees would have little recourse. Were employees allowed to decide whether they prefer to use biometrics, the overall system would be less secure and more difficult to administer. Therefore, IT security applications would likely require a slightly higher ATV.

In *e*-commerce applications, the general recommendation is for an ATV of at least 95%. This allows the large majority of one's customer base to partake in biometric authentication if so desired, while still allowing a variety of biometric solutions to be deployed. A merchant may choose to allow verification through different biometric technologies to increase customer convenience, with the understanding that some of these solutions may not have the highest ATV for specific populations.

IT security deployments often require an ATV of 97.5% or greater, and are well served by systems which can generate 99% ATV. Such an ATV would ensure that enrolment in network login-style applications can be nearly universal.

15.4.3 Value of ATV

When balanced with an acceptable False Match Rate, ATV can be extremely useful because it is has an impact on three key aspects of biometric deployments: cost, security, and convenience.

Cost.   One of the most expensive aspects of a biometric system is the costs involved with exception processing. Any user unable to be processed by the biometric needs to be processed by a 'fall-back' procedure, meaning that dual systems must be maintained. Whether an alternate biometric, a password, or a live verification, there is a need for a separate enabling and support infrastructure

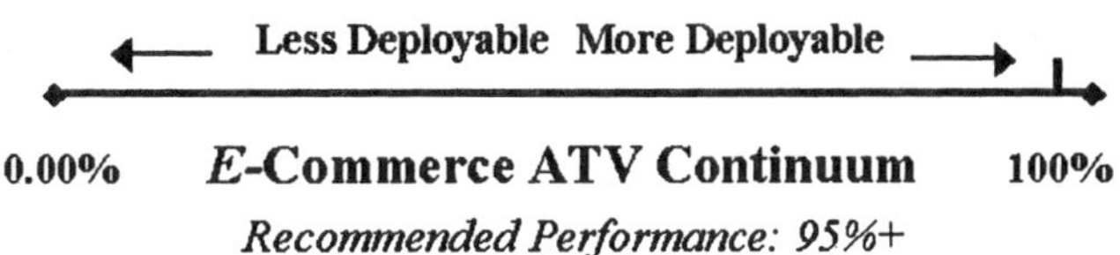

Figure 15.10. e-Commerce ATV Continuum

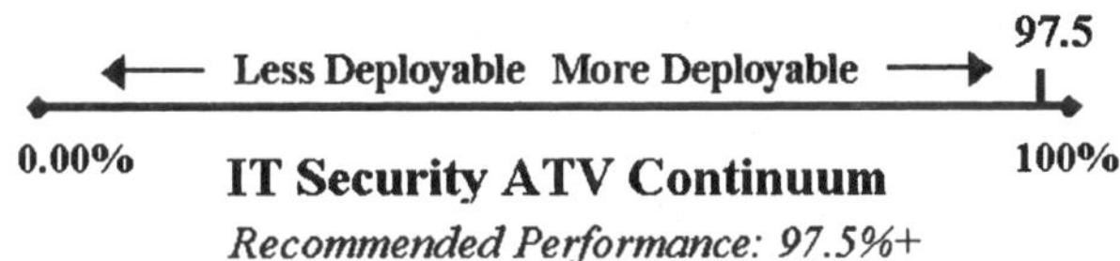

Figure 15.11. IT Security ATV Continuum

Security.   A low ATV means that a substantial percentage of users are not being verified by your system. The security provided by a system which can only verify 90% of its users may be acceptable for some deployments, but can be problematic in many others.

Convenience.   A low ATV may be a reflection of a difficult to use system. In situations in which user convenience is paramount, adjustments to enrolment and verification settings may be required to maximize the ATV rate.

Recall that comparison of biometric templates does not result in 100% matches, but instead results in some degree of correlation. A score is generated after template comparison, this score is then compared to a threshold, and a decision is rendered. Biometric systems return degrees of certainty, not 100% certainty.

The security, convenience, and fraud reduction that biometrics are expected to provide are based on the assumption that biometrics work: that they verify and identify users correctly and can enrol a high percentage of users. Just as defining the "best" biometric is fruitless without understanding the application, assessing biometric accuracy requires that the application be defined.

15.5.   Vendor-generated Test Results

There are several explanations for the discrepancy between vendor claims and the reality of most Comparative Test results, in particular long-term ATV. In many cases, vendor-supplied metrics are simply estimates of how robust the vendor perceives their algorithm to be. In other cases, vendors derive accuracy metrics from the distinctiveness of the underlying biometric data, although it is by no means a given that this data will (1) remain stable over time or (2) that the data will be acquired consistently from day to day. Those vendors who do generate their FMR and FNMR from testing (note that few vendors generate FTE rates) normally do so by feeding static or recorded images into their matching algorithm. While this is a reasonable test of an algorithm's capabilities, many other factors contribute to system accuracy, such as ergonomics, ease of use, the manner in which biometric data is acquired, and the level of training required for users to provide biometric data.

15.5.1   "Single" Error Rates vs. "System" Error Rates

The vendor-supplied accuracy metrics are usually generated from testing of static verification data. These results are indicative of a system's single false match rate, false non-match rate, or failure to enrol rate. They indicate the likelihood of a false match or false non-match from a single test of verification versus enrolment data. However, in real-world deployments, users may be able to submit several samples. For example, different fingers or different passphrases could be submitted. In real-world deployments, single error rates must be considered in conjunction with system error rates. These system error rates indicate the likelihood of system error in a real-world deployment where a user may be able (for better or worse) to provide different samples. In real-world applications, a person trying to break into a biometric system may be able to attempt more than one match; he or she may be able to try a series of matches. As a result, the actual odds of an imposter break-in are much higher. The likelihood of an imposter break-in for a given system is the system false match rate.

To illustrate, take a finger-scan system with a stated false match rate of 1/10,000. In this system, the likelihood of templates from two different people matching during a single match attempt is 1/10,000. Let's also assume that the system is not designed to lock a user out after a certain number of attempts. Next, John Smith enters Jane Doe's username, and places his index finger, and is rejected. John Smith can then try to break in with all ten fingers.

Each break-in attempt has a false match rate of 1/10,000, but the overall system false match rate is immediately higher. John does not break in against Jane, but he also happens to have Kris' username as well. John then attempts to break in ten more times, further increasing the false match rate. If the verification environment is unsupervised, this might continue unabated until the likelihood of a false match becomes dangerously high

As the example given above makes clear, a very important metric in real-world deployments is the system false match rate. Real-world users and deployers of biometric technology are concerned with how well biometrics will solve their identification and authentication problems. In most cases, the system false match is a much more useful expression of problem-solving capability than the single false match rate alone. To determine system false match rate, one requires knowledge of the single false match rate, the number of verification or identification attempts the user is allowed, the availability of usernames an imposter has access to, and other factors which can only be determined by looking at system process flow. Because ensuring a low system false match rate is a more complicated task than simply assessing a technology's false match rate, it becomes a requirement of deploying secure biometric systems.

System False Non-Match Rate.   Similarly, generating false non-match rates from a single presentation or verification attempt is inconsistent with real-world system usage. In operational deployments, it is rare that users have only one chance to present data to a biometric system. Instead, users are generally allowed to attempt verification a handful of times until an account or login name is locked. Therefore, the single false non-match rate, which represents the probably of a single user attempt resulting in a false non-match, does not reflect real-world usage. Instead, the **System False-Non-Match Rate** becomes a better indicator of how a system will perform in a real-world environment.

Utilizing the system false non-match rate is beneficial to biometric systems. This contrasts to system false match rate, which recasts the real-world FMR of biometric systems in a fairly harsh light. Because of the multiple factors which can contribute to false non-matching, some of which cannot be controlled or accounted for by biometric vendors, it is reasonable to assume that a user may need to attempt verification more than once in order to be verified. Though the user may be slightly inconvenienced by having to place a backup finger or recite a passphrase more than once, the inconvenience of being denied access would likely be more substantial.

As an illustration, consider a system with a single false non-match rate of 1% where 1% of verification attempts are incorrectly judged to not match.

For most deployments, this would be an unacceptably high rate. However, users normally have between 3-5 attempts to verify in logical and physical access situations, allowing for improved presentation and thereby reducing the effective FNMR. In addition, most finger-scan systems strongly recommend enrolling more than one finger to reduce FNMR. By attempting to verify with a second or third finger, and allowing multiple verification attempts, the system false non-match rate become much less than 1%.

System Failure to Enrol Rate.   There is much less discussion in the biometric industry of FTE than other accuracy metrics. Therefore, there is no consensus on what constitutes a failure to enrol. The strictest definition of a single failure to enrol rate would be the likelihood that a user is unable to enrol after one full enrolment sequence. However, in real-world applications, users have more than one chance to enrol. A user may simply be prompted to attempt enrolment a second time, or may be routed to a training and presentation sequence. A user may be prompted to place a second finger, or to choose a longer or shorter passphrase. Biometric systems are usually quite flexible in allowing for multiple enrolment attempts.

The **System Failure to Enrol Rate** represents the percentage of users who are deemed FTE after a reasonable number of attempts to enrol in a biometric system. This number will always be lower than the **Single Failure to Enrol Rate**, because many users only require one enrolment attempt to become acclimated to interacting with a given biometric system.

The point at which a user becomes a FTE is dependent on the application. In a network authentication system where enrolment takes place at a desktop, a user may be allowed to attempt enrolment several times. On the other hand, a deployer may require that enrolment be kept very brief – 2 full attempts, for example - so as to not reduce productivity. In another example, users who are unable to immediately enrol in a physical access system may be asked to re-attempt enrolment at a later time to avoid generating long lines. At some point in every application, a decision point is reached which concludes that a given user is, indeed, a failure to enrol. One must be aware that a user who requires 10 attempts to enrol is very likely to encounter high false non-match rates, as he or she is clearly unable to provide consistent biometric data. There is a point of diminishing returns when making multiple attempts to enrol a user.

15.6. Conclusions

IBG's Comparative Biometric Testing demonstrates the importance of testing for enrolment and verification over time. This testing is a strong indicator of the ability of biometric systems in an *e*-commerce and IT security environment to operate effectively in real-world environments.

Testing suggests that in order to determine whether a particular biometric technology can meet performance requirements, institutions must assess all three accuracy metrics: False Match Rate, False Non-Match Rate, and Failure to Enrol rate. Assessing anything less than all three metrics is not only of reduced value, but can be highly misleading. Using only selected performance metrics will generate a false sense of the system's actual capabilities. In particular, the use of Failure to Enrol rates and False Non-Match Rates – rendered collectively as Ability to Verify (ATV) – is a critical indicator of long-term system usability.

Furthermore, IBG testing shows that assessing System Error Rates as opposed to Single Error Rates gives the strongest indication of a biometric technology's real-world suitability for a given application. System rates are much more difficult to derive, as they are contingent on combining system design with Single False Match Rates, but they are essential to understanding the security, convenience, and cost savings that a biometric system provides.

References

[1]   International Biometric Group's Comparative Biometric Testing, Rounds I, II, III

[2]   Biometrics: Identity Verification in a Networked World. Samir Nanavati, Michael Thieme, and Raj Nanavati. John Wiley & Sons; ISBN: 0471099457

[3]   National Biometric Test Center Collected Works 1997 – 2000
        http://www.engr.sjsu.edu/biometrics/publications.html

[4]   The BioPrivacy Initiative
        http://www.bioprivacy.org

Chapter 16

AUTOMATED AUTHENTICATION USING HYBRID BIOMETRIC SYSTEM

Norman Poh

The School of Computer Science

University Science of Malaysia, 11800 Penang, Malaysia

poh@dpt-info.u-strasbg.fr

Jerzy Korczak

Université Louis Pasteur, LSIIT (UPRES-A CNRS-ULP 7005)

Bld. Sébastien Brant, Pôle API, F-67400 Illkirch, France

jjk@dpt-info.u-strasbg.fr

Abstract   A highly reliable biometric authentication system can be realised by using multiple biometric models. In this study, a framework that makes use of signal- and image-processing algorithms, together with pattern recognition techniques, is applied to solve the problem of biometric pattern recognition in a unified way. In general, this problem can be broken down into the following taxonomy: sensors, extractors, experts and the supervisor. Using this general schema, biometric systems with similar fundamental problem characteristics can be processed. According to the product law of reliability, a distributed (or parallel) system is more reliable than a linear system. Inspired by the idea of parallelism, ensemble methods and the notions of multi-sample and multi-model are studied. Based on the proposed framework, a hybrid biometric authentication prototype that makes use of upright frontal face-scans and text-dependent voice-scans is implemented. This prototype has been tested on a real-life database in our laboratory with encouraging results. We show that multi-sample multi-model biometric approach is more reliable than other existing combination models (single-sample single-model, single-sample multi-model or multi-sample single-model). From the application point of view, we have identified four categories of biometric application according to several criteria: security (or accuracy) versus convenience (ease-of-use and non-intrusiveness), traffic flow and cost. We propose that the hybrid biometric approach as an effective alternative when no other single-model biometric approach can satisfy both the user (i.e. ease-of-use and non-intrusiveness) and technical (i.e. cost and accuracy) constraints at the same time.

Keywords: Multi-model biometrics, face/voice authentication, integration, fusion, security, and pattern recognition

16.1.   The State of the Art

16.1.1   Introduction

Several studies show that multi-model biometric approach is superior to any single-model biometric approach [3,6,13,15,17-18,22]. Abstraction is considered the most important element in solving biometric pattern recognition because it is independent of any specific extraction or classification algorithm. Over the years, extraction algorithms, be they local or global, with prior knowledge or not, have also emerged. Morphological analysis, statistical analysis (e.g. principal component analysis), multi-level analysis (e.g. wavelets) and optimisation algorithm (e.g., genetic algorithm) are very common among extraction algorithms. Classifiers have also evolved and have been applied to biometric authentication. Among them are Bayesian-based networks [26], artificial neural networks [24], support vector machines [27] and most recently SNoW (Sparse Network of Winnows) [29]. Furthermore, recent advancement in ensemble methods, e.g. AdaBoost [9] and ECOC (Error-Correcting Output-Coding) [8], can further improve the classification result. It is therefore reasonable to believe that better classification algorithms will continue to emerge. However, there lacks a thorough study on how this seemingly separate algorithms can be integrated in a unified and hopefully optimised way to solve the problem of biometric pattern recognition.

The proposed framework should be generic, i.e., biometric-independent and modular. Biometric independence means that the framework established in one biometric model should be able to be applied to other biometric model. Modularity means that the taxonomy of modules should be well defined and that one module should be able to be replaced by another without affecting the whole system. This framework can easily lend itself to generic system architecture and implementation.

This chapter also aims to contribute to solving the problem of biometric pattern recognition based on the product law of reliability [30]. Based on this "rule of thumb", we introduce the following approaches for biometric pattern classification: (i) multiple-classifier, (ii) multiple-sample and (iii) multiple biometric model. The use of multiple classifiers is the basis in ensemble methods such as ECOC, boosting and bagging. The use of multiple-sample is motivated by Kittler [13] while the use of multiple biometric models is inspired by several authors Brunelli and Falavigna [3], Dieckmann et al. [6] and Maes et al. [15]. Using the results of experiments, we show how these notions can be established in a single framework.

Based on this framework, a prototype that uses voice and face biometric models is implemented. These two biometric models have been chosen to represent 1D and 2D biometric data respectively. 1D biometric model often deals with data sampled in time such as voice-scan and signature-scan. 2D biometric model often deals with space, viewpoint variation and elasticity of biometric data, such as face-scan, hand-scan, iris-scan and fingerprint. In the future, 3D biometric data such as head-scan may be integrated into the system as well.

Section 16.1.2 discusses the pattern recognition concept in the light of multiple biometric models. Section 16.1.3 will discuss several combination schemes that exist. Section 16.2 presents our prototype in such a way as to highlight some practical considerations. Tests based on our experiments can be found in Section 16.3. Section 16.4 discusses how a hybrid biometric model can consolidate different user and technology criteria to increase the security needed for a given application. It is followed by conclusions in Section 16.5.

16.1.2 Biometric Authentication Taxonomy

The pattern recognition concept is important because many biometric systems are based upon a similar series of processes. The main contribution of this study to the field of biometrics is to define the underlying processes so that having formalised the relationships in question, the model may be applied to any given biometric system. In terms of software architecture design, such generic representation can help create a system that can integrate new techniques or new biometric models without having to change the system design.

In the interest of explaining biometric authentication as a subset of the object recognition problem, we propose a generic biometric-independent framework, as shown in Figure 16.1.

A user's biometric data is captured using sensors. Examples of sensors are Charged Couple Device (CCD) camera, Infrared-Red (IR) camera, fingerprint scanner and microphone. Sensors have their standard data representation. These representations can be further grouped into 1D, 2D and even 3D data. For example, a microphone captures vocal passwords and stores them in a wave file as a 1D data. The output of a CCD camera can be stored in several file formats: bitmap, JPEG, PNG, etc. They can be grouped as 2D data. 3D data is not frequently used for recognition because devices to acquire 3D data are still relatively expensive compared to other devices.

More importantly, they are inefficient in sampling biometric data, thus making them impractical.

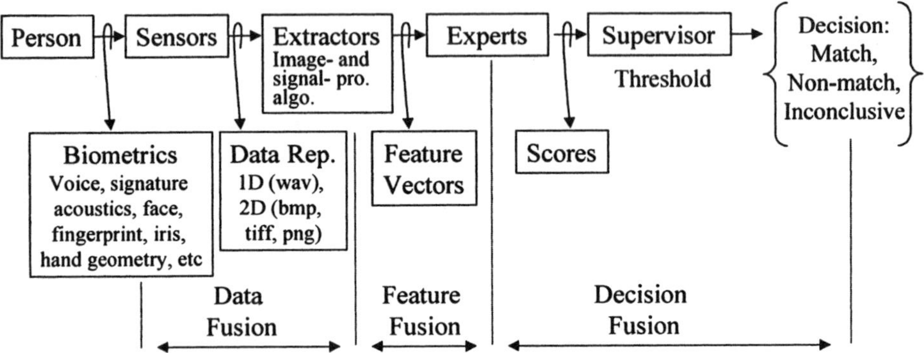

Figure 16.1.   A generic biometric authentication framework.

Having classified the data, the objective is to define a set of basic operations that work on 1D, 2D and 3D problems. These operations, often founded on signal- and image-processing algorithms, constitute the building blocks of *extractors*. Extractors have two functions: to detect and to extract user-discriminant information. Each extractor produces its own type of *vectors or feature vectors*, also called *templates* in BioAPI Specification Version 1.1 (or simply BioAPI) in a more generic setting. (A template is defined as data that represents the biometric measurement of an enrollee used by a biometric system for subsequent comparisons) We prefer the term *vectors* to *templates* because there is no template comparison during matching. *Experts* recognise the produced vectors. *Experts* or *classifiers* are a set of pattern-matching algorithms, which might be learning-based or template-based. Examples of learning-based pattern-matching algorithms are Multi-Layer Perceptron (MLP) and Support Vector Machine (SVM). Examples of template-based matching algorithms are dynamic time wrapping, Euclidean distance and normalised correlation. Experts serve to map a vector belonging to an associated identity. They do so with a certain degree of confidence commonly called a *score* or a *confidence measure*. It could be a scalar value or a vector when more information is supplied. A score could be interpreted as the estimated *a posteriori* probability that a given feature belong to the claimed class label. Therefore, an expert can be seen as a function that receives a vector and maps it to an identity with a certain level of confidence called score. When there are several experts, a *supervisor* merges different scores to obtain the final decision.

If the final decision is a match, then the system accepts the identity claim. If the decision is a non-match, then the system rejects the identity claim.

Finally, if the decision is inconclusive, fallback procedure should be activated.

The whole process from biometric acquisition to supervisor decision can be viewed as a serial system. Errors in each sub module accumulate along the way. The very first error introduced is during biometric acquisition. This could be due to errors in localisation, environmental interference, etc. In the next step, the biometric data may not be adequately represented. This is most evident during data discretisation or sampling. Information is further lost during the extraction process. Finally, the experts and the supervisor will each introduce certain errors. Currently, each individual error cannot be calculated [28]. Consequently, biometric test results are always dependent on the test environment and will not reflect errors in dissimilar application environments. The serial nature of the authentication process suggests that one way to improve the system is to introduce parallel modules to increase the overall accuracy of the system (see Section 16.1.3).

Many literature reviews give a very good coverage on face [4], voice [21], fingerprint [32] and other biometric recognition [31]. We made a survey of algorithms related to biometric feature extraction and classification based on the proposed framework[19].

16.1.3 Combining Framework

Why Hybrid Biometric Model can Increase Accuracy? A serial system is where one module concatenates in a serial manner to solve a problem. A distributed system is where two or more modules work in a parallel manner so that the error is distributed. According to the product law of reliability [30], the reliability of a *serial* system, R_s, in its generic form can be defined as:

$$R_s = \prod_{i=1}^{n} R_i \tag{16.1}$$

where R_i is the reliability of the sub-component i and $R_s, R_i \in [0..1]$

On the other hand, the reliability of a distributed system, R_d, is

$$R_d = 1 - \prod_{i=1}^{n} (1 - R_i) \tag{16.2}$$

where R_i is the reliability of the sub-component i and $R_s, R_i \in [0..1]$

In a multi-model biometric system, each module, e.g., face, voice, etc, can be seen as a parallel component of the whole distributed system. An example will clarify the idea. If i = 2 where there are 2 subsystems, e.g., face and voice modules, and if we assume that the reliability of each system is 0.97, then, the reliability of the distributed system is, $R_d = 1-(1-0.97)^2 = 0.9991$.

The reliability of a serial system, where one subsystem depends on the other, is $R_s = (0.97)^2 = 0.9409$. This implies that to increase the reliability of the system, a distributed system is always preferable over a serial system. However, the disadvantage of having a parallel component is the extra memory and the higher computational consumption required in a biometric authentication system.

To justify our approach formally, we must prove that the reliability of a distributed system is always greater than that of its most reliable sub-component. This hypothesis can be represented as: $R_d \geq \max_{i=1}^{n} R_i$. We can rewrite Eq. 16-2 as follows:

$$1 - R_d = \prod_{i=1}^{n} (1 - R_i),$$

Since $R_i \in [0..1]$ which implies that $1 - R_i \in [0..1]$ and

$$\prod_{i=1}^{n} (1 - R_i) \leq \max_{i=1}^{n} (1 - R_i).$$

Hence,

$$1 - R_d \leq \max_{i=1}^{n} (1 - R_i),$$

$$1 - R_d \leq \left(1 - \max_{i=1}^{n} R_i\right),$$

$$R_d \geq \max_{i=1}^{n} R_i.$$

We can therefore say that the reliability of a combined system organised in a distributed manner (or parallel manner, as contrary to a serial manner) can be more reliable than the most reliable sub-system that constitute the combined system. The consequence is that, in practice, two or more components arranged in parallel (therefore a distributed system) can strengthen the reliability of the whole system.

We can summarise the above discussion in the following statement:

"A distributed system can be more reliable than the most reliable individual subsystem that constitutes it, provided that the joint policy is chosen correctly."

In the discussion that follows, we will see how the product law of reliability can improve the biometric system via the multi-model concept. We can classify biometric system as (i) single-sample single-model (SSSM) system, (ii) multi-sample single-model (MSSM) system, (iii) single-sample multi-model (SSMM) system, and (iv) multi-sample multi-model (MSMM) system. This classification not only facilitates our discussion, but also provides several insights on how combinations can be made and how each model can be compared. Single-sample in this context means a life-scan of a biometric data; while multi-sample means several life-scan of a single-model biometric data. Single-model means the use of a biometric model; as apposed to multi-model where two or more biometric models are life-scanned.

Theoretically, the computation complexity increases in each category but the accuracy increases as well. We can expect a multi-model system to be more accurate than a single-model system because two completely independent biometric models are more robust against fraud or noise than a single-model system. We can also expect a MSSM system to perform better than a SSSM biometric system because it has the advantage of several life-scan samples. Furthermore, noise can be cancelled out by averaging the biometric life-scans [11] and/or their extracted feature vectors. In the following discussion, different fusion strategies will be discussed. This is followed by a survey of SSMM and MSSM systems. We then propose a MSMM system as a more reliable approach for authentication.

Different Fusion Strategies. In MSSM and SSMM systems, fusion design is an important issue. We divide the fusion into three categories: (i) data fusion, (ii) feature fusion, and (iii) decision fusion. (see Figure 16.1).

Data fusion is the process of combining streams of raw measurements as they come out of different sensors. These measurements could be pixel intensities generated by several cameras looking from different angles of a biometric model (as in a MSSM system) or a camera and microphone capturing both the audio and video information (as in a SSMM system).

Feature fusion is defined as a method of combining extracted features from the raw measurements. The fundamental assumption in our framework is that the feature should be in vector form. Two vector features can be combined by concatenation. This assumption is violated when biometric features are represented with a graph. This is because there is no operation to combine a graph and a vector. In that case, a graph cannot be combined with a vector representation and feature fusion is impossible, unless the graph is translated into vector format.

Finally, decision fusion is a method of combining the outputs of each expert. A decision fusion is implemented via a *supervisor*, according to a particular *decision policy* (a term used by Wayman [28]). A supervisor is a function that receives inputs from several classifiers and outputs a final decision. Hong and Jain [12] proposed three different levels of decision fusions, namely: (i) abstract level – where the output of each classifier is a set of possible labels without any confidence value associated with the labels; (ii) rank level – where the output of each classifier is a set of possible labels ranked by decreasing confidence values, but the confidence values themselves are not specified; and (iii) measurement level – where the output from each classifier is a set of possible labels with associated confidence values.

In a nutshell, in our framework, we have data fusion, feature fusion and three different levels of decision fusion, namely abstract, ranked and measurement.

Single-Sample Multi-Model Biometric System. The fusion of face and voice biometric models as proposed by Ben-Yaoub et al [2] falls into the measurement level decision policy. They call the fusion supervisor algorithm. They propose five different supervisor algorithms, namely the SVM (using both polynomial and Gaussian kernel), Fisher discriminant analysis, MLP, Bayesian classifier and C4.5. In their approach, the output score vector of each classifier is considered as a pattern and therefore a general learning-based vector classifier can be used. One important advantage of Ben-Yaoub's contribution is that the underlying decision function of the supervisor can be empirically estimated using "on-the-shelf" algorithms without any modification. This avoids the use of parameters to model the data.

Contrary to Ben-Yaoub's approach, Hong and Jain merge their fingerprint and face classification using a statistical approach based on a Poisson distribution [12]. A less accurate biometric model, i.e., face biometric model, is used to query a database and then the returned subset of possible candidates is verified by a more accurate biometric model, i.e., fingerprint model.

We generalise their approach in Eq. (16.3). H_i is the final hypothetical score of the class label (or identity) i. $Cl_{i,j}$ is the output of classifier i of biometric model j. Similarly, $w_{i,j}$ is a weight parameter of classifier i of biometric model j. There are n biometric models.

$$H_i = \prod_{j=1}^{n} Cl_{i,j} \times w_{i,j} \tag{16.3}$$

This is typically a product rule. In Hong and Jain's context, they use a product rule where the face classifier has a weight based on the Poisson distribution and the fingerprint classifier implicitly has a weight based on the Binomial distribution [12].

We further propose an alternative rule, i.e., the sum rule, which has the form:

$$H_i = \sum_{i=1}^{n} Cl_{i,j} \times w_{i,j} \tag{16.4}$$

From the viewpoint of the fundamental product rule (Eq. (16.3)) and sum rule (Eq. (16.4)), it can be seen that Ben-Yaoub et al use linear models (i.e., C4.5, Fisher discriminant function and linear-SVM), non-linear models (i.e.,

MLP and polynomial-SVM) and the Bayesian model. In linear models, a pattern can be mapped linearly into a score. This can be viewed as the multiplication of a pattern x of 1×p dimension to a weight matrix of p×1. A non-linear model requires multiplication, exponential operation, etc. Example of parametric models are Gaussian, Poisson distribution models, etc, as in Hong and Jain's approach [12].

Multi-Sample Single-Model Biometric System. Kittler et al propose a MSSM biometric system that life-scans several face biometric samples [13]. The fusion is done at the measurement level decision policy and is based on the Bayesian estimation theory.

During an authentication session, R instances of biometric samples are life-scanned. This gives R instances of raw biometric data and R instances of feature vectors, denoted as x_i, where $i = 1..R$. According to the Bayesian theorem, the *a posteriori* class probability is $P(w_j|x_i)$, $j = 1$ or 2 which denotes two events: acceptation or rejection of an identity claim. The *a posteriori* probability is proportional to the probability density function, $P(x_i|w_j)$ and the *a priori* probability is proportional to $P(w_j)$. The basic underlying assumption in Bayesian theorem is that each element in the feature vector x_i is independent. Violation of this rule means that the multiplication rule cannot be applied, i.e., $P(x_{i1}|w_j)$ $P(x_{i2}|w_j)$ ... $P(x_{in}|w_j)$ will be erroneous, where the feature vector x_i can be represented as $[x_{i1}, x_{i2}...x_{in}]$. Bayesian theorem has to be used with care because sometimes elements in the extracted feature are not completely independent from each other.

A classifier outputs an *a posteriori* probability when given a feature vector x_i. Kittler et al combined the final *a posteriori* probability, $P(w_j|x_i)$, for a given pattern x_i belonging to class w_j using four strategies, namely, the average, maximum, minimum and median rules. He found that the average rule works the best:

$$\hat{P}(w_j|x) = \frac{1}{R}\sum_{i=1}^{R} P(w_j|x_i) \qquad (16.5)$$

Multi-Sample Multi-Model Biometric System. We proposed the MSMM system of biometrics as a better solution [20]. Under this framework, two or more biometric models can be used to authenticate an identity claim. Whenever possible, as computation permits, as many samples from each biometric model should be obtained. This approach requires a mechanism to combine different biometric models. We propose to use the error-correcting output-coding (ECOC) [8,14]. The idea is to use an ECOC model for each biometric model.

Briefly, the ECOC provides a method to solve multi-class problem by reducing the problem to binary problems. It is a concept derived from the information theory. Dietterich and Bakiri suggest that classification can be modelled as a transmission channel [8]. Bit data can often be corrupted (or miss-classified in our context). A class is represented by a *code word* (a binary string). Any pair of code words has a large Hamming distance. This can be generated using the most popular BCH codes. When a set of code words is arranged by row, a code word matrix is formed. Each column bit in the codeword matrix is learnt by a classifier. Therefore, for a code word of n bits, n classifiers are needed. During identification, the n classifiers produce a vector score of n elements. Classical distance functions like Euclidean Distance or city-block distance can be used to match against each code word (or class/identity label) in the code word matrix. The winning class label is the code word that produces the minimum distance. During authentication, however, a threshold value has to be defined. An identity claim is accepted if the distance is smaller than the threshold and vice-versa.

The ECOC has the advantage of being independent from classifiers. Heterogeneous classifiers can work together. By dividing the problem into several independent sub-problems, it is now possible to optimise the performance of each sub-classifier, because each individual classifier is now responsible for solving parts of the problem.

If there are N persons in the database, then the ECOC approach will produce a vector of N elements, each corresponding to the ECOC distance of each possible claimed identity. This distance is inversely proportional to the probability of the true identity. Now, to work on several vectors coming from different biometric models, we propose that these vectors be added using the classical vector addition operation. For example, in a two-biometric model system that life-scans two samples of each model, there will be four vectors, to combine these vectors, we just add them. The identity claim can then be verified as usual, i.e., the ECOC distance of the claimed identity should be below a predefined threshold. Section 16.2.5 gives a formal description of this approach.

16.1.4   Summary

The biometric authentication problem is a special case of the typical object recognition problem. Therefore, the usual pattern recognition taxonomy can be used to conceive a biometric authentication system. By viewing the system as a chain of input-output modules, one can see that errors accumulate along the chain sensors-extractors-experts-supervisor. It is proven that by using the product rule of reliability, one can improve the system by adding parallel modules. Based on this concept, the notion of multi-samples and multi-models are introduced to categorise different types of hybrid biometric systems. By using this MSMM framework, we implemented a hybrid biometric person authentication prototype using face and voice biometric data. This is the subject of the next section. We further show that the combination of several biometric systems can actually improve the accuracy of the overall distributed system, despite of its weak sub-components.

16.2. A Hybrid Biometric Person Authentication Prototype

16.2.1 System Overview

Our prototype is designed to function in a workplace of about 30 people, where there is a need to distinguish authorised persons from unauthorised persons to access the workplace. The system has to function within a very fast response time (less than three seconds), with a very low false acceptance rate (near zero) and an acceptable false rejection rate. It should be economically feasible for small and medium industry. In terms of implementation, the system has to be modular and adaptable to changes in algorithm and be independent from any specific biometric model. The framework based on sensors, extractors, experts and the supervisor are the main modules of the system. The proposed framework prototype was implemented using C++ on Windows platform. For experimental purposes, Matlab is used because it has many numerical calculation functions.

We have implemented a face and voice biometric authentication system based on the sensors-extractors-experts-supervisor framework. These two biometric models were chosen due to their diversity in terms of dimensionality and fundamental problem characteristics. The face biometric model is in 2D and is a physiological measurement. Among problems dealt with are space, orientation, lighting variation and occlusion. The voice biometric model is in 1D and is a behavioural measurement. Common problems dealt with are time sequence, noise and change of tune. Their diversity can be generalised as much as possible to other biometric model, as defined in our framework. Another advantage is the low cost of sampling devices: video camera and microphones, both of which are commonly found devices in today's multimedia PCs. Finally, both biometric models have very high user acceptability, i.e., the user do not feel threatened when his/her biometric samples are life-scanned.

At present, we have developed several face extractors based on information around the eyes [18], Principal Component Analysis (PCA) and Fisher Discriminant Analysis [20]. We have also developed two voice extractors based on wavelets and LPC [18]. We have built classifiers using the ANN, the SVM, ECOC-based SVM ensemble (or simply ECOC-SVM ensemble) and ECOC-ANN ensemble [20]. The supervisor is discussed in Section 16.2.5 using multi-sample multi-model system.

16.2.2   Face Authentication: Sensors and Extractors

Firstly, a facial image is captured using a web camera. At present, the user has to move into a viewing area. A face is considered detected if the mean squared error between the viewing area and a face template is smaller than a certain threshold. This is a very simple temple-matching method. An alternative approach is to look for the minimum mean squared error of a series of images. This approach assumes that at this minimum point, an upright frontal image is present and that it fits the template perfectly.

We use PCA and Fisher Discriminant Analysis as extractors [19]. Detailed configuration and its test protocol will be discussed in Section 16.3. We build a database of 30 persons. Each person has 10 face-scans. Therefore, there are 300 images altogether. There is no particular effort to align the head position as long as the entire head, including hairlines, is present in the image. Although RGB colours are available, the average of the three RGB components are computed to reduce the memory consumption by a ratio of 3 [18].

The PCA covariance matrix is calculated based on the difference between each image with the average image. In PCA, the Eigenvectors of the covariance matrix are sorted in decreasing order of it corresponding Eigenvalues. 144 components are selected, roughly corresponding to 95% of the total variance. In short, the given 300 images, the PCA produces a linear transformation matrix, W_{PCA}, of 300×144 principal components in dimension.

When all 300 images are linearly transformed using the W_{PCA}, they are subjected to Linear Discriminant Analysis. This is the basic step in the Fisher Discriminant Analysis (FDA). FDA produces a linear transformation matrix W_{LDA} with a dimension of 300×50. Details of the algorithm can be referred to Belhumeur's work [1]. Briefly, FDA tries to maximise inter-class distance and minimise intra-class distance. On the other hand, PCA tries to reduce the data dimension without taking into account class labelling. Figure 16.2 shows the scatter plots of the PCA and Fisher components using their first two components. It can be observed that Fisher components are grouped more tightly, as shown on the bottom graph of Figure 16.2. In fact, we later found out that our linear-ECOC-SVM can classify the problem. This means that the Fisher components are linearly separable. On the other hand, features extracted using PCA are *not* linearly separable on this particular dataset. This behaviour comes with no surprise, as the scatter plot of PCA using the first two components is not well separated.

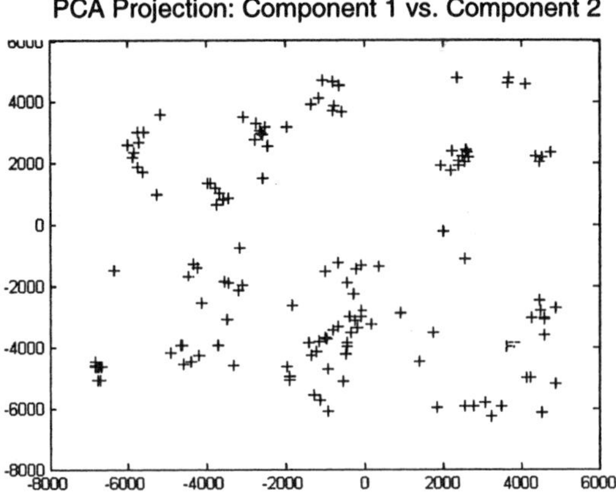

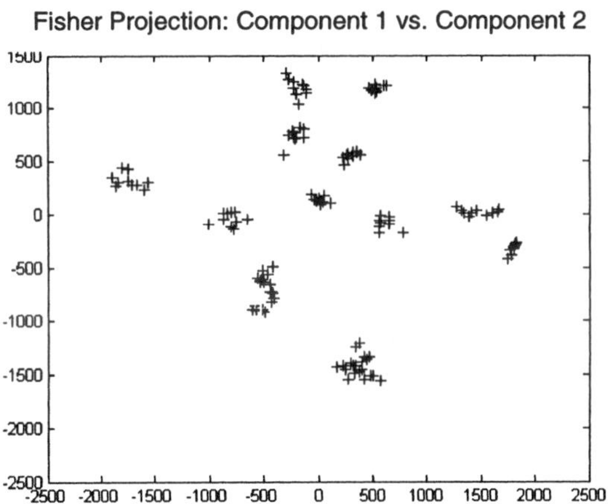

Figure 16.2. Scatter plots based on PCA (top) and FDA (bottom).

16.2.3 Text Dependent Speaker Authentication: Sensors and Extractors

The front end of the speech module aims to extract the user dependent information. It includes three important steps: speech acquisition, detection and extraction. In general, the user's vocal password is sampled via a microphone at 8 kHz over a period of 3 seconds. In the second step, the presence of speech is then detected and then extracted using Morlet wavelets [16].

In our experiments, a wavelet transform on a speech signal of 3 seconds gives 8 analysable scales. By using signal-to-noise analysis on the wavelet coefficients scale, we were able to determine that wavelets of scale-1, 2, 3 and 4 are more significant than other scales. Each of these scales is then truncated, normalised and then sampled before being merged to form a vector of 64 values. Through this sampling process, some important data could be lost. Such data reduction is necessary to make sure that the final vector is small enough to train the neural network [18].

16.2.4   Experts

Recall that the face feature extractors based on PCA and Fisher method produces vectors of 144 and 50 elements respectively. The voice feature extractor that is based on wavelets produces vectors of 64 elements. Each type of face and voice features is classified using its own Multi-Layer Perceptrons (MLP). The result of matching of these two MLPs are two scores. After applying thresholds on these scores, the final result (the supervisor) is joint by a logical AND operation. Of course, OR operation can also be used.

Instead of using a single classifier only, ensemble methods can be used to improve the classification result further. The basic idea of ensemble methods is to use a set of classifiers working on different partition of the problem. The ECOC approach is one such example. An ECOC matrix is typically generated using the BCH algorithm [8]. A standard BCH algorithm may produce columns with all zeros or ones. These columns are meaningless in classification problems so they are simply removed [10]. Kittler propose to use a set of neural networks arranged in ECOC [14] that we call ECOC-ANN here.

To further improve the classification result, we extend the idea of ECOC-ANN into Bagging-ECOC-ANN and Permuted-ECOC-ANN. This approach is motivated by the following observation: (i) Repeating columns in ECOC is useful for unstable classifiers like ANN [10]; This also implies that repeating columns in ECOC does not gain using stable classifiers like the SVM; (ii) Combining several ANN trained with different initial weights (termed *simple neural networks* by Dietterich [7]) can improve the overall classification result; and (iii) different binary classifiers solve different "parts" of the problems. The third motivation is the original goal of ECOC.

ECOC raises several questions: (i) What happens if several ECOC matrices are used with unstable ANN? This leads to our conception of *bagging*-ECOC-ANN. This can be done by simply repeating every column in an ECOC matrix. Each column may be learnt by ANNs of different initial weights [7]. We use a different number of hidden neurons instead to ensure that the approximation precision of the underlying function is different and that a different degree of generalisation is achieved. (ii) What happens if one randomly permutes the rows in an ECOC matrix so that new and *different* binary problems are created? This leads to the conception of *permuted-ECOC-ANN*. The combined result is simply a summation of the distance of several ECOC maps. Since each ECOC matrix is randomly permuted, each binary classifier now learns different parts of problem and thus guarantees the variation needed. Furthermore, by repeating the columns, the distance between any given row is also augmented.

Finally, we expect that between permuted-ECOC-ANN and bagging-ECOC-ANN, permuted-ECOC-ANN should work better because each individual classifier in permuted-ECOC-ANN really learns different parts of the problem while each individual classifier in bagging-ECOC-ANN learns the same problem, varied only by their degree of generalisation (e.g. different early stopping conditions) and/or approximation precision (e.g. different hidden neurons).

Of course, the disadvantage is the larger consumption of memory and the decrease of authentication speed. These factors, although important, are not taken into consideration in our experiments because one can overcome them by using PCs with faster processors and larger RAM.

16.2.5   Supervisor

Formally, we can summarise our hybrid approach as the following:
Assuming the followings:

N_{bio} the number of biometric models (n be the index)
N_s the number of samples (m be the index)
N_{ecoc} the number of ECOC matrices used (k be the index)
N_b the length of each ECOC binary string (i be the index)
N_c the number of identities/class labels (j be the index)

Let $f_{i,n}^k$ be a classifier for the i-th bit of the k-th ECOC for the n-th biometric model. Let x_m^n be the m-th sample of an extracted pattern of the n-th biometric model. Then the output score of the biometric pattern can be represented as $y_i^k(m,n)=f_{i,n}^k(x_m^n)$. The class hypothesis, H_j, i.e., the final score of supervisor is defined as:

$$H_j=\sum_{m=1}^{N_s}\sum_{n=1}^{N_{bio}}\sum_{k=1}^{N_{ecoc}}\sum_{i=1}^{N_b}\left|Z_{i,j}^k-y_i^k(m,n)\right| \tag{16.6}$$

H_j is the total ECOC distances across different biometric models and samples. During authentication, an identity claim is accepted if H_j is smaller than a predefined threshold. During identification, H_j is minimised.

This single formula shows three important notions, i.e., (i) the notion of multiple classifiers – indicated by the index i (this is the classical way how an ECOC ensemble of N_b classifiers is merged) and k (this is the extension of

ECOC: bagging- and permuted-ECOC [20]) (ii) the notion of multiple biometric models – indicated by the index n of N_{bio} biometric models and (iii) the notion of multiple samples – indicated by the index m of N_s samples. When $n=1$ and $m=1$, the system is a SSSM biometric model. When $n=1$ and m>1, the system is a MSSM biometric model. When n>1 and $m=1$, the system is a SSMM biometric model. Finally, when $n>1$ and $m>1$, the system is a MSMM biometric system.

16.3.   Database, Tests and Results

16.3.1   Database

Our database simulates the real-life environment of a moderate-size business. There are 30 persons. Each person has 10 face-scans and voice-scans respectively. Each biometric data is taken about the same time to cut down the cost of data collection.

A generic PC web cam, i.e. Creative WebCam Bluster II, is used for sampling 320×240 RGB image. Within this area of viewing, a face image is cropped out to the dimension 225×150. The cropped out image is saved in Windows' 24-bit bitmap (BMP) format. When taking the photo, the person is requested to move his face into the area of interest where the cropped face image is expected. The recorded image contains an upright frontal image without any time information available.

Under Windows' system, we sampled a 3-second voice password at 8K Hz on a mono-channel. The data is saved in a wave (WAV) file format with approximately 24K bytes. The password of each client could be any short word such as his name. Voice-scan is taken in the laboratory environment as well to model a typical indoor environment. As can be seen, no effort is made to create more challenging problem or to make the problem particularly easy.

16.3.2   Experiment Protocol

Briefly, there are 30 identities in the database ($N_c = 30$) and two types of biometric models: face and voice ($N_{bio} = 2$). For each type of biometric models (face and voice), 5 out of 10 samples of each person is used for training and the other 5 samples are used for testing ($N_s = 5$). Training and test sets are mutually exclusive. These samples are selected randomly on a per person basis. Therefore, for each biometric model, there are 5×30×1 = 150 positive examples and 5×30×29 = 4350 from a total of 5×30×30 = 4500 examples. Since our objective is to show the improvement of hybrid methods, and *not* the absolute accuracy based on the test data, we did not carry out cross-validation testing, which often requires very long computation.

We now introduce the notion of confusion matrix. Let $H_{j,l}$ be a confusion matrix of the j-th class label score with the l-th true class label. Therefore, when $j = l$, the identity is a genuine user and when $j \neq l$, the identity is an impostor. Using our hybrid approach $H_{j,l}$ is calculated exactly the same way as in Equation 6, with l as the true class label of the particular pattern in question. By using $H_{j,l}$ one can plot ROC curves and find EER for the particular confusion matrix.

The test procedures are as follow:

SSSM. With respect to Eq. (16.6), since only one biometric model and only one sample is used, $N_{bio} = 1$ and $N_s = 1$. This experiment is carried out on voice data only.

MSSM. With respect to Eq. (16.6) since there is only one biometric model, $N_{bio} = 1$. At first, one sample is used, i.e., $N_s = 1$. The experiment repeats with $N_s = 2$, $N_s = 3$, $N_s = 4$ and $N_s = 5$, i.e., until all 5 test samples of a single biometric model are exhausted. This experiment is conducted on both voice and face biometric models independently.

SSMM. With respect to Eq. (16.6), in multi-model setting, $N_{bio} = 2$, two for indicating both face and voice biometric models. In single-sample setting, $N_s = 1$. In other words, a sample of each model is combined for authentication.

MSMM. With respect to Eq. (16.6), in multi-model setting, $N_{bio} = 2$, two for indicating both face and voice biometric models. At first, one sample of each model is used, i.e., $N_s = 1$. The experiment repeats with $N_s = 2$, $N_s = 3$, $N_s = 4$ and $N_s = 5$, i.e., until all 5 test samples of each of the face and voice biometric model are exhausted.

16.3.3   Results

Single-Sample Single Model.   The objectives of testing SSSM are: (i) to be used as a baseline method for other methods, i.e., MSSM, SSMM and MSMM; (ii) to test the efficiency of bagging-ECOC and permuted-ECOC against the conventional one-versus-all method. We choose only the voice features for this test. One could expect that the result would be the same if the test were applied on face features. This is because in this SSSM problem, we are interested in finding out how the ECOC method can improve on the result of the basic one-versus-all method. The one-versus-all method is denoted as *combined*-1vsAll because we actually used a sum rule to combine three ensembles with different hidden neurons (4, 8, 16 hidden neurons; 64 input normalised feature neurons and one output neuron). The two other ECOC ensembles are denoted as bagging-ECOC and permuted-ECOC. These two methods have already been described in Section 16.2.4

Figure 16.3 plots the ROC curves of combined-1vsAll, bagging-ECOC and permuted-ECOC. Their EERs are 0.1970, 0.1631 and 0.1272, respectively. It can be summarised that the performance of experts in increasing order are: bagging-1vsAll, bagging-ECOC and permuted-ECOC. This confirms to the explanation in Section 16.2.4.

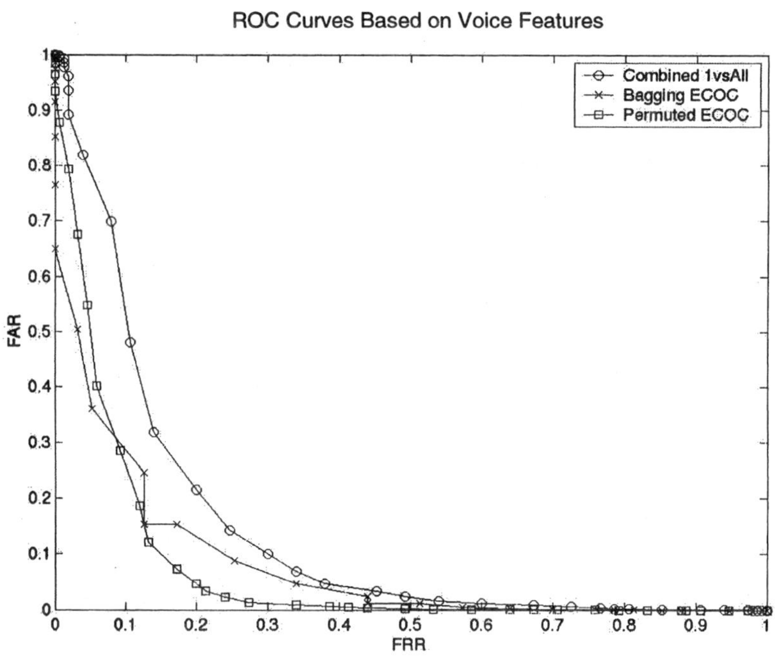

Figure 16.3. Comparisons of combined-1vsAll, bagging-ECOC and permuted-ECOC.

Multi-Sample Single-Model.   The objective of testing MSSM is to find out how accuracy is affected when the number of samples increases within a single biometric model. Since there are two biometric models, i.e., that of face and voice, this test is carried out on these two models separately.

As the number of samples increases, both the face and voice MSSM show a significant increase in accuracy, in terms of EER (see Table 16.1).

It can be concluded that as the number of samples used increases, a single-biometric model's accuracy also increases. This confirms Kittler et al's work [13].

Table 16.1. The corresponding EERs of face and voice biometric feature vectors in Figure 16.4 as the number of samples used increases gradually.

No. of samples used	Face EER	Voice EER
1	0.0885	0.0856
2	0.0621	0.0586
3	0.0466	0.0293
4	0.0397	0.0086
5	0.0351	0.0063

Single-Sample Multi-Model.   The objective of testing SSMM is to see how significant the improvement of a combined model is comparing to the case where each model is used separately.

The respective ROC curves of face, voice and the combined system are shown on the top graph of Figure 16.5. It can be observed that the ROC curve of the combined model is more efficient than any single biometric model. Before the combination, the *overall* EER of the face model is 0.1483 and that of the voice model is 0.1272. The combined EER is 0.0513. This increase in accuracy is significant.

Multi-Sample Multi-Model.   The tests in SSMM and MSSM have shown that both combination strategies can indeed increase the accuracy. The objective of using MSMM is to test how much and far MSMM can increase the accuracy further.

As the number of sample increases, i.e., from 1 to 5, the combined face and voice multi-sample shows very significant increase in accuracy. The ROC curves of using 1 to 5 samples, denoted as C1-C5, move closer and closer to the origin as the number of sample increases. Their corresponding EER are 0.0046, 0.0057, 0.0017, 0.0000 and 0.0000 respectively. In conclusion, the gain in accuracy in MSMM is very significant. This is shown on the bottom graph of Figure 16.5.

Discussion.   It has been shown that our ensemble method, which combines several ECOC matrices using permuted ECOC matrices can increase the performance of a biometric system. We have further shown that simple summation of class hypothesis scores (or distance scores), using multiple samples and/or multiple biometric models, can improve the overall performance. This improvement is due to the fact that errors from noisy extracted features cancel each other out during summation. The more independent the extracted feature is, the more random the error is. Independence can be achieved by combining several samples of a single biometric model (multi-sample) or combining different types of biometric models (multi-model). We further show that in combining these two ideas, i.e., multi-sample and multi-model, one can produce a very robust system achieving zero EER.

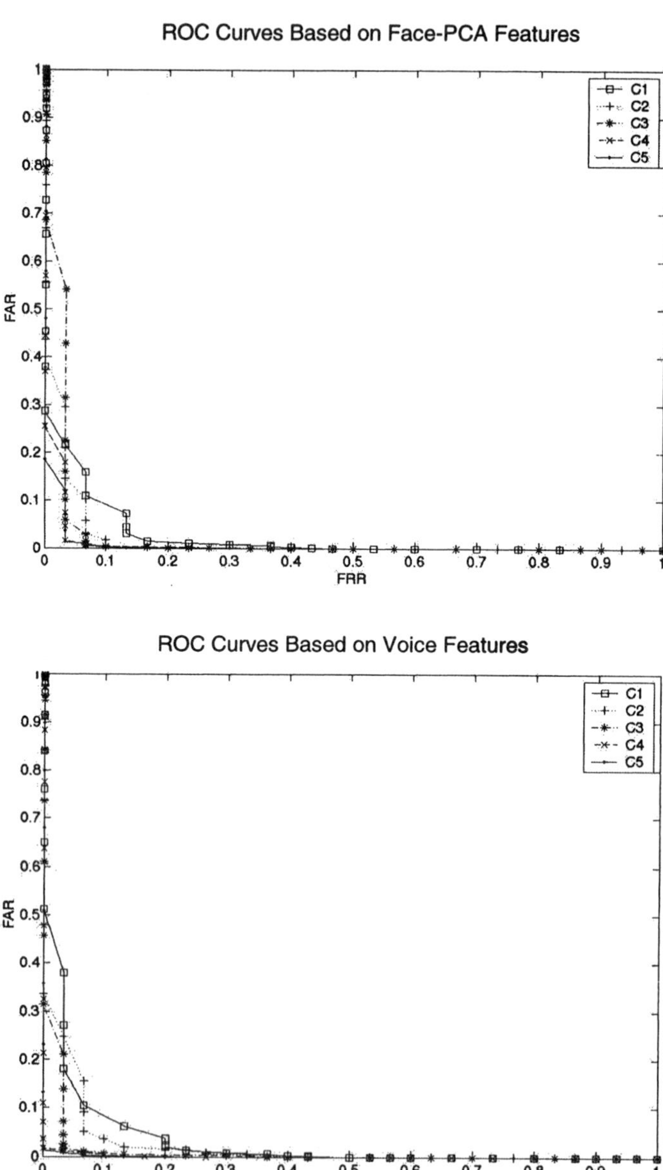

Figure 16.4. C1-C5 are ROC curves plotted using 1-5 face and voice samples respectively.

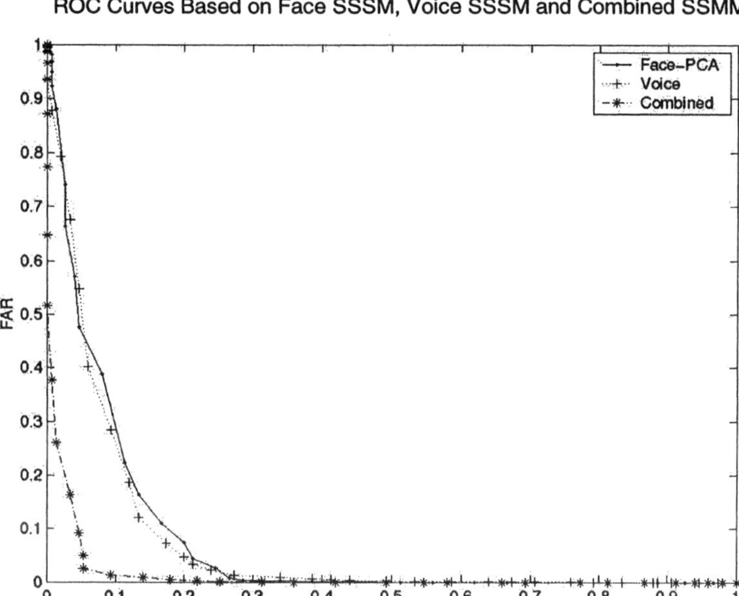

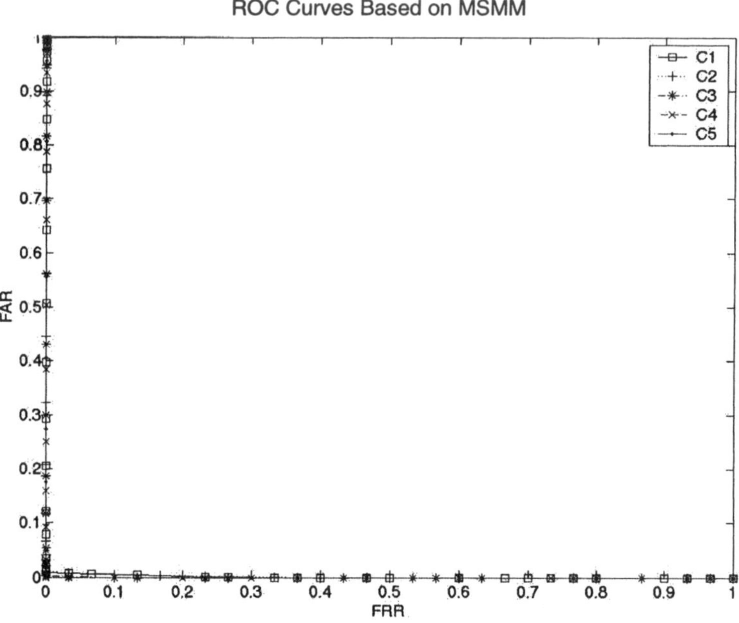

Figure 16.5. Top: The ROC curves of the face model, voice models and the combined models. Bottom: The ROC curves plotted using 1-5 samples of combined face and voice biometrics.

The next question is: instead of simply combining them by a summation rule (refer Eq. (16.4)), is there a better model for the supervisor? Our multi-classifier, multi-sample and multi-model approach as shown in Eq. (16.6), is a special case of Eq. (16.4), where the weights associated to each class label score $w_{i,j}$ equals to 1. The advantage of our model is that one does not need to estimate the weights. Consequently, no extra biometric data is needed to estimate the weights. If one wishes to estimate the weights, what is the suitable model for $w_{i,j}$? What degree of improvement can be achieved if $w_{i,j}$ can be estimated? This is where the idea of *stacked-generaliser* can come it.

Basically, one can consider the vector of class label scores as an input pattern to a stacked-generaliser (a stacked-generaliser can be a synonym for a supervisor). Then a standard classification algorithm, be it parameter-based or not, linear or not, can be used to classify the vector of class label scores. In doing so, however, the supervisor will become dependent on the pattern. Hong and Jain [12] used a probabilistic model to estimate w_i and claimed that their approach can increase the recognition rate. On the other hand, Ben-Yaoub et al [2] applied classical classification algorithms, e.g. C4.5, Fisher discriminant function, MLP, and SVM, and Bayesian model on the vector of class label scores. They showed that the SVM with polynomial and the Bayesian classifiers are among the most effective supervisors when tested on the XM2VTS database. Fundamentally, it is not clear how the stacked-generaliser can be trained in practice. Should another set of validation data be used to train the stack-generaliser? It is usually expensive to put aside a certain number of biometric data for this purpose because the number of biometric data is limited. The final question to address is how multiple samples and multiple models can be merged using the stacked-generaliser.

16.4.   Hybrid Biometric Applications

16.4.1   User and Technology Criteria in a given Biometric Model

So, how practical is a hybrid biometric authentication solution? In this section, we propose to categorise biometric systems according to a few selected criteria: user and technology criteria. All single-model biometric systems are then ranked according to these defined criteria. Four categories of biometric applications have been identified. Finally, the role of the hybrid biometric system and its applications are discussed in this context. The discussion ends with some practical considerations regarding real-life applications for biometric systems.

Biometric systems are normally employed in the following circumstances: (i) the current level of security does not match the specifications defined for the application; (ii) fraud in the current application is, or is feared to be, too high or uncontrollable; and (iii) current verification methods are too expensive, inconsistent or unreliable. The underlying motivation is to have greater accuracy than the existing system and to keep the cost low or reasonable. Biometric authentication is an alternative solution because it verifies the user based on his/her behavioural or psychological characteristics. However, because biometric authentication takes life-samples from the user directly, user criteria have to be taken into account, particularly the amount of time and effort that are required on the part of the user and the degree of intrusiveness of a given biometric model. In short, the four criteria influencing the choice of a biometric model are: (i) the accuracy of the biometric model, (ii) the cost of the biometric model, (iii) the ease-of-use and (iv) the degree of non-intrusiveness. The first two criteria are user-related criteria while the later two criteria are technology-related criteria. Based on these four criteria, the International Biometric Group (IBG) plotted Zephyr charts. We summarise the chart by ranking eight selected biometric models according to the four criteria stated above in Table 16.2.

Table 16.2. Rank of four biometric criteria versus biometric models in descending order of priority.

Ranking	Technology criteria		User criteria	
	Accuracy	Cost	Ease-of-use	Non-intrusiveness
1	Iris-scan	PIN	Iris-scan	Voiceprint
2	Retina-scan	Voiceprint	Face	PIN
3	Fingerprint	Signature	Signature	Signature
4	Face	Fingerprint	Voiceprint	Hand
5	Hand	Face	Fingerprint	Face
6	Voiceprint	Hand	Hand	Fingerprint
7	Signature	Retina-scan	PIN	Iris-scan
8	PIN	Iris-scan	Retina-scan	Retina-scan

PIN or password is used in Zephyr charts because this is the conventional authentication method and the competitor of biometric authentication system.

It should be noted that the concept of accuracy itself is influenced by the following characteristics by Jain [31]: (i) *universality*, which means that every person should have the characteristic, (ii) *uniqueness*, i.e., two persons should not have the same measurement of characteristic, (iii) *permanence*, i.e., the characteristic should be invariant with time, (iv) *measurability*, i.e., the characteristic can be quantified (that is the origin of the word metrics as in biometrics). The accuracy of a biometric model depends on the presence of these properties: the more they are present, the greater its accuracy.

Unfortunately, these properties are not really quantifiable. The conventional way to quantify accuracy is by using the FAR (False Acceptance Rate) and FRR (False Rejection Rate) measurements, which themselves are dependent on a threshold value. To compare different biometric models, the value that is frequently used is FAR=FRR, which is called the EER (Equal Error Rate) point. When comparing different biometric models based on EER, there is inevitably a certain bias because the number of test samples and protocols used to calculate the EER across biometric models is not uniform. In other words, EER is not a reliable measure of different biometric systems.

16.4.2   Classification of Biometric Applications Based on Security-Convenience Scale

Classifying applications according to the user and technology based criteria is difficult because biometric applications do not have the same priority regarding criteria. However, one can see that user criteria (ease-of-use and non-intrusiveness) are related to user convenience while technology based criteria are related to the level of security. In general, the higher the level of required security of a biometric model, the greater its accuracy. Also, the higher is the required level of security, the more it costs. In this discussion, the "soft assumption" is that security is proportional to accuracy and cost. This simplifies the classification of biometric applications.

We suggest classifying biometric applications scenarios according to the security-convenience scale. Each application scenario places different priority on its criteria, namely, security (or accuracy), user convenience (ease-of-use and non-intrusiveness), traffic, cost, etc. Several application scenarios are listed in Table 16.3, together with their respective level of requirements.

Applications in Category I place security as the most important criteria, differed only by the traffic, i.e., the number of people requesting to be authenticated within an interval (e.g. per hour). Convenience and cost are considered to be secondary priorities. For low traffic applications, retina-scan has been employed in very high security environments, e.g., nuclear research and weapons sites and communications control facilities [33]. In applications where the traffic is high, even a small false rejection rate can quickly become intolerable. For instance, in a biometric system with a 0.01% of FRR but with a traffic of 100 000 users per hour, there will be 10 genuine users to be falsely rejected every hour. On the other hand, when the traffic is high, convenience becomes more and more important because it involves a wide variety of demographic compositions. Applications that require high security and high traffic with emphasis on the user convenience are in high demand but not many biometric models can satisfy such demand. Fingerprint is one example that is now used in the border control, e.g., between Malaysia and Singapore border.

Table 16.3. Rank of biometric applications scenarios according to the security-convenience scale.

Category	Biometric application scenarios	Priority of criteria
I	Top secret agency, top-management	Very high security, low traffic
	Prison system	Very high security, moderate traffic
	Border control (airport), public identity, voting system	High security, high traffic, high user convenience
II	Banking system (ATM machines)	Very high user convenience, high security, high traffic
III	Tourism, Internet and telephone transaction, network access, welfare system	Very high user convenience, moderate security, high traffic, low cost
IV	Book-keeping of traffic flow (time-stamping)	Low cost, high traffic, low security

Applications in Category II are typically bank systems with ATM machines. Bank systems are a service-oriented industry but require high security at the same time. They have a big number of clients. High security (very low FAR) and high user convenience (very low FRR while requiring minimal efforts from the user) are very important in this category. Unfortunately, minimising FAR and FRR at the same time are not possible because FAR and FRR are, by the nature of the problem, inversely proportional, i.e., minimising one increases the other one and vice-versa. Furthermore, high traffic magnifies the FAR and FRR. Cost is not a factor that comes into play here because the abovementioned important criteria cannot be satisfied yet. As a result, not many biometric models are employed in the bank industry.

Contrary to applications in Category II, applications in Category III require less level of security. Otherwise, they share the same characteristics, i.e., high priority on high user convenience and high traffic. Cost comes into play in Category III applications because the organisations in this applications are commercially motivated and therefore much more cost-sensitive than the bank systems in Category II.

Finally, Category IV applications are very cost-sensitive. So, the cost factor is the priority. Other characteristics are the high traffic flow and low level of security. With the low level of security, many biometric models, particularly those with high user convenience are employed in this category of applications. For example, hand geometry for time-stamping systems are commonplace in factory settings with thousands of workers. These systems are used to prevent "time-clock buddy-punching" where one worker asks the other one to mark his/her attendance.

Category II and Category I applications with high traffic flow are two particular areas where very few biometric models can make their way to the market or can be successful in convincing their robustness in real-life applications. The fundamental obstacle with applications in Category II is the high user convenience with high security. For both categories, high traffic flow requires that biometric models to be scalable.

When no more single biometric models can satisfy these application requirements, one naturally looks for a hybrid solution. In multi-model biometric system, even another weak biometric model can boost the reliability of the whole distributed system. This has been formally proven using the product law of reliability. This is subject of the next section.

16.4.3 Hybrid Biometric System to Boost Accuracy

We define hybrid biometric system as the use of multi-model, multi-sample or multi-classifier to tackle biometric recognition problems. Until now, several hybrid models have been proposed: Brunelli and Falavigna proposed the use of face and voice [3]. Dieckmann et al proposed face, lip motion and voice [6]. Kittler et al proposed multi-sample biometric model using face features [13]. Maes et al proposed voice-scan, with non-biometric data i.e. smart card or password [15]. We proposed face and voice biometric models in an asynchronous way [17]. We further propose a multi-sample multi-model biometric system as a more robust solution [20].

The principal question is: ultimately, how does the hybrid biometric model fit into a given application? Hybrid biometric models offer an alternative solution to applications where no single biometric models can satisfy. Following the discussion in the previous section, the identified critical application demand are found in Category I with high traffic and Category II: banking systems.

A few related criteria imposed by the two categories are re-evaluated:

Security. In both categories, the cost of making a false acceptance mistake can be extremely high. With the hybrid approach, the system accuracy will be increased, such that the FAR of the hybrid system should be lower than its subcomponents.

User Convenience. In Category II applications, the subcomponents of the hybrid approach must both have high user convenience, i.e., the effort required by the user to get to use the system should be relatively low. Comparing to the single-model biometric system, the hybrid biometric model requires more efforts from the user because he/she has to learn to use multiple biometric models instead of just one. In terms of non-intrusiveness, the hybrid biometric model has the luxury of choosing the following models in decreasing order of priority: voiceprint, PIN, signature, hand and face (refer Table 16.2).

Traffic. If the traffic flow is measured in terms of the number of authentication request per unit time, the hybrid biometric model will take longer time to authenticate an identity claim then a single model. This implies that speed becomes a crucial factor if a biometric system is to be scaled-up to accommodate high traffic. One sensible way to get around this problem is to increase the number of biometric authentication machines to cater to the high traffic flow.

Cost. Cost is considered a secondary priority in Category I and II. However, the total cost of a hybrid biometric model should be less than a single biometric model, given a desired level of accuracy. If this condition is not satisfied, then a single model biometric is still preferable.

In a nutshell, a hybrid biometric model is a feasible solution to complement what a single-model biometric cannot achieve. In the following section, several practical considerations are proposed to ensure that a biometric system functions correctly and is properly maintained.

16.4.4 Several Practical Considerations on the Proposed Framework

Our suggested framework in Figure 1 shows that an authentication process is a concatenation of several processes: sensors, extractors, experts and a supervisor, unfortunately, in a serial manner. Due to this serial system configuration, errors tend to accumulate along the chain. To increase the reliability of the system, one can either reduce the error of each sub-component in a serial system or add a parallel module to minimise the error.

Several practical suggestions are given below:

Robust Detection Module. Badly life-scanned biometric samples contribute to the error called Data Collection Error [23]. This particular error is not available in laboratory environment where each sample is carefully collected, under survey or purposely simulated. One of the ways to avoid badly life-scanned biometric samples is to define a quality index. In automatic fingerprint recognition problem, when the quality of fingerprint is known, the respective enhancement can be used. Shen et al used Gabor WT to estimate the quality of sampled fingerprint [25]. The estimated quality index can then either be used to guide the enhancement module needed before proceeding to extraction module or to decide another life-scan. Such methodology can easily be generalised to other biometric module to estimate the noise model in the hope to achieve better recognition rate. Another way to increase robustness of the detection module, according to the product law of reliability, is by integrating two parallel detection modules.

Feedback Sensors. When taking a life biometric sample, it is important that the associated biometric device has some feedback information. For example, when using a camera, it is desirable that there are additional light source detection sensors. One can emulate a camera that is used for face detection as a light source sensor. For example, Choi et al applied two different face recognition modules for two different lighting conditions [5]. Although they do not have another sensor, using the same camera to capture and estimate environmental condition is an interesting approach. Although not extensively tested on a large database, they have shown that such feedback information can make a system more robust.

Extra Information. For example, if an ATM machine is to function at night, then, the associated camera should be adjusted to a higher threshold if there is a high probability of crime at night. Often, the Bayesian-based network fusion will fail because the conditional probabilities that it tries to model in the lab environment do not apply any more. Therefore, getting extra information as a function of threshold-based classifiers may improve its effectiveness.

Controlled Environment. To improve the detection reliability, environment should be controlled/constrained as much as possible. The constraints should not be imposed on the user but on the environment, e.g., lighting control, sound control, etc. One easy proposition is to put the biometric system in a protected room whenever possible, because the environment can be easily controlled. This will prevent life-scanned biometric data from being corrupted. An example of constraint imposed on the user is putting up emotionless face during life-scan. The key idea is that one should not expect a biometric system to recognise a noisy biometric data.

Similarity of Environment during Life-scan and Enrolment. A life-scanned biometric sample during enrolment should reflect that of the real-life situation. It should be sampled where it is used so that the biometric system picks up the same level of inevitable environmental noise whenever possible.

Surveyed Life-scan. It should be noted that unattended authentication system is more easily tempered with then an attended authentication system. For example, an amputated sample can be used to abuse the system. This suggests that a third-party automatic surveying system can be used to prevent such attempt. One proposal is to install a gesture recognition system in order to provide feedback to authentication system to detect any abnormal behaviour. Providing such feedback information can help fine-tune the threshold information.

Fallback Procedures. Last but not least, fallback procedures are a must because all system may fail in exceptional situations. As Murphy's law goes, "if something may happen, it will happen". 10% of fingerprint life-scan fails because of different problems [32]. It is a myth that fingerprint or iris-scan biometric models are solved problems, despite many vendors' claims, often based on laboratory experiments.

Surely it is important that biometric system be managed and maintained carefully. It can be easily hampered if put under hostile environments that are vulnerable to attack. Managing the server is one example of such issue. It is really out of what the algorithms can control. This is where the policy of handling biometric system should come in, typically in the form of "manuals" or guidelines. There are surely much to be done before the system can be delivered into real-world applications.

16.5. Conclusions

It is shown in this work that a highly secured biometric authentication system can be realised by using multi-sample and multi-model biometric systems. We propose a biometric framework based on the current signal- and image-processing algorithms, together with pattern recognition techniques. The proposed independent biometric framework is divided into sensors, extractors, experts and the supervisor. Several fusions, namely data, feature and decision fusions are explored.

The product law of reliability implies that the overall reliability of a distributed (or parallel) system is always better than the reliability of a serial system. This suggests that whenever possible one should create several parallel modules to increase the system reliability. The three areas where such parallelism is identified are the ensemble method, the notion of multiple samples and the notion of multiple models. The ensemble methods are a set of classifiers that work together to solve problems on a single model biometric system. We have employed the Error-Correcting Output-Coding method as our ensemble method. Because different classifiers solve different parts of the problems, experiments have shown that the ECOC-based classification outperforms the classical one-versus-all method. We have further extended the conventional ECOC method with bagging-ECOC and permuted-ECOC where we used artificial neural networks with different configuration in the first case and in addition to that, we used randomly permuted ECOC matrix in the second case. Permuted-ECOC turns out to be a more accurate ensemble method.

Under the notions of multiple samples and multiple models, four different hybrid biometric systems can be categorised as Single-Sample Single-Model, Multi-Sample Single-Model, Single-Sample Multi-Model and Multi-Sample Multi-Model. Both the theoretical and experimental results are coherent in showing that each system improves in recognition accuracy in the order the models are presented. The experiments are based on a small database of 30 persons. Each person has 10 upright frontal faces and 10 3-second passwords recordings.

With the established framework, many algorithms can be readily applied into it. Furthermore, our prototype has shown that the concept of parallelism could be integrated into the framework easily. Depending on the degree of parallelism, the gain of accuracy can be very significant. While the concept of parallelism has many advantages and practical values, one should be aware that such approach increases memory consumption and calculation complexity in a linear way. The future computing machines will overcome such a problem. More importantly, for the sack of security, robustness and reliability are the critical success factors in any high-security biometric authentication system.

From the application point of view, we have identified four categories of biometric applications according to several criteria: security (or accuracy) versus convenience (ease-of-use and non-intrusiveness), traffic flow and cost. These four categories of applications are ordered according to the security-convenience scale, varied only by other criteria with different priority. Category I applications require very high security, varied only by the quantity of traffic flow. These are used typically in top-secret agencies, prison systems and border control applications. Category II applications are used in bank systems that are characterised principally by their very high user convenience and very high security requirements at the same time. Category

III applications are used in service-oriented industries that require very high user convenience, moderate security and high traffic flow. Category IV applications are routine entry-exit bookkeeping systems that are typically characterised by high cost-sensitivity, high user convenience and low level of security comparing to other categories. We have identified that Category I applications with high traffic flow and Category II applications are highly demanded areas. Unfortunately, in these applications, no single-model biometric system can fully satisfy their challenging user (i.e. ease-of-use and non-intrusiveness) and technical (i.e. cost and accuracy) constraints. We propose that the hybrid biometric approach is an effective alternative approach when no other single-model biometric system can achieve the required constraints. Therefore, a hybrid system is a very feasible approach.

References

[1] P. Belhumeur, J. Hespanha and D. Kriegman. Eigenfaces vs. Fisherfaces: Recognition Using Class Specific Linear Projection. IEEE Trans. on PAMI, July 1997.

[2] S. Ben-Yacoub, Y. Abdeljaoued and E. Mayoraz. Fusion of Face and Speech Data for Person Identity Verification. IDIAP Research Report, 99-03, 1999.

[3] R. Brunelli and D. Falavigna. Personal Identification using Multiple Cues. IEEE Trans. on Pattern Analysis and Machine Intelligence, vol. 17, no. 10, pages 955-966, 1995.

[4] R. Chellappa and S. Sirohey. Human and Machine Recognition of Faces: A Survey. In Proc. of the IEEE, vol. 83, no. 5, pages 705-740, May 1995.

[5] J. Choi, S. Lee, C. Lee and J. Yi. PrimeEye: A Real-Time Face Detection and Recognition System Robust to Illumination Change. 3rd Int. Conf. on Audio and Visual Biometric Person Authentication, pages 360-365, Sweden, 2001.

[6] U. Dieckmann, P. Plankensteiner and T. Wagner. SESAM: A Biometric Person Identification System using Sensor Fusion. Pattern Recognition Letters, vol. 18, no. 9, pages 827-833, 1997.

[7] T. G. Dietterich. Ensemble Methods in Machine Learning. Multiple Classifier Systems, First Int. Workshop, MCS2000, Cagliari, Italy, pages 1-15, Springer-Verlag, 2000.

[8] T. G. Dietterich and G. Bakiri. Solving Multi-class Learning Problems via Error-correcting Output Codes. Journal of Artificial Intelligence Research vol. 2, pages 263-286, 1995.

[9] Y. Freund and R. Schapire. A Short Introduction to Boosting. Journal of Japanese Society for Artificial Intelligence, vol. 14(5), pages 771-780, September 1999.

[10] R. Ghaderi. Arranging Simple Neural Networks to Solve Complex Classification Problems. PhD Thesis, University of Surrey, U.K., 2000.

[11] R. Gonzalez and R. Woods. Digital Image Processing. 2nd edition, Addison-Wesley, 1993.

[12] L. Hong and A. Jain. Multimodal Biometrics. Chap. 16, Biometrics: Person Identification in Networked Society, Kluwer Academic Publishers, 1999.

[13]   J. Kittler, G. Matas, K. Jonsson, and M.U.R. Sanchez. Combining Evidence in Personal Identity Verification Systems. Pattern Recognition Letters, vol. 18(9), pages 845-852, 1997.

[14]   J. Kittler, R. Ghaderi, T. Windeatt, and J. Matas. Face Identification and Verification via ECOC. 3rd Int. Conf. on Audio and Visual Biometric Person Authentication, Sweden, pages 1-13, 2001.

[15]   S. Maes and H. Beigi. Open sesame! Speech, Password or Key to Secure Your Door? In Proc. of 3rd Asian Conference on Computer Vision, Hong Kong, pages 531-541, 1998.

[16]   T. Masters, Signal and Image Processing With Neural Networks: A C++ Sourcebook. Academic Press, 1994.

[17]   N. Poh and J. Korczak. Hybrid Biometric Authentication System Using Face and Voice Features. 3rd Int. Conf. on Audio and Visual Biometric Person Authentication, Sweden, pages 348-353, 2001.

[18]   N. Poh and J. Korczak. Biometric Authentication System. MSc Thesis, Penang, 2001. http://hydria.u-strasbg.fr/~norman/BAS/publications.htm

[19]   N. Poh and J. Korczak. Biometric Authentication: A Taxonomy Framework. Research Report of LSIIT, 2001.

[20]   N. Poh and J. Korczak. Biometric Authentication: A Hybrid Approach. Research Report of LSIIT, 2001.

[21]   L. Rabiner and B-H. Juang. Fundamentals of Speech Recognition. Prentice Hall, 1993.

[22]   A. Ross, A. Jain and J.Z. Qian. Information Fusion in Biometrics. 3rd Int. Conf. on Audio and Visual Biometric Person Authentication, pages 354-359, Sweden, 2001.

[23]   T. Ruggles. Comparison of Biometrics Techniques., 2001. http://biometric-consulting.com/bio.htm

[24]   D. E. Rumelhart, G. E. Hinton, and R. J. Williams. Learning Representations by Back-Propagation Errors. Nature, Vol. 323, pages 533-536, 1986.

[25]   L. L. Shen, A. Kot and W. M. Koo. Quality Measures of Fingerprint Images. 3rd Int. Conf. on Audio and Visual Biometric Person Authentication, pages 266-271, Sweden, 2001.

[26]   R. Viswanathan and P.K. Varshney. Distributed Detection with Multiple Sensors. Proc. of IEEE, 85:54-63, January, 1997.

[27]   V. N. Vapnik. Statistical Learning Theory. Springer, 1998.

[28]   J. L. Wayman. Technical Testing and Evaluation of Biometric Identification Devices. Chap. 17, Biometrics: Person Identification in Networked Society, Kluwer Academic Publishers, 1999.

[29]   M.-H. Yang, D. Roth, and N. Ahuja. A SNoW-based Face Detector. Advances in Neural Information Processing Systems, MIT Press, vol. 12, pages 855-861, 2000.

[30]   K. Trivedi. Probability and Statistics with Reliability, Queuing and Computer Science Application. Prentice Hall, 1993.

[31]   A. Jain, R. Bolle, S. Pankanti. Biometrics: Person Identification in Networked Society. Kluwer Academic Publishers, 1999.

[32] A. Jain, S. Pankanti and S. Prabhakar and A. Ross. Recent Advances in Fingerprint Verification. 3rd Int. Conf. on Audio and Visual Biometric Person Authentication, pages 182-191, Sweden, 2001.

[33] R. Hill. Retina Identification. Chap. 6, Biometrics: Person Identification in Networked Society, Kluwer Academic Publishers, 1999.

INDEX

Biometrics Solutions
For Authentication in an *e*-World

This book provides a collection of sixteen chapters containing tutorial articles and new material describing, in a unified way, the basic concepts, theories and characteristic features of integrating/formulating different facets of biometrics solutions for authentication, with recent developments and significant applications in an *e*-world. The book, which is unique in its characters, will be useful to graduate students and researchers in computer science, electrical engineering, systems science, and information technology as a reference book and a text book for some parts of the curriculum. The researchers and practitioners in industry and R&D laboratories working in the fields of security system design, biometrics, immigration, policeman, control, pattern recognition, and Internet will also be benefited.

David Zhang graduated in computer science from Peking University in 1974 and received his MSc and PhD degrees in computer science and engineering from Harbin Institute of Technology (HIT) in 1983 and 185, respectively. From 1986 to 1988, he was a postdoctoral fellow at Tsinghua University and became an associate professor at Academia Sinica, Beijing, China. He received his second PhD in electrical and computer engineering at University of Waterloo, Ontario, Canada, in 1994. Currently, he is a professor in Hong Kong Polytechnic University. He is Founder and Director of both Biometrics Research Centres in PolyU and HIT, supported by UGC/CRC, Hong Kong Government, and National Nature Scientific Foundation (NSFC) of China, respectively. In addition, he is Founder and Editor-in-Chief, *International Journal of Image and Graphics*, and an Associate Editor, *IEEE Trans. on Systems, Man and Cybernetics, Pattern Recognition, International Journal of Pattern Recognition and Artificial Intelligence, International Journal of Robotics and Automation* and *Neural, Parallel and Scientific Computations*. So far, he has published over 180 articles including seven books around his research areas.